The International Lesson Annual
1972-73

THE
INTERNATIONAL
LESSON ANNUAL

1972-73

A Comprehensive Commentary
on
The International Sunday School Lessons
Uniform Series

Edited by
HORACE R. WEAVER

Lesson Analysis by
CHARLES M. LAYMON

Nashville   **ABINGDON PRESS**   *New York*

THE INTERNATIONAL LESSON ANNUAL—1972-73

Copyright © 1972 by Abingdon Press

ISBN 0-687-19134-3
Library of Congress Catalog Card Number: 55-6961

Lessons based on International Sunday School Lessons; the International Bible Lessons for Christian
Teaching, copyrighted 1968, 1969 by the Committee
on the Uniform Series, and used by its permission.

Scripture quotations unless otherwise noted are from
the Revised Standard Version of the Bible, copyrighted 1946 and 1952 by the Division of Christian
Education, National Council of the Churches of
Christ in the U.S.A., and are used by permission.

Scripture quotations noted Phillips are from *The
New Testament in Modern English,* copyright 1958
by J. B. Phillips.

Scripture quotations noted TEV are from *Today's
English Version of the New Testament.* Copyright
© 1966 by American Bible Society.

MANUFACTURED BY THE PARTHENON PRESS AT
NASHVILLE, TENNESSEE, UNITED STATES OF AMERICA

Editor's Preface

The lessons for this eighteenth edition of THE INTERNATIONAL LESSON AN-NUAL are for the fifth year of the six-year cycle of the International Lesson Series (1966-74). The first quarter of thirteen lessons explores the relevance of biblical teachings and principles to problems growing out of the changing world of science and technology, interpersonal relationships, and national and international relations.

The second quarter of thirteen lessons is a study of four prophets in later Hebrew history: Jeremiah, Ezekiel, Haggai, and Zechariah. Emphasizing the historical background, the lessons help students to achieve better understanding of each of the four prophets and the problems and issues each faced as God's messenger, and to discover the relevance of the prophetic message for faith and action on the part of the people of God in our time.

The thirteen lessons of the third quarter provide for a study of some basic Christian beliefs, with the intention of helping persons realize a better understanding and experience of the Christian faith.

The fourth quarter lessons will help persons know what the laws of God are and challenge them to apply these laws in daily living. Lesson one deals with man's need for an ultimate authority and suggests reasons why this authority rests in God. Lessons two through ten deal with the Ten Commandments, with each lesson empasizing the vital truth on which the respective commandment is based. Each law is further examined in terms of its highest interpretation in the New Testament. Lesson eleven directs attention to the Great Commandment, which, said Jesus, sums up all the others. The last two lessons are devoted to a study of the problem of alcohol use and other forms of intemperance.

We would remind the reader of the basic conviction that undergirds the Uniform Lessons: "The Bible is a medium of God's self-revelation to mankind and . . . its truth is relevant to the life of growing persons." [1] The study of these lessons is intended to help persons become aware of the living God as seen through Jesus Christ and commit themselves in discipleship to him as co-workers with the risen Lord in making the will and purpose of God a reality in our time.

In line with the above educational goal the ANNUAL is so structured that the sections in each lesson help the teacher get into the heart of the matter, see the scriptural meaning and relevance, and use teaching techniques that create discussion and personal involvement with the major issues.

The first section, entitled "The Main Question," introduces a persistent life concern—alienation, faltering faith, discipleship—and a question basic to that concern that is suggested by the Scripture selected for the lesson.

"As You Read the Scripture," written by a biblical scholar, provides special background material for better understanding of the passages, including references to other translations, meaning of key words, and cross references to other portions of the Bible.

[1] From the introduction to the 1969–74 cycle of the Uniform Series, published in 1966 by the Division of Christian Education, National Council of the Churches of Christ in the USA, and the International Council of Religious Education under the title *International Sunday School Lessons; the International Bible Lessons for Christian Teaching.*

5

Following the printed Scripture—King James and Revised Standard Versions—is a section entitled "The Scripture and the Main Question." Here the main question is considered in light of the Scripture passage, thus making the Scripture contemporary, personal, concrete, and redemptive.

Teaching plans for the lesson are offered in the section "Helping Adults Become Involved." Topics under this heading include "Preparation of Self and Class," guidance necessary for preparing oneself to teach the lesson; "Presenting the Main Question," ways in which the teacher can help each group member see that the main question is a significant concern in his life; "Developing the Lesson," guidance for using many types of teaching-learning methods; "Helping Class Members Act," ways the class may respond by means of some types of creative action to the insights learned in the lesson; and "Planning for Next Sunday," the topic for the following lesson and suggestions regarding assignments to be made.

A feature of the ANNUAL is the inclusion of the audiovisual listings for the entire quarter in the introduction to the first unit of each quarter. Audiovisuals listed include the unit they are recommended to accompany. The teaching plans for particular lessons may include a reference to one of these audiovisuals. The teacher is encouraged to do unit planning in order to request audiovisuals in time for proper scheduling. The introductions to the first unit of each quarter also include suggestions of books that will provide additional knowledge for the teacher as he makes his plans for each unit of study in that quarter.

A valuable feature of previous ANNUALS retained in the current volume is the subject index. This index will be helpful in locating illustrations for talks or devotionals on various subjects. The Scripture index also makes the volume useful for many years.

The authorship of this issue maintains the same high level of distinction as its predecessors. Interdenominational in character, the list includes: Harry B. Adams, Clifton J. Allen, Glenn H. Asquith, Charles H. Copher, Floyd V. Filson, George W. Frey, George A. Hartman, John C. Irwin, Charles M. Laymon, Martin Rist, Ronald L. Schlosser, James S. Thomas, Claude H. Thompson, Howard E. Tower, Harlan R. Waite, and Harold R. Weaver.

We want to express our deep sense of loss in the death of Dr. Claude H. Thompson. The third quarter exegesis, "Affirmations of Our Faith," was written by Dr. Thompson. At the time of writing he was aware of the fact that he was facing death. So his lessons are a wonderful affirmation of his own way of life, one of deliberately seeking to live the life of Christ in his everyday relationships.

A special word of appreciation and indebtedness should be made to Miss Eleanor A. Moore, assistant editor of this volume. Her careful, thorough, and creative editing of the manuscripts is seen throughout. We appreciate also the work of Mrs. Irma Evans, who typed the manuscript. We would like to add a word of gratitude for the way our artist, Mr. Cliff Johnston, has carried out our verbal descriptions in his art work.

HORACE R. WEAVER, *Editor*

Contents

7

SECOND QUARTER

Prophets of Judgment and Hope: Jeremiah, Ezekiel, Haggai, Zechariah

UNIT V: PROPHETS OF JUDGMENT AND HOPE: JEREMIAH, EZEKIEL, HAGGAI, ZECHARIAH (DEC. 3–FEB. 25)

THIRD QUARTER

Affirmations of Our Faith

UNIT VI: OUR HUMAN SITUATION (MAR. 4–18)

FOURTH QUARTER

God's Laws for Man

10

The Bible Speaks to Issues of Our Time

UNIT I: INTRODUCTION
Horace R. Weaver

ONE LESSON   SEPTEMBER 3

The purpose of this quarter's study is to discover the relevance of biblical teachings and principles to problems growing out of the changing world of science and technology, interpersonal relationships, and national and international relations. The units in this quarter relate to these three issues in the order indicated.

In a world where mobility, mass communication, and increased urbanization bring persons closer together and at the same time threaten to depersonalize and exploit the individual, Christians—committed to a philosophy of the infinite worth of human personality—may find guidance in God's Word for spelling out that commitment in action. Intelligent, concerned search must be made for answers to the problems related to international relations, the theological and moral ferment so evident in our day, and the overthrow of traditional patterns long accepted.

Many modern conditions may have no specific counterparts in the biblical narrative; yet the principles of love and brotherhood and disciplined living are timeless. This study seeks to help us face realistically and honestly both man's situation and the eternal message found in God's Word for meeting human problems.

The introductory lesson for September 3, "The Bible in Our Changing World," emphasizes the fact that God will be with us in changing times as he was with Joshua, Isaiah, Daniel, and John. We can count on the unchanging love of God regardless of the changes that take place around us!

Helpful background reading for this quarter may be found in the following books: *Uncertain Men and Certain Change,* Allan R. Brockway; *Environmental Man,* William Kuhns; *Crisis in Eden,* Frederick Elder; *Science, Technology and the Christian,* Charles A. Coulson; *Protestant Thought and Natural Science,* John Dillenberger; *Truths Men Live By,* John A. O'Brien; *The Times of Our Lives,* Ralph Bugg; *Mass Communication,* Alan Hancock; *Morality and the Mass Media,* Kyle Haselden; *The Secular City,* Harvey Cox; *Urbanism and Urbanization,* Nels Anderson, ed.; *Sex and the Now Generation,* Scott N. Jones; *God and Human Sexuality; Let's Face Racism,* Nathan Wright, Jr.; *The Politics of Religion in America,* Fred Krinsky; *The State in the New Testament,* Oscar Cullmann; and *Strategy of Peace,* John F. Kennedy.

Listed below are several audiovisual resources that should be valuable as you prepare not only the lessons in this first unit but also the lessons in other units on "The Bible Speaks to Issues of Our Time." (Each item will include a reference to the particular unit it may accompany.) These resources have been carefully selected and correlated with the major themes of the lessons. Teachers who wish to use the aids should make plans sufficiently early to ensure proper scheduling and delivery. All prices are subject to change without notice. All these materials may be obtained from your denominational publishing house unless another source is denoted in the description. Because of the lapse of time between the printing of this book and the use of these materials some resources may not be available.

Hide or Go Seek. 35mm filmstrip, 94 frames, script, guide, 33 1/3 rpm record. How does a Christian meet the challenge of a new day? One way is through study of the Bible and the world—along with active Christian involvement in contemporary affairs. Sale: color, $8.95. (Unit I)

Homo Homini. 16mm film, 11 min. This film makes a deeply religious inquiry into where we are and where we are going in our world. It serves as a discussion starter for groups considering hunger, population explosion, change, technology, and many other topics. Rental: color, $7, from Board of Missions; The United Methodist Church; 475 Riverside Drive; New York, New York 10027. (Unit I)

Right Here, Right Now. 16mm film, 10 min. A simple janitor, by his total openness to everyone and everything, becomes, in death, a bond of love and a sign of revelation to those whose lives he touched. Rental: color, $12, from Saint Francis Productions; 1229 South Santee Street; Los Angeles, California 90015. (Unit I)

Very Nice, Very Nice. 16mm film, 8 min. This film is made up of dozens of still pictures that will seem similar, if not identical, to ones seen in newspapers, magazines, and on television. On the screen one fast cut succeeds another emphasizing the incongruities of modern life. Rental: black and white, $10, from Mass Media Ministries; 2116 North Charles Street; Baltimore, Maryland 21218. (Unit I)

Of Time, Work and Leisure. 16mm film, 30 min. Through dramatization, film clips, narration, and exposition, this film examines modern ideas about time, work, and leisure. It presents the problem of the enslavement of people in a society dominated by machines and clocks. What is leisure? What is man's real purpose in life? What is the difference between free time and true leisure? Rental: black and white, $5.40, from National Education Television; 10 Columbus Circle; New York, New York 10019. (Unit II)

Mr. Grey. 16mm film, 10 min. Mr. Grey is a suburbanite who only imagines that in his metropolitan white-collar world he is his own man. He is bought and sold in the marketplace and committed to an organization that cares very little about him as a person. Rental: color, $15, from Mass Media Ministries; 2116 North Charles Street; Baltimore, Maryland 21218. (Unit II)

My Own Yard to Play In. 16mm film, 10 min. Here is a charming film of children playing on the streets of New York City. The sound track records games, songs, and comments of children. The film stresses the need for better recreational facilities for children in large metropolitan areas. It shows, at the same time, that children will play in any place at any time. Rental: black and white, $6.50, from Contemporary Films/McGraw-Hill; 330 West 42nd Street; New York, New York 10036. (Unit II)

The Persistent Seed. 16mm film, 14 min., guide. This film shows how the forces of nature battle against man's mechanical monsters. Forces of ugliness in the city are brought up short by the contrast of frail beauty there. Rental: color, $15, from Henk Newenhouse; 1825 Willow Road; Northfield, Illinois 60093. (Unit II)

Science and Foresight. 16mm film, 25 min. This film examines a serious problem of our times—how to cope with the advances of modern science and technology. We must foresee the consequences—good and bad—of new discoveries. Rental: black and white, $20, from Peter Robeck and Company, Inc.; 230 Park Avenue; New York, New York 10017. (Unit II)

Super Up. 16mm film, 12 min. This film is a perceptive, provocative commentary on the conflict between the individual and advertising pressures. Signs, billboards, cars, pigeons, a thousand familiar images, make up a fascinating mosaic. One of the three protagonists who must make something of their relationship to this bewildering culture is a young Negro boy, intrigued and puzzled, enticed and prohibited. Rental: color, $15, from Brandon Films; 221 West 57th Street; New York, New York 10019. (Units II and III)

Urbanissimo. 16mm film, 6 min. This is a humorous animated film from Expo that shows man blithely going about littering, destroying, and fouling his nest. Rental: color, $10, from Contemporary Films/McGraw-Hill; 330 West 42nd Street; New York, New York 10036. (Unit II)

How Do You See Black America? 35mm filmstrip, 40 frames. Intended for non-black Americans, the filmstrip pictures the living conditions, the patterns of violence, and the sense of isolation and personal frustration that have inhibited black Americans; and it illustrates a few of the new opportunities for this race that lie ahead. Sale: color, $6.50, from The Seabury Press; 815 Second Avenue; New York, New York 10017. (Unit III)

I Wonder Why. 16mm film, 5 min. Based on a book by Shirley Burden, the film is a photographic essay in which the love of life is visually presented with the narration—the thoughts of a young Negro girl who likes all the things other people like and wonders why "people don't like me." Rental: black and white, $7.50, from Contemporary Films/McGraw-Hill; 330 West 42nd Street; New York, New York 10036. (Unit III)

Let the Rain Settle It. 16mm film, 15 min. Two adolescent boys, one Caucasian and one Negro, discover God's revelation in discovering each other. Rental: color, $10, from Saint Francis Productions; 1229 South Santee Street; Los Angeles, California 90015. (Unit III)

Time Piece. 16mm film, 10 min. With the steady tempo of a human heart beat, the forces of advertising, movies, and modern sex symbols are presented as a visual satire of a day in the life of contemporary man. Rental: color, $8, from Contemporary Films/McGraw-Hill; 330 West 42nd Street; New York, New York 10036. (Unit III)

Who Do You Kill? 16mm film, 58 min. This film deals with a young Negro family trapped by the hideous Harlem slum conditions in which they live and faced with anti-Negro job prejudice, frustration, and bitterness. Rental: black and white, $15, from Mass Media Ministries; 2116 North Charles Street; Baltimore, Maryland 21218. (Unit III)

A Matter of Conscience. 16mm film, 28 min. Two young Americans are pictured as they struggle with the problems created by the draft. Against war in all forms, one boy goes to Canada, the other to jail. Rental: color, $28, from Cathedral Films; 2921 West Alameda Avenue; Burbank, California 91505. (Unit IV)

Hypothese Beta. 16mm film, 7 min. A funny cartoon, this film winds up with a surprise ending that adds another dimension to the film. The moral of the piece is: in a world of nuclear power, accidents and misunderstandings can mean disaster. Rental: color, $12.50, from Contemporary Films/McGraw-Hill; 330 West 42nd Street; New York, New York 10036. (Unit IV)

The Hat. 16mm film, 18 min. Two soldiers in different armies, only a few feet apart, are on border patrol on a remote and nameless frontier. By accident the helmet of one of the guards falls across the line into the other's territory, and the plot proceeds from there. Rental: color, $15, from Mass Media Ministries; 2116 North Charles Street; Baltimore, Maryland 21218. (Unit IV)

The Hole. 16mm film, 15 min. Two workmen under the city streets begin discussing the cause of accidents and the possibility of an accidental nuclear explosion. Rental: color, $15, from Mass Media Ministries; 2116 North Charles Street; Baltimore, Maryland 21218. (Unit IV)

Overture. 16mm film, 9 min. Produced by the United Nations, this film is a pictorial study of humanity in war and peace, a poetic presentation of man's heroic renewal after conflict. Rental: black and white, $4. (Unit IV)

LESSON 1   SEPTEMBER 3

The Bible in Our Changing World

Background Scripture: Joshua 1:1-9; Isaiah 40:6-8; Daniel 1; John 8:12

The Main Question —Charles M. Laymon[1]

"Why should I read and study the Bible?" asked a college student. "It is an old book, written about events that happened centuries ago, and dealing with a world long past. Its characters have strange sounding names, and it is impossible to pronounce the names of some of the towns and cities. Why wouldn't a course in sociology or psychology be better to prepare me for living today?"

The youth might also have said that biblical man thought the world was flat and had four corners. Space for him was confined to a small area between the earth and the firmament above, across which the heavens were stretched like a curtain.

Youth are not the only persons, however, who are asking why they should read the Bible. Adults, caught up in the contemporary scene with all the changes, are asking the same questions: What does the Bible have to do with high-rise apartments? data processing? communism? race relations? Vietnam? the Middle East?

Yet the church is still saying that one should continue to read the Bible. Is this just a carry-over from the past, or are there up-to-date reasons for this emphasis on Bible reading? The biblical passages for this lesson will help to answer this question.

[1] Charles M. Laymon: chairman of the Department of Religion and professor of religion at Florida Southern College, Lakeland, Florida, and former editor of adult publications of The Methodist Church.

14

As You Read the Scripture —Martin Rist [2]

Joshua 1:1-9. *After the death of Moses:* The title of the Book of Joshua, the sixth book in the Old Testament, is most appropriate because Joshua (or Jeshua), the son of Nun (nothing else is known about Nun), is the heroic figure throughout the twenty-four chapters. Joshua, as is true of many Hebrew names, has a special meaning—"Jehovah is salvation." Joshua was Jesus' Hebrew name. Because Joshua son of Nun was a kind of redeemer of his people, he has been considered by some scholars to be a prototype of Jesus.

For the most part, the Book of Joshua deals with the conquest of Canaan (which became the Holy Land of the Jews) under Joshua's leadership and the allotment of the conquered territory to the various tribes of Israel. According to Numbers 27:18-23, Moses, at the Lord's command, laid hands upon Joshua and commissioned him to be his assistant. In Deuteronomy 31:23 we read that the Lord himself commissioned Joshua to lead the children of Israel into the Promised Land.

Following the death of Moses, recounted in Deuteronomy 34:5, the people of Israel obeyed Joshua, "full of the spirit of wisdom," as his successor (Deuteronomy 34:9). This new leader, who was to go over the Jordan into the Promised Land (Joshua 1:2), was to be a kind of second Moses: a) God would be with him as he was with Moses (verse 5) ; b) he was to be obeyed as Moses was obeyed (verse 17) ; c) he, as was true of Moses, sanctified Israel (Joshua 3:5) ; d) like Moses he was exalted before Israel (Joshua 3:7) ; e) the miraculous crossing of the Jordan (Joshua 1:2; 3:14-17) resembled the crossing of the Red Sea; and f) like Moses, Joshua was to be of good courage, an example to his people (Joshua 1:7).

Moses gave the Law to Israel, and Joshua was to be its guardian; for the "book of the law shall not depart out of his mouth." (verse 8) Indeed, he was to "meditate on it day and night"; and by doing what it commanded he would have "good success." (verse 8) These instructions concerning the Law remind me of the righteous man of Psalms 1 whose "delight is in the law of the LORD, and on his law he meditates day and night," with the result that "in all that he does, he prospers." Joshua, then, was a worthy successor to Moses as the leader of Israel; moreover, he was enabled to do what had been forbidden to Moses—to lead the chosen people of God into the land of promise, dispossessing its inhabitants.

Isaiah 40:6-8. *A voice says, "Cry!"* Chapters 40 and following of the Book of Isaiah are generally thought of as reflecting the period of the Babylonian Exile of the sixth century B.C. rather than the time of Isaiah of Jerusalem (742-701?). The Israelites were conquered by the Babylonians in 586 B.C., and many of them were deported. As captives and exiles the Jews in Babylon needed words of comfort and encouragement. Accordingly, Chapter 40 opens with the memorable words: "Comfort, comfort my people, says your God," and continues, "Speak tenderly to Jerusalem, . . . that her warfare is ended, that her iniquity is pardoned. . . . The glory of the LORD shall be revealed." These words of comfort (40:1-5) preface the verses of the lesson (40:6-8), in which a voice is heard uttering words that are pessimistic and disconsolate

[2] Martin Rist: professor of New Testament and Christian History at Iliff School of Theology, Denver, Colorado.

15

and that call attention to the transitory nature of human life: "All flesh is grass," which withers away. Even so there is something comforting and hopeful in the contrasting statement, "the word of our God will stand for ever." (verse 8)

John 8:12. *I am the light of the world; he who follows me will not walk in darkness, but will have the light of life:* According to Hebrews 4:8-10, Joshua, great leader though he was, had not given his people rest. Instead, God's Sabbath rest for his people will depend upon the redeeming work of Jesus Christ.

Selected Scripture

King James Version

Joshua 1:1-9

1 Now after the death of Moses the servant of the LORD it came to pass, that the LORD spake unto Joshua the son of Nun, Moses' minister, saying,

2 Moses my servant is dead; now therefore arise, go over this Jordan, thou, and all this people, unto the land which I do give to them, even to the children of Israel.

3 Every place that the sole of your foot shall tread upon, that have I given unto you, as I said unto Moses.

4 From the wilderness and this Lebanon even unto the great river, the river Euphrates, all the land of the Hittites, and unto the great sea toward the going down of the sun, shall be your coast.

5 There shall not any man be able to stand before thee all the days of thy life: as I was with Moses, so I will be with thee: I will not fail thee, nor forsake thee.

6 Be strong and of a good courage: for unto this people shalt thou divide for an inheritance the land, which I sware unto their fathers to give them.

7 Only be thou strong and very courageous, that thou mayest observe to do according to all the law, which Moses my servant commanded thee: turn not from it to the right hand or to the left, that thou mayest prosper whithersoever thou goest.

Revised Standard Version

Joshua 1:1-9

1 After the death of Moses the servant of the LORD, the LORD said to Joshua the son of Nun, Moses' minister, 2 "Moses my servant is dead; now therefore arise, go over this Jordan, you and all this people, into the land which I am giving to them, to the people of Israel. 3 Every place that the sole of your foot will tread upon I have given to you, as I promised to Moses. 4 From the wilderness and this Lebanon as far as the great river, the river Euphrates, all the land of the Hittites to the Great Sea toward the going down of the sun shall be your territory. 5 No man shall be able to stand before you all the days of your life; as I was with Moses, so I will be with you; I will not fail you or forsake you. 6 Be strong and of good courage; for you shall cause this people to inherit the land which I swore to their fathers to give them. 7 Only be strong and very courageous, being careful to do according to all the law which Moses my servant commanded you; turn not from it to the right hand or to the left, that you may have good success wherever you go. 8 This book of the law shall not depart out of your mouth, but you shall meditate on it day and night, that you may be careful to do according to all that is written in it; for

8 This book of the law shall not depart out of thy mouth; but thou shalt meditate therein day and night, that thou mayest observe to do according to all that is written therein: for then thou shalt make thy way prosperous, and then thou shalt have good success.

9 Have not I commanded thee? Be strong and of a good courage; be not afraid, neither be thou dismayed: for the LORD thy God is with thee whithersoever thou goest.

Isaiah 40:6-8
6 The voice said, Cry. And he said, What shall I cry? All flesh is grass, and all the goodliness thereof is as the flower of the field:

7 The grass withereth, the flower fadeth: because the spirit of the LORD bloweth upon it: surely the people is grass.

8 The grass withereth, the flower fadeth: but the word of our God shall stand for ever.

John 8:12
12 Then spake Jesus again unto them, saying, I am the light of the world: he that followeth me shall not walk in darkness, but shall have the light of life.

Memory Selection: **The grass withereth, the flower fadeth: but the word of our God shall stand for ever.** (Isaiah 40:8)

then you shall make your way prosperous, and then you shall have good success. 9 Have I not commanded you? Be strong and of good courage; be not frightened, neither be dismayed; for the LORD your God is with you wherever you go."

Isaiah 40:6-8
6 A voice says, "Cry!"
    And I said, "What shall I cry?"
All flesh is grass,
    and all its beauty is like the
    flower of the field.

7 The grass withers, the flower fades,
    when the breath of the LORD
    blows upon it;
    surely the people is grass.

8 The grass withers, the flower fades;
    but the word of our God will
    stand for ever.

John 8:12
12 Again Jesus spoke to them, saying, "I am the light of the world; he who follows me will not walk in darkness, but will have the light of life."

Memory Selection:
The grass withers, the flower fades; but the word of our God will stand for ever.   (Isaiah 40:8)

The Scripture and the Main Question —Charles M. Laymon

A NEW LAND AND A NEW LIFE
Change is difficult when we become entrenched in a certain place or way of life. Rufus Jones once told of a kindly man who summered on the coast of Maine and who decided he

would teach a church school class of children living on a nearby island. His first question as he sought to establish contact with them was, "How many of you have ever seen the Atlantic Ocean?" Not a hand went up. The ocean was all around them, yet they had never seen it. The only spot they knew was the rocky land where they placed their feet.

This example sounds extreme, but it is not at all uncommon to find people with nineteenth-century minds living in the second half of the twentieth century. They like life this way; their security lies in holding tight to the past. They have never heard of the Sea of Tranquillity.

Some of the Hebrews in this lesson had a similar attitude about life. Yet Moses was dead, and the Exodus was behind them. Their only hope lay in a new life and a new land. To this Joshua was calling them (Joshua 1: 1-7). For this new adventure they needed to be strong and to have courage (verses 6-7). Longing for the past would do no good.

The Bible continually calls upon men to move forward. The gentile world to which the early Christian missionaries took the gospel was a new world to them. Atlantic Oceans and Seas of Tranquillity are always ready to be explored. Not only must men adjust to new living areas but also to new ideas and understandings of God and his call to them. The prophets' messages were new to the men of their time; Jesus' message was new in his era; and the apostle Paul's presentation of the gospel was new. In the Bible there is an ever-widening circle of life opening up to the people. And, in this sense, the Bible provides guidance for persons of the present who are called upon to live a new kind of life in a new day.

A NEW LAND AND AN OLD BOOK

When Joshua called upon the Hebrews to move out with him into a new land, he urged them to take the book of the law with them: "This book of the law shall not depart out of your mouth, but you shall meditate on it day and night, that you may be careful to do according to all that is written in it." (verse 8) If the people will do this, they will prosper and know success.

Why were the Hebrews told to take an old book into a new land? This is the same as asking why persons today should read the Bible, an ancient writing, in this new age. One of the reasons is that in reading the Bible we are constantly discovering new truth that is relevant to our time. John Bunyan wrote *Pilgrim's Progress* while imprisoned in Bedford jail. During this time he read the Bible constantly. He said of his experience, "I never knew all there was in the Bible until I spent those years in jail. I was constantly finding new treasures."

One reason for our finding new treasures in the Bible, even though we have read it many times, is the vast area of history and life that it covers. If we date Abraham as early as 2000 B.C. and Second Peter about A.D. 150, we can see the tremendous sweep of time involved. In addition, many ideas and thoughts in its writings would take a lifetime to master. Still another reason is that the Holy Spirit takes the truths of the Bible as we read it and quickens our minds to perceive them.

THE ETERNAL WORD

Because new truths continue to be found as one reads the Bible, it has been called "The Eternal Word." This refers not only to the statements the Bible contains but also to the new ideas it inspires. The Bible not only says what it says; it also says what it leads you, the reader, to say as you read it. It is timeless because the truths that come home to the reader are timely.

Referring to the dynamic nature of

the Scriptures, Harry Emerson Fosdick wrote: "The Bible grows in their [those who are experiencing a crisis in their lives] apprehension with the enlarging of their life; new passages become radiant as, in a great landscape, hills and valleys lately unillumined catch the rays of the rising sun." [3] Human need draws new ideas from the Bible as we read it in our desperation.

The author of Isaiah 40, in a burst of insight, expressed the fact that the Word of God was eternal: "The grass withers, the flower fades; but the word of our God will stand for ever." (verse 8) Isaiah was thinking of God's Word alive in his mind and heart rather than of the Bible as such, but it is this same living word that lays hold of us today as we read the Bible.

JESUS THE LIGHT OF THE WORLD

Appropriately this lesson closes with John's reference to Jesus as the light of the world (8:12). John had previously said that the "Word became flesh" (1:14) in referring to the coming of Jesus into the world.

[3] *The Meaning of Faith* (Association Press, 1917), p. 144.

From first to last the Bible is a Jesus-centered book. The Old Testament looks to his advent as it anticipates the coming of the Kingdom; the Gospels tell the story of his ministry; and the epistles and later writings are centered on him as the exalted, living Lord.

Most important, in Jesus we can see the truths that are found throughout the Bible. In him we grasp the truths, not as we would grasp abstract ideas, but as we would embrace a person. The commandments, the insights of the psalmists, and the teachings of the prophets can all be given new meaning through our fellowship with Jesus Christ.

As the light of the world, Jesus would have us not just observe and behold his teachings but take them into our lives as we invite him to enter our hearts. The little girl who was looking at Holman Hunt's canvas "The Light of the World," which portrays Christ knocking at a door, caught the point of the picture. She simply asked, "Did he ever get in?" Jesus still is the Word of God for a changing world.

Helping Adults Become Involved —Ronald E. Schlosser[4]

Preparation of Self and Class

As you begin a new series of lessons for the quarter, it would be helpful to be aware of the four units into which the series is divided. Following today's introductory session, Unit II will deal with "The Changing World of Science and Technology" (sessions 2-6); Unit III will consider "The Changing World of Interpersonal Re-

[4] Ronald E. Schlosser: director, Department of Youth Publications, American Baptist Board of Education and Publication, Valley Forge, Pennsylvania.

lations" (sessions 7-8); and Unit IV will examine "The Changing World of National and International Relations" (sessions 9-13).

Today's session introduces the series by focusing on the place of the Bible in today's changing world. You might reflect on your own attitude toward the Bible and its relevance for your life. Do you honestly believe the Bible can help you meet the challenges of a fast-moving, highly complex society with all its problems and frustrations? Is the Bible a vital force and influence in your life? One can hardly convince others of the relevance of the Bible for their lives if he is not convinced first.

Among the resources and materials you will need for today's session are: several sheets of newsprint and a marking pen or a chalkboard and chalk, pencils and paper, and Bibles for everyone. If by chance you have access to back issues of *Time* magazine, the issue for December 26, 1969, would be a helpful resource to have on hand. It contains listings of the top news events of the 1960's, classified by year and subject area (national, international, medicine, sports, entertainment, and so forth).

As you prepare for today's session, as well as for the succeeding sessions in the quarter, spend some time considering the needs of your class members. This series of lessons may speak to them in a way that no other series in the past has. The issues to be dealt with are vital ones that affect each of us in our day-to-day lives. Pray for each student that he may encounter the truths of the Bible as God's living word for him now.

It is important to determine before the class session begins what you hope to accomplish during the teaching-learning experience. What new understandings and insights might the class gain? What issues do the students need to come to grips with? How might they respond to the main question? How can you help them respond in this way?

To get a hold on today's main question, you might aim for three learning goals:

1. To recognize the extent to which the world is changing.

2. To discern some of the problems brought on by change.

3. To see the Bible as a resource in facing problems in this changing world.

If these goals do not relate to the needs and interests of your class, do not hesitate to revise or rewrite them. It is important that you adopt goals that you feel are pertinent to the background and learning readiness of your own class members.

Presenting the Main Question

Begin the class session by asking the members to consider how the world has changed during the last ten years. Have them reflect back to the year 1962 and try to remember what the world was like then. Who was president? What were the burning issues? What was the international situation like? What books, movies, and television shows were popular?

Distribute pencils and paper and ask each class member to list some of the events or issues making news in the world of 1962. This may be a difficult assignment for some, so you may need to jog their memories a bit by mentioning a few of the following items: President John F. Kennedy; Cuban missile crisis; freedom riders in the South; Berlin Wall; oral polio vaccine; James Meredith at the University of Mississippi; U. S. observers and advisory personnel in Vietnam; Nuclear Test Ban Treaty; publication of Rachel Carson's *Silent Spring* (warning against pesticides); genetic code of the DNA molecule; stage production of Edward Albee's *Who's Afraid of Virginia Woolf?*; introduction of pop art; Pope John XXIII and the Second Vatican Council.

Ask members to share their lists with the total class. Use the chalkboard or newsprint to jot down the things mentioned. You probably will hear such statements as, "So much has happened in ten years that I can't remember back to 1962," or "I can remember some personal things that happened to me, but I can't remember what was going on in the world around me." Accept these statements as honest feelings and point out that the world is changing so rapidly that we can scarcely remember what it was like two years ago, let alone ten years back.

Discuss with the class some of the significant changes that have occurred during the past decade. Mention might be made of automation and cybernation, urbanization and pollution problems, the communications explosion, the sexual revolution, or the increase of crime and violence. How do the members of the class feel about these changes and problems? How do they as Christians expect to face the changes that the next decade will bring?

Developing the Lesson

Indicate that at the time of Moses' death the Israelites were facing changes that would have far-reaching effects in their lives. What were some of these changes? Have the class spend some time in Bible study, preferably in groups of twos. Ask each pair to read Joshua 1:1-9 and to discuss briefly what this passage says about the changes facing the Israelites. What advice did God give to the people through Joshua? (The Israelites would be moving into a new land with unknown dangers and hardships. Their whole way of life would change as they gave up a nomadic existence and settled down in their own land. There would be threats from the Canaanites, not only to their lives but also to their religion. For this reason Joshua urged the people to take the book of the law with them. God's Word would give them guidance and strength to carry on in their new life.) Call the class together and discuss

with the members what this passage reveals about the situation facing the Israelites. The notes by Dr. Laymon and the biblical exegesis will help you guide this part of the discussion.

Ask the class to compare the present day with Bible times. What conditions do we face today that are similar to those of Joshua's day? (Insecurity about the future; threats to our way of life; pressures to corrupt our religion; hope in God's guiding and strengthening care.)

Helping Class Members Act

Ask someone to read aloud Isaiah 40:6-8. Then ask the question: How can the Bible help us face the problems brought on by continual change? Explore with the class the hope brought to us by Christ, as revealed in the Scriptures. Meaning for life can be found in the life and ministry of Jesus Christ. There is no need to face a dark future if one lives in the light of Christ (John 8:12).

On the reverse side of the paper on which the class members listed the events of 1962 have them write some of the truths from God's Word that they feel can help them personally as they face the future. What do they know about Christ that will give them strength and courage? What promises does the Bible give to those who are concerned about finding meaning in life? How can love for God and for one another give one a firm foundation to stand on when values and standards seem to be changing all around?

Conclude with a period of silent prayer in which the class members may reflect on these truths.

Planning for Next Sunday

Ask class members to clip articles and pictures from current magazines and newspapers that describe or illustrate man's dominion over nature. The members are to bring these items to the session next week. | Scripture passages they may want to read and reflect on in advance include Genesis 1:26-28 and Psalms 8.

UNIT II: THE CHANGING WORLD OF SCIENCE AND TECHNOLOGY
Horace R. Weaver

FIVE LESSONS   SEPTEMBER 10–OCTOBER 8

There can be no question that we are in a changing world of science and technology. It is not so much that the world changes but that our knowledge deepens, and so our perspective is forced to change. I recall as a boy hearing that the atom was the last and basic unit of all matter. My father even laughed at the idea that we had dropped atomic bombs on Nagasaki and Hiroshima—the atom could not be split! And here we are in our day—not only have we split the atom but scientists have discovered over two hundred particles (classified in three categories, meson, lepton, and baryon) which make up the proton. So an atom is made up of electrons and protons (with their over two hundred kinds of particles). What a changing perspective science throws upon the physical things around us. And not only so, but scientists are talking about antimatter—a world very much like the one we have, and yet its absolute opposite.

The problem we are trying to face in this unit is to help adults realize that God and his truth do not change, but man's understanding of his truth changes. Man's mind must change as our understanding of God's world changes. Our problem then is to help modern man see the relevance of faith for an age in which great change is taking place in every area of human knowledge. The lesson for September 10, "Man's Dominion in God's World," deals with what it means for man to have dominion—in an age of pollution of water, air, and earth. The lesson for September 17, "Does Scientific Knowledge Threaten Faith?" seeks to help us realize that science is a discipline that leads us to discover the basic truths God created, by which he maintains and sustains our present world. There certainly is no conflict between science and faith—God is the author of both! The lesson for September 24, "Social Change: Work and Leisure," faces the fact that modern man must redefine the concepts of work and leisure. Too many adults have assumed that man's basic duty is to work, with little leisure time for creativity. Leisure time is now opening the doors for a new kind of life for mankind. We must let the insights of the Christlike God speak to these opportunities. The lesson for October 1, "The Battle for Men's Minds," raises the important question of truth, helping us to distinguish between truth and falsehood, distortion, brainwashing, false advertising, and that which is destructive of human understanding and knowledge. One of the basic concerns in this lesson is to help adult Christians face the great values of mass communication for the communication of the Christian gospel. The lesson for October 8, "Christianity and the Secular City," helps us think through the ruthlessness, anonymity, depersonalization, and social frustration of the city. Christian faith is found to speak to the challenge of urban materialism and commercialism.

Audiovisual resources appropriate for use with the lessons of this unit may be found in the introduction to Unit I, page 12. Listings for the entire quarter are given in one location to facilitate ordering well in advance of planned viewing dates.

LESSON 1   SEPTEMBER 10

Man's Dominion in God's World

Background Scripture: Genesis 1:24-31; 2:19-20; Psalms 8

The Main Question —Charles M. Laymon

A news commentator recently said, "When I think of the power in the hands of the President of the United States, I am afraid." When asked what he meant, he referred to the President's political decisions that mean life or death for millions throughout the world, his financial policies that could send the economy of the nation into a tailspin, and his capacity to push the button that could release rockets with atomic warheads. The President of this republic does have a dominion in God's world that is frightening.

Replying to the above statement, someone pointed out that the rest of us also have an area of dominion where our decisions can make a difference; the President is not the only one who is on the spot. What about our spending power, our use of the ballot, our guidance of our families, and our daily moral choices? We too can turn God's wonderful world into a mess. The daily newspapers sometimes seem to indicate that this is exactly what we are doing.

The issue of conservation, which involves our dominion of the earth, has become a very sensitive one in recent years. We are using up our water supply and, at the same time, are polluting it with the output of our sewers. Vessels have reported seeing debris from the land floating in the middle of the Atlantic Ocean. Smoke from cars, homes, and factories has made air unsafe to breathe in certain urban areas of the nation. Our soil is washing away into our streams and rivers so rapidly that in time it will be depleted for farming.

What do all these facts have to do with religion? Is personal responsibility toward God's creation a part of our Christian duty? Why should we discuss this issue in a church school lesson? The biblical passages that follow suggest answers to these questions.

As You Read the Scripture —Martin Rist

Genesis 1:26-28. *Then God said, "Let us make man":* A few years ago a lady phoned to ask me some questions about the creation "story" in Genesis.

23

When I replied, "Which one?" she was greatly astonished. For there actually are two accounts in Genesis, one in Chapters 1:1 through 2:4a and the other in 2:4b-25. According to the first account, mankind was created, both male and female (1:26-27), after the creation of the vegetation (verses 11-12) and animal life (verses 20-25). In the second account man was created first (2:7), then the trees (2:9), next the animals (2:19), and last of all, woman (2:21-23).

According to Genesis 1:27 man was created in the "image of God." This reflects an anthropomorphic concept of deity (ascribing human characteristics to God), corresponding to many other passages in the Old Testament referring to the bodily form of God (Exodus 33:17-23) and also to emotions that are somewhat human in nature (Hosea 11). To be sure, the Hebrews were forbidden to make images of God (Exodus 20:4-6); but it was exceedingly difficult, if not impossible, for these ancient peoples to conceive of God as having no body, devoid of any material form or substance, purely immaterial in nature.

Genesis 1:26 and 1:28b say that man is to have dominion over all the earth and over all the life in the sea, on the earth, and in the sky above. By implication this would also include vegetation. The world and all that is in it are God's, but man is the steward over it all.

Psalms 8. *O* LORD, *our Lord, how majestic is thy name in all the earth!* This short psalm is related to the Genesis accounts of creation and also to

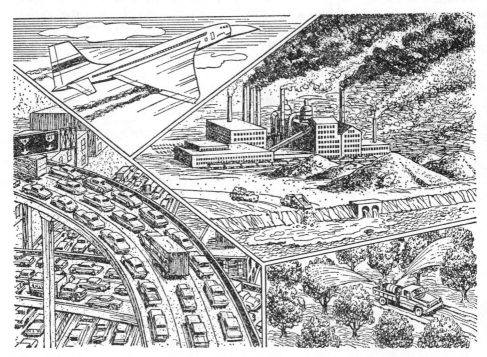

WHAT DOES THE FACT THAT MAN IS POLLUTING AIR AND WATER AT AN EVER-INCREASING RATE HAVE TO DO WITH RELIGION? IS PERSONAL RESPONSIBILITY TOWARD GOD'S CREATION A PART OF OUR CHRISTIAN DUTY?

Psalms 104. It is a beautiful hymn, opening with praise of God whose "name" (that is, God himself) is manifested in all the earth. The psalmist was likewise awed by the majesty of the heavens above (verse 3). I wonder to what extent this awe would have been magnified had he known as much about the universe around him as we today may learn from reading some popular book on astronomy?

But even with his very limited view of the universe the psalmist wondered about man's place in it. Indeed, overawed, he inquired, "What is man that thou art mindful of him?" (verse 4) On further reflection he stated (verse 5) that after all man is but a "little lower than the angels." (King James has a better translation here than the Revised Standard's "than God.") Man is not at all insignificant; for God has given him "dominion over the works" of his divine hands (verse 6), which brings up once more the question of stewardship.

Selected Scripture

King James Version	Revised Standard Version
Genesis 1:26-28	*Genesis 1:26-28*
26 And God said, Let us make man in our image, after our likeness: and let them have dominion over the fish of the sea, and over the fowl of the air, and over the cattle, and over all the earth, and over every creeping thing that creepeth upon the earth.	26 Then God said, "Let us make man in our image, after our likeness; and let them have dominion over the fish of the sea, and over the birds of the air, and over the cattle, and over all the earth, and over every creeping thing that creeps upon the earth." 27 So God created man in his own image, in the image of God he created him; male and female he created them. 28 And God blessed them, and God said to them, "Be fruitful and multiply, and fill the earth and subdue it; and have dominion over the fish of the sea and over the birds of the air and over every living thing that moves upon the earth."
27 So God created man in his own image, in the image of God created he him; male and female created he them.	
28 And God blessed them, and God said unto them, Be fruitful, and multiply, and replenish the earth, and subdue it: and have dominion over the fish of the sea, and over the fowl of the air, and over every living thing that moveth upon the earth.	
Psalms 8	*Psalms 8*
1 O LORD our Lord, how excellent is thy name in all the earth! who hast set thy glory above the heavens.	1 O LORD, our Lord, how majestic is thy name in all the earth! Thou whose glory above the heavens is chanted
2 Out of the mouth of babes and sucklings hast thou ordained strength	2 by the mouth of babes and infants,

because of thine enemies, that thou mightest still the enemy and the avenger.

3 When I consider thy heavens, the work of thy fingers, the moon and the stars, which thou hast ordained;

4 What is man, that thou art mindful of him? and the son of man, that thou visitest him?

5 For thou hast made him a little lower than the angels, and hast crowned him with glory and honour.

6 Thou madest him to have dominion over the works of thy hands; thou hast put all things under his feet:

7 All sheep and oxen, yea, and the beasts of the field;

8 The fowl of the air, and the fish of the sea, and whatsoever passeth through the paths of the seas.

9 O Lord our Lord, how excellent is thy name in all the earth!

Memory Selection: Thou madest him to have dominion over the works of thy hands; thou hast put all things under his feet. (Psalms 8:6)

thou hast founded a bulwark because of thy foes,
to still the enemy and the avenger.

3 When I look at thy heavens, the work of thy fingers,
the moon and the stars which thou hast established;
4 what is man that thou art mindful of him,
and the son of man that thou dost care for him?

5 Yet thou hast made him little less than God,
and dost crown him with glory and honor.
6 Thou hast given him dominion over the works of thy hands;
thou hast put all things under his feet,
7 all sheep and oxen,
and also the beasts of the field,
8 the birds of the air, and the fish of the sea,
whatever passes along the paths of the sea.
9 O Lord, our Lord,
how majestic is thy name in all the earth!

Memory Selection:
Thou hast given him dominion over the works of thy hands;
thou hast put all things under his feet. (Psalms 8:6)

The Scripture and the Main Question —Charles M. Laymon

A MAN GOD CAN TRUST

Did God take a risk when he created the universe and placed man within it? Knowing what capabilities all of us have for making mistakes and doing wrong, for shutting out the good from our lives and letting in (if

not actually promoting) the evil, we would have to conclude that God was risking a lot. He might even be said to have taken a gamble where we are concerned.

The reason God took such a long chance was not only because he had

26

plans for our lives but also because he made something special when he created man. God made us in his own image (Genesis 1:26-27) and only a "little less than God." (Psalms 8:5) The references here are to moral and spiritual likeness rather than to physical similarity. Our understanding of God's nature forbids us from limiting him with a physical body.

Because man is made in God's image, man is unique among all the creatures of earth. He can think God's thoughts after him and by choice enter into God's will. As Halford Luccock said, "There is a real sense in which every man *is* an island. Someone has called man the 'Isle of Man.' Each one has an inner life that is not a social affair, but an individual concern in the sight of God."

Yet this inner communion with God does not rule out interest in others or social concerns. Like God, man is concerned for all men. He is his brother's keeper. Such a man, God concluded, could be trusted *with* and *in* the universe.

WHAT DOMINION MEANS

Man was placed in the universe not only to enjoy it but also, within reason, to be responsible for it. We did not create the universe, but it will respond to our actions. And because life is responsive to our actions we can exercise dominion over what God has created (Genesis 1:26b-28; Psalms 8: 6-8).

G. A. Studdert-Kennedy was chaplain to George V of Great Britain. His service to the soldiers and the youth of his day was unexcelled. He once said that when he stood before God, the Almighty would ask him one question, "Well, what did you make of it?" Here is the basic question all who have dominion, great or small, will be asked.

Luther Burbank would be asked, "What did you make of the soil?" Charles Steinmetz would be asked, "What did you make of electricity?" Albert Einstein, "What did you make of mathematics?" Charles Darwin, "What did you make of life's species?" Phillips Brooks, "What did you make of your pulpit?" John Dewey, "What did you make of education?" Each of us will be asked his own question, related to his own situation.

A GREAT WORLD AND A GREAT GOD

What moves us to want to make the best use of this world, to conserve its resources and increase its productivity? Someone answers that the profit motive is the push behind high productivity. But having dominion over God's creation in the biblical sense is not a question of production and profits. Rather it is a matter of conservation and appreciation; it is a religious concern.

It is no accident that Psalms 8, which deals with creation, man, and dominion over the earth, should open and close with the words, "O LORD, our Lord, how majestic is thy name in all the earth!" (Psalms 8:1, 9) The author is excited over the wonders of the earth and is caught up in a moment of pure worship. True worship is not an empty emotion, without content or meaning. It is an act of deliberate praise, growing out of a deep realization of the greatness of God. In such an expression we forget ourselves and think only of God.

Too often in our time worship has gone out of our religious life. The reason is that we are more concerned with ourselves than with God. To use the words of Will Herberg, "Contemporary American religiosity is converting God into a great cosmic public utility which we find useful in *advanc-*

ing our purposes as individuals and as a nation." With this attitude our sense of responsibility in our sphere of dominion under God is lost. Recognizing our responsibility as stewards, having dominion over the earth, is being God-centered, not self-centered.

HUMILITY BEFORE GOD AND HIS CREATION

Worship of God is not the only response of a true conservationist who is concerned with dominion; he also becomes humble before God and his creation. Like the author of Psalms 8, he feels small and of no account before the greatness of God. "What is man that thou art mindful of him?" he asks (verses 3-4).

In our own time this humility has been a characteristic reaction of our astronauts and those among us who have followed the revelations of the space age. If the author of Psalms 8 were living today, he would more than ever feel insignificant in the presence of the Creator and his creation. The gospel hymn "How Great Thou Art" has taken on a deeper meaning since man has walked on the moon.

This feeling of insignificance, however, is not a downgrading of man so much as an upgrading of God. In our humility we must never forget that we were made in God's image and called to be his children in the Kingdom.

C. S. Lewis described his experience when as a student at Oxford he knelt in submission to God. "The demand," he said, "was simply 'All.' " He had not wanted to give in to God, yet he felt that night in his room that it was inevitable: "That which I greatly feared had at last come upon me. In the Trinity Term of 1929 I gave in, and admitted that God was God, and knelt and prayed." The psalmist of Psalms 8 was doing the same as he wrote.

Helping Adults Become Involved —Ronald E. Schlosser

Preparation of Self and Class

Plan to bring to the session today magazines and newspapers that contain articles or pictures illustrating man's dominion over nature. These items should show both man's use and misuse of his natural environment. Pictures of dams, irrigation canals, forest reclamation projects, underwater and space explorations, and the like would be positive illustrations. Items depicting air and water pollution, garbage disposal, strip mining, offshore oil drilling, and similar activities would be negative illustrations.

Also bring sheets of newsprint, brown wrapping paper, or shelf paper for mounting the various clippings supplied by the class. Scissors, glue, and felt-tipped markers (or crayons) should also be provided.

If you or members of your class have books in the *Life* Science or Nature Library series, bring these to the session also. Volumes dealing with weather, energy, water, earth, sea, and ecology would be particularly relevant.

A 16mm animated film entitled *Urbanissimo* would provide an unusual introduction to today's topic. A farmer, symbolic of non-urban man, is caught up in the blight brought about by urban development, personified by a "city monster." In six minutes' time the film depicts a number of major issues relating to man's use and misuse of the world's natural resources. (See page 13.)

28

To get at the main question raised in today's lesson you might focus your session on three learning goals:

1. To consider the nature and extent of man's dominion over God's world.

2. To investigate what man has learned about God through exploring his world.

3. To appreciate the responsibility God has given man as steward of the world and its resources.

Presenting the Main Question

As the class members arrive, have them mount on newsprint or large sheets of paper the clippings you asked them to bring to the session. If some have neglected to bring clippings on man's control or dominion over the natural world, have them look for such items in the magazines and newspapers you have provided.

The pictures and articles should be mounted in a way that highlights the good and bad effects man has had upon the natural world. One group of clippings might illustrate man's constructive harnessing of natural resources or his efforts at conservation. Another group of clippings could emphasize the harmful results of man's carelessness in nature.

If the animated film *Urbanissimo* is available, plan to show it early in the session. Following the showing, ask the class to list some of the problems depicted in the film. (Mechanization, overpopulation, air and water pollution, extinction of wildlife, depletion of natural resources.) What do these say about "man's stamp on nature"?

Developing the Lesson

Select two persons to read aloud today's Scripture lesson: Genesis 1:26-28 and Psalms 8. Then divide the class into small groups of three or

four members each and ask them to discuss these two questions:

1. Does man's God-given dominion over creation imply complete domination?

2. What should be the extent of man's dominion?

After about ten minutes call the class together and have each group report its response to the questions. The comments by Dr. Laymon and in the biblical exegesis can help guide the class as it grapples with the concepts of dominion and stewardship. Point out that the word *dominion* in Genesis 1:28 can be translated "mastery." Man was given mastery over the natural world. By virtue of the intelligence God has given him, man is able to understand more of the created world than any other living thing; and thus he is able to be master over it. "Being master" does not mean exploiting the earth, however. Rather, using his God-given gifts as a responsible steward, man has the ability to wield the world's resources for his own good.

Move next to consider what we have learned about God through man's explorations of his world. Ask the class to name some of the mysteries of creation that man's scientific research has unlocked. List the various suggestions on the chalkboard. These might include: the makeup of the atom; the genetic code of the DNA molecule; the discovery of quasars as the most distant objects in the universe; the composition of moon rocks; the spectacular array of living organisms in the ocean depths.

Discuss with the class what recent space explorations have revealed about the comparative paradise man has on earth. You might allude to the observations by our astronauts that the moon is like a dead, burned out cinder. In light of what we know about the moon and other planets in our solar system, what can we say about the creative nature of God and his provision for us on earth?

Consider next what man himself reveals about his Creator. What does man as a created being reveal about God, whose image he bears? Look again at Psalms 8 and the comments in the biblical exegesis. Man's glory is his own creative nature. What has man accomplished that has brought good to the earth and its inhabitants? Ask the class to mention some of man's contributions to the world. List these on the chalkboard. These would include advances in medical knowledge (vaccines against polio and German measles, heart transplants, artificial organs, treatments for leukemia and Parkinson's disease); environmental control (weather satellites, flood control, air conditioning, solar energy); industrial production (computers, automation, packaging); and other areas of scientific research (development of the laser, transistors, television, communications satellites, and so forth).

Refer to Dr. Laymon's illustration about G. A. Studdert-Kennedy and to the various men mentioned in the paragraph following the illustration. Pose the question: How are we using our talents to enhance the world in which we live?

If time permits, you might explore with the class the meaning of the name Adam. Possibly derived from the Hebrew word for earth (*dhamah*), this name for man (*adham*) might better be translated "earthling." Thus Genesis 3:19 might be paraphrased: "Remember, earthling, that you are earth. You were formed from earth; you are to care for earth; from earth will come your sustenance; and to earth you will ultimately return."

Man is not just *on* this earth; he is *of* the earth and *for* the earth. It is his responsibility to care for it as he cares for himself.

Helping Class Members Act

Call the attention of the class members to the clippings on display that illustrate man's despoiling of the natural world. Indicate that though Psalms 8 speaks of man's glory, these clippings give evidence of man's shame. Moreover, man is not only a despoiler of nature; he is also a despoiler of his fellow man. Because of sin, man has exploited persons as well as things.

Pose the question: How can man become what God meant him to be? Allow time for group discussion. The answer to this question, of course, is found in the person and work of Jesus Christ. Jesus is a perfect example of what God meant man to be.

Conclude the session by having the class suggest ways whereby man, in right relation to God and to his fellow man through Christ, can begin to recognize what his relation to the natural world around him should be. How one acts speaks eloquently of what one is. What implications does this have for man as a steward of God's earth and a spiritual heir with Christ?

Planning for Next Sunday

Ask for two volunteers to prepare to debate (or discuss) the following questions: Does scientific knowledge threaten faith? Ask one person to take the affirmative position and one the negative position.

Class members may want to read the background Scripture for the next session in advance: Job 38; 42; Proverbs 3:13-20; and 1 Corinthians 1 and 2.

Does Scientific Knowledge Threaten Faith?

Background Scripture: Job 38; 42; Proverbs 3:13-20;
1 Corinthians 1 and 2

The Main Question —Charles M. Laymon

The discussion in the class for young adults was a heated one, dealing with the relation between science and religion. One young salesman of data processing machines said, "By now everyone knows the new knowledge of the universe that science has given us. Why knock it?" A housewife with children in school who were just beginning their science studies replied, "It's not that simple; already my youngsters are bringing home questions that I can't answer from the Bible." A third member chimed in, "I solve the problem this way. I do my religious thinking with one part of my mind and my scientific thinking with another. And I keep the two separate." Still another member— this time a young science teacher in a junior high school—broke into the discussion. He asked, "If this is a universe with one God behind it, truth must be one. Right? There can be no basic conflict between the real truths of science and the real truths of religion."

What would you have said had you been a member of this class? Does scientific knowledge—if it is true knowledge—actually threaten faith? Would it not be a revelation of God as well as any other truth from whatever source it comes? Do all scientists agree in their conclusions? Do all biblical scholars agree in their interpretations of Scripture?

The biblical passages for this lesson will be helpful in answering these questions.

As You Read the Scripture —Martin Rist

1 Corinthians 2:6-16. *Yet among the mature we do impart wisdom:* The ancient Hebrews were not versed in science or philosophy, as were some of the peoples of their time. Apart from elementary instruction in reading, writing, and arithmetic, their education was limited to the study of Scripture, especially the Law and its interpretation; it was primarily religious education. This situation was even true of the rabbis, for they wanted little to do with pagan culture and learning.

This is not to deny that the Hebrews had wise men. Some of their wisdom, practical rather than philosophical and scientific, has been preserved in the wisdom literature of the Bible, such as Proverbs, Ecclesiastes, Job, certain psalms in the Old Testament, and Ecclesiasticus (which is well worth reading and pondering over) in the Apocrypha. In the main, Hebrew wisdom literature consisted of proverbial, pithy sayings, most of them in poetic form, dealing with morals, ethics, and everyday living against a background of Jewish monotheism.

A striking example of a somewhat different type of wisdom literature is

31

presented in one of the background Scripture selections, Job 38. This magnificent poem, which represents God as speaking out of the whirlwind as he recounts the creation of the world, the sea, the rain, the dew, the ice, the heavenly constellations, and the wild animals, emphasizes the mighty power and inscrutable wisdom of God in contrast to man's finite and limited power and wisdom.

An important development among the Jews was the rise of a professional class of teachers of the Law and its application to the various conditions of human living. Gamaliel was "a teacher of the law." (Acts 5:34) Ezra was traditionally considered to have been the first in a long line of these scribes, learned in the Jewish law (Nehemiah 8:1-8).

Paul, as we know, was the product of two cultures—the Jewish and the Greek. His Jewish background, however, was mainly that of the Dispersion, not that of Palestine. According to Acts 22:3, he sat "at the feet of Gamaliel"; but this need not mean that he was a rabbi. Paul states in Galatians 1:14 that he was "extremely zealous" for the "traditions" of the fathers, that is, for the Jewish law. Furthermore, he no doubt had some knowledge of Graeco-Roman wisdom, of philosophy and science; for he was a native of the Graeco-Roman city Tarsus. It is not necessary to suppose that Paul was extensively trained in the Tarsian schools; in fact, in his letters he displays little knowledge of the subjects that would be taught in such schools.

Some of Paul's knowledge may have been picked up incidentally. According to Acts 17:22-31, when he was in Athens, Paul engaged in discussions with the Jews in the synagogue. He also held disputations in the marketplace with those who passed by, including Epicurean and Stoic philosophers. In the speech attributed to him in the Areopagus he actually quotes with full approval from a poem attributed to Epimenides: "In him we live and move and have our being," and from Aratus, "For we are indeed his offspring." But these brief phrases could have been picked up in the marketplace.

However, in 1 Corinthians 2, Paul displays a negative attitude toward Greek wisdom, "the wisdom of this age." He was writing to a cosmopolitan church in a worldly city. Its members had been disturbed during Paul's absence by Apollos, a Hellenistic (Greek) Jewish Christian from Alexandria, the actual center of Greek learning. He was a smooth talker, well versed in Scripture and probably in philosophy.

This incident may account for Paul's rejection of wisdom in 1 Corinthians 1:20: "Where is the wise man? Where is the scribe? Where is the debater of this age? Has not God made foolish the wisdom of the world?" He continues in the beginning of Chapter 2: "I did not come proclaiming to you the testimony of God in lofty words or wisdom," as perhaps Apollos had done. He avers that he knew nothing "except Jesus Christ and him crucified." Actually, he does "impart wisdom"; but it is not the "wisdom of this age," which is transitory (verse 6). Rather it is a "secret and hidden wisdom of God," which was decreed for "our glorification," that is, for salvation and immortality. Paul seemingly quotes from Scripture to support his argument, "What no eye has seen, nor ear heard, nor the heart of man conceived, what God has prepared for those who love him" (verse 9); but actually this quotation is not from the Old Testament. No written source for it has been found to this day. God's saving wisdom is only revealed "through the Spirit" to those who "possess the Spirit" (verse 13); it is not taught by human means.

Since Paul is directing his words to a specific situation in Corinth, it may be that he had not given up the wisdom received from his Jewish and Greek background but is hoping to counteract the unsettling teachings presented by Apollos.

Selected Scripture

King James Version	Revised Standard Version
1 Corinthians 2:6-16	*1 Corinthians 2:6-16*

1 Corinthians 2:6-16

6 Howbeit we speak wisdom among them that are perfect: yet not the wisdom of this world, nor of the princes of this world, that come to nought:

7 But we speak the wisdom of God in a mystery, even the hidden wisdom, which God ordained before the world unto our glory:

8 Which none of the princes of this world knew: for had they known it, they would not have crucified the Lord of glory.

9 But as it is written, Eye hath not seen, nor ear heard, neither have entered into the heart of man, the things which God hath prepared for them that love him.

10 But God hath revealed them unto us by his Spirit: for the Spirit searcheth all things, yea, the deep things of God.

11 For what man knoweth the things of a man, save the spirit of man which is in him? even so the things of God knoweth no man, but the Spirit of God.

12 Now we have received, not the spirit of the world, but the spirit which is of God; that we might know the things that are freely given to us of God.

13 Which things also we speak, not in the words which man's wisdom teacheth, but which the Holy Ghost teacheth; comparing spiritual things with spiritual.

1 Corinthians 2:6-16

6 Yet among the mature we do impart wisdom, although it is not a wisdom of this age or of the rulers of this age, who are doomed to pass away. 7 But we impart a secret and hidden wisdom of God, which God decreed before the ages for our glorification. 8 None of the rulers of this age understood this; for if they had, they would not have crucified the Lord of glory. 9 But, as it is written,

"What no eye has seen, nor ear heard,
nor the heart of man conceived,
what God has prepared for those who love him,"

10 God has revealed to us through the Spirit. For the Spirit searches everything, even the depths of God. 11 For what person knows a man's thoughts except the spirit of the man which is in him? So also no one comprehends the thoughts of God except the Spirit of God. 12 Now we have received not the spirit of the world, but the Spirit which is from God, that we might understand the gifts bestowed on us by God. 13 And we impart this in words not taught by human wisdom but taught by the Spirit, interpreting spiritual truths to those who possess the Spirit.

14 But the natural man receiveth not the things of the Spirit of God: for they are foolishness unto him: neither can he know them, because they are spiritually discerned.

15 But he that is spiritual judgeth all things, yet he himself is judged of no man.

16 For who hath known the mind of the Lord, that he may instruct him? But we have the mind of Christ.

Memory Selection: **Prove all things; hold fast that which is good. (1 Thessalonians 5:21)**

14 The unspiritual man does not receive the gifts of the Spirit of God, for they are folly to him, and he is not able to understand them because they are spiritually discerned. 15 The spiritual man judges all things, but is himself to be judged by no one. 16 "For who has known the mind of the Lord so as to instruct him?" But we have the mind of Christ.

Memory Selection: **Test everything; hold fast what is good. (1 Thessalonians 5:21)**

The Scripture and the Main Question —Charles M. Laymon

SCIENTIFIC KNOWLEDGE

Science has accomplished so much in recent decades that the very word *science* has an almost magical tone to it. Yet scientific knowledge is not absolute; scientists disagree among themselves as much as theologians. For instance, at present there are two leading views concerning the origin of the universe. One is the "Big Bang" theory that the universe came into being by the explosion of a fireball some ten billion years ago. A rival theory is called the "Steady State" concept of continuous creation. It holds that although the universe has always been in a steady state, matter is continuously being fed into it, possibly one atom at a time. Thus the universe continues to expand. Which view is correct?

Science has more or less reached agreement in such areas as energy, motion, gravity, and matter; although even here there are often new breakthroughs of knowledge requiring a readjustment in conclusions. The main point here is that science seeks to base its conclusions on factual data that can be measured, analyzed, weighed, charted, and tested by scientific tools. Thus its conclusions lie mainly in the physical world.

Other areas of knowledge exist, however, where scientific tools are not adequate. Such concerns as beauty, values, motivation of persons, purpose, and ultimate meanings and causality belong to a different sphere or intellectual discipline. Here we find philosophy, religion, psychology, and sociology making their studies and drawing their own conclusions in line with their special abilities to discover truth.

Scientists should not seek to browbeat religionists; neither should religionists seek to browbeat scientists. Each should attempt to recognize the merits of the other, to listen thoughtfully to what the other says, and be free to draw his own conclusions. Neither discipline needs to "threaten" the other.

A BIBLICAL ILLUSTRATION

The situation behind the biblical section for this lesson provides an excellent illustration of the above issue. In this case it was not science versus religion but Greek philosophy versus Christian thinking. The philosophers in Corinth were poking fun at the Christians as those who were simple-minded compared to themselves. Christians, they said, did not use philosophical jargon or speak in "lofty words or wisdom." (1 Corinthians 2:1) This criticism was giving the Christians an inferiority complex.

Paul answered the Greek critics by saying that he came only to preach "Jesus Christ and him crucified." (verse 2) There was a wisdom here that went deeper than the high-sounding theories of the philosophers. Christian preaching may have seemed to some to be so much foolishness; but to those who understood the cross, it was both the power and the wisdom of God (1 Corinthians 1:22-24).

CHRISTIAN TRUTH

Christian truth can be understood only from the inside. We have to experience it in order to know it. Looking on from the outside, observing the church's practices, reading about its history—all this is good but not good enough. Only when one can say out of a personal realization *it was for me* Jesus died, can the cross have meaning. Spiritual truth must be spiritually perceived to be known.

Paul says just this in our passage from First Corinthians. The wisdom of the Christian is given to him by the Spirit of God: "God has revealed [it] to us through the Spirit." (2:10) He then adds, "Now we have received not the spirit of the world, but the Spirit which is from God, that we might understand the gifts bestowed on us by God." (verse 12)

Here is the point where scientists must understand Christian truth. It is personal and spiritual and cannot be measured by their physical instru-

ments. A laboratory in the science department is ill equipped to test Christian truth. Its sphere is the material order. Only here can it speak a final word.

Christian truth, on the other hand, is tested in the laboratory of human experience. Does life bear out the truths of the Sermon on the Mount? Does daily living demonstrate the validity of the Ten Commandments? What kind of character does genuine Christian discipleship produce?

The answers to these questions can be discovered only in personal and group experience. Bishop Gerald Kennedy, in expressing the need for a personal knowledge of Christianity if we are to witness to it with authority, quoted the answer some men in a Kentucky jail gave to a social worker who asked them why their families and friends had not taught them to write: "You can't teach what you don't know any more than you can go back to where you ain't been." How true of teaching Christian truth!

WHERE SCIENCE AND RELIGION MEET

The scientist approaches life from his particular bent and skill; the Christian also approaches life from his own insight and experience. Both are seeking for truth, each in his own way. This search naturally brings them together.

Harry Emerson Fosdick once wrote: "Wherever peace has come between science and religion, one finds a realm where the boundaries between the two are acknowledged and respected. Ask *now* the question, What makes it rain? There is a scientific answer in terms of natural laws concerning atmospheric pressure and condensation. There is also a religious answer, since behind all laws and through them runs the will of God." [5]

[5] *The Meaning of Faith*, p. 171.

The scientist *as a person* may be a practicing Christian, and the Christian as a person may be a brilliant scientist. Many of each have been and now are. A student came upon the great scientist Louis Pasteur bent over his microscope. He did not wish to disturb his teacher, so he quietly started to leave. Pasteur looked up, and the student said to him, "I thought you were praying." Pasteur replied, "I was," and returned to his microscope.

Helping Adults Become Involved —Ronald E. Schlosser

Preparation of Self and Class

More than likely there are persons in your class who could identify with the various points of view expressed in the illustration used by Dr. Laymon in the section "The Main Question." As you prepare for today's session, you ought to consider where your class members are in terms of their understanding of the relation between science and religion. If most of your class members have a predominate scientific bent, you may need to deal at some length with the nature and value of religious truth. On the other hand, if the majority of your members have a strong religious faith and a somewhat suspicious attitude toward science, you may need to help them gain a greater appreciation for the truths science can contribute to one's understanding of God's universe. In other words, be sensitive to your students' readiness to deal with issues that may cause controversy or bring about sharp differences of opinion.

During the week contact the class members who agreed to debate (or discuss) the question: Does scientific knowledge threaten faith? Be prepared to share with them the helps given by Dr. Laymon in the preceding section, "The Scripture and the Main Question." You may also have other resources that can provide helpful background information. The book *Science and Religion* by Harold K. Schilling examines the relationship between these two disciplines and attempts to show how each addresses itself to different sets of questions. Science seeks answers to such questions as What? When? and How? while religion responds to such questions as Why? Whence? and Whither? In a book aimed particularly at laymen, entitled *Faith That Makes Sense*, J. Edwin Orr gives a number of examples to demonstrate that religious faith can indeed stand the tests that scientific inquirers may bring to bear upon it. Chapter 1 in this book is especially relevant to today's theme.

The learning goal for today's session is to explore the relationship between scientific knowledge and religious faith. The opening debate (or discussion) should begin the process of exploration, and the other activities that follow ought to help your group come to some conclusions about the main question: Does scientific knowledge threaten faith? You might write this question on the chalkboard or on newsprint to keep the focus of today's session before the class.

Presenting the Main Question

Introduce the main question and the persons from the class who will be debating it. If a panel discussion seems to be a more appropriate way to present the main question, arrange a table and some chairs at the front of the room for use by the participants. You as teacher should act as moderator of the debate or the panel discussion.

Allow approximately ten minutes for whatever formal presentation is made and then ask for questions and comments from the rest of the class.

Developing the Lesson

At an early point in the discussion that follows the debate or panel presentation have the class members work on a definition of terms. What do the members understand *scientific knowledge* to be? How would they define *faith?* Dr. Laymon suggests that scientific knowledge is factual data that can be measured, analyzed, weighed, and tested. Hebrews 11:1 defines faith as "the assurance of things hoped for, the conviction of things not seen." Religious truth, which is comprehended by faith, can be understood only from the inside, says Dr. Laymon. Such truth is revealed to the believer by God, through his Spirit (1 Corinthians 2:10).

What are the dangers of accepting scientific knowledge without considering its religious implications? Ask half of your class members to consider this question and the other half to consider the following question: What are the dangers of clinging to a simplistic faith that belittles scientific knowledge? Allow two or three minutes for the members to think quietly about their respective question, and then discuss each in turn.

Concerning the first question, new scientific discoveries often create ethical problems having deep religious implications. For example, oral contraceptive pills have brought about a major re-evaluation of our society's sex mores and standards. The breakthrough in experiments with the DNA molecule has vast implications for parents who may want to determine and regulate the genes of their future

offspring. The ability to transplant hearts and other vital organs has far-reaching religious implications, as does science's ability to keep alive a human organism by means of highly sophisticated machines. Some scientists say that the religious or ethical implications of their discoveries are really not their concern. They maintain that their field is strictly science. Would your class members agree?

Concerning the second question, have your group ponder how valuable a simplistic, unthinking faith is in a highly complex, scientific world. Will such a faith help a person to function adequately in his world? How effective can this person's witness be to persons around him who need a relevant faith for themselves? Will the mind set of this person hinder his growth as a well-rounded human being?

A study of what the apostle Paul had to say about the wisdom of God and the wisdom of man may help the class come to grips with the issues brought into focus by the preceding questions. Have someone read aloud 1 Corinthians 2:6-16, and then ask the class members to try to summarize in one sentence the main point of this passage. Pass out pencils and paper and give the members about five minutes to do this assignment. They may work on it individually or informally in groups of two or three.

When you feel the members have spent an adequate amount of time working on their summaries, ask them to share their sentences with the rest of the class. Refer to the biblical exegesis for guidance in discussing the thrust of this passage.

Helping Class Members Act

In addition to the issues raised by the questions in the preceding paragraphs, there are several perennial problems Christians usually find themselves discussing whenever they confront the science-religion controversy. The biggest one seems to be the question of evolution versus literal creation. Since this issue can spark a heated discussion that can easily get out of hand if there are a number of highly vocal class members, care should be taken if you decide to examine it. However, if the class members have come to the conclusion that scientific knowledge ought not to threaten one's faith, then they should approach this last part of the session with open and seeking minds.

The book by J. Edwin Orr mentioned earlier, *Faith That Makes Sense,* has a helpful chapter on the evolution/creation question (Chapter 3). Other help can be found in Volume I of *The Interpreter's Bible,* pertaining to the early chapters of Genesis. In effect, these resources see no conflict between the theories of science and the claims of religion. The story of creation in Genesis is basically concerned with the question of *why* man began rather than with *how* he began. Science can speculate as to the how; religion affirms the why. Regardless of the method used, God created the world and all that is within it. Science can neither prove nor disprove this religious truth. It is a realm of knowledge outside the sphere of science. It is a realm comprehended by faith.

Your class members may wish to discuss other questions about the relation between science and religion. Approach these in the same manner as has been suggested above—with an open and receptive mind. Help the members see the distinction between scientific truth and religious truth. Remind members of the questions science can answer and those religion can answer. Then ask God to lead you to greater wisdom by his Spirit.

Planning for Next Sunday

Ask the class members to think about this question: Should Sunday (or Sabbath) laws be strengthened and enforced? Some members may wish to gather the opinions of friends and acquaintances and report these at the next session.

The background Scripture is Genesis 3:17-19; Exodus 20:8-11; Ecclesiastes 2:1 through 3:9; and Colossians 3:17, 23.

LESSON 3   SEPTEMBER 24

Social Change: Work and Leisure

Background Scripture: Genesis 3:17-19; Exodus 20:8-11;
Ecclesiastes 2:1 through 3:9; Colossians 3:17, 23

The Main Question —Charles M. Laymon

An elderly gentleman put down his paper and said to his son, who held an office in the local labor union, "Boy, you have got it all wrong. All you men want is less hours, larger benefits, and more pay." He had been reading about the union's proposed demands of the automobile industry.

The son replied, "Dad, you are the one who has got it all wrong. Life was not intended to be a grind. Men are supposed to *live* as well as to work. We are due a larger share in the profits that come from our work. We need more time to be with our families, more leisure to be ourselves; and that's what it is all about. Times have changed."

Another young man of my acquaintance said to his father, "Dad, you were fortunate that your work gave you deep personal satisfaction. I work mainly to provide security and enjoyment for my family. What I do is just a job to me." This young man was successful, but his motivation in his work was providing a good life for his family rather than working for the joy of working.

By contrast, Dr. Charles Mayo of the famous clinic kept the following motto on his office wall: "There is no fun like work." Commenting upon it, he said, "To be without work is almost to be without life. For it is work which creates interest in life."

These contrasting statements raise the question of the place and purpose of work in life. Should work be a burden or a blessing? What about leisure? The biblical passages that follow will be helpful in facing this issue.

As You Read the Scripture —Martin Rist

Exodus 20:8-11. *Remember the sabbath day, to keep it holy:* Even though labor was implied to be a curse on man for Adam's sin ("In toil you shall eat of it [the ground] all the days of your life," Genesis 3:17), actually work of all kinds, and especially manual labor, was highly esteemed by the Jews. By contrast indolence and sloth were a curse ("Through sloth the roof sinks in, and through indolence the house leaks," Ecclesiastes 10:18). The lazy man was urged to take the ever busy ant as an example: "Go to the ant, O sluggard." (Proverbs 6:6) Or, "a little folding of the hands to rest, and poverty will come upon you like a vagabond." (Proverbs 6:10-11)

In Jesus' day a Jewish boy was taught some manual craft, even though he might be studying to be a rabbi. Jesus learned the skill of a carpenter, and Paul was a tentmaker (or possibly a leather worker) ; and both without shame. In contrast to the Jewish attitude the Greeks and Romans tended to look upon manual labor with disfavor. This was in part because in the days of Jesus and Paul much of the manual labor and even some of the skilled craftsmanship were performed by slaves, who were very numerous as the result of wars of conquest. Consequently, a free man was reluctant to labor lest he be disgraced.

In Exodus 20:8-11 the Sabbath was to be kept holy, was to be a day of rest, because God himself rested on the seventh day following six days of creative work. (Deuteronomy 5:12-15 says that the command was in remembrance of the Exodus.) Accordingly, the Sabbath (from sunset on Friday to sunset on Saturday) was blessed and hallowed; and all unnecessary work was forbidden on this day of rest.

Yet the Sabbath was by no means a day for idleness and indolence. It was especially set apart for prayer and meditation, for the reading and studying of the Law, for attendance upon the synagogue services, and for Temple worship and sacrifices. The Sabbath was a meaningful day, one when the family joined in religious activities of one kind or another, including the Sabbath meal. It was a day of joy and feasting, not of sadness and fasting.

Attention is usually directed to the command to abstain from work on the Sabbath to the neglect of the injunction in Exodus 20:9: "Six days you shall labor, and do all your work." Jews were to work in imitation of God, who worked during the six days of his creative activity. Consequently, not only in antiquity but down to our day, the Jews have been characterized by their industry, whether in manual trades, in business, in the arts and professions, or in their studies.

Ecclesiastes 2:4-11, 24-25. *I made great works:* For the Jews productive labor was honorable and excellent; but the storing up of wealth for its own sake was evil, as was luxurious living. This is the meaning of these verses. The man who had stored up many goods and much wealth and who lived in luxurious idleness became sated with his many possessions and pleasures; for all this "was vanity and a striving after wind, and there was nothing to be gained under the sun." (verse 11) Everything is temporary; death overtakes both the wise man and the fool (2:16). A man cannot take his wealth with him but must leave it to someone who did not earn it to enjoy. Finally, whatever a man does have and enjoys is "from the hand of God." (verse 24)

This reminds me of the parable of the rich fool (Luke 12:16-21). He had filled his barns with grain and other goods, and then said to himself, "Take your ease, eat, drink, be merry." (verse 19*b*) But he died that very night. So it is with one who "lays up treasure for himself, and is not rich toward God." (verse 21)

Selected Scripture

King James Version

Exodus 20:8-11

8 Remember the sabbath day, to keep it holy.

9 Six days shalt thou labour, and do all thy work:

10 But the seventh day is the sabbath of the LORD thy God: in it thou shalt not do any work, thou, nor thy son, nor thy daughter, thy manservant, nor thy maidservant, nor thy cattle, nor thy stranger that is within thy gates:

11 For in six days the LORD made heaven and earth, the sea, and all that in them is, and rested the seventh day: wherefore the LORD blessed the sabbath day, and hallowed it.

Revised Standard Version

Exodus 20:8-11

8 "Remember the sabbath day, to keep it holy. 9 Six days you shall labor, and do all your work; 10 but the seventh day is a sabbath to the LORD your God; in it you shall not do any work, you, or your son, or your daughter, your manservant, or your maidservant, or your cattle, or the sojourner who is within your gates; 11 for in six days the LORD made heaven and earth, the sea, and all that is in them, and rested the seventh day; therefore the LORD blessed the sabbath day and hallowed it."

Ecclesiastes 2:4-11, 24-25

4 I made me great works; I builded me houses; I planted me vineyards:

5 I made me gardens and orchards, and I planted trees in them of all kind of fruits:

6 I made me pools of water, to water therewith the wood that bringeth forth trees:

7 I got me servants and maidens, and had servants born in my house; also I had great possessions of great and small cattle above all that were in Jerusalem before me:

8 I gathered me also silver and gold, and the peculiar treasure of kings and of the provinces: I gat me men singers and women singers, and the delights of the sons of men, as musical instruments, and that of all sorts.

9 So I was great, and increased more than all that were before me in Jerusalem: also my wisdom remained with me.

10 And whatsoever mine eyes desired I kept not from them, I withheld not my heart from any joy; for my heart rejoiced in all my labour: and this was my portion of all my labour.

11 Then I looked on all the works that my hands had wrought, and on the labour that I had laboured to do; and, behold, all was vanity and vexation of spirit, and there was no profit under the sun.

. . . .

24 There is nothing better for a man, than that he should eat and drink, and that he should make his soul enjoy good in his labour. This also I saw, that it was from the hand of God.

25 For who can eat, or who else can hasten hereunto, more than I?

Memory Selection: **Whether therefore ye eat, or drink, or whatsoever ye do, do all to the glory of God. (1 Corinthians 10:31)**

Ecclesiastes 2:4-11, 24-25

4 I made great works; I built houses and planted vineyards for myself; 5 I made myself gardens and parks, and planted in them all kinds of fruit trees. 6 I made myself pools from which to water the forest of growing trees. 7 I bought male and female slaves, and had slaves who were born in my house; I had also great possessions of herds and flocks, more than any who had been before me in Jerusalem. 8 I also gathered for myself silver and gold and the treasure of kings and provinces; I got singers, both men and women, and many concubines, man's delight.

9 So I became great and surpassed all who were before me in Jerusalem; also my wisdom remained with me. 10 And whatever my eyes desired I did not keep from them; I kept my heart from no pleasure, for my heart found pleasure in all my toil, and this was my reward for all my toil. 11 Then I considered all that my hands had done and the toil I had spent in doing it, and behold, all was vanity and a striving after wind, and there was nothing to be gained under the sun.

. . . .

24 There is nothing better for a man than that he should eat and drink, and find enjoyment in his toil. This also, I saw, is from the hand of God; 25 for apart from him who can eat or who can have enjoyment?

Memory Selection: **Whether you eat or drink, or whatever you do, do all to the glory of God. (1 Corinthians 10:31)**

The Scripture and the Main Question —Charles M. Laymon

THE SACRAMENT OF LABOR

An unknown author wrote:

This for the day of life I ask:
Some all-absorbing useful task;
And when 'tis wholly, truly done,
A tranquil rest at set of sun.

The philosophy of labor in these lines embraces more than first meets the eye. One's work should absorb his entire being; it should be useful and thus contribute to the welfare of others. Work should be carried out with high standards, and it should lead to personal satisfaction. Under these conditions, work is a kind of sacrament; it is a calling or vocation.

This philosophy of work is in line with the commandment: "Six days you shall labor, and do all your work." (Exodus 20:9) God intended that men should work. From first to last the Bible takes this position.

On one occasion Jesus said, "My Father is working still, and I am working." (John 5:17) God works; Christ works; man works. Here is another kind of trinity, joining God and man. Even before Jesus began his ministry of proclaiming the kingdom of God, he was a carpenter and known as a carpenter's son.

The Scriptures also make clear that a workman should be paid for his services. The apostle Paul told the Corinthians that he had a right to require a contribution from them for his work, although he did not press for pay, fearing that they would conclude he was a professional with ulterior motives. He said that Jesus himself "commanded that those who proclaim the gospel should get their living by the gospel." (1 Corinthians 9:14)

A DAY FOR REST

Leisure is important along with work. It is part of the rhythm of life —work and leisure alternating with each other. The Sabbath was a seventh day, set apart for God. It was a day of rest for man, even as God "rested on the seventh day." (Genesis 2:2) The Sabbath was to be kept holy since it was a segment of time that belonged to God.

Many think of leisure only as time away from work. During this period any activity that brings restoration of mind and body is proper and good. For them the Sabbath is an occasion for leisure. The intention of the commandment to keep the Sabbath as a day when no work shall be done, however, is that it should provide a kind of leisure that renews life *because it is focused upon the things of God.*

A friend of mine was pastor of a suburban church in a city where excellent fishing and boating could be had. Both of these provided leisure opportunity for his members, and they made the most of their situation. Late celebrations after the football games on Saturday night kept them from attending church on Sunday morning in the fall, and weekends at the lake took them away from church in the spring and summer. There was plenty of leisure, but little of it was centered in God.

A BROADER QUESTION

The broader question of how to use the large segments of leisure time a computerized society will enjoy will be facing us in the near future. What we now do in a five-day workweek may be accomplished through the use of computers in a three- or even two-

42

day workweek. Society must provide incentives and profitable means for spending the extra time off from work, or we may degenerate into a generation of sluggards.

A religious issue is involved here because this problem involves the enrichment of personal life or its impoverishment. Growing wealthy, we may become poor because our energies are not being used creatively. Already chambers of commerce and civic organizations are projecting their plans for a meaningful use of leisure time.

The church also is beginning to face the question of what more free time will mean for the spiritual life of the nation. Will there be a place for additional study opportunities during the week? What new church-sponsored community programs will be needed? Will the church buildings be opened for activities the whole week through?

Currently there is a dearth of prepared leaders in the church. Capable people do not have time to assume responsibilities. Securing an adequate staff of church school teachers is becoming ever more difficult, according to reports coming from directors of Christian education. Perhaps more leisure time will be the answer to this predicament.

Nothing Apart From God

The biblical answer to the question for today and tomorrow is that work and leisure both must find their focus in God.

The Book of Ecclesiastes is a writing in which a "preacher" philosophizes about life. His words concerning labor are significant. He looks back on his days of toil and says, "I hated all my toil in which I had toiled under the sun, seeing that I must leave it to the man who will come after me." (Ecclesiastes 2:18) He could not be sure that his successor would carry on the good work he had done.

This is the concern of a man who had put his heart into his work and who cared about the outcome of his labor. Many a father would like to see his son continue his profession. A dentist of my acquaintance said to me one day, "I wish my son had wanted to go into dentistry. I have a clinic of my own and a large practice I would like to turn over to him. But he chose internal medicine instead. Now who will continue my work?" He knew that his son must choose the kind of work he liked most. Yet he was troubled about the future of his own professional interests.

Even though the preacher of Ecclesiastes had this same concern about the future of his work, he said, "There is nothing better for a man than that he should eat and drink, and find enjoyment in his toil." (verse 24a) Labor and leisure are bound together here.

The final conclusion the "preacher" draws is that apart from God no one can eat and have enjoyment (2:25). All life, involving work and leisure, is rooted and grounded in God. From God alone come wisdom, knowledge, and joy. Even the humblest task when performed to God's glory becomes a spiritual sacrament, the preacher says. Centuries later Brother Lawrence discovered this as he washed his pots and pans to the glory of God in the monastery kitchen.

Helping Adults Become Involved —Ronald E. Schlosser

Preparation of Self and Class

In preparing for today's session read the articles on *Sabbath* and *Lord's Day* in a Bible dictionary. Think through the meaning that the concept of the Sabbath has for you. Review some of Jesus' teachings about the Sabbath (Matthew 12:1-14; Mark 2: 23 through 3:6). Consider to what extent Christians are called upon to keep Sunday—their Sabbath—holy.

You might consider using the film *Of Time, Work and Leisure* to get at the various implications of today's main question. The thirty-minute motion picture presents modern ideas about leisure and free time by means of dramatization, film clips, and commentary. (See page 12.)

Prior to the session, duplicate enough copies of the following opinion poll so that each member may have his own set to respond to:

OPINION POLL

After each statement write whether you agree or disagree. If you have mixed feelings, write "unsure."

1. A person should find meaning and purpose for his life primarily through his work.

2. Work is a blessing rather than a curse.

3. Anybody who really wants to work can find a job.

4. Idleness makes a man grow lazy and leads to his ruin.

5. It is good that man is gaining increasing amounts of leisure time.

Read through the introduction to the main question by Dr. Laymon. Today's session might aim at achieving the following learning goals:

1. To evaluate the changing concepts of work and leisure brought about by scientific technology.

2. To consider the place of work and leisure in the life of modern man.

3. To explore the meaning of Sabbath observance in biblical times and its implications for Christians today.

Presenting the Main Question

If you plan to use the audiovisual mentioned above, schedule its showing at the beginning of the session to insure time for adequate follow-up discussion. Explore with your class the various questions the film raises in relation to today's theme. Then move to the Bible study activity described below in the section "Developing the Lesson."

Another way to begin the session is to distribute copies of the opinion poll, asking your class members to respond to the statements as directed. Allow about five minutes for the members to do their individual work and then discuss the statements as a total group. The comments by Dr. Laymon, plus the following notes pertaining to each statement, can guide your discussion.

1. This first statement may seem a lofty ideal in view of the fact that so many jobs in today's automated, assembly line society do not give one a personal sense of satisfaction in doing them. A monotonous job in a noisy, dirty factory; long working hours on the night shift; and bitter management/union relations hardly contribute to one's sense of meaning and purpose for life. Yet someone has to do these jobs. Should such persons seek meaning for life apart from their work?

2. The person who has found meaning in his work would probably agree with this statement, while the person who has a dull or exhausting job would surely disagree. Many a re-

tired person, who has not planned to use his newly acquired leisure time creatively, has found himself slipping both mentally and physically. For him work may have been a blessing even if he viewed it as a burden or a curse.

3. This idea is the great American middle-class myth. As men are increasingly being replaced by machines, the job market seems to be drying up. This is particularly true of unskilled and semi-skilled jobs, but it is also true of jobs requiring a high degree of training and specialization. In recent years highly trained engineers, scientists, and teachers have either joined the ranks of the unemployed or are working at jobs that have caused them to feel a great sense of futility and loss of dignity.

4. A distinction needs to be made between idleness and relaxation and between loafing and leisure. One can be idle when he relaxes, or he can relax by being active. He can waste his free time by idleness or use it creatively by relaxing. His leisure activities can prevent relaxation as well as encourage it.

5. How we respond to this statement depends on our understanding of the place of leisure in a work-oriented society. We have extolled the virtue of work and have criticized both the affluent "jet setters" and the perennially unemployed. We are now living in a day when we need to re-examine our traditional concepts about work and leisure. This examination might begin with a study of what the Bible has to say about the subjects.

Developing the Lesson

Focus first on Exodus 20:8-11. Have someone read the passage, and then ask the class members to comment on their understanding of what the Sabbath meant to the Hebrew people. What was the purpose of the Sabbath?

(Refer to the comments in the biblical exegesis printed above.)

Introduce the question of how Christians ought to observe their Sabbath, which is Sunday. Call for reports from the class members who carried through on last week's assignment: to gather the opinions of various people as to whether or not Sunday laws ought to be strengthened and enforced.

Use the following questions and comments to stimulate discussion:

1. Should everyone be compelled to observe one day a week as a day of rest? Are the rights of persons being disregarded when laws are established to limit certain activities on Sunday? (It is interesting to note that a United States Supreme Court decision has upheld the constitutionality of three state laws prohibiting the operation of retail stores on Sunday. However, this decision viewed Sunday "blue laws" as welfare, not religious, legislation. Would your class members agree that a "closed" Sunday is primarily for the welfare of citizens [to give employees an assured day of rest] rather than an aid to their religious observances?)

2. What of those who must work on Sunday—telephone operators, dairy farmers, those in public utilities? How can we justify this work in light of strict Sunday observance? What limits would you allow on justifiable Sunday employment?

3. God ordained the seventh day to be kept holy. How literally should Christians observe this commandment?

Have your class members study silently Matthew 12:1-14 and Mark 2:23 through 3:6, asking them to try to pinpoint the reasons Jesus gave in justifying his Sabbath activity. Jesus indicated that the Sabbath is to be used by man (Mark 2:27). This was

God's intent. Jesus affirms the goodness of God's creation and sees the Sabbath as man's opportunity to rejoice in this creation. It is not a time for turning one's back upon the created order but for enjoying it as one acknowledges the God who made it and is sovereign over it. God himself rejoiced in the goodness of his creation on the seventh day (Genesis 2:2-3).

Helping Class Members Act

Conclude the session by asking class members to suggest ways that various leisure-time activities may provide meaning for their lives. Younger persons may wish to examine the kinds of things they do on weekends or vacations. Older persons may like to explore activities that can become part of their retirement pace of life. The method of brainstorming—that is, listing as many ideas as possible without discussing each—could be used here. Jot down the ideas on a chalkboard or newsprint. After the class has developed a rather long list, encourage the members to select those ideas from the list that seem to have particular relevance for giving meaning to life. Consider again the question of whether or not a person can find meaning for his life outside his work. What might this say to the person who is unemployed? to the person whose workweek is shortened? to the person who is forced to retire at an early age?

Planning for Next Sunday

Ask class members to compare what their children or grandchildren are now studying in high school with what they studied. How great would they say is the knowledge explosion over the past several decades?

Also ask members to analyze the various political advertisements being presented in the mass media to determine the kind of appeal they are making to the electorate.

Background Scripture passages that members may want to read in advance include: Ephesians 4:11-16, 25-32; Philippians 4:8-9; 2 Timothy 4:1-5; and James 3:1-12.

LESSON 4   OCTOBER 1

The Battle for Men's Minds

Background Scripture: Ephesians 4:11-16, 25-32;
Philippians 4:8-9; 2 Timothy 4:1-5; James 3:1-12

The Main Question —Charles M. Laymon

The committee on social concerns in an urban church was disturbed by the showing of an "X" rated movie at the local theater. All attempts to influence the manager of the movie house were fruitless. He had to secure his films on a block booking basis, and his theater was one of a chain owned by an absentee corporation. Besides this, the interpretation of the constitution that was current had opened the way for new standards in distinguishing between pornography, art, and education.

"It isn't only the movies; it's television and the magazines as well," said a member of the committee who had teen-age children. "Mass communications," he continued, "have gotten out of control."

A young mother added, "There seems to be so little that a parent can do. Our children are bombarded on all sides with false values and images of life that give them a distorted view of right and wrong."

What is the real problem with mass communication? What means do we have of being selective so that its tremendous opportunities for education and entertainment will not be lost? Does the church have a stake in this situation? Is it largely a question of censorship? Are the producers in charge of the media of communication open to public opinion, including the views of the church?

The biblical passages that follow undergird the importance of this issue.

As You Read the Scripture —Martin Rist

2 Timothy 4:1-5. *I charge you . . . preach the word:* Mass communication, by means of which a person may make his message or views known to large groups of people within a brief period of time, is a modern phenomenon. It began with the development of printing with movable type some five hundred years ago. Instead of a book being laboriously written or copied by hand on leather, papyrus, vellum, or paper, it became possible for hundreds, thousands, tens of thousands of copies of a handbill, a pamphlet, a book, a newspaper, or a magazine to be produced quickly for publication and circulation. Today, with improved methods, it is possible to produce a limitless number of copies of a given periodical or book. Within the memory of many people other means of mass communication have been invented and come into common use: the moving picture, radio, tape recorders, and television.

In ancient times methods of mass communication, as we know them, were undreamed of. Furthermore, they were not needed; for the population of most cities and nations was very small. Indeed, even then it was not necessary to communicate with the populace but only with their leaders. According to Exodus 19:7, Moses at first addressed the elders of the people alone and then later the people as a whole.

The early prophets, such as Elijah and Elisha and probably Amos, relied upon the spoken word alone; consequently, they could not reach many people with their oracles at a given time. Later on, the sayings of Amos, which had been transmitted orally, were written down to form the book given his name in the Old Testament. There were probably very few copies of this book, and they undoubtedly had a limited circulation.

Insofar as we know, Jesus used only the spoken word. He spoke to small groups and to larger groups; one is said to have consisted of more than five thousand people (Matthew 14:13-21). Since he was accustomed to traveling from place to place, speaking as he went, Jesus thereby increased the number of people who heard his message of repentance and the kingdom of God. Quite possibly his expectation that he might preach to still more people in Jerusalem at the Passover festival induced him to go there. Later

47

How can Christians be helpful about the ways in which mass communication media are used for educational and entertainment purposes? What stake does the church have in this situation?

records of his deeds and words were written in what we call Gospels; at any given time probably very few copies of any Gospel were in circulation.

We read in Acts that the early Christian missionaries went from place to place preaching the good news. We are well aware of the missionary journeys of Paul from city to city; other apostles were using the same means. Paul, as a Jew, could use a Jewish synagogue as a platform for his message; or he could rent a hall, like the hall of Tyrannus, where he spoke daily during his stay in Ephesus (Acts 19:8-10). For the most part, the missionaries worked in the towns and cities, where there were more people than in the countryside.

Paul and other missionaries also wrote letters. Paul's letters were not addressed to the masses but to individual churches or groups of churches, for example, the "churches of Galatia" (Galatians 1:2). The author of the Book of Revelation addressed his book (actually in letter form) to seven churches in Asia Minor (Revelation 1:4). He apparently expected his book to be read aloud in each of the churches (Revelation 1:3). But even this method of reaching people was far removed from that provided by printed books.

The lesson from 2 Timothy 4:1-5 consists of valuable advice for the preacher-evangelist, who is told to preach the word urgently, in season and out of season, and unfailingly.

Philippians 4:8-9. *Finally, brethren, whatever is true:* These verses have relevance for those in control of mass communication media. Paul's list of

Christian virtues deserves repeated consideration as program content is planned: "Whatever is honorable, whatever is just, whatever is pure, whatever is lovely, whatever is gracious, . . . think about these things."

Selected Scripture

King James Version	Revised Standard Version
2 Timothy 4:1-5	*2 Timothy 4:1-5*

2 Timothy 4:1-5

1 I charge thee therefore before God, and the Lord Jesus Christ, who shall judge the quick and the dead at his appearing and his kingdom;

2 Preach the word; be instant in season, out of season; reprove, rebuke, exhort with all longsuffering and doctrine.

3 For the time will come when they will not endure sound doctrine; but after their own lusts shall they heap to themselves teachers, having itching ears;

4 And they shall turn away their ears from the truth, and shall be turned unto fables.

5 But watch thou in all things, endure afflictions, do the work of an evangelist, make full proof of thy ministry.

Philippians 4:8-9

8 Finally, brethren, whatsoever things are true, whatsoever things are honest, whatsoever things are just, whatsoever things are pure, whatsoever things are lovely, whatsoever things are of good report; if there be any virtue, and if there be any praise, think on these things.

9 Those things, which ye have both learned, and received, and heard, and seen in me, do: and the God of peace shall be with you.

Memory Selection: **Putting away lying, speak every man truth with his neighbour: for we are members one of another. (Ephesians 4:25)**

2 Timothy 4:1-5

1 I charge you in the presence of God and of Christ Jesus who is to judge the living and the dead, and by his appearing and his kingdom: 2 preach the word, be urgent in season and out of season, convince, rebuke, and exhort, be unfailing in patience and in teaching. 3 For the time is coming when people will not endure sound teaching, but having itching ears they will accumulate for themselves teachers to suit their own likings, 4 and will turn away from listening to the truth and wander into myths. 5 As for you, always be steady, endure suffering, do the work of an evangelist, fulfil your ministry.

Philippians 4:8-9

8 Finally, brethren, whatever is true, whatever is honorable, whatever is just, whatever is pure, whatever is lovely, whatever is gracious, if there is any excellence, if there is anything worthy of praise, think about these things. 9 What you have learned and received and heard and seen in me, do; and the God of peace will be with you.

Memory Selection: **Putting away falsehood, let every one speak the truth with his neighbor, for we are members one of another. (Ephesians 4:25)**

49

The Scripture and the Main Question —Charles M. Laymon

SPREAD THE NEWS

When the writer of Second Timothy said that the church should "preach the word" (4:2), he was urging that the gospel be spread to others. He was reemphasizing Jesus' "Great Commission" to go into all the world and proclaim the good news (Matthew 28: 19-20).

In that day, when there were no electronic devices by which to reach and teach others, men were limited to speaking and to some writing. Today we are confronted with mass media for spreading ideas: radio, television, records, tapes, movies, newspapers, magazines, and so forth. Telstar circles the globe; cables span the seas; and the air waves are crowded with messages. It is possible to reach others almost instantly in the most distant places.

Who will make use of these avenues of communication? They are open to all who can pay for them. Truth as well as falsehood can be transmitted; persons can be led or misled, ennobled or degraded, helped or harmed by what they see and hear through these channels. Which shall it be?

We usually think of God as speaking through the Holy Spirit when he communicates his will to us today. What if, in addition to spiritual speaking, God could have placed at his disposal these new opportunities? Would he make use of them?

William F. Fore, a United Methodist minister, is a specialist in the areas of broadcasting and films. In his book *Image and Impact* he says, "God never stands still. He is always ahead of us, speaking where we least suspect. . . . He speaks through whatever channels are used the most, and in our time this includes the mass media of communication." [6]

WHAT THEY WANT TO HEAR

Whether or not God finds an opportunity to speak through the mass media depends upon who gains control. In a free society this usually means those who can pay. Since the mass media are very expensive to use, the church and educational agencies are often outbid by other groups. To illustrate, for the most part advertising interests determine the programing on the television networks. They pay the bill; and by buying or not buying viewing time, they can control the output.

The above situation can be good, but it can also be bad. Advertisers seek to please the public, and systems of viewer ratings have been devised to determine what the people want to see and hear. If the taste of the public is low, the programs will drop to a low level.

The biblical passage for this lesson refers to times "when people will not endure sound teaching, but having itching ears they will accumulate for themselves teachers to suit their own likings, and will turn away from listening to the truth and wander into myths." (2 Timothy 4:3-4) Sometimes just this happens in the case of television.

Eventually, through the mass media, what the people like they get. In the mid-1960's a sociological series called "East Side/West Side" was aired on television. It depicted living conditions in the slums realistically and won the National Television Critics' Best Film Series Award. Audiences, however, began to turn the show off because they did not want to view

* (Friendship Press, 1970), pp. 12-13.

50

misery. CBS lost $2,184,000 in unsold commercial spots on this show that season. The series was cancelled the next season.

WHEN MEDIA CREATE THE NEWS

When a prominent television newscaster left his post two years ago, it was reported he regretted the fact that, for many, television was their chief source of news. Some persons would agree with the sentiment attributed to him and go one step farther. They hold that television not only presents but also creates the news, making its use as the only source of news for thousands of Americans twice as dangerous.

When the television cameras pictured the Chicago police moving against the New Left radicals at the time of the 1968 Democratic Convention, an event many thought was blown out of proportion by the networks, those looking on chanted: "The whole world is watching! The whole world is watching!" And it was!

Does watching such violence create a taste for violence? Will such visual images impressed on the mind of a disturbed person tend to create the pattern of violence? Can the whole truth be communicated through the projection of a picture of a news event? Will reasons for what is seen, motives behind the action, and its implications for our society be grasped by unthinking persons who only see and are inflamed?

GOVERNMENT AND MASS MEDIA

Creating and enforcing standards for mass media are difficult in a free society. "Pass a law," someone says. But this is easier said than done. The rights of free speech and free assembly make it possible for a democracy to operate. How do we determine the point where governmental control of mass media becomes a denial of these rights.

"Let the public taste decide," is another statement that is often made. But what if the public taste becomes immoral? How far can the government go in these matters within the framework of a democracy?

Yet if the government is ruled out entirely in the area of controlling what people see, hear, and read, many persons will be helpless. Currently, advertising slogans are constantly being checked by federal agencies to see if their claims are honest. Pure food and drug laws are on the records to protect the public against being misled. The well-being of the citizen is a concern of the state and must be. But how much regulation can a free society permit?

WHAT CAN THE CHURCH DO?

Obviously something has to be done in the area of mass media to make certain its potential shall be used for good. The lives of persons should be enriched and not degraded, strengthened and not weakened, by these media. And in this the church has a responsibility.

What can the church do? The first answer is that those who are Christian should, through their spiritual influence and moral character, permeate the atmosphere of society with a concern for living the fullest and highest life possible. This is what Jesus had in mind when he said that his followers were to be the "salt of the earth" and that they were to let their light "shine." (Matthew 5:13-16) The apostle Paul was saying the same thing when he urged Christians to think about whatever is true, honerable, just, pure, lovely, and gracious (Philippians 4:8).

A major part of "thinking" about

the enrichment of mass media is being concerned. If people do not care, no change can come about. Concern, however, needs to be based on knowledge. We must be informed about the problems of mass media, know how each medium operates and who is in charge. Personal contacts with those who produce and write the materials presented through mass media can be helpful. Civic organizations can be contacted for action and our lawmakers alerted to the issues. In addition, the church itself should make a more frequent use of mass media for spreading the gospel.

Helping Adults Become Involved —Ronald E. Schlosser

Preparation of Self and Class

As you prepare for this week's session, gather news stories and articles about this summer's political conventions. Appraise the television coverage and estimate the impact that this coverage made on the millions of viewers around the country. Plan to bring to the class session newspaper advertisements of various political candidates. You may also wish to tape-record some political commercials from radio or television and play these during your session.

A book that ought to be on your reading list this fall is Joe McGinniss' *The Selling of the President 1968.* The book is a fast-paced, fascinating, and somewhat frightening account of how professional advertising agencies, public relations firms, and television promoters work to sell political candidates to the public. The implications are vast, particularly in light of the increasing influence the mass media are having in molding public opinion.

Probably the easiest and most relevant way of getting at today's main question is to focus on the influence the mass media are having on the current political campaign. Most members of your class will have some opinions on what is happening in this area, which should spark lively class discussion.

However, you may wish to focus on mass communications in general, without highlighting the political scene. The session will later move to a consideration of modern evangelistic methods, so you may wish to concentrate on this area from the start.

The following learning goals are suggestive of the kind you might formulate to guide the development of your session.

1. To recognize the influence of the mass media in shaping one's ideas and opinions.

2. To contemplate our Christian responsibility for integrity in speech and communication.

3. To evaluate the effectiveness of modern evangelistic methods.

Presenting the Main Question

If you wish to focus on the political implications of the mass media, begin the session by displaying a variety of news stories, articles, and editorials about the current election campaigns. Play a sampling of the radio and television commercials of the various candidates if you were able to record them. Analyze newspaper advertisements. Ask your class members for their opinions of these advertisements and commercials. Do they feel the mass media have too great an influence in shaping public opinion? What are the very real dangers in giving the mass media such a prominent role in a national election? What are some values?

Another way to begin the session, particularly if you do not want to deal with the political scene, is to play a word association game with the class. Read the following list of words and ask the members to write down on a sheet of paper another word they associate with each:

Bread	Trip
Grass	Long hair
Rap	Fuzz
Pot	Dig

Compare the modern meanings with the traditional dictionary definitions. (You may need to substitute newer words for any of the words in the above list that are no longer in vogue. When this was written, bread meant money; pot and grass referred to marijuana. Trip was a drug experience; rap meant to discuss; fuzz was a policeman; dig meant to understand; and long hairs were hippie types, not classical musicians.)

Discuss how words and their meanings change. How does this affect communication, particularly between older and younger generations? Can class members give any examples from personal experience that illustrate the problems of communication between the generations? If some of your members have compared what their children or grandchildren are studying in school with what they themselves studied, ask for reports from these persons. What implications does such change have for us in this age of mass communication?

Developing the Lesson

Since much of mass communication is one-way communication, there is great danger that the communications media will become vehicles for prop-

aganda techniques. What are some of these techniques?

1. *Name-calling:* using emotionally toned words to color one's perception and evaluation of whatever is being talked about. Words like *radical, fundamentalist, capitalist, imperialist,* and the like are examples.

2. *Glittering generalities:* glowing slogans or statements that sound wonderful but reveal very little. A political candidate might be introduced as "a man with a heart who has a program with a soul." What, in fact, is being said about either the man or his program?

3. *Endorsement transfer:* identifying the object, idea, or product to be sold with someone or something highly respected and admired. A pro football player endorses a shaving lather; a beautiful blonde drools over a new sports car; a political candidate stands in front of an American flag—these are examples of the transfer technique.

4. *Appeal to the people:* a number of techniques whereby persons are influenced into a certain line of action because it is identified with an attractive group of people. The "in crowd" drinks a certain soft beverage; the individualist smokes a certain brand of cigarettes; the common man votes for a particular political candidate.

5. *Card stacking:* a rigging of facts or circumstances to get a desired outcome. For instance, a pharmaceutical company sends free samples of its mouthwash or toothpaste to a representative group of dentists, who are later asked what brand they use. The answers are placed on a chart of impressive-looking statistics, and we are led to believe that nine out of ten dentists recommend this brand.

6. *Bandwagon:* an appeal to the instincts of people who like to be with

the majority. Politicians, for example, try to convince people that their candidates are on the winning side and that everyone should get on board and share in their victory.

Have the class analyze the various political advertisements (or regular commercial advertisements) in magazines and newspapers, as well as on radio and television, trying to identify some of the above propaganda techniques. Discuss with your group the need for Christians to detect and reveal distortions of truth, false advertising, and other methods of manipulating people used in the mass media.

Follow this discussion with an in-depth study of some of the background Scripture suggested for today. You might divide the class into three groups, assigning each of the groups one of the following passages: Ephesians 4:25-32; 2 Timothy 4:1-5; James 3:1-5. Ask each group to study its respective passage and discuss what the passage says about person-to-person communication and its implications for mass communication. Allow about ten minutes for these small group discussions, and then call the class together for a time of general sharing.

An alternate approach to Bible study might be to ask each person in the class to study 2 Timothy 4:1-5 and to write a one- or two-sentence statement that lifts up one striking idea or insight from the passage. Have the members share these with the whole group. An example of such a statement might be: In an age when people are being influenced by all kinds of propaganda, when conflicting philosophies are battling for men's minds, it is important—indeed, urgent—that Christians faithfully proclaim the gospel of Jesus Christ in all its truth and power, regardless of the consequences.

Helping Class Members Act

Use the last part of the session to discuss and evaluate modern evangelistic methods in light of the influence the mass media are having in our world today. Ask the class members to name as many evangelistic methods as they can think of and list these on the chalkboard. Then, using a scale of one (highly effective) to five (least effective), have the class rate each method. Discuss the reasons for giving the method the rating indicated. Consider the potentialities and problems each method has for communicating the gospel.

The following methods should be among those the class considers: large crusades and rallies, street corner preaching, Christian radio or television programs, tract distribution, two-by-two visitation, evening gospel services, Christian films and records, halfway houses or drug rehabilitation centers, dial-a-prayer services, individual witnessing in public places. This list is by no means comprehensive, but it suggests the wide variety of methods that might be discussed.

Planning for Next Sunday

Ask your members to visit the downtown shopping area of a large city during the week and, if possible, engage in conversation with some of the people they meet. What are their reactions to city life? Do they find it to be exciting and stimulating, or are they aware mostly of its problems and frustrations?

Passages of Scripture that members may want to study in advance for next week include: Genesis 11:1-8; Zechariah 8:3-5; John 17:15-18.

Christianity and the Secular City

Background Scripture: Genesis 11:1-9; Zechariah 8:1-8; John 17:15-18; Acts 19:23-41; 1 John 2:15-17; Revelation 21:10, 22-27

The Main Question —Charles M. Laymon

A friend of mine recently said, following a trip to Europe, that if one wanted to see Europe as it really was he would need to see it soon. Why? The reason is that contemporary high-rise apartments and factories are springing up everywhere. Built alongside ancient historical sites, these modern structures are changing the face of the past. "It is a secular effrontery to culture," he said.

Someone, hearing my friend, commented, "It is the same with the church. The city is taking over. Everything is wide open on Sunday, and secular activities are smothering us." He then cited figures to show an alarming decrease in church attendance. Membership is shrinking in all the larger denominations.

What should be done in the face of these challenges? Is retrenchment the answer? Can the church recapture the city for Christ? Is modern culture a substitute for Christianity?

Jesus once spoke of the church as built on a rock and said that "the powers of death [the gates of Hades] shall not prevail against it." (Matthew 16:18) Here is a picture of the church standing firm in the presence of secular encroachment, marching against the forces of evil in the world and gaining victory over them. Does the church have marching orders today? What are they?

The following biblical passages will help us understand the church's calling in the world.

As You Read the Scripture —Martin Rist

Genesis 11:1-8. *Now the whole earth had one language and few words:* This passage is not the story of a city but of the planning for a city. Nor was the city to be secular; on the contrary, its most notable structure was to have been a tower on top of which was to be built a temple. Actually, this familiar story attempts to explain the cause for the variety of languages in the world. The story answers a very natural question: Why are there so many languages in the world, instead of one that everyone might understand?

The setting for the account of the Tower of Babel was Babylonia. The story begins with the assumption that there was but one language in the world, with a limited vocabulary everybody understood. Some migrants (place of origin unstated) found a suitable plain in the land of Shinar (a name for Babylonia). They decided to build a city of burnt bricks with a temple-

55

tower that would reach the heavens (verses 2-4). The writer no doubt was referring to a ziggurat, a high, square, pyramidal structure rising upwards in seven terraces with a shrine on its top. Marduk was the chief Babylonian deity, but the seven terraces probably represented the seven planets, considered to be deities, who mediated between earth and heaven. The shrine was thought of as the entrance to heaven. Ascending the tower was considered to be a meritorious act, ascending to the gods, as it were.

According to the Hebraic view, the religious aspects of this astrological tower would be most offensive to their god, Yahweh, who prevented its completion by confusing the language of the builders so that they could not understand one another. Since this handicap prevented them from continuing with their work, they left and were scattered abroad, becoming migrants once more. Consequently, the city's name became Babel (Babylon), which the writer, in a play on words, erroneously derived from the Hebrew word *balal*, to mix or to confuse. Babylon actually means "gate of God."

Zechariah 8:3-5. *Thus says the* Lord: *I will return to Zion:* The oracle in Chapters 7 and 8 of Zechariah may be dated at 518 B.C.; hence it was composed during the Exile in Babylonia. The rebuilding of the Temple had begun in 520 B.C.; Zechariah looked forward to its completion as the prelude to the coming of a messianic period of peace, good will, and prosperity. Chapter 8:3-5 reflects the prophet's ardent expectation that the Lord will return to Jerusalem to dwell in its midst at that time.

John 17:15-18. *I do not pray that thou shouldst take them out of the world:* This section from the High Priestly Prayer of John 17:6-26 reflects a period when there was disunity in the Christian church; consequently the prayer urges among the Christians that they, who are consecrated, "may all be one." (verse 21) It is a reversal of the disunity of "babel" into the unity of Christ.

Selected Scripture

King James Version	Revised Standard Version
Genesis 11:1-8	*Genesis 11:1-8*
1 And the whole earth was of one language, and of one speech.	1 Now the whole earth had one language and few words. 2 And as men migrated in the east, they found a plain in the land of Shinar and settled there. 3 And they said to one another, "Come, let us make bricks, and burn them thoroughly." And they had brick for stone, and bitumen for mortar. 4 Then they said, "Come, let us build ourselves a city, and a tower with its top in the heavens, and let us make a name for ouselves, lest we be scattered abroad upon the face of the whole earth." 5 And the Lord
2 And it came to pass, as they journeyed from the east, that they found a plain in the land of Shinar; and they dwelt there.	
3 And they said one to another, Go to, let us make brick, and burn them throughly. And they had brick for stone, and slime had they for mortar.	
4 And they said, Go to, let us build us a city and a tower, whose top may reach unto heaven; and let us make us a name, lest we be scattered	

abroad upon the face of the whole earth.

5 And the LORD came down to see the city and the tower, which the children of men, builded.

6 And the LORD said, Behold, the people is one, and they have all one language; and this they begin to do; and now nothing will be restrained from them, which they have imagined to do.

7 Go to, let us go down, and there confound their language, that they may not understand one another's speech.

8. So the LORD scattered them abroad from thence upon the face of all the earth: and they left off to build the city.

Zechariah 8:3-5

3 Thus saith the LORD; I am returned unto Zion, and will dwell in the midst of Jerusalem: and Jerusalem shall be called a city of truth; and the mountain of the LORD of hosts the holy mountain.

4 Thus saith the LORD of hosts; There shall yet old men and old women dwell in the streets of Jerusalem, and every man with his staff in his hand for very age.

5 And the streets of the city shall be full of boys and girls playing in the streets thereof.

John 17:15-18

15 I pray not that thou shouldest take them out of the world, but that thou shouldest keep them from the evil.

16 They are not of the world, even as I am not of the world.

17 Sanctify them through thy truth: thy word is truth.

18 As thou hast sent me into the world, even so have I also sent them into the world.

came down to see the city and the tower, which the sons of men had built. 6 And the LORD said, "Behold, they are one people, and they have all one language; and this is only the beginning of what they will do; and nothing that they propose to do will now be impossible for them. 7 Come, let us go down, and there confuse their language, that they may not understand one another's speech." 8 So the LORD scattered them abroad from there over the face of all the earth, and they left off building the city.

Zechariah 8:3-5

3 Thus says the LORD: I will return to Zion, and will dwell in the midst of Jerusalem, and Jerusalem shall be called the faithful city, and the mountain of the LORD of hosts, the holy mountain. 4 Thus says the LORD of hosts: Old men and old women shall again sit in the streets of Jerusalem, each with staff in hand for very age. 5 And the streets of the city shall be full of boys and girls playing in its streets.

John 17:15-18

15 I do not pray that thou shouldst take them out of the world, but that thou shouldst keep them from the evil one. 16 They are not of the world, even as I am not of the world. 17 Sanctify them in the truth; thy word is truth. 18 As thou didst send me into the world, so I have sent them into the world.

Memory Selection: Be not conformed to this world: but be ye transformed by the renewing of your mind, that ye may prove what is that good, and acceptable, and perfect, will of God. (Romans 12:2)	*Memory Selection:* Do not be conformed to this world but be transformed by the renewal of your mind, that you may prove what is the will of God, what is good and acceptable and perfect. (Romans 12:2)

The Scripture and the Main Question —Charles M. Laymon

THE MIXED VOICES OF THE CITY

When everyone is talking at once, who will be heard? Is it the person who talks the loudest, or the one who talks the fastest, or the one who makes the most sense? If we are to be honest, must we not conclude that sometimes the answer is one of these and again it is another? This much is certain; in the city today all three types of voices are being raised, and the resulting sound is often garbled.

New forms of city government are arising in which whole counties become cities. Neighborhood lines are broken as schoolchildren are "bussed" to different parts of the city. Persons are crowded together in living situations where natural beauty is all but gone. Day nurseries are substituted for home life as mothers bring in added income. Pollution is found in the air, the water, and the soil. Constant noises jar the nerves. These are but a few of the mixed voices of the city.

These many voices speaking loudly at one time are like the babble of tongues when God confounded the speaking of the people while they were attempting to build a tower that would reach from earth to heaven (Genesis 11:1-8). In the confusion that followed, all building stopped because the workers could not understand one another.

Who is going to bring order out of the confusion of mixed voices in the city today? It is not enough to say,

"I don't know what to make of it all. Everything seems to be changing. I don't feel that I belong." As we think of the future of the city, why not take, instead, the attitude of Robert Kennedy, who closed one of his speeches with words adapted from a statement by George Bernard Shaw: "Some men see things as they are and say 'Why?' I dream things that never were and say 'why not?' "

THE DREAM OF A CITY RENEWED

Ancient biblical cities were not like modern cities. Life was much simpler within their walls. Even so, here the people congregated, bought and sold, loved, labored, won, and lost. Narrow streets brought them close together, and the common need to protect the city from attack welded them into a fraternity.

Then as now, some cities became more than an aggregation of persons. As a city, Jerusalem stood for something; it was Zion, the city of God. In a special way it was believed that God dwelled there. Because of this, the prophet Isaiah taught that Jerusalem was inviolable (Isaiah 37:33-35). His belief did not, however, turn out to be true; for the Babylonians conquered it in 586 B.C. They razed the walls, destroyed the Temple, and burned large portions of the city.

When Zechariah prophesied, the Jews had recently returned to the burned-out rock pile that had been Jerusalem—Zion, city of the great king. He called upon the people to rebuild. Once more God would dwell in Jerusalem; it "shall be called the faithful city, and the mountain of the LORD of hosts, the holy mountain." (Zechariah 8:3) The aged will relax and be at home, while the streets will ring again with the laughter of boys and girls (verses 4-5). The city will be renewed.

At the particular moment when Zechariah was proclaiming the renewal of Jerusalem, however, the city was far from the ideal community the prophet had in mind. His expectations were in the dream stage. But the dream was real, and dreams are a preface to reality. Zechariah would not have understood the expressions "City Planning" and "Urban Renewal." Yet he was advocating the very thing these words imply. And whenever any modern city undertakes such programs, it is entering into the prophet's dream of a city renewed.

THE CHURCH IN THE CITY

At Bradenton, Florida, a youthful director of Christian education saw an abandoned building on a wharf. Eager to reclaim youth from the stifling influences of the secular city, she was struck with the idea that here would be the perfect site for a youth coffee house. The task called for cooperation of other churches in the community. The youth themselves took over the task of cleaning, decorating, and furnishing the building. Fish nets now hang festooned from the ceiling where spider webs had been; candlelight, discarded furniture, and the aroma of coffee, well mixed with the laughter of teen-agers, now fill the once vacant building. Here is one instance of how to beat secularism at its game. And the church had a hand in it.

What is the place of the church in a secular city—a city in which goals and motives are materialistic and temporal? This question is being asked more than any other today by those who are concerned that the church be relevant. Remembering Jesus' prayer: "I do not pray that thou shouldst take them out of the world" (John 17:15), alert Christians are continually looking for ways to make daily living more fully Christian.

To distinguish this active, life-centered or person-centered ministry from the otherworldly, ingrown type, Dietrich Bonhoeffer used to call it "Worldly Christianity." Langdon B. Gilkey goes a step further when he spells out the task of the church in the city: "There is so clearly a need for a ministry of reconciliation and of reform to areas and issues untouched by, and seemingly closed to, the local residential church—the labor unions, the inner city, the slums and tenements, racial problems, and so on— that it may well seem that the congregational community of Word and Sacrament, which has been the classical form for the church, is now irrelevant, too captive to its own smug residential milieu to spread the gospel or live it out in human reality." [7]

CAN THE CHURCH REMAIN SPIRITUAL?

When the church marshals its energies to go out into the city and challenge its degrading secular forces, there are usually those who say the church is engaged in worldly interests. "Why doesn't the church stay at home and tend the store?" they say. And then they may add, "If you play with fire, you will get burned. The church will lose its spirituality."

However, in seeking to renew the city so that persons may have an op-

[7] Langdon B. Gilkey, *How the Church Can Minister to the World Without Losing Itself* (Harper & Row, 1964), p. 26.

portunity to develop their God-given potential, the church is not playing with fire; it is putting out the fires that consume the spirits of men. In the upper room Jesus prayed, "As thou didst send me into the world, so I have sent them [his followers] into the world." (John 17:18) He was well aware of the dangers they would encounter, but he sent them forth just the same.

Bill Holman is a minister in Tarrytown, New York, who combines activity in today's world with spirituality. A nonprofit corporation of Protestant, Catholic, and Jewish leaders is constructing a three-million-dollar, integrated, low- and middle-income housing project that will obliterate the slum area. The project is under Bill's direction, so much so that Bishop Lloyd Wicke of New York said, "There should be a plaque on the building that says: 'To the glory of God—and the tenacity of Bill Holman.'" Here is a minister who understands the "power structure of modern society and knows how to work within it without being destroyed or turned off by it." [8]

[8] Jane D. Mook, *Probe-Probe* (Friendship Press, 1970), pp. 23, 27.

Helping Adults Become Involved —Ronald E. Schlosser

Preparation of Self and Class

Look through back issues of newspapers and news magazines for articles about life in the city. What are some of the problems facing urban centers? What about the largest city in your state? How is this city coping with social change? What kind of education are children getting in its schools? Are there any plans for urban renewal? How is the housing situation? the job market? Seek to gather this kind of information as a way of increasing your understanding of today's main question.

Two helpful paperback books that could give you a portrait of city life and the problems that gnaw at its base are *The City as a Community* and *The Negro in the City*. The latter book would also make a good background resource for the lesson for October 22. Both books contain very readable articles, a large number of dramatic photographs, and penetrating questions for thought and discussion.

An old but still fascinating film that could be used as a discussion starter is the ten-minute motion picture *My Own Yard to Play In.* (See page 12.) Photographed on the streets of New York, the film gives a revealing glimpse into the world of children at play. It captures the songs, thoughts, and fantasies of the city's youngsters as they adapt their play to their environment.

As your class grapples with today's question, its aim ought to be twofold:

1. To become familiar with some of the characteristics of urban culture.

2. To consider how the church can minister to, and in, an increasingly urban world (building on the suggestions that may have been discussed on February 6).

Presenting the Main Question

If you plan to use the film *My Own Yard to Play In,* show it at the beginning of the session. You might introduce it by reading Zechariah 8:5. Following its showing, discuss such questions as:

1. Do the children seem to enjoy

playing on the sidewalk and in the street?

2. How would you evaluate the kind of games they play? What does this tell us about the children?

3. What is the significance of the film's title? How do you interpret the wish of the child who wanted "my own yard to play in"?

If you are not using the film, begin the session by asking the class members to mention all the words that come to their minds when they think of the word *city*. List these words on the chalkboard as they are mentioned. Negative words, such as *rootlessness, depersonalization, anonymity, frustration, social injustice,* may be suggested, as well as positive words, such as *togetherness, excitement, movement, encounter,* and *community*. Note how many negative words are mentioned. How does this list compare with the positive words suggested? What does this say to the class members about the characteristics of the city and the implications for working and/or living in an urban center?

Developing the Lesson

Move to a discussion of some of the problems brought on by the increasing urbanization of society. Analyze the list of words formulated in the preceding activity (or have the class suggest some if they have just viewed the film). Consider what problems are the cause of the conditions or symptoms described by these words. For example, what has brought on loneliness? Why are people frustrated? How does the fast pace of city living contribute to the despair that is often felt by the elderly, the poor, or the racially oppressed? Try to isolate some of the "mixed voices of the city" that Dr. Laymon talks about in his commentary on the main question.

Discuss with the class members some of the specific problems faced by persons in the city nearest to where they live, if in fact they do not live in the city themselves. What plans are being made, or steps already being taken, to solve some of these problems? Is it the responsibility of Christian citizens to cooperate with civic officials in these programs? Should the church take the lead in giving its support to a city government that is trying to cope with urban problems?

It may be well at this point to look at some of the background Scripture for study today. Have the class members consider four passages in particular: Genesis 11:1-9; Zechariah 8:1-8; John 17:15-18; and Acts 19:23-41. Assign each passage to a number of members for individual study and reflection. Ask the members to consider what their respective passage might say to persons who are facing urban problems today. Allow about five or six minutes for individual study and then enter a period of general discussion and sharing.

Briefly, the Genesis passage might suggest the confusion that results when persons begin a project without considering God's place in it; the Zechariah passage speaks of the hope that a renewed city can bring to its inhabitants; the John passage reminds us of our commission as Christians to be in the world but not of it, and yet to serve it; the Acts passage raises the question of what should be our approach to the secular world as witnesses, being faithful to the gospel and yet sensitive to potentially dangerous, emotionally charged situations. All these passages have some relevance to our style of life as spiritually oriented persons living in a complex, secular society.

Helping Class Members Act

With the preceding Scripture study as a framework, lead the class into an exploration of how the church can minister in and to the urban world in which it finds itself. If this concern was discussed last February when you dealt with "Christ in the City," take it one step further now and consider how your own local church can minister in and to an urban setting.

There may be a tendency on the part of some class members to minimize the effect of urban culture upon them, particularly if they live in a suburban, rural, or small town location away from any large metropolitan area. They will need to be reminded that urban culture has a profound influence on their lives whether they realize it or not. If they watch television, go to the movies, read the newspaper, or buy manufactured goods, some aspects of urban culture are there to pervade their thinking. Can anyone say, in this day of mass communication when the world has become a global village, that violence, slums, race problems, war, and poverty are of no concern to him and do not touch his life? Help your class members to be sensitive to the underlying causes of problems. But do not dwell on problems and causes; seek to reach some solutions and plans for action.

Refer to the two illustrations given by Dr. Laymon in his commentary about the coffee house ministry in Bradenton, Florida, and the housing project in Tarrytown, New York. What does your class think of these examples of Christian ministry and outreach? How are they meeting the needs of the people for whom they are intended?

As another illustration of concerned Christians ministering to people's needs in an urban society, you might mention the program known as Operation Fish. The name Fish is taken from an ancient symbol for Christ. In communities around the country where this program is in operation a group of volunteers make themselves available around the clock to offer aid and assistance to people in trouble. Requests for aid come into a local telephone answering service and are passed on to the volunteer on duty. He in turn determines what type of help is needed and contacts a member of the Fish group who can best meet the need.

You might inquire whether such a program is available in your own community. If it is, some of your class members may wish to sign up as Fish volunteers. If no such program is operating, your members might investigate the possibility of beginning one themselves.

Planning for Next Sunday

Ask your class members to bring to next week's session newspaper stories or magazine articles dealing with the so-called sex revolution going on in our society today. Each person should be able to state what he feels is a characteristic of this sex revolution.

Background Scripture for the next session includes Exodus 20:14; Proverbs 7; Matthew 5:27-30; 1 Corinthians 7; and 1 Thessalonians 4:1-8.

World Order Sunday

(OCTOBER 15)

GLENN H. ASQUITH [9]

World order was spoken of with great assurance when the United Nations was formed in 1945. Indeed, men and women who were living at that time put a period after the words *world order,* or even an exclamation point. But now we are inclined to speak uncertainly—*world order?* Is the world any nearer peace and brotherhood than it was twenty-seven years ago? What has happened to the dreams of men and nations since the guns were finally silent following World War II? Have all the sessions of the United Nations been in vain?

We of the church have yet a more particular question to ask, Has World Order Sunday contributed anything toward the unity of all God's children? Prayers have been offered; literature has been printed and distributed; announcements have been made; sermons have been preached; classes have held discussions; communities have come together for United Nations Day observances. Has all this faithfulness been of no avail? With this question before us, we could make no better use of *this* World Order Sunday than that of taking stock of the worthwhileness of our efforts.

In the first place, World Order Sunday guarantees that we shall give attention at least once a year to the urgency of living together and solving our problems without recourse to war. The apostle Paul did not advise the Philippians to take "whatever is true, whatever is honorable, whatever is just" for granted but commanded them to "think about these things." (See Philippians 4:8.) The very thinking about war has brought such a revulsion against it that no nation can deal violently with another without a great protest arising around the world. The protest is heard within the warring nation as well as from outside. Citizens can no longer be depended upon to endorse a political decision that involves death and destruction at home or abroad. Our annual focusing on world order in the churches has been a factor in the thoughtfulness with which our young people are weighing the pros and cons of national and international military actions.

Also growing out of this annual "thinking" has come a close survey of the causes of war. The classic reasons for war taught in the history books until recently—balance of power, imperialism, religious differences, dynastic struggles, assaults on national honor—no longer satisfy our minds and hearts. During the past twenty-seven years we have dug deeper until we have come to the basic causes of misunderstandings and conflicts. We have uncovered the festering sores of hopeless poverty, racial discrimination, and outrage to human dignity.

In the matter of poverty we of the church have been taking a new and close look at the judgment story in Matthew 25:31-46. We have looked at the condemning words, "I was hungry and you gave me no food." (verse 42) Statistics showing that a minority in the world owns the preponderance of the world's goods no longer bring a satisfied glow to those of us who happen to

* Glenn H. Asquith: former director, Division of Christian Publications, American Baptist Board of Education and Publication.

be of that minority. We can no longer hide behind the false notion that we have what we have simply because *we* are good and ambitious, while *they* are bad and lazy. Recent articles on the wealth of the churches cause us great concern. During a study trip to Mexico in 1964 the writer was taken with his group to visit a village within easy driving distance of Mexico City. In that village (which was so poor we were forbidden to take pictures) were *two* large churches of the same faith. The buildings were ornate, and the altar materials were evidently costly. This was a good illustration of what we of the church have done and the image we must have among the poor. Our intentions have been excellent, but our "thinking" has been faulty. We know now that as long as there are in the world both desperate "have-nots" and fortunate "haves," fearful of losing their favored position, wars and revolutions can occur.

Going on to our new understanding of racial discrimination as a cause of war, we have been able to come to a late realization of the cleavage that exists between and among the races of men. Wherever a race sets itself up as a "master race" or "superior people," there are the seeds of war. This has been evident in the United States, in South Africa, and in Rhodesia; but it is also true wherever man is found. Add the anti-Semitism found in many places, and it is not difficult for us to foresee future wars. Long, long ago God taught Peter in a vision that all men are dear to their creator. He said, "What God has cleansed, you must not call common." (Acts 10:15) After this vision Cornelius, an Italian, sent for Peter; and the two men met as brothers in Christ.

The third basic reason for war that we mentioned as a fruit of our study on World Order Sundays is the outrage to human dignity, keeping a man in a menial spot and curtailing his liberty. Due to the spread of the teaching of man's worth by churches, missionaries, and books, it is possible for the great majority of mankind to know something of the sacredness of personality and the inalienable right of the individual to choose his destiny. In a poem written about a Mississippi steamboat it is said that in order to win a race the captain had a boy sitting on the safety valve to avoid losing steam. Under these circumstances, of course, the boat eventually caught fire and was destroyed. Similarly, for too many generations the privileged classes have been trying to suppress the natural strivings and ambitions of the underprivileged; and riots and insurrections have been the common result. Perhaps our study of the problem of human dignity is reminding us that we are all in the same boat when disaster strikes. A rereading of the prophetic books discloses to us terrible indictments against all who oppress their brothers. (See Amos 4:1-3; Micah 2:1-2.)

This brings us back to our listing of the reasons World Order Sunday has been and can be useful. We have seen, in the first place, that it draws our attention to the fact that man has a choice of peace or war; and World Order Sunday provides a splendid opportunity for ferreting out the *real* causes of war apart from any inherited romantic ideas and blind nationalism.

A second encouraging thing about this particular observance is the sharing of information on our progress toward world order. We take heart in remembering that World War III is taking a long time to get around that corner where pessimists have been telling us it is lurking. Despite the failures listed against it, the United Nations still serves as a great deterrent to war, with men of many nations gathering to talk to one another about their problems. Through the telecasts of UN deliberations the world has come to know something about the struggling little countries of Africa and Asia as well as the wealthy nations of long standing. We are heartened to note the disappearance of "colonies" one after the other and the appearance of small states determined to take their place among the nations of men. We hear of the dispatch of relief materials to stricken nations and the cooperative work among children done through the United Nations International Children's Emergency Fund.

So, as we talk today and tell one another that this is World Order Sunday, shall we put a question mark after world order? Were the men of twenty-seven years ago who drew up the charter for the United Nations too optimistic? Or were they God-inspired? Is our acceptance of the discipline of this special study part of our obedience to God's Word: "Seek peace, and pursue it"? (Psalms 34:14) Our reward for diligence in this project will be that held out by Jesus: "Blessed are the peacemakers, for they shall be called sons of God." (Matthew 5:9)

UNIT III: THE CHANGING WORLD OF INTERPERSONAL RELATIONS

Horace R. Weaver

TWO LESSONS   OCTOBER 15-22

This third unit on our quarter's theme ("The Bible Speaks to Issues of Our Time") deals with interpersonal relationships. Perhaps the challenge to sexual patterns and to brotherhood among the races was never so explosive and divisive in point of view as it is today. Some young adults in communes are living as if they were in the days of the patriarchs—in pre-prophetic and pre-Christian days! Overt racism among persons of different pigmentation is rampant and is dividing the church as well as the world into groups of mutual distrust and bitterness. The Christian faith calls for a study in depth of the purposes and intentions of God for our changing world of human relations.

The lesson for October 15, "The Sexual Revolution," helps us speak to sexuality as basic to God's purpose for man. October 22, "The Racial Revolution," offers opportunity to speak to the basic brotherhood of the sons of God. Love for one's neighbor must be translated in terms of service, sacrifice, and suffering.

Audiovisual resources appropriate for use with the lessons of this unit may be found in the introduction to Unit I, page 13.

The Sexual Revolution

Background Scripture: Exodus 20:14; Proverbs 7; Matthew 5:27-30;
1 Corinthians 7; 1 Thessalonians 4:1-8

The Main Question —Charles M. Laymon

David Reuben has written a book that was widely read. Some persons thought it was long overdue; such a frank approach to sex was badly needed. Others regarded it as brash and sensational. The book is titled *Everything You Always Wanted to Know About Sex—But Were Afraid to Ask*. This book is an index to the sexual revolution all about us—and within us. The author holds that it is nobody's business what an American adult does in the privacy of his or her own home—with another consenting adult. Society should, the book advocates, provide compassion and understanding where sex is concerned instead of rejection and moral judgment. Do you agree?

On the one hand, there is a sensational side to the issue of sexual freedom today. Although claiming to be a sociological study, the movie *I Am Curious Yellow* was an open portrayal of sex acts lacking in moral concepts, artistry, and good taste. After its release came a whole series of "X" movies. The results of these portrayals in stimulating unrestrained and demoralizing sex acts would be difficult to measure.

On the other hand, there are serious attempts to introduce sex education in the public schools and to place abortion with a doctor's recommendation within the law. In addition, many are urging the abandonment of discriminating laws against consenting homosexuals and the open distribution of the pill or similar contraceptives to unmarried youth.

What do you think? What stand should the church take on these issues? What is a Christian response in these areas? The biblical selections for this session suggest some answers to these questions.

As You Read the Scripture —Martin Rist

1 Corinthians 7:1-7. *Now concerning the matters about which you wrote:* Not long after the death of Jesus the apostles began to organize churches, first in Palestine, and soon afterward in the gentile world. Before long the churches in the various towns and cities of the Roman Empire began to be increasingly composed of gentile Christians. Throughout the empire, and especially in the towns and cities, there was a great deal of sexual laxity, liberty, and promiscuity. Premarital sex by the male was a normal expectancy in this period. In general, a woman was expected to be somewhat chaste; certainly a married woman was more faithful to her husband than her hus-

66

band was to her. There also was a considerable amount of homosexuality among the gentiles. (See 1 Corinthians 6:9-10 for Paul's opinion.) Abortion was commonly practiced, as well as infanticide. Unwanted babies, especially girls, might be "exposed" on rubbish heaps to die or to be picked up alive by persons who enslaved them, frequently raising the girls to become prostitutes. Epictetus, a Stoic contemporary of Paul, dramatically protested "exposure" by rescuing a baby, though he himself was unmarried, and hiring a woman to raise the infant. He and other moralists criticized the prevalent immorality of their times but without much effect.

The Jews, on the whole, were more moral than their gentile contemporaries. To be sure, in ancient times the Hebrews did engage in the fertility cult rites, which involved sacred prostitution, a practice the prophets sternly condemned as sin. Homosexuality and other sexual perversions were strongly prohibited by the Law. The seventh commandment forbade adultery, but this may have been in part to assure the husband that his wife's children were also his. There is little evidence of the practice of abortion; the strong desire for children was a preventive. Infanticide was practiced in the more ancient times in connection with fertility cult rites but not in order to get rid of unwanted children.

Again, the Jews had a high regard for marriage and the bearing and rearing of children. Indeed, this was a divine command: "Be fruitful and multiply, and fill the earth and subdue it." (Genesis 1:28) Normally a young man would be married by the time he was twenty. To be sure, a husband could readily divorce his wife, according to Deuteronomy 24:1; but she could scarcely divorce him. One deterrent to such action by the husband, however, was the requirement that he return the wife's dowry to her if he divorced her.

Some persons in the gentile world looked upon all sexual relationships as evil. They practiced and encouraged celibacy—a pattern that survived in Christian monasticism and, later, in the priesthood. The Jews, however, seemingly did not share this negative attitude toward sex.

All this information forms a background—somewhat mixed—for an appreciation of Paul's views. Personally, contrary to the Jewish norm, he preferred celibacy (1 Corinthians 7:1). However, he viewed marriage as the lesser of two evils: marriage or immorality (verse 2). Yet Paul wished that all were as he was (verse 7). According to Mark 10:11-12 and Luke 16:18, Jesus forbade divorce for any cause; but according to Matthew 5:31-32 and 19:9, a man may divorce his wife for unchastity. Paul advised against the divorce of Christian couples (1 Corinthians 7:10-11), but he permitted it in the case of mixed marriages when the non-Christian partner desired it (verse 15).

1 Thessalonians 4:1-8. *Finally, brethren, we beseech and exhort you:* In verse 3 Paul warns his readers against immorality, for they are sanctified. In the next verse he displays a higher regard for marriage than he does in First Corinthians; for he states that "each one of you know[s] how to take a wife for himself in holiness and honor," which seemingly is an approval of marriage. Paul also warns against adultery, for "the Lord is an avenger." (verse 6) The observation in verse 7, "For God has not called us for uncleanness, but in holiness," is similar to what Paul states in 1 Corinthians 6:19-20, the memory selection for this lesson.

Selected Scripture

King James Version

1 Corinthians 7:1-7

1 Now concerning the things whereof ye wrote unto me: It is good for a man not to touch a woman.

2 Nevertheless, to avoid fornication, let every man have his own wife, and let every woman have her own husband.

3 Let the husband render unto the wife due benevolence: and likewise also the wife unto the husband.

4 The wife hath not power of her own body, but the husband: and likewise also the husband hath not power of his own body, but the wife.

5 Defraud ye not one the other, except it be with consent for a time, that ye may give yourselves to fasting and prayer; and come together again, that Satan tempt you not for your incontinency.

6 But I speak this by permission, and not of commandment.

7 For I would that all men were even as I myself. But every man hath his proper gift of God, one after this manner, and another after that.

1 Thessalonians 4:1-8

1 Furthermore then we beseech you, brethren, and exhort you by the Lord Jesus, that as ye have received of us how ye ought to walk and to please God, so ye would abound more and more.

2 For ye know what commandments we gave you by the Lord Jesus.

3 For this is the will of God, even your sanctification, that ye should abstain from fornication:

4 That every one of you should know how to possess his vessel in sanctification and honour;

5 Not in the lust of concupiscence, even as the Gentiles which know not God:

Revised Standard Version

1 Corinthians 7:1-7

1 Now concerning the matters about which you wrote. It is well for a man not to touch a woman. 2 But because of the temptation to immorality, each man should have his own wife and each woman her own husband. 3 The husband should give to his wife her conjugal rights, and likewise the wife to her husband. 4 For the wife does not rule over her own body, but the husband does; likewise the husband does not rule over his own body, but the wife does. 5 Do not refuse one another except perhaps by agreement for a season, that you may devote yourselves to prayer; but then come together again, lest Satan tempt you through lack of self-control. 6 I say this by way of concession, not of command. 7 I wish that all were as I myself am. But each has his own special gift from God, one of one kind and one of another.

1 Thessalonians 4:1-8

1 Finally, brethren, we beseech and exhort you in the Lord Jesus, that as you learned from us how you ought to live and to please God, just as you are doing, you do so more and more. 2 For you know what instructions we gave you through the Lord Jesus. 3 For this is the will of God, your sanctification: that you abstain from immorality; 4 that each one of you know how to take a wife for himself in holiness and honor, 5 not in the passion of lust like heathen who do not know God; 6 that no man transgress, and wrong his brother in this matter, because the Lord is an avenger in all these things, as we

6 That no man go beyond and defraud his brother in any matter: because that the Lord is the avenger of all such, as we also have forewarned you and testified.
7 For God hath not called us unto uncleanness, but unto holiness.
8 He therefore that despiseth, despiseth not man, but God, who hath also given unto us his holy Spirit.

Memory Selection: Know ye not that your body is the temple of the Holy Ghost which is in you, which ye have of God, and ye are not your own? For ye are bought with a price: therefore glorify God in your body. (1 Corinthians 6:19-20)

solemnly forewarned you. 7 For God has not called us for uncleanness, but in holiness. 8 Therefore whoever disregards this, disregards not man but God, who gives his Holy Spirit to you.

Memory Selection: **Do you not know that your body is a temple of the Holy Spirit within you, which you have from God? You are not your own; you were bought with a price. So glorify God in your body.** (1 Corinthians 6:19-20)

The Scripture and the Main Question —Charles M. Laymon

SEX IS A FACT OF LIFE

"Let's face it, sex is a fact of life," said a high school teacher of biology in arguing for a course in sex education for the public school. "I know, but . . . ," came the reply from a member of the schoolboard. The question of sex education in the public schools was not an issue in biblical times because they had no schools as we know them today. The people did, however, talk openly about sex, more openly by far than our fathers did. All one has to do is read the Bible to discover this fact. Not only the usual "acceptable" sex acts are mentioned but also homosexuality and sodomy.

The point here is that the Bible recognizes sex as a fact of life. Some forms of sex it brands as immoral, but others it accepts as not only proper but also necessary to a meaningful marriage.

In our passage from First Corinthians (7:1-7) the apostle Paul was

arguing in behalf of a happy marriage for those who chose to be married. Most likely Paul was unmarried, probably because he needed to give his whole time to his calling as a missionary (verse 7). We also know that on the whole he thought others should not marry because he believed the end of the world was near and they should be "free" to prepare for it (1 Corinthians 7:29-31). He faced the fact, however, that the sex instinct is very strong; and he concluded it was sometimes better for people to marry if they could not control their passions (1 Corinthians 7: 9).

Persons today may or may not agree with Paul's line of reasoning, but it is clear he was facing the fact of sex rather than sweeping the issue under the rug and being hush-hush about it. Our puritan silence is dead in today's sexual revolution; sex is going to be openly discussed from now on. The real issue is *what* we are going to say and *how* we are going to say it. Are we going to talk sense or nonsense? Is our discussion to be Christian or unchristian?

IN HOLINESS AND HONOR

The first-century world was full of sexual license and immorality. At this stage the sexual revolution of our day resembles this period. It is difficult for some persons, now as then, to tell the difference between freedom and license. They want freedom in sexual expression without responsibility.

In contrast to this attitude Paul wrote to the Thessalonians urging them to "abstain from immorality" and telling each man to "take a wife for himself in holiness and honor." (1 Thessalonians 4:3-4) To combine sex relations with holiness and honor may seem strange to some who view all sex as dirty and obscene. Not so to Paul, who saw persons as filled with the Holy Spirit (verse 8). On this basis sex relations are spiritual relations.

Albert Schweitzer was more than a medical missionary. He was also a distinguished musician, a theologian of repute, a highly esteemed New Testament scholar, and a skilled philosopher. In all these disciplines he discovered a single thread running throughout that gave meaning and value to his activities. He called it "reverence for life." In his autobiography *Out of My Life and Thought* Schweitzer wrote, "Let a man once begin to think about the mystery of his life and the links which connect him with the life that fills the world, and he cannot but bring to bear upon his own life and all other life that comes within his reach the principle of Reverence for Life. . . . The ethic of Reverence for Life is the ethic of Love widened into universality."

Is not reverence for life the very same principle Paul had in mind when he wrote of a man's regarding his wife "in holiness and honor"?

SEX AND LOVE

Sex is more than a physical experience. David Reuben, whose views were referred to in "The Main Question" section for this lesson, holds that, broadly considered, sex is more than intercourse. He would also include caressing, hugging, reassurance, and "above all, love."

The potential of love makes it the greatest thing in the world. When, therefore, it is cheapened, prostituted, and treated only as a "kick," a "charge," or a passing pleasurable sensation, the loss is irreparable.

Some persons do not know how to express their love. It is bottled up within, and they act as though they did not feel it. Others have loved and lost and been hurt by the experience; they may reject love when it comes again. Still others are denied love because their family life has been cold and cruel. The hunger for love exists, but they do not know how to satisfy it; and they may settle for a cheap substitute. Whenever any one of these things occurs, it is a tragedy; for life is unfulfilled.

A THEOLOGY OF SEX

A fire at Leyden United Church of Christ in Brookline, Massachusetts, made it necessary to redesign the altar of the church. When the building committee faced the question of what they should have carved on the wooden panel above the altar, they decided that a carving of the Holy Family would be best because, since God was a loving father, the family was the heart of our Christian faith.

In commenting upon this decision a member of the church said, "Someone ought to write a theology of sex."

At first the idea seemed unreal, if not preposterous. But why should not sex have a theological foundation? This would remove it from the emotional flotsam and jetsam of daily living and give it a firm foundation in the nature of existence. Did not God create persons male and female and command them to be fruitful and multiply?

What should be included in a theology of sex? Does the existence of sex say anything about the nature of God and the nature of man? What does it say? Does the fact that we speak of God as a father imply anything that would illumine the nature of the sex act that leads to offspring? What kind of God would place the sex drive in man? Is man more than a creature of sex? How much more?

If questions such as the above were introduced into discussions on the modern sexual revolution, we might discover answers that were basic. We would then view sex as God views it.

Helping Adults Become Involved —Ronald E. Schlosser

Preparation of Self and Class

One needs look no further than the movie advertisements in a large city newspaper to get an idea of the extent to which sex is being peddled in the marketplace. To be sure, this is not the whole, or even the major part, of the sexual revolution going on in our country today; but it does serve as a barometer for measuring the kind of "sex pressure" being exerted on our society by forces seeking to take advantage of—even to mold—the so-called new morality. Here are advertising blurbs from a recent film "direct from Denmark": "A bold film that goes as far as possible . . . mass of nudity and intimacy . . . high-powered lesbian drama . . . sex and quality combined . . . totally revealing." Undoubtedly you will find similar advertisements in your local newspaper. You might cut these out and paste them on a piece of poster paper, making a collage for display in your classroom.

If in your reading this week you come upon any newspaper stories or magazine articles dealing with some aspect of the sexual revolution— whether relating to birth control advice, abortion laws, campus morality, or the like—clip these also and bring them to the class session. If a particularly pertinent article appears in a publication readily accessible to the members of your class, call their attention to it during the week and ask them to read it by Sunday. Such an article might serve as a good discussion starter for your session.

In focusing on today's main question Dr. Laymon suggests a number of issues that have been churned up in the backwash of the sexual revolution. Although the session plan that follows offers one way of approaching the main question, you may wish to delve into some other aspect of the topic, particularly if you feel there is class interest and concern. For instance, your group might consider the pros and cons of sex education in public schools, or the ethics of abortion, or the need for a theology of sex.

Whichever direction you take, the following two learning goals might provide a foundation for your study:

1. To identify the nature of the

sexual revolution going on in our society.

2. To evaluate New Testament standards of morality in light of the increasing permissiveness in our secular culture.

Presenting the Main Question

Exactly what is the nature and extent of the sexual revolution going on in today's society? Begin the session by asking this question and having each class member state what he feels is a characteristic of this revolution. If some are of the opinion that there is no major revolution taking place, have them indicate why they think this is so.

A number of your members may mention news stories or articles they have read recently that illustrate their position. You might refer to the kind of movies being shown currently in theaters and drive-ins. If you have prepared a collage of movie advertisements, this might be displayed. Frankness in films and television, more open talk about sex in schools and in the home, increasing pressure to liberalize homosexual laws and abortion laws, the ready availability of contraceptive information and devices, the new moral attitude and standards among the young—these are some of the characteristics of the sexual revolution going on in our society.

Developing the Lesson

Discuss with the class some of the benefits and dangers of the sexual revolution. One of the benefits is the demise of the "conspiracy of silence" about sex. *Sex* is no longer considered a word to be whispered about only in the shadows of the bedroom. Yet with the increasing availability of erotica in the open marketplace, there is the danger that sex is being viewed only

as "fun and games," which is a graver distortion than the previous false Victorian inhibitions. And while it is good that repression and fear are being replaced by a completely open and honest attitude toward sex, a new form of dread is now developing—a dread that one will be a social misfit if he does not adopt a liberal outlook and liberal behavior patterns concerning sexual matters. Rather than the pressure to conform to a narrow set of moral standards, the pressure now is to conform to a broader set of standards, whether one feels he should or not.

Raise this question, Is New Testament morality as old-fashioned as some people claim? To deal with this question, divide the class members into two groups. Assign one group 1 Corinthians 7:1-7 and the other group 1 Thessalonians 4:1-8. Ask the members of each group to read their respective passage and discuss it in light of the question you have raised. Allow about ten minutes for this discussion in groups, then call the members together for reporting and a general sharing of opinions. You might refer to the material in the biblical exegesis above as it relates to the class discussion.

One important concept ought to be shared with the class members somewhere in the discussion. This is the need to distinguish between *sex* and *sexuality*. To understand sex means to be aware of the body and the physical and emotional responses between persons because of their bodies. To understand sexuality means to go beyond the physical-emotional processes in order to discover what these mean in the total life of a person, to his personality and to his behavior in society. Sexuality is a medium of personal expression, an important way of revealing who we are and how we think and feel. Thus the biblical view of sexual morality is more than a series of statements about what we should or should not do as Christians. The Bible sees us as sexual beings created by God, redeemed by Christ, and commanded to live a life of love in which respect for the personhood of others is a prime prerequisite. A Christian life style, which includes one's sexuality, might well be described by the insight expressed by Hendrik Kraemer, the noted Dutch clergyman, "I will not tell you what you should do, but I *will* tell you who you are."

Helping Class Members Act

Conclude the session by having the class members consider one or two of the following problem situations, as time allows.

1. You discover that your teen-age child has seen a restricted film (under seventeen not admitted) by lying about his age. What should you do? See the film yourself and then discuss it with your child? Punish your child for lying and going to "dirty" movies? Discuss with your child why he went to see the film and instruct him not to go again without asking permission? Start a campaign for stricter enforcement of the movie rating system at the local theater? Some other action?

2. Your daughter, away at college, freely admits she has slept a number of nights at the apartment of a boy living off campus and feels she has not done anything wrong. She says she loves the boy and that he loves her. What should you do? Insist she transfer to a local college where she can live at home under your supervision? Put the pressure on the young couple to get married immediately? Talk to your daughter and try to convince her that what she is doing is indeed wrong? Petition the college administration to adopt stricter controls for dormitory and off campus living? Some other action?

3. You are close friends with your next-door neighbor, a woman who is raising her two children—ages eight and ten—herself because her husband left her a year ago to have an affair with another woman. Since that time he has gone from woman to woman, but now he wants to return to his wife. She asks your counsel. What would you advise? What information would you like to know before giving counsel? Do you feel you ought to give counsel? What other persons might give counsel to this woman? If you were in this woman's place, what might you do? Why?

One way of dealing with these problem situations is to role play them for a brief period of time. If none of the situations seem pertinent to your group members, you might use another one more relevant to their concerns and interests. For example, you could role play a PTA meeting in which the issue of sex education in the schools is raised. Try to discover where your class members really need to come to grips with the implications of the sexual revolution for their lives and then plan this concluding activity accordingly.

Planning for Next Sunday

Ask your members to come prepared next week to indicate ways in which minority groups have been exploited—either on the basis of race, religion, or national origin—in your community or region.

Passages of Scripture that members may want to read in advance include: Luke 10:25-28; Colossians 3:11; and James 2:1-9.

The Racial Revolution

Background Scripture: Genesis 1:26-27; Luke 10:25-37;
Ephesians 2:11-18; Colossians 3:1-11; James 2:1-9

The Main Question —Charles M. Laymon

When James Forman the black militant leader walked into the pulpit of Riverside Church in New York City and delivered his Black Manifesto, charging the church with wrongs against the blacks and demanding a half billion dollars as reparations for past injustices, the church was in turn shocked, angered, put on the defensive—and thoughtful. In a brief time several major denominations reacted to the Manifesto by assigning funds to areas of need within the black community. These funds were not given to Forman and his group to administer but were mostly distributed through and by black groups within the denominations.

No single denomination, to my knowledge, agreed with Forman's militant views. Nor did any approve of the way in which he made his demand. The whole idea of reparations seemed extreme. How then are we to account for the response that followed?

During the period of heated reaction after the Forman incident, a young adult class was discussing the claims made and the response by official church groups. One young father said heatedly, "It is blackmail, pure and simple. Even if the claim were true, which it isn't, I wouldn't have given the blacks a cent at the point of a gun." A mother replied, "I think we should forget that the demand was made by a militant black and consider the charge on its merits alone." "That's just it," spoke up another, "the case has no merits at all." At this a high school teacher interjected a question, "Where does conscience come in? Shouldn't we face up to our complacency in the past? I don't like the word *reparations,* but I think we should do something." "But we have done something and are doing something," chimed in a woman on the back row.

This real life situation brings us face to face with the question of race relations. The Scripture passages that follow do likewise.

As You Read the Scripture —Martin Rist

Luke 10:25-28. *And behold, a lawyer . . . saying, "Teacher, what shall I do to inherit eternal life?"* Cyrus, King of Persia and conqueror of the Jews, was an enlightened ruler who attempted—and not without success—to remove barriers of race, nationality, and religion. Later, Alexander the Great, who conquered the Persians, was similarly motivated and worked toward a marriage of the culture of the West (Greece) and the East (Persia). Even so, racial antagonisms peristed in the first-century Mediterranean world.

This tendency toward racism had been evident among the Hebrews from an early period of their history; they considered themselves an exclusive

74

people, chosen by God himself. This exclusiveness was implemented by the Mosaic law, which covered almost every aspect of human life. Regulations concerning food prevented Jews from eating with non-Jews. Various rules and rites of purification curtailed relationships with other peoples. Their peculiar celebration of a holy day, the Sabbath, prevented trade one day a week. Their rite of circumcision was a unique sign of their covenant with God. Above all, the Jews practiced strict monotheism, which precluded any religious fellowship with non-Jews. Even in the early days of Christianity this exclusive bent was in evidence, for Jewish Christians set themselves apart from the uncircumcised gentile Christians, even refusing to eat at the same table with them (see Galatians 2:11-12).

DOES THE PASSING OF LAWS SOLVE THE PROBLEM OF RACISM? MUST THERE NOT ALSO BE A CORRRESPONDING CONVICTION IN THE HEARTS AND CONSCIENCES OF PEOPLE?

A part of this racism was a strange, but somewhat understandable, hostility between two very similar peoples, the Jews and the Samaritans. Apparently the enmity was mutual. Even so, they both worshiped the same God; were circumcised; had the same books of the Law (however, the Samaritans did not accept the other books of the Old Testament); celebrated the Sabbath and certain other festivals in common; and looked for a deliverer, one for a Davidic Messiah, the other for a Taheb (Restorer) like Moses. On the other hand, they had different holy mountains (Zion and Gerizim), different priesthoods, and different temples. The Jews considered the Samaritans a mixed race of people, not pure "Hebrew"; also they thought the Samaritans had at times assisted their enemies. Perhaps even more basic to this animosity was the fact that the antagonisms that existed between the Southern and the Northern Kingdoms in the time of the Divided Kingdom (935-721 B.C.) had survived.

This complicated but little known background gives point to the parable of the good Samaritan. The parable is prefaced with a dialogue concerning the Great Commandment. In Mark 12:28-30 (paralleled by Matthew 22:34-40) the conversation occurs during the last week of Jesus' life, and the teaching is given by Jesus. However, in Luke the setting is earlier in the career of Jesus; and the teaching is given by a lawyer. In either account the greatest commandment is a quotation of Deuteronomy 6:5, which is part of the basic Jewish creed or *Shema* avowing the oneness of God. (Both Matthew and Luke leave out the crucial statement, "Hear, O Israel: the LORD our God is one LORD.") The commandment that follows, "You shall love your neighbor as yourself," is also from the Old Testament (Leviticus 19:18).

This answer raised the question, "And who is my neighbor?" Jesus replied with the now familiar parable about a man (obviously a Jew) who had been beaten, robbed, and left for dead on the road to Jericho. A priest, who theoretically should have helped a fellow Jew, passed him by without offering aid, as did another Temple official, a Levite. However, a third traveler, a Samaritan, a traditional enemy of the Jews who might well have imitated the priest and Levite, stopped and gave the wounded man invaluable aid. The teaching of this parable is self-evident; elaboration usually spoils it.

Colossians 3:11. *Here there cannot be Greek and Jew:* Paul, who lived in three worlds, Jewish, Greek, and finally Christian, was constantly confronted with the barriers of race, religion, and sex. In part, he sums up his view about the all-inclusiveness of Christianity in this passage. A similar statement in Galatians 3:28 adds the equal status of women: "There is neither Jew nor Greek, there is neither slave nor free, there is neither male nor female; for you are all one in Christ Jesus." We may wonder why he failed to mention the Samaritans, a number of whom had become Christians.

James 2:1-9. *My brethren, show no partiality:* This section from the Book of James is not specifically related to the racial problem, but the author is concerned about the partial treatment given in a church to a rich man in contrast to that accorded to a poor man. This partiality does not "fulfill the royal law," that is, "You shall love your neighbor as yourself." (verse 8)

Selected Scripture

King James Version	Revised Standard Version
Luke 10:25-28	*Luke 10:25-28*
25 And, behold, a certain lawyer stood up, and tempted him, saying, Master, what shall I do to inherit eternal life?	25 And behold, a lawyer stood up to put him to the test, saying, "Teacher, what shall I do to inherit eternal life?" 26 He said to him, "What is written in the law? How do you read?" 27 And he answered, "You
26 He said unto him, What is written in the law? how readest thou?	

27 And he answering said, Thou shalt love the Lord thy God with all thy heart, and with all thy soul, and with all thy strength, and with all thy mind; and thy neighbour as thyself.
28 And he said unto him, Thou hast answered right: this do, and thou shalt live.

Colossians 3:11
11 Where there is neither Greek nor Jew, circumcision nor uncircumcision, Barbarian, Scythian, bond nor free: but Christ is all, and in all.

James 2:1-9
1 My brethren, have not the faith of our Lord Jesus Christ, the Lord of glory, with respect of persons.
2 For if there come unto your assembly a man with a gold ring, in goodly apparel, and there come in also a poor man in vile raiment;
3 And ye have respect to him that weareth the gay clothing, and say unto him, Sit thou here in a good place; and say to the poor, Stand thou there, or sit here under my footstool:
4 Are ye not then partial in yourselves, and are become judges of evil thoughts?
5 Hearken, my beloved brethren, Hath not God chosen the poor of this world rich in faith, and heirs of the kingdom which he hath promised to them that love him?
6 But ye have despised the poor. Do not rich men oppress you, and draw you before the judgment seats?
7 Do not they blaspheme that worthy name by the which ye are called?
8 If ye fulfil the royal law according to the scripture, Thou shalt love thy neighbour as thyself, ye do well:
9 But if ye have respect to persons, ye commit sin, and are convinced of the law as transgressors.

shall love the Lord your God with all your heart, and with all your soul, and with all your strength, and with all your mind; and your neighbor as yourself." 28 And he said to him, "You have answered right; do this, and you will live."

Colossians 3:11
11 Here there cannot be Greek and Jew, circumcised and uncircumcised, barbarian, Scythian, slave, free man, but Christ is all, and in all.

James 2:1-9
1 My brethren, show no partiality as you hold the faith of our Lord Jesus Christ, the Lord of glory. 2 For if a man with gold rings and in fine clothing comes into your assembly, and a poor man in shabby clothing also comes in, 3 and you pay attention to the one who wears the fine clothing and say, "Have a seat here, please," while you say to the poor man, "Stand there," or, "Sit at my feet," 4 have you not made distinctions among yourselves, and become judges with evil thoughts? 5 Listen, my beloved brethren. Has not God chosen those who are poor in the world to be rich in faith and heirs of the kingdom which he has promised to those who love him? 6 But you have dishonored the poor man. Is it not the rich who oppress you, is it not they who drag you into court? 7 Is it not they who blaspheme that honorable name by which you are called?

8 If you really fulfil the royal law, according to the scripture, "You shall love your neighbor as yourself," you do well. 9 But if you show partiality, you commit sin, and are convicted by the law as transgressors.

| *Memory Selection:* If ye fulfil the royal law according to the scripture, Thou shalt love thy neighbour as thyself, ye do well: But if ye have respect to persons, ye commit sin. (James 2:8-9) | *Memory Selection:* If you really fulfil the royal law, according to the scripture, "You shall love your neighbor as yourself," you do well. But if you show partiality, you commit sin. (James 2:8-9) |

The Scripture and the Main Question —Charles M. Laymon

LAWS ARE NOT ENOUGH

When the Supreme Court in 1954 interpreted the United States Constitution as requiring more than separate but equal education for Negro children and youth, major adjustments in the laws of the land were made. The social legislation that has followed has spread into the areas of housing, employment, entertainment, and straight down the line wherever discrimination has been practiced against Negroes. Each new law has been hailed as a step forward.

This attempt to seek a change through law has also spread into the churches. Changes in organizational structures have been made in major denominations. The merging of Negro and white groups on national, regional, and local levels has taken place. In one Protestant denomination, for instance, some areas have Negro bishops presiding over predominantly white ministerial and lay groups.

We are so law minded in America, and justly so, that we conclude that all we need do is to pass a law and all will be well. Isn't it true, however, that laws only take us part of the way? First of all, they must be enforced; and second, there must be a corresponding conviction in the hearts and consciences of the people. If this latter aspect is lacking, the laws of the land cannot be made effective. Law alone cannot make us love one another.

For instance, it is claimed by Major J. Jones of Gammon Theological Seminary that in the future, in spite of the new church legislation, "black people will be getting together more and more at unofficial levels within the context of white annual conferences." The reason for this is that in spite of the legislation enacted black people remain a minority group in church organizations. They have discovered a new image of themselves in which they take pride, and they remain apart by choice. In addition, whites have not always wanted or known how to unite with them in Christian brotherhood.

LOVE MAKES THE WORLD GO ROUND

The only foundation for Christian interracial fellowship that will succeed is found in what we call the "Great Commandment" (Luke 10:25-28). Here we are told to love God completely and man fully. These words of Jesus are a summons to invincible good will, to show respect for all persons.

During these years of racial adjustment one frequently hears the expression "second-class citizens." It suggests that blacks, or any other minority group, and whites should be treated alike. There should not be one kind of citizenship for whites and another kind for other groups.

The Christian expression would be

78

there should be no "second-class persons." We get our citizenship from the state, but we were created persons by God. In the final analysis our self-respect comes from God. We should love and accept ourselves and one another because God made us; he loved and accepted us in our creation as well as in his coming to help us through Jesus Christ.

SEGREGATION IN REVERSE

When black groups become militant against white groups, it is just as reprehensible as when the reverse is true. Then you have segregation in reverse. There is a real threat of this happening today. The experience is a black backlash; and even though it is to be regretted, it bears witness to the fact that the repressed blacks are discovering their own image and that they like what they see. Note their pride in the Afro hair style.

What a change from the days when black people were owned, bred, and sold like cattle! An early United States newspaper reported that in certain states "as much attention is paid to the breeding and growth of Negroes as to that of horses and mules. . . . We raise them both for use and for market."

Black people find it difficult to forget these segments from their past. Much of their vehemence against whites stems from the fact that today all this history is held before them by militant blacks to stimulate their continued fight for freedom.

WHEN BARRIERS DIVIDE

When one actually stands before the Berlin wall, the tragedy of barriers that separate people from one another bears down upon you. It is a depressing experience. One woman in our party said, "I wish I hadn't seen it; it will haunt me in my sleep." And it does.

Still other barriers separate people besides physical ones. *Psychological barriers*, where all communication is blocked; *cultural barriers*, where value systems are in conflict; *social barriers*, where class consciousness keeps persons apart; *economic barriers*, where the "haves" and the "have-nots" are separated; *religious barriers*, where creeds divide—all these are tragically real.

Paul found a way to bridge these barriers. In Christ they simply did not exist. Jew–gentile, free–slave, male–female, rich–poor—all were one in Christ (Colossians 3:11). For instance, the only race with which Christ is concerned is the human race in its strength and weakness as well as in its glory and depravity. We all belong to him, and he shares himself with us.

The bond that binds all men together in Christ is more than the holding of a common thought or creed. It is a personal attachment to him that makes us a family—his family. This is the reason why the church is the body of Christ, and in this body there can be no separations if it is to continue to live.

Helping Adults Become Involved —Ronald E. Schlosser

Preparation of Self and Class

The parable of the good Samaritan is such a familiar story that sometimes people need to hear it from a new or different translation of the New Testament. Two such modern translations—actually, paraphrases—that put the story into a contemporary setting are found in *God Is for Real, Man* by Carl F. Burke and *The*

Cotton Patch Version of Luke and Acts by Clarence Jordan. The Burke paraphrase, entitled "A Cool Square Comes to the Rescue," sets the story on the streets of the inner city; while the Jordan version happens on the road between Atlanta and Albany, Georgia. Both accounts use the language of the locale in which they are set, providing a powerful commentary on what Jesus' parable is really all about.

As was mentioned in the session plan for October 8, the paperback book *The Negro in the City* would be a helpful resource to have in preparing for today's session. In a series of articles and photos leading black voices speak out about life in the ghetto, the deep scars of racism, and the new mood of the black people.

Dr. Laymon introduces the main question by referring to the Black Manifesto issued by James Forman several years ago. If this incident can still spark discussion among your class members, you might wish to refer to it (or to some similar, more recent event) as a way of beginning your session. Care should be taken, however, when using a controversial incident such as this lest your class members spend all their time expressing their negative feelings and neglect dealing positively with the broader issue under consideration. You will need particularly to be alert to persons who may voice displeasure over some current minority group movement or program. Are these persons really cloaking their prejudices by denouncing the movement rather than the people? Help them focus on the people involved (what they are seeking and why) rather than on the methods these people are using. Analyze the cause of their grievances.

To guide your study of today's main question you might aim at the following learning goals:

1. To become aware of the ways people of minority groups have been and still are being exploited.

2. To consider how Christians can effectively work as individuals and as groups toward eliminating such exploitation.

Although today's session focuses primarily on race relations, the background Scripture certainly applies to the treatment of people of other minority groups as well, particularly those of different religions and nationalities. Keep this thought in mind as you pursue your study today.

Presenting the Main Question

If you do not begin your session by discussing a current issue such as the one mentioned above, read to the class a modern paraphrasing of the story of the good Samaritan. The one by Clarence Jordan in *The Cotton Patch Version of Luke and Acts* is particularly good. Ask your members what they think of it. Is it an accurate interpretation in terms of meaning and intent? Why, or why not? What setting and characters might your members suggest to make the parable relevant to their time and situation?

Developing the Lesson

Move now to a reading of Luke 10:25-37 from a standard version or translation of the Bible. Ask the class members to indicate what they see as the main point Jesus is trying to make. Refer to the comments on this passage in the biblical exegesis. Help the members to recognize that the *neighbor* in this parable was not the victim of the robbery but the man who helped him—the Samaritan. Jesus seems to be saying that a neighbor is not someone else but ourself. We are the neighbor to others. This is a fine but important distinction. It sees *neighbor* more as a verb than as a noun. We are to *neighbor* others— to be concerned about them, to help them, to love them. Rather than viewing them as neighbors to us, we should see ourselves as neighbors to them—indeed, "neighborers" to them.

Have the class members next mention examples, either from the present or from history, of people who have been mistreated or exploited because of their race, religion, nationality, or economic status. Here are a few such examples; the class members certainly will be able to add others to the list.

1. *Slum housing.* Absentee landlords charge exorbitant rent and make no improvements to the dwelling.

2. *Price markups in ghetto supermarkets.* The excuse given is that losses need to be recouped because of excessive shoplifting and theft.

3. *Treatment of Indian Americans.* When the government of the United States forcibly removed the Indian tribes from their ancestral lands to the territory of Oklahoma, it promised them that the land would be theirs "so long as the grass shall grow and the rivers shall flow." History attests to the sorry record of broken promises, and present conditions confirm the shameful neglect that has been the lot of these people.

4. *Treatment of Mexican Americans.* The exploitation of migrant farm laborers continues, despite recent efforts to improve their working and living conditions.

5. *Job discrimination.* Closed door policies in construction unions, unequal pay for equal work in non-union shops, lack of opportunity for promotion on the job, inability to procure employment in certain specialized fields—these are but a few examples of job discrimination.

Discuss some of the barriers that keep people apart, that tend to cause the exploitation or mistreatment of certain groups of people by others. Refer to the sections headed "Segregation in Reverse" and "When Barriers Divide" in Dr. Laymon's commentary.

Move on to consider what role the church has played in these matters. When and where has the church contributed to or condoned exploitation of minority groups? How has it fought to end exploitation and bring social justice to oppressed people? What part has your local church had in dealing with these concerns? What yet needs to be done?

Helping Class Members Act

To help the class members consider this last question, have them turn to two passages of Scripture: Colossians 3:1-11 and James 2:1-9. Suggest that half the class members look at the Colossians passage and the other half the James passage. The members might pair off to do their study, or they could do it as individuals. They are to consider what their respective verses say about the stance that individual Christians and the church as a whole should take in dealing with the exploitation of people, particularly minority groups, that is still being carried on in our society. What implications do these verses have for individual and group action? Ask your members to be as specific as possible.

Allow time at the end of the session for the sharing of insights and ideas. If there is some obvious injustice existing at the moment in your community, now is the time to call it to the attention of the public. Election time often makes local government officials more sensitive to the voices of the electorate. Plan, however, to work *with* the persons whose cause you are championing. People who have been mistreated and exploited so long often are quite wary of "do-gooders" who come on strong on their behalf. Work through already established channels. If no such channels exist, get counsel from responsible citizens as to how you and your group might get something moving.

Planning for Next Sunday

Ask for three volunteers to serve on a panel next week to discuss the subject, "Civil Disobedience: How Much and When?" One panel member is to take the position that we must obey the law at all times, even if it is unjust. The second panel member is to defend the right of people to disobey a law if they, out of conscience, deem it unjust. The third member of the panel is to uphold the right to dissent through peaceful means, such as mass demonstrations, marches, picketing, sit-ins, and the like.

Background Scripture for the next session includes: 2 Chronicles 10:1-16; Romans 13:1-7; and 1 Peter 2:11-17.

Unit IV: The Changing World of National and International Relations
Horace R. Weaver

FIVE LESSONS   OCTOBER 29—NOVEMBER 26

Hundreds of thousands of people throughout the world are becoming accustomed to flying halfway around the world—breaking the time zones so that night only has two or three hours' duration and day seems to stretch out to twenty-two hours. Because of this, the distances between Cairo and New York, Boston and Borneo, are becoming exceedingly small. The relationships between governments and people, between church and state, between the great powers of the world and the smaller powers all become of significant concern for the Christian today.

The lesson for October 29, "Freedom Under Authority," helps us face the tension between individual freedom and increasing governmental control. What attitudes should Christians have as they seek to make the kingdoms of this world become the kingdoms of our Christ? November 5, "The Church in the Secular State" helps us face the questions of what is Caesar's and what is God's and what does it mean to "obey God rather than men." November 12, "All Nations Under God" raises a basic question as to the relationship of all men to one another and also the question as to whether God is actually moving in the history of our time with a divine plan. November 19, "Living on the Brink" presents biblical examples of persons who dealt with the tensions between militarism and pacifism so that adults can develop a Christian attitude toward internationalism that will help bring "peace on earth, good will toward men." The lesson emphasizes the place of Christian faith and hope as opposed to helpless fatalism. November 26, "What Kind of Peace?" points us to the biblical faith that peace can come in only one way—the way of God's methodology, the way of suffering for others (the way of the cross).

Audiovisual resources appropriate for use with the lessons of this unit may be found in the introduction to Unit I, page 13.

Freedom Under Authority

Background Scripture: 2 Chronicles 10:1-16; Romans 13:1-7; 1 Peter 2:11-17

The Main Question —Charles M. Laymon

During recent years protest movements have almost reached epidemic proportions. More than once a state of national emergency has been in the making. Month after month the theme song of the protesters has been "Everything is wrong."

At the heart of this protest activity has been a reaction against authority. Persons used to call authority the status quo. Now young people are calling it the establishment. Freedom from the controls of government, freedom from the supervision of college administrations, freedom from all censorship in mass media, freedom from anything and everything that sets limits on self-expression—these have been and still are the dominant demands we hear.

Are we a free people? What does freedom mean? Does the absence of all restraint guarantee freedom? Freedom for what? Is there a difference between freedom and license? Is man ever completely free? Is freedom always good?

Czechoslovak statesman Jan Masaryk, speaking to an American audience, once said, "Raised in liberty, most Americans accept their freedom as a matter of course. Sometimes it seems to me you free people don't realize what you've got. . . . You can wake up in the morning free to do as you choose, to read what you wish, to worship the way you please, and to listen to a lovely piece of music."

Is the above statement still true? Does authority guarantee these freedoms or threaten them? The following biblical passages shed light on the issue between freedom and authority.

As You Read the Scripture —Martin Rist

Romans 13:1-7. *Let every person be subject to the governing authorities:* Paul, as we know, was a Hellenistic (Greek-speaking) Jew of the Dispersion; a native and citizen of a Hellenistic city, Tarsus; and apparently a Roman

83

citizen by birth (Acts 21:39; 22:25-28). It is significant that Paul's clearest statement about the relationship of a citizen or subject to the Empire is stated in his letter to the Christians of Rome, which he wrote as a kind of introduction of himself before visiting them. This mainly gentile church was no doubt composed of people from various parts of the Empire, persons of differing racial and religious backgrounds; for all roads led to the capital city. We may but conjecture what their attitudes toward the Roman government might have been; Paul himself may not have known, but he apparently thought that it was important to share his views with them.

Paul opened his religio-political comment by observing that every person should *be subject to the governing authorities,* that is, to the Emperor and the Roman officials under him. This has nothing to do with church leaders, which Paul deals with in other contexts. In accord with traditional Jewish teaching, which regarded a king, Jewish or otherwise, as God's agent, Christians should obey the authorities because "they have been instituted of God." They are his servants. By obeying them Christians are obeying God. It follows, then, that "he who resists the authorities" is actually resisting God himself, who has appointed them, and by doing so will incur judgment, possibly that of God himself (verse 2). Those who do good need not fear, but wrongdoers should be fearful. They will be punished, for an official of Rome is a servant of God (verses 3-4).

Another reason for being subject to these officials is for the "sake of conscience." (verse 5) What is *conscience?* Paul does not define the term, which was used by Greek thinkers long before his day. Indeed, it is difficult to define; for it is intangible, subjective, so much so that one man may decide to follow a given course because of "conscience," another a quite different, even opposite, course for the sake of "conscience."

As was true of Jesus' teaching, Paul declared that persons should pay taxes; for the Roman authorities are agents ("ministers" is a misleading translation) of God. They should also be accorded "respect" and "honor." (verses 6-7)

1 Peter 2:11-17. *I beseech you . . . to abstain from the passions of the flesh:* First Peter was written shortly before or after A.D. 100 during a period of persecution. Perhaps it was during the reign of Trajan, around A.D. 110; for Trajan persecuted Christians in Bithynia, which is mentioned in 1 Peter 1:1 among the churches addressed. In places First Peter seems to be dependent upon the Book of Romans, especially upon Romans 13:1-7.

The author, whoever he was, urged Christians to "maintain good conduct among the Gentiles, so that . . . they may see their good deeds and glorify God." (verse 12) He charged them to "be subject for the Lord's sake to every human institution," which of course meant the Empire; "to the emperor as supreme"; and to his "governors." (verses 13-14) Christians are to live as "free men"; but, of course, within the framework of Roman law. Accordingly, their freedom should not become a "pretext for evil." They are to live as "servants of God." (verse 16)

In a period when emperor worship was required of all peoples (save the Jews) under penalty of death the advice in verse 17 is especially significant. Christians are, of course, to "honor all men." They are to "love the brotherhood" (their fellow Christians). Moreover, they are to "fear God," that is, they are to worship him and him alone. At the same time, they are to "honor the emperor"; but, by implication, they are not to worship him, regardless of consequences.

Selected Scripture

King James Version	Revised Standard Version

Romans 13:1-7

1 Let every soul be subject unto the higher powers. For there is no power but of God: the powers that be are ordained of God.

2 Whosoever therefore resisteth the power, resisteth the ordinance of God: and they that resist shall receive to themselves damnation.

3 For rulers are not a terror to good works, but to the evil. Wilt thou then not be afraid of the power? do that which is good, and thou shalt have praise of the same:

4 For he is the minister of God to thee for good. But if thou do that which is evil, be afraid; for he beareth not the sword in vain: for he is the minister of God, a revenger to execute wrath upon him that doeth evil.

5 Wherefore ye must needs be subject, not only for wrath, but also for conscience sake.

6 For for this cause pay ye tribute also: for they are God's ministers, attending continually upon this very thing.

7 Render therefore to all their dues: tribute to whom tribute is due; custom to whom custom; fear to whom fear; honour to whom honour.

Romans 13:1-7

1 Let every person be subject to the governing authorities. For there is no authority except from God, and those that exist have been instituted by God. 2 Therefore he who resists the authorities resists what God has appointed, and those who resist will incur judgment. 3 For rulers are not a terror to good conduct, but to bad. Would you have no fear of him who is in authority? Then do what is good, and you will receive his approval, 4 for he is God's servant for your good. But if you do wrong, be afraid, for he does not bear the sword in vain; he is the servant of God to execute his wrath on the wrongdoer. 5 Therefore one must be subject, not only to avoid God's wrath but also for the sake of conscience. 6 For the same reason you also pay taxes, for the authorities are ministers of God, attending to this very thing. 7 Pay all of them their dues, taxes to whom taxes are due, revenue to whom revenue is due, respect to whom respect is due, honor to whom honor is due.

1 Peter 2:11-17

11 Dearly beloved, I beseech you as strangers and pilgrims, abstain from fleshly lusts, which war against the soul;

12 Having your conversation honest among the Gentiles: that, whereas they speak against you as evildoers,

1 Peter 2:11-17

11 Beloved, I beseech you as aliens and exiles to abstain from the passions of the flesh that wage war against your soul. 12 Maintain good conduct among the Gentiles, so that in case they speak against you as wrongdoers, they may see your good

they may by your good works, which they shall behold, glorify God in the day of visitation.

13 Submit yourselves to every ordinance of man for the Lord's sake: whether it be to the king, as supreme;

14 Or unto governors, as unto them that are sent by him for the punishment of evildoers, and for the praise of them that do well.

15 For so is the will of God, that with well-doing ye may put to silence the ignorance of foolish men:

16 As free, and not using your liberty for a cloak of maliciousness, but as the servants of God.

17 Honour all men. Love the brotherhood. Fear God. Honour the king.

Memory Selection: [Live] As free [men], and not using your liberty for a cloak of maliciousness, but [live] as the servants of God. (1 Peter 2:16)

deeds and glorify God on the day of visitation.

13 Be subject for the Lord's sake to every human institution, whether it be to the emperor as supreme, 14 or to governors as sent by him to punish those who do wrong and to praise those who do right. 15 For it is God's will that by doing right you should put to silence the ignorance of foolish men. 16 Live as free men, yet without using your freedom as a pretext for evil; but live as servants of God. 17 Honor all men. Love the brotherhood. Fear God. Honor the emperor.

Memory Selection: **Live as free men, yet without using your freedom as a pretext for evil; but live as servants of God. (1 Peter 2:16)**

The Scripture and the Main Question —Charles M. Laymon

FREEDOM UNDER GOD

That God has created us free men is a general assumption in our democratic society. We claim God-given rights that belong to us by birth— rights to life, liberty, and the pursuit of happiness. These rights have been extolled by poets, statesmen, preachers, and politicians.

When we come down to reality, however, we discover that our freedoms are conditioned by the way we live, think, and act. The electrical engineer knows that power is made available only when certain conditions are met; the physicist knows that atomic energy is available only when specific controls are provided; the physician knows that bodily vigor is present only when the laws of health are kept; and the preacher knows that happiness and wholeness are present in our lives only when we are following God's will. This series of "only whens" could be extended to every area of experience.

Thoughtful persons will probably agree that freedom is conditioned by certain structures God has built into his universe. Sometimes we call these the laws of nature. The author of First Peter would probably not have understood this expression, but he did know that personal life was conditioned by moral laws. He realized also that true freedom was possible only when God's ways were followed. Thus he tied freedom and loyalty to God together: "Live as free men, . . . live as servants of God." (1 Peter 2:16)

GOVERNMENT INSTITUTED BY GOD FOR MAN'S GOOD

Paul held that government was a divine institution. The apostle's general conviction was that everything necessary for fullness of life is rooted and grounded in God. Benjamin Franklin was approaching Paul's outlook when he said, "We have been assured, sir, in the sacred writings that except the Lord build the house, they labor in vain that build it. I firmly believe this; and I also believe that without his concurring aid we shall succeed in this political building no better than the builders of Babel."

The apostle Paul would not have been popular among some protesting groups today because he regarded government as instituted by God for man's good. At first glance it appears that Paul is saying that government can do no wrong. But this is not what he meant. Instead, he saw the institution of government as created by God to provide law and order within which persons could experience the freedom of the sons of God. It is in this light that Paul's statement in Romans should be read: "Let every person be subject to the governing authorities. For there is no authority except from God." (13:1)

The opposite of no government or a weak government is anarchy—every man for himself regardless. This would bring chaos. All our most significant institutions would be destroyed. Home life, freedom of movement and assembly, economic development, educational opportunities, and religious freedoms would be impossible if anarchy existed in the nation. This kind of freedom would be no freedom at all. It would be no less than slavery.

OBEDIENCE TO GOVERNMENT AND THE DEMANDS OF CONSCIENCE

If government is regarded as instituted by God, does it follow that all governments are good? What about the government that executed Paul? In the Book of Revelation the Roman state was viewed as an agent of Satan and as such was seen as the source of great evils among men. Christians were advised to resist Rome unto death.

While the institution of government is of God's making, certain specific governments may prostitute their purpose and be evil in intent. Under these circumstances the Christian conscience may feel called upon to protest, rebel, or even disobey the edicts of the state.

The founding fathers of our country, who refused to obey the orders of the British king, were considered traitors and lawbreakers by the Crown. If they had failed in the Revolutionary War, men like George Washington, Thomas Jefferson, Alexander Hamilton, and John Adams quite likely would have been hanged. They did not fail, however, and as a result established a new free nation, becoming national heroes instead.

Today we refer to a person's refusal to obey the law on the grounds of conscience as civil disobedience. Conscientious objectors whose sincerity is clearly evident are usually relieved from military duty. The law provides for this. Some major denominations officially support such dissenters, even providing funds to argue their cases before a court of law. These bodies do not sanction violent dissent but support freedom of conscience as a Christian principle.

How far should freedom of conscience be allowed to express itself within the state? What if such freedom threatens to destroy the state that guarantees it? What about draft card burning and other acts of protest? Whom does this help? Whom does it hurt? Where does one draw the line? Or does one draw the line? What if one's way of expressing his freedom of conscience threatens the freedom of others? These are knotty questions both the state and the conscientious objector must seriously consider.

DOES GOVERNMENTAL CONTROL ENDANGER FREEDOM?

George Bernard Shaw once said, "Unless human beings make the State their servant, it soon becomes their master." Are we in danger of letting this happen?

In our highly organized society it is becoming increasingly easy to say, "Let the government do it." The cost of education, public health agencies, social work, anti-poverty programs, and so forth, is so staggering that it often seems that only the government has the means to support these services. Income taxes make it impossible for individuals to accumulate fortunes sufficient to care for these needs. In turning so consistently to the government for aid, are we not running the risk of losing our freedom? "Whoever controls the purse strings will soon control the people," said a political candidate. Was he correct?

A balance must be found between the need for governmental assistance on the one hand and the freedom and responsibility of the individual on the other. This is a Christian concern because it involves the well-being of persons.

Helping Adults Become Involved —Ronald E. Schlosser

Preparation of Self and Class

Sometime during the week plan to meet with those who volunteered to serve as panel members for this session. Share with them the comments by Dr. Laymon on the preceding pages and the information contained below in the section "Presenting the Main Question." Have them suggest how they would like to make their presentations—formally from behind a table at the front of the classroom or informally from where they will be sitting (if the class is in a circle or semicircle). Indicate that after their presentations the class members will have an opportunity to question them and to discuss the points they make.

To lend atmosphere to the classroom, you might make several posters on which are printed slogans of current protest groups and resistance movements. Display these around the classroom at appropriate spots.

If you sense that your group would have particular interest in discussing the issues related to the draft resistance movement, you might plan to show the twenty-eight-minute motion picture A Matter of Conscience. (See page 13.) The film documents the personal struggles of two young Americans against war and the draft. One chooses to go to jail for his beliefs; the other decides to go to Canada. Regardless of their own opinions, viewers certainly will become more aware of the painful decisions today's youth are facing as they struggle with the issue of freedom and authority.

In today's session you should help your class do at least two things:

1. Explore the meaning of Christian freedom.

2. Determine what attitudes Christians should have toward secular authority.

If for some reason you are not able to arrange a panel presentation, you might introduce the main question by means of an opinion poll. Duplicate and distribute the following series of statements and have the class members indicate whether they "strongly agree," "partially agree," "partially disagree," or "strongly disagree" with each.

1. A Christian should obey all civil laws, whether or not he feels they are just or unjust.

2. A Christian should follow his conscience and feel free to disobey unjust laws, if necessary.

3. Demonstrating with a large group for a just cause, even without a police permit, is justified at times.

4. Mass demonstrations are ineffective ways of making known one's point of view as a Christian.

5. Circulating petitions of protest is a more effective way to express dissent than picketing peacefully at a public gathering.

Presenting the Main Question

Write the topic of the panel discussion on the chalkboard ("Civil Disobedience: How Much and When?") and introduce the members of the class who will serve on the panel. Each of the members is to represent a different point of view. A brief summary of each viewpoint is presented below.

Panel member number one is to take the position that a person must obey the law at all times, regardless of whether it is just or unjust. He could refer to Paul's words in Romans 13:1-7 to support his position. At the time of his writing, Paul viewed the Roman government as friendly and just, a source of order in society.

Christians, said Paul, should be good citizens and "be subject to the governing authorities." Since government was instituted by God, those who resist these authorities resist God.

Panel member number two is to defend the position that a Christian has a sacred obligation to follow his God-given conscience in the matter of obeying laws. If he believes a certain law is unjust, he will, like Peter in Acts 5:29, respond by saying, "We must obey God rather than men." Martin Luther King, Jr., once wrote, "A just law is a man-made code that squares with the moral law or law of God. An unjust law is a code that is out of harmony with the moral law. . . . Any law that uplifts human personality is just. Any law that degrades human personality is unjust." [10] Of course, Christians who hold this position should be prepared and willing to take whatever consequences may come their way because of their disobedience, as indeed Dr. King did through his life and death.

Panel member number three is to uphold the position that the right to dissent is one of the privileges of a free society and that this dissent may often be demonstrated by nonviolent but forceful means. A number of Old Testament prophets relied on public demonstrations to put across their message. (See Isaiah 20; Jeremiah 19:1-13; Ezekiel 5:1-12; 12:1-7.) Jesus himself rather forcefully demonstrated his displeasure by chasing the money-changers out of the Temple (Matthew 21:12-13).

Developing the Lesson

Following the presentations of the panelists, encourage the class members to ask them questions or to comment on the various viewpoints

[10] *The Christian Century*, June 12, 1963, p. 769.

expressed. There are alternative actions other than the three presented by the panelists. What does your class think of violent resistance to oppressive laws—such as the open rebellion of the American colonists against the British in 1776? When one's personal liberty is at stake, is revolt against the oppressor justified? If some young men feel they are being forced to fight an immoral war and kill innocent women and children, as has been the argument of the peace demonstrators in recent years, are they justified in seeking to overthrow a system that allows such injustice (in their opinion) to exist?

As a total class you might study in some depth the two major Scripture passages for consideration today. Look first at Romans 13:1-7. On what basis did Paul advise the Christians to support the government authorities? Compare Paul's statement with that of Jesus in Mark 12:17. Are they basically in agreement? What connection if any is there between the question of paying one's taxes and the question of obeying authority? How are Christians to decide whether or not the authority deserves respect or honor? Use these questions and the comments by Dr. Laymon and the writer of the biblical exegesis to guide your study of this passage.

Turn next to 1 Peter 2:11-17. Is the author's position similar to that of Jesus and Paul? What does the statement "Live as free men" mean? (See the comments in the biblical exegesis.) In the context of today's society what does *freedom* mean? Is man ever completely free? (See the comments by Dr. Laymon in the section "Freedom Under God.") Focus on the relationship between human freedom and Christian freedom. Help the class members to see the distinction between the two.

Helping Class Members Act

During the session the class members have had an opportunity to express their opinions about the meaning of freedom, authority, and dissent. Plan to spend the last part of the session helping the members organize ideas and opinions into a sort of summary statement of guiding principles. In other words, on the basis of what has been said about freedom, authority, and dissent, how would members state the principles that guide their actions in these areas? If responses are slow in coming, suggest the following to stimulate their thinking:

1. One's exercise of freedom, including freedom to dissent, should be done responsibly. One is not free to deprive another of his freedom. For example, a massive sit-down demonstration in a public thoroughfare blocks the free flow of traffic and deprives others of the right of free movement.

2. The form a protest takes should be directly related to the unjust law or action being protested. A bus boycott against the unfair practices of a bus company seems a valid kind of protest, whereas a march on a newspaper office to intimidate the paper into taking up the cause seems unrelated to the injustice being protested.

3. One should be willing to take the consequences of willful civil disobedience. If conscience dictates that one should disobey a law because it is unjust, he must be ready to accept the consequences of that action.

These are a few examples of the kind of principles your group might formulate. Seek to get consensus but do not disregard minority points of view. Encourage members to think through the implications of whatever they suggest.

Planning for Next Sunday

Ask your class members to come prepared to identify and discuss what they think is the most pressing church-state problem today. You might also consider inviting to the session a special resource person, such as a lawyer, civil official, or community leader, to share his views about church-state relations.

Ask members to read in advance Matthew 22:15-22 and Acts 5:27-29.

LESSON 2   NOVEMBER 5

The Church in the Secular State

Background Scripture: Daniel 6; Matthew 22:15-22; Acts 5:17-29

The Main Question —Charles M. Laymon

The issue of church and state might not seem to be a live one in the United States. Our constitution commits us to a separation between the two. The founding fathers, in setting up this arrangement, did so because they were concerned that the church should not attempt to assume the rights of the state. The so-called state church had proved to be a problem in Europe and had sometimes led to the domination of the church over government.

By contrast in our time there have been attempts by the state in totalitarian countries to control the church. This was true in Germany during the time of the Nazis. Albert Einstein wrote of those days: "I never had any special interest in the Church before, but now I feel a great affection and admiration because the Church alone had the courage and persistence to stand for intellectual truth and moral freedom."

Sometimes the church today is accused of withdrawing into itself and showing little concern with affairs of state in Washington. "The church isn't relevant when it comes to what is going on in Congress," said a political science major. Should it be? Must the church "stick to its own knitting" (whatever that might be), or is it called upon to be the conscience of the state? Should idealistic politicians look to the church for support in their efforts for the improvement of the nation or just for votes when election time is at hand? Can the church be an effective lobbying force when national issues are being decided? Should it be? The biblical passages that follow will be helpful in answering these questions.

As You Read the Scripture —Martin Rist

Matthew 22:15-22. *Then the Pharisees went and took counsel how to entangle him in his talk:* This account of the tribute money is derived from Mark 12:13-17. Actually, it is not directly concerned with the church and the secular state (for there was no Christian church at the time) but rather with the Jews and the Roman Empire. It should be recalled that after about a century of national independence under their own rulers the Jews were conquered in 63 B.C. by the Romans under Pompey. The Romans then became the rulers of Palestine and of the Jews living there, as well as of the Jews dispersed throughout the Empire.

In the main the Romans were tolerant rulers. First of all, since Judaism was an ethnic religion (the traditional religion of a people), the Romans granted the Jews religious liberty to worship their God as their fathers had done. They exempted Jews from the worship of the emperor, and the Jews were asked to pay temple sacrifices *for* the emperor but not *to* him. Jews were also exempted from military conscription. Although the Romans were tax hungry, they allowed the Temple to collect the yearly half-shekel tax from male Jews twenty years old and older throughout the Empire. However, as conquerors the Romans did expect political loyalty. They required the maintenance of peace and order, and they insisted upon the payment of taxes. Finally, the Romans allowed the Jews a considerable degree of self-government under their Sanhedrin (Council).

Jewish views about the Empire were divided. Many Jews, of course, were unconcerned. Although the Romans exercised some control over the appointment of the high priest, lest the office be used for political purposes, the priestly party, the Sadducees, were not averse to Roman rule as long as the status quo of the priesthood was insured. The Pharisees, though not actually content with being a subjugated people, considered that the Romans, like previous conquerors, were agents of God punishing his people for their sins. They were concerned with religious liberty, which had been granted. We do not have any evidence of discontent among the Samaritans. However, another and militant group, the Zealots, were fanatically against Roman control. They constantly plotted against the Romans, at times were involved in revolt, and in A.D. 66 were successful in causing the Jews to rise up against Rome with tragic results, including the destruction of the Temple and the liquidation of the priesthood.

These historical facts prepare the way for the interpretation of the account of the tribute money. The tax in question, a poll or head tax, was to be paid with a small silver coin, smaller than our quarter, called a *denarius*. The Jews resented this tax more than any other because it was a visible symbol of their subjugation by Rome. The question as asked was "loaded" and potentially politically dangerous. Had Jesus said the tax should not be paid, he would have been accused of siding with the Zealots. On the other hand, had he said, "Pay this poll tax, for this is God's will," he would have alienated an untold number of his disciples and potential followers. As it was, he adopted a middle course: "Render unto Caesar the things that are Caesar's," that is, civil obedience including the payment of this obnoxious tax, and render to "God the things that are God's," that is, according to the Jewish practice and the rights accorded by Rome to worship God and him alone.

Acts 5:27-29. *When they had brought them, they set them before the council:* This passage deals with the relationship of the Christians to the Jewish authorities (the Sanhedrin or Council) and not to the Romans. The Sanhedrin was thoroughly Jewish, being composed of some seventy leading men (Sadducees, Pharisees, and their scribes). It was convened and presided over by the high priest. As stated before, the Jews had been granted a great deal of local autonomy, with authority over matters that were controlled by their Jewish religious and civil laws, including, of course, control of the Temple. Accordingly, the disciples, who had violated no Roman law but who were apparently displeasing the Temple authorities by preaching in the Temple, were brought before the Sanhedrin. They were beaten (both a Jewish and Roman custom) and released with injunctions that they should no longer proclaim their message about Jesus, injunctions that they disobeyed, saying, "We must obey God rather than men."

Selected Scripture

King James Version	Revised Standard Version
Matthew 22:15-22	*Matthew 22:15-22*

King James Version

Matthew 22:15-22

15 Then went the Pharisees, and took counsel how they might entangle him in his talk.

16 And they sent out unto him their disciples with the Herodians, saying, Master, we know that thou art true, and teachest the way of God in truth, neither carest thou for any man: for thou regardest not the person of men.

17 Tell us therefore, What thinkest thou? Is it lawful to give tribute unto Caesar, or not?

18 But Jesus perceived their wickedness, and said, Why tempt ye me, ye hypocrites?

19 Shew me the tribute money. And they brought unto him a penny.

20 And he saith unto them, Whose is this image and superscription?

21 They say unto him, Caesar's. Then saith he unto them, Render therefore unto Caesar the things which are Caesar's; and unto God the things that are God's.

22 When they had heard these words, they marvelled, and left him, and went their way.

Acts 5:27-29

27 And when they had brought them, they set them before the council: and the high priest asked them,

28 Saying, Did not we straitly command you that ye should not teach

Revised Standard Version

Matthew 22:15-22

15 Then the Pharisees went and took counsel how to entangle him in his talk. 16 And they sent their disciples to him, along with the Herodians, saying, "Teacher, we know that you are true, and teach the way of God truthfully, and care for no man; for you do not regard the position of men. 17 Tell us, then, what you think. Is it lawful to pay taxes to Caesar, or not?" 18 But Jesus, aware of their malice, said, "Why put me to the test, you hypocrites? 19 Show me the money for the tax." And they brought him a coin. 20 And Jesus said to them, "Whose likeness and inscription is this?" 21 They said, "Caesar's." Then he said to them, "Render therefore to Caesar the things that are Caesar's, and to God the things that are God's." 22 When they heard it, they marveled; and they left him and went away.

Acts 5:27-29

27 And when they had brought them, they set them before the council. And the high priest questioned them, 28 saying, "We strictly charged you not to teach in this name, yet

in this name? and, behold, ye have filled Jerusalem with your doctrine, and intend to bring this man's blood upon us.

29 Then Peter and the other apostles answered and said, We ought to obey God rather than men.

Memory Selection: **Render therefore unto Caesar the things which are Caesar's; and unto God the things that are God's. (Matthew 22: 21)**

here you have filled Jerusalem with your teaching and you intend to bring this man's blood upon us." 29 But Peter and the apostles answered, "We must obey God rather than men."

Memory Selection: **Render therefore to Caesar the things that are Caesar's, and to God the things that are God's. (Matthew 22:21)**

The Scripture and the Main Question —Charles M. Laymon

UNDER TWO FLAGS

The Christian citizen is a person who lives under two flags, both of which call to him for loyalty and obedience. The state expects him to vote, pay taxes, and serve in the defense of his country. On the other hand, the church summons him to obedience to Christ, support of the institution, and devotion to the Kingdom.

This dual relationship is easier to assume in some countries than in others and at some times than at others. The tradition is deep seated in our nation that it is Christian to be a good citizen and that when one is a good American he will be a good Christian. We traditionally refer to ourselves as a Christian nation.

One of the reasons for the above is that when our nation came into being there was felt and expressed an idealism that made the identification of the nation with Christian principles logical. The documents of state that our forefathers wrote are filled with Christian idealism. As a nation we had a mission under God.

Not by chance were certain words from "The New Colossus" by Emma Lazarus inscribed on the base of the Statue of Liberty:

Give me your tired, your poor,
Your huddled masses yearning to breathe free,
The wretched refuse of your teeming shores.

These words sound like Jesus' sermon at Nazareth when he spoke of his mission as proclaiming release to the captives and setting at liberty those who were oppressed (Luke 4:18-19).

We called ourselves the "melting pot" of the world and gloried in the opportunities for fullness of life that our nation held out to all mankind.

GIVE TO EACH WHAT IS OWED

In one of the Scripture passages for this lesson an attempt was made to trap Jesus with a question regarding the payment of taxes to the Roman government. This had been a touchy issue among the Jews for some time. Why should they support a pagan government, they argued, since they were the people of God? For this reason they hated tax collectors who were in the service of Rome.

Jesus' reply has become a classic: "Render therefore to Caesar the things that are Caesar's, and to God the things that are God's." (Matthew 22:21*a*) At first it might seem that

Jesus' answer was a clever piece of footwork to get out of a tight corner. If he had said outright, "Yes, pay taxes to Caesar," the Pharisees would have said to the people, "How can he be your Messiah when he supports a foreign power?" If he had said, "No, do not pay your taxes," they would have reported him to the authorities. When Jesus was brought before Pilate, you will recall, one of the charges they leveled at him was that he perverted the nation and forbade the Jews to give tribute to Caesar (Luke 23:2). Actually, Jesus' answer was not sidestepping the issue. He was saying that Rome should be paid for services rendered the nation and that God also should be given what was due him. The state provided law and order, protection, roads, and a court system intended to bring justice to the people. God too showered his gifts upon the people by giving them life, fruitful seasons, and the blessedness of a new life in the Kingdom. To him also the nation was deeply indebted. In short, Jesus was saying that men should pay their debts—to the state and to God.

THE ULTIMATE OBLIGATION

In spite of the insistence that men should be law abiding and pay their debts to the state, there can be no doubt but that Jesus put God first. To recognize God was the ultimate obligation. This places upon the church the responsibility to insist upon God's sovereign right to our obedience. We can never forget Peter's words before the council, "We must obey God rather than men." (Acts 5:29)

The church should always be in the position of calling the state to task, in the name of Christ, when it becomes unjust, materialistic, militaristic, and irresponsible in its calling under God. Martin Niemöller was a distinguished German hero as a submarine commander in World War I. Afterwards he became an outstanding Lutheran minister. When the Nazis came into power, he would not call upon the church to support this godless totalitarian state. Consequently he was arrested and imprisoned. In a rare letter, written to his wife after he had spent six months in jail, Niemöller said, "I think my imprisonment belongeth to the holy humor of God. First the mocking joke, 'Now we have got that fellow!' and then the imprisonment; and what are the consequences? Full churches, a praying community! To get bitter about such things would be shameful ingratitude."

The church is not being disloyal to the state when it refuses to support some of the state's actions. Instead, because the church is interested in the highest ideals of government it cannot "rubber-stamp" every decision in Washington. If, as a church, we remain informed, dedicated, and vocal, our voice raised in support of better government for the well-being of all the people will be heard. But if we become subservient, complacent, and a silent majority, we not only will not be true to our calling but we will have missed our opportunity to contribute to the improvement of the nation.

CHURCH AND STATE TOGETHER

Whenever the church becomes the state or the state becomes the church, there is a great loss on both sides. We have only to recall how dissolute, worldly, and corrupt the Holy Roman Empire became to realize the truth of this statement. In this same vein, whenever the church becomes a state church supported by the government, it tends to lose its soul and voice and becomes subservient to the state rather than to God.

The togetherness the church and the state may share focuses upon the recognition by both that each has a responsibility to the people and before God. The story is told of Marshal Foch's coming to kneel at the altar of a church during World War I. A peasant woman, already praying there, rose to leave. The marshal restrained her, saying, "We are all equal here." Here the church and the state were bound together in the presence of God.

Helping Adults Become Involved —Ronald E. Schlosser

Preparation of Self and Class

As you prepare for this week's session, be alert to the issues that have been highlighted in the current election campaign, both on the local and the national level. What issues should be of particular concern to Christians? Or should all issues be of concern to Christian citizens? Are there any issues that lift up the question of church-state relations? If so, what are the various points of view expressed? Would one of these issues make a good starting place for the class discussion?

If there is such an issue currently in the news, plan to highlight it in your session. Otherwise, use the case studies described below to bring today's main question into focus. Prior to the session, copy on 3″ x 5″ cards the following short case studies involving some aspect of church-state relations. These studies will serve as discussion starters for small groups during the session.

CASE STUDY 1

A small religious sect, the Old Order Amish, believes it must separate itself from the worldliness of modern society. The people of this group dress plainly and avoid the use of such modern conveniences as electricity, telephones, and automobiles. They also refuse to send their children to "worldly" public schools. Although the Amish operate their own schools, using their own members as teachers, they have been ordered by the courts to send their children to public schools because their own teachers are not certified. The Amish have consistently objected to this order and, although heavily fined, have refused to comply with what they feel is an unfair state law. They have also refused, on religious grounds, to employ certified teachers. Questions: Is the state government interfering with the religious freedom of the sect? Can the state forcibly require persons to go against their consciences, especially if the matter seems to be basic to their deep religious beliefs?

CASE STUDY 2

Over the years, questions have been raised as to the extent to which state and city governments may use tax funds to support schools operated by church-related organizations. Some states use tax revenues to pay transportation costs of parochial schoolchildren. Others provide free text books to all schoolchildren, public and private. For years church-related colleges have benefited from government grants and loans. Questions: Should secondary and primary schools operated by religious groups receive federal financial aid? Does government aid to church-related schools violate the principle of the separation of church and state?

CASE STUDY 3

Religious and charitable groups have always enjoyed a special tax-exempt or tax-sheltered status in our country. Real estate, buildings, and other property owned by churches and church-related agencies are essentially tax free holdings. Special exemptions, such as a housing allowance, are given members of the clergy on their income tax form. A local church can benefit from community services such as police and fire protection and yet not be required to pay for these services through taxes. Questions: Is the church and state really separate if the state grants special privileges to the church? What obligations, if any, does the church have to the state?

Three learning goals may be aimed for in today's session, if time allows:

1. To consider certain conflicts that arise between church and state.

2. To examine what the Bible says about church-state relations.

3. To explore areas in which church and state may cooperate.

If you have invited a special resource person to be with you today, let him suggest the direction the class session might take. A lawyer may want to discuss the legal aspects of certain legislation pertaining to a church-state question; a civic official may wish to explore areas in which church and state may be mutually helpful; a community leader could suggest how a group of churches might work together with other community agencies on a particular project. Plan to use the resource person in a way that will help the whole class benefit from his knowledge and skills.

Presenting the Main Question

Begin the session by having the class identify as many church-state questions or issues as it can. Among those that might be suggested are: prayer and Bible reading in the public school; religious celebrations in the public school, such as Christmas and *Hanukkah;* the use of chaplains in the military services; Sunday sales laws; religious lobbies or pressure groups to influence legislation; special tax privileges for church groups; financial aid to parochial schools. Your members may be able to suggest other issues. List all those suggested on the chalkboard.

Developing the Lesson

Divide the class members into three groups and have the groups discuss either several of the church-state issues just mentioned or the three case studies above. If you will be dealing with the case studies, assign one to each group, giving the conveners of the groups the cards containing the description of the situation and the discussion questions.

Allow about ten minutes for this small group discussion and then call the class members together to share findings and opinions. Do not try to pin down definite conclusions, however, until the members have had an opportunity to look at the Scripture passages for study today.

Ask someone to read aloud Matthew 22:15-22 and another person to read Acts 5:17-29. Ask your members to review the questions they discussed in their small groups. Do the passages give any additional insight into issues that were considered?

You might ask various members to indicate how they would interpret these passages. Use the comments by Dr. Laymon and the writer of the biblical exegesis to guide the group's study of these verses. Record on newsprint general ideas or principles that may be drawn from the Scripture references. See particularly the sections "Give to Each What Is Owed" and "The Ultimate Obligation" by Dr. Laymon.

Helping Class Members Act

Conclude the session by exploring with the class the areas in which the church and state may cooperate. Are there ways the state can give support to the work of the church without violating the principle of churchstate separation? (The state can give police and fire protection; guarantee the right of peaceful assembly; provide resources and facilities for supplemental ministries such as health care, education, recreation, and the like.) In what ways can the church give support to the work of the state? (Provide facilities and personnel for community-oriented programs; serve the community through child-care centers, low-cost housing, nursing and retirement homes, hospitals, and rehabilitation centers; provide counseling and chaplain services to state-run institutions.)

If time allows and there is interest, consider with your class members how much influence the church should attempt to exert in state affairs. What responsibility do the church as a whole and its members as individuals have in speaking out either for or against legislation being considered at the local, state, or national level? Should the church take an active role in pressing for specific legislation or government action in such matters as civil rights, equal employment, the welfare system, and selective service? Why, or why not?

Ask the class to suggest guidelines that might form the basis for mutually acceptable church-state relations. Some of the following might be considered.

1. Recognize that we live in a pluralistic society. The rights and feelings of all people must be considered.

2. Get the facts. Do not operate on a rumor or hearsay level.

3. Determine what is right for you. Do not insist that everyone must believe and act as you do.

4. Make your voice heard but do it constructively, not destructively.

5. Practice love in all encounters with persons in government positions.

Planning for Next Sunday

Ask each person in your class to bring to next week's session a newspaper clipping that highlights a trouble spot in the world.

Background Scripture includes: Isaiah 45:1-6; Amos 9:7-8; Jonah; and 1 Timothy 2:1-5.

LESSON 3   NOVEMBER 12

All Nations Under God

Background Scripture: Isaiah 45:1-6; Amos 9:7-8; Jonah; 1 Timothy 2:1-5

The Main Question —Charles M. Laymon

The speaker at a service club luncheon was discussing the national economy in America. He was concerned because the balance of trade between imports and exports was changing; other nations were "poaching" in our markets abroad. "And to think," he added, "we financed the recovery of these competing nations after the war."

In the question period that followed a man in the group asked the speaker, "But doesn't the health of our national economy depend upon the health of world economy?" It was a pointed question. Can any nation exist alone in the modern world? Are we not forced into internationalism because of economics?

If economics in today's world requires an international approach, what about religion? Does not the Christian faith also push us beyond national boundaries? Where does the love of God begin? How far does it go? Where does it stop? Is isolationism in any form Christian?

It has been estimated that there are more than one hundred thousand billion stars in the universe. Conditions for humanlike life may exist on other heavenly bodies. Will the time ever come when we will need to extend our brotherhood into outer space?

Our definition of neighborhood is growing larger by leaps and bounds. Science, economics, and the Christian faith alike are driving us into a broader outlook and association than at any previous time in history. The biblical passages in this lesson will prove helpful as we face these new experiences.

As You Read the Scripture —Martin Rist

Isaiah 45:1-6. *Thus saith the* LORD, *to his anointed, to Cyrus:* Cyrus the Great, a Persian king and enlightened conqueror, had added Palestine to his realm in 539 B.C. when he became the master of the Babylonian Empire. A lenient and tolerant ruler, he permitted the Jews to return to Jerusalem from Babylonia and encouraged them to rebuild their Temple. He was admired by various peoples whom he conquered, both as a liberator from their tyrannical rulers and as one who respected their traditional customs and religions.

Cyrus was praised by the author of Isaiah 40 through 55 because of his friendliness toward the Jews and his assistance to them. The writer called him the Lord's "shepherd," who will rebuild Jerusalem and the Temple (Isaiah 44:28). Also, in Chapter 45:1 he entitles Cyrus the anointed of the Lord, which is to say, the "Messiah." This is the only occasion when a pagan ruler, and a conqueror of the Jews as well, had been given this honorific title. God, accordingly, had called Cyrus to be his agent as the chosen, anointed ruler of God's people Israel, whom Cyrus had liberated from the hated Babylonians. However, lest Cyrus boast in his own power, God reminded him that it was God who had chosen and girded him and that there was no other God (verses 4-6), which is a strong reminder of the unqualified monotheism of Judaism.

Under Cyrus a kind of internationalism developed in the eastern part of the Mediterranean world. There was one ruler, Cyrus, and one kingdom, the Persian Empire, composed of many nations. To be sure, the people of this area had been conquered by the Persians; but even though subjugated they enjoyed a measure of freedom, peace, and prosperity under an enlightened

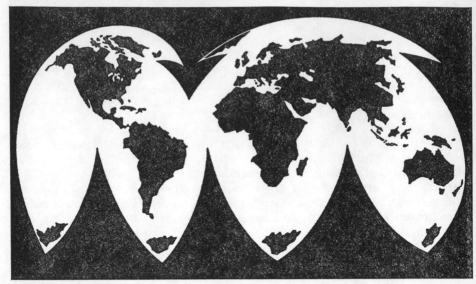

ruler. During the next two centuries or so, until Alexander defeated the Persians at Issus in 333 B.C., the Jews lived in comparative peace under Persian rule.

Amos 9:7-8. *Are you not like the Ethiopians to me, O people of Israel?* Amos was a prophet of the eighth century B.C. when the Jews were divided into two nations, Israel to the north and Judah to the south. Amos emphasized that only when the people of a nation dealt justly with one another could that nation be truly called a covenant people of God, his chosen ones. The avarice of merchants and landowners, the dishonesty and injustice of the judges, and the immorality of the people in general were betrayals of God. He urged the Jews to be imitators of God, who is just, holy, and pure.

Consequently, according to the printed lesson, the Jews, who relied upon their status as the chosen people of God, should know that because of their sins they may not continue to enjoy this unique relationship. For God has favored the (dark-skinned) Ethiopians, the Philistines (traditional enemies of the Jews), and the powerful Syrians as well. No one people, not even the Jews, has an exclusive relationship with God; and the Jewish kingdoms face destruction because they are sinful.

1 Timothy 2:1-5. *First of all, then, I urge that supplications . . . be made for all men:* It is increasingly believed that the so-called Pastorals, First Timothy, Second Timothy, and Titus, were composed sometime during the first half of the second century. This period was marked by repeated difficulties with the Roman authorities, who considered that Christianity was an illegal cult and that the Christians, who by now were for the most part gentiles not Jews, should participate in the worship of the imperial gods. Consequently Christians were subject to persecution unto death. Despite the dangerous tensions between Christianity and the Empire, the author of First Timothy urged his readers to pray for all men, especially for kings, emperors, and others in high position (verses 1-2). He further exhorted them to lead peaceable and godly lives and emphasized that there was but one God and but one mediator, Jesus Christ, between God and man (verses 3-5).

Selected Scripture

King James Version

Isaiah 45:1-6

1 Thus saith the LORD to his anointed, to Cyrus, whose right hand I have holden, to subdue nations before him; and I will loose the loins of kings, to open before him the two leaved gates; and the gates shall not be shut;

2 I will go before thee, and make the crooked places straight: I will break in pieces the gates of brass, and cut in sunder the bars of iron:

3 And I will give thee the treasures of darkness, and hidden riches of secret places, that thou mayest know that I, the LORD, which call thee by thy name, am the God of Israel.

4 For Jacob my servant's sake, and Israel mine elect, I have even called thee by thy name: I have surnamed thee, though thou hast not known me.

5 I am the LORD, and there is none else, there is no God beside me: I girded thee, though thou hast not known me:

6 That they may know from the rising of the sun, and from the west, that there is none beside me. I am the LORD, and there is none else.

Amos 9:7-8

7 Are ye not as children of the Ethiopians unto me, O children of

Revised Standard Version

Isaiah 45:1-6

1 Thus says the LORD to his anointed, to Cyrus,
whose right hand I have grasped,
to subdue nations before him
and ungird the loins of kings,
to open doors before him
that gates may not be closed:

2 "I will go before you
and level the mountains,
I will break in pieces the doors of bronze
and cut asunder the bars of iron,

3 I will give you the treasures of darkness
and the hoards in secret places,
that you may know that it is I, the LORD,
the God of Israel, who call you by your name.

4 For the sake of my servant Jacob, and Israel my chosen,
I call you by your name,
I surname you, though you do not know me.

5 I am the LORD, and there is no other,
besides me there is no God;
I gird you, though you do not know me,

6 that men may know, from the rising of the sun
and from the west, that there is none besides me;
I am the LORD, and there is no other.

Amos 9:7-8

7 "Are you not like the Ethiopians to me,

Israel? saith the LORD. Have not I brought up Israel out of the land of Egypt? and the Philistines from Caphtor, and the Syrians from Kir?

8 Behold, the eyes of the Lord GOD are upon the sinful kingdom, and I will destroy it from off the face of the earth; saving that I will not utterly destroy the house of Jacob, saith the LORD.

1 Timothy 2:1-5
1 I exhort therefore, that, first of all, supplications, prayers, intercessions, and giving of thanks, be made for all men;
2 For kings, and for all that are in authority; that we may lead a quiet and peaceable life in all godliness and honesty.
3 For this is good and acceptable in the sight of God our Saviour;
4 Who will have all men to be saved, and to come unto the knowledge of the truth.
5 For there is one God, and one mediator between God and men, the man Christ Jesus.

Memory Selection: [He] hath made of one blood all nations of men for to dwell on all the face of the earth. (Acts 17:26)

O people of Israel?" says the LORD.
"Did I not bring up Israel from the land of Egypt,
and the Philistines from Caphtor and the Syrians from Kir?
8 Behold, the eyes of the Lord GOD are upon the sinful kingdom, and I will destroy it from the surface of the ground;
except that I will not utterly destroy the house of Jacob,"
says the LORD.

1 Timothy 2:1-5
1 First of all, then, I urge that supplications, prayers, intercessions, and thanksgivings be made for all men, 2 for kings and all who are in high positions, that we may lead a quiet and peaceable life, godly and respectful in every way. 3 This is good, and it is acceptable in the sight of God our Savior, 4 who desires all men to be saved and to come to the knowledge of the truth. 5 For there is one God, and there is one mediator between God and men, the man Christ Jesus.

Memory Selection: He made from one every nation of men to live on all the face of the earth. (Acts 17:26)

The Scripture and the Main Question —Charles M. Laymon

ONE GOD—ONE WORLD

David Livingstone's heart is buried in Africa, but his bodily remains rest in Westminster Abbey, marked by a large black stone. Gold letters on the stone spell out the words, "Other sheep I have, which are not of this fold." Behind these words of Jesus is the fact that the Good Shepherd is the Lord of all the earth, and the people of every land compose his flock. This is a divine internationalism.

In science we refer to the universe; in our religion we call ourselves monotheists. Both references essentially say the same thing. The universe is a single system of life; monotheistic faith is belief in the existence of one God only.

Isaiah, writing in the period when the Hebrews were exiled in Babylonia, spoke for God in monotheistic terms when he said:

I am the LORD, and there is no other,
  besides me there is no God;
  I gird you, though you do not know me,
that men may know, from the rising of the sun
  and from the west, that there is none besides me;
I am the LORD, and there is no other.
                          (Isaiah 45:5-6)

Here is one of the most outspoken and eloquent statements of belief in the existence of one God to be found in the entire Old Testament. As such it provides a theological foundation for internationalism. If there is only one God in the universe, then all nations are his concern; and each nation has a relationship, under God, to every other nation.

THE LORD OF HISTORY

International relations is a live issue in today's world. With the sounding board provided by the United Nations, television coverage, and the press, there is no reason why any of us should not be informed about world affairs. We wait for the pronouncements of international conferences, SEATO, NATO, and other agencies of similar scope. When the governments of Western Germany and the Soviet Union confer, we listen with bated breath for the reports.

Typical of the questions we ask are, What is Russia doing? What is Communist China up to? What will the United Arab Republic do next? Will Israel provoke a war with Egypt over Suez? What stance will our Congress and the President take? The questions come, fast and furious.

Another question was asked by the biblical prophets, and perhaps we too should seek an answer to it: What is God doing right now in the affairs of men and nations? Is he at work in his world in the interests of peace, justice, and righteousness?

Isaiah asked this question at a time when the Hebrews were captives in Babylonia, with Jerusalem in ruins and the future of the people of God at the mercy of pagan powers. And he was given an answer! God was going to use the rising young Persian conqueror Cyrus to overcome the Babylonians and free the Hebrews, so that they could return home, re-establish their institutions, and once more take up their calling (Isaiah 45:1-4).

God was in control of history; he had not abdicated his concern for the nations or his purpose which he was working out through the Hebrew people. What answer would God give today if he were asked what he was doing on the scene of international history? Who has the answer here? We need a vertical answer from God and not simply a horizontal answer from men.

GOD IS COLORBLIND

When Charles Evers became the first black mayor of Fayette, Mississippi, he made a speech that *The New Yorker* magazine printed. In it Evers said, "You can't blame the kids for what is happening in this country, and you can't blame the blacks. It is the system which has kept *us* in the corner. But the black mayor and the black aldermen of Fayette are going to behave the same to everyone: young, in-between, old; black, white; rich, poor." [11]

Charles Evers' statement here is in line with the prophet Amos' statement in today's Scripture passage,

[11] June 14, 1969, p. 29.

"Are you not like the Ethiopians to me, O people of Israel?" (9:7) What Amos, speaking for God, was saying is that God is colorblind. He cares for all alike; none are his favorites. God is not a racist. How can he be since he created all the races? No special treatment of any particular race should be expected.

PRAY FOR THE NATIONS

The implications of God's creation of all men, his concern for all nations, and his love for all races lead us into an international outlook that is inescapable. They call for a way of life together that goes beyond the limits of geography, nation, and race.

What this truth means for international justice in the areas of economics, social opportunities, immigration laws, trade barriers, and so forth needs to be spelled out afresh in every age. The technology that has brought us all together into a world neighborhood forces certain decisions upon us that cannot be postponed.

As the popular song puts it, "What the world needs now is love, sweet love." In First Timothy we find an admonition from the writer along this same line. He says, "I urge that supplications, prayers, intercessions, and thanksgivings be made for all men." (2:1) He then goes on to mention "kings and all who are in high positions." (verse 2)

The responsibilities of government are tremendous today. More than at any other time in history a sound, Christian foreign policy is demanded. Those who must carry out these programs need the prayers, deep and fervent, of all men.

Helping Adults Become Involved —Ronald E. Schlosser

Preparation of Self and Class

Last week you asked your class members to bring to the session newspaper clippings about the trouble spots in the world today. In case some of your members forget to follow through on this assignment, plan to bring in recent issues of your local newspaper that contain the kind of stories you called for. Have colored construction paper and glue available for mounting the clippings. This will make them easier to handle as the class passes them around at the beginning of the session.

If you have access to a tape recorder (a small cassette type would be particularly good), record about four or five minutes of news from a radio or television broadcast. Try to get a good sampling of national and international news.

Review the projects suggested at the end of this session in the section "Helping Class Members Act." Bring to the session a sample of the items needed for undertaking any of these projects. This would include a map of the world with assorted pins; a copy of a world almanac or similar resource, containing information about countries of the world; and a list of the missionaries of your denomination or church (or the address of your denominational offices where such a list may be obtained). In addition, a dictionary ought to be available to aid the class in defining such terms as *nationalism, internationalism, colonialism,* and *imperialism.*

The main question for today can be approached from a number of directions. You may wish to deal with the three points suggested by Dr. Laymon—God's creation is for all men; his concern is for all nations;

104

and his love is for all races. Or you may wish to explore the ecumenical dimensions of the question; that is, how can the many and varied branches of the Christian church around the world cooperate in their primary mission to proclaim the gospel of Jesus Christ in word and deed?

The following session plan has been developed yet another way with these learning goals in mind:

1. To identify some of the national and international tensions in the world today.

2. To compare these with the kinds of problems encountered in Bible times.

3. To discover ways we can display Christian concern for the needs of people around the world.

Presenting the Main Question

As the class members arrive, have them mount their newspaper clippings on construction paper and pass them around. The members are to read the headlines of the various clippings and scan the stories to discern what problems seem to be the most pressing in the world today.

If you have taped a radio or television news broadcast, you might play it shortly after the session begins. Ask the class members to make a mental note of the items highlighted in the news. Are they mostly national or international concerns?

(An interesting discussion might be conducted concerning the emphasis given in this country to most news from abroad. Usually this news is presented in a way that interprets what implications it has for the United States. Such and such happened in the Middle East and has this effect on us in America. On the other hand, news broadcasts in Europe, when they focus on foreign news, usually do not

interpret it from their own country's perspective but give an objective reporting of the story as it happens, where it happens. If any of your class members have traveled abroad, you might ask them if they concur in this observation. What does this say about our own image of international importance here in the United States?)

Developing the Lesson

After the class has discussed the various news items presented, spend some time in analyzing the cause of each problem mentioned. How much of it is rooted in the spirit of nationalism? (Ask for a definition of *nationalism*.) Has colonialism either in the past or in the present been a contributing factor? (Define colonialism.) Some nations accuse others of imperialism. What is this? What role has a disputed boundary, or a treaty commitment, or the desire for independence played in the troubled situation?

Distrust, misunderstanding, pride, and arrogance often are blamed for modern international crises. But these are not new attitudes. Even in Bible times problems arose that could be traced to these basic causes. Have the class members examine today's background Scripture to get an idea of the kind of problems faced by the Jews and early Christians.

Divide the class into four sections and assign each section one of the following passages: Isaiah 45:1-6; Amos 9:7-8; Jonah 4:6-11; 1 Timothy 2:1-5. Ask the members to study their respective Scripture passages to identify the national-international concern described and the lesson it might have for us today. The members should do their study in small groups of two or three if possible. Allow about five or six minutes for this study and then have the members from the various sections share their findings and insights.

The comments by Dr. Laymon and the biblical exegesis should help guide the total class discussion. In brief the main point of each reference might be noted as follows. *Isaiah 45:1-6—* God does not limit his activity to any one nation but works through all of them to accomplish his purposes in his world. *Amos 9:7-8—*God is concerned about all nations. They are under his providential care. *Jonah 4: 6-11—*Jonah's narrow nationalism and his hatred for his nation's enemy Ninevah are countered by God's revelation of his love for all people and his desire that none should perish. *1 Timothy 2:1-5—*Christians should pray for all governments and their leaders and work for reconciliation among all peoples.

You might summarize this period of Bible study by referring to the observation made by Dr. Laymon: "If there is only one God in the universe, then all nations are his concern; and each nation has a relationship, under God, to every other nation." This means that each of us, because we are related to God in Jesus Christ, has a special responsibility to work for understanding and harmony among all nations.

Helping Class Members Act

We often feel helpless when contemplating what we can do as individual Christians to meet the challenges presented by a large and complex world. How can we tackle the problems that are international in scope from where we sit in a very tiny corner of the world? Pose this question for your class to discuss, and ask for practical suggestions as to how we can become more sensitive to the needs of our neighbors around the world.

Add to the suggestions offered by the class the following four ideas, some of which might be used by individual members who would like to undertake a personal project.

1. Display in some prominent place at home a map of the world. On the basis of current news reports, or for some other personal reason, place a pin on a particular nation each day (or group of days) and pray for the leaders and people of that nation. Find out as much information as possible about that nation and its people from an almanac, encyclopedia, or other resource.

2. For a period of two or three weeks try to discover the national origins of the families of your friends. Discover what you can about the rich heritage of the people of these lands. Pray for them.

3. After hearing a radio or television news broadcast, spend five minutes in prayer for the people and nations mentioned in the news.

4. Find out who your missionaries are—those who are serving your church or denomination at home and abroad. Put their names on a special prayer list and remember several of them in prayer each day. Perhaps you may be able to discover their birthdays and remember them with a card or note. Such information probably is available from your denomination's mission board.

Planning for Next Sunday

Look ahead to the session next week and notice the listing of films, books, and records that would make good resources. Seriously consider getting one or two of these items to provide variety and interest for your session.

Ask the class to contemplate the following question during the week and come prepared to discuss it at the next session, Will God allow man to destroy himself? Scripture passages they may also want to read include: Psalms 33:13-17; Isaiah 31:1-3; and Jeremiah 21:8-10.

Bless the Lord!
(THANKSGIVING, NOVEMBER 23)
HAROLD R. WEAVER [12]

Can a man living at the end of the twentieth century reach back to a man who lived a thousand years before Christ and say with him, "Bless the LORD, O my soul; and all that is within me, bless his holy name!" (Psalms 103:1)? The answer is that all men, in all cultures—nomadic, agricultural, or industrial—need times set aside to thank God.

Thanksgiving wells up from the heart of man as naturally as a helium-filled balloon floats upward. It often springs unbidden but spontaneously to our lips. Thus years ago I was riding with a college debate team on a snow-covered road in Ohio. Our car spun around in the road. We teetered on the edge of a precipice. I remember the words of one youth in the back seat as he shouted, "God help us!" I also recall the words of another who said, as our car came safely to rest at a point of near-disaster, "Thank God." No one stopped to ask whether God actually had anything to do with our safety; we simply drove on, when we could, with those words ringing in our ears, "Thank God."

Having said this much, it seems only fair to add that when we offer our thanks to God we do not thank him for everything. Certainly evil does not come directly from the hand of God. Who amongst us would thank God for the tidal wave that inundated East Pakistan two years ago, killing hundreds of thousands of persons? If we thought God sent the wave, then we should not have sent aid to the victims; for we would be frustrating God's purposes. Nor does it occur to us today to view a cholera epidemic as due to the explicit will of an angry God. Venereal diseases are sweeping this country and have, indeed, become epidemic; but we do not blame God. Rather, we are likely to insist that God will not do evil things. We recall a man named Jesus who suggested that if human fathers know how to do good, refusing to give stones to children asking for bread, then how much more will the heavenly Father express his goodness to his children (Matthew 7:7-12). We may not understand the evil about us, but we do not feel God is responsible for it. Indeed, we are more prone to side with John Greenleaf Whittier in his poem "The Eternal Goodness":

Yet, in the maddening maze of things,
And tossed by storm and flood,
To one fixed trust my spirit clings;
I know that God is good!

[12] Harold R. Weaver: pastor, Wauwatosa United Methodist Church, Wauwatosa, Wisconsin.

Such is our faith. We lift our prayers of thankfulness to a good and loving God.

For what do we thank God? What do we mean when we say, "Bless the LORD, O my soul"? First of all, we bless God for his steadfast love. How it flows over our lives with cleansing when we turn to him. God's love has a healing for human emotions far beyond what we have ever begun to imagine. He wants to meet our flaring anger with love's understanding; he wants to displace our feeling of inferiority and sense of worthlessness with his own affirmation of our lives. We are made in his own image. Say to yourself, "*I* am made in his image!" Affirm it; rejoice in it; live humbly and gladly in it. His loving presence is with us at all times. We can turn our cup upward and find it overflowing with love.

Secondly, we bless God for freedom. We remember that when the Pilgrims called for thanksgiving, it was not merely to be a time of celebrating life, of giving thanks for food and drink. Rather, it was to be a time to thank God that they were still alive, that they lived in a country as yet unexplored but that seemed filled to overflowing with a bounty beyond imagining. Even more, they wanted to thank God that they could worship in freedom; for they had fled the establishment that insisted on doing all things, especially worshiping God, in a traditional way. They were innovators. They wanted their own style, their own new form of worship. This means that they wanted not to abandon worship but rather to recast it in such a way that it was *their* worship, freely given at a time of their own choosing and with the people whom they invited to share their goods and their joy. The Pilgrims wanted to say in their own way, "Bless the LORD, O my soul; and all that is within me, bless his holy name!"

Finally, we bless God because of the bountiful world he has prepared for us. The hills are stuffed like Christmas stockings with coal, gold, silver, and zinc. Below the ground too is liquid gold in the form of oil, the product of millions of years of evolution, waiting for man's questing spirit and inventiveness. Likewise the crust of the good earth awaits man's coming to plow and plant in it. Fresh streams teem with fish, and the oceans are alive with millions more. What a world God has given us! Yet only lately we have come to see that he has given us responsibility for keeping the air fresh, the water clear, and the soil unpoisoned so that the good earth can continue to be a home for living creatures of land, sea, and air. Never have we seen more clearly than now the awesome task God has placed before us. But even for this responsibility we should bless God. He has given us work to do and the strength and intellect to do it.

Let us lift our hearts and voices and say, "Bless the LORD, O my soul; let all that is within me, bless his holy name!" He loves us; he made us free; and he gives us responsibility!

Living on the Brink

Background Scripture: 2 Kings 14:8-14; Psalms 33:13-17; Isaiah 31; Jeremiah 21; 27; 2 Peter 3:8-13

The Main Question —Charles M. Laymon

I talked recently with a woman seated next to me in a compartment of a railway car on the Flying Scotsman train enroute to Edinburgh. She had lived in London during the blitz when the Germans flew over the city almost nightly to bomb it. "How did you stand it," I asked, "never knowing if, and when, and to what extent a bomb would strike your home?"

She replied, "Prayer and a sense of humor brought us through." She went on to recount the humorous things that occurred, like the loss of one shoe, a suitcase that landed on the top of a church steeple, or a donkey marooned on a patch of pavement in the midst of a destroyed area. "We each had our story to relate in broad daylight after a night of terror," she said. "But of course it was the prayers that brought us through," she added. "We learned that we were not forgotten by God, even though the worst might happen."

Truly these Londoners had been living on the brink. How can a person live when faced with disaster? What are his options? This is the question we must face.

A friend once said to me that in every situation, no matter what, there is always a Christian thought to think, a Christian word to speak, and a Christian act to do. This was his formula for living on the outer edge of destruction. Do we believe this? Do we practice this?

The biblical passages that follow depict situations in which disaster threatens and various options for meeting it are presented.

As You Read the Scripture —Martin Rist

Throughout the Old Testament the writers have a good deal to say about war and peace. In some passages Jehovah is a warrior deity, in others a god of peace. We should recall that the Hebrews acquired the Holy Land through a warfare of aggression. This was a "holy war." After obtaining possession, they believed that any military resistance to an aggressor was also a "holy war" and trusted in God to bring his wrath upon any invader and destroy him. The exception, for the prophets, was when God was using an invader and conqueror to punish his people for their sins. The prophets were against the alliance of Israel—who occupied the strategic corridor between the Nile valley and Mesopotamia—with one powerful neighbor or another to ward off such an attack. This, of course, would not be a holy war.

Psalms 33:13-17. *The Lord looks down from heaven:* This passage from a liturgical hymn of praise to God as the savior and defender of his people depicts him on his heavenly throne looking down upon the inhabitants of the earth and observing them and their deeds (verses 13-15). Previously, verse 10 states that God had brought "the counsel of the nations to nought," a theme that is repeated in verses 16-17, which begin, "A king is not saved by his great army." Indeed, no human power is able to save men from divine penalties for attempting to thwart God's purposes.

Isaiah 31:1-3. *Woe to those who go down to Egypt for help:* These verses reflect a historic situation, namely the sending of a Jewish delegation or embassy to the Egyptians to obtain military help in a proposed rebellion against the Assyrians. This proposal seemed to bear promise of success with the death of Sargon II in 705 B.C. Isaiah 30:1-5 relates the situation in some detail, with the warning against seeking aid from Pharaoh. This theme is repeated in the printed lesson, 31:1-3. The Egyptians are men, not gods. "When the LORD stretches out his hand, the helper [Egypt] will stumble, and he who is helped [Israel] will fall."

Jeremiah 21:8-10. *I set before you the way of life and the way of death:* Likewise, in Jeremiah's day the Jews, living in their strategic corridor, were caught in the international power play between the Egyptians and the rulers of Mesopotamia, in this case the Babylonians. In the year 605 B.C. Nebuchadnezzar, the mighty king of the Babylonians, had defeated the Egyptians in the battle of Carchemish. Jehoiakim, king of the Jews, who had previously been allied with the Egyptians, made a strategic shift in alliance and began paying tribute to the Babylonians in order to save his kingdom and his throne. However, he vacillated; and contrary to the advice of Jeremiah, who curiously enough considered Nebuchadnezzar to be an agent of God, began a revolt against the Babylonians. Jehoiakim died in 598. His son Jehoiachin continued his policy, whereupon Nebuchadnezzar besieged Jerusalem. The king followed Jeremiah's advice to surrender. He was taken captive, and his life was spared. He was replaced by Zedekiah, the last king of Judah, who in 587 was put to death by Nebuchadnezzar, who then sent the Jews into exile.

Jeremiah 21:8-10 apparently reflects the period when Jerusalem was besieged. The people of Jerusalem have a choice between life and death (verse 8). If they continue the defense of the city, they will die "by the sword, by famine, and by pestilence." It will be far better to go out and surrender to the Chaldeans (Babylonians), thereby saving their lives (verse 9). This will be in accord with God's will (verse 10).

Selected Scripture

King James Version	Revised Standard Version
Psalms 33:13-17	*Psalms 33:13-17*
13 The LORD looketh from heaven; he beholdeth all the sons of men.	13 The LORD looks down from heaven, he sees all the sons of men;
14 From the place of his habitation he looketh upon all the inhabitants of the earth.	14 from where he sits enthroned he looks forth on all the inhabitants of the earth,

15 He fashioneth their hearts alike; he considereth all their works.

16 There is no king saved by the multitude of an host: a mighty man is not delivered by much strength.

17 An horse is a vain thing for safety: neither shall he deliver any by his great strength.

Isaiah 31:1-3

1 Woe to them that go down to Egypt for help; and stay on horses, and trust in chariots, because they are many; and in horsemen, because they are very strong; but they look not unto the Holy One of Israel, neither seek the LORD!

2 Yet he also is wise, and will bring evil, and will not call back his words: but will arise against the house of the evildoers, and against the help of them that work iniquity.

3 Now the Egyptians are men, and not God; and their horses flesh, and not spirit. When the LORD shall stretch out his hand, both he that helpeth shall fall, and he that is holpen shall fall down, and they all shall fail together.

Jeremiah 21:8-10

8 And unto this people thou shalt say, Thus saith the LORD; Behold, I set before you the way of life, and the way of death.

9 He that abideth in this city shall die by the sword, and by the famine, and by the pestilence: but he that

15 he who fashions the hearts of them all,
   and observes all their deeds.
16 A king is not saved by his great army;
   a warrior is not delivered by his great strength.
17 The war horse is a vain hope for victory,
   and by its great might it cannot save.

Isaiah 31:1-3

1 Woe to those who go down to Egypt for help
   and rely on horses,
who trust in chariots because they are many
   and in horsemen because they are very strong,
   but do not look to the Holy One of Israel
   or consult the LORD!
2 And yet he is wise and brings disaster,
   he does not call back his words,
   but will arise against the house of the evildoers,
   and against the helpers of those who work iniquity.
3 The Egyptians are men, and not God;
   and their horses are flesh, and not spirit.
When the LORD stretches out his hand,
   the helper will stumble, and he who is helped will fall,
   and they will all perish together.

Jeremiah 21:8-10

8 "And to this people you shall say: 'Thus says the LORD: Behold, I set before you the way of life and the way of death. 9 He who stays in this city shall die by the sword, by famine, and by pestilence; but he who goes out and surrenders to the Chaldeans

goeth out, and falleth to the Chaldeans that besiege you, he shall live, and his life shall be unto him for a prey.

10 For I have set my face against this city for evil, and not for good, saith the LORD: it shall be given into the hand of the king of Babylon, and he shall burn it with fire.

Memory Selection: We look not at the things which are seen, but at the things which are not seen: for the things which are seen are temporal; but the things which are not seen are eternal. (2 Corinthians 4:18)

who are besieging you shall live and shall have his life as a prize of war. 10 For I have set my face against this city for evil and not for good, says the LORD: it shall be given into the hand of the king of Babylon, and he shall burn it with fire.' "

Memory Selection: We look not to the things that are seen but to the things that are unseen; for the things that are seen are transient, but the things that are unseen are eternal. (2 Corinthians 4:18)

The Scripture and the Main Question —Charles M. Laymon

WHEN ARMAMENTS FAIL

Thomas Hardy wrote a poem entitled "Christmas, 1924." The song of the angels announcing "peace on earth" was in his mind as he contemplated the meaning of the birth of Christ. The memories of World War I were still fresh in his mind. In this poem he mentioned the "million priests" whose task is to work for peace and the "two thousand years of mass" since Christ died. Yet, in spite of all this, he concluded: "We've got as far as poison gas."

If Hardy were writing today, no doubt he would be even more pessimistic. Since 1924 we have had World War II, the Korean War, and the war in Vietnam. Priests have continued to labor, and masses by the thousands have been celebrated; yet war still remains a live option when nations are faced with living on the brink.

As far back as the time when the psalms were written men had learned the futility of war. The author of Psalms 33 wrote:

A king is not saved by his great army;
a warrior is not delivered by his great strength.
The war horse is a vain hope for victory,
and by its great might it cannot save.
(verses 16-17)

Times have changed considerably since the psalmist wrote of kings and their war horses. Has the value of war as a promising option for those who live on the brink also changed?

Suppose the psalmist had used the words *jet fighter bombers* in place of *horses of war.* Do you think he would have drawn the same conclusion as before, or have modern armaments assured us of a peaceful and life-enriching outcome for war?

WHEN MILITARY ALLIANCES MISLEAD

Military alliances are sometimes regarded as another effective option when men are living on the brink. Nonaggression pacts are still popular in international diplomacy. But these have often turned out to be scraps of paper.

Adolf Hitler and Joseph Stalin

made a nonaggression pact during World War II; but when it suited Hitler's purposes, he marched against Russia, forgetting the alliance completely. The value of a military alliance depends upon the integrity of the nations entering into it. Living on the brink places great pressures upon national integrity because self-interest comes to the front and overshadows alliances.

Military alliances are finally not effective for another reason. In the very beginning most of them are made for self-centered reasons. They are not usually instruments of generosity. The prophet Hosea saw this in the case of Israel. He said of her alliances with the nations: "Ephraim is like a dove, silly and without sense, calling to Egypt, going to Assyria." (Hosea 7: 11) These were her neighbors to the south and to the north. Israel made an alliance with each, seeking promises of protection against the other. Her imagined security was like chaff in the wind, however, when the crisis came in 722 B.C. as Assyria conquered her forever.

Isaiah made a similar denunciation of military alliances when he said of Judah, "Woe to those who go down to Egypt for help and rely on horses." (Isaiah 31:1) Chariots of war seemed more tangible than faith in God. Therefore they "consulted" Egypt rather than the Lord, the Holy One of Israel.

WHEN YOU CAN DO NOTHING

Sometimes when brought to the outer edge of the brink of disaster there is nothing that one can do but submit to what is before him. We are familiar with the saying, "What cannot be cured must be endured." Endurance may be the only option left; and if accepted in the right spirit, it may save the day. E. Stanley Jones

called this "evangelizing the inevitable."

In his sermon "Overwhelmed?" J. Wallace Hamilton says to men on the brink: "Remember, you are not God. Resign as soon as you can the office of General Manager of the universe." This is what Jeremiah urged the Hebrews to do when threatened by Babylonia. Judah was helpless before the military might of Babylonia, and to attempt to match blow with blow would have destroyed her.

So strongly did Jeremiah feel this that he called upon the nation to submit to Babylonia; any other course he regarded as a "way of death." Then he added, "He who goes out and surrenders to the Chaldeans who are besieging you shall live and shall have his life as a prize of war." (Jeremiah 21:9b)

Deliberately submitting, because it was God's will that they should, would enable the Hebrews to break the back of defeat and turn it into victory. Although outwardly they would be enslaved, within they would be free men. Was this not what Jesus did when he went to the cross? It seemed as though the Jewish leaders had won the day when the sun set upon Golgotha, but Easter proved otherwise.

WHEN FAITH TAKES OVER

Faith is the answer—God's answer given to man—for meeting situations in which we find ourselves living on the brink. The illustrations from the biblical passages for this lesson refer to the desperate times when men are tempted to turn to war as they face a crisis in their national existence. But there are also other times when it seems that life for us has reached a dead-end street. Here too faith is called upon to take over.

Peter Forsyth once said, "Unless

there is *within* us that which is *above* us, we shall soon yield to that which is *about* us." Was this not what the apostle Paul had in mind when he wrote, "We look not to the things that are seen but to the things that are unseen; for the things that are seen are transient, but the things that are unseen are eternal." (2 Corinthians 4:18)

Helping Adults Become Involved —Ronald E. Schlosser

Preparation of Self and Class

Special effort should be made this week to use a Bible commentary for help in understanding the context of today's background Scripture. Interpretive comments, of course, are provided by Dr. Laymon and the biblical exegesis elsewhere in this session; but you may wish to explore more fully the historical situation out of which the psalmist and the prophets Isaiah and Jeremiah speak. Volumes IV and V of *The Interpreter's Bible* would be especially good for your background study.

Today's main question has been explored in a great many ways by modern media. Films, records, and books have focused on the threat of world calamity from a variety of angles; and you ought to consider how you might be able to use some of these resources to open up the subject in a way that will speak to your class. Books such as *On the Beach, Fail-Safe,* and *Nineteen Eighty-Four* are modern works on the theme. Each has also been made into a feature-length motion picture that some persons in your class may have seen. Be alert to any other modern novels or motion pictures that have for their theme the threat of world calamity. One of these could probably provide a good starting place for class discussion.

A number of short films dealing with today's theme would also prove to be good discussion starters. The fifteen-minute, animated cartoon entitled *The Hole* tells the story of two workmen below the city streets who get into a somewhat humorous discussion about the cause of accidents and the possibility of an accidental nuclear explosion. Behind their humor, however, is the stark reality that what they are saying makes a lot of sense. (See page 14.) A similar approach to the possibility of an accidental nuclear attack is provided in another whimsical cartoon, *Hypothese Beta*. In this seven-minute film a nonconformist perforation on a computer punchcard delights in bothering the other perforations until the card is read by an electronic device and flashes a warning light that signals the release of a nuclear missile. (See page 13.) A third animated film, entitled *The Hat*, examines how a trivial incident like a sentry's hat falling across an international borderline can be blown up to gigantic (and ridiculous) proportions and be the cause of an international dispute. (See page 14.)

There may be a current hit song that can be used to introduce today's main question (such a song as "The Eve of Destruction"). The song, however, need not be one of despair or futility; it might speak words of assurance and hope. A great many religious songs and hymns do this. Later in the session you will be asking your members to suggest some. Have hymnals available for their use when this time comes.

A number of suggestions have been

given for introducing today's main question. Select the approach that you feel will be the most appropriate for your class. The learning goals for the session are twofold:

1. To determine how real the threat is of an impending world disaster.

2. To consider how one can live with hope in the face of an unknown and ominous future.

Presenting the Main Question

Begin the session by using one of the resources suggested above—a film, a book, a record—or some current incident that lifts up the threat of a devastating world calamity. The headlines of the morning paper may provide just such an illustration. If not, read to the class the first two paragraphs of the section entitled "When Armaments Fail" in Dr. Laymon's comments. Ask such questions as: Is the possibility of a major war closer now than it was a year ago? Why, or why not? What are the chances that war will be started by accident—some human frailty, some minor misunderstanding, some mistake in pushing a wrong button or throwing an unlocked switch?

Developing the Lesson

Move into considering the question you asked your members to think about during the week: Will God allow man to destroy himself? At the outset of the discussion you might ask for a show of hands. Those who definitely feel that man has the power to destroy himself should raise their hands first; then those who feel that God will intervene directly in history before man can annihilate his world should lift their hands; finally those who have no strong feeling one way or the other should raise their hands. Ask persons representing each point

of view to give reasons for their opinion. Do they base their feeling on instinct, a study of history, an analysis of present trends, an understanding of some biblical teaching, or some other reason?

There is no one "right" answer to this question. Students of history, as well as students of the Bible, are divided as to the direction present world affairs are going. Some people are quite optimistic, while others are equally pessimistic. Yet despite differences of opinion, we do have some word from the Scripture about what *not* to put our trust in if we want a secure future.

Have the class members turn to three passages in their Bibles: Psalms 33:13-17; Isaiah 31:1-3; Jeremiah 21: 8-10. Ask someone to read aloud each one, and then ask the members to indicate what these passages say to them about the search for a secure future. After they have had a chance to express their understanding, share with them the comments by Dr. Laymon and the writer of the biblical exegesis as they interpret these passages. The verses in Psalms 33 indicate that ultimate national security does not rest in the might of armaments; the Isaiah passage sees military alliances to be useless also; and the Jeremiah passage seems to say that there are times when resistance to superior military power should be considered futile.

The question facing Christians, and which your class members should face at this point in the session is, Is there any hope? If the countries of the world, including our own, continue to rely on armaments and alliances to settle their differences, what does the future hold? The answer we often give is in words that for some have the sound of glibness, yet they are undeniably true—we may not know what the future holds, but we know who holds the future. Have your class turn to 2 Peter 3:8-13, and ask someone to read these verses aloud. What do they say to your members about the future and about hope? (In a time when total destruction threatens, Christians should continue to live lives that are characterized by patience and faith.) You might refer to the comments by Dr. Laymon in the section "When Faith Takes Over" to guide this part of the discussion.

Helping Class Members Act

The passage in Second Peter is only one of many such verses in the Bible that refer to the hope Christians can hold onto as they face a perilous future. Move to the concluding part of the session by asking your class members to read or quote verses from the Scripture that say something to them about hope in troubled times. Encourage them to suggest hymns and gospel songs that speak of this kind of hope. Pass out hymnals for them to look through to aid their memories. If there is time and the class has an inclination, sing a stanza or two of some of the hymns that are particularly meaningful to your members.

Close the session by reading aloud in unison the memory selection for today: "We look not to the things that are seen but to the things that are unseen; for the things that are seen are transient, but the things that are unseen are eternal." (2 Corinthians 4:18) A time for individual sentence prayers might also be appropriate here.

Planning for Next Sunday

Arrange a debate or panel discussion on the topic: "Resolved, the United Nations can be an effective organization to bring world peace." Ask for volunteers to take the affirmative and negative positions, and spend some time with them during the week to help research their respective positions.

If there is not much interest in this particular topic or activity, ask each member of the class to come next week with a written definition of *peace*.

Background Scripture for the session includes: Micah 4:1-4; Matthew 24:3-14; and James 4:1-10.

LESSON 5   NOVEMBER 26

What Kind of Peace?

Background Scripture: Micah 4:1-4; Matthew 24:3-14; James 4:1-10

The Main Question —Charles M. Laymon

Franklin D. Roosevelt was writing down his thoughts concerning war and peace the night before he died. Included in his statements were these words: "We seek peace—enduring peace. More than an end to war, we want an end to the beginnings of all wars—yes, an end to this brutal, inhuman, and thoroughly impractical method of settling differences between governments."

116

Since President Roosevelt wrote this statement we have continued to be at war almost constantly. Why? Do we really want peace? Do we enjoy fighting? If we promoted peace as desperately as we pursue war, would it become a reality; or are we by nature doomed to desire war? Some persons hold that the ideal of peace is contrary to human nature and that peace movements run against the grain of our being. "Look at the animal kingdom," they say. "A twenty-four-hour watch at a water hole in Africa will prove that it is natural to fight for survival," they conclude.

On the other hand, there are those who point to man's higher nature. He is not simply a "naked ape" as a popular book title has claimed. He can be both rational and loving at his best. Therefore he can overcome war if he tries. Do you agree?

The biblical passages for this lesson are helpful in answering these questions.

As You Read the Scripture —Martin Rist

Micah 4:1-4. *It shall come to pass in the latter days:* Micah, a contemporary of Isaiah's, uttered most of his oracles during the reign of King Hezekiah, 715-687 B.C. Shortly before Hezekiah's reign began, in 722/721 B.C., Sargon II, king of Assyria, captured Samaria, deported thousands of captives, and brought the Northern Kingdom to an end. Micah, duly impressed by this disaster, warned Judah of a similar tragic fate unless the rulers and the people repented of their many sins. In contrast to this gloomy prediction Micah 4 and 5 consist of oracles, in poetic form, depicting the messianic hope, with Bethlehem named as the birthplace of the expected deliverer (Micah 5:2-4).

Micah 4:1-4 is a poetic oracle, prophesying a period of universal peace for all nations under God, that is, under the God of the Jews, of course. Some scholars ascribe this messianic poem to a later period than that of Micah, to the closing days of the Babylonian exile, which usually is considered to have ended in 515 B.C.

Uttered by Micah or by someone else, the picture is one of strange geological changes, with Mount Zion, the mount of the Temple, "the house of the LORD," becoming the highest of all mountains (verse 1). All peoples will ascend the holy mount to the Temple to be taught the ways and the law of the Lord (verse 2). The God of the Hebrews will be the judge (and ruler) of all the nations of the earth. Weapons of war will be changed into tools of peace, and there will be no more war (verse 3). During this era of universal peace each man will sit under his own vine and fig tree (verse 4) and be unafraid, because "the mouth of the LORD of hosts has spoken."

Matthew 24:6-8. *And you will hear of wars:* Both the Little Apocalypses of Matthew 24 and Luke 21 are based upon Mark 13, with changes to be sure. They all bear some resemblance to portions of the Book of Revelation. Not all scholars are in agreement that these passages reflect the actual views and teachings of Jesus. Rather, some believe that they represent an early Christian view that Jesus Christ would soon appear from heaven with his angels in power and glory to bring this present evil age to a catastrophic end, after

117

which the new age under God would be inaugurated. The Second Coming would be preceded by signs, heavenly and terrestrial. The sun and moon would be darkened; stars would fall from heaven; there would be earthquakes and famines; and there would be "wars and rumors of wars" (verse 6), with nation rising against nation (verse 7).

James 4:1-3. *What causes wars?* This little book of Christian wisdom deserves repeated reading. Written around A.D. 125-150 when some persons of affluence had become members of the Christian church, it contains over fifty commands in its one hundred and eight verses. This alone reveals the earnestness of the author.

In answer to the question, "What causes wars, and what causes fightings among you?" the author states that our passions are the cause (verse 1). People desire what others have; they are covetous. They do not have, either because they do not ask or because they ask in the wrong manner. To sum up, the cause of war is the constant struggle between the "have-nots" and the "haves." To be sure, this problem causes difficulties between individuals, between groups of individuals, and between nations. However, the author has given no solution for solving the problem so that the "have-nots" will become the "haves." But who has given us the answer to this puzzle? We should also recall that there are other causes of wars, among them racial antipathies, religious differences, and so on, which also defy solution. Is this why so many people become frustrated and look for divine intervention?

MICAH SPOKE OF A TIME IN WHICH ALL MEN WOULD BE AT PEACE. WHAT MUST CHRISTIANS DO TO BRING SUCH A TIME INTO BEING? WHAT ARE THE PREREQUISITES FOR PEACE?

Selected Scripture

King James Version	Revised Standard Version

Micah 4:1-4

1 But in the last days it shall come to pass, that the mountain of the house of the Lord shall be established in the top of the mountains, and it shall be exalted above the hills; and people shall flow unto it.

2 And many nations shall come, and say, Come, and let us go up to the mountain of the Lord, and to the house of the God of Jacob; and he will teach us of his ways, and we will walk in his paths: for the law shall go forth of Zion, and the word of the Lord from Jerusalem.

3 And he shall judge among many people, and rebuke strong nations afar off; and they shall beat their swords into plowshares, and their spears into pruninghooks: nation shall not lift up a sword against nation, neither shall they learn war any more.

4 But they shall sit every man under his vine and under his fig tree; and none shall make them afraid: for the mouth of the Lord of hosts hath spoken it.

Matthew 24:6-8

6 And ye shall hear of wars and rumours of wars: see that ye be not troubled: for all these things must come to pass, but the end is not yet.

7 For nation shall rise against na-

Micah 4:1-4

1 It shall come to pass in the latter days
　that the mountain of the house
　　of the Lord
shall be established as the highest
　of the mountains,
　and shall be raised up above the
　　hills;
and peoples shall flow to it,

2 and many nations shall come,
　and say:
"Come, let us go up to the mountain of the Lord,
　to the house of the God of Jacob;
that he may teach us his ways and
　we may walk in his paths."
For out of Zion shall go forth the
　law,
　and the word of the Lord from
　　Jerusalem.

3 He shall judge between many peoples,
　and shall decide for strong nations afar off;
and they shall beat their swords into plowshares,
　and their spears into pruning
　　hooks;
nation shall not lift up sword
　against nation,
　neither shall they learn war any
　　more;

4 but they shall sit every man under
　his vine and under his fig tree,
　and none shall make them
　　afraid;
for the mouth of the Lord of
　hosts has spoken.

Matthew 24:6-8

6 And you will hear of wars and rumors of wars; see that you are not alarmed; for this must take place, but the end is not yet. 7 For nation will rise against nation, and kingdom

tion, and kingdom against kingdom: and there shall be famines, and pestilences, and earthquakes, in divers places.
8 All these are the beginning of sorrows.

James 4:1-3
1 From whence come wars and fightings among you? come they not hence, even of your lusts that war in your members?
2 Ye lust, and have not: ye kill, and desire to have, and cannot obtain: ye fight and war, yet ye have not, because ye ask not.
3 Ye ask, and receive not, because ye ask amiss, that ye may consume it upon your lusts.

Memory Selection: Blessed are the peacemakers: for they shall be called the children of God. (Matthew 5:9)

against kingdom, and there will be famines and earthquakes in various places: 8 all this is but the beginning of the sufferings.

James 4:1-3
1 What causes wars, and what causes fightings among you? Is it not your passions that are at war in your members? 2 You desire and do not have; so you kill. And you covet and cannot obtain; so you fight and wage war. You do not have, because you do not ask. 3 You ask and do not receive, because you ask wrongly, to spend it on your passions.

Memory Selection: Blessed are the peacemakers, for they shall be called sons of God. (Matthew 5:9)

The Scripture and the Main Question —Charles M. Laymon

IS WAR INEVITABLE?

I once attended what was called a convention on prophecy. A speaker declared it was futile to work for peace because to do so was to be working against God. He then quoted one of the Scripture passages in this lesson that states that before the end of the world "nation will rise against nation, and kingdom against kingdom." (Matthew 24:7)

Some persons interpret the above words as meaning God has decreed wars shall be. Others, however, regard this passage as a realistic description of the fact that men do fight when they are outside God's kingdom. And they will continue to fight unless they come to know and practice the love of God.

Jesus' birth was announced with a song of peace. In the Beatitudes he called the peacemakers blessed. When Jesus rode into Jerusalem on what we know as Palm Sunday, he chose a humble ass, a beast of burden, instead of a horse of war to carry him. The whole tenor of his message is on the side of peace, not war.

Jesus' followers through the centuries have been men of peace. George Fox the Quaker was offered the office of captain by the Puritans in their struggle against Parliament. He refused to take part in war, however, and said that he "lived in virtue of that life and power which took away the occasion of all war."

What if men took the attitude of George Fox today regarding the primacy of a life of good will among all men? Would this, in his words, take away "the occasion of all war"?

WHAT CAUSES STRIFE?

One of Abraham Lincoln's neighbors in Springfield, Illinois, Roland Diller, reported that one day he heard some cries of children in the street. When he went to the door to check, he saw Lincoln striding along with two of his boys who were wailing loudly. Diller asked what the trouble was; and Lincoln said, "Just what's the matter with the whole world. I've got three walnuts, and each wants two."

How like the statement of James in one of the biblical passages for this lesson: "What causes wars, and what causes fightings among you? . . . You desire and do not have; so you kill. And you covet and cannot obtain; so you fight and wage war." (James 4:1-2)

This statement may seem at first to be an oversimplification. Self-defense is not always the same thing as self-desire. And the support of small and oppressed peoples is not always for ulterior purposes. On the other hand, James's statement is a demand that we examine our motives. Wars easily cloak themselves in the mantle of righteousness. There are those who make material gains out of wars, and they have sometimes even sought to create and prolong a war so that their profits will not cease. If there were no money to be made nor power to be gained in war, we would not have had many of the wars of history.

AN INSTRUMENT OF PEACE

George Bernard Shaw was known as a person who spoke his mind bluntly. Even when he seemed to be speaking with tongue in check, he was often taking a crack at one of society's cherished ideals. Toward the close of his life, as Shaw made the following statement, his words were direct and to the point. He said, "After reviewing the world of human events for sixty years I am prepared to say that I see no way out of the world's misery except the way that Christ would take if he should undertake the work of a modern statesman."

What way would Christ take? Would he organize a movement and establish an institution as an instrument of peace? He did neither of these when he lived on earth in Galilee and Judea. But that was a different day and in a different setting.

In the modern world the need for organized institutional efforts seems necessary if we are to make an impression. This would include the organized church. Other structured peace efforts have come into existence such as the United Nations. Some feel it is not adequate, that it has become a sounding board for propaganda only. Yet the ideal of peace among the nations lies at the heart of the UN.

The prophet Micah had a dream of peace, even as we do. He envisioned all the nations of the world coming to Jerusalem to learn the law of the Lord. When they returned to their homes, they would live in harmony together, following a way of life that was based upon the Law (Micah 4:2). How contemporary all this sounds!

THE GOALS OF PEACE

Are the goals of peace attainable? This is like asking whether or not the Kingdom can come on earth even as it is in heaven. Jesus told his followers to pray for the coming of the Kingdom. Would he have invited us to pray thus if there was no likelihood the goal could ever be reached?

In words of startling realism Micah pictured the goals of peace: that men would "beat their swords into plowshares, and their spears into pruning hooks." He then portrayed a peaceful setting when every man would sit under his vine and fig tree and not be afraid. As a seal to the promise he added, "For the mouth of the LORD of hosts has spoken." (Micah 4:4)

The goal of peace is laid out before us in this and other biblical passages. We cannot in despair or disillusionment turn from it without losing something that lies at the very heart of the Christian faith. Our calling is to dream of peace, to pray for peace, and to work for peace.

Helping Adults Become Involved —Ronald E. Schlosser

Preparation of Self and Class

If several members of your class volunteered to debate or discuss the topic: "Resolved, the United Nations can be an effective organization to bring world peace," meet with them prior to the session to help them work on their presentations. Material on the United Nations should be available from your local public or high school library. The children of some of your members may be able to procure resources from their history or social studies teacher.

As an alternate approach to today's session you might consider showing the nine-minute film entitled *Overture*. (See page 14.) Produced by the United Nations over a decade ago, it still has strong emotional impact and dramatic punch. A performance of Beethoven's "Egmont Overture" by the Vienna Philharmonic Orchestra serves as the background sound track for scenes depicting the effects of war and the UN's efforts to aid recovery and reconstruction. Without using a word of narration or dialogue the film makes an impressively moving statement about the oneness of mankind. A helpful little book on the subject of peace is Culbert Rutenber's *Peace Keeping or Peace Making?* Only sixty-three pages in length, it can be quickly read and should provide teacher and student alike with some solid theological food for thought.

To lend atmosphere to the classroom for today's study, you might make some colorful posters to hang around the room. Use slogans and sayings related to the subject of peace. Some suggestions are: Peace now; War is not healthy for children and other living things; "The first and fundamental law of Nature . . . is, to seek peace and follow it"—Thomas Hobbes; "Peace is the healing and elevating influence of the world"—Woodrow Wilson; "Where there is peace, God is"—George Herbert; "Peace cannot be kept by force. It can only be achieved by understanding" —Albert Einstein. Of course, the familiar Micah 4:3 and Matthew 5:9 should also be included.

Whether you begin the session with a debate, a discussion, a film, or some other activity, you ought to aim for at least two major learning goals:

1. To consider what kind of peace is possible in today's world in light of present-day conditions.

2. To explore what role Christians have as peacemakers.

Presenting the Main Question

As has been suggested the main question may be presented in a number of ways. If you have planned for a debate or a discussion on the topic of the United Nations' effectiveness as a peacemaker, introduce the participants who will be giving leadership and let them guide the exploration of the theme. If you plan to use the film *Overture*, discuss some of these questions after its showing:

1. What is the central premise of the film? (War leaves innocent victims in its wake, and all people are related in need.)

2. What emotions do you see traced on the faces of the people in the film? (Confusion, fear, grief, courage, need —and the striking absence of resentment or hatred.)

3. What were some of the rehabilitation activities depicted? (Literacy programs, land reclamation, physical rehabilitation, the learning of agricultural skills, bridge building— literally and figuratively.)

Developing the Lesson

How would your class members define *peace*? Call for suggestions. Note the differences in emphases. Some may see peace as something personal—a quietness of soul and spirit, a peace of mind. Others may define peace as the absence of war. Statistics are sometimes given as to the comparatively few years of peace this world has known, referring of course to the years when no war was being waged. Urban dwellers may be concerned about peace in the streets—the absence of violence. Still others may talk about "heavenly peace" or "peace that passes all understanding." This again is a personal kind of peace.

Ask the question, What kind of peace does the Bible speak about? Is it realistic to look for this kind of peace in the twentieth century, or is this peace only for the hereafter?

Have the class members turn to the three Scripture passages for study today: Micah 4:1-4, Matthew 24:3-14, and James 4:1-10. Divide the class members into three groups and assign each group one of the passages to study and discuss. They should consider what their passage says about the subjects of war and peace. What is the nature of peace promised by the prophet? What are the causes of war? How should Christians view the constant threat of war? How should they act in the midst of war?

Allow about ten minutes for these small group discussions and then call the class members together to share findings. Use the comments by Dr. Laymon and the biblical exegesis to guide your class discussion and interpretation of the background Scripture.

Move to a consideration of the memory selection (Matthew 5:9). Ask these questions: What should be the Christian's role as a peacemaker? How can he work for peace? Should he become involved in an organized peace movement? Should he join a pacifist group? Ought he to participate in peace demonstrations? Should he write regularly to his congressmen supporting disarmament, demilitarization, and other peace legislation? What *should* the Christian do to be an effective peacemaker?

You might share this true story with your class as an example of what one concerned young man did. Captain Colin P. Kelly, Jr. was America's first World War II hero. On December 9, 1941, Captain Kelly died in the flaming crash of his bomber after he destroyed the Japanese battleship *Haruna* off Luzon in the Philippines. Captain Kelly was posthumously awarded the Distinguished Service Cross for his heroism, and President Franklin D. Roosevelt wrote a letter "to the President of the United States in 1956," asking that Kelly's nineteen-month old son, Colin III, be considered at that time for appointment to West Point.

When the younger Kelly grew up,

he did go to West Point; but he did it on his own, taking the examinations and declining the presidential nomination. After graduation from the academy he went on to become a captain in the tank corps; but even then he felt a strong conviction that he should be helping men, not learning how to kill them. He considered becoming an Army chaplain.

His convictions grew until in 1967 Kelly took a five-year leave of absence from the Army and entered the Divinity School of the Protestant Episcopal Church in Philadelphia. He graduated in May of 1970 and, as a deacon of the church, worked with teenagers in a New Jersey community.

Then, in December, 1970—exactly twenty-nine years to the month since the death of his famous father—Colin P. Kelly III was ordained an Episcopal priest. As he anticipated his return to the Army as a chaplain, Father Kelly observed, "It's going to be hard, but it's what I want to do." His dream of being a peacemaker in this turbulent age was being fulfilled.

Helping Class Members Act

What can your class members do to be peacemakers? One thing might be to write a letter to the editor of their local paper on the subject "What Makes for Peace." If possible, the letter should tie in with some current issue in the news or a pertinent bill before Congress. Pass out pencils and paper and ask the members to compose such a letter (or if time is limited, outline some thoughts) about prospects for peace. If some members feel they just are not good letter writers, suggest that several of them get together and list ideas that someone else in the class might use in preparing a composite letter.

The purpose of this concluding activity is to encourage your members to become involved in something tangible that makes for peace. Here is a specific thing they can do—now—to give them a sense of participating in the work of peace. If letter writing is not a practical activity, suggest something else for them to do. Make this an opportunity to put their Christian convictions into action.

You might close the session by singing together a hymn that relates to the theme of peace.

Planning for Next Sunday

Next Sunday begins a study on the topic "Prophets of Judgment and Hope: Jeremiah, Ezekiel, Haggai, and Zechariah." The first session introduces the prophet Jeremiah. Your class members may want to read all the background Scripture (2 Chronicles 36; Jeremiah 1; 26) as a preparation for the study.

Prophets of Judgment and Hope: Jeremiah, Ezekiel, Haggai, Zechariah

UNIT V: PROPHETS OF JUDGMENT AND HOPE:
JEREMIAH, EZEKIEL, HAGGAI, ZECHARIAH
Horace R. Weaver

THIRTEEN LESSONS   DECEMBER 3–FEBRUARY 25

How similar our days are to those of the sixth century B.C. Some people in that time were saying that God was dead; others were saying that the old moral laws were obsolete—a new moral system was needed; old nations were falling, while new ones were arising; other people were asking if there was anything that was stable or permanent in life. Doesn't that sound like 1972-73?

In the same century that Jeremiah, Ezekiel, Haggai, and Zechariah prophesied, Buddha of India was claiming that he had sought God but could not find him—because he did not exist. Confucius of China was declaring the need for a new moral code. The philosophers of Miletus (in modern Turkey) were declaring that there is no certainty of anything that is permanent. Yet the prophet Isaiah of Babylonia declared that there is one thing everybody can count on: the Lord God lives. He has given an enduring moral code. His Word endures forever. What a period of turmoil and uncertainty and affirmation! What a time for the voice of the Lord to be heard by men who knew God and were willing to lay their lives on the line (regardless of costs) in order that men might hear of his purposes!

This quarter we seek to understand the messages of these men—Jeremiah, Ezekiel, Haggai, and Zechariah. Their messages, we will discover, are exceptionally relevant to our contemporary world.

Six lessons are taken from the words of the prophet Jeremiah. December 3, "A Man for the Hour," helps us sense that God sometimes calls a youth to speak his message. Perhaps this suggests that we should be more open to the concerns of contemporary youth through whom God just might be speaking.

December 10, "A Nation Against God," speaks of Jeremiah's conclusion that the people of his time were stubborn in their thinking ("hearts") and so missing the opportunity of aligning their purposes with those of God. December 17, "Convictions Can Be Costly," is illustrated through Jeremiah's sufferings: a "burning fire" within him; imprisonment with little or no food offered him; confinement in a miry cistern with the promise of slow starvation (and his being saved through the love of a black man).

December 24, "The Promised Messiah," is based on Jeremiah's reference to the "Branch" who would rule with justice and mercy, seen as fulfilled in Matthew 2:1-12. December 31, "The Reshaping of Life," reflects on the difficulty that even God has when a nation is useless as far as its contribution to his purpose of bringing in the kingdom of God on earth. January 7, "The New Covenant," helps us as Christians to see our rootage in the old covenant

—yet a covenant etched in the attitudes and motives of persons rather than on tablets of stone.

Next, four lessons are taken from the Book of Ezekiel. While Jeremiah faced problems of a nation in an impossible war, Ezekiel faced the problems of persons who had lost the war and were captives and exiles in a foreign land (Babylonia).

January 14, "Prophet to Displaced People," portrays the prophet as having to find a new approach to getting his message across. He stopped preaching and turned to symbolic prophecy, such as displaying a make-believe siege against Jerusalem. His action suggests that we might try different techniques to communicate the gospel in our day—ways different from anything we have ever tried in our churches. January 21, "God Really Cares!" includes a statement of condemnation for those shepherds (pastors and teachers) who "feed themselves" (are nourished on meat) while not nourishing the sheep on similar solids, giving them only milk. God's condemnation on such misguided leaders is very strong. January 28, "No Alibis With God," shows the integrity with which God judges all men. February 4, "A New Heart and Spirit," promises a new era—a new society based on new ideas, godly attitudes, kindness, and love.

One lesson is taken from the Book of Haggai, "God's House and Yours." When Haggai and Zechariah returned to Jerusalem from captivity, they restored the Temple. It was not an elaborate restructuring, for that would wait until the days of King Herod. But the point was clear: men need a clean, well-kept place for assemblage for corporate worship.

The last two lessons of this quarter are based on the Book of Zechariah. February 18, "More Than Human Power," emphasizes the method by which God (and the Risen Christ in our midst) works to achieve his purpose. February 25, "The Shape of Things to Come," is based on a dream like that of Hosea (2:16-20). These two men prophesied of a time to come when those who were *Lo Ammi* (not my people) would become *Ammi* (my people), and they would accept the Lord as their God. So the future of man would fulfill God's purposes in creation.

Helpful background reading for this quarter may be found in the following books: *Jeremiah*, Elmer A. Leslie; *Jeremiah, Prophet to the Nations*, Walter J. Harrelson; *Prophets of Israel* (2), William Neil; *Prophetic Religion*, J. Philip Hyatt; *The Prophets Tell Their Own Story*, Elmer A. Leslie; *The Relevance of the Prophets*, R. B. Y. Scott; *The Beacon Lights of Prophecy*, Albert C. Knudson; *Prophets in Perspective*, B. Davie Napier; *The Prophets on Main Street*, Jack E. Corbett; and *The Everlasting Covenant*, Horace R. Weaver.

Listed below are several audiovisual resources that would be valuable as you prepare the lessons on the prophets of judgment and hope. These resources have been carefully selected and correlated with the major themes of the lessons. Teachers who wish to use the aids should make plans sufficiently early to ensure proper scheduling and delivery. All prices are subject to change without notice. All these materials may be obtained from your denominational publishing house unless another source is denoted in the description. Because of the lapse of time between the printing of this book and the use of these materials some resources may not be available.

Adventures of an *. 16mm film, 10 min. The maturation of a man, symbolized by an *, is visualized in animation. As a child, he enjoys the richness of seeing, doing, and questioning all about him. His father, however, has lost much of such joy in life. As the boy approaches manhood, he begins to slip into such a trap but in time rediscovers through his own son the wealth of childhood. Rental: color, $10, from Mass Media Ministries; 2116 North Charles Street; Baltimore, Maryland 21218.

The Antkeeper. 16mm film, 27 min. The overseer of a lush jungle is angered by ants who invade his private garden, so he destroys their wings. Smitten by compassion, he sends his son into the jungle in the form of an ant to live with the insects. The son is killed by them; but because of the death of the human ant, the other ants are able to be born again with their wings restored. Rental: color, $25, from Mass Media Ministries; 2116 North Charles Street; Baltimore, Maryland 21218.

A Scrap of Paper and a Piece of String. 16mm film, 6 min. This film is a comment on the place of humility in the building of friendship. The two items mentioned in the title are close companions. They are made in such a way as to be able to pretend they are something else. All goes well until the paper becomes jealous of the string's elastic prowess. The paper boasts of its self-sufficiency and decides it no longer needs the piece of string. Not until the boat into which the paper has formed itself begins to capsize and the string acts as a lifeline to come to the rescue are the two reconciled. Rental: color, $10, from Mass Media Ministries; 2116 North Charles Street; Baltimore, Maryland 21218.

Come Back. 16mm film, 10 min. A man's struggle with his own responsibility and guilt in a traffic accident forms the basis for this dramatic interpretation of the key elements of repentance—acceptance of guilt, sorrow, and forgiveness. Rental: color, $8, from St. Francis Productions; 1229 South Santee Street; Los Angeles, California 90015.

The Coming of the Stranger. 16mm film, 27 min. A parable about the meaning of Christmas, this film involves five persons—an old candlemaker, his wife, their young grandson, a friend, and his daughter—living in a lonely, isolated village, unchanged for generations—until the Stranger arrives with an unusual gift. Rental: color, $15.

The Human Race. 16mm film, 5 min. The lone Everyman whom the film portrays is startled out of his siesta on a grassy knoll by the screaming voice of a woman in distress. But our Everyman's dash in the unknown victim's direction instantly loses the pace of desperation and turns into a jaunty jog down a country road, accompanied on an excellent soundtrack by the voice of Phil Ochs singing "A Small Circle of Friends." Rental: color, $15, from Mass Media Ministries; 2116 North Charles Street; Baltimore, Maryland 21218.

In Faith and Love. 35mm filmstrip, 12 min. This filmstrip is to aid persons and churches to become the people of God on mission in his world. Sale: color, $3.50.

Our Old Testament Heritage. 35mm filmstrip, 67 frames, script and guide. Five major areas of the Old Testament are outlined. Part I carries the story of Abraham; Part II documents Moses. The formation of Israel and its subsequent division are shown in Part III. Part IV deals with Jeremiah;

Part V tells the story of Habakkuk. The filmstrip highlights the beliefs contributed by each man and period to contemporary Christianity. Sale: color, $5.50.

Out of the Land of Egypt. 35mm filmstrip, 73 frames, 33⅓ rpm record. Throughout the Old Testament man seems to be alternately entering into relationship with God and then rejecting him. But even in those times of man's rebellion, God's love remains firm; and man is called to repentance. Sale: color, $4.95.

The Pusher. 16mm film, 17 min. This film is a satirical biography of an egocentric pusher who elbows his way into a job and then elbows himself onward and upward until he is elbowed out in turn. Rental: black and white, $15, from Mass Media Ministries; 2116 North Charles Street; Baltimore, Maryland 21218.

Right Here, Right Now. (See page 12.)

Sounds of Christmas. 33⅓ rpm record, 48 min. This record album brings to the listener an impression of Christmas as it is lived by an American in the 1970's. Through the use of dramatic episodes, music, and contemporary happenings related to Christmas, it presents the message of Christmas as it is found in today's marketplace and compares it with the traditional biblical Christmas message. Sale: $4.25.

Spokesmen for God. 35mm filmstrip, 75 frames, script. This filmstrip deals with three Old Testament prophets, the background of their time, and their messages. The prophets selected for this study are Elijah, Micah, and Haggai. Sale: color, $5.50.

The Trap. 35mm filmstrip, 90 frames. This filmstrip presents a dramatic picture of one of the most dangerous problems facing the United States today—the immediate and long-range effects of poverty in an affluent society, a society that purports to respect the dignity and worth of each individual and the freedom of the individual for self-realization. Sale: color, $15, from The Ben Rinaldo Company; 6917 Melrose Avenue; Hollywood, California 90038.

LESSON 1   DECEMBER 3

A Man for the Hour

Background Scripture: 2 Chronicles 36; Jeremiah 1; 26

The Main Question —Charles M. Laymon

A business executive was talking with his personnel officers just before they began their yearly visits to college campuses to recruit young men for the corporation. He had reviewed the specific openings in the company, listed the types of preparation that were needed, and projected the business cycle for the future as he saw it. "One final word," he said. "It is the person who counts most. Any reasonably intelligent young man can learn what he needs to know. It is what is inside him that matters."

These remarks raise the question as to just what it is that makes a person the man for the hour. Is it his ancestry? his home background? his preparation? his particular talents? his personality? his character? his drive? his dedication?

When Zane Grey was asked his recipe for greatness, he replied, "To bear up under loss; to fight the bitterness of defeat and the weakness of grief; to be victor over anger; to smile when tears are close; to resist disease and evil men and base instincts; to hate hate, and to love love; to go on when it would seem good to die; to look up with unquenchable faith in something ever more about to be. That is what any man can do, and be great."

The above would be an excellent description of the prophet Jeremiah, whose career we shall discuss for six lessons.

As You Read the Scripture —Floyd V. Filson[1]

By ancestry Jeremiah was a priest (Jeremiah 1:1), but what marked all his career was God's call to him to speak the divine message. That call came in the thirteenth year of the reign of Josiah, King of Judah. (Josiah reigned from 640-609 B.C.; his thirteenth year as king was 628-627 B.C.)

Jeremiah lived in Anathoth, about two miles northeast of Jerusalem. His career as a prophet extended from his call in 628-627 B.C. through the reigns of Jehoiakim (609-598 B.C.) and Zedekiah (598-587 B.C.) . (See Jeremiah 1:1-3.) Actually, as Chapters 40 through 44 indicate, Jeremiah prophesied several years after 587 B.C., the year in which Jerusalem was captured and destroyed by the Babylonian king Nebuchadnezzar. Against his will, Jeremiah was taken to Egypt (Jeremiah 43:1-7) and there continued his prophetic utterances.

Jeremiah 1:4-5. *Before I formed you in the womb I knew you:* In a way not clearly explained to us the Lord speaks directly to Jeremiah. Before Jeremiah was born God knew him, that is, chose him for a special mission and consecrated him, that is, set him apart for a specific mission as God's prophet. He is to be God's "prophet to the nations." Actually, Jeremiah spoke almost always to his own people; but what went on among surrounding nations, especially Babylonia and Egypt, was part of the situation Jeremiah faced. He spoke repeatedly of the activities of these neighboring nations.

Verse 6. *Behold, I do not know how to speak:* Jeremiah shrinks from the call that he hears God giving to him. His reasons: (1) He does not *know how to speak;* he fears he could not speak worthily for God. (2) He feels too young for such a responsible task; he is "only a youth," which means not a mere boy but a very young man.

Verses 7-8. *But the* LORD *said to me:* Jeremiah's excuses are rejected. When God calls, youth does not justify refusal. God's appointment is what counts. God's chosen spokesman must go and speak God's word. God will give him his

[1] Floyd V. Filson: professor emeritus of New Testament literature and history, McCormick Theological Seminary, Chicago, Illinois.

message, and he must utter it. He must not be afraid of those who reject and oppose his words. He must speak plainly and remember that the Lord is with him and can deliver him from enemies of the truth.

Verses 9-10. *Then the* LORD *. . . touched my mouth:* In his inaugural vision Jeremiah is vividly aware of God's presence. God gives him the words he must proclaim. His message will have meaning and authority, not merely for the leaders and people of Judah but also for nations and kingdoms on whom Jeremiah pronounces judgment.

Jeremiah's sermon to his people in Chapter 7:1-15 appears in shorter form in Jeremiah 26:1-6. These passages show the basic content of Jeremiah's repeated preaching: the threat of disastrous judgment on Judah if it does not repent, the promise of divine blessing if it does repent. His hearers did not agree on the proper response to such preaching. The priests and false prophets declared, "This man deserves the sentence of death." (Jeremiah 26:11) They thought it was blasphemous for Jeremiah to announce the impending destruction of Jerusalem and its Temple.

Chapter 26:12-15. *The* LORD *sent me to prophesy:* Jeremiah begins and ends with the earnest testimony that the Lord has sent him (verses 12, 15). But he adds that the verdict of doom on Jerusalem, its Temple, and its people is provisional. If they amend their ways and obey God's voice speaking through Jeremiah, "the LORD will repent," that is, change his attitude. He will not bring the threatened doom on them. God wants their good. He wants to bless them, but disobedience will bring deserved disaster.

The officials may do as they like with Jeremiah; his fate is not the important thing. What really counts is that people listen to his message. Not to listen to Jeremiah and heed his message will bring disaster upon Jerusalem and its people.

Selected Scripture

King James Version	Revised Standard Version
Jeremiah 1:4-10	*Jeremiah 1:4-10*
4 Then the word of the LORD came unto me, saying,	4 Now the word of the LORD came to me saying,
5 Before I formed thee in the belly, I knew thee; and before thou camest forth out of the womb I sanctified thee, and I ordained thee a prophet unto the nations.	5 "Before I formed you in the womb I knew you, and before you were born I consecrated you; I appointed you a prophet to the nations."
6 Then said I, Ah, Lord GOD! behold, I cannot speak: for I am a child.	6 Then I said, "Ah, Lord GOD! Behold, I do not know how to speak, for I am only a youth." 7 But the LORD said to me,
7 But the LORD said unto me, Say not, I am a child: for thou shalt go to all that I shall send thee, and whatsoever I command thee thou shalt speak.	"Do not say, 'I am only a youth'; for to all to whom I send you you shall go, and whatever I command you you shall speak.

8 Be not afraid of their faces: for I am with thee to deliver thee, saith the LORD.

9 Then the LORD put forth his hand, and touched my mouth. And the LORD said unto me, Behold, I have put my words in thy mouth.

10 See, I have this day set thee over the nations and over the kingdoms, to root out, and to pull down, and to destroy, and to throw down, to build, and to plant.

Jeremiah 26:12-15

12 Then spake Jeremiah unto all the princes and to all the people, saying, The LORD sent me to prophesy against this house and against this city all the words that ye have heard.

13 Therefore now amend your ways and your doings, and obey the voice of the LORD your God; and the LORD will repent him of the evil that he hath pronounced against you.

14 As for me, behold, I am in your hand: do with me as seemeth good and meet unto you.

15 But know ye for certain, that if ye put me to death, ye shall surely bring innocent blood upon yourselves, and upon this city, and upon the inhabitants thereof: for of a truth the LORD hath sent me unto you to speak all these words in your ears.

Memory Selection: Be not afraid of their faces: for I am with thee to deliver thee, saith the LORD. (Jeremiah 1:8)

8 Be not afraid of them,
for I am with you to deliver you,
says the LORD."

9 Then the LORD put forth his hand and touched my mouth; and the LORD said to me,
"Behold, I have put my words in your mouth.

10 See, I have set you this day over nations and over kingdoms,
to pluck up and to break down,
to destroy and to overthrow,
to build and to plant."

Jeremiah 26:12-15

12 Then Jeremiah spoke to all the princes and all the people, saying, "The LORD sent me to prophesy against this house and this city all the words you have heard. 13 Now therefore amend your ways and your doings, and obey the voice of the LORD your God, and the LORD will repent of the evil which he has pronounced against you. 14 But as for me, behold, I am in your hands. Do with me as seems good and right to you. 15 Only know for certain that if you put me to death, you will bring innocent blood upon yourselves and upon this city and its inhabitants, for in truth the LORD sent me to you to speak all these words in your ears."

Memory Selection:
Be not afraid of them,
for I am with you to deliver you,
says the LORD.
(Jeremiah 1:8)

The Scripture and the Main Question —Charles M. Laymon

BORN TO SERVE

Some men stumble into greatness; others are pushed into greatness; still others are called by God into greatness. Jeremiah belonged to the latter group. As a young man he experienced a summons from God to become a prophet. He was even told that before he was born God had picked him out to be his special servant: "Before I formed you in the womb I knew you, and before you were born I consecrated you; I appointed you a prophet to the nations." (Jeremiah 1:5) The belief that God is behind the births of great men—men of destiny —is thoroughly biblical. From Genesis to Revelation this conviction is asserted over and over again. When greatness showed itself in a man, the Hebrews invariably exclaimed, "What hath God wrought!" What some today might regard as a biological accident, the Bible considers as an act of God.

The conviction that God had brought his life into existence for a great work gave Jeremiah the needed strength to confront and rise above the many obstacles he faced. J. Wallace Hamilton quoted a medical doctor from the University of Vienna as saying, "There is nothing in the world which helps a man surmount his difficulties, survive his disasters, keep him healthy and happy, as the knowledge of a life task worthy of his devotion." Jeremiah possessed this knowledge.

HESITANT TO SERVE

The significance of great events sometimes escapes us. Perhaps our vision is dim, or what we are witnessing seems too marvelous to be true. Neither of these alternatives explains Jeremiah's hesitancy to move out with God into the future. On the contrary, he was overcome by the enormity of the call, since he was but a youth and the call to serve required tremendous resources. What Jeremiah said was "I do not know how to speak, for I am only a youth."

"How unlike many youth today," someone says. This is the day when young people speak out in protest against whatever they consider to be unjust. They organize demonstrations, and some of them engage in violence. Hesitancy is not their dominant mood.

Youth have done remarkable things in every age. John Henry Newman was only thirty-two when he wrote "Lead, Kindly Light." Samuel F. Smith was twenty-four when he wrote "My Country, 'Tis of Thee," and John Milton was but fifteen when he wrote "Let Us With a Gladsome Mind." We should add that Jesus was about thirty years of age when he began his public ministry.

We should not, therefore, conclude that Jeremiah was timid just because of his age. He was probably unusually sensitive. At the moment, he felt the tremendous pressure of a prophetic ministry in which he would be called upon to cry out against the establishment of his day.

THE PROPHET'S AUTHORITY

A wise minister once told a youth who was called to the ministry that God never calls a person into his service without knowing in advance how he will be able to serve. This is what God told Jeremiah.

Thus Jeremiah's hesitancy was short-lived. God assured him that he would be with him, saying, "Behold, I have put my words in your mouth." (verse 9) The prophet was not to speak what was merely a personal opinion; he was not to deal with temporary truth. Instead, Jeremiah would speak forth none other than the word of God.

If one is certain that what he has to say is God's own word, he possesses an authority that goes beyond himself and his personal limitations. The congregation knows whether the preacher is urging his own ideas or proclaiming a word that God has given him to preach.

Whether it is Jeremiah or someone else, the prophet speaks for God; the

132

prophet speaks as one called by God; the prophet speaks as one empowered by God. As he stands in the pulpit with every eye in the congregation fastened upon him, the preacher wonders how he, being a man, can speak the word of God. And yet he must! It is sheer effrontery, if not actual blasphemy, to do anything else. Yet how can he speak? It is because, like Jeremiah, he has been called by God. God's words have been placed in his heart and on his lips. He is a man possessed by God.

Such a person need not be an ordained minister. God frequently speaks through lay persons—businessmen, teachers, statesmen, editorialists, college presidents, scientists, and others who do not follow white-collar professions. Anyone may be tapped by God as his person for the hour.

JUDGMENT AND HOPE

What was the word of God that Jeremiah was called upon to proclaim? In some ways this is like asking what God's word is for today. His word is always on the side of justice, good will, righteousness, love, hones-ty, purity, and truth. Whatever the circumstances, the man of God takes his stand here.

In doing this he is sometimes called upon to proclaim God's judgment, while on other occasions he brings hope and joy. In this vein, Jeremiah was told that he was "to pluck up and to break down," as well as "to build and to plant." (verse 10)

We too easily conclude that we are speaking for God only when we are negative and critical, bold in denunciation, and forthright in judging. Like Jonah, we rejoice in condemning our Ninevahs. But proclaiming the grace and forgiveness of God is also to bring the divine word to men. This Jeremiah did, in the case of Judah, when he said, "The LORD sent me to prophesy against this house and this city." (Jeremiah 26:12) Then he added, "Now therefore amend your ways and your doings, and obey the voice of the LORD your God, and the LORD will repent of the evil which he has pronounced against you." (verse 13) There was still hope for the nation. Judgment is preached in order that repentance will divert it.

Helping Adults Become Involved —Harlan R. Waite[2]

Preparation of Self and Class

This is the first lesson in a series of thirteen on the general theme "Prophets of Judgment and Hope." Since six of these lessons will deal with the prophet Jeremiah, it is very important that the teacher read the entire Book of Jeremiah. Only relatively few passages from the book will be dealt with in the class sessions, but the

[2] Harlan R. Waite: minister of education, First United Methodist Church, Glendale, California.

background that can be gained from reading the remaining passages will be indispensable.

Of special importance to this lesson also are 2 Chronicles 36, which gives the general historical setting, and Jeremiah 1 and 26. Other resources for use in your preparation should include *The Interpreter's Bible*, the materials in your denominational student quarterlies, and other translations of Jeremiah, such as *Moffatt's* or *The New English Bible.* Keep the needs of your class members in mind as you plan. For example, if they are complacent, they may need to be challenged to new sensitivity. If they are unaware of the Bible's vital relationship to the living issues of life, they may need clarification at this point.

Presenting the Main Question

It may be helpful for you to start the session with the showing of the color filmstrip *Our Old Testament Heritage* (see page 127), which outlines five major periods of Old Testament history: Abraham, Moses, the formation and division of Israel, Jeremiah, and Habakkuk. Following the showing of the filmstrip, let the class members discuss how each of the men considered was, in his own way, "a man for the hour." One of the values of this filmstrip is that it sets Jeremiah in the context of the total history of Israel, to which he refers (2:1-8).

The members of your class should understand Jeremiah as vitally related to the burning issues of his own day. Background studies, such as those in *The Interpreter's Bible,* will help you develop an accurate picture. Help the class members to understand that Israel was caught in the power-play of nations (Assyria, Egypt, and Babylonia) much as peoples are today. Jeremiah became unpopular because he counseled against an alliance with Egypt and recommended surrender to the king of Babylonia. Underscore the fact that he considered this to be God's will for his country.

Developing the Lesson

An understanding of the role of the prophet and of the meaning of the word itself is of crucial importance to an adequate understanding of Jere-miah (and of the other prophets to be considered in this series). The word *prophet* comes from two Greek words: *pro* ("on behalf of") and *phemi* ("to speak"). Combined, they mean "to speak on behalf of"; and in biblical usage this is understood to mean that the prophet speaks on behalf of God.

Ask your class members to contrast this meaning with other more common meanings for the word. Undoubtedly, for some of your class members, *prophecy* will have the meaning of forecasting the future. However, this is only a secondary meaning of the word. The prophet, who speaks on behalf of God, is a man of deep insight. On the basis of this insight he is able to see the consequences of human behavior. He understands the meaning and nature of God in sufficient measure to enable him to warn of impending peril or give assurance of future well-being. Thus foresight grows out of insight. It is not some kind of magical gift but a function of deep spiritual sensitivity.

For a further development of the role of the prophet refer to "As You Read the Scripture" and "The Scripture and the Main Question" for this lesson.

Ask a member of the class to read Jeremiah 7:1-11; then discuss what Jeremiah has seen in the life of his nation that is out of favor with God. Do not hesitate to add your own thoughts if there are significant points that have been overlooked by the class members. Among the sins of the nation are the failure to execute justice; oppression of the alien, the fatherless, and the widow; the shedding of innocent blood under the protection of religious pretext ("in this place"—verse 6); idolatry; stealing;

134

murder; adultery; false witness; and the service of false gods.

Finally, ask the class members to discuss the meaning of "den of robbers" in verse 11. Do they recall where else they may have read these words in the Bible? If not, refer them to Matthew 21:13; Mark 11:17; and Luke 19:46. In this passage in Jeremiah there seems to be no money involved. Why are the people called "robbers"? Did the leaders of the church, in overlooking these matters of private and public morality, really rob men of the kind of sensitive faith God wanted them to have? Are churchmen of today guilty of similar crimes?

Now ask the class members to read quietly the printed Scripture from Jeremiah 1:4-10. After a few moments of silent reading, ask them to describe Jeremiah, using only the information from these verses. They may mention his youth, his feeling that God had called him to be a spokesman (prophet), his feeling of insecurity about his youthfulness, and his fear of the consequences.

Then ask the class members this second question, How does the Scripture passage describe Jeremiah's mission? Pay special attention to verse 10, with its contrasting references to building and planting. Follow this discussion with related questions, such as: When does it become necessary in the reform of a nation to "pluck up"? How can a nation avoid letting a crisis become so severe that the only way out is "to destroy and to overthrow"? What would Jeremiah have thought of the demonstrations and protests of our times? What changes can we Americans make to bring our dream of "liberty and justice for all" to full realization?

In discussing these questions help the class members to avoid mentioning only what others can do. This discussion will be most helpful if your class members will deal with what they and their particular segment of society can do to contribute to the good of the whole.

An American "Jeremiah" is to be found in William Lloyd Garrison. An opponent of slavery, he spoke in strong language not unlike Jeremiah and some of the other prophets. Listen to some of his words: "Let Southern oppressors tremble—let their secret abettors tremble—let their Northern apologists tremble—let all the enemies of the persecuted blacks tremble."

The priests and the false prophets of Jeremiah's time also have their counterparts in American history. Even as people had tried to silence Jeremiah in the sixth century B.C., so America passed a series of "gag rules" from 1836 to 1844, with provisions under which the House of Representatives automatically shelved all abolitionist petitions without debate.

Just as it was disastrous for Judah not to heed Jeremiah, it proved disastrous for the United States not to deal constructively with the slavery question in the quarter century prior to the Civil War.

Let your class members discuss this question: Do we serve God well by refusing to listen to one another and to face basic issues?

Helping Class Members Act

Let the members of your class discuss practical ways in which they may implement this lesson. One possibility would be to have small subgroupings meet in the homes of members to discuss the revitalization and renewal of your church and to find practical ways of making the ministry of your church more like the ministry of Jeremiah than the ministry of the priests who opposed him. Specific requests may be addressed by each group to the council on ministries, the official board, or the administrative body of your church. Beyond this, some groups may wish to write letters to community or national leaders, warning them of the consequences of allowing certain specific injustices to persevere in our society.

Planning for Next Sunday

Call the attention of your class to the theme for next Sunday: "A Nation Against God." State that the main question will be What does the worship of God in the life of a nation contribute to its character? Ask class members to read Jeremiah 2:1-19 and 3:6 through 5:31.

LESSON 2   DECEMBER 10

A Nation Against God

Background Scripture: Jeremiah 2:1-19; 3:6 through 5:31

The Main Question —Charles M. Laymon

A teen-age boy on his first trip to Washington, D.C. was enthralled by what he saw. The great sweep of the Capitol dome, the height of the Washington Monument, the stately dignity of the Supreme Court Building—all these impressed him greatly. But the memorials to Abraham Lincoln and Thomas Jefferson moved him most of all. In telling his friends about these memorials he said, "It was like being in a church."

And it is! The solemnity of the setting and the strength of the tall pillars take hold of you as you enter. You feel you are in a sanctuary; and if you speak, it is in a muffled whisper. Besides this, when you read the carved inscriptions of Lincoln's Gettysburg and second inaugural addresses, as well as excerpts from the words of Jefferson, you find the name of God occurring over and over again. The nation's destiny and its recognition of God are tied together so that they cannot be separated.

Several attempts have been made in recent years, in the name of democracy, to remove the recognition of God from our life as citizens. Even Frank Borman's reading of the creation account of Genesis from outer space was criticized as an effrontery to atheistic citizens.

All this raises the question of a nation's relationship to God. Does freedom of worship carry a bias against recognition of God? Is a nation without God no different from one with God? What does the worship of God in the life of a nation contribute to its character?

The biblical passages that follow will be helpful in answering these questions.

136

As You Read the Scripture —Floyd V. Filson

Jeremiah 5:21. *Hear this, O foolish and senseless people:* The people of Jeremiah's time show no intelligence or judgment. They have the capacity to learn the truth about their evil ways, if only they would open their eyes to their moral failure and their ears to Jeremiah's earnest message. In other passages Jeremiah indicts and rebukes the religious leaders of his people. But the failure of these leaders does not excuse the common people.

Verse 22. *Do you not fear me?* The Lord of nature is the Lord of men. He has power in the moral and spiritual world as well as in the world of nature. Men cannot break or destroy God's moral order; they will come under condemnation if they try. So Jeremiah's hearers should listen to the message that God has given him; they should have a wholesome fear of the divine judgment on those who try to break God's moral order.

THE MEN THESE MONUMENTS HONOR SPOKE WORDS FULL OF REFERENCES TO GOD AND HIS RELATIONSHIP TO THE UNITED STATES. ARE A NATION'S DESTINY AND ITS RECOGNITION OF GOD TIED TOGETHER? WHAT DOES THE WORSHIP OF GOD IN THE LIFE OF A NATION CONTRIBUTE TO ITS CHARACTER?

Verse 23. *But this people has a stubborn and rebellious heart:* The Hebrew word for heart does not refer merely to one's emotions. It refers to the total conscious life of the person, including his thoughts and decisions. Jeremiah indicts his people because their whole life direction is stubbornly rebellious against God. They have turned aside from what God wants of them; they have set their outlook and life against God's will.

137

Verses 24-25. *They do not say . . . "Let us fear the* LORD *our God":* These stubborn and rebellious people fail to fear the Lord. Note the word *fear.* Here it does not mean a wild and frantic flight before real or imagined danger. Nor does it mean paralyzing panic in the face of some terrifying threat. Fear rather refers to a wholesome awe and respect toward man's Creator, Lord, and Redeemer. In that sense of the word, men who are alert to the truth and alive to their duty will say in their hearts, *"Let us fear the* LORD *our God."* What Jeremiah sees in his fellow countrymen is not such fear but callous indifference to God's claim.

Evidently drought and crop failure have plagued the people of Judah. Jeremiah sees this as God's judgment upon his people for failure to listen to his prophet. Palestine has two rainy seasons, one in the autumn and one in the spring. But "the weeks appointed for the harvest" have proved deeply disappointing, and Jeremiah is sure that the crop failure is punishment for his countrymen's sins.

In Jeremiah 5:26-28 the prophet gives examples of the sins he has just mentioned. He describes how ruthless, treacherous, unjust rich men prey upon their fellow countrymen.

Verse 29. *Shall I not punish them for these things?* The words *these things* refer especially to the wickedness and social injustice denounced in verses 26-28. Using for emphasis the solemn formula "says the LORD," Jeremiah declares that divine judgment will certainly punish such a nation. The people must not think that because God has shown special favor to them in the past he will not notice and judge present wrongdoers.

Verses 30-31. *An appalling and horrible thing has happened in the land:* The situation is shocking to Jeremiah—*an appalling and horrible thing,* almost unbelievable. Three groups are condemned here.

The basic fault Jeremiah sees is in the popularly recognized prophets. They predict smooth things and pleasant prospects with no ability or willingness to pronounce judgment on the moral sickness of his people.

The priests rule at the direction of the prophets. They take their cue and get their message from the comfortable but false message of the prophetic group.

The astounding thing to Jeremiah is that his "people love to have it so." They raise no protest. They see no convincing word in the condemnation Jeremiah pronounces on the sins of God's people. They are complacent and contented when they ought to be quick to repent for their sins.

Jeremiah closes his condemnation of these three groups with the ominous question, "What will you do when the end comes?" There will be a reckoning. It is inescapable. Jeremiah implies that it will bring doom and disaster; there will be no escape from the divine judgment and penalty.

Selected Scripture

King James Version	Revised Standard Version
Jeremiah 5:21-25, 29-31	*Jeremiah 5:21-25, 29-31*
21 Hear now this, O foolish people, and without understanding; which	21 "Hear this, O foolish and senseless people,

have eyes, and see not; which have ears, and hear not:

22 Fear ye not me? saith the LORD: will ye not tremble at my presence, which have placed the sand for the bound of the sea by a perpetual decree, that it cannot pass it: and though the waves thereof toss themselves, yet can they not prevail; though they roar, yet can they not pass over it?

23 But this people hath a revolting and a rebellious heart; they are revolted and gone.

24 Neither say they in their heart, Let us now fear the LORD our God, that giveth rain, both the former and the latter, in his season: he reserveth unto us the appointed weeks of the harvest.

25 Your iniquities have turned away these things, and your sins have withholden good things from you.

.   .   .   .

29 Shall I not visit for these things? saith the LORD: shall not my soul be avenged on such a nation as this?

30 A wonderful and horrible thing is committed in the land;
31 The prophets prophesy falsely, and the priests bear rule by their means; and my people love to have it so: and what will ye do in the end thereof?

Memory Selection: **My people have committed two evils; they have forsaken me the fountain of living**

who have eyes, but see not,
who have ears, but hear not.
22 Do you not fear me? says the LORD;
Do you not tremble before me?
I placed the sand as the bound for the sea,
a perpetual barrier which it cannot pass;
though the waves toss, they cannot prevail,
though they roar, they cannot pass over it.
23 But this people has a stubborn and rebellious heart;
they have turned aside and gone away.
24 They do not say in their hearts, 'Let us fear the LORD our God,
who gives the rain in its season,
the autumn rain and the spring rain,
and keeps for us
the weeks appointed for the harvest.'
25 Your iniquities have turned these away,
and your sins have kept good from you.

.   .   .   .

29 Shall I not punish them for these things?
says the LORD,
and shall I not avenge myself on a nation such as this?"

30 An appalling and horrible thing has happened in the land:
31 the prophets prophesy falsely, and the priests rule at their direction;
my people love to have it so,
but what will you do when the end comes?

Memory Selection:
My people have committed two evils: they have forsaken me,

waters, and hewed them out cisterns, broken cisterns, that can hold no water. (Jeremiah 2:13)

the fountain of living waters,
and hewed out cisterns for themselves,
broken cisterns,
that can hold no water.
(Jeremiah 2:13)

The Scripture and the Main Question —Charles M. Laymon

THE SOVEREIGN GOD

The Hebrews considered the recognition and worship of God to be a political as well as a religious concern. Their very existence as a nation was an act of God.

In the Bible the God who created the universe and man is the same God who called Abraham to seek out a new country. He is the same God who made a covenant with this ancient patriarch, delivered the Hebrews from Egypt, and gave them the Law on Mount Sinai. Thus the God of creation, the God of the nation, and the God of Hebrew religion were one and the same.

As over against this listen to J. B. Phillips as he says, "The trouble with many people today is that they have not found a God big enough for modern needs." [3] He goes on to state that, in the face of changing world events and mounting scientific discoveries that have enlarged our view of the universe, our ideas of God have remained largely static.

What a shot in the arm then are Jeremiah's words concerning God's creation of the universe! God laid out its borders, and these will hold "though the waves toss, . . . though they roar, they cannot pass over it." (Jeremiah 5:22) God is sovereign.

Such a view of God will give meaning not only to our existence as a nation but also to our personal lives.

Even though the waves of strife toss and roar, we can be confident that if we remain faithful to such a God we shall not be overthrown from within or without.

WHEN A NATION CEASES TO FEAR GOD

The nation of Israel had sufficient reason for a sound faith in God; yet there were times when the people ceased to fear him. Jeremiah diagnosed the problem thus, "They do not say in their hearts, 'Let us fear the LORD our God . . . '" (verse 24) To "fear" God in the Bible means to hold him in reverence, to respect his power, and to recognize his holiness. Without these reactions, God is only a name.

If one had asked these Hebrews whether or not they believed in God, they would have answered, "Yes, of course, we do. Ours is the God of Abraham, Isaac, and Jacob." Yet this affirmation would have been an empty one because *they did not live as though they believed in God.* Here is the most deceptive kind of atheism. The people who practice it think they are religious, but their profession is empty because they do not carry through. They know and use all the right words, but that is the end of it.

An illustration of this same emptiness is a group of Americans singing "My Country, 'Tis of Thee," with the last stanza ending "Great God our King," but not meaning what they say. We do the same thing when we mouth the words of the Lord's Prayer

[3] *Your God Is Too Small* (The Macmillan Co., 1952), p. vii.

140

and do not enter into its meaning by really praying.

Such action is deadly because it has the face of religion, but the face turns out to be only a mask. Irreligion or even no religion at all seems almost preferable.

WHEN OFFICIAL RELIGIOUS LEADERS MISLEAD

Much of the false religion of the people that was weakening the nation in Jeremiah's day stemmed from the irresponsibility of the religious leaders. "The prophets prophesy falsely, and the priests rule at their direction." This to Jeremiah was "an appalling and horrible thing." (verses 30-31a)

Self-centeredness on the part of the priests and prophets stood in the way of their experience of God and their love for the people of the nation. Ministers are those whose function is to bring God to men and men to God. They must be self-effacing; it is their glory to be "used up" personally in this service.

Harry Emerson Fosdick, in *The Meaning of Service*, tells of a lighthouse keeper on an isolated reef. "Are you not lonely out here?" he was asked. The reply came fast and firm, "Not since I saved my first man." This is the way a true priest would have spoken.

The priests of a modern nation are not limited to the ministers in the churches. Men in public life—educators, lawyers, statesmen, labor leaders, all who are responsible for the welfare of the nation—serve in a priestly role. In the concept of the character of this nation those who would serve the people as their leaders must do so as persons "under God." Thus this particular phrase was added to the pledge of allegiance to the American flag.

WHEN PEOPLE LOVE EVIL

The picture Jeremiah gives of his time includes not only irresponsible priests but also irresponsible people. The religious leaders misled; the people followed without protest. As the prophet put it, "My people love to have it so." (verse 31b) This situation was doubly deplorable.

A minister once delivered a powerful sermon based on these words of Jeremiah. He went straight down the line, pointing out the evils of the day —war, injustice, bad housing, poverty, poor working conditions, insincere worship, immorality—and after describing each he would say, "My people love to have it so." What a message for a day in which the people have a vote!

The people have a responsibility to make any nation Christian. What is important is not how much evil they will tolerate but how much good they will set in motion, not just when they will put on the brakes but in what direction they will point the car.

Helping Adults Become Involved —Harlan R. Waite

Preparation of Self and Class

The main theme of this week's lesson is the relationship between Christian worship and national behavior. The background Scriptures paint a poignant picture of God's concern for Israel and its conduct as a nation. Read Jeremiah 2:1-19 and 3:6 through 5:31. Spend some time letting the poetic images and figures of speech become real.

As you read, you will realize that there are different needs among the members of your class. Some resent hearing our nation criticized, while others feel that we should face up to some of our own sins. Some feel that our nation is doing God's will, while others feel it is not. Determine how you will use the material in this lesson by considering which emphases will be most helpful to your class members.

Consult *The Interpreter's Bible* and the materials in your denominational quarterlies as you prepare.

Presenting the Main Question

Begin by asking the class members to discuss what difference religion has made in the life of America. There will, of course, be immediate references to the fact that our forebears came, in part, seeking religious freedom. There will also be references to great national documents, especially the Declaration of Independence. The protection of freedom of religion in the First Amendment to the United States Constitution may also be mentioned.

Note that religion has made another kind of difference as well, not always positive. There have been conflicts between religious groups, with prejudice becoming so strong at times that it has broken out into mob violence. Your class members will know something about the Catholic-Protestant conflict, denominational rivalries, and other religious struggles.

A more positive way in which religion has affected American life is revealed in literature, politics, reform movements, and other aspects of American life. Draw on your class members' knowledge of some of the events of our history.

Developing the Lesson

Part of this week's Bible reading recalls God's faithfulness to Israel in its pilgrimage through history. Have someone in the class read aloud Jeremiah 2:2-13, and ask the class members to listen for the poetic words that paint pictures and suggest feelings. For example, in verse 2 there is profound meaning and warm emotion in the phrases "the devotion of your youth" and "your love as a bride." What is there in Israel's history that led Jeremiah to use these phrases? Could we use similar phrases about the history of our country?

Then ask the class members to identify specifically the historical episodes mentioned, such as the wandering in the wilderness, the settlement in the land of Canaan, and the acceptance of certain pagan customs and concepts that watered down their faith.

Next point out the reference in verse 18 to the fact that there were political factions within Israel that thought they could solve their problems by entering into alliances either with Egypt or with Assyria. In poetic imagery Jeremiah describes this activity as their desire to drink the waters of the Nile or the Euphrates. Are we apt to rely more upon international alliances for our security than on building a nation that everyone will recognize as just and trustworthy? This was one of Jeremiah's concerns.

Summarize this section of the lesson by reading Jeremiah 5:30-31. Ask the class members to identify the three groups of people (prophets, priests, and citizens) who have failed in their own unique roles. Note that the prophets reassure the people that everything is all right, the priests are defensive against anything that threatens the established institution of religion, and the people like it that way. Raise the question as to whether we prefer a false sense of security to having to struggle with the real issues of life. How does worship help us to be realistic?

At this point in the lesson recall the oft-heard claim that if we are to get anywhere in life we must be realistic. Ask the members to discuss what this means. In the discussion choose some specific problem to focus on, such as poverty or urban redevelopment. Then divide the class into small buzz groups and ask each group to list the factors that are important in reaching a solution to the problem. Emphasize that they are to be realistic.

After approximately five minutes let the groups report to the entire class. List the responses on the chalkboard. Do the responses indicate that our goal is to have a just society that respects the dignity of every human being, a community that expresses compassion and human concern, and a nation of opportunity for every man to fulfill his own potential as a human being? What were Jeremiah's goals? What were the standards that led him to criticize his nation?

Close this section of the lesson by noting that worship in the life of a nation contributes to the nation's character by helping it have the right goals. National integrity is more than a matter of economics, politics, and international relationships. It is a commitment to the good life for all of its citizens and the expression of this commitment in the economic, political, and other aspects of the life of the nation.

A second effect of the worship of God in the life of a nation is that it raises up prophets. Recall last week's discussion on the role of the prophet and the meaning of the word. Suggest that a prophet cannot speak on behalf of God unless God has spoken to him. Ask the class members to recall how God spoke to Jeremiah. You may want to refer to Jeremiah 1:11-13 and observe that God can speak to us through the commonplace things of life (such as a rod of almond or a boiling pot), which, as we reflect on them, have symbolic meaning for us. Perhaps your class members will recall that God spoke to Amos through a basket of summer fruit, a plague of locusts, and a wall that was not true with the plumbline (Amos 8:1-3; 7:1-3, 8-9).

Not only is insight deepened but commitment is strengthened through events in our lives. Recall how Abraham Lincoln was affected by the sight of a slave being sold at auction. Worship can sensitize the life of a nation and make it more open to God's wisdom and power, as it helps us discover and serve God in our day-to-day experiences.

Refer once again to Jeremiah 5:31, noting that the people love to have the prophets prophesying falsely and the priests ruling at their discretion. Is this an apt description of us too? Do we prefer to listen to the preachers who tell us everything is all right? Are we satisfied when our priests simply run a good show and keep the ecclesiastical machinery well oiled?

Illustrating the tendency to turn a deaf ear to negative judgment is the omission from most hymnals I have seen of a verse from the famous Christmas carol "It Came Upon the Midnight Clear." Written at the time of the Mexican War (1846-48), the hymn originally contained a reference to the events of history that drown out the pleas of God:

But with the woes of sin and strife
  The world has suffered long;
Beneath the angel-strain have rolled
  Two thousand years of wrong;
And man, at war with man, hears not
  The love song which they bring:
O hush the noise, ye men of strife,
  And hear the angels sing!

Helping Class Members Act

Since the original Christmas was not a beautiful abstraction but a flesh and blood event set in the world of innkeepers, emperors, cruel kings, and indifferent neighbors, the members of your class may want to help your congregation become more aware of how the meaning of Christmas relates to the hard realities of contemporary life. Duplicate the verse of the carol quoted above, and ask your congregation to sing it. The story of the author, Edmund Hamilton Sears, and a description of American affairs at that time can be found in *The Gospel in Hymns* by Albert Edward Bailey.

Planning for Next Sunday

Next week we will be talking about involvement. Read the story of the involvement of Jeremiah and Ebedmelech in Jeremiah 20 and 21; 37 and 38; and 39:15-18. Read "Helping Adults Become Involved" for next week's lesson, and note certain suggestions that can be prepared in advance by some of your class members. In particular, ask someone to read Thomas Paine's pamphlet entitled *Common Sense* and prepare a report for the class. Ask someone else to prepare a report on Washington Gladden—his public witness and his hymn "O Master, Let Me Walk With Thee."

Convictions Can Be Costly

Background Scripture: Jeremiah 20 and 21; 37 and 38; 39:15-18

The Main Question —Charles M. Laymon

In recent years we have heard a great deal about the silent majority. Many persons feel that here lies the strength of the nation. This group can swing any election, effect any civic change, and surmount any crisis.

But why are these persons silent? Why are they not outspoken day by day, making their convictions heard? Some hold that there is sufficient explosive talk already; with protests, marches, sit-ins, and hold-outs, more voices are not needed. Others are fearful that if they speak out they may be falsely identified with the new left or with some facist group. Still others do not want to face the consequences of being vocal, and so they "keep their counsel." Is such silence always a virtue?

I was in the home of a young married couple recently when this issue came into the discussion. The husband said, "We are getting out of the silent majority. Too long we have given the microphone to the radicals. We are going to write letters to the editor; speak up in class discussions at church; and politic in local, state, and national elections."

Across the street from City Road Chapel in London is a cemetery where a number of famous persons are buried, including Susanna Wesley, the mother of John and Charles Wesley. Among others buried there are Isaac Watts, the hymnwriter; Daniel Defoe, author of *Robinson Crusoe;* and John Bunyan, author of *Pilgrim's Progress.* This cemetery is called the "Dissenters' Cemetery" because of the outspokenness of those buried there. They could not be buried in a churchyard or a place consecrated by the church because of their views. But what a glorious company!

The Scripture passage that follows also tells of a dissenter who was an outcast because of his views.

As You Read the Scripture —Floyd V. Filson

Jeremiah denounced his people's sinfulness and injustice. He said that God would hand his sinful people over to the king and army of Babylonia (Jeremiah 37:8, 17). Jerusalem would be captured and destroyed, and Zedekiah the king of Judah would be taken captive.

Such predictions by Jeremiah, we can easily understand, aroused indignation among his people's leaders, especially their military leaders. They were fighting a desperate but losing battle to save Jerusalem from capture and destruction. They feared—and with reason—that the city and its people, and especially its leaders, would, if captured, suffer severely at the hands of Nebuchadnezzar king of Babylonia. They knew only one plan of action for besieged Jerusalem—fight to the finish. Against this policy the prophet Jeremiah raised a dissenting voice.

Jeremiah 38:2-3. *He who stays in this city shall die:* Things were getting desperate for Jerusalem's defenders. Jeremiah was telling the people that to continue the fight would only mean violent death, famine, and pestilence; the thing to do was to go out and surrender to the army of the Chaldeans (that is, the Babylonians). The people would become slaves of the Chaldeans, but at least they would save their lives.

Verses 4-6. *Let this man be put to death:* The leaders of the "fight-to-the-bitter-end" war party were determined to silence Jeremiah. Death, disease, and desertion were decimating their defending forces; but just possibly, they thought, they might drive off the besieging army if Jeremiah could be stopped from weakening the morale of their army and people. They considered him guilty of treason. He must *be put to death,* they told King Zedekiah.

The king lacked the independence and courage to stand up against the war-party leaders. He dared not oppose them. He gave them permission to put Jeremiah to death. They did not execute him; perhaps they thought this would cause too hostile a reaction among the people. Instead, they put him in a cistern used to hold water channeled there in the rainy season. When they put Jeremiah there, in the summer of 587 B.C., it was empty except for some mire at the bottom. They lowered Jeremiah into the cistern and left him to sink in the mire and die.

Verses 7-9. *Ebed-melech . . . heard that they had put Jeremiah into the cistern:* Ebed-melech means "servant of the king." He was not an Israelite but an Ethiopian, a eunuch with a rather important position in the household or court of the king. Ebed-melech heard what had been done to Jeremiah. He went to the king, who was sitting in the Benjamin Gate, the north gate of the city, where the city wall was most open to attack. He told the king what had happened and asked him to save the prophet's life. It is odd that Jeremiah was said to be facing death from hunger; if he was sinking in the mire of the cistern, he would be smothered to death long before he could die of hunger. In any case, Jeremiah was facing death.

Verses 10-13. *Take three men . . . and lift Jeremiah . . . out of the cistern:* King Zedekiah, who had given the princes permission to execute Jeremiah, now thinks better of it. He directs Ebed-melech to rescue Jeremiah from the cistern before he dies in the mire. He tells Ebed-melech to *take three men* with him and rescue the prophet. Some ancient manuscripts of the Book of Jeremiah say Ebed-melech was to take thirty men (see KJV). Yet three men would be sufficient to pull Jeremiah out of the cistern. Just possibly the king sent thirty men because he feared some attempt might be made to prevent rescue of the prophet.

Ebed-melech took old rags and worn-out clothes from a storehouse, let them down to Jeremiah by ropes, had the prophet put the rags and clothes under his armpits so the ropes would not cut into the flesh, and pulled Jeremiah out of the cistern. Jeremiah remained in the court of the guard, apparently protected by the soldiers on duty.

Selected Scripture

King James Version

Jeremiah 38:2-13

2 Thus saith the Lord, He that remaineth in this city shall die by the sword, by the famine, and by the pestilence: but he that goeth forth to the Chaldeans shall live; for he shall have his life for a prey, and shall live.

3 Thus saith the Lord, This city shall surely be given into the hand of the king of Babylon's army, which shall take it.

4 Therefore the princes said unto the king, We beseech thee, let this man be put to death: for thus he weakeneth the hands of the men of war that remain in this city, and the hands of all the people, in speaking such words unto them: for this man seeketh not the welfare of this people, but the hurt.

5 Then Zedekiah the king said, Behold, he is in your hand: for the king is not he that can do any thing against you.

Revised Standard Version

Jeremiah 38:2-13

2 "Thus says the Lord, He who stays in this city shall die by the sword, by famine, and by pestilence; but he who goes out to the Chaldeans shall live; he shall have his life as a prize of war, and live. 3 Thus says the Lord, This city shall surely be given into the hand of the army of the king of Babylon and be taken." 4 Then the princes said to the king, "Let this man be put to death, for he is weakening the hands of the soldiers who are left in this city, and the hands of all the people, by speaking such words to them. For this man is not seeking the welfare of this people, but their harm." 5 King Zedekiah said, "Behold, he is in your hands; for the king can do nothing against you." 6 So they took Jeremiah and cast him into the cistern of Malchiah, the king's son, which was in the court of the guard, letting Jeremiah down by

6 Then took they Jeremiah, and cast him into the dungeon of Malchiah the son of Hammelech, that was in the court of the prison: and they let down Jeremiah with cords. And in the dungeon there was no water, but mire: so Jeremiah sunk in the mire.

7 Now when Ebed-melech the Ethiopian, one of the eunuchs which was in the king's house, heard that they had put Jeremiah in the dungeon; the king then sitting in the gate of Benjamin;

8 Ebed-melech went forth out of the king's house, and spake to the king, saying,

9 My lord the king, these men have done evil in all that they have done to Jeremiah the prophet, whom they have cast into the dungeon; and he is like to die for hunger in the place where he is: for there is no more bread in the city.

10 Then the king commanded Ebed-melech the Ethiopian, saying, Take from hence thirty men with thee, and take up Jeremiah the prophet out of the dungeon, before he die.

11 So Ebed-melech took the men with him, and went into the house of the king under the treasury, and took thence old cast clouts and old rotten rags, and let them down by cords into the dungeon to Jeremiah.

12 And Ebed-melech the Ethiopian said unto Jeremiah, Put now these old cast clouts and rotten rags under thine armholes under the cords. And Jeremiah did so.

13 So they drew up Jeremiah with cords, and took him up out of the dungeon: and Jeremiah remained in the court of the prison.

ropes. And there was no water in the cistern, but only mire, and Jeremiah sank in the mire.

7 When Ebed-melech the Ethiopian, a eunuch, who was in the king's house, heard that they had put Jeremiah into the cistern—the king was sitting in the Benjamin Gate—8 Ebed-melech went from the king's house and said to the king, 9 "My lord the king, these men have done evil in all that they did to Jeremiah the prophet by casting him into the cistern; and he will die there of hunger, for there is no bread left in the city." 10 Then the king commanded Ebed-melech, the Ethiopian, "Take three men with you from here, and lift Jeremiah the prophet out of the cistern before he dies." 11 So Ebed-melech took the men with him and went to the house of the king, to a wardrobe of the storehouse, and took from there old rags and worn-out clothes, which he let down to Jeremiah in the cistern by ropes. 12 Then Ebed-melech the Ethiopian said to Jeremiah, "Put the rags and clothes between your armpits and the ropes." Jeremiah did so. 13 Then they drew Jeremiah up with ropes and lifted him out of the cistern. And Jeremiah remained in the court of the guard.

Memory Selection: They shall fight against thee; but they shall not prevail against thee; for I am with thee, saith the LORD, to deliver thee. (Jeremiah 1:19)

Memory Selection: They will fight against you; but they shall not prevail against you, for I am with you, says the LORD, to deliver you. (Jeremiah 1:19)

The Scripture and the Main Question —Charles M. Laymon

POLITICS OR RELIGION?

Jeremiah lived in a difficult day. The Babylonians were threatening the nation of Israel. Jerusalem was facing destruction, and the people were in danger of losing their homes. The prophet urged the people to surrender to Nebuchadnezzar. He believed it was the Lord's will: "Thus says the LORD, He who stays in this city shall die by the sword, by famine, and by pestilence; but he who goes out to the Chaldeans shall live; he shall have his life as a prize of war, and live." (Jeremiah 38:2)

Jeremiah's advice was grounded in the belief that the nation would not lose its identity if it submitted to Babylonia. The people would be allowed to stay in Jerusalem, maintain their religious institutions, and keep their homes intact.

The other alternative was to resist the Babylonians. This seemed to be the brave and patriotic decision. The enemy, however, was so much greater militarily than Israel that defeat seemed inevitable. Jeremiah knew that the citizenry would be transferred as slaves to a foreign land and their life as a people disrupted, if not destroyed.

What Jeremiah advised, therefore, was political realism. At the time, however, it seemed fanciful. Jerusalem would never fall.

The prophets spoke out on political issues on many occasions. They did this because the welfare of God's people was involved. Men have done so ever since. Wendell Phillips was an abolitionist who was often criticized for his stand against slavery. However, his invalid wife would say, as he was leaving for a lecture, "Now, Wendell, don't you shilly-shally."

This type of response to a social question is thoroughly biblical.

LOOK FOR THE MOTIVE

The political situation Jeremiah faced was further complicated by the fact that there was a pro-Egyptian group in the nation who opposed the prophet's position that it would be better to submit to the Babylonians and live. They were blinded to his logic because they saw only their own political position. If the nation of Israel submitted to the Babylonians, Egypt would lose her chances in Israel.

This pro-Egyptian group had the ear of King Zedekiah, a vacillating ruler without religious depth. They convinced him that the prophet's advice was bad. More than this, they said Jeremiah was a traitor: "This man is not seeking the welfare of this people, but their harm." (verse 4b)

If only Zedekiah had been a more perceptive person, he could have detected the false motives of the pro-Egyptians. They really did not care for the welfare of the Hebrews but clothed their true motives in high-sounding words. The pro-Egyptian group said they sought to do away with the prophet in the interest of the well-being of the people, yet there was a hidden personal political motive. We would all do well to examine the motives for our actions more closely.

A PRICE TO BE PAID

King Zedekiah gave in to the pro-Egyptian group that wanted to still the voice of Jeremiah. He said, "Behold, he [Jeremiah] is in your hands; for the king can do nothing against you." (verse 5) How like Pilate, who, after washing his hands, handed over Jesus to be crucified, saying, "I am

148

innocent of this man's blood; see to it yourselves." (Matthew 27:24)

Jeremiah was placed in a cistern, which, although empty of water, was miry with mud on the bottom. The biblical author stresses this fact by adding, "Jeremiah sank in the mire." (38:6) The prophet was again discovering that convictions can be costly. Once before he had been beaten, put in stocks, and publicly humiliated (Jeremiah 20:2). He had even decided that he would resign from the ministry, that he would "hold in" because his messages were so filled with judgment. But Jeremiah could not do this. A fire burned in his bones and heart, and he could not keep silent (20:9). He must speak out regardless of the consequences.

In our own day there have also been those who have discovered that convictions can be costly. These were not morbid men without hope. Martin Luther King, Jr. was such a man; ultimately he paid for his views with his life. On one occasion he said, "The dawn will come. Disappointment, sorrow, and despair are born at midnight, but morning follows." There is a midnight, but it does not have the final word.

DELIVERANCE COMES

As Martin Luther King, Jr. said, surely the dawn will come. In fact, only by holding to convictions that are costly can we experience the dawn that confirms our adventurous faith. The cross was the price of the Resurrection. Night ushers in the day.

Jeremiah must have felt deep despair as he stood in the mire of the cistern where he was imprisoned. Zedekiah no doubt planned to kill him as a traitor. But Jeremiah also knew God was going to make his move too. The faith that God will make the final move in any situation gives a structure to life when it is about to fall apart.

It is interesting, almost ironical, to note that a foreigner, an Ethiopian by the name of Ebed-melech, interceded for Jeremiah before the king and secured his release from the cistern prison. A rope, cushioned by rags and old clothes, was placed under Jeremiah's armpits; and he was pulled from the dark hole into the light.

The prophet's ministry was not finished. The king continued to call upon him for advice—advice which unfortunately he did not follow. Yet Jeremiah continued to give it, cost or no cost.

Helping Adults Become Involved —Harlan R. Waite

Preparation of Self and Class

The background Scriptures for this lesson are Jeremiah 20 and 21; 37 and 38; and 39:15-18. The verses printed in the student quarterlies are Jeremiah 38:2-13. Read these passages carefully to get a picture of what Jeremiah was saying and what was happening to him. As you read, try to think of men and women who have taken unpopular positions in our time.

Keep your class members in mind as you read. Some may need to be sensitized to the real issues and challenged to action. Others may need support and encouragement in expressing their convictions more freely and effectively. In any event, gear your lesson to the needs of your class members.

CONVICTIONS CAN BE COSTLY

Presenting the Main Question

During the American Revolution it was difficult to get persons very deeply involved in the struggle. Probably at no time were even one-half the citizens of the colonies actively in support of the war. In 1776, Thomas Paine wrote a pamphlet entitled *Common Sense,* in which he offered a very persuasive argument for involvement in the American cause. Introduce this lesson by reading some of his words: "These are the times that try men's souls. The summer soldier and the sunshine patriot will, in this crisis, shrink from the service of his country; but he that stands it *now,* deserves the love and thanks of man and woman." In one important respect, of course, the situation is the opposite of that of Jeremiah; for Jeremiah opposed a war and Thomas Paine favored one. However, the principle of involvement is the same. The colonists who would not support the Revolution did not get involved enough even to oppose it. Thomas Paine's words and the popular attitudes that made those words seem necessary to him highlight a basic human problem: convictions can be costly, and we are often held back from acting on our convictions because of the cost involved.

Above, the main question has been identified as this: Why is the silent majority silent? Ask your class members to rephrase the question so that it becomes more personal for them. For example, the question may be restated this way, Why are we, or why am I, a part of the majority that is more inclined to be silent than to get involved?

Developing the Lesson

Observe that the main question is a question of our basic motivations. Lead the class members into a discussion of the different levels of motivation. For example, some motivations are purely physical. Pain causes us to do that which will bring us comfort. This is true not only in a strictly physical sense but in other ways as well. "Pain" in the pocketbook will cause us to buy less, to look for bargains, to complain about taxes, to oppose certain government programs, or to vote for certain political candidates. Fatigue, fear, and feelings of insecurity are other examples of factors that motivate us on a rather elemental level.

Another motivational level your class members may deal with is that of interest or taste. We do some things and avoid doing other things because we like or dislike doing them. Our decision is simply a matter of personal taste.

Certain social factors also enter into our motivation. Whose favor and approval are we seeking? Who will support us or oppose us?

Finally, there are the deeper motivations springing out of one's sense of morality, of responsibility, of ultimate relationship to God and to man. The basic questions of one's life, then, are Why am I here, and what is the goal of my life?

In the light of these levels of motivation ask the class members to deal with a second question that flows out of the first: How would you explain the failure of the people of Jeremiah's day to face the real issues and to become involved in the solution of the crucial problems faced by Jerusalem? Then proceed to another question: How do you explain Jeremiah's sense of involvement? Suggest to the class members that they review what they know of the story of Jeremiah, including the facts that he was born into a priestly family and that, as his words clearly indicate, he was a sensitive

150

person. Consider also the fact that many people saw an almond rod or a boiling pot, but it was Jeremiah who saw something more profound in these commonplace things. Why would he say, despite his deep desire to avoid suffering, that he could not hold in the "burning fire" in his heart (20:9)?

Ask the class members this question: Can we really escape all involvement with others? Do we really want to? To pinpoint the issue, ask your class members to consider the interdependence of all human beings. Let them list the ways in which we are involved with one another, whether we choose to be or not: in the family; in education; in the securing of food, clothing, and other necessities of life; in the area of health (we give someone our cold or some other disease; we take medicine discovered and developed by someone else; we are cured by doctors). By the very nature of our creation we belong to one another and interact with one another.

Review the story of Jeremiah. To what extent was his involvement automatic, and in what ways was it deliberate? Ask the class members to describe his internal struggle and the way in which fact, feelings, and values each played a part in his commitment.

Finally, ask your students to report on certain individuals who have paid a price for their convictions: politicians, ministers, and other public leaders who have taken unpopular positions on controversial issues; persons who have given liberally of time, energy, money, and other personal resources to render a service or serve a cause they have believed in; or others who have given up opportunities for personal benefit to help others.

Washington Gladden's life is an example of how a man can pay a heavy price for his involvement. Deeply concerned—as was Jeremiah—about applying God's justice to the social, political, and economic life of his nation, Gladden preached with boldness and conviction. Also, like Jeremiah, he became the object of bitter attack; and his motives were twisted and distorted. Gladden's aim was to bring reason and Christian conscience into larger areas of American life. Ironically he became the object of bitter criticism and misrepresentation. He was twice prevented from becoming president of large universities because of his spiritual convictions, and he was almost repudiated at one time by his own denomination for condemning a gift of "tainted money."

Helping Class Members Act

Refer the members of your class to Washington Gladden's hymn "O Master, Let Me Walk With Thee"; and ask them to read it in a devotional mood and to relate it to the outspoken, often hard-hitting proclamation of the gospel by Dr. Gladden. Social activist though he was, he revealed in this hymn the sources of his faith and his strength for witness.

The original stanzas three and four have been omitted from most hymnals on the rather shallow ground that the words are not suitable for worship services. Some of your class members may be interested in going to the library to research this hymn. If so, let them share the words of these omitted stanzas with the class and make their own evaluation of whether or not they could be used in worship. A source for this investigation is *The Gospel in Hymns* by Albert Edward Bailey.

Planning for Next Sunday

As you go to class this week, you will want to be prepared to make assignments for the Christmas Sunday lesson. The main question will be

What is the true meaning of Christmas? Read through the section "Helping Adults Become Involved," and assign key questions to some of your students to think about and answer in advance. Ask someone in the class to compare Isaiah 9:6-7 and 11:1-5 with Jeremiah 33:14-16. Ask someone else to read John 1:1-18 and to be prepared to report briefly on what it says about the true meaning of Christmas.

Christmas—When God Invades the Commonplace

(DECEMBER 24)

JAMES S. THOMAS[4]

The second chapter of Luke's Gospel gives us abundant reason to think of Christmas as the time when God invades the commonplaces of life. A decree was issued by the Emperor, Caesar Augustus, providing the occasion for Joseph and Mary to go to Bethlehem to be enrolled. Coming to the time of delivery, Mary "gave birth to her first-born son . . . and laid him in a manger, because there was no place for them in the inn." (Luke 2:7)

That Jesus, the Christ, could be born in this way continues to be somewhat amazing. The birth of a king is no small event, and the place for such a birth is usually in a palace. But this king was born in a small town, in a manger, of humble parents, and with no royal hosts to greet him. Jesus was of the common people, but he was also the Son of God—the long-awaited Messiah. He was born in a manger, but he was also "born this day in the city of David." (Luke 2:11) He was the son of Joseph and Mary, but he was also "of the house and lineage of David." (Luke 2:4) He was a descendant of Israel's kings.

This strange mixture of the glorious and the commonplace has not always been easy for the church to accept. Throughout Christian history there have been those who refused to acknowledge the humanity of Jesus. Their faith was based upon a Christ who was too divine to come into such humble circumstances. Others could not admit the reality of Jesus' suffering and agony. The Docetists set forth the doctrine that he was too divine for such suffering as was apparent on the cross. In a much more complex way Christian Gnosticism tended to make Jesus only an apparition. His death was apparent, not real. According to the Gnostics, all the earthy and quite human developments of the Gospels had to be repudiated.

While such efforts to protect Jesus' divinity are understandable, they seriously miss the main point of the Incarnation. "The central claim of the Christian Gospel," writes Gordon Kaufman, "is that God comes to man." [5] This fact is no glorious illusion that must forever be veiled in mystery. God comes to man in a way that cannot be denied: he comes in human form, in human history, and in the ordinary circumstances of human life.

Colin Morris once said, "The Incarnation was an operation in cosmic

---

[4] James S. Thomas: resident bishop, Iowa Area, United Methodist Church, Des Moines, Iowa.
[5] *Systematic Theology: A Historical Perspective* (Charles Scribner's Sons, 1968), p. 41.

152

simplification or it was nothing." [6] It is one thing to have God come to us in ways that are great but distant; it is quite another to have God enter into our human condition in such a way that we cannot miss his presence. When Jesus came in the simplicity of human conditions, God became inescapably real. That is why Christian preachers could say, "Have this mind among yourselves, which you have in Christ Jesus, who, though he was in the form of God, did not count equality with God a thing to be grasped, but emptied himself, taking the form of a servant, being born in the likeness of men." (Philippians 2:5-7)

We also find a combination of the glorious and the commonplace in the Christmas celebration. While we observe Christmas on December 25, the reason for this date is certainly not clear. It can be said, without disrespect, that Christmas might have been observed on any other day of the year. Indeed, little interest seems to have been shown in this observance until the third century. Dates proposed for the observance of Jesus' birth included May 20, April 19 or 20, November 17, and March 25 or 28. For some time Christmas was observed on January 6. Some of these dates will sound strange to those who cannot understand a Christmas observance without the natural scenery and weather of winter. We sing a popular song entitled, "I'm Dreaming of a White Christmas." This idea is fitting for a particular setting in the northern part of the United States, but there is nothing sacred about snow. The point is that the glory of the Christmas observance can and does come on all kinds of days, in all kinds of settings, and to all kinds of people.

For many Christians the observance of Christmas becomes a hopelessly secular affair. There are the tinsel and the holly, the shopping and the crowds, the heavy advertising and the traffic. Every store has a Santa Claus, a merchant trying to make a profit, and customers trying to save money. Becoming cynical about this commercialism, which usually begins in November and lasts until mid-January, is easy. Is it possible for Christ to come to man through all this commercialism?

We must look beneath this commercial activity for the real spirit of Christmas. Families are caught up in the frenzy of Christmas shopping, yet many families do come closer together at this time of year than at any other time. If one is willing to walk slowly enough, he will see men and women standing on the edge of the sidewalk ringing small bells. They are calling attention to the needs of others who have nothing with which to shop. This, too, is Christmas. The imaginative person can also see many people who make a special point of making someone else happy at Christmastime. Food is carried to the hungry; prisoners are visited in jail; strangers are invited for dinner. All these acts of generosity express the true spirit of Christmas.

Finally, however, the glory of Christmas invades our commonplace life in a much more disturbing way. Just as the birth of Jesus greatly disturbed King Herod, his coming to man at Christmastime still greatly disturbs those who understand its meaning. For Christmas is not simply a time of gentle exchange of gifts and lighthearted enjoyment. It is a time to ponder what it means to have a God of justice come to a world of injustice. It is a time to

[6] *Include Me Out* (Abingdon Press, 1968), p. 18.

assess the shallowness of our self-centered love before Christ, who reveals the holy love of God.

When Mary praised God for the child who was coming to her, she told of the mighty acts of God:

> He has shown strength with his arm,
> he has scattered the proud in the imagination of their hearts,
> he has put down the mighty from their thrones,
> and exalted those of low degree;
> he has filled the hungry with good things,
> and the rich he has sent empty away.
>
> (Luke 1:51-53)

Here is the kind of God who comes to man in Jesus Christ. Such a God not only wills that the poor be fed at Christmastime; he also wills that there must be a just society in which the fruits of the earth will be fairly shared with all men every day. God's will is that the foundations of peace on earth will be so sound that Christmas will be a continuing reality in the lives of men.

LESSON 4   DECEMBER 24

The Promised Messiah

Background Scripture: Jeremiah 23:5-6; 33:14-16; Matthew 2:1-12

The Main Question —Charles M. Laymon

Someone has said that the problem with Christmas is that it is so yearly. What he meant was that once a year there was a big splurge—and then it was over, leaving us gasping, tired, and grateful. A certain feeling comes when we put away the decorations, take down the Christmas tree, fit the presents into the bureau drawers, and rearrange our social calendar. "Whew!" we say, with a sigh of relief, "I won't have to go through all this for another year."

Riding in a department store elevator last Christmas season, and faced with the sign "5 more shopping days until Christmas," I was startled to hear a lady say, "I hate Christmas." What did she mean? Why did she say it? What had happened to Christmas to call forth such a remark as this? These were some of the questions that went through my mind.

Could it be that we have lost the true meaning of Christmas? Perhaps we have never really grasped it. Has the modern celebration, so elaborate and stylized, obscured what happened so long ago in a distant land where there were no organized programs, no sales propaganda, no round of social engagements, and no fatiguing religious exercises?

The biblical passages for this lesson provide us with an opportunity to bring the true meaning of Christmas into focus.

154

As You Read the Scripture —Floyd V. Filson

Jeremiah 33:14. *The days are coming . . . when I will fulfil the promise I made:* The prophet sees the days of fulfillment coming. He recalls *the promise* God made to the house of Israel, that is, the ten northern tribes, and to the house of Judah, now facing judgment for its wicked ways. It was a promise of righteous leadership and rule, as the next verse shows.

Verse 15. *I will cause a righteous Branch to spring forth for David:* Essentially the same promise is made in Jeremiah 23:5-6; it was thought so important in Jeremiah's message that it is repeated here. (For other similar promises read Isaiah 11:1-5 and Zechariah 6:12-13.) *Branch* refers to the coming righteous ruler who will be a branch of the tree or family line of David. God will raise up this righteous ruler to "execute justice and righteousness in the land."

WITH OUR EMPHASIS ON COMMERCIALISM SURROUNDING THE MODERN OBSERVANCE OF CHRISTMAS, HOW CAN WE RETAIN THE DEEPER MEANING OF THE DAY? TO WHOM DID THE SHEPHERDS AND WISE MEN GIVE GIFTS? TO ONE ANOTHER? TO WHOM DO WE GIVE GIFTS?

Verse 16. *Judah will be saved and Jerusalem will dwell securely:* In verse 14 the promise includes Israel as well as Judah. Verse 16 centers on Judah, which has been overrun by the army of the king of Babylonia, and Jerusalem, which Jeremiah has predicted the enemy will capture and destroy. In those coming days the now-harassed Judah will be saved, and the now-besieged and doomed city of Jerusalem will dwell securely under God's protection. This will be achieved by God's action. He is the very embodiment of righteousness,

155

and in Jeremiah 23:6 this title is used of him. Here, however, it seems to be Jerusalem that is called "our righteousness." The two ideas do not conflict. God's character, action, and new order are all the perfect expression of righteousness.

Matthew 2:1-2. *Now when Jesus was born in Bethlehem:* Wise Men, called Magi, were considered expert interpreters of dreams and star movements. They were not Jews but gentiles from the East; and in the Gospel of Matthew, often regarded as simply a Gospel for the Jews, they foreshadow and point to the coming response of the gentile world to Christ.

Verses 3-4. *Herod . . . was troubled, and all Jerusalem with him:* The Wise Men knew the expectation that a king would be born to rule God's people. They asked, "Where is he who has been born king of the Jews?" They thought, in part at least, of a political leader. (Herod thought even more in such terms.) But they sensed a divine purpose and power in the birth of this child.

Herod saw in the newborn child a threat to this rule of Palestine. To get information to guide him, he called in the Jewish religious leaders, the chief priests and scribes, to learn where the Christ, the anointed leader of God's people, was to be born. His aim was to find and kill the child quickly.

Verses 5-6. *They told him, "In Bethlehem of Judea":* The Jewish leaders cited Micah 5:2, which speaks of a ruler of Judah who is to be born in Bethlehem. From Bethlehem was expected to come "a ruler who will govern my people Israel." That is why, in the genealogy in Matthew 1:2-16, David is mentioned with such emphasis. The early church and the writer of the Gospel of Matthew held that this Old Testament expectation was fulfilled in the birth and work of Jesus; he was the expected king of God's people, even though his coming and kingship had a spiritual depth and a world outreach that was not clearly grasped in the earliest days of the Christian church.

Selected Scripture

King James Version	Revised Standard Version
Jeremiah 33:14-16	*Jeremiah 33:14-16*
14 Behold, the days come, saith the LORD, that I will perform that good thing which I have promised unto the house of Israel and to the house of Judah.	14 "Behold, the days are coming, says the LORD, when I will fulfil the promise I made to the house of Israel and the house of Judah. 15 In those days and at that time I will cause a righteous Branch to spring forth for David; and he shall execute justice and righteousness in the land. 16 In those days Judah will be saved and Jerusalem will dwell securely. And this is the name by which it will be called: 'The LORD is our righteousness.'"
15 In those days, and at that time, will I cause the Branch of righteousness to grow up unto David; and he shall execute judgment and righteousness in the land.	
16 In those days shall Judah be saved, and Jerusalem shall dwell safely: and this is the name wherewith she shall be called, The LORD our righteousness.	

Matthew 2:1-6

1 Now when Jesus was born in Bethlehem of Judaea in the days of Herod the king, behold, there came wise men from the east to Jerusalem,

2 Saying, Where is he that is born King of the Jews? for we have seen his star in the east, and are come to worship him.

3 When Herod the king had heard these things, he was troubled, and all Jerusalem with him.

4 And when he had gathered all the chief priests and scribes of the people together, he demanded of them where Christ should be born.

5 And they said unto him, In Bethlehem of Judaea: for thus it is written by the prophet,

6 And thou Bethlehem, in the land of Judah, art not the least among the princes of Judah: for out of thee shall come a Governor, that shall rule my people Israel.

Memory Selection: **Blessed be the Lord God of Israel; for he hath visited and redeemed his people. (Luke 1:68)**

Matthew 2:1-6

1 Now when Jesus was born in Bethlehem of Judea in the days of Herod the king, behold, wise men from the East came to Jerusalem, saying, 2 "Where is he who has been born king of the Jews? For we have seen his star in the East, and have come to worship him." 3 When Herod the king heard this, he was troubled, and all Jerusalem with him; 4 and assembling all the chief priests and scribes of the people, he inquired of them where the Christ was to be born. 5 They told him, "In Bethlehem of Judea; for so it is written by the prophet:

6 'And you, O Bethlehem, in the
    land of Judah,
are by no means least among the
    rulers of Judah;
for from you shall come a ruler
who will govern my people
    Israel.' "

Memory Selection:
Blessed be the Lord God of Israel, for he has visited and redeemed his people.   (Luke 1:68)

The Scripture and the Main Question —Charles M. Laymon

A GOD OF PROMISES

The first question to ask at this season of the year is: What kind of God does Christmas call upon us to worship? God makes Christmas, CHRISTMAS. God makes Christmas, CHRISTIAN. Whether the "in" color this season is pink, orchid, or red; whether candles for the table should be long, medium, or short, it is what God has done for the world—what God is doing for the world at Christmastime—that is the issue.

Christmas presents us with a God who makes promises and keeps them. The Old Testament is filled with promises of a coming Savior. Its authors again and again present the picture of a new day that will dawn through the advent of a person whose entrance into life will renew and remake life. Jeremiah wrote, "Behold, the days are coming, says the LORD, when I will fulfil the promise I made to the house of Israel and the house of Judah." (Jeremiah 33:14)

A God who makes and keeps promises is a special kind of God. The gods of the pagan world were gods who acted on impulse. Because they were gods, they felt free to do as they pleased, to change their pattern of action according to their mood. They owed no man anything and did not need to be consistent in their relations with man.

Not so the God of the Hebrews. He is a promise-making and a promise-keeping deity. There is integrity in his relations with his created children. He can be counted on to keep his word. This is what he was doing when the Christ child was born.

A RIGHTEOUS BRANCH FROM DAVID

The Person in whom the promises of God would have their fulfillment was to be born of the line of King David. Jeremiah called this One a "righteous Branch." (33:15a) This meant that he would be a part of God's purpose in history that was made known in the rule of David. Of the lineage of David, whom God chose to be king, would be born this One who would become the King of kings.

No king in the history of the nation was revered and honored like David. He brought to the nation the realization that they were a special people, the people of God. They realized during his reign as never before that they had a place under the sun. Thus since David's time, whenever they dreamed of a new day to come, they envisioned it as an extension and enlargement of his kingdom.

We all need guidelines by which to adjust our sights. Whether we are building a road, erecting a house, planning a life, or improving the social order, there must be a blueprint or a pattern to follow. This is what the reign of David provided. With the example of this king before them the Hebrews could have faith in the coming of the Messiah.

SECURITY BASED UPON JUSTICE

Christmas is more than a date on the calendar, more than a celebration; it is the promise of better days to come when peace and good will shall be on earth. Jeremiah was anticipating this utopia when he described the Coming One as executing "justice and righteousness in the land." Looking ahead he said, "In those days Judah will be saved and Jerusalem will dwell securely." (33:15b-16) This security will be based upon justice.

This vision is an ideal; it is also to be a fact. Paul A. Schreivogel was pointing this out when he wrote: "In the Good News we discover God working through the ordinary affairs of man. His Son takes on human form. . . . In the Good News we have the record of God working in historical events, using the lives of men and the actions of a people to reveal himself." [7]

God is at work in his world. The birth of Jesus says this; the Gospel says this; the church says this; the Holy Spirit says this; every new man in Christ says this. God's promises will be fulfilled.

CHRIST IS BORN

In the fullness of time Christ was born (Matthew 2:1-6). The Gospel writers, especially Matthew, regard him as the One promised—the One whom prophets believed would come (Matthew 1:23; 2:6; Luke 1:54-55, 70-75). The dreams of the past had come true. Phillips Brooks expressed this belief in "O Little Town of Bethlehem":

The hopes and fears of all the years
Are met in thee tonight.

When we stop to think of it, there were only a few who knew of Jesus' birth at the time. Several shepherds and Wise Men were all who were

[7] "The World of Art—The World of Youth" (Joint Youth Publications Council, 1968), p. 33.

158

aware of his coming. No trumpet blasts and no special editions of the newspapers announced the birth. Again, as Phillips Brooks said, "How silently, how silently/The wondrous gift is given!" (Angels sing softly, you know.)

Today we make a great thing of Christmas. Weeks before, the store decorations and the newspaper advertisements make their appearance. It is known as the period of the holidays. But with all this hoopla, how many of us really are aware of the deeper meaning of Christmas? In the sentiments of Mary Tatlow, do we overlook this sacred hour "when love unnoticed came to earth"?

Helping Adults Become Involved —Harlan R. Waite

Preparation of Self and Class

Read Jeremiah 23:5-6; 33:14-16; and Matthew 2:1-12. You will also find it of interest to read Isaiah 9:6-7 and 11:1-5, comparing these with the passages from Jeremiah. To supplement your study, read the commentary in *The Interpreter's Bible* and the materials in your denominational quarterlies.

Keep in mind as you read that Christmas is far more than a sentimental moment in the Christian year. It is an opportunity for us to rediscover in very practical terms how God's presence is felt in human life. The doctrine of the Incarnation is not irrelevant, even though it seems to be sophisticated theology. It is practical in a very direct way, and it gives us a chance to make theology applicable to the world into which God sent his son.

Many of your class members will be feeling the fatigue of the Christmas season. Others will find the time intensely lonely (there are more suicides at this time of the year than at any other). Be sensitive to the needs of your class members, and select from the resources available to you those that will be most genuinely helpful to your particular class.

Presenting the Main Question

Dr. Laymon has identified the main question as this: What is the true meaning of Christmas? Somewhere beyond our frustration, our fatigue, our frenzy, there is a fulfillment in Christmas for all of us—the vindication of our deepest yearnings and hopes. Observe that the answer to the question is not as easily stated as the question itself. Only part of the meaning can be found in the story that can be told. Most of the meaning can be found only in our own personal experience of the presence of God in our lives. This lesson will not answer the question entirely, but it can point the way to where answers may be found.

Share with the class members any common contrasts in the attitudes people have about Christmas. Dr. Laymon tells about one reaction, which is to say in effect, "Thank goodness Christmas comes only once a year." On the other hand, some feel like the man whom I heard say recently, "Thank goodness Christmas comes every year; we need to be reminded."

Have the class members suggest where to look for answers to the main question. Certainly the Christmas literature says much about the impact of Jesus upon human life, as do the carols of many nations. The immediate effect of the season upon each one of us and even upon warring nations who declare a truce at Christmastime supplies another insight into the meaning of Christmas.

Scripture is, of course, basic to our understanding—the familiar Christmas stories in Matthew and Luke, the *Magnificat* and the *Benedictus* (two early Christian hymns found in Luke 1:46-55 and 68-79), and the Old Testament passages mentioned by Dr. Filson. Another important passage is John 1:1-18, which interprets the meaning of the event of Christ's coming.

Developing the Lesson

Point out to the class members that the printed Scripture passage, Jeremiah 33:14-16, is very nearly identical to Jeremiah 23:5-6. Scholars believe the former passage was originally part of an independent document, which quoted the earlier passage of Jeremiah and added a commentary found in 33:17-26. This document was included in a later edition of the Book of Jeremiah, partly because it was recognized as a quote from him and partly because the post-exilic Jewish state needed the kind of encouragement it could give. Also note that the name to be given Jerusalem is "the LORD is our righteousness," a play on the name of the king in Jeremiah's time, Zedekiah (righteousness of Jehovah).

The deep yearning expressed in the prophets as they looked toward the coming of the Messiah was basically the yearning of all men for security and salvation. Ask the class members to discuss how modern man goes about his search for security and salvation. What evidence do we see to indicate that security is a very basic need of man? Where are we looking for the answers? Then ask the class members what the story of the Wise Men may suggest about where we look. Do we look to our own culture for salvation? Do we look to the political and military structure (symbol-ized by Herod) for security? Where did the Wise Men look?

Suggest that maybe we are hunting for the wrong thing. Are security and salvation our ultimate goals, or are they by-products of a deeper search for justice and righteousness? How does Jeremiah answer this question? How did Jesus answer this question (see Matthew 6:25-33, especially verse 33)?

As a next step, ask the class members to answer this question: What are the sources of a just society? Some say law; others say education; still others say welfare programs. The Bible seems to emphasize, however, a deep faith in God expressed in the various social systems and services (law, welfare, and so forth) as the real source. What kinds of attitudes are at the root of a just society?

Ask the class members to reconsider the passage from Jeremiah. Look at the word *righteous*. Let the class discuss why Jeremiah did not use some other adjective, such as *powerful, mighty, proud,* or *great.* Why *righteous?* Then ask the class members to evaluate this statement: Salvation and security are basically not political matters; they are matters of morality. The values that guide men to the truly free and abundant life are not economic values or material values but human (spiritual) values. At the same time, they must be expressed in our economic, legal, political, and social structures.

Observe that the Christian gospel does not convince most people. Christians are still a minority group. As was the case with Herod, many are disturbed when people take Jesus seriously. Ask the class members to discuss why this is true. To what extent does loyalty to Christ transcend or conflict with other loyalties that are important to us?

The story of the visit of the Magi to Bethlehem (Matthew 2:1-12) underscores a fundamental truth: God's love is not reserved for one segment of humanity but embraces all mankind. The Fourth Gospel says it simply, "God so loved the world." In Jeremiah's day God's love for Israel was uppermost; with the advent of Christ, however, the circle of faith became all-inclusive and universal.

Ask the class members to note the various national cultural sources of Christmas carols. A quick look at your hymnal will suffice. There are carols from England, France, Germany, Poland, and America, to say nothing of many familiar carols heard each year that have other origins. Recall also the portrayals of the madonna and child in so many different cultural settings, both occidental and oriental. Perhaps you might display some of these paintings in your classroom or prepare a worship service based on carols from different countries.

Discuss the implications of this emphasis for today's world. What attitudes and practices keep the church from being truly universal? What is the Christian church doing, and what more can it do, to fulfill the spirit of all-inclusive love so central to the gospel?

Helping Class Members Act

Christmas is more a time of celebration than a time of logic. Feelings of joy, love, peace, gratitude, and hope should dominate the season. Let your class members plan a celebration type service. If possible, use not only traditional stories and music but also some contemporary experiences of Christmas. Slides expressing these feelings (love, joy, peace, and so forth) in the everyday experiences of persons you know can help bring the meaning of Christmas closer to your students.

Planning for Next Sunday

Announce next Sunday's theme to your class members, noting that the main question will be Which is the true view of life, the optimistic or the pessimistic? Assign the reading of Jeremiah 18:1-11 and 32:1-25. Ask your class members to come prepared to report on some parables they find in the commonplace experiences of life. Beyond this, some may wish to read and report on the life stories of some Christian martyrs who, despite their suffering, were upheld by an optimistic view of life.

LESSON 5   DECEMBER 31

The Reshaping of Life

Background Scripture: Jeremiah 18:1-11; 32:1-25

The Main Question —Charles M. Laymon

The teacher held up a sizable piece of paper covered with black and white splotches. She asked her students whether it was a white paper with black figures or a black paper with white markings. Some held that the paper had been black in the beginning; others insisted it had been white.

This exercise in judgment is typical of two views of life. One is that this is a good world in which evil sometimes breaks through. The other is that it is an evil world with flecks of goodness here and there. Which is the true view? How can one tell? Does it make any difference in the end? Will the answer we give to this question affect our attitude toward life?

The philosopher Arthur Schopenhauer, who died over a hundred years ago, was a pessimist who saw all events as ultimately in the grip of blind, insatiable Will. Life was like a black piece of paper marked here and there with white. Ralph Waldo Emerson, on the other hand, was an optimist. He was a contemporary of Schopenhauer but took a very opposite view. Life was a white paper temporarily invaded by black. He wrote, "The whole of what we know is a system of compensations. . . . Every suffering is rewarded; every sacrifice is made up; every debt is paid." [8]

Who is correct, Schopenhauer or Emerson? The teaching of Jeremiah in this lesson will be helpful in answering this question.

As You Read the Scripture —Floyd V. Filson

Jeremiah 18:1-2. *Arise, and go down to the potter's house:* The prophet Jeremiah is led to see that the potter and his work can illustrate and emphasize a teaching God wants to give his people. (For other passages that draw an illustration from the potter's work see Jeremiah 19:1-11 and Isaiah 64:8.) *The potter's house* or workshop probably was located in the valley of Hinnom, on the southwest side of Jerusalem. Jeremiah had seen the potter there, busy at his craft, many times; and he found a message to his people in the way the potter worked.

Verses 3-4. *I went down to the potter's house, and there he was working at his wheel:* The prophet watched the potter *working at his wheel,* which he used to help shape the clay into the vessel he wanted to make. Jeremiah got his message for his people when he saw what the potter did when the vessel was spoiled in his hand. The potter did not discard the clay. Instead, he reworked it into another vessel.

In this experience Jeremiah saw a parable. We often think of Jesus as the only teacher to use parables. He was the master teacher by parables, but the use of events of daily life to teach spiritual truth is found also in the Old Testament. Perhaps the most famous Old Testament parable is 2 Samuel 12:1-6.

Verses 5-6. *O house of Israel, can I not do with you as this potter has done?* Jeremiah is certain that what he has seen the potter do contains a lesson from God that his people should take to heart. The house of Israel is in the hands of God just as the clay was in the potter's hand, to use as he thinks best. Even if God's original intention for Israel has not worked out, God can and does have a second plan. He can rework his people into the kind of nation he chooses to make. Their failure to realize God's original purpose does not end the story. They are still in God's hand; he can work out the plan he now wishes to adopt.

[8] *The Heart of Emerson's Journals,* ed. Bliss Perry (Dover Publications, 1958), p. 30.

Verses 7-8. *If at any time I declare concerning a nation:* The parable of the potter and his revised plan here fades from view; attention centers more directly on what God will do when a nation changes its attitude and action. What is said refers not merely to Israel but more generally to any nation or kingdom. Suppose God has declared he will "pluck up and break down and destroy" a nation or kingdom. Suppose the condemned nation or kingdom turns from its evil ways. Will God hold to his declared intention to destroy that nation or kingdom? No. He will repent of the evil he intended to do to it.

This does not mean that God has done wrong and now must repent and reform. There is always a provisional character in God's declared purpose. He is always ready to take into account the change in attitude and action of a condemned people (see the Book of Jonah).

Verses 9-10. *If . . . I declare . . . that I will build and plant it:* These verses spell out the opposite possibility. Suppose God has declared that he will *build and plant* a nation or kingdom, that is, bless and prosper it. Suppose, then, the nation does evil in God's sight, refusing to follow his declared will. Will God keep on blessing it in spite of its turn for the worse? Not at all. He will repent of the good he had intended to do. He will bring judgment on that nation.

Verse 11. *Behold, I am shaping evil against you:* Israel no longer deserves God's promised blessing. So Jeremiah urges sinful Judah and Jerusalem to "return, every one from his evil way, and amend your ways and your doings." God through the prophet denounces the evil ways of the people, calls them to repent, and implies that if they repent he will not bring disaster. If they do not repent, complete disaster faces them.

Selected Scripture

King James Version

Jeremiah 18:1-11

1 The word which came to Jeremiah from the LORD, saying,

2 Arise, and go down to the potter's house, and there I will cause thee to hear my words.

3 Then I went down to the potter's house, and, behold, he wrought a work on the wheels.

4 And the vessel that he made of clay was marred in the hand of the potter: so he made it again another vessel, as seemed good to the potter to make it.

5 Then the word of the LORD came to me, saying,

6 O house of Israel, cannot I do with you as this potter? saith the

Revised Standard Version

Jeremiah 18:1-11

1 The word that came to Jeremiah from the LORD: 2 "Arise, and go down to the potter's house, and there I will let you hear my words." 3 So I went down to the potter's house, and there he was working at his wheel. 4 And the vessel he was making of clay was spoiled in the potter's hand, and he reworked it into another vessel, as it seemed good to the potter to do.

5 Then the word of the LORD came to me: 6 "O house of Israel, can I not do with you as this potter has done? says the LORD. Behold, like the

LORD. Behold, as the clay is in the potter's hand, so are ye in mine hand, O house of Israel.

7 At what instant I shall speak concerning a nation, and concerning a kingdom, to pluck up, and to pull down, and to destroy it;

8 If that nation, against whom I have pronounced, turn from their evil, I will repent of the evil that I thought to do unto them.

9 And at what instant I shall speak concerning a nation, and concerning a kingdom, to build and to plant it;

10 If it do evil in my sight, that it obey not my voice, then I will repent of the good, wherewith I said I would benefit them.

11 Now therefore go to, speak to the men of Judah, and to the inhabitants of Jerusalem, saying, Thus saith the LORD; Behold, I frame evil against you, and devise a device against you: return ye now every one from his evil way, and make your ways and your doings good.

Memory Selection: **But now, O LORD, thou art our father; we are the clay, and thou our potter; and we all are the work of thy hand. (Isaiah 64:8)**

clay in the potter's hand, so are you in my hand, O house of Israel. 7 If at any time I declare concerning a nation or a kingdom, that I will pluck up and break down and destroy it, 8 and if that nation, concerning which I have spoken, turns from its evil, I will repent of the evil that I intended to do to it. 9 And if at any time I declare concerning a nation or a kingdom that I will build and plant it, 10 and if it does evil in my sight, not listening to my voice, then I will repent of the good which I had intended to do to it. 11 Now, therefore, say to the men of Judah and the inhabitants of Jerusalem: 'Thus says the LORD, Behold, I am shaping evil against you and devising a plan against you. Return, every one from his evil way, and amend your ways and your doings.' "

Memory Selection:
Yet, O LORD, thou art our Father; we are the clay, and thou art our potter; we are all the work of thy hand. (Isaiah 64:8)

The Scripture and the Main Question —Charles M. Laymon

FINDING PARABLES IN LIFE

Jesus was a master in the use of parables. He turned to the events of daily life and found illustrations of how God was at work. A farmer sowing seed, a merchant buying pearls, a builder constructing a house, a woman looking for a lost coin, a father forgiving a wayward son—all these situations spoke to him of God and the Kingdom. Joseph Klausner, a Jewish scholar, commenting upon this fact, said, "Jesus was a poet and skilful story-teller and, therefore, he made use of poetical descriptions drawn from everyday life."

Jeremiah was also a poetic person who dramatically illustrated his teachings. He found examples of how God worked with men in the things he saw happening around him. He could say with Elizabeth Barrett Browning,

Earth's crammed with heaven,
And every common bush afire with God.[9]

Not everyone, however, discovers God in the events of daily living. Instead, they speak of coincidences, lucky breaks, or the way the cookie crumbles. In such matters much depends upon what we were taught to see as we were growing up. Those who are familiar with the Bible are more likely to have their eyes open to God's presence in the universe than those who do not know or read it. A biblically illiterate generation is apt to be blinded to the deeper meaning of human events.

A personal experience of God will also open our eyes to his work among us. Now we can see where before we could only observe. All of life becomes a parable to the man who is committed to God.

THE MENDER OF MEN

In today's Scripture passage Jeremiah tells of observing a skillful potter turning a spoiled vessel into a different design: "He reworked it into another vessel." (Jeremiah 18:4) This action immediately reminded the prophet of God's relation to men and nations. When lives break down, God renews and refashions them into something new and fine.

God mends lives as the potter remolded the vessel. Sometimes he turns brokenness into a witness for his and our glory. The psychiatrist Viktor E. Frankl lived through incarceration in four concentration camps. For two and a half years of bare survival he saw persons around him treated like animals. Yet he came through the fire

of persecution restored and renewed, and his writings have inspired thousands.

Frankl saw others who in their brokenness and death were also restored to heights of heroism. Many a man, he said, "entered those gas chambers upright with the Lord's Prayer or the *Shema Yisrael* on his lips." [10] Even though these persons died in the gas chambers, their lives had been reshaped by God.

Leslie Weatherhead once referred to the breakdowns in life as occasions for God to demonstrate his omnipotence. He said that God can use evil "in his overall plan . . . for our final well-being and the establishment of his kingdom. . . . Omnipotence means that nothing that is allowed to happen has within itself the power finally and ultimately to defeat God." Should we not also add, or to defeat us if we meet life with faith?

A PHILOSOPHY OF HISTORY

What God does in renewing and reshaping persons, he also does in working with nations. Jeremiah believed that what happens to the people of a nation depends upon their attitudes and characters. God will pluck them up and destroy them or build and plant them, depending on their obedience. It is a question of whether or not they turn a deaf ear or listen to his voice (18:7-10).

The fate of nations is morally conditioned; God is like a potter here also. He shapes and reshapes nations according to their righteousness. The old adage that righteousness exalts a nation and that evil destroys it is thoroughly biblical (Proverbs 14:34). From first to last, the prophets taught this belief.

When Jeremiah proclaimed this

[9] From "Aurora Leigh."

[10] Viktor E. Frankl, *Man's Search for Meaning* (Washington Square Press, 1963), p. 214.

165

truth, he was speaking to a nation tottering on the brink of destruction. The Babylonians were breathing down Judah's neck, and her fate hung in the balance. What was it to be? The prophet was saying that finally it was up to Judah herself. If only she would listen to God!

An old Chinese proverb simply and directly states the truth that the destiny of a nation depends upon moral attitudes. It says, "If there is righteousness in the heart, there is beauty in the character. If there is beauty in the character, there will be harmony in the home. If there is harmony in the home, there will be order in the nation. When there is order in the nation, there will be peace in the world."

Note how this proverb bases even world peace upon the attitude of individual persons. In this vein we can say, "My righteousness exalts the nation, or my sin will destroy it." How promising! How frightening!

A CALL TO REPENTANCE

We are studying this lesson on the very eve of a new year. At midnight 1973 will begin. Such a time is always an occasion for serious thinking—never more so than now—and many of us will go to our churches for a watchnight service as we usher in the new year. Now is a time for taking stock and for beginning again. New Year's resolutions are in order.

The message God told Jeremiah to give to the nation is most appropriate for such an occasion. He said, "Return, every one from his evil way, and amend your ways and your doings." (18:11b) The Hebrew people did not take Jeremiah's summons to repentance seriously. They said, "That is in vain! We will follow our own plans, and will every one act according to the stubbornness of his evil heart." (verse 12) This decision led to the destruction of Judah. Is this what the people of our nation will say also?

Helping Adults Become Involved —Harlan R. Waiteʿ

Preparation of Self and Class

Begin your preparation by reading the background Scripture: Jeremiah 18:1-11; 32:1-25. Pick out the most important emphases and develop your own aim in teaching this lesson. Then consult the materials in the student quarterlies. Background material in *The Interpreter's Bible* will be helpful.

For illustrative material consult the genealogy of Jesus in Matthew 1:1-16. Note such men as "Judah the father of Perez and Zerah by Tamar" in 1:3; David, "the father of Solomon by the wife of Uriah" in verse 6; and Manasseh, one of the most evil kings of Judah, in verse 10. You may want to research these and other persons mentioned by using a concordance. The point of the study will be to show that Jesus' family tree was like the vessel Jeremiah saw spoiled in the potter's hand and reworked into another vessel.

Presenting the Main Question

Open by noting the subject of this lesson, "The Reshaping of Life," and referring the class members to the illustration of the main question above. Let them discuss the contrast between Schopenhauer and Emerson. Note that it raises this question: Which view of life, the pessimistic or the optimistic, is more compatible with the biblical point of view? Then ask the class members to recall and retell the stories in Jeremiah 18:1-11 and 32: 1-25, noting what the Scriptures say about pessimism and optimism. Is it really true that a poor vessel can be recast? What is the meaning of Jeremiah's purchase of the land at Anathoth? How do our reactions to difficult times compare with Jeremiah's reaction?

Since this is the Sunday after Christmas, relate the message specifically to the birth of Jesus by asking, What does Christmas say about optimism? Discuss its meaning as good news to a world that is unhappy, fearful, mistrustful, and discouraged. Report at this point on your study of the genealogy of Jesus as suggested above in "Preparation of Self and Class." In what ways may the reshaping of the potter's vessel take place today?

Developing the Lesson

Despite man's moral failures, the potential for goodness is always there. Ask the class members to recall biblical affirmations of this truth. They may mention the creation story, which affirms that creation itself is good. Your students may also recall the long history of Israel, a story of moral ups and downs in which God's people often turned away from him only to find that he continued to love them and to re-create them (review Jeremiah 2:1 through 3:25).

At this point have the class look at Christian history. In what way did the coming of Jesus reshape life? What happened to the disciples as a result of their meeting Jesus? In what way does the development of the early Christian church reveal God's power to reshape life? How has the church, "the body of Christ," reshaped life at different times in history?

If possible, lead your class members from this general and more objective discussion of the theme to a closer look at their own lives. Ask your students to share their own experiences of how God has reshaped their lives. The lesson will become most significant at this point if your class members can witness to changes in attitudes, understandings, values, and behavior that have taken place as a result of their Christian experience. The high point of this lesson can be the acknowledgment of specific ways in which they seek to have their lives reshaped by God.

Other members of your class may feel helplessly hemmed in by what has happened in the past. Ask your students to discuss ways in which the past has influenced their lives for good and for ill. How deeply influenced are we by the thought that what happens in our childhood determines what we are as adults? What effect has our scientific understanding of cause and effect had upon our understanding of our present circumstances and upon our hope for the future? To what extent can we rise above past mistakes and start over again? What reasons do your students have for believing that the Christian doctrine of hope makes sense?

Observe that there has been a strong reaction against determinism in psychology and sociology, that is, the idea that we are simply the products, or the victims, of what has happened to us in the past as individuals and as members of society. Ask your class members to evaluate this statement: As Jeremiah's experience with the potter's vessel clearly says, we do not need to be bound by the mistakes of the past. According to the Bible, realism demands not only that we recognize, acknowledge, and accept the existence of evil in our experience but that we also recognize and seek new opportunities to "shape up."

The secret of optimism is the long look. Let the class members discuss this question: To what extent are we as Americans able to recognize evil in the life of our nation? We often attack persons who criticize what they feel is immoral in our country's behavior. Suggest that the first step in taking the long look is to take an honest look at the present moment.

Divide the class members into small buzz groups. Ask each group to describe as specifically as possible some critic or criticism of our society or country, to state why the critic feels the way he does, and to describe the general reaction of the public to the criticism.

The groups may also analyze the bumper sticker, "America, Love It or Leave It." What does this say about one's feelings toward critics and criticism? Does a critic offer criticism because he hates his country or because he loves it? How did Jeremiah feel about his own country, which, of course, he criticized? You may want to note his agonizing concern for the welfare of his country expressed in Jeremiah 4:19. After seven or eight minutes of such discussion bring the groups together again, and ask them each to report on their discussion. Follow this with the question, When is criticism an expression of patriotism, and when is it unpatriotic?

Suggest that the redeeming feature in our negative observations about present life is precisely what Jeremiah saw when he recognized that a vessel may be spoiled but the very same material may be used to create a new vessel. If we are honest, we recognize devastating restrictions of freedom; yet we build on the strength of the American ideal that all men shall be free. We are painfully aware that there are many injustices in our American society, but we build on the American dream of "justice for all." We cannot escape glaring examples of inequality, but there is strength and hope in our basic commitment to the proposition that "all men are created equal," and there is encouragement in the advances we have already made in this direction.

What evidence is there that Jeremiah had the same kind of hope for his country? What does his purchase of the land at Anathoth say about his hope for the future of Israel?

Helping Class Members Act

An activity members of your class may find helpful in following up this lesson would be to hold a conversation with someone who is critical of the church, the country, or some other respected institution to discover the motivation behind his criticisms. Is there a long-range hope by the critic that the "vessels will be reshaped" and his criticism will have the redeeming effect of bringing the kind of change God would like to see?

Note that Jeremiah's long look was vindicated by history. As he predicted, the Babylonians (Chaldeans) did conquer Jerusalem and carry its inhabitants into exile. As this series will lead us to discover later, the Exile gave birth to the development of the synagogue and the migration of Jews to many cities of the then known world. Those cities and the synagogues that sprang up in them later became the bases of operations for Paul the apostle, and hence the springboards that Christianity used to launch its mission to the gentiles and ultimately to the entire world.

Planning for Next Sunday

Announce the theme for next Sunday, "The New Covenant," and ask your class members to read the background Scriptures: Jeremiah 31; 32:

36-41. Ask one of your class members to prepare a report on the covenant idea. Resources for this report may be found in biblical dictionaries. In addition, ask your reporter to read the account of the establishment of the covenant in Deuteronomy 29 and 30.

He should also read some of the salvation history songs that recount the faithfulness and unfaithfulness of Israel in the covenant relationship. These may be found in Deuteronomy 32:1-43; Psalms 78; and Jeremiah 2: 1-12.

The New Covenant

Background Scripture: Jeremiah 31; 32:36-41

The Main Question —Charles M. Laymon

The pastor of a church appointed a committee and called it his renewal committee. At their first meeting the members sat in a circle and, looking one another in the face, tried to decide what it was they were to do. They wrote the word *renewal* on the chalkboard. What did it mean? What did it say to the church? Where should they begin?

One of the members said, "I think we need a new choir director. The music has gone stale." Another said, "It's the organization that creaks. If modern business methods were like ours, we couldn't stay alive." Still another added, "Look at our sanctuary; it's out-of-date. We should have more contemporary styling."

At this point, a woman member of the committee said, "You may all be right. But what about a new heart? Doesn't renewal work from the inside out?"

Is renewal needed in the church? This is a leading question. Where? Why? How? These questions follow fast upon the heels of the first. In the Scripture passage for this lesson Jeremiah has some significant words to say relevant to this issue.

As You Read the Scripture —Floyd V. Filson

The idea of covenant is prominent in the Bible. Covenants were well known in the life of the ancient world. One form of covenant was that between the sovereign of a nation, on the one hand, and his subjects and servants on the other. The Old Testament speaks of such a covenant between God and his people. The covenant was made at Mount Sinai (Exodus 19:5-6; 24:3-8). But even at Mount Sinai, and repeatedly later, the Israelites broke the covenant by their disobedience to God.

Jeremiah 31:31-32. *Behold, the days are coming . . . when I will make a new covenant:* We often think of the Old Testament as telling of a time when keeping the law of God was the basis of the people of Israel's relation to their God. But, in fact, the Old Testament tells of continual failure by the Israelites to give to God the obedience they had pledged at Mount Sinai. Only by God's grace could they continue to worship him and live as his people. Something better than this record of repeated failure was needed. This passage in Jeremiah looks forward to a new act of God to bind his people to himself and lead them to true obedience.

The word *behold* calls special attention to the new relationship promised in this passage. *The days are coming* looks forward to God's new acts and blessings for his people. "Says the LORD" occurs four times in Jeremiah 31: 31-34 to give assurance that God will really fulfill the promise expressed in these verses.

Verses 33-34. *I will put my law within them, and I will write it upon their hearts:* Three emphases mark this new covenant: (1) Since Israel is sinful, the new covenant can only be established if God first forgives her sin. This God promises to do. (2) Since the written commandments had not won the loyalty and obedience of his people, God promises to put his law within them and to write it upon their hearts. (3) This privilege and blessing will not be God's special gift to a chosen few; no one will have to depend on his neighbor to tell him about God. "They shall all know me, from the least of them to the greatest."

Chapter 32:36-37. *Now therefore thus says the* LORD: "This city" refers to Jerusalem, whose defeat and captivity in Babylonia, Jeremiah had predicted. As Jeremiah had foreseen, the city had suffered "by sword, by famine, and by pestilence"; God had driven his sinful people into exile in his anger and wrath and great indignation. But now he will gather them and bring them back to their own land from all the countries to which he had driven them, and especially from Babylonia. He will see that henceforth they dwell in safety.

Verses 38-39. *They shall be my people, and I will be their God:* All the people will have "one heart and one way" of obedient and dedicated living. They will fear God. This does not mean that they will suffer panic and terror before God but that they will recognize his greatness and their duty of loyalty, reverence, and gratitude to him.

Verses 40-41. *I will make with them an everlasting covenant:* God's promise is that never will he "turn away from doing good to them." Likewise, in their wholesome fear of him, they will not turn from him. He will rejoice in doing them good, and he will plant them in their homeland. With all his heart and soul God will seek their good.

Selected Scripture

King James Version	Revised Standard Version
Jeremiah 31:31-34	*Jeremiah 31:31-34*
31 Behold, the days come, saith the LORD, that I will make a new covenant with the house of Israel, and with the house of Judah:	31 "Behold, the days are coming, says the LORD, when I will make a new covenant with the house of Israel and the house of Judah, 32 not like the
32 Not according to the covenant that I made with their fathers in the day that I took them by the hand to	covenant which I made with their fathers when I took them by the hand to bring them out of the land of

bring them out of the land of Egypt; which my covenant they brake, although I was an husband unto them, saith the LORD:

33 But this shall be the covenant that I will make with the house of Israel; After those days, saith the LORD, I will put my law in their inward parts, and write it in their hearts; and will be their God, and they shall be my people.

34 And they shall teach no more every man his neighbour, and every man his brother, saying, Know the LORD: for they shall all know me, from the least of them unto the greatest of them, saith the LORD: for I will forgive their iniquity, and I will remember their sin no more.

Jeremiah 32:36-41

36 And now therefore thus saith the LORD, the God of Israel, concerning this city, whereof ye say, It shall be delivered into the hand of the king of Babylon by the sword, and by the famine, and by the pestilence;

37 Behold, I will gather them out of all countries, whither I have driven them in mine anger, and in my fury, and in great wrath; and I will bring them again unto this place, and I will cause them to dwell safely:

38 And they shall be my people, and I will be their God:

39 And I will give them one heart, and one way, that they may fear me for ever, for the good of them, and of their children after them:

40 And I will make an everlasting covenant with them, that I will not turn away from them, to do them good; but I will put my fear in their hearts, that they shall not depart from me.

41 Yea, I will rejoice over them to do them good, and I will plant them in this land assuredly with my whole heart and with my whole soul.

Egypt, my covenant which they broke, though I was their husband, says the LORD. 33 But this is the covenant which I will make with the house of Israel after those days, says the LORD: I will put my law within them, and I will write it upon their hearts; and I will be their God, and they shall be my people. 34 And no longer shall each man teach his neighbor and each his brother, saying, 'Know the LORD,' for they shall all know me, from the least of them to the greatest, says the LORD; for I will forgive their iniquity, and I will remember their sin no more."

Jeremiah 32:36-41

36 "Now therefore thus says the LORD, the God of Israel, concerning this city of which you say, 'It is given into the hand of the king of Babylon by sword, by famine, and by pestilence': 37 Behold, I will gather them from all the countries to which I drove them in my anger and my wrath and in great indignation; I will bring them back to this place, and I will make them dwell in safety. 38 And they shall be my people, and I will be their God. 39 I will give them one heart and one way, that they may fear me for ever, for their own good and the good of their children after them. 40 I will make with them an everlasting covenant, that I will not turn away from doing good to them; and I will put the fear of me in their hearts, that they may not turn from me. 41 I will rejoice in doing them good, and I will plant them in this land in faithfulness, with all my heart and all my soul."

Memory Selection: I will put my law in their inward parts, and write it in their hearts; and will be their God, and they shall be my people. (Jeremiah 31:33)

Memory Selection: I will put my law within them, and I will write it upon their hearts; and I will be their God, and they shall be my people. (Jeremiah 31:33)

The Scripture and the Main Question —Charles M. Laymon

NEW LIFE FOR OLD

When William Stidger wrote that he had seen "God wash the world last night" and "hang it out to dry," [11] he was expressing man's universal longing for renewal. Every religion has some expression of this inner drive for resurrection. Rituals calling for sacred bathing, pilgrimages to appointed shrines, revival meetings, and rededication services of various kinds all speak of it.

The old must pass away, and the new must take its place. This is what was happening when Martin Luther challenged the basic position of the Roman Catholic Church, when John Wesley opened the doors of Christian fellowship to the factory workers in England, when Washington Gladden called upon the church to meet its obligations to society, and when Karl Barth lifted high before us the centrality of the Word of God. In every case a new plateau had been reached and new heights of Christian experience were brought within man's grasp.

Such a breakthrough is found in this lesson when Jeremiah announces: "Behold, the days are coming, says the LORD, when I will make a new covenant with the house of Israel and the house of Judah." (Jeremiah 31:31) A time of renewal, reconstruction, and resurrection lay ahead. God would carry his people to a new level of fellowship with himself. A new kind of personal life was to be theirs.

[11] "I Saw God Wash the World."

LET THE HEART SPEAK!

Roger Shinn in his book The Sermon on the Mount wrote, "Nothing seems much older than the pancakes that were fresh yesterday." What Dr. Shinn was saying was that most things in our modern world go out of style. We are always looking for a new model television set, dress, or suit. The old becomes stale.

Some things in life, however, are evergreen; they do not age with the passing of time or dull with the wear and tear of living. These are the inner feelings of the heart, such as love, joy, and peace. They are always in style whether they are packaged in a brown paper bag or sealed in cellophane.

Sometimes we hear a woman say, "I feel so depressed. I think I will buy a new hat. That will perk me up." Again, a man will say, "I'm down in the dumps; what I need is that new sports car I saw at the automobile show." But how short-lived is the renewal that such acquisitions bring.

Is it not the same with renewal in the church? When we speak of making improvements in the plant, staff, or grounds, we are not really getting to the root of the matter. These may be needed, but they are not the cause of our difficulties. Our trouble comes from within.

Jeremiah was saying this when he contrasted the old covenant of the law of Moses, written on tablets of stone, with the new covenant written on the heart (31:32-33). The new life would henceforth come from within.

172

UNIVERSAL KNOWLEDGE OF GOD

When Frank Borman read from the creation story as he sat in his spaceship, the whole earth could hear. As I listened, entranced at what was happening and humbled by its immensity, I thought of the words Jeremiah spoke for God: "And no longer shall each man teach his neighbor and each his brother, saying, 'Know the LORD,' for they shall all know me, from the least of them to the greatest." (verse 34)

A direct connection exists between this universal knowledge of God and the fact that God's law is written within men's hearts. The commandments written on tablets of stone were cold, impersonal, and remote; but the law written within the heart is warm, personal, and near. This law does not command us to be good but draws us toward godliness.

The language of the heart spreads from individual to individual with great contagion because it is personal. Why do they put people in television advertisements to sell shaving cream, soap, and automobiles? The reason is obvious; they really are selling happy, satisfied, and attractive persons. The product just goes along as part of the good feeling.

Another and deeper reason for the universal spread of the law when it is written in the heart is that it is God who is speaking within. We are dealing not with a legal system but with the loving, living God. And love spreads like wildfire.

FORGIVENESS AND RENEWAL

A recent United Fund drive took as its slogan "Have a Heart." How close this is to Jeremiah's message concerning God's covenant with man that was written within man's heart. From the heart we give and forgive.

A religion of the heart is one in which personal relationships are central—relationships between man and God and between man and man. When personal relationships grow cold or are broken, they can be rekindled. Forgiveness can restore and renew. This is what Jeremiah envisioned as taking place between God and the nation of Israel. He heard God saying, "I will forgive their iniquity, and I will remember their sin no more." (31:34b; see also 32:36-41)

Forgiveness is not a legal matter. No code of law can forgive. But persons can—persons in whose hearts God has written his witness of love.

Helping Adults Become Involved —Harlan R. Waite

Preparation of Self and Class

Read the background Scripture for this lesson: Jeremiah 31; 32:36-41. Think about the meaning of the covenant relationship and how it has affected the understanding of both the Israelites and the Christians as to their relationship to God. Read Deuteronomy 29 and 30 to get a picture of the covenant as made originally through Moses. Spend some time reading the songs of salvation history as found in Deuteronomy 32:1-43 and

Psalms 78. Compare this with the words of Jeremiah in Chapter 2. Consult some Bible dictionaries for further information regarding the idea of the covenant.

Presenting the Main Question

Note that this is the concluding session of a series on Jeremiah—one of four prophets of judgment and hope to be studied in this quarter. List on the chalkboard the themes you have considered: Jeremiah's call, the rebellion of a nation, the cost of loyalty to God, the promised Messiah, and the possibility of having our lives reshaped. Indicate that today's lesson deals with the new covenant. It is both a climax of the study of Jeremiah and an excellent introduction to the forthcoming study of Ezekiel.

Call for the report previously assigned, or personally review the entire history of Israel's covenant with God. You may find it helpful to use *Out of the Land of Egypt,* a sound filmstrip in color (see page 128). Turning to biblical history for clarification of the covenant idea, this filmstrip points out that throughout the Old Testament man seems to be alternately entering into relationship with God and then rejecting him. But even in those times of man's rebellion, God's love remained firm and man was called to repentance.

Ask your class members to discuss the filmstrip or report on the covenant and to restate the basic principles that bound God and Israel together. Note that God adopted Israel as his chosen people and that Israel agreed to abide by the law (expressed by the Ten Commandments—see Deuteronomy 5:1-21). In essence, the covenant was Israel's response of commitment to God's act of creation (of a special nation).

Now ask the class members to discuss this question: In Jeremiah's mind what relationship did the covenant have to the invasion and impending defeat of Jerusalem by the armies of Babylonia? As the class members discuss this question, be sure they cover the following points: (1) The Exile was evidence of God's punishment; for Israel had not been true to the covenant, its ideals of social justice and its demand for moral integrity. (2) The Exile, then, was caused by disobeying the terms of the covenant

—the code of social morality that was the basis of a just society ordained by God to protect the rights of his people. (3) The covenant had an obvious external reference to economic, political, and social affairs; but beneath all these external considerations was the conviction that the health of the nation rests upon a moral and spiritual base expressed in the covenant relationship.

Let the class members discuss the several meanings of the word *exile.* What did it mean to Jeremiah? What does it mean to us today? Start with the definition of exile as a geographical removal of people from their own land. Thousands of Jews were carried off by the Babylonians. A modern illustration is the way in which millions of persons have been displaced and dispersed by war. Such movement of peoples uproots them psychologically and spiritually as well as physically, and the shock is demoralizing.

Next, have the class members discuss the social, cultural, and spiritual definitions of the term *exile.* Socially, exile means broken relationships, barriers between persons and groups of persons, inaccessibility to certain circles of human association, and ostracism by persons who disagree with you. There is also a cultural exile, in which persons brought up in minority cultural groups feel themselves discriminated against, rejected, and refused the privileges of free association with other members of society. They cannot buy property or build homes in certain places; they are confined to ghettos that do not permit the usual kind of association with others that many of us find in schools, clubs, lodges, and other social groupings.

Finally, exile has a spiritual meaning. It is the sense of being alienated from one's fellow man or from life itself by personal or social turmoil.

Let the class members discuss the circumstances of their lives, individually and socially, which give evidence of one or another of these kinds of exile: for example, civil strife, poverty, the generation gap, international suspicion and fear. What effect do these kinds of exile have on our life as a nation in such areas as taxes, voting, and welfare?

Helping Class Members Act

What does it mean to be the people of God today? Let the class members discuss the question, drawing on their knowledge of Israel's history. Help them understand the covenant idea as (1) a sense of relationship to God, who has given us life and all its resources, and (2) a sense of responsibility that makes us accountable to God for everything we do as individuals and as nations. Contrast this idea of accountability with the thought that sometimes we use God as a tool to achieve our own ends. Let the class members illustrate ways in which we use God as a tool.

Then ask the class members to discuss this question: How does our relationship to God affect our relationships to our fellow human beings? Highlight the spirit of compassion and the experience of community. Illustrate this by a reference to early Christian history. In the fourth century Christianity became the official religion of the Roman Empire. This fact has often been explained in an oversimplified manner by saying that it was accomplished because the Roman Emperor Constantine declared Christianity to be the official faith. Christianity's wider acceptance, however, rested upon a reputation it had developed for compassion and community. Because they took their covenant with God seriously, the Christians were always to be counted on in times of disaster (epidemics, floods, and so forth). Thus the depth and reality of the covenant relationship were expressed in community relationships.

End the lesson by recalling the need to renew and internalize our commitment. Judge Learned H. Hand, who spoke on "The Spirit of Liberty" to a New York audience in the latter days of World War II, has said that liberty lies in the hearts of men and women. When it dies there, no constitution, no law, no court can save or even help it. The only true hope for our time lies in the compassion we express in our community as we pursue the ideal of liberty and justice for all.

Planning for Next Sunday

Ask your class members to read the background Scripture: Ezekiel 1:1-3; 2 through 4; and 33:1-9. Assign one of your students a special report on Ezekiel's role as a watchman. To prepare this report, he should read Ezekiel 3:16-21 and 33:1-9. Suggest that the class come prepared to discuss who Ezekiel was, where and when he prophesied, to whom he was speaking, what his hearers were like (see especially Ezekiel 2:3-7), what he had to say, and how he communicated his message (see especially 4:1-3).

Prophet to Displaced People

Background Scripture: Ezekiel 1:1-3; 2 through 4; 33:1-9

The Main Question —Charles M. Laymon

"What does it mean to be a displaced person?" asked a church school teacher. The answers coming from his class were varied. One member said a displaced person was a war casualty who had been bombed out and had no place to live. Another added that a displaced person was someone like Albert Einstein, who fled to America to escape the Nazis.

"What about displaced persons in this country?" asked a high school teacher in the group. When pressed to explain what he meant, he referred to the migrants who travel from crop to crop, to the blacks who still crowd into Chicago and Detroit, and to the hippies who take to the country and set up colonies of their own for communal living.

"But can't you be a displaced person at home in a situation where you feel not wanted, or that you no longer belong?" asked a young housewife. "I know what you mean," said the man sitting in the circle next to her. "Life seems to be passing you by, and there is no place for you in the parade."

Then the teacher came back to the original question: What is a displaced person? When is one displaced? What does one do when he is displaced?

The people to whom Ezekiel spoke in the following biblical passages were displaced. His words may help us answer these questions.

As You Read the Scripture —Floyd V. Filson

Ezekiel 1:1-3. *The heavens were opened, and I saw visions of God:* The date of Ezekiel's call, at first sight, seems exact; actually two datings are given. The first is not clear because we do not know from what earlier date the thirtieth year is reckoned. Fortunately, the second date is clear. The fifth year of the exile of King Jehoiachin was 593 B.C. Nebuchadnezzar took Jehoiachin captive to Babylonia (see 2 Kings 24:10-17). "The land of the Chaldeans" was Babylonia.

Verse 1 is in the first person singular: "I was among the exiles, . . . I saw visions." Verse 3 speaks of Ezekiel in the third person singular, "the word . . . came to Ezekiel the priest, . . . the hand of the LORD was upon him." The former may have been written by the prophet and the latter by an editor.

The river Chebar was really a canal. It branched off from the Euphrates River upstream from Babylon, ran southeast, passing through Nippur, and rejoined the Euphrates near Erech. Some of the captives brought from Palestine were living by this canal. They were called exiles because they no longer were allowed to live in their native land.

Like Jeremiah, Ezekiel was a priest; but—again like Jeremiah—what made

176

him significant was not his priestly ancestry but his role as a prophet. Ezekiel differed from Jeremiah in personal traits. He saw strange *visions of God* in which *the heavens were opened.* The hand of the Lord was upon him, compelling him to see and report his strange visions and words of doom.

Chapter 3:14-15. *The Spirit . . . took me away, and I went in bitterness:* The visions Ezekiel saw dealt with God's message to the Israelite exiles. At times Ezekiel, though in Babylonia, saw vividly scenes of people and events in Jerusalem. Once he saw a moving throne-chariot, which to Ezekiel was a picture of the glory of God (1:4-28). In his vision the throne-chariot rose from its place in the Temple in Jerusalem. Ezekiel realized the glory of the Lord was leaving the Temple (3:12). Then he (the prophet), in his vision, was lifted up and swiftly taken back to his exile home in Telabib by the river Chebar (verse 15).

Ezekiel was by no means happy over the vision. He sensed that it contained a call to become God's spokesman. Like Jeremiah, who argued with God before he finally accepted his role as prophet, Ezekiel was reluctant to take the task. He *went in bitterness* and only because the hand of the Lord was strong upon him. When his vision was over, Ezekiel came back to the exiles at Telabib and "sat there overwhelmed among them seven days."

Verses 16-17. *At the end of seven days: At the end of seven days* the Lord gave Ezekiel explicit appointment as his prophet. The Lord called him *son of man.* This title occurs eighty-seven times in Ezekiel. It refers to him as human in weakness and duty to God. God appoints him to be a watchman, to warn sinful Israel that the people must repent or suffer disaster.

Chapter 4:1-3. *Take a brick and lay it before you:* Several times in the Book of Ezekiel the prophet feels instructed by God to perform some symbolic act. In this passage Ezekiel predicts the siege of Jerusalem. The enemy will besiege the city by familiar methods. A siege wall will cut off the city from connection with the rest of Judah; a mound will be made from which stones can be thrown at the city's defenders; camps of military forces will be set up around it; battering rams will be brought up all around it to break down the walls. The prophet is to put an iron plate, as an iron wall, between him and the city as a sign that Jerusalem is cut off and is cast off by God. Ezekiel explained the symbolism. He was portraying and predicting the siege of Jerusalem; its destruction drew near. It was not a pleasant message to the exiles, but it was a true picture of what soon took place.

Selected Scripture

King James Version	Revised Standard Version
Ezekiel 1:1-3	*Ezekiel 1:1-3*
1 Now it came to pass in the thirtieth year, in the fourth month, in the fifth day of the month, as I was among the captives by the river of Chebar, that the heavens were opened, and I saw visions of God.	1 In the thirtieth year, in the fourth month, on the fifth day of the month, as I was among the exiles by the river Chebar, the heavens were opened, and I saw visions of God. 2 On the fifth day of the month (it was

2 In the fifth day of the month, which was the fifth year of king Jehoiachin's captivity,

3 The word of the LORD came expressly unto Ezekiel the priest, the son of Buzi, in the land of the Chaldeans by the river Chebar; and the hand of the LORD was there upon him.

the fifth year of the exile of King Jehoiachin), 3 the word of the LORD came to Ezekiel the priest, the son of Buzi, in the land of the Chaldeans by the river Chebar; and the hand of the LORD was upon him there.

Ezekiel 3:14-17

14 So the spirit lifted me up, and took me away, and I went in bitterness, in the heat of my spirit; but the hand of the LORD was strong upon me.

15 Then I came to them of the captivity of Telabib, that dwelt by the river of Chebar, and I sat where they sat, and remained there astonished among them seven days.

16 And it came to pass at the end of seven days, that the word of the LORD came unto me, saying,

17 Son of man, I have made thee a watchman unto the house of Israel: therefore hear the word at my mouth, and give them warning from me.

Ezekiel 3:14-17

14 The Spirit lifted me up and took me away, and I went in bitterness in the heat of my spirit, the hand of the LORD being strong upon me; 15 and I came to the exiles at Telabib, who dwelt by the river Chebar. And I sat there overwhelmed among them seven days.

16 And at the end of seven days, the word of the LORD came to me: 17 "Son of man, I have made you a watchman for the house of Israel; whenever you hear a word from my mouth, you shall give them warning from me."

Ezekiel 4:1-3

1 Thou also, son of man, take thee a tile, and lay it before thee, and portray upon it the city, even Jerusalem:

2 And lay siege against it, and build a fort against it, and cast a mount against it. This shall be a sign to the it, and set battering rams against it round about.

3 Moreover take thou unto thee an iron pan, and set it for a wall of iron between thee and the city: and set thy face against it, and it shall be besieged, and thou shalt lay siege against it. This shall be a sign to the house of Israel.

Ezekiel 4:1-3

1 "And you, O son of man, take a brick and lay it before you, and portray upon it a city, even Jerusalem; 2 and put siegeworks against it, and build a siege wall against it, and cast up a mound against it; set camps also against it, and plant battering rams against it round about. 3 And take an iron plate, and place it as an iron wall between you and the city; and set your face toward it, and let it be in a state of siege, and press the siege against it. This is a sign for the house of Israel."

Memory Selection: Son of man, I have made thee a watchman unto the

Memory Selection: Son of man, I have made you a watchman for the house of Israel: therefore hear the word at my mouth, and give them warning from me. (Ezekiel 3:17)

house of Israel; whenever you hear a word from my mouth, you shall give them warning from me. (Ezekiel 3:17)

The Scripture and the Main Question —Charles M. Laymon

A DISPLACED PEOPLE

Throughout most of their history the Jews have been a displaced people. Even when they lived in Palestine, they were mostly under the domination of foreign peoples—Babylonians, Persians, Greeks, Syrians, Romans, Turks, and so forth. Not until the United Nations created the nation of Israel in 1948 have the Jews had a land to call their own for more than two thousand years. And they have had a hard time keeping it.

More than anything else, it was their religion that held the Jews together as a people under these circumstances. Where other groups have been absorbed, they have been able to keep their identity while displaced throughout the world. No group has been persecuted over such a long period of time. In the present century alone ten million Jews lost their lives in the gas furnaces of Adolf Hitler. And anti-Semitism is still here.

As far back as the time of Ezekiel the Jews were beginning to learn how to live as displaced persons. They discovered that God was with them wherever they went. He even sent his prophet to be with them in exile.

In our time too we are often displaced as life around us falls apart. As Hamlet put it, "The time is out of joint." At such times God continues to send his servants among us to help us set our houses in order.

A HOPE AND A DREAM

Robert Wingard was the young pastor of a United Methodist Church

in Pensacola, Florida. His bishop asked him why he did not stop complaining about what was wrong with the church and, instead, begin to do something about it. He took up the challenge and led his church into a new community outreach program that included tutoring help in the schools, a "halfway house" for teenage boys who were dropouts and delinquents, and summer recreation assistance in a federal housing project. In each of these areas persons were displaced, out of touch, and wrongly related.

Commenting upon these accomplishments of his church, Bob said, "Every significant thing that I have seen happen in the church has happened because some person had a hope or a dream!" [12] If Ezekiel had been saying this, he would probably have added the word *vision*. This is because he was an ecstatic, and God spoke to him through the images of his visions.

Describing his experience, Ezekiel said, "The heavens were opened, and I saw visions of God." (Ezekiel 1:1) As far as the earth was concerned, the prophet was probably in Babylonia with the group of Hebrews who had been deported from Jerusalem in 597 B.C. He was definitely a displaced person. Yet he rose above his fate by looking above and beyond it.

We continue to turn to our prophets today for their visions of our fu-

[12] *Risk and Reality* (Women's Division, Board of Missions, The United Methodist Church, 1970), p. 48.

ture. They too must see more than the current scene; they must help us see ourselves as God sees us. God's hope and dream for our generation is in the keeping of his loyal followers.

SITTING WHERE THEY SAT

Ezekiel, even though he was a man of visions, was not looking at the situation his people were facing from afar. He did not pontificate at a distance but sat where they were sitting in exile: "I came to the exiles at Telabib, who dwelt by the river Chebar. And I sat there overwhelmed among them seven days." (3:15)

A famous poem expresses the desire of the author to "live in a house by the side of the road/And be a friend to man." [13] For all its lovely sentiment something seems to be lacking. If we are to help others, we must get out into the moving crowds and live with them. Unless we are shoulder to shoulder, we cannot be heart to heart.

This has been the genius of the Peace Corps. Young and old have journeyed to the ends of the earth to work alongside others who were building roads, planting and harvesting crops, and performing the humblest of daily chores. On this same basis some of the churches have sponsored short-term missionary programs in which youth might get the feel of service both at home and abroad by actually working with the people.

[13] Sam Walter Foss, "The House by the Side of the Road."

Isn't this what God did in the Incarnation? In Christ he lived among men and lifted them by actually identifying with them and their needs. He ate their bread and drank their cup, even to suffering on the cross. He sat where they sat.

A MODEL OF THE FUTURE

Some scholars think that parts of Ezekiel were written in Jerusalem before any of the Hebrews had been sent into exile in Babylonia. Others conclude that the prophet sent messages from Babylonia back to Jerusalem, warning those who remained in the city of the destruction that lay ahead. In either case, when the prophet constructed a model of a city under siege, he was speaking directly to the political situation the nation was facing.

There is something dramatic in scale models of buildings to be built, parks to be laid out, and automobiles to be constructed. Architects frequently build a "set" to demonstrate their plan for a campus or church plant. These seem to fix the future in our thinking. Ezekiel did this in his model of a besieged city (4:1-3). This was what would happen to Jerusalem, he said. And it did.

Some persons do not wish to know their future. What lies ahead may frighten them. The prophets did not feel this way. It was important to learn what God was going to do. Even if the future meant being displaced, the sure confidence that God would be with his people brought strength and stability.

Helping Adults Become Involved —Harlan R. Waite

Preparation of Self and Class

This lesson introduces a series on Ezekiel, the second of the "prophets of judgment and hope" considered in this quarter's lessons. The background Scripture for this session is

180

Ezekiel 1:1-3; 2 through 4; and 33: 1-9. Even though only a portion of this material is printed (Ezekiel 1: 1-3; 3:14-17; and 4:1-3), it is important that you become thoroughly familiar with all the background material.

You will find it helpful to read a portion of the introductory study of Ezekiel found in Volume VI of *The Interpreter's Bible*. Although much of this material is for more extensive study than is required here, you will find genuine help in the sections entitled "Ezekiel in Exile," "Jerusalem and Judah," and "Sketch of Ezekiel's Message" (pages 56-59, 60-62).

Prepare to give some explanation of certain terms that occur in the background Scriptures. For example, the term *son of man* is used several times. Although in Daniel and the New Testament the term has a special messianic significance, it refers here simply to a human being. Psalms 8:4, which equates *man* and *son of man*, supports this definition. Thus Ezekiel was an ordinary man picked out by God to be his special spokesman.

Research the meaning of "sweet as honey" by turning to Psalms 119:103 and Psalms 19:9b-10. Note that Ezekiel is simply saying that the sweet taste of the scroll indicated it did indeed contain the Word of God.

Finally, review the role of prophets in pronouncing judgment upon a nation. Amos 8:1-3 and Isaiah 6:11-13 (see also Chapter 1) point up this function of a prophet. Review the discussions you have had during the past six weeks regarding Jeremiah. Reread Jeremiah 1 and the lesson for December 3.

As you prepare, give thought to how this lesson may deal with some of the needs felt by members of your class. Often persons respond to tur-moil and crisis in a mood of bitterness, in a state of confusion, or with feelings of despair. In today's lesson and in the lessons that follow try to relate Ezekiel's message to the needs of your students as they attempt to make sense out of current national and international events and the ways these events affect their lives. Beyond this, lead them to accept a new role for their lives in helping their fellow citizens understand the spiritual causes underlying life's crises, and to accept responsibility for making, in their own lives and in the life of the nation, those changes that will end the "exile."

Presenting the Main Question

The main question has been described above as What does it mean to be a displaced person? There is also another major question for this lesson: What does it mean to be a prophet to displaced people? Ask the class members to review the scriptural content for the lesson and to consider that these two questions belong together.

Next, describe the displaced persons portrayed by Dr. Laymon; and ask the class members to add to his descriptions whatever firsthand knowledge they have of such groups. Are there any displaced persons in your community? What can you do to become more sensitive to their needs?

Note, at the same time, that the displaced persons to whom Ezekiel was speaking were not necessarily the innocent victims of oppression. The exiles in Babylonia, as described by the prophets, were former political, social, intellectual, and religious leaders of the nation. Indeed, King Jehoiachin was among them (1:2). In Ezekiel's mind these were the persons who had sinned against God and who were thus responsible for the sorry plight of the deported Israelites.

This observation raises another question: Is it possible that the most significantly displaced persons in our society today are those who have failed to appreciate, or have even ignored, the implications of God's law of love, even though they may continue to occupy positions of prestige and power? Today, irresponsible leaders among us are not carried into exile in a literal sense; but biblical thought certainly would term them spiritual exiles living out of contact with the reality of God, who ordains righteousness and justice among men.

Does this not call God's church to a new sense of mission in these times? If you would like to pursue this thought, you may find it helpful to use the color filmstrip *In Faith and Love* (see page 127). This filmstrip is designed to aid persons in churches to become the people of God on mission in his world. It discusses the implications of the gospel for the congregation "in mission" for Christ, using such terms as *mission, witnessing,* and *discipleship* in relationship to the world.

Developing the Lesson

Undertake a review of the role of the prophet and his function in pronouncing judgment on a nation (see the suggestions in "Preparation of Self and Class"). Next, explain some of the key terms used in the background Scripture, also suggested above.

Ask your class members to tell what they know of Ezekiel as a result of reading the background Scriptures, especially Ezekiel 1:1-3; 2:1-3. They may also be able to describe something of his style of prophecy by referring to the printed materials from Ezekiel 4:1-3. Chapter 5 and the passages in 12:1-16 and 21:18-23 also reveal his style. The discussion will identify where and when Ezekiel prophesied, to whom he directed his prophecy, and the way in which he communicated his message.

Call for the special report, assigned at the end of last week's lesson, on Ezekiel's role as a watchman. The basic Scriptures for this report are Ezekiel 3:16-21 (verses 16-17 are printed) and 33:1-9. Have the class members discuss this question: Over whom was Ezekiel to be a watchman, and what was their relationship to him? Note that Ezekiel was not asked to criticize the Babylonians, despite the fact that they had been the invaders and conquerors of his nation. Rather he was to speak to the people of his own nation and call them to a recognition of their own guilt as contributing to their national distress.

Then ask this question: How does Ezekiel picture the responsibility of the prophet? Discuss the application of this insight to our life as Christians in today's world. Should we, as a matter of fact, warn our nation if we feel its behavior is destructive? If we fail to do so, do we bear the burden of responsibility for whatever social upheaval our nation may experience? In the light of current and recent upheavals, how do we evaluate the Christian church as a prophet?

At appropriate points, illustrate this lesson by noting that John Wesley spoke out against social evil in his day, in sharp contrast to a church that was apathetic and silent. Martin Luther was doing the same thing when he nailed the ninety-five theses to the door of the church at Wittenberg. It is significant to note that, like Ezekiel, these men were priests. They did not aim to destroy the institution, but they certainly did aim to point out the moral failures of a church

182

they loved and to make it more responsive to the righteousness of God.

Helping Class Members Act

Have some of your class members research your hymnal to find hymns that call a nation to moral accountability. Suggest that others, as they read the daily papers, make note of the efforts of men and women in our society to keep our nation faithful to the highest in moral and human values.

Planning for Next Sunday

Announce the theme for next week: "God Really Cares!" Ask your class to read Ezekiel 34 for background study. Recruit three volunteers to report on the following themes: (1) the faith of Dietrich Bonhoeffer and how he could affirm that God really cares while he and the world were suffering so deeply; (2) the shepherd image in Ezekiel 34 compared with the references to the shepherds in John 10 and 21; and (3) the judgment scene in Ezekiel 34 compared with the parable of the last judgment in Matthew 25. Finally, ask your class members to watch the newspaper during the following week for illustrations of the false use of power in our society.

LESSON 8   JANUARY 21

God Really Cares!

Background Scripture: Ezekiel 34

The Main Question —Charles M. Laymon

Everybody meets on the same level at a laundromat. Each person comes with a bundle of dirty clothes; each wears his worst outfit (no Sunday best for this job). The smells of hot clothes from the dryer and perfumed soap powders mingle with the screams of young children or parents, who have just run out of patience.

Some down-to-earth conversation frequently develops in these places—including discussions of religion. A brokenhearted mother burst into tears at a laundromat recently. She had just had the word, the tragic word, from the War Department that began: "We regret to. . . ." In an attempt to comfort this woman another said, "My son would be better off dead; he has multiple sclerosis, and I can see him decline steadily. You don't know what it's like to watch day by day."

Standing by, one could not help but raise the questions: Does God care? Just what is God doing in today's world? How can we live like Christians with all that is going on around us and happening to us?

If anyone had good reason to ask such questions, Dietrich Bonhoeffer did. The Nazis finally executed him after he had endured months of imprisonment in which he saw persons going to pieces all around him. And he both asked the questions—and answered them. In *The Cost of Discipleship,* Bonhoeffer said that it is clearer every day that the most urgent problem of our church is how persons can live the Christian life in the modern world. How can we?

The biblical passages that follow contain some answers to this question.

As You Read the Scripture —Floyd V. Filson

Ezekiel 34:1-2. *Son of man, prophesy against the shepherds of Israel:* Here *the shepherds* means the rulers of Israel. Perhaps the prophet includes among the shepherds the religious leaders, the priests; but his main attention seems directed toward the civil rulers.

Shepherds were prominent in Israel. Their concern for their flocks was a good illustration of kindly, faithful care. Consequently the Bible frequently

EZEKIEL LIKENS RELIGIOUS LEADERS (SUCH AS TEACHERS) TO SHEPHERDS. SOME SHEPHERDS "FEED THEMSELVES" . . . READ HELPFUL IDEAS THAT BRING MATURITY, BUT FOR MANY REASONS (FEAR, JEALOUSY, GREED) DON'T FEED THE "SHEEP" THE SAME IDEAS. TEACHERS ARE RESPONSIBLE FOR HELPING ADULTS MATURE IN FAITH . . . GROW BEYOND ADOLESCENT CONCEPTS OF GOD, SALVATION, AND HOPE.

refers to God's people as a flock and God's rulers as shepherds. In the Old Testament, for instance, see Psalms 23:1: "The LORD is my shepherd"; Psalms 95:7: "We are the people of his pasture, and the sheep of his hand"; Jeremiah 23:1: "Woe to the shepherds who destroy and scatter the sheep." The same usage occurs in the New Testament: Luke 15:3-7: the parable of the lost sheep; John 10:7, 11: "I am the door of the sheep. . . . I am the good shepherd"; Hebrews 13:20: "Our Lord Jesus, the great shepherd of the sheep"; 1 Peter 2:25: "the Shepherd and Guardian of your souls."

Raising sheep and caring for them were so much a part of Israel's life that it was natural to use the shepherd and his flock as a figure for leader and people in Israel. Evidently there were not only good shepherds, who took the best possible care of their flocks, but also careless indifferent shepherds, who took good care of themselves but had no concern for the safety and proper care of the sheep entrusted to them. They illustrated well the rulers of Israel who had no conscience about the way they treated their people. These shepherds fed themselves but did not feed the sheep. They did not see that the sheep had good pasture, water, and protection from theft and attack by wild animals. Every good shepherd feeds his sheep. It was an outrage that the leaders of Israel did not show such care for the common people. But Ezekiel saw just such neglect among his people.

Verses 7-8. *Therefore, you shepherds, hear the word of the* Lord: With stern indignation Ezekiel denounces the careless leaders; he feels certain his message is the authentic *word of the* Lord. Sheep unguarded and uncared for become prey and food for all the wild beasts. The sheep wander away, are lost, and face all sorts of dangers unless their shepherds search for them and bring them back to the flock. Shepherds who have fed themselves and not the sheep are to be condemned; so it is with the leaders, the shepherds, whom God has placed in charge of his people Israel.

Verses 9-10. *Behold, I am against the shepherds:* God is against such leaders. They will have to answer to him for their evil conduct. He will put a stop to their feeding the sheep, for they have fed themselves and neglected the sheep.

Here a new point is added. The false shepherds not only feed themselves, they actually devour the sheep they are supposed to feed and protect. To this God will put a stop; he will rescue his sheep from the very mouths of the ravenous false shepherds.

Verses 11-15. *Behold, I, I myself will search for my sheep:* As a shepherd seeks out his flock when some of them have been scattered, God will search for his sheep—the people of Israel. He will seek out and rescue his people from all the places where they have been scattered in exile. He will bring them back to their own land and feed them on its good pasture, by the fountains where they will find fresh water. Their pasture will be on the mountains of Israel.

The Lord God declares through the prophet: "I myself will be the shepherd of my sheep."

Selected Scripture

King James Version	Revised Standard Version
Ezekiel 34:1-2, 7-15	*Ezekiel 34:1-2, 7-15*
1 And the word of the Lord came unto me, saying,	1 The word of the Lord came to me: 2 "Son of man, prophesy against the shepherds of Israel, prophesy, and say to them, even to the shepherds,
2 Son of man, prophesy against the shepherds of Israel, prophesy, and	

say unto them, Thus saith the Lord
GOD unto the shepherds; Woe be to
the shepherds of Israel that do feed
themselves! should not the shepherds
feed the flocks?

. . . .

7 Therefore, ye shepherds, hear the
word of the LORD;

8 As I live, saith the Lord GOD,
surely because my flock became a
prey, and my flock became meat to
every beast of the field, because there
was no shepherd, neither did my
shepherds search for my flock, but the
shepherds fed themselves, and fed not
my flock;

9 Therefore, O ye shepherds, hear
the word of the LORD;

10 Thus saith the Lord GOD; Behold, I am against the shepherds; and
I will require my flock at their hand,
and cause them to cease from feeding
the flock; neither shall the shepherds
feed themselves any more; for I will
deliver my flock from their mouth,
that they may not be meat for them.

11 For thus saith the Lord GOD;
Behold, I, even I, will both search
my sheep, and seek them out.

12 As a shepherd seeketh out his
flock in the day that he is among his
sheep that are scattered; so will I seek
out my sheep, and will deliver them
out of all places where they have
been scattered in the cloudy and dark
day.

13 And I will bring them out from
the people, and gather them from the
countries, and will bring them to
their own land, and feed them upon
the mountains of Israel by the rivers,
and in all the inhabited places of the
country.

14 I will feed them in a good pasture, and upon the high mountains
of Israel shall their fold be: there
shall they lie in a good fold, and in a
fat pasture shall they feed upon the
mountains of Israel.

15 I will feed my flock.

Thus says the Lord GOD: Ho, shepherds of Israel who have been feeding
yourselves! Should not shepherds feed
the sheep?

. . . .

7 "Therefore, you shepherds, hear
the word of the LORD: 8 As I live,
says the Lord GOD, because my sheep
have become a prey, and my sheep
have become food for all the wild
beasts, since there was no shepherd;
and because my shepherds have not
searched for my sheep, but the shepherds have fed themselves, and have
not fed my sheep; 9 therefore, you
shepherds, hear the word of the LORD:
10 Thus says the Lord GOD, Behold,
I am against the shepherds; and I
will require my sheep at their hand,
and put a stop to their feeding the
sheep; no longer shall the shepherds
feed themselves. I will rescue my
sheep from their mouths, that they
may not be food for them.

11 "For thus says the Lord GOD: Behold, I, I myself will search for my
sheep, and will seek them out. 12 As
a shepherd seeks out his flock when
some of his sheep have been scattered
abroad, so will I seek out my sheep;
and I will rescue them from all places
where they have been scattered on a
day of clouds and thick darkness. 13
And I will bring them out from the
peoples, and gather them from the
countries, and will bring them into
their own land; and I will feed them
on the mountains of Israel, by the
fountains, and in all the inhabited
places of the country. 14 I will feed
them with good pasture, and upon
the mountain heights of Israel shall
be their pasture; there they shall lie
down in good grazing land, and on
fat pasture they shall feed on the
mountains of Israel. 15 I myself will
be the shepherd of my sheep."

Memory Selection: Ye my flock, the flock of my pasture, are men, and I am your God, saith the Lord GOD. (Ezekiel 34:31)

Memory Selection: You are my sheep, the sheep of my pasture, and I am your God, says the Lord GOD. (Ezekiel 34:31)

The Scripture and the Main Question —Charles M. Laymon

WHEN LEADERS LAG

What does one say to a leader who will not lead? This was the question the prophet Ezekiel faced in Babylonia with the exiled Hebrews. The kings had misled the people. They had proved to be "false shepherds." (Ezekiel 34:1-2)

The term *shepherd* for one who leads is used frequently in the Bible. God himself is the shepherd in Psalms 23, and Jesus is the good shepherd in John 10. Here the kings were called shepherds—only they were not shepherding. They were leaving the people as a prey for the enemy, not feeding them, and allowing them to wander. The leaders had nourished, clothed, and looked after themselves while sadly neglecting the people.

Did God care? This question came painfully to the minds of the people in their desolation. Yes, obviously God did care. He instructed Ezekiel to say to these false leaders, "The weak you have not strengthened, the sick you have not healed, the crippled you have not bound up, the strayed you have not brought back, the lost you have not sought, and with force and harshness you have ruled them." (verse 4)

These words of the prophet offer a schedule for social action today. This is what anti-poverty programs, adequate housing measures, the Peace Corps, concern for drug abuse, movements for world peace, and efforts for racial justice are all about. Even though these come largely under the function of the government, they should be a concern of God's church and its leaders.

Yet what happens to persons also is my concern under God. In a very real sense I am the church, and I am society; and I am the one who must take a stand.

WHEN GOD LEADS

When shepherds cease to care for the sheep or leaders fail to lead, God takes over; he acts when men refuse to do so. Not all of us are aware of this fact, and in despair we draw dark conclusions.

A scientist engaged in cancer research told me that in five years Russia would invade the United States. He was not an extremist but a person who had been born in Leningrad and had come to our country to seek freedom for scientific study. The reason for his dark prophecy of the future was that he believed we were weakening ourselves as a nation with drugs, riots, and lack of discipline. "Russia is just waiting for us to collapse," he said. "Then they will make their move."

My friend made a gloomy prediction. Do you agree with him? Need you agree? Is he dangerously near a possibility?

Ezekiel in his dark hour believed that God would not allow his people to be lost: "Behold, I, I myself will search for my sheep, and will seek them out. As a shepherd seeks out his flock when some of his sheep have been scattered abroad, so will I seek

187

out my sheep; and I will rescue them. . . ." (verses 11-12)

How like Jesus' teaching concerning the shepherd who went out to find the one sheep that was lost (Luke 15:3-7) ! Not just for "some" but for "one" will he seek and continue the search until he finds it.

Does this reassuring truth relieve us of our necessity to be responsible leaders? Is this teaching only for men who are at the end of their rope? And do not leaders, even at their best, still need God?

GOD'S PROVIDENTIAL CARE

A Christian has a special way of looking at life. His perspective is unique, and his standard of values is extraordinary. He has his own slant on things, or at least he should have.

Edward Farley in *Requiem for a Lost Piety* said, "The most prominent fact in the life of the Christian is the fact of the gospel, the claim that the final word about man and the world is not a word of condemnation and despair but a word of grace and hope. . . . This means that the Christian looks upon himself and the world through a particular lens." [14]

Ezekiel was doing this when he spoke to the exiles in Babylonia. The prophet had a special view of God's role in history. He would not let go of God, nor should the nation release its hold, because God would not let go.

God's creating presence, his caring

[14] (Westminster Press, 1966), p. 124.

presence, and his calling presence would not depart from the Hebrews (34:13-14). They would know "good pasture"; even on the tops of the mountains they would find fountains of water and lush grass. This is an incredible feat, but those who believe in God are often called upon to believe the impossible.

GOD THE TRUE SHEPHERD

When God told Ezekiel that He would be the shepherd of his sheep (verse 15), he was affirming that he was the living God. A poem, by an unknown author, that appeared in *motive* states this truth in a startling way:

I know my God to be—
What He knows me to be—
Alive.
Have you never wrestled with Him,
Never felt the muscle of His arm
In wind or tide of mountainsteep?
Never striving drawn strength from Him?
Have you never matched minds with Him,
Never searched His secret in atom or in star,
Never known the pain of infinite thinking?
Have you never been still,
Never been aware, before Him,
As He breathed an ideal
In on your soul?
Go to your God:
Ask Him to come to you
Alive. [15]

Ezekiel had just such a God in mind in his message to the exiles.

[15] December, 1943, p. 14.

Helping Adults Become Involved —Harlan R. Waite

Preparation of Self and Class

The background Scripture for this week's lesson is Ezekiel 34. Read the passage carefully, recalling as you read

the use of the metaphors of the shepherd and the sheep elsewhere in your Bible. Specifically, read John 10 and 21; Matthew 25; Acts 5:36-37; and

Psalms 23. Note the parallelism, and refer to "Developing the Lesson" below for suggestions.

Read the student materials in your denominational quarterlies and consult *The Interpreter's Bible* for further help.

Presenting the Main Question

Dr. Laymon lifts up the main question in simple terms: Does God care? This question, and the related questions that he mentions, are well illustrated in the heart-rending losses of the two mothers he describes. Also, how could Dietrich Bonhoeffer, imprisoned and facing death, believe that God cares? Ask the member of your class who accepted the assignment to report on Bonhoeffer's faith and his answer to the main question.

Perhaps your class members will recall discussions that were common during the days of World War II. Families were losing their husbands and sons; widespread devastation brought tragedy to millions. Many people ceased asking whether God cared and simply declared that he did not. How could a loving God permit such cruelty? Yet there were some, faced with the very same circumstances, who declared that the war itself was a proof of God's care. Even as a parent expresses his love and care by permitting a child to suffer the consequences of wrong actions so that he will learn and be strengthened, so these affirmers of faith believed that through the war God was chastening people who had forgotten, or rebelled against, basic spiritual values. Indeed, only an uncaring and unloving God would deny his children the opportunity to discover the consequences of their foolishness. Summarize by noting that in the Scripture for this Sunday, God expresses his care by pronouncing judgment, by letting

Israel learn her spiritual lessons through suffering the consequences of her rebellion, and by offering his "flock" a secure pasture in the future.

Developing the Lesson

Next ask the class to identify the separate units in Chapter 34: the condemnation of the shepherds (verses 1-10), the determination to rescue the sheep (verses 11-12), the return of the sheep to the mountains of Israel (verses 13-16), the judgment between "sheep and sheep" (verses 17-24), and the covenant of peace (verses 25-31).

Next, ask those who have agreed to give reports to compare these passages. The first reporter should note that the metaphor of the shepherd and the sheep is used at many places in the Bible to characterize God's relationship to man. Contrast the shepherds who feed themselves rather than the sheep (verse 2) with the picture of the good shepherd in John 10, and note the injunction of Jesus in John 21:15-17 to "feed my sheep." Observe that, in John, feeding the sheep involves great cost, even death (21:18-19; see also John 10:15).

As your other reporter will undoubtedly note, the element of judgment is strongly present in both Ezekiel 34 and Matthew 25. Through discussion, help the class members complete the picture painted in Ezekiel 34:17-24. In verse 17 God is pictured as judging "between sheep and sheep," and this is explained in verse 20 in the reference to "fat" and "lean" sheep. Note the strong descriptive verbs: *push, thrust,* and *scattered.* Notice also in verse 18 that they tread down the pasture and foul the water. Did the people of Ezekiel's time have an ecological problem? Did the few who controlled the natural resources use them only to their own advantage and destroy their usefulness for the common welfare?

Refer again to the story of the good shepherd in John 10. This story reflects the fact that people of the early Christian community suffered at the hands of false shepherds. John may be talking about such men as Theudas and Judas the Galilean, who are reported in Acts 5:36-37. Jeremiah, a contemporary of Ezekiel, also refers to false shepherds (23:1-4). Ask the class to look at the passages in Ezekiel 34 and characterize the shepherds. They may describe them as privileged, irresponsible, self-seeking, calloused, and insensitive; as men who pretended to seek the welfare of all but who really sought their own good. To modify a familiar metaphor, they were wolves in shepherds' clothing.

Ask the class members to apply the metaphor to life today. Are there areas of human experience in which we find false shepherds? Ask your class members to report on what they found in newspapers regarding the misuse of power. They may report on indictments of persons in public office who take advantage of their position and, through unethical behavior, defraud the public. They may read of bribery, exorbitant charges by professional or business people, or the efforts of certain high-pressure special interest groups to gain legislation that benefits only a part of our society.

A striking illustration of the problem of misuse of power has been widely discussed in recent years, as residents of ghetto neighborhoods have pleaded for good police protection and an end to an abuse of police power. Or consider the misuse of power by other institutions of society. For example, in 1914 the Congress of the United States recognized the abuse of economic power and passed the Clayton Act, which strengthened the Sherman Anti-Trust Law. It sought to control such abuses of power as deliberate and ruinous price cutting, trade-restraining tying contracts, intercorporate investments, and interlocking directorates between large corporations and banks. In a certain sense, then, our own Congress has been a kind of "watchman for the house of Israel" (Ezekiel 3:17), hence performing its law-making function in a prophetic spirit.

Summarize the lesson by reviewing the evidence that God does care. In the first place, he pronounces judgment on leaders who exploit people. He does care that justice shall prevail, and justice is an expression of love. Secondly, he calls man to the responsible service of others, hence to a life of stewardship in which God's care is expressed in tangible ways. Thirdly, he promises restoration for Israel; and in so doing reinforces our faith that both our chastening in disobedience and our service in obedience will result in the good life.

Helping Class Members Act

Psalms 23 has been suggested as the devotional reading in connection with this week's lesson. Ask your class members to follow up this lesson by taking ample time to read the twenty-third psalm in the light of Ezekiel 34. Note the contrast between shepherds and false shepherds, between green pastures and trodden down pastures, between still waters and foul waters, between righteousness for his name's sake and prosperity for the sake of personal gain. Read Psalms 23 in the light of the experiences of deportation and death through which the exiles passed, their fear of evil because they were separated from God, their humiliating sense of defeat, and their hopeless frame of mind. The metaphors of death, rod and staff, table and oil have new meaning; and the conviction that, no matter where they are, they "shall dwell in the house of the LORD forever" dispels hopelessness.

Planning for Next Sunday

Announce to your class the theme for next Sunday: "No Alibis With

God." Ask your class to read Ezekiel 18 and to outline its content. Secure two volunteers to prepare the following reports: (1) a description of the exiles' behavior and attitudes as revealed in Psalms 137 and (2) an analysis of the causes of the exiles' plight as described in Ezekiel 22:23-31.

No Alibis With God

Background Scripture: Ezekiel 18

The Main Question —Charles M. Laymon

When a group of young adults met at the church one Sunday night, the meeting promised to be routine. But when the leader read Psalms 104, about the beauty of the earth and the harmony God had built into nature between need and supply, something happened. The group began to talk about pollution and what man had done to the beautiful earth. "Total irresponsibility!" said one. Another added that refuse had been found in the middle of the Atlantic Ocean.

A young woman reporting on the meeting said, "What a discussion, all those people talking about how to enforce the present laws and why the mayor of this town lets that factory dump all that junk into the river. Wow, I'll try that again."

This young woman's supportive comment raises the question, Are we responsible to God for the way we live? She responded to the challenge of the church to persons in the area of contamination. This is but one issue. What are some of the others in which God would hold us to the line—his line?

The biblical passage from Ezekiel dramatizes the issue of man's responsibility under God.

As You Read the Scripture —Floyd V. Filson

Ezekiel 18:1-4. *The word of the* LORD *came to me again:* The proverb "the fathers have eaten sour grapes, and the children's teeth are set on edge" means that children were held guilty and punished for sins their fathers committed.

Compare Exodus 20:5 about God "visiting the iniquity of the fathers upon the children to the third and the fourth generation of those who hate me," and Lamentations 5:7: "Our fathers sinned . . . and we bear their iniquities." Ezekiel protests against using this proverb and declares to his fellow Israelites that it "shall no more be used by you in Israel." The father and the son are on the same level before God; each must answer for his own sin. The basic principle Ezekiel states is "the soul that sins shall die."

Ezekiel spells out his meaning by giving five illustrations: (1) Verses 5-9. The righteous man "shall surely live." (2) Verses 10-13. His son who sins shall not live. "His blood shall be upon himself." (3) Verses 14-18. His son's son who obeys God's statutes "shall surely live." Father and son shall each answer for his own conduct. (4) Verses 21-23. A wicked man who turns away from his sins and does right shall surely live. (5) Verse 24. A righteous man who turns away and commits iniquity shall die.

Verses 25, 29. *Yet you say, "The way of the Lord is not just":* Ezekiel answers the protest he has heard among the Israelites. They say that *the way of the Lord is not just.* Ezekiel reports in the name of the Lord that it is the ways of Israel that are not just. This vigorous defense of God's justice, given first in verse 25, is repeated for emphasis in verse 29.

Verses 26-28. *When a righteous man turns away from his righteousness:* These verses answer a possible objection to what Ezekiel says, namely, that a man should be judged not solely by what he does at the very end of his life but rather by the dominant character of his whole life. To take an extreme case, a man might live an upright life for 95 per cent of his life and only in the last 5 per cent turn to evil. He had lived well most of his life; would it be right to condemn him for that last brief time of evil living?

Take the opposite example. A man lives an evil life for a time, perhaps for almost his entire life. If after this long bad record he turns and does what is right, should not his record, especially if the bad part was the longer part, be reckoned on the basis of his entire career? Is he not getting off too easy if he is given clearance and life in spite of that earlier bad record?

Ezekiel is convinced that in such a mixed record the final attitude is decisive. When a man, after knowing the meaning and blessing of a good life, turns to evil ways, it is his final attitude, Ezekiel holds, that is decisive. And when a man, after a life of wrong attitudes and actions, sees that this is the wrong way to live and turns from it to do the will of God, this final decision on the basis of experience is the one that counts. The man who sees his error and turns to God's way for him "shall save his life."

Verses 30-32. *Therefore I will judge you . . . every one according to his ways:* The righteous God will judge Israel, *every one according to his ways.* Since Israel has sinned, it is urgently important for her to repent for all the transgressions she has committed.

But it is not enough to regret past sins. An inner renewal and dedication are necessary. The very word *repent* involves an inner change of attitude. What Israel needs is "a new heart and a new spirit." The good style of life God wants for each of us can only result from an inner renewal that will be expressed in outer obedience to God's will. God does not want anyone to be condemned and die; he has no pleasure in the death of anyone. So the prophet closes discussion of this theme with the urgent words, "turn, and live."

Selected Scripture

King James Version	Revised Standard Version
Ezekiel 18:1-4, 25-32	*Ezekiel 18:1-4, 25-32*

King James Version

Ezekiel 18:1-4, 25-32

1 The word of the LORD came unto me again, saying,

2 What mean ye, that ye use this proverb concerning the land of Israel, saying, The fathers have eaten sour grapes, and the children's teeth are set on edge?

3 As I live, saith the Lord GOD, ye shall not have occasion any more to use this proverb in Israel.

4 Behold, all souls are mine; as the soul of the father, so also the soul of the son is mine: the soul that sinneth, it shall die.

.   .   .   .

25 Yet ye say, The way of the Lord is not equal. Hear now, O house of Israel; Is not my way equal? are not your ways unequal?

26 When a righteous man turneth away from his righteousness, and committeth iniquity, and dieth in them; for his iniquity that he hath done shall he die.

27 Again, when the wicked man turneth away from his wickedness that he hath committed, and doeth that which is lawful and right, he shall save his soul alive.

28 Because he considereth, and turneth away from all his transgressions that he hath committed, he shall surely live, he shall not die.

29 Yet saith the house of Israel, The way of the Lord is not equal. O house of Israel, are not my ways equal? are not your ways unequal?

30 Therefore I will judge you, O house of Israel, every one according to his ways, saith the Lord GOD. Repent, and turn yourselves from all your transgressions; so iniquity shall not be your ruin.

31 Cast away from you all your

Revised Standard Version

Ezekiel 18:1-4, 25-32

1 The word of the LORD came to me again: 2 "What do you mean by repeating this proverb concerning the land of Israel, 'The fathers have eaten sour grapes, and the children's teeth are set on edge'? 3 As I live, says the Lord GOD, this proverb shall no more be used by you in Israel. 4 Behold, all souls are mine; the soul of the father as well as the soul of the son is mine: the soul that sins shall die.

.   .   .   .

25 "Yet you say, 'The way of the Lord is not just.' Hear now, O house of Israel: Is my way not just? Is it not your ways that are not just? 26 When a righteous man turns away from his righteousness and commits iniquity, he shall die for it; for the iniquity which he has committed he shall die. 27 Again, when a wicked man turns away from the wickedness he has committed and does what is lawful and right, he shall save his life. 28 Because he considered and turned away from all the transgressions which he had committed, he shall surely live, he shall not die. 29 Yet the house of Israel says, 'The way of the Lord is not just.' O house of Israel, are my ways not just? Is it not your ways that are not just?

30 "Therefore I will judge you, O house of Israel, every one according to his ways, says the Lord GOD. Repent and turn from all your transgressions, lest iniquity be your ruin. 31 Cast away from you all the transgressions which you have committed against

transgressions, whereby ye have transgressed; and make you a new heart and a new spirit: for why will ye die, O house of Israel?

32 For I have no pleasure in the death of him that dieth, saith the Lord GOD: wherefore turn yourselves, and live ye.

Memory Selection: Again, when the wicked man turneth away from his wickedness that he hath committed, and doeth that which is lawful and right, he shall save his soul alive. (Ezekiel 18:27)

me, and get yourselves a new heart and a new spirit! Why will you die, O house of Israel? 32 For I have no pleasure in the death of anyone, says the Lord GOD; so turn, and live."

Memory Selection: Again, when a wicked man turns away from the wickedness he has committed and does what is lawful and right, he shall save his life. (Ezekiel 18:27)

The Scripture and the Main Question —Charles M. Laymon

TO EACH HIS OWN

The expression "to each his own" is usually used to refer to our rights and privileges. It may also include our punishments and judgments, as when one says that person is getting his "just deserts."

The issue Ezekiel was facing when he said that each generation should suffer for its own sins was the teaching that the sins of the fathers are visited upon their children. Instead of the fathers' eating sour grapes and the children's teeth being set on edge, the prophet urged that each man himself should have his own teeth set on edge because he ate the sour fruit (Ezekiel 18:1-4). This is just recompense for one's own acts.

The fact remains, however, that future generations often must pay the price of the sins of the fathers. Babies may be born with syphilitic blindness because of the social sins of their parents.

In another sense, we adults sometimes pass on to our children a social

order that is weakened by our injustice and neglect. The seeds of present strife are usually sown in the unjust peace that was made in the settlement of past wars. For instance, youth today did not create a divided Germany; we, their fathers, did this. And neither was the situation in the Far East made by the young men who are called upon to fight on foreign soil. Similarly, the economic instability of our age that youth must try to correct when they assume adult responsibilities was not of their own making. We handed it to them.

MY BROTHER'S KEEPER

Many centuries ago Cain asked God if he were his brother's keeper. He was trying to sidestep his murder of Abel, but God's answer was a resounding "yes." The voice of his brother's blood cried out to God from the ground (Genesis 4:8-10).

If we were our brother's keeper and felt responsible for future generations, to use Ezekiel's language, we would then do our best to see to it that their teeth would not be set on edge because we have eaten sour grapes. We would be socially responsible persons.

Montesquieu was a wise political philosopher, one of the world's greatest. In urging our responsibility to all in the present and the future he once said, "If I knew something advantageous to my family but injurious to my country I would try to forget it. If I knew something profitable to my country but detrimental to the human race, I would consider it a crime."

The outreach in Montesquieu's words is worthy of the Christian's responsibility to love all men. God sent Christ because he loved the world (John 3:16), and we cannot turn off our social responsibility this side of the most distant shores of the earth. Even from a selfish standpoint, the sickness of any part of the world will bring sickness to our own shores. No nation can resign from the world and retreat into narrow isolationism. No man can become a solitary island. We all belong to the family of God.

IT's UP TO YOU

Having one's own teeth set on edge because one has eaten sour grapes, as Ezekiel said, places the responsibility upon each person individually. If future generations are not to be held responsible, we must bear the blame or know the blessing. The old game of "passing the buck" is out.

A tradition of ancient Locris illustrates the principle of individual responsibility most dramatically. It is said that if a man introduced a law in the popular assembly, he must do so while standing upon a platform with his neck in a noose. Off came the noose if his law passed, but out came the platform beneath his feet if it failed. Whether this is true or not,

it highlights the idea that responsibility is an individual matter.

Harry Emerson Fosdick once put it this way, "Every Christian truth, gracious and comfortable, has a corresponding obligation, searching and sacrificial." And this obligation falls upon me. To the extent of my ability and opportunity it is mine.

Ezekiel has his own way of pointing to such responsibility: "When a righteous man turns away from his righteousness and commits iniquity, he shall die for it; for the iniquity which he has committed he shall die." (18:26) There is nothing soft or sentimental in Ezekiel's teaching here; it is realistic and uncompromising. There are no alibis with God.

TURN AND LIVE

Other religions also do not let men off without punishment. Both the Hindus and the Buddhists teach what is known as the principle of karma. It sounds very much like what Ezekiel is saying concerning ethical responsibility, since the principle holds that the consequences of one's acts fix his destiny. As popularly stressed this idea of course leads to fatalism.

Ezekiel's view, however, is not finally fatalistic. There is something that we can do if we have been irresponsible and evil. We can repent. "When a wicked man turns away from the wickedness he has committed and does what is lawful and right, he shall save his life. . . . He shall surely live, he shall not die." (verses 27-28) Therefore the prophet calls upon men to "turn, and live." (verse 32)

Although the prophets of Israel bore down with unrelenting insistence upon the fact that sin brings God's judgment, they invariably held the way open for a change of heart. Repentance will reverse the picture. God's grace is open to all.

Helping Adults Become Involved —Harlan R. Waite

Preparation of Self and Class

Read Ezekiel 18, the background Scripture for this lesson, and outline its several units. The content of the outline is suggested below. Consult *The Interpreter's Bible* for help in interpreting the Scripture passage. Read your denominational quarterlies for further help.

Presenting the Main Question

Daniel Webster said that the most important thought he ever had was that of his individual responsibility to God. This is a direct illustration of how many leaders in American history have given strength to democracy by their own insistence upon responsible individualism. Contrast this with the opposite tendency, which has also been present in American life, to carry a doctrine of "rugged individualism" to such an extreme that it became socially irresponsible. Emphasize that the teaching of the Bible relates the freedom of the individual to the well-being of the community. Healthy religion has two poles—the individual and the social: "Thou shalt love the Lord thy God . . . and . . . thy neighbour as thyself." (Mark 12:30-31, KJV)

Refer to Dr. Laymon's statement of the main question: Are we responsible to God for the way we live? Note his contemporary illustration.

To illustrate the question from a different perspective, note the changes that have been taking place over the past few years with reference to the psychological understanding of human behavior. Undoubtedly some of your class members will be able to describe these changes. Either through your own statement or through class discussion, note that classical psychoanalytic theory has held that our deepest feelings and our behavior are due to childhood influences that make us what we are. Other schools of psychology have emphasized the importance of social and cultural conditioning as the determinant of our behavior. Today, however, without denying the large elements of truth in earlier understandings, many leading psychologists and psychiatrists are stressing the importance of the will, decision, and deliberate choice. They affirm that within certain limitations that our past does put upon us we are free to modify old behavior patterns, to change attitudes, to experience and express feelings in a new way, and to create new modes of behavior.

Their findings reinforce Ezekiel's insistence that we shall no longer use the old proverb, "The fathers have eaten sour grapes, and the children's teeth are set on edge." (18:2) Modern psychology holds that there is, indeed, a certain kind of truth in the proverb; but the great emphasis is on the affirmation of real freedom for the individual to determine the way his life shall go and, therefore, real responsibility to God as we make the basic decisions of our lives.

Developing the Lesson

Following the assignment you gave your class last Sunday, ask your students to outline the contents of Ezekiel 18. Use the chalkboard to list the main divisions. You will want to note that verses 1-4 recall the proverb and state the principle of individual responsibility before God. Before proceeding refer the class members to Exodus 20:5, which underscores the importance of the second commandment ("You shall not make yourself a graven image. . . ."), "for I the LORD your God am a jealous God, visiting the iniquity of the fathers upon the children to the third and the

196

fourth generation of those who hate me."

Then let the class members identify the next three units: verses 5-9, verses 10-13, and verses 14-20. Note that these illustrate the principle of individual responsibility by applying it to three generations: a righteous father, an unrighteous son, and a righteous grandson. This three-generational illustration reflects the sense of relationship this proverb bears to the second commandment.

Let the class members complete the outline of this chapter, noting that in verses 21-24 Ezekiel speaks of the repentant wicked and the backsliding righteous, that the theme of verses 25-29 is the declaration of God's fairness, and that in verses 30-32 God pleads for repentance. ("Get yourselves a new heart and a new spirit" anticipates next week's lesson, with the same phrase appearing in Ezekiel 11:19 and 36:26.)

Ask your class members to discuss this question: What made it necessary for Ezekiel to bring up the subject of individual responsibility? The first part of the answer, of course, is obvious: the exiles were avoiding responsibility by quoting the old proverb. But pursue this with a further question: With what situation were the exiled Israelites attempting to deal when Ezekiel confronted them with this message? The answer, again probably obvious, is the Exile, with all its disruption of normal life, its hardships, its separation from familiar people and places, and its sense of hopelessness.

At this point, call for the report on Psalms 137, which you assigned last week. The psalm pictures the exiles as taunted by their captives, weeping by the Euphrates River, spiritually devastated, and bitterly vindictive. No wonder they would quote the proverb,

feeling that their sad plight was due to the failures of earlier generations who had precipitated this crisis.

Call for the report, assigned last week, on some of the causes of Israel's downfall, as described in Ezekiel 22:23-31. The passage highlights the responsibility of princes, priests, prophets, and the people. Following the report, ask the class members to discuss what bearing this has on Ezekiel's emphasis on individual responsibility. Must the individual really bear all the responsibility for his own sins or the sins of his generation? Is there not some sense in which the ills that befall us are really caused by others?

Note at this point that in criticizing the princes, the priests, the prophets, and the people Ezekiel was pointing the finger of judgment at Israel, his own nation, not at Babylonia. In the social sense, then, the principle of personal responsibility still holds. We must do something about *our* sins and let God worry about *their* sins. Perhaps the heart of the matter, then, is to respond to God's judgment in the first person, whether it be singular or plural, and not in the third person. Thus we are accomplishing the spiritual objective, which is to refrain from giving alibis or blaming others and to accept responsibility for ourselves.

Today we have many problems in our society. Some of them are caused by others; some of them we cause ourselves. Basically, Ezekiel's principle means that we must face the facts as they are. Although we are not called upon to bear guilt that is not ours, we are called upon both to accept guilt where we should bear it and, even more important, to make our own responsible contribution to a healthy society.

We are too easily given to blaming one another, and in so doing we avoid taking responsibility ourselves. For example, we blame the wicked, the communists, and our political opponents. We are far more apt to condemn people who protest rather than people who create injustice. Let the class members discuss and evaluate these and other tendencies to blame others for our troubles.

Helping Class Members Act

Ask your students to spend some time in self-evaluation and to list defense mechanisms by which they attempt to justify their own behavior. Alibis may be one way, but there are other ways just as serious. Suggest, for example, that we defend ourselves by denying that anything is wrong; by rationalizing our behavior with excuses; by blaming our behavior on heredity, environment, or unhealthy influence; by diverting attention from our weakness to others' sins through counterattack; or by withdrawing. Contrast these with the positive response to crisis pictured by Ezekiel: an honest acceptance of responsibility, an openness to judgment, repentance, and trust in God's love.

Ask members to close by reading Psalms 139:1-12.

Planning for Next Sunday

Announce next week's theme, "A New Heart and Spirit"; and assign the reading of the background Scripture: Ezekiel 11:14-21; 36. Ask a class member to make a detailed comparison of the two passages. Ask a second class member to read and report on Mark 10:35-45.

LESSON 10   FEBRUARY 4

A New Heart and Spirit

Background Scripture: Ezekiel 11:14-21; 36

The Main Question —Charles M. Laymon

The legends that surround Leonardo Da Vinci's painting of the Last Supper are numerous. One of the more dramatic is that the person he chose as the model for Christ was later found so degraded that Da Vinci also selected him as the model for Judas. I have also heard the legend the other way around. This time the man who modeled for Judas was converted and later posed for the painting of Jesus.

The reason these stories continue to be told is that both are possible. The former haunts men with the fear that they might not be able to hold out in the fight to live as Christians, and the latter gives men hope that they can not only hold out but also mature and grow in Christ.

The question follows: Can men be changed for the better? Books continue to come from the press that keep before our eyes the dreams of renewal. From Harold Begbie's *Twice-born Men* to David Wilkerson's *The Cross and the Switchblade* this story of new birth is repeated over and over. And before us always is the Bible with its insistence that in Christ all things can be made new.

The biblical passage from Ezekiel also urges us to believe in the new heart and spirit.

198

As You Read the Scripture —Floyd V. Filson

This passage in Ezekiel clearly recalls the closing portion of the Scripture used in the last lesson. In Ezekiel 18:30-32, Israel was earnestly urged to repent and adopt a new attitude of willing loyalty to God. To avoid the judgment and condemnation Israel deserved, she was told, "Get yourselves a new heart and a new spirit," a heart and attitude earnestly dedicated to doing God's will.

The passage now to be studied, Ezekiel 36:22-32, speaks to Israel in exile and tells how God intends to act to carry out his purpose for his people. He plans to bring the house of Israel back to its own land in Palestine. As Ezekiel 36:16-21 states, her defeat and exile were God's punishment of Israel for her wrongdoings. But that was not God's last word for Israel. The passage we now study tells what his purpose and promise are.

Ezekiel 36:22-23. *It is not for your sake, O house of Israel, that I am about to act:* This message Ezekiel is instructed to tell his people, who are now in exile. But God will not act for the sake and honor of Israel. The people have been guilty of sin, first in their homeland and then while in exile, where they have profaned (dishonored) God's name by their sinful conduct. Just what their sin was is not clearly stated; probably, as verse 25 suggests, the exiles joined in pagan worship in Babylonia instead of worshiping only the Lord their God. Yet, God will act to vindicate his holy and great name by bringing his people back from exile and settling them firmly in their homeland.

Verses 24-25. *For I will take you from the nations, . . . and bring you into your own land:* Ezekiel's main concern is for his people in Babylonia and their coming restoration to their former home in Palestine. But in this passage Ezekiel seems to think of his people as scattered even more widely than throughout the region of Babylonia. God, he promises, will take Israel *from the nations;* he will gather the people from all the countries and bring them into their *own land.* Perhaps the prophet thinks in part here of the earlier captivity of Samaria under the king of Assyria (2 Kings 17:1-6).

In large or small groups the Israelites had become widely scattered, and in their various places of captivity they had become contaminated by polytheism (worshiping many gods) and moral faults that deserved God's judgment. They had lost their faith in the one true God.

So Israel needs cleansing. As a symbol of the spiritual and moral cleansing God will make effective in the lives of the captives, Ezekiel speaks of sprinkling them with clean water. God will graciously make them clean from all uncleannesses.

Verses 26-27. *A new heart I will give you:* (See Jeremiah 31:27-34 and Ezekiel 18:30-32.) Here is further evidence that the Old Testament has a prominent place for grace; it is far from being a law book. God will give his people the needed new heart and new spirit. The Hebrews have so nearly lost their full loyalty to God that instead of a God-directed heart of flesh they now have a heart of stone (callousness toward God's will for them). But God will act to change that; he will put his spirit within them and cause them to walk faithfully as he requires.

Verses 28-30. *You shall dwell in the land which I gave to your fathers:* The

199

Israelites will dwell safely in the land God gave to their ancestors. They will be glad to be God's people and acknowledge him as their God. From all the uncleannesses of wrong living he will deliver them. Abundant grain and fruit, the abundant increase of the field, will bless their life under God. They will never again suffer the disgrace of famine that would suggest God does not care for them.

Verses 31-32. *Then you will remember your evil ways:* Brought home and blessed by God, the Israelites will remember their *evil ways,* not in pride but in shame and with loathing of their former iniquities and abominable deeds. In that promised day they will regret and avoid their former sinful ways.

But Israel is reminded that God will not act because she has deserved such good treatment. The house of Israel in that day of obedience to God will recognize that this blessed life is not what she has deserved. God has acted to vindicate himself and demonstrate in the life of his people his goodness and holiness.

Selected Scripture

King James Version	Revised Standard Version
Ezekiel 36:22-32	*Ezekiel 36:22-32*
22 Therefore say unto the house of Israel, Thus saith the Lord GOD; I do not this for your sakes, O house of Israel, but for mine holy name's sake, which ye have profaned among the heathen, whither ye went.	22 "Therefore say to the house of Israel, Thus says the Lord GOD: It is not for your sake, O house of Israel, that I am about to act, but for the sake of my holy name, which you have profaned among the nations to which you came. 23 And I will vindicate the holiness of my great name,
23 And I will sanctify my great name, which was profaned among the heathen, which ye have profaned in the midst of them; and the heathen shall know that I am the LORD, saith the Lord GOD, when I shall be sanctified in you before their eyes.	which has been profaned among the nations, and which you have profaned among them; and the nations will know that I am the LORD, says the Lord GOD, when through you I vindicate my holiness before their eyes. 24 For I will take you from the nations, and gather you from all the
24 For I will take you from among the heathen, and gather you out of all countries, and will bring you into your own land.	countries, and bring you into your own land. 25 I will sprinkle clean water upon you, and you shall be clean from all your uncleannesses, and from all your idols I will cleanse
25 Then will I sprinkle clean water upon you, and ye shall be clean: from all your filthiness, and from all your idols, will I cleanse you.	you. 26 A new heart I will give you, and a new spirit I will put within you; and I will take out of your flesh the heart of stone and give you a heart of flesh. 27 And I will put my
26 A new heart also will I give you, and a new spirit will I put within you: and I will take away the stony heart out of your flesh, and I will give you an heart of flesh.	spirit within you, and cause you to
27 And I will put my spirit within	

you, and cause you to walk in my statutes, and ye shall keep my judgments, and do them.

28 And ye shall dwell in the land that I gave to your fathers; and ye shall be my people, and I will be your God.

29 I will also save you from all your uncleannesses: and I will call for the corn, and will increase it, and lay no famine upon you.

30 And I will multiply the fruit of the tree, and the increase of the field, that ye shall receive no more reproach of famine among the heathen.

31 Then shall ye remember your own evil ways, and your doings that were not good, and shall loathe yourselves in your own sight for your iniquities and for your abominations.

32 Not for your sakes do I this, saith the Lord GOD, be it known unto you: be ashamed and confounded for your own ways, O house of Israel.

Memory Selection: A new heart also will I give you, and a new spirit will I put within you: and I will take away the stony heart out of your flesh, and I will give you an heart of flesh. (Ezekiel 36:26)

walk in my statutes and be careful to observe my ordinances. 28 You shall dwell in the land which I gave to your fathers; and you shall be my people, and I will be your God. 29 And I will deliver you from all your uncleannesses; and I will summon the grain and make it abundant and lay no famine upon you. 30 I will make the fruit of the tree and the increase of the field abundant, that you may never again suffer the disgrace of famine among the nations. 31 Then you will remember your evil ways, and your deeds that were not good; and you will loathe yourselves for your iniquities and your abominable deeds. 32 It is not for your sake that I will act, says the Lord GOD; let that be known to you. Be ashamed and confounded for your ways, O house of Israel."

Memory Selection: A new heart I will give you, and a new spirit I will put within you; and I will take out of your flesh the heart of stone and give you a heart of flesh. (Ezekiel 36:26)

The Scripture and the Main Question —Charles M. Laymon

WHAT'S IN A NAME?

One of the desperadoes in the saga of the opening of the West was John Wesley Hardin. Little is known about his family, but the fact that his first two names were *John Wesley* indicates that his parents held an ideal for their son. They wanted him to grow up to be like the founder of Methodism whose name he carried. That this did not happen might lead one to ask, "What's in a name?"

The ancient Hebrews would reply

to such a question that a name means everything, for it stands for a person's character. Was not Jacob's name changed to Israel when he wrestled all night with the angel and prevailed (Genesis 32:28). And did not the name *Israel* mean "he who strives with God"?

Similarly, in giving God a name we are defining his character. When the Westminster Assembly was preparing the *Shorter Catechism,* the members had difficulty in arriving at a definition of God. One of their number was asked to lead them in prayer. He began his prayer with the words, "O God, thou who art a spirit infinite, eternal, and unchangeable in thy being, wisdom, power, holiness, justice, goodness, and truth." With one voice those present said, "This is it! Here is our definition of God."

In Ezekiel we find God saying that he would lead Israel back from Babylonia to Palestine for the sake of his holy name: "I will vindicate the holiness of my great name." (Ezekiel 36: 23) He would forever act as God, and to be God meant that he would save his people. His name and his character were one. It was not that his people deserved to be saved but that he was the Lord.

AN ACT OF CLEANSING

Yet God's act in bringing his people back to Jerusalem would not be simply an arbitrary move to prove that he was God. It would be a redemptive move, because in doing this he would cleanse them from their sins: "I will sprinkle clean water upon you, and you shall be clean from all your uncleannesses, and from all your idols I will cleanse you." (verse 25)

The Bible abounds in such references to washing away sins. One of the most famous of these is God's call for men to be cleansed in Isaiah 1:16. Then, Isaiah adds, "Though your sins are like scarlet, they shall be as white as snow." (verse 18) These references probably reflect the washings practiced by the Jews in ceremonial cleansing.

Charles Wesley used this same theme in one of his hymns:

Wash me, and make me thus Thine own;
Wash me, and mine Thou art;
Wash me, but not my feet alone:
My hands, my head, my heart.

The loving God, the forgiving God, the cleansing God—this is the God of the Bible; and this is the God of the church. When this emphasis is missing, Christianity is no longer a redemptive religion.

A HEART OF FLESH

Household cleansers promise great and wonderful things today. At their best, however, they cannot equal the results Ezekiel claimed for the cleansing of God. The "heart of stone," he said, would be replaced with the "heart of flesh." (36:26)

When I was a young boy, a visiting evangelist came to our church. On the pulpit beside the Bible he placed an object and covered it with a handkerchief. My curiosity was aroused to the boiling point. What was under the cloth? The minister said that he would show us before the sermon ended. At one place in the sermon the results of sin were being described. Dramatically, the minister lifted the handkerchief from the object. There it was in all its hardness—a stone. "This is the heart of the sinner," he said. For a long time afterward, every time I saw a stone I thought of this acted parable.

If it is true that sin changes persons, it is equally true that God changes men also. Nicodemus was told by Jesus that he needed to be "born anew." (John 3:3) And the apostle Paul announced that if anyone is in Christ, he is a "new creation." (2 Corinthians 5:17)

The change from the heart of stone to the heart of flesh is God's doing. He puts a new spirit within us, *his very own spirit;* and the miracle of the transformation occurs (Ezekiel 36:27). Ezekiel reaches a New Testament level of thought in this passage. The gospel of the changed heart is the very center of our Christian life.

Whatever we call it—renewal, redemption, rebirth—it means new lives for old.

GOING HOME AGAIN

Thomas Wolfe wrote a famous novel with the title *You Can't Go Home Again*. He was referring to the impossibility of recapturing the past. In his own life Wolfe found it difficult to return to Asheville, North Carolina, where he had grown up. Too much had happened since he left. Hometown folks resented his placing them as characters in his novels; at least they thought they recognized themselves in his writings.

Ezekiel, on the other hand, promised the Jews that one day they would return to Jerusalem from their exile in Babylonia. He said to them, "You shall dwell in the land which I gave to your fathers; and you shall be my people, and I will be your God." (36:28) What this meant to them we can readily imagine. Jerusalem was the land of promise, their land, God's land.

However, Ezekiel's words really were telling the Jews that they should return to God in faithfulness and trust. The home of the soul is in God himself. We do not find ourselves until we find God; we do not really discover who we are until we learn who God is and what our relationship to him is.

Augustine said the same thing, "Thou hast made us for Thyself, and the heart of man is restless until it finds its rest in Thee." A touching incident in the life of the famous theologian further underscores this truth. He was at Ostia with Monica, his mother. They were on their way home, and she was very ill. Augustine expressed the fear that she would die far from home. His mother replied, "No one, my son, is ever far from God."

Helping Adults Become Involved —Harlan R. Waite

Preparation of Self and Class

Read the background Scripture for this week: Ezekiel 11:14-21; 36. Then turn to *The Interpreter's Bible* and the student materials for further resources. Drawing upon these and the materials provided by Dr. Laymon and Dr. Filson, answer for yourself the question, Why did the exiles need a new heart and spirit? Certainly many of them were discouraged; and apparently large numbers had given up, thinking that God had deserted them. In their resignation they turned to Babylonian cults for help.

Think of the needs of your class members and of the whole society of which they are a part. Have we been captivated by "gods" unworthy of our faith? In what ways do these gods manifest themselves in our personal conduct and in the life of our nation?

Presenting the Main Question

The main question for today's lesson is Can men change? If so, how? I once served a church in a racially changing community. Sentiment in the church was heavily weighted in the direction of white exclusiveness. However, taking its faith seriously, the church made a conscious decision not to move out of the community but to become all-inclusive in its fellowship. The result was that the church soon included substantial numbers of non-Anglo persons. In the experience individuals discovered that some of the things they imagined about other persons were not true and that their fellowship with persons across ethnic lines could be rich and rewarding. They learned that men can be changed for the better. Christian history is full of many illustrations of how men can change: the twelve disciples, Paul, Saint Francis, Saint Augustine, Martin Luther, and John Wesley. Choose some examples from this list. Best of all, ask some of your class members to contribute their own testimonial as to how they have changed as a result of their Christian faith.

Developing the Lesson

Call for the report assigned last week on the comparison of the two passages in Ezekiel: 11:14-21 and 36. Following the report, ask the class members to discuss the focus of each passage. Note that both passages refer to the gift of a new heart and spirit, which means a new obedience to the statutes and ordinances of God and a new sense of relationship to God as his people.

Beyond this, however, the emphases differ. In the first passage God is promising to gather up the exiles and give them the land of Israel once again, in the faith that they will re-create it as the nation of God. The second passage, concerned with the effect of the Exile on other nations, insists that the restoration of the house of Israel is to take place not for the sake of the Israelites but for God's sake. The nations had drawn the conclusion that since a nation that professed belief in God had suffered exile, their God could not be very effective. The purpose of the return of the exiles would be to let the nations "know that I am the LORD . . . when through you I vindicate my holiness before their eyes." (36:23) Call the attention of your class

members to Ezekiel 36:25 and its reference to the idols from which Israel would be cleansed. Suggest that this raises an important question for us: What has captivated our hearts? What are the idols of modern, affluent America? Remind the class members that the prophets were all hard-hitting men who pulled no punches. They got at the heart of the matter, even though it was painful for all concerned. Suggest that the class members approach this question with the same kind of seriousness. Essentially the question has to do with the conflict between certain American values and the central values of Christ's gospel.

Divide the class members into buzz groups of five or six persons each. Ask each group to have a reporter prepared to share their discussion with the rest of the class regarding several questions to be assigned. The first is this: What are we really most concerned about in our daily life as Americans? You will not, of course, control the answers groups make to this question; but you may anticipate some. For example, persons may mention our obsession with being the biggest and best country in the world. Perhaps people of all nations are given to this kind of national loyalty, but the Christian gospel clearly rejects this kind of arrogance. We can demonstrate factually that we do excel in certain scientific and technical ways. However, we are far from the best so far as infant mortality is concerned; and many nations have a higher literacy rate than we do. There is room within the Christian spirit to know, be grateful for, and share one's strengths; but it is hardly in keeping with the mind of Christ to be arrogant and boastful. Call for the report assigned last week on Mark 10:35-45.

Is "Bigger-and-Better" the name of our pagan idol?

A high material standard of living is another obsession of modern man. We have come to place a great value on physical conveniences, external appearances, superficial luxuries, and an almost indulgent desire for comfort. This value system leads us to want things that are really not essential to the good life as the Christian faith defines it. This is a spiritual problem, but it has many practical ramifications. In fact, we are experiencing what Ezekiel would have called the judgment of God; for our inflation is a direct result of our desire for more material goods, and the ecological problems we are facing today stem from the materialism expressed in our basic value system. Is this materialism one of our pagan idolatries?

The groups may also want to discuss such things as our drive for status and prestige, the high value we place on power, our near worship of tradition, and our exaltation of the idea of competition.

Next, ask the buzz groups to define what it means to have a new heart. Are there Christian alternatives to the idol worship that has been discussed? What about the goals of our country? Is the imposition of law and order enough, or are we really interested in a thoroughgoing system of justice for all? Are we going to continue to seek wealth as a primary goal, or is life more truly a search for human fulfillment? In any event, a new heart means a new set of goals that are in keeping with the Christian gospel.

Can we redeem our interest in "bigness and betterness"? The new heart may mean a new set of standards for what is really better.

A new heart may mean new relationships and a new style of relating to other human beings. For example, America has often been considered a "melting pot"; but there are many in our society today who, concerned with healthy individualism, resist the idea of having one's identity lost in a mass phenomenon known as Americanism. What about the "salad bowl" concept, a blending of different ingredients that retain their individuality while contributing to the whole, as an ideal for American society?

As the final bit of spiritual exploration ask the buzz groups to discuss *how* we may change. For example, despite the claim that morality cannot be legislated, we teach our children morality by certain disciplines. On a larger scale, fair employment practice laws have made it necessary for people to work with members of other races; and often they have made the surprising discovery that they not only need not fear one another but can enjoy one another. We can change therefore by developing both personal and social disciplines.

As you call the buzz groups back together to report, consider each of their observations; and offer the above suggestions for class reaction.

Helping Class Members Act

We also change because people believe in us. Suggest that each one of us may have a vital role in producing change in one another. That role is simply to trust in the capacity of other persons to grow spiritually. Consider some practical ways to demonstrate this kind of trust among the members of the class or toward some person who remains on the fringes of the class.

Planning for Next Sunday

Ask your class members to read the entire Book of Haggai (only thirty-eight verses in length), and explain that Haggai was interested in rebuilding the Temple. Ask one of your class members to report on the historical background, using materials in *The Interpreter's Bible*. Ask two or three others to interview some church members on why they think a church building is important and how much money should be invested in it.

God's House and Yours

Background Scripture: Haggai

The Main Question —Charles M. Laymon

President Calvin Coolidge became famous for his quick, off-the-cuff, taciturn remarks. He was once asked whether or not it was necessary to go to church in order to worship God. "Cannot I worship God in the green fields?" was the question put to him. He answered almost curtly, "You can, but you don't."

When I reported this incident to an adult class, one of the members said to me, "Coolidge was wrong. As I play golf I often look up and think of God." Another spoke up in agreement: "Yes, why not? Who was it that said, 'The groves were God's first temples'?"

Then came a rebuttal from another class member, "President Coolidge was right. You may think of God once in a while on the golf course, but that is not the same thing as spending an hour in a worship service in a church that has been dedicated to God."

All this raises the question as to whether or not we could get along without church buildings. Why build a church in a community? How much money should be spent? Should it be lavish and beautiful or plain and functional?

The cathedrals of Europe cost billions of dollars; and when they were built, people were starving. Is this Christian? Does God expect us to erect churches? Is it possible to build too many churches?

The biblical passages from Haggai may suggest helpful answers to such questions.

As You Read the Scripture —Floyd V. Filson

Haggai occupies a rather modest place among the Old Testament prophets. We know nothing of his personal background and family ties. We do know the time and core message of his career. Jerusalem had fallen in 587 B.C., as Jeremiah and Ezekiel had said it would. Decades later, in 539 B.C., Cyrus of Persia conquered Babylonia; and in 538 B.C. he issued a decree permitting peoples exiled by the kings of Babylonia to return to their ancestral homes. Many Jews, especially those led by Ezra and Nehemiah, did return. But they lacked resources; they had no military or political power. They may have worshiped at the ruins of the Jerusalem Temple, destroyed in 587 B.C.; but they took no real steps to rebuild it.

The prophet Haggai was concerned with this question of whether to push for prompt rebuilding of the Temple. He felt led by God to insist that God's people must act at once to rebuild God's house. His four prophetic utterances are clearly dated. They all fall in the year 520 B.C., under the Persian ruler Darius I. They cover a period of about four months, running from late summer through the fall season.

Haggai 1:1. *In the second year of Darius the king:* This second year was 520 B.C. Darius became king about 522 B.C. The sixth month was the latter part of August and early part of September; the new year then began in the spring.

WHY DO CHRISTIANS NEED CHURCH BUILDINGS? SHOULD BUILDINGS BE LAVISH AND BEAUTIFUL OR PLAIN AND FUNCTIONAL?

Note that the Persian ruler was using leaders of the Jews for government administration in Judah; this was intended to win the Jews' voluntary support for the Persian rule. Zerubbabel was of the royal line of the kings of Judah and so of the line of David. His grandfather Jehoiachin had been king of Judah when the Babylonians captured and destroyed Jerusalem (2 Kings 24:8-17). Though the Temple had not been rebuilt, Joshua the son of Jehozadak was high priest (see 1 Chronicles 6:14-15). The Persians permitted the Jewish priestly leadership to be in the hands of persons of real stature. But note this about these two leaders. They evidently had not been pushing for the rebuilding of the Jerusalem Temple. Yet, they were the people to see, if one wanted, as Haggai did, to urge prompt rebuilding.

Verse 2. *This people say the time has not yet come to rebuild the house of the* LORD: Haggai quoted the position of the people: it is not yet the time to undertake such a rebuilding project. To this delaying tactic Haggai—convinced that his retort is truly the word of the Lord—presents a twofold rebuttal (verses 4-7).

Here, and four other times in this short book, Haggai gives emphasis to his message by saying *thus says the* LORD *of hosts;* eight other times we find *says the* LORD *of hosts;* and in seven other cases we find *says the* LORD. Haggai wants to make it clear that his message is not his personal whim but is really God's word to his people.

Verses 3-4. *Then the word of the* LORD *came by Haggai the prophet:* Haggai says that the people even enjoy the luxury of paneled houses, while the house of God, which should be a concern for all God's people, lies in ruins. How, the prophet asks, can they defend the difference between their own living standards and their neglect of the Temple?

Verses 5-6. *Consider how you have fared:* The people should consider what it means that they have lean harvests, insufficient food and drink, inadequate clothing, and wages that slip away. Is not God trying to tell them something about their neglect of the Temple?

Verses 7-8. *Go . . . build the house, that I may take pleasure in it:* If they really consider how things have been going with them, and why, the people will go up to the hills and bring wood (stone, also needed, would be abundant right at hand) and build the house of God. There they could count on meeting him and enjoying his pleasure in them.

Verses 12-15. *All the remnant of the people, obeyed the voice of the* LORD *their God:* The leaders, with *all the remnant of the people* (the returned exiles), heard and heeded Haggai the prophet. They set to work to rebuild the Temple. When this happened, the prophet spoke with approval and gave them the Lord's message: "I am with you." There was more delay to come, but for the time being the people worked to rebuild the Temple as a worthy place of worship.

Selected Scripture

King James Version	Revised Standard Version
Haggai 1:1-8, 12-15	*Haggai 1:1-8, 12-15*
1 In the second year of Darius the king, in the sixth month, in the first day of the month, came the word of the LORD by Haggai the prophet unto Zerubbabel the son of Shealtiel, governor of Judah, and to Joshua the son of Josedech, the high priest, saying,	1 In the second year of Darius the king, in the sixth month, on the first day of the month, the word of the LORD came by Haggai the prophet to Zerubbabel the son of Shealtiel, governor of Judah, and to Joshua the son of Jehozadak, the high priest, 2 "Thus says the LORD of hosts: This

2 Thus speaketh the Lord of hosts, saying, This people say, The time is not come, the time that the Lord's house should be built.

3 Then came the word of the Lord by Haggai the prophet, saying,

4 Is it time for you, O ye, to dwell in your ceiled houses, and this house lie waste?

5 Now therefore thus saith the Lord of hosts; Consider your ways.

6 Ye have sown much, and bring in little; ye eat, but ye have not enough; ye drink, but ye are not filled with drink; ye clothe you, but there is none warm; and he that earneth wages earneth wages to put it into a bag with holes.

7 Thus saith the Lord of hosts; Consider your ways.

8 Go up to the mountain, and bring wood, and build the house; and I will take pleasure in it, and I will be glorified, saith the Lord.

. . . .

12 Then Zerubbabel the son of Shealtiel, and Joshua the son of Josedech, the high priest, with all the remnant of the people, obeyed the voice of the Lord their God, and the words of Haggai the prophet, as the Lord their God had sent him, and the people did fear before the Lord.

13 Then spake Haggai the Lord's messenger in the Lord's message unto the people, saying, I am with you, saith the Lord.

14 And the Lord stirred up the spirit of Zerubbabel the son of Shealtiel, governor of Judah, and the spirit of Joshua the son of Josedech, the high priest, and the spirit of all the remnant of the people; and they came and did work in the house of the Lord of hosts, their God,

15 In the four and twentieth day of the sixth month, in the second year of Darius the king.

people say the time has not yet come to rebuild the house of the Lord."

3 Then the word of the Lord came by Haggai the prophet, 4 "Is it a time for you yourselves to dwell in your paneled houses, while this house lies in ruins? 5 Now therefore thus says the Lord of hosts: Consider how you have fared. 6 You have sown much, and harvested little; you eat, but you never have enough; you drink, but you never have your fill; you clothe yourselves, but no one is warm; and he who earns wages earns wages to put them into a bag with holes.

7 "Thus says the Lord of hosts: Consider how you have fared. 8 Go up to the hills and bring wood and build the house, that I may take pleasure in it and that I may appear in my glory, says the Lord. . . ."

12 Then Zerubbabel the son of Shealtiel, and Joshua the son of Jehozadak, the high priest, with all the remnant of the people, obeyed the voice of the Lord their God, and the words of Haggai the prophet, as the Lord their God had sent him; and the people feared before the Lord. 13 Then Haggai, the messenger of the Lord, spoke to the people with the Lord's message, "I am with you, says the Lord." 14 And the Lord stirred up the spirit of Zerubbabel the son of Shealtiel, governor of Judah, and the spirit of Joshua the son of Jehozadak, the high priest, and the spirit of all the remnant of the people; and they came and worked on the house of the Lord of hosts, their God, 15 on the twenty-fourth day of the month, in the sixth month.

Memory Selection: Be strong, all ye people of the land, saith the LORD, and work: for I am with you, saith the LORD of hosts: . . . my spirit remaineth among you: fear ye not. (Haggai 2:4-5)

Memory Selection: Take courage, all you people of the land, says the LORD; work, for I am with you, says the LORD of hosts. . . . My Spirit abides among you; fear not. (Haggai 2:4-5)

The Scripture and the Main Question —Charles M. Laymon

WHEN THE TIME IS RIGHT

The old adage "strike while the iron is hot" goes back to the horseshoe days when the village blacksmith heated the metal to a certain temperature to make it soft. Then he struck it, blow by blow, and, while the sparks flew, fashioned it into the familiar shape. The blows must be struck at just the right time. A little sooner or a little later and the metal would have been too hard.

This is a kind of parable. In life's decisions there is also a period or even a moment when the time is right to act. To be premature is to lose out; to procrastinate is to fail.

Abraham Lincoln signed the Emancipation Proclamation in a scrawly script. He had been through a difficult day and was tired. Receiving calls and shaking hands had made his arm stiff and numb. He said, "Now this signature is one that will be closely examined, and if they find my hand trembled they will say, 'He had some compunctions.' But anyway, it is going to be done." And he signed the paper. The time was right; postponement could have been fatal for the cause.

This same urgency was in the words of Haggai as he spoke for God concerning the rebuilding of the Temple. The Jews had procrastinated, and the prophet said, "This people say the time has not yet come to rebuild the house of the LORD." (Haggai 1:2) But the time had come, and God wanted the Temple to be erected immediately. The building of the house of worship was all-important.

OUR NEEDS AND GOD'S

The real reason the Jews had not rebuilt the Temple was not that it was not the proper time but that they had spent too much on themselves. There was no time or money left for God. Therefore Haggai asked them, "Is it a time for you yourselves to dwell in your paneled houses, while this house [the Temple] lies in ruins?" (verse 4)

Haggai was insisting that the way we spend our money is a religious concern. Is not this the reason Jesus had more to say about money than any other subject? That our needs are great cannot be denied. Certainly proper housing is one of them. The question the prophet asked, however, implied that excessive sums had been spent on paneled houses while the Temple lay in ruins.

The story is told of a Jew who was visiting in the home of a wealthy Christian. All about were signs of luxury. When the visitor, who was usually a brilliant conversationalist, remained rather silent, his irritated hostess asked, "Why are you so dumb?" He answered, "I am studying a problem which I cannot solve. I have been looking at these gold dishes, this fine linen, these splendid waiters, your great diamonds, and wondering what you Christians are going to do with the camel question."

Jesus' word that it is as difficult for a camel to pass through the eye of a needle as for a rich man to enter the Kingdom has stumped Christians for centuries. Impossible? No—*difficult*. The temptation to spend upon ourselves first and to spend upon God second remains to this very day.

GIVING AND GETTING

Haggai taught that there was a law of commensurate return at work in the area of giving to God. Because the Jews had spent much upon themselves and neglected the Temple, they would be rewarded in kind: "You have sown much, and harvested little; you eat, but you never have enough; you drink, but you never have your fill; you clothe yourselves, but no one is warm; and he who earns wages earns wages to put them into a bag with holes." (verse 6)

The generous spirit attracts generosity. By contrast, in time the Scrooges get the Scrooge treatment themselves. Sowing and reaping in kind is a principle of life that can be seen all about us.

This principle of commensurate return is well illustrated by George Frederic Watts's famous painting *"Sic Transit Gloria."* On the edge of the canvas, which pictures a man stretched out on his bier, are the words, "What I spent I had; what I saved I lost; what I gave I have." In the latter case there were no bags with holes.

Which shall it be, the house of God or my own house? Is there not room for both? Is Haggai asking us to neglect our own homes, or is he warning us against the excesses of selfishness at the expense of God's church?

A HOUSE FOR GOD'S GLORY

Why was God interested in the rebuilding of the Temple? Haggai answers this question eloquently. The new building would make it possible for God to appear in his glory (1:8, 12-15).

Churches are temples where men may come to find God and experience fellowship with him. To be sure, God is everywhere; but if we do not find him somewhere, we will not find him anywhere. For this reason we dedicate our churches in a formal service for God's indwelling and use.

Willard R. Sperry told of a priest who was found scrubbing a remote spot in the church that no one could see. When asked why he was doing this task, which seemed like a waste of precious time since no one ever saw the place, he replied, "No, no one ever comes in here. We keep this place clean for the eye of God."

The holiness of the sanctuary brings home to us a sense of God's presence. The church structure is not an assembly hall. We must enter it with the awe that grows out of our expectation to meet God there. This attitude will make all the difference in the world in our experience of worship and in the quality of our listening. Even the sermon will take on a new meaning for both the minister and the congregation if we believe that the glory of God is to be found in his holy temple.

Helping Adults Become Involved —Harlan R. Waite

Preparation of Self and Class

Although only twelve verses are printed, the entire Book of Haggai (thirty-eight verses) should be read in preparation for this session.

Acquaint yourself with the historical background of Haggai's prophecy. Since Haggai and Zechariah were contemporaries, the background material for this lesson will also serve for the remaining lessons of this series. *The Interpreter's Bible* is a good source for this information. Highlights include the fall of the Babylonian Empire to the Persians under Cyrus, the encouragement given to conquered peoples to pursue their religious traditions, and the return of some of the exiles to Jerusalem.

Also, read the Book of Ezra for general background. Haggai and Zechariah are mentioned in Ezra 5:1 and 6:14.

Note that although Ezra indicates the rebuilding of the Temple began very shortly after the return of the exiles to Jerusalem, Haggai and Zechariah both date it some seventeen years later. Scholars are agreed that Haggai and Zechariah are more accurate in their dating than Ezra, who wrote approximately two hundred years after the event. Note the reasons given for the delay: (1) remnants of the foundations of the old, burned-out Temple remained, and the people had grown accustomed to this makeshift arrangement; (2) war between Egypt and Persia brought Persian armies to Palestine, and this was a distressing and disruptive influence; and (3) the returning exiles were very poor (Haggai 1:5-6, 10-11), and they were so preoccupied with the difficulties of making a living that they did not give attention to the rebuilding of the Temple.

Pay special attention to the messianic hope expressed by Haggai. Two events seemed especially important to Haggai in this respect. In the first place there were many revolts against the rule of the Persians. This led Haggai to think that in their shifting loyalties the nations were ripe for the coming of the messianic age. Second, Zerubbabel, appointed by King Darius as governor of Judah, was of the royal house of David. Haggai seemed certain that he was indeed the long-expected Messiah.

Presenting the Main Question

Dr. Laymon states the main question this way: Why build a church in a community? Two men were discussing the building of a new sanctuary. One asked the other, "Why are you so interested in building a new church here?" His friend replied, "It is an important way to make my faith visible. No matter how much I may try, my personal witness is expressed directly to relatively few people. Those who know my faith and are affected by it are, for the most part, members of my family, my circle of friends, and my associates at work. However, through participation in the building of a church, I can join with many others in affirming my Christian faith and the importance of the Christian life style in a way that speaks dramatically to an entire community." Relate this story as an illustration of the main question.

Another way of presenting the main question is to show your class a filmstrip entitled *Spokesmen for God* (see page 128). This filmstrip deals with three Old Testament prophets, the background of their time, and their messages. The prophets selected for this study are Elijah, Micah, and Haggai. Contrasting Haggai with the other two prophets will in itself help your students understand Haggai more easily.

Developing the Lesson

Review briefly what has been said about the role of the prophet in the introductory lessons to the studies of Jeremiah and Ezekiel. Point out to the class members the special irony in the contrast between the messages of the prophets. Jeremiah and Ezekiel, although they were confident of the re-establishment of Israel, declared it to be God's will that Jerusalem, including the Temple, would be destroyed. Now Haggai declares that it is God's will that the Temple be built up. Recall Jeremiah 1:10, which indicates that in such crises God is in both the destruction and the rebuilding, the plucking up and the planting.

At this point, call for the report on the historical background that you assigned last week. Then call for a report on the interviews assigned last week. List the reasons those interviewed feel a church building is important. Pose this question to the class as well and let the members add their reasons to the list.

How do these reasons compare with Haggai's reasons for rebuilding the Temple? Note that in 1:8 Haggai suggests that he wants Israel to be ready for God's coming. Even though he had in mind the coming of the Messiah in a political sense, his motivation may be suggestive to us. Is the church building a tool by which we help persons prepare to receive God in their individual and community lives? Observe that there is a well-established principle in education, namely, that children learn better when they have had certain experiences that make them ready to learn. For example, among children who are beginning to read, the child who has seen a cow is better able to understand the meaning of the word *cow* than the child who has never seen one. Reading readiness has its religious counterpart. The church building is a tool to be used by the Christian community to provide Christian experiences on which children, youth,

and adults can base their continuing education in the Christian faith.

Recall the example of the man who was interested in the church building because it made his faith visible. Ask your class members to explore the ways in which we give visibility to many things we believe in. We erect national monuments; we display the flag; we wear lapel buttons; we erect magnificent buildings to house the headquarters of our business enterprises; we make or buy attractive clothing to express our own personalities. What does this have to say about making our faith visible in a church building?

Conclude the discussion by moving beyond the building to the church as a community. Recall Paul's point of view that the true building is made up of the people in the church. How much of ourselves do we invest in this redeeming fellowship?

Helping Class Members Act

Ask your class members to spend some time in the coming week exploring their own motivations: Why do they support their church? Or why do they not support their church more than they do? Have them consider the fact that most churches are in financial difficulty today. Point out that both economic and spiritual factors are involved and that neither stands in isolation. Have them consider such questions as: How much importance do I attach to my church? Is it my primary commitment? Have I considered a tithe of my money, time, and talent? What are my real life priorities? Would Haggai have been speaking to me?

Planning for Next Sunday

Read Zechariah 1:1-6; 4, the background Scriptures for next Sunday's lesson. Read also Amos and Micah, with special reference to Amos 5:21-24. Compare the messages of these earlier prophets with those of Haggai and Zechariah.

Ask your students to collect news clippings from a local newspaper that illustrate how people use or misuse power today.

LESSON 12   FEBRUARY 18

More Than Human Power

Background Scripture: Zechariah 1:1-6; 4

The Main Question —Charles M. Laymon

Our age has been referred to as the Power Age. Almost in the same breath it has been called the Atomic Age. Again men have aptly named it the Space Age. We can take our choice of these names because each points to the fact of power.

The big question, however, is how are we going to use this power? Unused, it is simply a potential this or that. Employed badly, it is destructive and deadly; employed well, it is life, joy, and peace.

When President Harry S. Truman gave the order to drop the first atomic bomb, the world was suddenly thrust into a new era. Like a great divide, it created a new before and a new after. Just as we have a B.C. and an A.D. in relation to the Christian era, scientifically speaking we now have a B.A.B. (before atomic bomb) and an A.A.B. (after atomic bomb).

Albert Einstein has pointed out our dilemma: "The objective of avoiding total destruction must have priority over any other objective." [16] The scientist was thinking of the power threat that hangs over us.

It takes character to control the use of such power as we possess today. How shall we build this character? Is our own will-power sufficient? Do we need God's power to do this?

The biblical passage that follows deals helpfully with the power issue, even though it was written centuries before our time.

As You Read the Scripture —Floyd V. Filson

Zechariah 1:1. *In the eighth month, in the second year of Darius:* Zechariah's prophetic messages date from 520 to 518 B.C. Zechariah thus was a contemporary of Haggai. God's call to Zechariah to become a prophet came *in the second year* of the reign of Darius I over the Persian Empire, which included Palestine. The *eighth month,* called Bul, fell in the latter part of October and the early part of November.

[16] *Out of My Later Years* (Philosophical Library, 1950), p. 175.

214

Zechariah is named with Haggai in Ezra 5:1 and 6:14. They were earnestly concerned for the rebuilding of the Temple at Jerusalem. Zechariah probably was the son of Iddo, as Ezra 5:1; 6:14 and Nehemiah 12:16 suggest, though here he is called the son of Berechiah and grandson of Iddo.

The Book of Zechariah has two parts, Chapters 1 through 8, which deal with the situation and work of Zechariah the prophet, and Chapters 9 through 14, which are best understood as a later addition to the book and as the work of a different writer. Characteristic of Chapters 1 through 8 are the eight visions they contain. The fifth one, reported in Chapter 4, is discussed below.

Verses 2-3. *The* LORD *was very angry with your fathers:* The word of the Lord comes to Zechariah and reminds him that *the* LORD *was very angry with your fathers,* and so he let them be defeated and taken into exile. Presumably this anger has continued; for even though the exiles who wanted to return to their homeland have been permitted to do so, the word of the Lord begins with an urgent call to them to repent and return in loyalty to their God. If they do so, he will return to them; that is, he will again show them his favor and bless them.

Chapter 4:1. *And the angel . . . waked me:* The angel calls Zechariah to see the fifth of the eight visions the book contains. Such references to the angel seem intended to emphasize the lofty and superior nature of God as compared with finite, sinful men.

Verses 2-3. *And he said to me, "What do you see?"* The vision is not at first explained; however, in verse 10b the seven lamps on the lampstand are said to be "the eyes of the LORD, which range through the whole earth," so that nothing men do escapes his notice. In verses 11-14 the two olive trees are said to be "the two anointed who stand by the LORD of the whole earth." This seems to be a reference to the two leaders of God's people, Zerubbabel the governor and Joshua the high priest (3:1; 4:7-10; 6:11).

In this passage, however, the attention is centered not on the high priest Joshua but on Zerubbabel. In verses 1-10a we find a group of several short sayings concerning him. It often is thought that this group of sayings is a later insertion by an editor and not part of the original account of the fifth vision. The main point, however, is that these sayings center on Zerubbabel and his role in carrying out God's plan.

Verse 6. *This is the word of the* LORD *to Zerubbabel:* The realization of God's purpose by Zerubbabel will be due not to human might and power but to the powerful working of the Spirit of God.

Verse 7. *What are you, O great mountain?* Difficulties as formidable as a great mountain will become a plain before Zerubbabel, and he will put the keystone of the Temple in place while the people cry out how beautiful the building is.

Verse 9. *The hands of Zerubbabel have laid the foundation of this house:* The prophet reports that *the hands of Zerubbabel have laid the foundation* of the Temple and promises that "his hands shall also complete it." The rebuilding project will be fully realized. When the building work is completed, the people will know that the Lord of hosts has really sent the prophet to foretell the completion of the rebuilding program.

Verse 10a. *For whoever has despised the day of small things shall rejoice:* There had been skeptics. During the early and hesitant stages of the rebuilding of the Temple, which evidently was not carried out without a lull, they had thought that the rebuilding program would never be completed and had looked with scorn on *the day of small things*. But the lull was to prove only temporary, and even the skeptics would rejoice when they saw Zerubbabel put the last stone of the sacred building into place.

Selected Scripture

King James Version	Revised Standard Version

Zechariah 1:1-3

1 In the eighth month, in the second year of Darius, came the word of the Lord unto Zechariah, the son of Berechiah, the son of Iddo the prophet, saying,

2 The Lord hath been sore displeased with your fathers.

3 Therefore say thou unto them, Thus saith the Lord of hosts; Turn ye unto me, saith the Lord of hosts, and I will turn unto you, saith the Lord of hosts.

Zechariah 4:1-10a

1 And the angel that talked with me came again, and waked me, as a man that is wakened out of his sleep,

2 And said unto me, What seest thou? And I said, I have looked, and behold a candlestick all of gold, with a bowl upon the top of it, and his seven lamps thereon, and seven pipes to the seven lamps, which are upon the top thereof:

3 And two olive trees by it, one upon the right side of the bowl, and the other upon the left side thereof.

4 So I answered and spake to the angel that talked with me, saying, What are these, my lord?

5 Then the angel that talked with me answered and said unto me, Knowest thou not what these be? And I said, No, my lord.

6 Then he answered and spake unto me, saying, This is the word of the Lord unto Zerubbabel, saying, Not

Zechariah 1:1-3

1 In the eighth month, in the second year of Darius, the word of the Lord came to Zechariah the son of Berechiah, son of Iddo, the prophet, saying, 2 "The Lord was very angry with your fathers. 3 Therefore say to them, Thus says the Lord of hosts: Return to me, says the Lord of hosts, and I will return to you, says the Lord of hosts.

Zechariah 4:1-10a

1 And the angel who talked with me came again, and waked me, like a man that is wakened out of his sleep. 2 And he said to me, "What do you see?" I said, "I see, and behold, a lampstand all of gold, with a bowl on the top of it, and seven lamps on it, with seven lips on each of the lamps which are on the top of it. 3 And there are two olive trees by it, one on the right of the bowl and the other on its left." 4 And I said to the angel who talked with me, "What are these, my lord?" 5 Then the angel who talked with me answered me, "Do you not know what these are?" I said, "No, my lord." 6 Then he said to me, "This is the word of the Lord to Zerubbabel: Not by might, nor by power, but by my Spirit, says the Lord of hosts. 7 What are you, O great mountain? Before Zerubbabel you shall become a plain; and he shall

216

by might, nor by power, but by my spirit, saith the LORD of hosts.

7 Who art thou, O great mountain? before Zerubbabel thou shalt become a plain: and he shall bring forth the headstone thereof with shoutings, crying, Grace, grace unto it.

8 Moreover the word of the Lord came unto me, saying,

9 The hands of Zerubbabel have laid the foundation of this house; his hands shall also finish it; and thou shalt know that the LORD of hosts hath sent me unto you.

10 For who hath despised the day of small things? for they shall rejoice, and shall see the plummet in the hand of Zerubbabel.

Memory Selection: Not by might, nor by power, but by my spirit, saith the LORD of hosts. (Zechariah 4:6)

bring forward the top stone amid shouts of 'Grace, grace to it!' " 8 Moreover the word of the LORD came to me, saying, 9 "The hands of Zerubbabel have laid the foundation of this house; his hands shall also complete it. Then you will know that the LORD of hosts has sent me to you. 10 For whoever has despised the day of small things shall rejoice, and shall see the plummet in the hand of Zerubbabel."

Memory Selection: Not by might, nor by power, but by my Spirit, says the LORD of hosts. (Zechariah 4:6)

The Scripture and the Main Question —Charles M. Laymon

A CALL TO RETURN

When the Hebrews returned to Jerusalem, they found a burned out shell of a city. In their eagerness to rebuild their homes they forgot the reconstruction of the Temple. The prophet Haggai, as we saw last week, summoned them to complete the restoration of this house of the Lord. But the work continued to remain undone; the people had lost heart for it.

Zechariah, a contemporary of Haggai, took up the cause. He talked of the messianic age and even regarded their leader, Zerubbabel, as the Messiah. In this high office Zerubbabel would complete the task of rebuilding the Temple.

What was needed most in this situation was power—soul power. More than returning to Jerusalem, the na-

tion needed to return to God. Hence Zechariah cried out: "Thus says the LORD of hosts: Return to me, says the LORD of hosts, and I will return to you, says the LORD of hosts." (Zechariah 1:3) If the people would do this, they would have both the incentive and the power to rebuild.

These words fairly burn with God's longing to be joined to his people. But they must first turn in his direction. Repentance must precede restoration. Then, as air rushes in to fill a vacuum, God would fill them with his spirit, presence, and power. He would forgive them and restore them to himself.

Forgiveness is a kind of miracle. Mark Twain once said that it is "the fragrance the violet sheds on the heel that has crushed it." Forgiveness is fragrant and tender but strong as steel bonds.

THE WORLD COMMUNITY OF GOD

The outreach of Zechariah's dream of a restored Jerusalem moved beyond the walls of the city and envisioned a world community. God's presence would be in the whole earth. The seven lamps with seven lips on the golden lampstand, which he saw in his vision, carried this idea, seven being a number that symbolized completeness (4:2).

The building of a world community does not happen easily. A brief look at the problems of the League of Nations and the United Nations will show this. Even the regional organizations of SEATO and NATO find it difficult to hold together. A dream is one thing; making it come true is another.

The prophets, including Zechariah, knew that such dreams as that of the world community of God would not come true by themselves. To them it was God's dream and would require God's power.

God does not waste his power; only those who really need it may be given it. As Halford E. Luccock, in *Marching Off the Map*, has reminded us, "He gives it to those who have tackled something so big, so overwhelming, that their own resources are quite insufficient." But when men have actually tackled such a task, Luccock continues, "there comes the rushing of the mighty wind of the spirit." [17]

GOD'S POWER AND MAN'S

Man has power—no doubt about it! His power to destroy or to build is greater during this century than in all the other centuries put together. He can make the desert blossom as a rose and turn arid plains into a Gar-

[17] (Harper & Brothers, 1952), p. 147.

den of Eden. At his bidding projectiles can circle both the earth and the moon. On the other hand, at the touch of a button man can destroy himself.

But there are limits. We have not yet learned to control ourselves and to live at peace with the rest of the world. The world community of God of which Zechariah dreamed remains to be built. It rests stillborn in the womb of history. We have not succeeded in bringing into being the kingdom of God. Why not? The answer is sobering yet simple; we cannot do it in our own strength, and we have not yet completely trusted God.

The famous French philosopher and satirist Voltaire once remarked, "To whatever side you turn, you are forced to acknowledge your own ignorance and the boundless power of the Creator." Although these words were spoken in another age, nothing has been discovered since to cancel their truth.

Centuries earlier Zechariah said it in another and unforgettable way, "Not by might, nor by power, but by my Spirit, says the LORD of Hosts." (4:6) The prophet was speaking to Zerubbabel, who had been called upon to rebuild the nation's life at Jerusalem. An impossible task! But was it really impossible with the power of God's Spirit?

THE POWER PROBLEM

The problem facing those persons who have power is that they either take it too seriously or do not take it seriously enough. To take power too seriously leads to self-intoxication. A friend of mine once said that if you visited a business executive and saw a statue of Napoleon sitting on his desk, you should get yourself out as gracefully and as hurriedly as possible. Such an executive could not be trusted to be just. Too much ego! Not to take power seriously, however, is to be irresponsible. Whether it is a simple assignment as a committee member or the performance of an act of trust on a national or international level, as long as the power to act is in our hands, we are stewards under God. This is the Christian view.

Human power takes many forms—political, social, physical, military, emotional, intellectual, and moral. There is also power that is more than human—spiritual power that comes from God. Some power corrupts, but other power ennobles. Such is the power of God.

Helping Adults Become Involved —Harlan R. Waite

Preparation of Self and Class

The background Scripture for this lesson is Zechariah 1:1-6; 4. Read these passages carefully, and make note of the ideas expressed as you read. Consult *The Interpreter's Bible* and the materials in your denominational student quarterlies for additional help.

Give some thought to the way in which power expresses itself in today's world. If your class is at all typical, there will be a deep feeling of powerlessness among your students. What can we do to help solve some of the pressing problems that beset the world and from which we all suffer? How do we counter the power plays of special interest groups in our society that seem to be thinking only of themselves?

As you think about these needs of your students, be aware of our natural inclination to resent the power tactics of others while we defend our own. One of the needs your students undoubtedly have in common with other Christians is the need to recognize how they themselves employ power in managing their lives, even in manipulating other people.

Presenting the Main Question

If your class is in the habit of singing to open its session, use the hymn "O Worship the King." It has several references to God's power and might, but it puts God's power in the context of his gentle use of his might to express his loving concern. Here is one of the keys to the meaning of this lesson, which stresses that our accomplishments are "not by might, nor by power, but by my Spirit." (Zechariah 4:6)

Illustrate the problem of power by recounting the American ideal for the use of power in a democracy. One of the fundamental tenets of faith for a democratic people is that power shall be distributed as broadly as possible. The first step was to wrest the power of government from a king and place it in the hands of a body representative of the people. From that time to this the history of America has been characterized by attempts to broaden the base of power. In our early days power was the exclusive possession of people with education and wealth. Later, certain groups of poor people received political power. Then power was granted to women and to members of ethnic minorities. Today's power struggles are a continuation of the effort to broaden not only the base of power but the areas over which that power can be applied. Use newspaper clippings gathered this past week to illustrate this point.

Summarize the main question, and hence the central point of this lesson, by suggesting that our responsibility as Christians in a democratic society is threefold: give the power to the people; give the people to God; and thus give the power to God.

Developing the Lesson

Through discussion, review the historical situation that provided the context for Zechariah's prophecies. Remind the class that he was a contemporary of Haggai, and review the historical material covered in last week's lesson. Highlight especially the return of the exiles to Jerusalem, the attempt by Haggai and Zechariah to encourage the people to rebuild the Temple, and the pronouncement that the Messiah was indeed present in the person of Zerubbabel. In this latter connection recall Haggai 2:6-7, 21-23. There was unrest among the nations, rebellion against the Persian overlords; and this was seen as preceding the advent of the Messiah.

Notice that Zechariah describes the Messiah as "the Branch" (3:8; 6:12). Inform your class that the same term was used in Isaiah 4:2 and Jeremiah 23:5; 33:15. This is one of the demonstrations that the expectation of a Messiah was a long-term and deeply rooted hope in Israel.

Spend a few moments talking about the concern of both Haggai and Zechariah that the Temple be rebuilt. Contrast this with the attitudes of Amos and Micah (the reading assigned last week), for example, who had little use for the Temple. Refer the class to the classic statement in Amos 5:21-24: "I take no delight in your solemn assemblies. . . . But let justice roll down like waters." Observe that although Haggai had little

of the moral and ethical message of the earlier prophets, Zechariah combined an interest in rebuilding the religious institution with a sense of its moral responsibility in social matters. Sin must be eliminated from the community before the Messiah comes. Read Zechariah 5:1-4 for an illustration of this concern.

Zechariah was interested in having the right kind of church. Recall that Amos felt power had been considered by the Temple authorities to be an end in itself. The institution, often referred to today as the establishment, seemed to exist for its own sake. It used power to control people for its own institutional purposes. The institution was more concerned with its own image than with the image of God that might be seen in its work. Contrast this attitude with the attitude of Jesus. He had the same idea about the Temple that Amos had had. He realized that the needs of God's children were being made secondary to the importance of the religious institution. Jesus expressed this prophetic moral concern on one specific occasion when he said, "The sabbath was made for man, not man for the sabbath." (Mark 2:27) Ask the class members to discuss this question: Are we concerned with using power for the achievement of social justice, or is our real goal in life simply to achieve power?

At this point, focus the discussion directly on the main question: How do we build the character necessary to control power? Is our will-power sufficient? Do we need the help of God's power? Refer to Dr. Laymon's discussion of this question above. Then read aloud Zechariah 4:6: "Not by might, nor by power, but by my Spirit, says the LORD of hosts."

Ask the class members to discuss the ways in which the use of power is

220

most visible today. War is perhaps the most obvious, with its use of armed might. Police protection utilizes the power of physical restraint, and courts apply the power of legal restraint. The power of public opinion is wielded by special interest groups: employee organizations, political campaigners, women's rights groups, ethnic minorities, and so forth. Less visible to the public, yet very real, is the political power exerted on legislative bodies by organized groups representing the entire spectrum of American life. Behind the scenes, hosts of inconspicuous citizens exert their power for good or ill through a threat or a promise, a good or a bad example, a vindictive or a forgiving spirit, an act of hostility or an act of love. Recall Dr. Laymon's quotation from Mark Twain, who described forgiveness as "the fragrance the violet sheds on the heel that has crushed it." This is real power.

Have the class members discuss these questions: How does one tell whether the power that all of us wield is of God or of man? Among the uses of power suggested above, and as identified by the class members through discussion, which ones fall in the class of "might" or "power" as conceived by Zechariah and which ones fall in the "power of the Spirit"? What standards does Christianity have to offer for making this distinction (for example, the Sermon on the Mount, the ideal of sacrificial service, the concept of love as expressed in 1 Corinthians 13)?

Helping Class Members Act

Ask your class members to take some time during the following week to read and reflect upon Ephesians 6:10-20. What does this passage have to say about power and its use?

Planning for Next Sunday

Inform the class that next week's topic is "The Shape of Things to Come." Ask them to read Zechariah 8. Since only a portion of the chapter is printed, ask one of your students to read Zechariah 8:9-10, 14-23, and be prepared to report. Recruit someone to present a report on Katherine Lee Bates and why she wrote "O Beautiful for Spacious Skies." An excellent source is *The Gospel in Hymns* by Albert Edward Bailcy. Ask this reporter to be sure to note the social conditions prevailing in the city of Chicago that contrasted so dramatically with "the alabaster city" Miss Bates saw at the Columbian Exposition.

The Shape of Things to Come

Background Scripture: Zechariah 8; 13; 14:9

The Main Question —Charles M. Laymon

Whither America? This is the question we are asking ourselves today. Some persons look back to the glory we once knew; others look ahead to the new order that shall be—must be. We cannot remain static. Growth and change are our only hope of survival.

These were the sentiments expressed in a young adult group that had been discussing Christian citizenship. The members were concerned for the nation they would be leaving to their children.

One of their number quoted words from Gunnar Myrdal, taken from his work *An American Dilemma:* "Mankind is sick of fear and disbelief, or pessimism and cynicism. It needs the youthful moralistic optimism of America." [18]

"Right," said another, "but where is this moral optimism? After two world wars, with Korea and Vietnam in addition, I've just about used up all the hope I ever had for the future."

At this point a young mother interjected, "You have left out something— rather Someone. If we believe in God, don't we just have to believe in better things to come?"

Do we? Is God right now concerned with the shape of things to come? What is he doing about it? What can we do about it?

The biblical passage for this lesson contains some guidelines for answering these questions.

As You Read the Scripture —Floyd V. Filson

Zechariah 8 contains nine sections introduced by the formula *Thus says the* LORD *of hosts.* Five other times we find shorter forms—*says the* LORD *of hosts* or *thus says the* LORD or *says the* LORD. These formulas emphasize that the prophetic utterances come from the Lord; they are not merely human ideas.

Zechariah 8:1-2. *I am jealous for Zion with great jealousy:* The term *Zion* is a name for Jerusalem. The Lord is *jealous* and full of wrath when Zion is not faithful and loyal to him. But part of God's being jealous is that if Zion puts faith in him, as the prophet expects her to do, God will be zealous for her good (see Joel 2:18).

Verse 3. *I will return to Zion:* God's presence and power will bring blessing to the city, which is to be renamed "the faithful city" and "the mountain of the LORD of hosts." The renamed city will express in its life and worship the holiness of God.

Verses 4-5. *Old men and old women shall again sit in the streets of Jerusalem:* At that time, when there was no clear faith in a rich life beyond the grave, long life was considered a special blessing, a sign of God's goodness (see Exodus 20:12; Isaiah 65:19-20). The prophet assured the people that the aged will sit safely in the streets of Jerusalem. Another picture of peace and freedom from danger will be the streets full of children playing happily together.

Verse 6. *If it is marvelous in the sight of the remnant:* Such a blessed life in Jerusalem may seem marvelous, especially to those to whom this verse is directed. They have seen disaster and hardship. So the picture of coming peace and blessing can easily seem marvelous and even too difficult to them. But not to God. He surely will bring that happy time.

Verses 7-8. *I will save my people from the east country and from the west*

18 (Harper & Row, 1967), p. 1021.

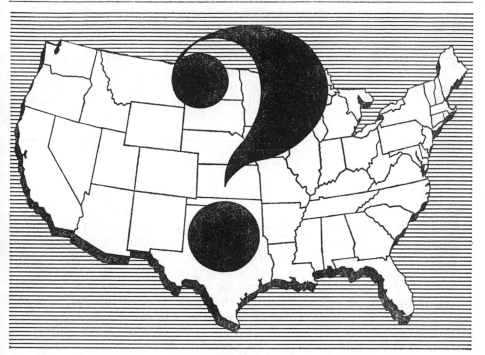

country: God will save his people and bring them back *from the east country
and from the west country.* The *east country* must be Babylonia and all places
east of Palestine where captured Israelites had been settled. There is no country just west of Palestine; on that side lies the Mediterranean Sea. Probably
Egypt, southwest of Palestine, is meant by this reference to the *west country.*
The meaning evidently is that in the coming days described by Zechariah the
exiles from Jerusalem and nearby cities will be brought back to their homeland. There they will dwell in Jerusalem, a hint that no huge numbers of
exiles are expected to return, or they would also be promised other places to
live throughout Palestine. In their faithful, upright, and loyal life in Jerusalem the returned exiles will gladly be God's people; and he will graciously be
their God. His covenant with his people will be renewed. (Compare Isaiah
43:5-6; Jeremiah 31:33.)

Verses 11-13. *I will not deal with the remnant of this people as in the
former days:* The reference to *the remnant* of God's people recalls the loss of
life when Jerusalem fell and many of her people were taken into exile. It recalls also that when the Persian rulers permitted the exiles to return home,
only part of them chose to do so. War, exile, and life in a foreign land were
hard; so was the long journey to their homeland. But now God will not deal
with his people *as in the former days.* In the new day, it is predicted, his people will have peace, abundant crops, and dew needed to produce such harvests.

In the past times of captivity and hardship God's people had been referred to in cursing; they were despised as people deserving contempt. But now they will be referred to by others as a favored people of the God who enriches their life with good things. They will not only be saved and called blessed; they will also be a blessing to others. They will live in security, gratitude, and plenty. This promise is not only for the house of Judah, exiled in 587 B.C., but also for the house of Israel, the northern tribes of Samaria who had been taken into exile in 721 B.C. They will live without fear, with strong hands to carry on their new life in their own land.

Selected Scripture

King James Version

Zechariah 8:1-8, 11-13

1 Again the word of the LORD of hosts came to me, saying,

2 Thus saith the LORD of hosts; I was jealous for Zion with great jealousy, and I was jealous for her with great fury.

3 Thus saith the LORD; I am returned unto Zion, and will dwell in the midst of Jerusalem: and Jerusalem shall be called a city of truth; and the mountain of the LORD of hosts the holy mountain.

4 Thus saith the LORD of hosts; There shall yet old men and old women dwell in the streets of Jerusalem, and every man with his staff in his hand for very age.

5 And the streets of the city shall be full of boys and girls playing in the streets thereof.

6 Thus saith the LORD of hosts; If it be marvellous in the eyes of the remnant of this people in these days, should it also be marvellous in mine eyes? saith the LORD of hosts.

7 Thus saith the LORD of hosts; Behold, I will save my people from the east country, and from the west country;

8 And I will bring them, and they shall dwell in the midst of Jerusalem: and they shall be my people, and I will be their God, in truth and in righteousness.

Revised Standard Version

Zechariah 8:1-8, 11-13

1 And the word of the LORD of hosts came to me, saying, 2 "Thus says the LORD of hosts: I am jealous for Zion with great jealousy, and I am jealous for her with great wrath. 3 Thus says the LORD: I will return to Zion, and will dwell in the midst of Jerusalem, and Jerusalem shall be called the faithful city, and the mountain of the LORD of hosts, the holy mountain. 4 Thus says the LORD of hosts: Old men and old women shall again sit in the streets of Jerusalem, each with staff in hand for very age. 5 And the streets of the city shall be full of boys and girls playing in its streets. 6 Thus says the LORD of hosts: If it is marvelous in the sight of the remnant of this people in these days, should it also be marvelous in my sight, says the LORD of hosts? 7 Thus says the LORD of hosts: Behold, I will save my people from the east country and from the west country; 8 and I will bring them to dwell in the midst of Jerusalem; and they shall be my people and I will be their God, in faithfulness and in righteousness. . . ."

11 But now I will not be unto the residue of this people as in the former days, saith the LORD of hosts.

12 For the seed shall be prosperous; the vine shall give her fruit, and the ground shall give her increase, and the heavens shall give their dew; and I will cause the remnant of this people to possess all these things.

13 And it shall come to pass, that as ye were a curse among the heathen, O house of Judah, and house of Israel; so will I save you, and ye shall be a blessing: fear not, but let your hands be strong.

Memory Selection: They shall call on my name, and I will hear them: I will say, It is my people: and they shall say, The LORD is my God. (Zechariah 13:9)

11 "But now I will not deal with the remnant of this people as in the former days, says the LORD of hosts.

12 For there shall be a sowing of peace and prosperity; the vine shall yield its fruit, and the ground shall give its increase, and the heavens shall give their dew; and I will cause the remnant of this people to possess all these things. 13 And as you have been a byword of cursing among the nations, O house of Judah and house of Israel, so will I save you and you shall be a blessing. Fear not, but let your hands be strong."

Memory Selection:
They will call on my name,
    and I will answer them.
I will say, "They are my people";
    and they will say, "The LORD is
    my God."   (Zechariah 13:9)

The Scripture and the Main Question —Charles M. Laymon

WHEN LIGHTS ARE LOW

A pessimistic scientist said in 1893 that all the great discoveries had been made. He believed that no new phenomena would be found, only more exact measurements of the old remained to be made. Yet it was after that time that the discoveries of X-rays, radioactivity, and the electron were made.

The Jews in Zechariah's day were not scientists, but many were in the same mood as the scientist discussed above. They expected nothing new. Discouragement lay heavy upon them. To rebuild Jerusalem and the Temple, as well as to re-establish the life of the nation, seemed out of the question.

Such are the times when lights are low. What is needed is something to hold to. False optimism will only irri-

tate, and Pollyanna platitudes will only lead to more discouragement.

Only God can lift man from such depression as the Jews were experiencing in this interim period following their return from Babylonia. The delegation that came to Zechariah (Zechariah 7:1-3) to consult the prophet concerning fasts as a means of restoring their spirits was told by the prophet that what God wanted instead was to show justice, kindness, and mercy toward the widows, the fatherless, the strangers, and the poor (verses 9-10). Here was their renewal, and here was the key to their future.

THE FAITHFUL AND HOLY CITY

I asked my students this question recently: What do you think God is doing today? They seem startled at my question; it had not occurred to them to think along these lines. After all, who among us would be able to say what God is doing today?

In discussing the matter we did agree on the following: Wherever there is injustice, God is working for justice; wherever there is cruelty, God is working for kindness; wherever there is war, God is working for peace; and wherever there is ignorance, God is working for truth. These same conclusions would apply to God's work in the renewal of the city of Jerusalem.

When God told Zechariah that he was working to make Jerusalem a faithful and holy city, he was referring to a small community at best—simple in structure and almost rural in character. Compared to a modern city with its high-rise apartments, tall office buildings, intricate traffic patterns, and political involvements, this city that David had founded was a relatively small community. The forces within her walls that affected the lives of persons were nothing compared to the erosion that works upon persons in a modern city.

Does this mean that God's call to make Jerusalem a faithful and holy city does not apply to our cities today? Not at all. Our need is even greater. Truman B. Douglass in *The New World of Urban Man* faces up to the challenge of urban life today and concludes: "In short, the success or failure of the city must be judged by what it does to and for this creature, man. . . ." [19]

A Family Portrait

A man of my acquaintance said that when he retired he wanted to live in a typical community where there were children, youth, young adults, middle adults, and older adults. He did not want to be segregated among older people.

The restored Jerusalem was to be just like the city my friend desired. It was to be a community where "old men and old women shall again sit in the streets [no automobiles], . . . each with staff in hand for very age. And the streets of the city shall be full of boys and girls playing in its streets." (8:4-5)

Zechariah seems to have been picturing the new Jerusalem as a city of families. The family is still with us. Modern life has made great demands upon it. Yet there is no institution to take its place, because none can do what the family does to enrich life. Here, as Ross Snyder says in *On Becoming Human*, "All ages profit. There could be no worse world for adults than one without young people or children, nothing worse for young people than a world only of teenagers—with no adults or children around." [20]

What will happen to the family in the future remains to be seen. Whatever changes may come, the new world will continue to need the tenderness of childhood, the adventurous spirit of youth, the strength and stability of adults, and the wisdom of old age.

Peace and Plenty

The ingredients of the shape of things to come as Zechariah presented them included the building of a faithful and holy city and the restoration of normal family living. But this was not all; there was also to come a time of peace and plenty: "There shall be a sowing of peace and prosperity; the vine shall yield its fruit, and the ground shall give its increase, and the heavens shall give their dew." (8:12)

The Hebrews did not look to Nature, spelled with a capital *N*, for their sustenance; instead, they looked

[19] (United Church Press, 1965), p. 46.

[20] (Abingdon Press, 1967), p. 90.

to the God of nature. They personalized the source of supply. This brought them an increased sense of closeness to God and made the growing of crops and the raising of herds sacramental. It has sometimes been said that rural people feel the closeness of God more acutely than those who live in the city. They deal not with the systems of nature but with the God of nature.

Sir Walter Scott was a great lover of the outdoors. His home was nestled among the hills of Scotland. On his drives to Edinburgh there was one spot from which he could see across the countryside. He stopped there so frequently that on the occasion of his funeral his horses, pulling the family carriage, stopped automatically when they came to this site.

Scott found God in nature and once wrote in "On the Setting Sun":

We often praise the evening clouds,
And tints so gay and bold,
But seldom think upon our God,
Who tinged these clouds with gold.

Zechariah thought constantly upon God's handiwork in nature and made this a part of his dream of the future.

Helping Adults Become Involved —Harlan R. Waite

Preparation of Self and Class

The background Scripture for this week's lesson is Zechariah 8; 13; and 14:9. Read these passages, and make note of the basic themes.

Keep the attitudes of your class members in mind as you prepare. Are they inclined to be defensive of the shortcomings of our nation that other nations find so offensive? Are they hunting for some way to improve the character of this nation so that we can be more persuasive to the nations around us?

With the content of the Scripture passages and the needs of your students in mind read the commentaries on the lesson in the student materials in your denominational quarterlies. Turn also to The Interpreter's Bible for additional help.

Presenting the Main Question

Dr. Laymon has identified the main question in two words: Whither America? There are several secondary questions: Is God concerned with the shape of things to come? What is he doing about the future? What can we do about it?

Suggest that the first step in moving out toward a better future is to recognize what life is like now and to acknowledge that improvement is necessary. This is not always as simple as it may seem, for we are given to defending ourselves against critics. Recall that Amaziah the high priest ran Amos out of town because of the criticisms Amos had directed toward Temple worship (Amos 7:10-14). Have the class members recall from earlier discussions in this unit what happened to Jeremiah at the hands of the priests, the false prophets, and the people. Observe that we do not like to look at the ugliness in our lives; but if we are simply going to pretend that the ugliness is beautiful, there is no place for America to go. A brighter future must start with honest recognition of where we are, however lovely or ugly.

The mood of the lesson, however, should be kept on the positive side. While there is a certain moral sternness to Zechariah, the mood is basically promising. You may even consider using one of our national hymns as an occasion to celebrate our national heritage and our future, while at the same time recognizing its need for improvement. "O Beautiful for Spacious Skies" is an uplifting hymn that expresses gratitude for the blessings we enjoy in this country; but, at the same time, it offers a prayer to God to help us grow in spiritual integrity. The singing of this hymn is one way to open up the question of where America is going.

Developing the Lesson

Have the class members discuss the message of Zechariah in the passages of Scripture printed in the quarterlies. Since some verses from Chapter 8 are missing, ask the volunteer who accepted the assignment given last week to report on Zechariah 8:9-10, 14-23. Use the chalkboard to write down the major affirmations. As a clue, note that there are some nine passages introduced by the words "Thus says the LORD of hosts." You will find the following emphases: God, because of his close identification with Israel, is jealous for Zion. He promises to return, set the city up as a "mountain of the LORD" in the midst of the nations, and restore it to a free and happy state. Israel will be his people, and Yahweh (Jehovah) will be Israel's God in faithfulness and in righteousness. The antagonisms between people will cease, and there shall be peace and prosperity. This will require, however, that they meet the moral requirements of truth and justice and that they neither devise evil against one another nor indulge in false oaths. There is a wonderful climax to the chapter: men of other nations shall want to follow Israel because it is clear that God is with them. Following the analysis of Zechariah

8, ask your students to turn in their hymnals to "O Beautiful for Spacious Skies." At this point call for the report on the life of Katherine Lee Bates that you assigned last week. Be sure there is an emphasis in this report on the experience of Miss Bates's visit to the Columbian Exposition in Chicago in 1893, an "alabaster city" that presented a picture of what America at its most beautiful could be. The city appealed strongly to her feelings of patriotism mentioned in the last stanza. Following her visit to Chicago, Miss Bates went to the top of Pike's Peak in Colorado. The panorama of "purple mountain majesties" and the vista of golden wheat fields through which she passed on her way to Colorado gave her the inspiration for the first stanza. Both of these experiences moved her profoundly. She also thought of the thousands upon thousands who had not only crossed the Atlantic but also crossed the plains and the mountains to settle the land under difficult conditions. But Miss Bates was also thinking of those who led the search for a greater freedom—freedom from poverty, from voting restrictions, from ignorance, from slavery, and from many other circumstances that restricted the experience of liberty. These are the "pilgrims" and the "heroes" in the second and third stanzas.

Ask the class members to indicate the points at which the hymn suggests our need to improve. Note that in the fourth stanza the "patriot dream" is still unrealized and that human tears mar the vision. What is wrong with our cities? Perhaps the clues to the answers are in the refrains for each stanza. We need the grace to realize true brotherhood; flaws in our freedom need to be corrected by self-control and law; impurities in our success need to be purged by nobleness. When the class members have pointed these ideals out, discuss what they mean in terms of today's social problems.

In dealing with "the shape of things to come" this lesson emphasizes the social dimension of religion. Note that both Haggai and Zechariah are saying that we cannot experience healthy religion simply by living as individuals in our own homes, going about our own concerns. Religion finds its fulfillment as we become a community (symbolized by the Temple) and as we build the life of our nation upon the laws of God. Quote Zechariah 7: 9-10, which parallels Zechariah 8:16-17. Note that none of these laws is strictly individual. All are concerned with the way in which an individual relates to other individuals; thus they are matters of social relationship. Ask the class to recall the Ten Commandments (Deuteronomy 5:6-21 or Exodus 20:2-17). With the possible exception of the first three commandments, the commandments are social. All of them involve one's behavior in relation to other people. The fact that an individual, under God, is a member of a community is an unavoidable and essential article of faith. Although the Bible speaks much of one's personal inner life, the fulfillment of faith and life is to be found in love: "Thou shalt love the Lord thy God . . . and . . . thy neighbour as thyself." (Mark 12:30-31, KJV)

Close the lesson by singing once again the great national hymn that has been discussed in the lesson. Our focus is not so much on our sinfulness as on God's power to restore and redeem those who acknowledge their sins and who are committed to do something about them. In the singing of this hymn your class members can celebrate the blessings of God and his promises for the future.

Helping Class Members Act

Suggest that your class members have an extra meeting, perhaps in someone's home, to talk about some specific problems they could tackle in the attempt to create a new and better future. Suggest that the group may want to view a color filmstrip entitled *The Trap* (see page 128) and discuss its implications. The filmstrip presents a dramatic picture of one of the most dangerous problems facing the United States today—the immediate and long-range effect of poverty in an affluent society, a society that purports to respect the dignity and worth of each individual and the freedom of that individual for self-realization.

Planning for Next Sunday

Next Sunday's lesson will be the first in a unit entitled "Our Human Situation." The unit is one of three in a quarter's study on the theme "Affirmations of Our Faith." Ask your class members to read in advance the background Scripture for the first lesson: Genesis 1:1-26, 31; Psalms 24: 1-2; 104:24-30.

THIRD QUARTER
Affirmations of Our Faith

UNIT VI: OUR HUMAN SITUATION
Horace R. Weaver

THREE LESSONS

MARCH 4–18

It is probably a truism that never before in history has mankind been in greater need of affirmations of faith. Christians, as well as non-Christians, spend a great deal of their time saying what they do not believe. Saying why we do not believe in someone else's doctrinal statement is easy. It is always easy to destroy; it is difficult to build. Yet we are living in a time when persons of all ages want to know what other persons believe. Persons are searching for affirmations of faith. This does not mean that we need no longer raise questions about conflicting faiths. On the other hand, formulation of affirmations encourages the raising of questions—not to destroy faith, but to make way for precise, clear statements of our faith.

The thirteen lessons in this quarter present some basic Christian beliefs. The purpose of this study is to help persons achieve a better understanding and experience of the Christian faith. We need clarity and precision in thought, but we also seek to help persons commit themselves to their Christian faith. We want persons to experience the abundant life. We approach the "Affirmations of Our Faith" through three units of study. Unit VI includes three lessons on "Our Human Situation." Unit VII, "Christian Redemption," emphasizes man's need of redemption from the human situation in which he finds himself. Unit VIII deals with affirmations about "The Christian Life."

Unit VI, "Our Human Situation," seeks to help adults to be honest about our human situation today. As we listen to the news on radio and television and read about events in our newspapers and periodicals, we see that the motives that direct most of the decisions of our corporate and individual lives include selfishness, pride, greed, and hate. All mankind, and especially Christians, should be aware of those things that are at the heart of human nature. For only if they see these things to which all too many men and women are dedicated, can they point the way to the higher life in Christ.

The lesson for March 4, "This Is God's World," begins the quarter in a logical way, pointing out the fact that the good God made a good world. The Christian is guided to an understanding of the meaning and purpose of the world that God made. The lesson for March 11, "Man Is a Responsible Being," points out that the good God made man in his image—suggesting that man was created for goodness through right relationships with God and man. The lesson for March 18, "Man Has Gone Astray," helps us face the fact of man's refusal to abide by his God-given instincts and understandings. Man rebels against the good God and his purposes and in that rebellion separates himself, not only from God, but also from his fellow man.

Helpful background reading for this quarter may be found in the following books: *Since Silent Spring*, Frank Graham; *On Being Responsible*, edited by James M. Gustafson and James T. Laney; *From the Apple to the Moon*, Annie Vallotton; *God With Us*, Van Bogard Dunn; *Jesus, Man for Today*,

230

T. Ralph Morton; *The Renewal of Hope*, Howard Clark Kee; *Who Trusts in God*, Albert Outler; *Who Is This Jesus?* Daniel T. Niles; and *Faith in Search of Understanding*, John B. Magee.

Listed below are several audiovisual resources that would be valuable as you prepare not only the first unit but also lessons in other units on the affirmations of our faith. These resources have been carefully selected and correlated with the major themes of the lessons. Teachers who wish to use the aids should make plans sufficiently early to ensure proper scheduling and delivery. All prices are subject to change without notice. All these materials may be obtained from your denominational publishing house unless another source is denoted in the description. Because of the lapse of time between the printing of this book and the use of these materials some resources may not be available.

The Human Race. (See page 127.) (Unit VI)

The Late Great God. 16mm film, 27 min. An attempt is made to impeach God at a Malibu Beach party. Is God: dead or alive? out there or in here? aloof or involved? tyrannical or loving? The different notions of God are explored, and man's need for the real God of Scripture emerges. Rental: color, $16; black and white, $10, from Association Instructional Materials; 600 Madison Avenue; New York, New York 10022. (Unit VI)

Run! 16mm film, 16 min. This film presents an allegorical suggestion of destructive tendencies in high-pressure modern society and self-centered modern man. Panicked and unthinking, a harried man runs blindly through life, pausing for sustenance and tranquilizers, until he falls into a grave he has dug and buries himself. Rental: black and white, $12.50, from Mass Media Ministries; 2116 North Charles Street; Baltimore, Maryland 21218. (Unit VI)

Syzygy. 16mm film, 27 min. The story concerns a group representing a variety of segments in contemporary North American society who meet to discuss reconciliation. Rental: color, $12. (Unit VI)

The Antkeeper. (See page 127.) (Unit VII)

The Gift. 16mm film, 23 min. Produced almost in "animated painting," this film traces God's prime act of giving his Son. Next follows a sequence on the post-Resurrection history of the church, plus treatment of the many tensions of today's world. A final sequence then approaches the requirement of reconciliation of the whole man as our response to "The Gift." Rental: color, $9. (Units VII and VIII)

Parable. 16mm film, 22 min. This film views the world as a circus. A clown the central character, changes the life and attitudes of those around him by his deeds. He is quiet, loving, understanding, and constantly offering himself for others. In the end he redeems the circus community by his life and actions. Rental: color, $15, from Mass Media Ministries; 2116 North Charles Street; Baltimore, Maryland 21218. (Unit VII)

The Red Kite. 16mm film, 17 min. A young father is preoccupied with questions about life, death, and God. This film is a provocative examination of modern man, his society, and his search for security and faith. Rental: color, $8. (Unit VII)

Almost Neighbors. 16mm film, 34 min. This film shows family concerns for persons of varying racial, social, and economic groups. Rental: black and white, $10. (Unit VIII)

Come Back. (See page 127.) (Unit VIII)
Members One of Another. 35mm filmstrip, 59 frames, script. This filmstrip is an allegory showing that life is good when persons enter into one another's world. Sale: color, $5.50. (Unit VIII)
Right Here, Right Now. (See page 12.) (Unit VIII)
These Four Cozy Walls. 16mm film, 55 min. The setting of this film is a church in Dallas, Texas. The church is not a model but one where persons are struggling to discover meaning and mission in today's changing world. Rental: black and white, $20. (Unit VIII)

LESSON 1   MARCH 4

This Is God's World

Background Scripture: Genesis 1:1-26, 31; Psalms 24:1-2; 104:24-30

The Main Question —Charles M. Laymon

The story of Hart's Woods in Fairport, New York, will long be remembered in the struggle to save our natural resources from the inroads of commercialization. Here a group of concerned citizens fought to preserve a twenty-acre tract of land that had achieved an ecological balance taking more than a thousand years to produce. In this self-perpetuating forest, plant, insect, and animal life were sustaining one another. The large apartment complex that was to be built on the property would despoil a part of God's world.

The issue was brought to a referendum, calling for the town to buy the land. "Too much money—too high taxes" was the cry, and the group that was seeking to preserve the area lost. But the fight to preserve Hart's Woods achieved national notice and inspired other groups across the nation to take up similar conservation issues.

At the height of the struggle a junior high student said, "How can they destroy God's beautiful world? Don't they know that he cares?" His remark poses the question of whether this is God's world or man's. Are we owners or stewards of what God has made? Will we have to give an accounting to God for what we have done with his created world? What is our view of the universe in which God has placed us?

The following biblical passages will be helpful in facing these questions.

As You Read the Scripture —Claude H. Thompson[1]

The Scripture passages for today show that God created the world and placed man in it as his special servant. Two other passages may well be read:

[1] Claude H. Thompson: until his recent death professor of systematic theology, Candler School of Theology, Emory University, Atlanta, Georgia.

Isaiah 42:5-9 and 45:8, 12, 18. These verses show the relation of man to God's purpose in creating the world.

Genesis 1:1. *In the beginning God created the heavens and the earth:* This statement means God created everything. The Bible does not say *how* God did it, only *that* he did it. There is no conflict between a scientific view of how things came to be and the biblical claim that, however it was done, God did and does create all things.

Verse 26. *Then God said, "Let us make man in our image, after our likeness":* Throughout the Bible a kinship between man and God is reported. *Image,* of course, does not refer to physical likeness but refers to a moral and spiritual similarity. The perfection of this kinship is seen in Jesus Christ who "is the image of the invisible God." (Colossians 1:15)

Man is also the climax of creation, the highest product in the universe—personal life. Man's role is to "have dominion." That is, he is to control all that is below him—in nature. But he is, in turn, to bow before and worship the Creator-God alone.

THIS IS GOD'S WORLD

Both Genesis 1 and Genesis 2 should be read for comparison of the two creation accounts. In one, man is created *after* God has finished his other creation; in the other, man is created *before* other things. But in either case man is seen as the most significant aspect of the whole creative process. To date nothing has appeared in history that surpasses the moral responsibility of human life. Thus when God chose to enter history in person, he could do so in man without doing violence to his own nature.

Verse 31. *And God saw everything that he had made, and behold, it was very good:* This early creation story includes no suggestion of evil, of disease, or of trouble of any kind. Whether such an ideal condition ever existed is a question. But the result of his creative activity was such that God was pleased with what he saw.

Psalms 24:1-2. *The earth is the* LORD's *and the fulness thereof:* These two verses express in poetry the Hebrew claim that the whole world belongs to God. Nothing is beyond his control. However man may abuse the earth, or sin against it, still the possessive hand of God is upon it. And man is seen as responsible, not only for human relations, but also for caring for the very material form of the earth.

This truth is especially important now that man has so polluted God's world that it may soon be unfit to support human life. If the ancient Hebrew felt this responsibility for the world, how much more should we. This passage shows that man has a responsibility for his fellow man since "the world and those who dwell therein" are all creatures of the same God. Even the physical universe implies a brotherhood among all people.

Psalms 104:24-30. *O* LORD, *how manifold are thy works!* This psalm continues the thought found in Psalms 24. It is interesting that no mention is made of man as creature. The sea, small and great living things, and ships are evident—but no human beings. Man's presence is implied, but concern for human life is left for other psalms. (See Psalms 8 and 144.)

Selected Scripture

King James Version	Revised Standard Version
Genesis 1:1, 26, 31	*Genesis 1:1, 26, 31*
1 In the beginning God created the heaven and the earth.	1 In the beginning God created the heavens and the earth.
. . . .	. . . .
26 And God said, Let us make man in our image, after our likeness: and let them have dominion over the fish of the sea, and over the fowl of the air, and over the cattle, and over all the earth, and over every creeping thing that creepeth upon the earth.	26 Then God said, "Let us make man in our image, after our likeness; and let them have dominion over the fish of the sea, and over the birds of the air, and over the cattle, and over all the earth, and over every creeping thing that creeps upon the
. . . .	earth." . . . 31 And God saw every-
31 And God saw every thing that he had made, and, behold, it was very good. And the evening and the morning were the sixth day.	thing that he had made, and behold, it was very good. And there was evening and there was morning, a sixth day.
Psalms 24:1-2	*Psalms 24:1-2*
1 The earth is the LORD's, and the fulness thereof; the world, and they that dwell therein.	1 The earth is the LORD's and the fulness thereof, the world and those who dwell therein;

2 For he hath founded it upon the seas, and established it upon the floods.

Psalms 104:24-30

24 O LORD, how manifold are thy works! in wisdom hast thou made them all: the earth is full of thy riches.

25 So is this great and wide sea, wherein are things creeping innumerable, both small and great beasts.

26 There go the ships: there is that leviathan, whom thou hast made to play therein.

27 These wait all upon thee; that thou mayest give them their meat in due season.
28 That thou givest them they gather: thou openest thine hand, they are filled with good.

29 Thou hidest thy face, they are troubled: thou takest away their breath, they die, and return to their dust.

30 Thou sendest forth thy spirit, they are created: and thou renewest the face of the earth.

Memory Selection: The earth is the LORD'S, and the fulness thereof; the world, and they that dwell therein. (Psalms 24:1)

---

2 for he has founded it upon the seas, and established it upon the rivers.

Psalms 104:24-30

24 O LORD, how manifold are thy works!
In wisdom hast thou made them all;
the earth is full of thy creatures.

25 Yonder is the sea, great and wide, which teems with things innumerable,
living things both small and great.

26 There go the ships,
and Leviathan which thou didst form to sport in it.

27 These all look to thee,
to give them their food in due season.

28 When thou givest to them, they gather it up;
when thou openest thy hand, they are filled with good things.

29 When thou hidest thy face, they are dismayed;
when thou takest away their breath, they die
and return to their dust.

30 When thou sendest forth thy Spirit, they are created;
and thou renewest the face of the ground.

Memory Selection:
The earth is the LORD'S and the fulness thereof,
the world and those who dwell therein.   (Psalms 24:1)

The Scripture and the Main Question —Charles M. Laymon

"IN THE BEGINNING GOD . . ."

Gilbert K. Chesterton, the English sage and writer, said that when he went to rent lodgings, instead of asking the usual questions dealing with the property and charges, he first inquired of the landlady, "Madam, what is your view of the universe?" Chesterton believed that this was the prior question that determined the rightness or wrongness of a person's views about everything else.

The Bible launches out into this sea of inquiry about the universe by saying, "In the beginning God created the heavens and the earth." (Genesis 1:1) If we accept this statement as true, it gives profound meaning to life. Here philosophy identifies the Ultimate Cause. Here science accounts for the wonderful process and order of life. Here religion summons us to bow in recognition of our creation. Here ethics insists that we consider our origin in God as we seek to find his will for daily living.

A world that did not have its roots and development in God would be cold, heartless, and impersonal. All the warmth and beauty of life would be a contradiction. This is why atheism is a most illogical and unsatisfying view.

GOD'S HANDIWORK IS GOOD

John Cowden sits outside Ogle's store in Gatlinburg, Tennessee, carving horses, dogs, mountain men, and birds from wood. He has been carving all his life, as did his father before him. Mr. Cowden loves wood, with its fragrant and colorful grain. When he has finished a piece of carving, he rubs his fingers caressingly over it. Then he will look up and smile. His creation is good, and it makes him happy.

How like the picture of God the Creator in the first chapter of Genesis: "And God saw everything that he had made, and behold, it was very good." (verse 31) Some might regard this description as too human a portrait of God. But is it not this very quality that makes it great?

Here is a God who feels as we feel, who is inspired to create, and who rejoices in his handiwork. Science has taught us much, and we are ever in its debt; but it is no substitute for the religious view of the value of life, nor is it intended to be. Albert Einstein's mathematical formula for relativity is useful in understanding the relationships of the physical order, but it does not speak to man of God's personal enthusiasm and appreciation for his universe. The first chapter of Genesis does.

If God appreciated his world, must we not also find delight in the world and love it because it is "precious in his sight"? Children tend to value what they see their parents valuing. A sloppy and slovenly attitude toward the things in the home will breed a shoddy feeling for surroundings. But an appreciative regard for beauty in the home on the part of parents will inspire children to grow up desiring beauty in their own homes. God's feeling for what he has created should produce a similar feeling on the part of his children.

ALL IS GOD'S

W. E. Orchard wrote some of the most beautiful prayers of this century. They are prayers that can be not only read but also *prayed*. As such they give wings to the longings and convictions of others, enabling them to get what they feel "off their hearts" and on its way to God. In one of these prayers Orchard wrote: "We thank Thee for all the gentle and healing ministries of life; the gladness of the morning, the freedom of the wind, the music of the rain, the joy of the sunshine, and the deep calm of the night."

In a prayer such as this, nature does not seem to be our enemy. Instead, she is friendly; more than this, she is loving and ministers to our deepest needs. This aspect of nature is what the psalmist had in mind when he wrote, "The earth is the LORD's and the fulness thereof." (Psalms 24:1) God made the earth; it is good; it is his very own.

You and I are tenants in God's good world. We have both the privilege of living in it and the responsibility of caring for it. Thus pollution and destruction are sins against God. They are also social sins against all our brothers who must live in the world with us. Ecology, in its stress upon preservation of the balance of nature, is a religious issue.

GOD SUSTAINS THE WORLD

The creation of the world was only the beginning. The universe must be continually sustained. We take this process for granted, as though by some mechanical means season follows season and day follows night. The comment that the sun rose in the eastern sky this morning because God said "Do it again!" is truer than we realize. Our scientific minds have impersonalized the natural processes, when they are really the activity of a personal, wise, and loving God.

The constant care of God for his world greatly impressed the writer of Psalms 104. Here we read how God maintained the sea so that Leviathan (the sea monster) could have a place to swim. He also opened his hand to feed all life and renewed the face of the ground (verses 24-30). Our scientific prowess must not prevent us from remembering that in every way this is still God's world, and he is daily working to sustain it.

Helping Adults Become Involved —Harry B. Adams[2]

Preparation of Self and Class

For the next three months class members will be considering some of the major affirmations of the Christian faith. In preparing this first lesson, it will be helpful to take a quick look at the material and structure of the whole quarter.

The first three lessons deal with the human situation, pointing up that man is a responsible creature in God's world who has misused the freedom God gives him. The next group of lessons consider how God has acted in Jesus Christ on behalf of man. The final section of the quarter's work explores the possibilities of the Christian life.

In preparing this lesson, you will want to keep in mind what the Christian affirmation of God as creator of the world means for the day-by-day

[2] Harry B. Adams: associate dean, Yale Divinity School, New Haven, Connecticut.

situation in which you and the other members of the class are involved.

Presenting the Main Question

An article in The New Yorker described a camping trip in the Cascade Mountain Range in the state of Washington. The author made the trip with two other men. One of the men was a geologist, adept at finding minerals in the earth. He was convinced that wherever minerals were found they should be mined by man and used to provide the lights, the wires, the tubes, the steel beams, the television sets, and the computers that make the contemporary world what it is.

The other man was one of the leading conservationists in the country. He believed that the wilderness and natural beauty that remain in this country must be protected against the mining interests, the logging industry, and all others who would ravage the landscape.

For days the men tramped through the wilderness area, the one man arguing that the mineral wealth was there to be used by man to maintain his standard of living, the other arguing that man was misuing the earth if he did not preserve and protect nature, not only its balance but its beauty.

You may want to begin the lesson by describing the situation of the men in the wilderness, and then enable the class to raise the issues involved in one of the following ways:

1. Divide the class members into two groups, and have one group develop the view of the conservationist and the other the view of the geologist.

2. Invite persons to present the views of each man, and then let the class members discuss the problem.

3. List on chalkboard or newsprint the arguments persons might make on behalf of the geologist or the conservationist.

Developing the Lesson

Next, consider with the class members the various responses that can be made to the question of G. K. Chesterton, "Madam, what is your view of the universe?" Some possible responses are indicated below:

1. The universe is a big machine that just happened.

2. The whole universe finally has no meaning and no purpose.

3. Many powers are at work in the world beyond the understanding or control of man.

4. The world was put here solely for man to use for his own ends.

5. The universe was created and is sustained by a purposeful and loving God.

6. The universe was created by a Power, and now runs according to

rigid and unchanging natural laws.

7. The universe is a "closed system" in which nothing new really happens but in which everything is caused by some prior condition.

Give the members of the class opportunity to express their own convictions as they indicate how they would answer for themselves the question of Chesterton. Then raise the further question of why they have this particular view of their world. What kinds of experiences have led them to view the universe as they do? What evidence about the nature of the universe have they found? What kinds of arguments count as men try to decide about the true character of their world?

You may want to point out that such basic issues as a man's view of his universe are not open to proof. Man has learned a great deal about how the physical world functions. He has gotten some glimpses of the vastness of space and of the complexity of the atom. But there is no *proof* that the universe is ultimately meaningful or meaningless, purposeful or purposeless, a creation of God or an inexplicable accident. A man's view of the universe is a commitment of faith.

Look at the biblical witness to the creation and character of the universe. The comments by Dr. Thompson and Dr. Laymon lift up the major assertions in the Scripture passages for this session. Have the members of the class read the passages and then indicate how the Bible has shaped their views of the universe, or how the biblical view differs from their own.

Discuss with the class members how the biblical view of the universe should influence the way a person uses the world and views his own life. Questions such as the following may be considered:

1. What does it mean to say that man was created in the image of God? How should this conviction affect the way a man deals with other men, including those of other nations and other races?

2. If a person believes that God found his creation good, how will he look upon the world around him? What evidence is there in the world to support the biblical assertion that God found his creation good? What evidence seems to counter the judgment that creation is good? Why have some men believed that to be "good" or "spiritual" they should detach themselves from the physical world?

3. How should man use the world if it is God's creation? In the situation of the geologist and the conservationist described at the beginning of the lesson, how might a biblical perspective on creation affect the judgments each of them makes about the proper use of the world?

4. How is man held accountable for the use he makes of God's world? What are some ways in which man has misused the world? What evidence is there that God indeed is judging man for his failure to be a good steward of nature?

Helping Class Members Act

One result of this lesson might be that the members of the class become more sensitive to the evidences of God's care for this creation. Suggest that they make a conscious effort to look at their world each day during the coming week to discern the power and the providence of God in a new way.

Members of the class may also be encouraged to support the efforts being made to use the world more responsibly, as men struggle with the problems of pollution and waste.

Planning for Next Sunday

This lesson focused on the character of the universe in which man finds himself. The lesson next week will consider the character of the human species that inhabits this earth. Ask the members of the class to observe closely people they meet and talk with during the week and to develop their own description of who man is. Suggest that members read Genesis 1:27-30 before the next lesson.

A Time of Preparation

(THE FIRST SUNDAY IN LENT, MARCH 11)

JOHN C. IRWIN [3]

Lent is a time of preparation. In the first centuries of Christianity, Lent was a time of preparation for baptism. As an underground movement the church had to screen its membership with great care. A time of intensive instruction was appointed during which the applicant could be evaluated as well as taught. This period came to involve forty weekdays (not counting Sundays) in memory of the fast and temptation of Jesus. The preparation culminated on Easter morning when the successful candidates were baptized.

[3] John C. Irwin: emeritus professor of preaching and dean of the faculty, Garrett Theological Seminary, Evanston, Illinois.

239

After the legal recognition of Christianity in A.D. 313, when secrecy was no longer necessary, Lent became a time of preparation for all Christians.

But preparation for what? The church has often centered its Lenten observance on the sufferings and crucifixion of Jesus, thus robbing Holy Week of its special significance. As early as the fifth century Pope Leo the Great found it necessary to remind Christians that Lent was appointed to prepare them for a fruitful commemoration of *Easter*—"as a time of inner purification and sanctification, of penance for sins past, of breaking off of sinful habits, of the exercise of virtues, especially almsgiving, reconciliation and the laying aside of enmity and hatred." This counsel might still serve to guide us in meaningful observance of Lent. A Scripture text for the season is found in Colossians 3:1—"If then you have been raised with Christ, seek the things that are above, where Christ is." The central fact we remember in Lent is that Christ rose from the grave and "brought life and immortality to light." (2 Timothy 1:10) Our quest then is to discover what this fact means to us.

Lent is a time for self-examination. Paul believed that the Christian at his baptism died to sin and was raised to a new life in Christ that began at once, not after physical death sometime in the future. (See such passages as Romans 6:3-11 and Colossians 2:12.) Therefore Lent is an opportunity to ask to what extent we are experiencing a quality of life that might properly be called eternal. Are we truly seeking "the things that are above," or do we waste our energies grubbing for the things we must leave below? This is not only a biblical question; it is the question our dissident young people continually ask their elders.

One of the recent translations of the New Testament provides a penetrating catechism for such self-examination: "Does your life in Christ make you strong? Does his love comfort you? Do you have fellowship with the Spirit? Do you feel compassion and love for one another?" (Philippians 2:1, *Today's English Version*) Read the entire passage, Philippians 1:27 through 2:4, for new understanding of what is involved in "life in Christ." How do we measure against the yardstick suggested in these verses? Lent, then, challenges us to take inventory of our spiritual condition.

Lent is a time for discipline. Much as we rebel against discipline, we know in our hearts that nothing worthwhile is achieved without it. The concert pianist still practices his scales. The athlete does his push-ups and wind sprints. Authoritative scholarship is won by thousands of hours of study. Good parents subordinate their own desires to the welfare of their children. And Christians cannot realize the life of love without submitting to the discipline of their Lord.

When we were young, we gave up candy for Lent. When we were a little older, we quit smoking. But now that we are mature, we know that such exercises are only symbols. Christ's will for our lives is positive, not negative. He wants us to do, not to refrain from doing. When John Wesley wrote the General Rules for his societies, he called upon them to "do no harm" and followed with a list of examples; but this was to clear the way for the more important directive to do good—"by being in every kind merciful after their power; as they have opportunity, doing good of every possible sort, and, as far as possible, to all men."

An appropriate discipline for Lent, then, will be to set ourselves consciously to practicing acts of love, bearing one another's burdens, sharing with those in need, and seeking reconciliation with the alienated. We are not surprised to discover from our dictionaries that *disciple* and *discipline* come from the same root word. A disciple is one who accepts the teaching (discipline) of his master.

Finally, *Lent is a time of renewal*. It is no accident that *Lent* is derived from the Anglo-Saxon word for spring, the season of renewal. Old lives made new—this has always been the miracle of the Christian faith. As we contemplate the life and teachings of Jesus, we discover anew what God intended human life to be. As we engage in honest self-examination, we discover in contrast our shortcomings. As we gladly accept the discipline of Christian commitment, we find our lives made new.

In the Letter to the Colossians, Paul lists the characteristics of the "new nature" that the Colossians have received from Christ. As God's people they are to put on "compassion, kindness, lowliness, meekness, and patience, forbearing one another and . . . forgiving each other. . . . And above all these put on love, which binds everything together in perfect harmony." (Colossians 3:12-14) These are the Christian virtues we can expect to be renewed in our lives as we prepare for Easter.

LESSON 2   MARCH 11

Man Is a Responsible Being

Background Scripture: Genesis 1:27-30; 4:1-9; Matthew 25:31-46; Acts 17:30-31; Romans 14:10-12

The Main Question —Charles M. Laymon

When Tarzan of the Apes was taught to say "Me Tarzan; you Jane," he was learning the difference between man and animals. In this same way when man learns to say, in the words of the philosopher Martin Buber, "I—Thou," he is becoming aware of the difference between God and man.

Identity is the word. Who am I? What am I? Where did I come from? Where am I going? When we begin to ask these questions, we are probing our own nature. And the answers we give to them will make all the difference in the world as to what we think about God, the universe, ourselves, and society in general.

Definitions of man have been given by many through the centuries. Aristotle referred to man as a political animal; Sir Thomas Browne called him a noble animal; Edmund Burke said that he was a religious animal; and Benjamin Disraeli once asked if man were an ape or an angel.

What are we to think about ourselves in view of our self-experience and the findings of science, psychology, and sociology? What does the Bible say about the identity of man?

The passages of Scripture that follow contain some enlightening answers.

241

As You Read the Scripture —Claude H. Thompson

The Scripture last week told of the creation of the world, including man's origin as the climax of that creation. Today a further element is introduced— man's moral responsibility.

Genesis 1:27-30. *So God created man in his own image:* This verse repeats the statement of the previous verse with one addition. It applies to both man and woman: "male and female he created them." Genesis 2:20-25 describes pictorially *how* God created woman. This is one of the differences between the two creation stories—Genesis 1:1 through 2:4a and 2:4b-25. But the basic truth is still there: God is the creator of man no less than of the world.

The key thought in this passage is that man will "have dominion." This is not only a privilege, it is a responsibility. The passage shows the exalted position of man—the climax of God's creative genius—and that man must honor that position by obedience. While nothing is said about the multiplication of animals and growing things, man is given direction to "multiply, and fill the earth." Whatever happens to the creation below man, God is concerned that man, made "in his own image," shall be in a position of authority and assume responsible stewardship.

Note the areas that man is to control: fish, birds, plants, trees, animals. But God does not give man authority to dominate other men. Even in this early account it is implied that each man has his own special role to play in God's plan.

Acts 17:30-31. *The times of ignorance God overlooked, but now he commands all men everywhere to repent:* These are the closing words of Paul's speech on Mars' Hill in Athens. He is attempting to speak to the minds of the intellectuals of Greece. *The times of ignorance* that *God overlooked* refer to the kindergarten period of man's development. Man's moral responsibility must always be measured by the degree of his understanding. We may say that God is always seeking the education of his people—a growing grasp of what is right.

Paul is persuaded that God *commands all men everywhere to repent,* since all men—Jews and non-Jews alike—have failed their moral responsibility. In the process of educating man in his moral task God has brought a final lesson in Jesus Christ. He is the standard by which the whole world is to be judged—already *is* judged.

Three things combine to indicate man's moral responsibility: (1) the norm for all judgment is a person, Jesus; (2) the judgment is in *righteousness,* a term that the non-Jewish audience would understand, since it implied justice in the Greek tradition; and (3) the authority for that judgment is the Resurrection. Here was a contrast to the Greek idea of immortality. The people on Mars' Hill could have understood the idea of survival after death. That was part of the ancient Greek tradition. But they knew nothing of resurrection. So the reaction, for the most part, was negative.

Romans 14:10-12. *Why do you pass judgment on your brother?* What is implied in Genesis 1:28-30 is here stated: every man is to stand before God, judged by him and by no other. This, of course, is the ideal purpose of God. By virtue of evil in the life of man, judgments within society have to be made. But always the norm for righteousness is God's revelation of his will in Christ.

Selected Scripture

King James Version	Revised Standard Version
Genesis 1:27-30	*Genesis 1:27-30*

Genesis 1:27-30

27 So God created man in his own image, in the image of God created he him; male and female created he them.

28 And God blessed them, and God said unto them, Be fruitful, and multiply, and replenish the earth, and subdue it: and have dominion over the fish of the sea, and over the fowl of the air, and over every living thing that moveth upon the earth.

29 And God said, Behold, I have given you every herb bearing seed, which is upon the face of all the earth, and every tree, in the which is the fruit of a tree yielding seed; to you it shall be for meat.

30 And to every beast of the earth, and to every fowl of the air, and to every thing that creepeth upon the earth, wherein there is life, I have given every green herb for meat: and it was so.

Acts 17:30-31

30 And the times of this ignorance God winked at; but now commandeth all men everywhere to repent:

31 Because he hath appointed a day, in which he will judge the world in righteousness by that man whom he hath ordained; whereof he hath given assurance unto all men, in that he hath raised him from the dead.

Romans 14:10-12

10 But why dost thou judge thy brother? or why dost thou set at nought thy brother? for we shall all stand before the judgment seat of Christ.

11 For it is written. As I live, saith the Lord, every knee shall bow to me,

Genesis 1:27-30

27 So God created man in his own image, in the image of God he created him; male and female he created them. 28 And God blessed them, and God said to them, "Be fruitful and multiply, and fill the earth and subdue it; and have dominion over the fish of the sea and over the birds of the air and over every living thing that moves upon the earth." 29 And God said, "Behold, I have given you every plant yielding seed which is upon the face of all the earth, and every tree with seed in its fruit; you shall have them for food. 30 And to every beast of the earth, and to every bird of the air, and to everything that creeps on the earth, everything that has the breath of life, I have given every green plant for food." And it was so.

Acts 17:30-31

30 "The times of ignorance God overlooked, but now he commands all men everywhere to repent, 31 because he has fixed a day on which he will judge the world in righteousness by a man whom he has appointed, and of this he has given assurance to all men by raising him from the dead."

Romans 14:10-12

10 Why do you pass judgment on your brother? Or you, why do you despise your brother? For we shall all stand before the judgment seat of God; 11 for it is written,

"As I live, says the Lord, every
    knee shall bow to me,

and every tongue shall confess to God.

12 So then every one of us shall give account of himself to God.

Memory Selection: Every one of us shall give account of himself to God. (Romans 14:12)

and every tongue shall give praise to God."

12 So each of us shall give account of himself to God.

Memory Selection: Each of us shall give account of himself to God. (Romans 14:12)

The Scripture and the Main Question —Charles M. Laymon

MADE IN GOD'S IMAGE

The most famous words in literature on the subject of man are those of William Shakespeare that begin with Hamlet's exclamation, "What a piece of work is a man!" Shakespeare then describes man as being "noble in reason" and "infinite in faculty." More than this, man is "express and admirable" in form and movement, "like an angel" in action and "like a god" in apprehension. Finally, he is "the beauty of the world! the paragon of animals!"

The bard of Avon must have written these words in a burst of enthusiasm. Was he too optimistic? Was he gilding the lily? All of us have felt this way about our fellow human beings when we have been touched by the actions of some noble and gracious person. Great heights of heroism and deep depths of sacrificial love are not uncommon where man is concerned.

On the other hand, man's cruelty can exceed that of the wildest animals. The gas furnaces in which ten million Jews were executed by the Nazis and the massacre at My Lai tell the tale of man's inhumanity to man. What a contradiction!

The point in all this, however, is that man's potential for greatness and nobility is as real as his potential for cruelty and evil. God created man this

way, so that his goodness would not be that of a puppet but of a free human spirit. Man's moral choices are genuine. As Benjamin Disraeli intimated, man can choose to be an angel or an ape.

The author of Genesis said that God created man in his own image (1:27). Like God, man can think, decide, create, and love. He can enjoy communion with God and experience the call to righteousness and discipleship in Christ. And he can know the forgiving love of God that restores his relationship to God when sin has ruptured it. Yes, "What a piece of work is a man!"

MADE TO MULTIPLY

John Fiske, the American thinker and historian, once visited the English philosopher Herbert Spencer. He showed Spencer a picture of his picnic wagon with the children inside. As he watched this bachelor's expression when he looked at the picture, Fiske pitied him and thought, That wagonload of youngsters is worth more than all the philosophy ever concocted from Aristotle to Spencer inclusive.

The two most basic drives of man are hunger and sex. No assessment of his nature and worth can neglect this fact. The celibate life, which denies to man his creative sexual urges as

244

God intended them to be expressed, is contrary to God's intention. This intention is clearly spelled out in Genesis, where we read, "God said to them, 'Be fruitful and multiply.'" (1:28)

Yet sex is directed toward family life and not to an indiscriminate free expression of instinct. The continuation of the race, the birth of new souls, and the creation of a family are what God had in mind when he created man as a sexual being. Thus man is responsible for the uses of this drive. What does this need for responsibility say about the increasing concern with overpopulation and the misuse of sex as lust rather than an act of love?

SUBDUE THE EARTH

Gerald Heard, in *Gabriel and the Creatures*, has said, "Man . . . is the master of all beasts and not only the crown but the promise of all life." In this vein Charles Swinburne also wrote in his *Hymn of Man*, "Glory to Man in the highest! for Man is the master of things."

Their sentiments are in line with what we read in Genesis. Man was not only made in God's image but was also instructed to subdue the earth "and have dominion over . . . every living thing that moves upon the earth." (1:28) This places man at the peak of all creation, as though the earth was made for man.

Accordingly, man has fished the earth's oceans, lakes, and streams; mined its coal, minerals, and precious stones; cut its timber; farmed its fields; and grazed his animals on its moors and pastures. In some cases he has furiously taken over nature, even to the point of devastating her resources. This, he felt, was his right and privilege.

GIVE AN ACCOUNTING

Yet since God is a responsible creator, man must be a responsible creature. The two go hand in hand. Being endowed with God's very nature, being made in his image, our freedom to act carries with it the necessity of giving an accounting of our handling of ourselves and of our stewardship over the earth.

This is what Paul was saying when he preached at Athens that God had fixed a day of judgment and that Christ would be the judge (Acts 17: 31). Again in writing to the Romans the apostle gave notice that "we shall all stand before the judgment seat of God." (Romans 14:10)

The present interest in ecology, in which we are shocked by what we have done to the earth God has given us, belongs in this picture, as do racism and injustice. In many areas of responsibility we have not done too well—not well at all.

But there is hope. The Holy Spirit is making us aware of our mismanagement of things and of our sinful attitudes toward persons made in God's image. And "the day of march has come." It is not too late to change the tide; God's power and grace are available.

Helping Adults Become Involved —Harry B. Adams

Preparation of Self and Class

The lesson last week dealt with the nature of the universe as man understands it and as it is interpreted in the Bible. This lesson gives attention to man's view of himself, as that view grows out of his own experience and out of the biblical witness.

As you make your plans for this lesson, you will want to think about the views and the needs of each of the persons in your class. How do you think each person in the class sees himself? What kind of understanding of who he is does each person seem to have? How can this lesson help each person in his quest for an identity that will enable him to become what God intends for him?

Two films would be useful in raising the issues to be dealt with in this lesson: *Run!* and *The Human Race.* (See page 231.)

Presenting the Main Question

Begin the lesson by giving the members of the class the experience of explaining who they are and finding out who others are. This may be done in one of several ways:

1. Divide the group into pairs, and have each person learn as much as he can about who the other person is.

2. Ask each person to write a short statement saying who he is.

3. Arrange before the lesson for two persons to have a conversation in front of the class in which each tries to find out who the other is.

4. Have someone pretend to be a new member of the class, and have the class members find out who that new person is by asking questions that can be answered by *yes* or *no.*

After the members of the class have shared some kind of experience in telling who they are or learning who another person is, have them look at what they have done in order to consider the kinds of things people talk about when they attempt to say who they are. What really gives a person his identity? When a person is asked who he is, he usually answers by relating some of the following: what his name is, who his family is, where he works, where he lives, where he came from, where he went to school, what his hobbies are, how long he has been living here.

Persons also find their own identity and are identified by others in terms of the various roles they play in a complex network of relationships. A man is a father, a son, a homeowner, a husband, an employee.

In establishing an identity, persons usually do only what is necessary for the occasion. A casual meeting at a party will not call for exhaustive interpretation of who each person is. An identity for the credit bureau will call for more extensive information.

Most answers persons give when asked about who they are can be pressed further than they are normally taken. For example, a person lives on a certain street. But where is the street? In which city? In which state? In which nation? On which continent? On which planet? In which solar constellation?

Go back and look at some of the other ways persons identify themselves to see how far they can be carried. Try to see the total complex in which each individual finds himself and in which he must try to figure out who he is, why he is here, where he is going, and what it means to be a person and to find an identity.

Developing the Lesson

Examine some of the views of man various persons have held. Dr. Laymon suggests a number of ways in which different persons have defined man. Give members of the class opportunity to indicate which of these definitions they find meaningful and helpful. Then invite members to share their insights as they thought about who man is during the past week.

Encourage the group to think about the nature of man, not only in the abstract, but in terms of who they are as individuals. Do they see themselves as political animals? as noble animals? as religious animals?

Explore the biblical assertions about the character of man. Use the insights of Dr. Thompson and Dr. Laymon as you help the class members understand what the Bible is saying about man. As you look at the text, the following questions might be considered.

1. How does the Bible help a person deal with the question, Who am I?

2. How does the biblical view of man agree with or differ from the way men see themselves today?

3. Which of the following comes closest to describing the biblical understanding of man? Explain your answer.

Man is a highly developed animal.
Man is a noble being.
Man is a responsible being.
Man is fundamentally good.
Man is fundamentally evil.
Man is a free being.
Man is a godlike creature.

Consider what it means to affirm that man is responsible. Two words may be put on chalkboard or newsprint to help the class members focus on two significant elements in any consideration of responsibility. The words are *freedom* and *accountability*. Give the class members opportunity to discuss what these two words mean

and why they are important concerns in any consideration of responsibility. Also, ask the members to reflect on what the Bible says about *freedom* and *accountability*.

Unless a creature is free, he cannot be held responsible for what he does. As the Bible describes man, he does have this freedom. He has dominion over the earth and its creatures, which means that he has certain powers to use in the world. As one made in God's image, he has the freedom to decide what use he will make of the world. Beyond that, man has the freedom to set the goals and shape the values that will determine the style and direction of his life. Of course, man's freedom is conditioned by many factors—physical limitations, environmental influences, natural laws. Yet man cannot finally escape responsibility for who he is and what he has done by claiming that he has no choice.

As the texts from Acts and Romans make clear, man is held accountable by God for what he does with his life. The idea of a day of judgment looks into the future; but when Paul talks of the world being judged by one whom God has raised from the dead, it suggests that man is *now* under the judgment of a living Lord. The present judgment of God comes upon man in that when man misuses his freedom to pollute his world, to harm his brother, to degrade himself, he does not become what God in Christ intends and enables him to become.

Who is man? He is one made in the image of God, free and accountable before God.

Helping Class Members Act

Have the class members suggest how they think an understanding of who they are before God will be helpful to them the next time they are discouraged, or arrogant, or tempted, or defeated, or successful, or perplexed.

Planning for Next Sunday

Suggest that the members of the class read Genesis 3 and Psalms 51. Neither of these passages is to be discussed extensively next Sunday, but both give a background for the situation of man that is to be looked at. Also ask each person in the class to be prepared with an illustration, from their own experience or from the newspaper, of the sinfulness of man.

LESSON 3   MARCH 18

Man Has Gone Astray

Background Scripture: Genesis 3:1-19; Psalms 14:1-3; Jeremiah 10:23; 17:9-10; Romans 1:28 through 2:24

The Main Question —Charles M. Laymon

The lost and found column of the classified advertisement section of the daily paper is a truly human document. The entire gamut of man's daily life sooner or later appears there. Lost pets, lost jewelry, lost gifts from loved ones, lost billfolds, lost life savings, lost cameras, lost business papers, lost briefcases, lost book manuscripts of hopeful writers—the list could be extended indefinitely. When you add to all this the reports from the Bureau of Missing Persons, you are doubly impressed with the fact that life breaks down, gets out of joint, is misplaced and disarranged.

But even more tragic are the news stories on the front page of most any newspaper any day in the week. Murder, dope addiction, embezzlement, sexual perversion, drunken driving, and so forth are depicted in column after column. Is there no end in sight?

Why is evil so persistent? Why hasn't education made a greater difference than it has? Why haven't science and organized religion with all their marvelous potential changed human behavior more radically?

The biblical passages that follow help to answer these questions.

As You Read the Scripture —Claude H. Thompson

Man's responsibility, described last week, has not been faithfully discharged. Today's Scriptures tell the story: the whole human race has turned away from God. We are all part of a sinful society.

Psalms 14:2-3. *The* LORD *looks down from heaven upon the children of men:* Paul quotes these lines in Romans 3:10-12. He discovered what the psalmist knew so well: there is perversity at the center of personal life. (Read

248

Romans 6 and 7 to get a full picture of this inner contradiction in human life.) Not every person acts in a vile, degenerate sort of way; but the drift in human life is away from God. Put into other words, it is easier to turn away from the right than to struggle for it. To do right seems like struggling up-hill; to do wrong is like coasting down a ski run.

But even in his moral failure man is not lost to God: "*The LORD looks down from heaven.*" Verse 2 shows God's concern to find even one righteous human being. The psalmist is clear that this is no unkind judgment but a sorrowing search for goodness on earth. But God is disappointed. His creation has failed. "There is none that does good, no, not one." Yet the psalmist implies, and Paul affirms, that God has not left man in this moral predicament. What man is unable to do—untangle his moral mess—God has done.

MAN HAS GONE ASTRAY

Jeremiah 10:23. *I know, O LORD, that the way of man is not in himself, that it is not in man who walks to direct his steps:* The prophet Jeremiah repeats the theme of man's inability to remake his own morally ruined life.

These words imply the creative origin of man as from God, as seen in the lesson for March 4. If man's way *is not in himself,* where is it? It is found only in God. This is a rejection of any sort of humanism—in which man affirms his own ability to direct his life. As J. B. Phillips paraphrases Romans 7:18: "I often find that I have the will to do good, but not the power." The history of human sin is the history of man's refusal to acknowledge this utter inability to manage his own life.

Chapter 17:9-10. *The heart is deceitful above all things, and desperately corrupt:* The prophet is sure that the trouble is not essentially what man *does* but what he *is*. Jesus accented this insight so vividly in the Sermon on the Mount. There he puts his judgment, not first of all upon man's actions, but upon twisted inner motivations.

"Who can understand it?" Understand what? The heart of man. And Jesus again has the answer. He knew what was in man. Again and again it is reported that Jesus grasped the inner motivations of people—and spoke to their need. (See Matthew 9:4; Luke 5:22; 6:8; 9:47; 11:17.) One thing is sure: unless the inner life of man can be remade, the outer life will continue to gravitate away from the right.

Romans 1:28 through 2:1. *And since they did not see fit to acknowledge God, God gave them up:* Three times in a few verses Paul says that *"God gave them up."* (See 1:24, 26, 28.) Perhaps there is no more serious judgment upon man's failure to be faithful to his created purpose than these words. For if God gives a man up, he surely appears beyond hope. Notice the vicious condition of those whom God has turned over to their own inner desires and appetites. No more tragic list of evils exists in the New Testament than this description of how people live when they reject God.

This condition is not something God inflicts upon the disobedient. He simply permits their inner attitudes to be manifested in outward conduct. Thus sin carries its own judgment. It is not merely something imposed upon the wrongdoer; rather man becomes what he is within. The older discussion of hell as a place misses the point. Hell is more truly the condition of the person who has no place for God in his life. He becomes what his inner desires are—the "man who has gone astray."

Selected Scripture

King James Version

Psalms 14:2-3
2 The Lord looked down from heaven upon the children of men, to see if there were any that did understand, and seek God.

3 They are all gone aside, they are all together become filthy: there is none that doeth good, no, not one.

Jeremiah 10:23
23 O Lord, I know that the way of man is not in himself: it is not in man that walketh to direct his steps.

Revised Standard Version

Psalms 14:2-3
2 The Lord looks down from heaven
upon the children of men,
to see if there are any that act wisely,
that seek after God.

3 They have all gone astray, they are all alike corrupt;
there is none that does good,
no, not one.

Jeremiah 10:23
23 I know, O Lord, that the way of man is not in himself,
that it is not in man who walks
to direct his steps.

Jeremiah 17:9-10

9 The heart is deceitful above all things, and desperately wicked: who can know it?

10 I the LORD search the heart, I try the reins, even to give every man according to his ways, and according to the fruit of his doings.

Romans 1:28 through 2:1

28 And even as they did not like to retain God in their knowledge, God gave them over to a reprobate mind, to do those things which are not convenient;

29 Being filled with all unrighteousness, fornication, wickedness, covetousness, maliciousness; full of envy, murder, debate, deceit, malignity; whisperers,

30 Backbiters, haters of God, despiteful, proud, boasters, inventors of evil things, disobedient to parents,

31 Without understanding, covenant-breakers, without natural affection, implacable, unmerciful:

32 Who knowing the judgment of God, that they which commit such things are worthy of death, not only do the same, but have pleasure in them that do them.

1 Therefore thou art inexcusable, O man, whosoever thou art that judgest: for wherein thou judgest another, thou condemnest thyself; for thou that judgest doest the same things.

Memory Selection: **All we like sheep have gone astray; we have turned every one to his own way. (Isaiah 53:6)**

Jeremiah 17:9-10

9 The heart is deceitful above all things,
and desperately corrupt;
who can understand it?

10 "I the LORD search the mind and try the heart,
to give to every man according to his ways,
according to the fruit of his doings."

Romans 1:28 through 2:1

28 And since they did not see fit to acknowledge God, God gave them up to a base mind and to improper conduct. 29 They were filled with all manner of wickedness, evil, covetousness, malice. Full of envy, murder, strife, deceit, malignity, they are gossips, 30 slanderers, haters of God, insolent, haughty, boastful, inventors of evil, disobedient to parents, 31 foolish, faithless, heartless, ruthless. 32 Though they know God's decree that those who do such things deserve to die, they not only do them but approve those who practice them.

1 Therefore you have no excuse, O man, whoever you are, when you judge another; for in passing judgment upon him you condemn yourself, because you, the judge, are doing the very same things.

Memory Selection:
All we like sheep have gone astray;
we have turned every one to his own way.   (Isaiah 53:6)

The Scripture and the Main Question —Charles M. Laymon

GOD'S WATCHFUL EYE

The first death in our family that I recall was that of my grandfather. I was ten years old. One of my reactions to his death was that, believing he was in heaven, I felt certain he could see everything I did. This particularly bothered me when I had done something I knew to be wrong. How could I keep his good favor?

From this line of thinking as a boy, I needed to take only a step to arrive at the realization that God knows all about me all the time. In turn, he knows all about everyone, what we do and do not do. We call this attribute the *omniscience* (total knowledge) of God.

When we consider sin and the breakdown of life, we note with assurance that the Bible asserts these do not take God by surprise. God's watchful eye misses nothing. This may be terrifying to the wicked, but it is strengthening to those who would find meaning in life and seek to do God's will.

The psalmist was assured that even though it sometimes seemed God was dead or had temporarily abdicated, this was not so. He was certain that the Lord looks down from heaven upon his children "to see if there are any that act wisely, that seek after God." (14:2)

DIFFICULT TO BE GOOD

Rufus Jones, the great Quaker mystic who taught for many years at Haverford College, used to tell a legend concerning Moses. This intrepid leader had had a difficult time with the Hebrews after he had led them out of Egypt. They had rebelled, worshiped idols, and lost their enthusiasm during the days of the wilderness wanderings. Finally, on the top of Mount Pisgah, Moses was given a glimpse of the Promised Land. This was all he ever had; he never entered that sought after place.

God, according to the legend, said to Moses: "Moses, . . . you lost faith in yourself, in the powers of your own leadership, and I could forgive you that. But then you lost faith in these people and in their divine possibilities. That I cannot forgive."

In observing men and their evil behavior, Jeremiah, unlike Moses in the legend, never gave up his faith in their possibilities. He knew, however, that it was difficult to be good. As he put it, "The way of man is not in himself." (10:23) Man needs God's direction to reach his best and to fulfill his highest potential.

LOOK TO THE HEART

Jeremiah is known as the father of personal religion because of his vision that a day would come when God would write his law in the hearts of men. Henceforth they would need to look, not to the tables of stone for the Ten Commandments, but to the new covenant of the heart (31:31-34). Here God would write his law afresh so that religion would be a personal and not a legal matter.

It may seem contradictory, but just as spirituality comes from within the heart so also does evil. Jeremiah said, "The heart is deceitful above all things, and desperately corrupt; who can understand it?" (17:9) For this reason God searches and tries the heart (verse 10).

A famous novelist was once asked if he did not want God to forgive his sins. "No," he replied, "I like my sins." How honest! How tragically revealing. In his heart of hearts the writer was egocentric and selfish. He wanted to follow his own will rather than God's.

252

Isn't this the reason evil has such a hold on man? Sin is putting our own desires above God's; we love evil, and therefore we do evil.

God asks man to seek God's forgiveness and to give his heart to God in love. Then man will choose to do God's will. And only then will the front page of the newspaper tell a different story.

WHEN MEN DENY GOD

Robert Browning was a poet both of faith and intellect. In *A Death in the Desert* he wrote:

I say, the acknowledgement of
God in Christ
Accepted by thy reason, solves
for thee
All questions in the earth and
out of it.

Paul was saying the same thing in reverse when in the Book of Romans he explained the sin of man as rooted in his failure to acknowledge God. Because men "did not see fit to acknowledge God," sin bore a harvest in their lives (1:28 through 2:1).

Our modern world is quite different from those of Paul and Browning. Neither would recognize it as the same place were they to return. On every hand there is newness. We acknowledge the new science, the new math, the new psychology, the new housing, the new economics of deficit spending, the new ecumenical movement, the new atomic age, and the new space era.

Yet light and sound still travel at the same rate of speed. Some things continue to hold true even in the midst of dramatic changes. The need to acknowledge God, the need for hope and holiness, and the need for a heart made new in Christ remain.

Helping Adults Become Involved —Harry B. Adams

Preparation of Self and Class

This is the third lesson in the unit, which is designed to "tell it like it is." The first lesson looked at the world as the creation of God. The second looked at man as a responsible creature who has freedom and who is going to be held accountable.

But what has man done with his world and his freedom? The material to be dealt with today is intended to help persons take an honest look at the condition of man. The second unit of this quarter, which begins next Sunday, explores what God has done on behalf of man; but before man is ready to accept what God has done, he has to face honestly his own plight.

In preparing for this lesson, you will need to try to assess how the various persons in the class can be helped to deal with their sin and thus their need for God's reconciling love. For some, the whole notion of sin may be meaningless. For others, sin may be defined so that it does not get too close to their own lives. For any person genuinely to acknowledge his own sin is not easy.

Presenting the Main Question

Begin the lesson by asking members of the class to give illustrations of things persons have done that indicate these persons are sinners. You may want to bring in some clippings from the newspaper to show what you consider to be the evidence that man does act in sinful ways.

List on chalkboard or newsprint the actions class members point out as being the result of sin. Then raise with the class the question of what it is about these actions that makes them sinful. Your list may look like the following:

An action is sinful if

it hurts another person.

it destroys something another person values.

it violates the commandments of God.

it breaks a law that society has set to guide the behavior of men.

it does harm to the person himself.

it goes against what men generally accept as proper behavior.

Developing the Lesson

Explore with the class members what the Scripture means when it declares:

They have all gone astray, they are all alike corrupt;
there is none that does good,
no, not one.   (Psalms 14:3)

Have members look again at the examples they offered of persons who are sinful, and then ask them to discuss whether such examples include everyone or whether there are persons who are not sinful in the way the examples indicate. Then look again at the list of things that make an action sinful. Raise with the class members the question of whether there are persons who can avoid all sinful acts if sinful acts are defined the way their list defines them.

Read the following statements to the class and ask members why they agree or disagree:

1. All men have missed the goal for which their lives were intended.

2. All men have corrupted and distorted their lives.

3. No man does what is good.

In the biblical view of man all men are sinful. Whether persons in the class accept that view or not at the moment, help them to see that distinctions between persons can still be made even if all men are sinners. To say that all men are sinners is not to say that all men are equally bad. There is certainly a difference between the man who regularly beats up his wife and the man who treats his wife with respect and tenderness. There is a difference between the man who embezzles from his employer and the man who does not. There is a difference between the murderer and the doctor who uses his skill to heal another.

The Bible asserts that all men are sinful, but the Bible does make discriminations between men. The author of Psalms 1, for example, draws sharp contrast between the way of the righteous and the way of the wicked, declaring that "the LORD knows the way of the righteous, but the way of the wicked will perish." (verse 6)

Consider the biblical understanding of sin. The Bible pictures all men as sinners. Some persons just do not accept the notion that all men are sinners. Perhaps part of the difference is in the understanding of what it means to say that a man is a sinner. Sin may be defined in terms of the kinds of things that make the front pages of the newspapers—a vicious murder, a spectacular bank robbery, a dastardly kidnapping. Or sin may be defined as any violation of the law.

Look with the class at some of the biblical interpretations of sin. Jeremiah talks about the deceitfulness and the corruption of the heart (17:9). He says that the Lord searches the mind of a man. Not only the external actions of a man are to be tested. God's measure of a man is not based on whether he has violated some law of society. God tests the heart and the mind. He probes the motives, the intentions, the secret desires, the hidden passions, the petty jealousies, the smoldering hates, the blind prejudices. The hidden matters of the heart and mind do not appear on the front pages of the newspaper, but they make the man. It is on the basis of what is within a man that the Bible makes judgments about his sin. "I the LORD search the mind and try the heart." (Jeremiah 17:10)

Paul also points to the inner dimension of a man's life when he writes of man's sin. Using the list in Romans 1:29-31, consider the following questions with the class members.

1. Which of these items were offered as evidences of man's sinfulness at the beginning of the lesson?

2. Which of these would you say were evidences that man is a sinner?

3. Which of these are really not very significant in indicating the true character of a person?

4. Do you think it is meaningful to put murder and gossip in the same list? Why, or why not?

5. Why do you agree or disagree with Paul when he says that "those who do such things deserve to die"?

Discuss with the class members what they think the basic problem of man is. Few persons would want to argue that everything is all right with man and the world. But what is the problem? Why don't things go better? Some views are indicated below. Give the class members opportunity to express their opinion about each interpretation.

1. Man's problem is ignorance. Better education is needed.

2. Man's problem is poverty. More production and better distribution are needed.

3. Man's problem is selfishness. Ways to motivate man to share with others are needed.

4. Man's problem is the social structures. Better laws and more rigorous enforcement are needed.

Paul says that men have their problems because "they did not see fit to acknowledge God." (Romans 1:28) Because man has broken his relationship with God, he corrupts his own life, hurts his brother, and even threatens to destroy God's creation.

Helping Class Members Act

Suggest that during the coming week the members of the class be especially alert when they find themselves passing judgment on someone else. Paul suggests that "in passing judgment upon him you condemn yourself, because you, the judge, are doing the very same things." (Romans 2:1) Ask the class members to test Paul's statement in their own experience.

Planning for Next Sunday

In spite of what man is and what man has done, the Bible affirms the good news of God's constant love for his people. Ask the class members to be ready next Sunday to indicate evidence of God's care for them and for others they have seen during this week.

UNIT VII: CHRISTIAN REDEMPTION
Horace R. Weaver

SIX LESSONS   MARCH 25–APRIL 29

The past three lessons have dealt with the creation of a good world by a good God, whose intent was that his creatures should live in harmony with one another and with him. God's intention was thwarted by man's refusal to live in Godliness (Christlikeness), desiring to live by his own man-made rules rather than those offered by God. Into this state of rebellion and alienation, Unit VII, "Christian Redemption," brings the promises of God to a broken and alienated mankind.

In an age of mechanization, dehumanization, and depersonalization it is of the greatest importance for every person to know that the God who made us loves us. The lesson for March 25, "God Loves Us," enlarges on the prophetic teaching of Hosea (11:1-9) that God has always loved his people. The gospel, of course, expands this prophetic insight and shows the truth of this statement incarnate in the life and teaching of Jesus Christ. The purpose of this lesson is to help people become alive and find meaning and purpose as they realize that God does love them.

The lesson for April 1, "God Speaks Through Christ," is to help adults see, not only that God cares (which could be a philosophical note), but that he also has expressed his concern and loving intent in a life (Jesus Christ), so that all may read for themselves the truth that God does love.

The lesson for April 8, "Christ Suffered for Us," emphasizes the suffering servant role by which and through which Jesus Christ draws men unto God. Jesus Christ came that he might draw (as the suffering servant of Isaiah 53) the hate and venom from others into himself. This spongelike attitude is to be incarnated into each of his followers that they may truly be Christians. To be spongelike is to absorb the hate, the verbal stings, the bitterness, and the selfishness of others that they may be free of these and may find forgiveness and enter the new life in Christ that comes from being free from a life of hell. The kingdom of heaven is opened by those who suffer to all who are in need.

The lesson for April 15, "Jesus Christ Is King," retells the story of the triumphant entering into Jerusalem by Jesus, riding on the ass, rather than a great, white, military charger. Even so Christ still comes into our lives in lowly ways.

The lesson for April 22, "Christ Conquered Sin and Death," celebrates the resurrection of Jesus Christ. The offer of the resurrected life to Christians now is a part of the perennial offer of eternal life to all men.

On April 29 we are challenged with the title "Man Responds Through Faith." We have faced the fact that unless a man hears and sees the challenge of Christ's love and sacrificial acts and makes a decision to respond in faith and love, he will miss the abundant life Christ offers.

Audiovisual resources appropriate for use with the lessons of this unit may be found in the introduction to Unit VI, page 231. Listings for the entire quarter are given in one location to facilitate ordering well in advance of planned viewing dates.

God Loves Us

Background Scripture: Psalms 103:8-14; Hosea 11:1-9;
John 3:16-17; Ephesians 1:3-10

The Main Question —Charles M. Laymon

A bishop of a major denomination was talking to me recently. He said that his son was leaving the ministry after only one year and going into law. "Why is he doing this?" I asked. His father replied sadly, "He feels that he can do more to help God in the legal profession than through the church."

This young minister was having an apparently successful ministry but felt that something was lacking. The people were too deeply entrenched in tradition and did not want to reach out to meet the community need. Their church was for themselves, and they felt too comfortable in it.

Someone may say that this was just one young man and that his temperament was not right for the ministry; he was too impatient. But the fact is that there are many young pastors who are leaving the ministry, Catholic and Protestant alike. The reason for this exodus is that they do not find the institution of the church adequate for effectively demonstrating the love and care of God.

Those who leave the church's service do not see themselves as turning from God. They are in search of a more direct way to express God's love in the world. We need to ask ourselves afresh what we mean by the love of God. Cannot we both find and express God's love through the church?

The biblical passages that follow will help us answer this question.

As You Read the Scripture —Claude H. Thompson

It would be surprising, even tragic, were God to leave us in the condition described in last week's lesson. Gratefully, he has not forsaken his creation. He is the God who cares—cares until the hurt of man becomes his hurt as well. Calvary is evidence of that.

Psalms 103:8. *The* LORD *is merciful and gracious, slow to anger and abounding in steadfast love:* The words *mercy, grace,* and *steadfast love* describe beautifully the faithful character of God. *Mercy* pertains to the covenant God made with his people. Though they often rejected him, God remained forgiving and compassionate. There was mercy even for those so prone to accept other gods. Thus divine mercy is seen in contrast to man's waywardness. Even when man must come under needed judgment, God always tempers judgment with mercy. "Goodness and *mercy* shall follow me all the days of my life." (Psalms 23:6) And what was available for the psalmist is available for every man.

Grace is one of the most meaningful words in the Bible. We speak of a graceful person, a graceful piece of art, or a gracious action. The Bible portrays God as gracious in spite of man's ingratitude. While it is occasionally

257

found in the Old Testament, as in this passage, *grace* is characteristically a New Testament term. It describes the love of God extended to persons who do not deserve it. Jesus' forgiveness of the woman caught in adultery was an act of sheer grace. Here was God in action.

Steadfast love, often translated as *mercy* in the Authorized Version, is commonly used in the Revised Standard text. It expresses not simply God's overflowing love for sinful man but the very character of God. "God is love." (1 John 4:8) His is a love that suffers to convey worth upon sinful, rebellious creatures.

Verses 9-10. *He will not always chide:* God does *chide,* and he does express his anger. If we ever think that mercy, grace, and love completely displace divine judgment, we miss the point of God's concern for a moral universe. But even in our lostness, God does not measure us "according to our sins." *Sins* and *iniquities* here apparently mean the same thing.

Verse 11. *For as the heavens are high above the earth:* The psalmist tries to show the greatness of God's love by comparing it with the heavens, which are higher than the earth. This picture helps us see the measureless quality of divine love. "Those who fear him" are those who are concerned to serve and obey God.

Verse 12. *As far as the east is from the west:* Our sins are removed *as far as the east is from the west,* not as far as the north is from the south. We may go so far north (or south) as to be going in the opposite direction. But we can never go so far east as to go west.

Verses 13-14. *As a father pities his children:* God is seen as a father who knows both the weakness and the worth of his children. This idea of God as father finds its fullest expression, of course, in the life of Jesus.

John 3:16. *For God so loved the world:* This is the best known verse in the Bible. Someone has said if we lost every other part of the Bible, this one verse would be sufficient to proclaim the gospel. Now, when love often is thought of as mere sentimentality or sensuality, God's love needs to be understood. His love suffers in order to save. It has no boundaries—even enemies are embraced. The love expressed from Calvary, "Father, forgive them," was love for a world that had disappointed God. Christ came to save the world in spite of its failure.

The contrast between "perish" and "eternal life" shows the danger confronting every man. These are the only options. But whatever lostness there may be cannot be the primary will of God. He has done all he can do to provide life abundant for every man.

Verse 17. *For God sent the Son into the world:* Three ideas are clear: (1) Christ came into history for a purpose; (2) Christ's purpose was not condemnation; and (3) his chief purpose was to redeem.

The simplicity of this affirmation shows the profound depth of the gospel. It is breathtaking to think that the Creator-God would and could become so involved in man's sinfulness and death as to experience the alienation they produce. But this is the good news. What we do with this message determines our destiny—now and forever.

Selected Scripture

King James Version	Revised Standard Version

Psalms 103:8-14

8 The LORD is merciful and gracious, slow to anger, and plenteous in mercy.

9 He will not always chide: neither will he keep his anger for ever.

10 He hath not dealt with us after our sins; nor rewarded us according to our iniquities.

11 For as the heaven is high above the earth, so great is his mercy toward them that fear him.

12 As far as the east is from the west, so far hath he removed our transgressions from us.

13 Like as a father pitieth his children, so the LORD pitieth them that fear him.

14 For he knoweth our frame; he remembereth that we are dust.

John 3:16-17

16 For God so loved the world, that he gave his only begotten Son, that whosoever believeth in him should not perish, but have everlasting life.

17 For God sent not his Son into the world to condemn the world; but that the world through him might be saved.

Memory Selection: The LORD is merciful and gracious, slow to anger, and plenteous in mercy. (Psalms 103:8)

Psalms 103:8-14

8 The LORD is merciful and gracious, slow to anger and abounding in steadfast love.

9 He will not always chide, nor will he keep his anger for ever.

10 He does not deal with us according to our sins, nor requite us according to our iniquities.

11 For as the heavens are high above the earth, so great is his steadfast love toward those who fear him;

12 as far as the east is from the west, so far does he remove our transgressions from us.

13 As a father pities his children, so the LORD pities those who fear him.

14 For he knows our frame; he remembers that we are dust.

John 3:16-17

16 For God so loved the world that he gave his only Son, that whoever believes in him should not perish but have eternal life. 17 For God sent the Son into the world, not to condemn the world, but that the world might be saved through him.

Memory Selection: The LORD is merciful and gracious, slow to anger and abounding in steadfast love. (Psalms 103:8)

The Scripture and the Main Question —Charles M. Laymon

GRACE ABOUNDING

The love of God cannot be defined in so many words. It is best seen in deeds and actions. In the presence of some magnificent and sacrificial act we say, "There goes the love of God." The word that best describes God's love in action is *grace*. One benediction that sends us on our way from church begins with the words *"May the grace of our Lord Jesus Christ. . . ."* What follows is a prayer that we may be kept in God's love. It is almost as though the minister was praying, "May God's love *happen* to you."

We find a similar sensitivity to God's love in some words of Robert Louis Stevenson: "Why not the grace of your Maker and Redeemer? He who died for you, he who upholds you, he whom you daily crucify afresh? There is nothing but God's grace. We walk upon it; we breathe it; we live and die by it: it makes the nails and axles of the universe."

God's love in action, freely given, is what holds the world together (*nails*) and makes the world go around (*axles*). This is what Stevenson is saying. Can such love be kept within the walls of the church? Does it not carry us out into the world, where death, suffering, cruelty, and anger are destroying God's children? Can we find love for ourselves and our own comfort unless we give it away to others by loving day by day?

FORGIVENESS WITHOUT LIMIT

The psalmist was describing God's love as grace when he said that we are dealt with not according to our sins or iniquities but according to God's "steadfast love." This love is as high as the heavens above the earth (103:10-11). To him the heavens were only a mile or a mile and a half above the earth. Yet this was the highest he knew. For us there is no limit to height in the universe. These words, therefore, carry an even greater meaning today than when they were first written.

Of all the works of God that demonstrate his gracious love, the psalmist singles out forgiveness. Had he personally been recently forgiven by God, and was he living in the glow of grati-

tude when he wrote: "as far as the east is from the west, so far does he remove our transgressions from us"? (103:12)

Man's forgiveness of others is often limited. We say, "I'll forgive but I will not forget." Sometimes we even forgive grudgingly. It is said that before his death Frederick the Great was told that he must forgive his enemies. He then said to Queen Dorothy, "Write to your brother that I forgive him all the evil he has done to me; *but wait till I am dead first."*

Not so with God, who forgives freely and forever. God's love rushes like a Niagara to heal and restore whenever we ask him to forgive us. How can the church demonstrate this truth to the world?

LIKE A FATHER

The Hebrews did not refer to God in abstract terms. Sometimes they spoke of him as Creator, King, or Lord of battle (hosts). These were not simply names to identify his person but references to his activity. God acted in the capacity of Creator, King, or Lord of battle, therefore these were proper ways of referring to him.

When the psalmist spoke of God as a father who "pities his children" (103:13), he was asserting that God loves like a father, that he is a father to his children. This truth was proved in history instead of through theological formulation or philosophical speculation.

Jesus, as we can see, did not originate the term *Father* for God. But he gave it a new depth of meaning. As the Son, God was *his* father. God was the father of such a Son. Thus we can see the fatherhood of God through the sonship of Jesus.

But the analogy does not stop here because God is the father of *all men.* He is "our Father who art in heaven," and *our* includes every man on earth.

Racial distinctions, social differences, economic levels, political affiliations, and geographical loyalties, while real to men, are of no significance where the love of God is concerned.

Brotherhood is the inevitable corollary of fatherhood. How can we call God "father" and take an unbrotherly attitude toward our fellow men? Inhumanity to man is a denial of God's character.

LOVE IN ACTION

The love of God as known in his mighty deeds for men is pre-eminently seen in the coming of Jesus Christ into history. God gave his Son that men might have eternal life (John 3:16). Here is the challenge to the church to remain the CHURCH. We have something to give to men—the Son of God and through him eternal life.

We must find a way, the best way, to give this gift in the present day.

At this point, Robert Raines's criticism of the church stabs us to the quick: " 'Come weal or woe, the status quo' is the gospel of many lately-revived ecclesiastical ghettoes which sold their evangelical birthright for a mess of pot-bellied respectability. . . . Let us say it quite clearly: refusal to change traditional patterns simply because they are traditional is a basic form of ecclesiastical idolatry. . . . Flexibility and experimentation should receive top priority in the church today." [4]

Are we emphasizing form and failing to present the gospel, the story of how much God cares for man, to the world? If so, how? What can we do to change this situation? If we can answer these questions, the exodus of young pastors from the ministry may be halted before it is too late.

[4] Robert Arnold Raines, *New Life in the Church* (Harper & Row, 1961), p. 139.

Helping Adults Become Involved —Harry B. Adams

Preparation of Self and Class

This lesson begins the second unit in this quarter. The first unit set forth the character of creation and the nature of man. In the concluding lesson of the unit last week the plight of man as sinner and as separated from God was described.

Although man has rebelled against God, corrupted the world God made, and distorted the life God gave to him, God does not cut himself off from man. The six lessons of this unit will explore the character of God as it is revealed in his actions—actions expressing God's love toward man and enabling man to find the life God intends for him.

This lesson looks at the profound expression of God's love in the psalm-ist's affirmation and in Jesus' witness. In preparing yourself for the lesson, you will want to reflect on what it means in your own life to know that God loves you.

Presenting the Main Question

Begin the lesson by describing the following situations, and then ask the members of the class how they would respond to the person in each instance.

Jane W. had only one child, a little girl who died of leukemia when she was five years old. Although the girl died two years ago, Jane has still not been able to put her life back together in any meaningful way. She has continued to attend church fairly regularly, but she is deeply troubled about how one can talk about a loving God who allows a five-year-old child to die.

The chaplain in the state prison talks with Jim frequently. Jim has been in prison for nearly ten years, convicted of the murder of his wife and child. He has appreciated talking with the chaplain and during his time in prison has become interested in religious questions and in what it means for a man to believe in God. Jim would like to believe but repeatedly raises with the chaplain the question of whether God could love a man who has done the things he has done.

Tom's father was an official in a large company. He made a lot of money, but his job was very demanding of his time and energy. From the time he was in the eighth grade, Tom was sent away to boarding school during the academic year and to camp during the summer. When he was home for vacations, his parents seemed to be glad to see him but were always so busy they did not seem to have much time to spend with him. Tom grew up very much a "loner" who just did not have any desire or capacity to relate in a significant way to other persons. At one stage in his college career he took several courses in religion and struggled with the questions of his own identity. But he could never quite figure out how God related to his life.

Developing the Lesson

Give the class members opportunity to share out of their experiences the ways in which they have known the love of God. You may want to list on chalkboard or newsprint the evidence that indicates to members of the class that it is possible to affirm God's love for his world and his people. Such things as the following may be indicated:

1. Through the resources of the world God provides for the needs of men.

2. God has made persons as creatures who are capable of expressing love for one another.

3. God has set men in a world in which there is beauty to nurture their spirits.

4. God has declared his love for men through the Scripture.

5. In the Holy Spirit men know the immediate presence of God in their lives.

6. God sustains men when they fail, when they are hurt, and when they are lonely.

7. God has created the church in which men's lives are sustained.

8. God has sent his son Jesus Christ to witness.

Look at the witness of the psalmist to the love of God. The material of Dr. Laymon and Dr. Thompson will help the class members explore the affirmation of God's love made by the author of Psalms 103. As the class members study this psalm, have them consider the following questions.

1. What keeps the psalm from being soft and sentimental?

2. Some men might think that if God loves them he will be easy on them no matter what they do. What evidence is there that the psalmist would or would not agree with that way of thinking?

3. What verse or verses in the psalm are most meaningful to you personally.

4. What experiences in your own life sustain or contradict what the psalmist is saying?

Consider what kind of people can know the love of God. Raise with the class members the question of whether there are men who are so evil or have done such terrible things that God no longer loves them. You may want to give some examples of persons who have been in the news recently because of the wrong they have done. Does God love the man who beats an old man to death on the street in order to take his wallet? Does God love the man who swindles people out of their life savings? Does God love the woman who beats her two-year-old daughter until she has to be taken to the hospital?

The biblical witness to God's love is that a man does not have to earn that love by being good. The psalmist talks of the mercy and the grace of God. Mercy and grace come to those who have no claim on God's love and forgiveness. As the previous lessons have made clear, no man has a claim on God's love because he is good enough to merit that love. God loves his people, whatever they are.

This is not to say that God will leave men as they are. He seeks to remove their transgressions, not so they will be free to sin again, but so they will try to show love for God and for their neighbor.

Not all men will know the love God has for them. In the words of the psalmist, it is "those who fear him" who know his steadfast love and his pity. God does not force his love on those who resolutely turn from him. Instead, he stands ever ready to receive those who turn toward him in fear and in expectation.

Listen to the affirmation of God's love made by the writer of the Gospel of John (3:16-17). As has been indicated in this lesson, there are many witnesses to God's love for his people, but the most compelling and moving witness is in the life and person of Jesus Christ. John 3:16 is one of the best known and best loved verses in all of Scripture, but try to help the class members to hear it anew in all its wondrous affirmation of God's love for them. Give members of the class opportunity to say what this verse means to them.

Indicate that the coming lessons will explore more fully what it means to affirm God's love in Jesus Christ in our kind of world.

Helping Class Members Act

Dr. Laymon raises the question of how God's love is expressed through the church. Consider with the class members how their church expresses God's love toward the world, and how it might do so more effectively.

Planning for Next Sunday

One of the verses in the Scripture for next Sunday declares that "the Word became flesh and dwelt among us, full of grace and truth." (John 1:14) Ask the members of the class to reflect on that assertion during the week and to indicate next Sunday what it means to them.

God Speaks Through Christ

Background Scripture: John 1:1-8, 14-18; Acts 10:34-43; Hebrews 1:1-4

The Main Question —Charles M. Laymon

When Mahatma Gandhi was leading the people of India to a new level of freedom and self-respect, he won the admiration of many Christians. Here was a man who, in his protest movement, advocated spirit-force rather than material violence. During those days a Hindu said to E. Stanley Jones, "Why do you preach on the second coming of Christ? He has already come—he is here—Gandhi!"

Such thoughts about Gandhi led many to ask, What is unique about Jesus Christ? This same line of thinking was even taken to include Buddha and Confucius. Students in the colleges were tempted to conclude that all religions were alike, equally good for those who really practiced them.

Is the idea that all religions are equally good tenable? Is it a sound judgment? Are we required by open-mindedness and tolerance to draw this conclusion?

Does it not finally come down to these questions: What is special about Jesus Christ? What is special about the Christian religion? Is God's revelation in Jesus unique?

The biblical passages that follow will help us in facing these issues.

As You Read the Scripture —Claude H. Thompson

The theme of last week, "God Loves Us," is now spelled out in life. Jesus comes into history as the personification of God's love.

Hebrews 1:1. *In many and various ways God spoke of old to our fathers by the prophets:* The Christian faith was not really new. Back of it was the ancient Hebrew religion. The Hebrew prophets were the spokesmen for God *par excellence.* This goodly heritage, although nearly lost in Jesus' day, was enshrined in the Bible of the time—the Old Testament. The prophetic message was adapted to current needs and was only partial. Each prophet had his own truth, but all the messages blended into the one theme of God's love and concern for men in their life situation.

Verse 2. *He has spoken to us by a Son:* While the prophetic message was *spoken,* that of the Son was *lived:* "The Word became flesh and dwelt among us." (John 1:14) God had to show us his will lived out in a man, his only son. What the prophets said in part, Jesus said fully—and more. What they anticipated of God's grace, Jesus portrayed. The prophets had a message *from* God; Jesus was the message *of* God. Note that Christ is said to have been involved in the very creation itself. This means that he was *pre-existent* —having a life within the divine community prior to his birth into history.

Verse 3. *He reflects the glory of God:* Note the cluster of high claims for

Christ: he reflects the very image of God; he bears "the flawless expression of the nature of God" (Phillips); he sustains the universe by his own power; he provides atonement for man's sin; and he occupies the position of authority in heaven. If these claims are not true, they are pious blasphemy. If they are true, Christ calls for our devoted obedience and worship.

GOD SPEAKS THROUGH CHRIST

Verse 4. *Having become . . . superior to angels:* Christ's is the most excellent rank in the universe, opening up the way into the very presence of God. He could do this because of his divineness and because he took upon himself the nature of man.

John 1:1. *In the beginning was the Word, and the Word was with God, and the Word was God:* The term *Logos* or *Word* indicates that Jesus was the very reason, wisdom, or mind of God. *Logos* was a profound term in Greek, and there is actually no completely satisfactory way to translate it. (Study carefully "The Word" in *The Interpreter's Dictionary of the Bible,* Vol. R-Z, pp. 868-72.) But the term at least means that the life of Jesus was the expression within history of God himself.

Verse 2. *He was in the beginning with God:* In simple language this means that Jesus is as eternal as God; that is, he was pre-existent, alive within the divine life before coming into history.

Verse 3. *All things were made through him:* The creative function of Jesus is asserted. His touch is upon everything that exists. Thus everything is made to perform his will; and when anything does not, it denies its own origin and nature.

Verse 4. *In him was life:* His life is Life—with a capital *L*—and it is so luminous as to enlighten every man who turns to the light.

Verse 5. *The light shines in the darkness:* But the enemy of light is there—darkness. Here is the perpetual conflict of light/darkness, good/evil, right/wrong, life/death. But even a tiny light can never be smothered by the dark.

Verses 6-8. *There was a man sent from God, whose name was John:* John the Baptist is introduced as pointing to Jesus as the Word of God.

Verses 14-18. *The Word became flesh and dwelt among us:* These words overwhelm us, so loftily do they represent Jesus. *The Word became flesh.* Here was no ghostly apparition. He was a *real* man—the only authentic man. He lived in the same sinful, messy world that we know but with "grace and truth." There was nothing phony about Jesus. His presence always uncovered the counterfeit.

The Fourth Gospel presents a series of witnesses to the significance of the life and mission of Jesus. Verse 15 has John the Baptist making the first witness.

Note the relation of law and grace (verse 17). The law, the most honored fact of the Hebrew religion, is attributed to Moses. But one greater than Moses has come. He provides not regulations and codes but a quality of life. *Grace* is a Greek term—meaning harmony, beauty, excellence, and, in the Christian faith, God's unselfish gift of his mercy to undeserving sinners. *Truth* is a Greek concept also; but here it is embodied in a life, a life that was lived among men to demonstrate the suffering love of God.

Since God is spirit, he cannot be seen. But Jesus has disclosed him—the fullest and most perfect revelation of God ever given to men. Thus "God Speaks Through Christ" an insistent message both of judgment and of reconciliation.

Selected Scripture

King James Version	Revised Standard Version
Hebrews 1:1-4	*Hebrews 1:1-4*
1 God, who at sundry times and in divers manners spake in time past unto the fathers by the prophets,	1 In many and various ways God spoke of old to our fathers by the prophets; 2 but in these last days he has spoken to us by a Son, whom he appointed the heir of all things, through whom also he created the world. 3 He reflects the glory of God and bears the very stamp of his nature, upholding the universe by his word of power. When he had made purification for sins, he sat down at the right hand of the Majesty on high, 4 having become as much superior to angels as the name he has obtained is
2 Hath in these last days spoken unto us by his Son, whom he hath appointed heir of all things, by whom also he made the worlds;	
3 Who being the brightness of his glory, and the express image of his person, and upholding all things by the word of his power, when he had by himself purged our sins, sat down on the right hand of the Majesty on high;	

4 Being made so much better than the angels, as he hath by inheritance obtained a more excellent name than they.

John 1:1-8, 14-18
1 In the beginning was the Word, and the Word was with God, and the Word was God.

2 The same was in the beginning with God.

3 All things were made by him; and without him was not any thing made that was made.

4 In him was life; and the life was the light of men.

5 And the light shineth in darkness; and the darkness comprehended it not.

6 There was a man sent from God, whose name was John.

7 The same came for a witness, to bear witness of the Light, that all men through him might believe.

8 He was not that Light, but was sent to bear witness of that Light.

. . . .

14 And the Word was made flesh, and dwelt among us, (and we beheld his glory, the glory as of the only begotten of the Father,) full of grace and truth.

15 John bare witness of him, and cried, saying, This was he of whom I spake, He that cometh after me is preferred before me: for he was before me.

16 And of his fulness have all we received, and grace for grace.

17 For the law was given by Moses, but grace and truth came by Jesus Christ.

18 No man hath seen God at any time; the only begotten Son, which is in the bosom of the Father, he hath declared him.

more excellent than theirs.

John 1:1-8, 14-18
1 In the beginning was the Word, and the Word was with God, and the Word was God. 2 He was in the beginning with God; 3 all things were made through him, and without him was not anything made that was made. 4 In him was life, and the life was the light of men. 5 The light shines in the darkness, and the darkness has not overcome it.

6 There was a man sent from God, whose name was John. 7 He came for testimony, to bear witness to the light, that all might believe through him. 8 He was not the light, but came to bear witness to the light.

. . . .

14 And the Word became flesh and dwelt among us, full of grace and truth; we have beheld his glory, glory as of the only Son from the Father. (15 John bore witness to him, and cried, "This was he of whom I said, 'He who comes after me ranks before me, for he was before me.'") 16 And from his fullness have we all received, grace upon grace. 17 For the law was given through Moses; grace and truth came through Jesus Christ. 18 No one has ever seen God; the only Son, who is in the bosom of the Father, he has made him known.

Memory Selection: No man hath seen God at any time; the only begotten Son, which is in the bosom of the Father, he hath declared him. (John 1:18)

Memory Selection: No one has ever seen God; the only Son, who is in the bosom of the Father, he has made him known. (John 1:18)

The Scripture and the Main Question —Charles M. Laymon

IN MANY AND VARIOUS WAYS

God's revelation to man is sometimes divided into general or natural revelation and special revelation. Paul the apostle recognized the first when he insisted that the gentiles had received a revelation of God in nature through "the things that have been made." (Romans 1:20) Special revelation, on the other hand, would refer to the truths that God has uniquely revealed in Christ. Paul also believed in this second channel of truth. He said of Jesus Christ that "in him the whole fulness of deity dwells bodily." (Colossians 2:9) Of none other could or would Paul say this.

Natural revelation has impressed men for centuries. In worshiping sun, fire, and water, early man was responding to what he saw in nature. Later the wonder and beauty of the natural order convinced man that there was a God. Alfred Lord Tennyson, in his "Flower in the Crannied Wall," took up a single blossom and musing said that if he could understand it, he would "know what God and man is."

A student once interrupted his science teacher, who was looking at a living cell tissue through his microscope, with the question, "Professor, do you believe in God?" The teacher replied without even looking up from the eyepiece, "Can't you see I am praying to him?" He was experiencing fellowship with God.

When the lunar module of Apollo 14 reached its destination only two minutes late, landed but sixty feet from the chosen spot, and redocked with the main rocket just two seconds off schedule, many said, "How wonderful is man!" Others added, "How majestic is God!" Here was a revelation of the divine integrity.

THE SON OF GOD

In spite of the wonders of God's revelation in nature, however, it is in the Son that we see him most truly. John said that the Word was made flesh in Jesus and that in him the glory of God was made manifest (1:14). The author of Hebrews also referred to the Son as reflecting the glory of God (1:3).

The material world, even in all its marvelous structure and beauty, does not have the warmth and significance of the personal touch that the Son, Jesus, had. He was the friend of sinners and the comforter of the sorrowing. Because of this, John Greenleaf Whittier, the poet, could refer to Jesus as one who was warm, sweet, and tender in the hymn "Immortal Love, Forever Full."

Most of us began to find God in the love with which our parents surrounded us. Here was security; but even more, here was heart-to-heart closeness. In this same way those who knew Jesus were encircled by the love of God. His words, deeds, countenance, and bearing—all spoke of God. When he was near, God was near. When he was present, they felt that God himself was at work in their lives.

To no other person could man plead as Charles Wesley did, "Jesus, lover of my soul,/Let me to thy bosom fly." Name the heroes of the Bible. Which of them would fit these words? Could we say "Moses, lover of my soul" or "Jeremiah, lover of my soul"? Why not? Is it because only in Jesus do we find the Son of God?

THE COSMIC CHRIST

Both John and the author of the Book of Hebrews were so convinced that what men found in Jesus was true of the character of the universe that they could refer to him as the one through whom God made the world (John 1:3; Hebrews 1:2). Some of the Greek philosophers of that day envisioned intermediary beings between heaven and earth who were active in creation. The philosophers regarded matter as evil and therefore believed that God could not have come into contact with it directly. In this setting it was a stroke of insight for the Christians to conclude that there was only one mediator between heaven and earth and that this mediator was the Word or the Son. He was the agent of creation.

We today are not so much concerned with the philosophical explanations of the Greeks, but we are eager to discover the nature of the universe. Is it friendly? More than this, is the universe good? Is love at the heart of all things?

The biblical authors in today's lesson were affirming that the universe is friendly, that it is good, and that love is at the heart of it. The Word —the Son—was active in its making. In Jesus we find the very purpose of existence—the world's and our own.

A CHRISTLIKE GOD

Whether he invented the expression or not I do not know, but Bishop Francis J. McConnell gave meaning to the idea of a Christlike God. In essence he asserted that if we find God revealed in Christ, then God himself is Christlike.

When, therefore, we think of God, we are to see him not as cold, impersonal Will but as a warm and active Being. Like Jesus he is personal; he knows; he cares; he acts in love. Since Jesus Christ has made him known, we are no longer in doubt as to God's character.

More than this, if God is this kind of being, we are expected to be his kind of person and to act in line with his character. George Bernard Shaw, the distinguished writer and winner of the Nobel Prize, did not consider himself a Christian. But he said that he preferred Jesus of Nazareth to Amos or Caiaphas, and added that he saw "no way out of the world's misery but the way which would have been found by his will." Is not this true because God is Christlike?

Helping Adults Become Involved —Harry B. Adams

Preparation of Self and Class

The conclusion of the previous lesson mentions the affirmation from the Gospel of John that "God so loved the world that he gave his only Son." The assertion of a God of love is not unique with the Christian faith.

There is testimony to God's steadfast love in the Old Testament. The Islamic faith affirms a God who cares for his people. Christianity as a religion shares many of its practices and tenets with other religions of the world.

But there is something unique about the Christian faith, pointed to in the affirmation that God "gave his only Son." Jesus Christ gives the distinction and crucial character to the faith of the Christian.

This lesson begins the exploration of who Jesus Christ was and what he did. As you begin your preparation for this lesson, you will want to consider what the church and the Scriptures have said about Jesus. You will also want to reflect on who Jesus has been to you and what he has meant in your own life. You might try to imagine how your life, and the lives of the people in your class, would have been different if they had never known Jesus.

Presenting the Main Question

A recent poll conducted in this country asked people to name the person they admired most in the history of the United States. You might begin the lesson by taking a poll of the class on the following questions:

1. What person has had the greatest influence in shaping the history of this nation, whether for good or bad?

2. What person has been most influential in helping the nation achieve whatever greatness or goodness it has achieved?

3. What person in American history do you think would be most admired by people in other nations?

4. What American has made the greatest contribution to mankind?

Incidentally, the poll mentioned above indicated that Abraham Lincoln was the most admired person in American history. After the class members have given their answers to the questions, ask them to consider not simply the history of this nation but the history of the whole world, and to reflect on whether they think Jesus would be the person most peo-

ple would suggest in responding to some of the questions.

Discuss with the class the following questions:

1. What qualities in Jesus do persons admire?

2. What impact has he had on the ways in which men understand who they are and how they should live?

3. If a person who had never heard of Jesus asked you to describe him, what would you say?

4. How has your own life been changed or influenced because you have known Jesus?

Developing the Lesson

Consider the factors that influence the views men have of themselves and of the meaning of their lives. Every man has to answer some basic questions about what it means to be a person and about how he is going to use his life. He may not articulate precise answers to all these questions, but he will answer them nonetheless by the way in which he lives.

Invite the class members to indicate what they think the most basic questions of life are. They might include some of the following:

1. What is the goal of life?

2. What are the values men seek to realize?

3. How does a person fulfill what he was intended to be?

4. What gives real joy or satisfaction to a person?

Once the class members have identified for themselves what the fundamental issues are, raise the question of the influences that shape the way in which men deal with these issues. What experiences have an impact on ·he way in which a person views the meaning of his life? Such things as books, magazines, television, the values of his parents, the ideas of his peers, the perspective of the culture, immediately come to mind as influences that play on each individual.

For the Christian, Jesus embodies man as he was intended to be. Give the class members opportunity to discuss two questions:

1. What is the meaning of life as Jesus expressed it?

2. How has Jesus helped you deal with the basic questions of your life?

Consider the factors that influence the views men have of God. If there are varied experiences that shape the way in which men look at themselves, it can also be noted that men's views of God are not formed in a vacuum. Or to put the issue in other terms, God has revealed himself to man in various ways.

Give the class members opportunity to express their ideas of how God comes to men and to share experiences that seemed to make God known to them. The section "In Many and Various Ways" in Dr. Laymon's material will provide a resource for this discussion.

As the Christian finds that Jesus embodies what man ought to be, he also sees in Jesus the embodiment of God, or God-become-flesh. Give the class members the opportunity to share their insights on the meaning of the assertion that "the Word became flesh and dwelt among us."

Using the material prepared by Dr. Laymon and Dr. Thompson, study the passages in Hebrews and John indicated as the resource for this lesson. Both of these passages are rich in imagery and compress profound assertions into a few words. As the passages are studied, give the class members opportunity to indicate in what way Jesus has been an active presence in their lives. For example, in what way has their experience of Jesus given meaning to the image that he is the light who has come into the dark-

ness? How do they feel about the assertion that from Jesus "have we all received, grace upon grace"?

Listen with the class members to what God is saying to men today, if he does speak through Jesus Christ. Ask the class members to indicate which of the following statements seem to them to express who God is and what he is doing, if the author of Hebrews is right that "he has spoken to us by a Son."

1. God does forgive men for their sins and offers them the possibility of a new start.

2. God is best described as the First Principle.

3. It is meaningful to discern God's involvement in the daily affairs of human existence.

4. God's power is expressed in ways men interpret as loving.

5. The power and wonder and beauty of nature are the most adequate expression of the nature and work of God.

Helping Class Members Act

Every action of men is distorted and tainted with self-interest. Yet men seek to act and live in accord with the purposes of God as he has expressed those purposes in Jesus Christ. Suggest that the members of the class look at their own actions during the coming week to determine what they do during their daily life that they believe to be in accord with God's will for them and for their world.

Planning for Next Sunday

In preparation for the lesson next Sunday ask the members of the class to consider what happens in the relationship between persons when one person hurts another and what possible ways a broken relationship can be restored.

Christ Suffered for Us

Background Scripture: Isaiah 52:13 through 53:12;
Matthew 26:1-5, 26-29; 1 Peter 2:21-25

The Main Question —Charles M. Laymon

Dr. J. Robert Oppenheimer, distinguished scientist at the research center at Los Alamos, was reported in *Time* magazine as saying that when the first atomic bomb was set off in the desert to test its potential, he immediately thought of a passage from the *Bhagavad-Gita* (a Hindu writing): "I am become death, the shatterer of worlds." Oppenheimer then commented, "In some sort of crude sense which no vulgarity, no humor, no overstatement can quite extinguish, the physicists have known sin: and this is a knowledge which they cannot lose." [5]

The words of this sensitive scientist placed the sin question at the center of modern life. Man knew sin all along, but a new feature had been added to its face and a new dimension to its evil character. Like the psalmist who said "My sin is ever before me" (51:3), we cannot forget the enormity of the destruction we are capable of bringing upon the world.

What is to be done about the sin question? What has been done about sin and sinners? What can I do about my own sins? A whole cluster of questions confront us when we begin to think deeply about sin.

Some basic answers to these questions are given in the biblical passages that follow.

As You Read the Scripture —Claude H. Thompson

God not only "speaks *through* Christ"; God acts *in* Christ. "God was in Christ reconciling the world to himself." (2 Corinthians 5:19) This reconciliation discloses the cost to God to bring a rebel people to their sanity—and salvation.

Isaiah 53:4. *Surely he has borne our griefs and carried our sorrows:* Isaiah 53:4-9 is part of at least four passages in Second Isaiah known as the "Servant Songs." All show suffering as God's way of redemption. (See Isaiah 42:1-4; 49:1-6; 50:4-9; and 52:13 through 53:12—in which occurs the passage for our lesson.)

Grief and sorrow are the common lot of man, sufficiently serious to require help from beyond man's own abilities. But who can help? Our fellow men can do a little, but they too labor under the common needs of humanity. The Christian faith has interpreted this passage as prophesying the coming of Christ, the Messiah, who alone has been adequate for man's grief and

[5] In "The Eternal Apprentice," *Time,* November 8, 1948, p. 77.

sorrow. There may be a question that the author precisely foresaw Jesus of Nazareth in this role, but we may be sure that Jesus identified his mission with the Suffering Servant of Second Isaiah. Jesus not only was the incarnation of God in history, but he also made the Suffering Servant a reality for men to see —and worship.

This verse also says the Servant was "smitten by God." At least it was the will of the Father, and Jesus' will, for Jesus to identify his life with man's sin, sorrow, and suffering. He actually experienced our sensations—even through death.

Verse 5. *He was wounded for our transgressions:* This verse should be read devotionally—with deep gratitude for such love. But it should also be heard in judgment, since in every pain of our time Jesus still bears the agony. "He always lives to make intercession." (Hebrews 7:25) I write this in the midst of the protest against the war in Cambodia. By the time it comes from the press, we trust, God willing, the tragedy in Southeast Asia will be over. But remember this: It was not America, not Cambodia, not Vietnam which suffered most; it was Jesus Christ, who has gone through it all while he intercedes at the high throne of heaven for his children who learn so slowly.

In Hebrew poetic parallelism the idea of Jesus' substitution for us is repeated several times in the verse for emphasis. The verse should be read aloud to get the feel of pain, yet of triumph. Listen: "Bruised for our iniquities"; "upon him was the chastisement"; "with his stripes we are healed." Read these words until they become a hymn of victory for the God who loves until it hurts.

Verse 6. *All we like sheep have gone astray:* The theme of man's waywardness is again introduced. We want to do our own will. And upon him has been laid "the iniquity of us all." Our waywardness led to his faithfulness.

Verse 7. *He was oppressed:* This verse shows the patient endurance, under the pain of death and rejection, of our Lord. He was silent, like the lamb or sheep about to be sacrificed.

Verse 8. *By oppression and judgment he was taken away:* Through treachery Jesus was killed, but who of those living in his time ever knew it was for their sins that he died? Only after reflection did even his closest followers realize he died for the very people who executed him—as well as for them.

Verse 9. *They made his grave with the wicked:* Jesus experienced the common death of the wicked man and the rich man alike in a democracy of the grave. Yet he died guiltless, condemned by those who hated him, misunderstood by the masses, and forsaken by his friends.

1 Peter 2:24-25. *He himself bore our sins:* These words are taken almost verbatim from Isaiah 53:5-6 and 53:12. The passage shows how the Christian mind, now with the career of Jesus in the past, could find no better language than these Old Testament words to describe the purpose of his coming: to suffer for the sins of the whole world.

Selected Scripture

King James Version

Isaiah 53:4-9

4 Surely he hath borne our griefs, and carried our sorrows: yet we did esteem him stricken, smitten of God, and afflicted.

5 But he was wounded for our transgressions, he was bruised for our iniquities: the chastisement of our peace was upon him; and with his stripes we are healed.

6 All we like sheep have gone astray; we have turned every one to his own way; and the LORD hath laid on him the iniquity of us all.

7 He was oppressed, and he was afflicted, yet he opened not his mouth: he is brought as a lamb to the slaughter, and as a sheep before her shearers is dumb, so he openeth not his mouth.

8 He was taken from prison and from judgment: and who shall declare his generation? for he was cut off out of the land of the living: for the transgression of my people was he stricken.

9 And he made his grave with the wicked, and with the rich in his death; because he had done no violence, neither was any deceit in his mouth.

1 Peter 2:24-25

24 Who his own self bare our sins in his own body on the tree, that we, being dead to sins, should live unto

Revised Standard Version

Isaiah 53:4-9

4 Surely he has borne our griefs
  and carried our sorrows;
yet we esteemed him stricken,
  smitten by God, and afflicted.

5 But he was wounded for our transgressions,
  he was bruised for our iniquities;
upon him was the chastisement
  that made us whole,
  and with his stripes we are
  healed.

6 All we like sheep have gone astray;
  we have turned every one to his
  own way;
and the LORD has laid on him the
  iniquity of us all.

7 He was oppressed, and he was
  afflicted,
  yet he opened not his mouth;
like a lamb that is led to the slaughter,
  and like a sheep that before its
  shearers is dumb,
  so he opened not his mouth.

8 By oppression and judgment he was
  taken away;
  and as for his generation, who
  considered
that he was cut off out of the land
  of the living,
  stricken for the transgression
  of my people?

9 And they made his grave with the
  wicked
  and with a rich man in his death,
although he had done no violence,
  and there was no deceit in his
  mouth.

1 Peter 2:24-25

24 He himself bore our sins in his body on the tree, that we might die to sin and live to righteousness. By his

righteousness: by whose stripes ye were healed.

25 For ye were as sheep going astray; but are now returned unto the Shepherd and Bishop of your souls.

Memory Selection: He was wounded for our transgressions, he was bruised for our iniquities: the chastisement of our peace was upon him; and with his stripes we are healed. (Isaiah 53:5)

wounds you have been healed. 25 For you were straying like sheep, but have now returned to the Shepherd and Guardian of your souls.

Memory Selection:
He was wounded for our transgressions,
he was bruised for our iniquities;
upon him was the chastisement
   that made us whole,
and with his stripes we are
   healed.   (Isaiah 53:5)

The Scripture and the Main Question —Charles M. Laymon

THE FACT OF SIN

Some persons seem to enjoy confessing their sins in public. In personal testimony they list the evil deeds they have done and try to outdistance their neighbor's record of sinful practices. Equally pathological are those who are so hush-hush about their sins that they give the impression of wearing a halo. The Bible avoids both of these extremes as it insists that sin is real. Isaiah says, "All we like sheep have gone astray." (Isaiah 53:6)

It is sobering to realize that by the time we are able to distinguish right from wrong we discover that we are already sinners in need of forgiveness. This gives significance to the doctrine of original sin. We all fall short of the ideal, everyone of us. The fact of sin is inescapable.

When we get down to the basics in our thinking about sin, one fact emerges as being true of all sin and sinning. Man places his own will first, even above God's will, when he sins. The words *I, me,* and *mine* loom large in our vocabulary. And when they take over fully, both God and others come in as second best.

Archbishop William Temple, in *Christianity and Social Order,* said of sin, "I put myself in God's place. This is my original sin." Was this not what Adam and Eve did in the Garden of Eden when they ate the forbidden fruit? We want what we want when we want it. This is true whether we sin secretly or openly. A drag away from goodness and a drive toward evil seem to be at work within us constantly.

GETTING RID OF GUILT

The so-called pleasures of sin are short-lived. They bear a bitter fruit. Paul Laurence Dunbar was one of the first black writers to gain recognition. One of his verses of special insight was titled "The Debt" and had to do with sin and its consequences:

This is the debt I pay
Just for one riotous day,—
Years of regret and grief,
Sorrow without relief.

The guilt feelings that follow sinning are very real. Ask any psychiatrist or minister who has counseled persons in trouble. Guilt feelings may last throughout life if nothing is done about them.

How can we get rid of guilt feelings? Modern man has tried many remedies. I saw a popular magazine on the rack at the check-out counter of the supermarket. The cover carried the title of the lead article: "Forgive Yourself." Such action may bring temporary relief, but somehow we do not stay forgiven on this basis.

Sometimes we attempt to atone for our sins by smothering them with a rash of good deeds, but they will not stay smothered. Again, we may try to psychologize our guilt away only to discover that mental gymnastics will not work either. In extreme cases we may subconsciously punish ourselves by becoming accident prone or depressed.

None of these ways of handling guilt are finally effective. But there is a way through this agonizing maze.

Where Christ Comes In

Here Christ comes into the guilt problem. In both of the biblical passages for today Christ's relation to sin and guilt are stressed. First Peter says, "He himself bore our sins in his body on the tree." (2:24) Isaiah tells of a suffering servant, who seems to prefigure the Christ. The prophet states, "He was wounded for our transgressions, he was bruised for our iniquities; . . . and with his stripes we are healed." (53:5)

That Christ died for man's sins is written into the "warp and woof" of the entire New Testament. If we remove this teaching, much of the message of its writings will not make sense. Christ's suffering on the cross and our forgiveness are inseparably bound together here.

Theologians have written many volumes to explain how Christ's death and man's forgiveness relate to each other. This theme is referred to as the atonement. Some of the explanations stress the debt side of sin, emphasizing that on the cross Jesus paid our debt and died in our stead. Others emphasize the death of Christ as a sacrificial shedding of blood for our sin. He is presented as the sacrificial lamb in line with the Hebrew background of blood sacrifice. How to describe the cross, how to explain it, how to interpret it—these theological formulations are attempting to do just this.

Christ the Savior

Lay Christians sometimes find it difficult to follow the intricate lines of theological reasoning. The most helpful and simple way that I have found to demonstrate the truth that Christ died for man's sins is to break apart the word *atonement* so that it will read at-one-ment. This is what looking at the cross with faith and, in repentance, responding to Christ's death for man brings about; the guilt for sin is lost in the love of God that touches our lives from the cross.

Where sin and guilt have separated us from God, his love on the cross draws us to him again. We have realized our at-one-ment with him. Once more we can know communion with God—in the assurance of forgiveness. The burden of guilt is lost in the love of God in Christ as demonstrated in his suffering for us.

But it does not end here; the acceptance of what Christ has done for us is but the beginning of a life of discipleship with Christ. First Peter says that Christ is the "Shepherd and Guardian" of our souls (2:25). Christians find this to be true as they lead lives of service in his name.

Helping Adults Become Involved —Harry B. Adams

Preparation of Self and Class

The third lesson of this quarter looked at the biblical interpretation of the nature and character of man. Though created in the image of God, man has corrupted and distorted his life. In short, he is a sinner. He and his world bear the consequences of his sin.

In spite of man's sin, God continues to express his love—a love evidenced in God's care and above all in his sending of Jesus Christ into the world. This lesson deals specifically with how the suffering and the death of Christ are related to the plight of man as a sinner.

Two films may serve as resources for this lesson: *Parable,* a depiction of the world as a circus with the clown as its redeemer, and *The Antkeeper.* (See page 231.)

No simple explanation or neat formula will grasp what the suffering and death of Christ mean for men. This lesson is dealing with a mystery, one which takes on meaning as persons reflect on it and respond to what God has done for them.

Presenting the Main Question

Ernest Gordon, in his book *Through the Valley of the Kwai,* tells of an incident in a Japanese prison camp during World War II. A guard accused a group of prisoners of stealing a shovel and selling it. He demanded that the guilty one step forward, but no one moved. Finally he declared that he would kill the whole group. Just as he was about to fire his rifle at the first man in the line, a soldier stepped forward. The guard jumped on him and beat him with his rifle until he was dead. When they got back to the guardhouse and count-ed the shovels again, they found that no shovel was missing.

This was one of a number of incidents that somehow changed the whole situation of the prisoners. They had been reduced almost to animals by their suffering and deprivation. Men fought one another for scraps from the garbage cans and pushed the weak off to die. But some acts of giving for others and bearing the burdens of others by a few of the prisoners brought a whole new life style to the camp. By acts such as that of the innocent soldier who gave his life so that his fellow prisoners would not be killed, men regained their humanity, their capacity to think about another even in the midst of their own terrible need.

Give the class members opportunity to share out of their experiences what happens to a group or to individual persons when one person is willing to give or to suffer for another.

Developing the Lesson

Explore with the class members what happens when sin corrupts and distorts the relationship between men. You might begin this discussion by asking three persons to take three roles. The first person is one who hurts or sins against another in some way. The second person is the one who is hurt by the first. The third person is a friend concerned about both.

Ask each person to indicate what he might do to help or to harm the situation in which the three find themselves because of the hurt the first man has done to the second.

For example, the first man might try to blame someone else; or he might try to deny that he had done any wrong. He might apologize, or he might try to make good for the damage he had done.

The second man might try to get revenge, or he might simply refuse to have anything to do with the other. He might hate the other, or he might forgive the other.

The third man might try to ignore the whole situation, or he might side with one of the men against the other. He might try to persuade the one to apologize and the other to forgive, or he might seek to help the man who had been hurt.

If you asked the class members to think during the week about what sin does to relationships between persons, give them an opportunity to share their insights.

Consider how sin breaks the relationship between man and God. When a person does something to hurt another out of greed or selfishness or indifference or hate, the bond between the two is seriously disrupted. In a similar way, the relationship between man and his God is strained when man sins against God and against his fellow man.

Let the class members share out of their experiences or insights their awareness of how sin separates men from God. Look also at some of the dynamics present when man violates his relationship with God. Some of the following might be indicated:

1. God is concerned, not only with external deeds, but also with the motives and intentions behind these deeds.

2. Before God's goodness and holiness even the best of men are revealed to be corrupt.

3. If man were acceptable to God only when he fulfilled completely what God wanted him to be, then no man would be acceptable.

4. God judges a man, not as an-other man who shares his sinful state, but as the holy and righteous one.

Explore the way in which God has dealt with men who have rebelled against him and sinned against one another. The passages from Isaiah and First Peter speak of the one who came to suffer for others and on behalf of others. Study these passages with the class members, using the guides prepared by Dr. Laymon and Dr. Thompson.

For the Christian, the suffering of Christ is inseparably tied to his own relationship to God, to his own sin and God's forgiveness. The meaning of Christ's suffering can never be grasped fully by any person. Some suggestions of the meaning of Christ's suffering as it relates to man's situation are given below. Give the class members opportunity to indicate which of these suggestions are meaningful to them.

1. Christ's suffering indicates the seriousness of man's sin, for it was the sin of man that put him on the cross.

2. Christ's suffering shows the depth of God's love for man, even when man has rebelled against him.

3. By his suffering, Christ paid the penalty that man should have paid because of his sin.

4. Christ's suffering is evidence of the costliness of God's forgiveness.

5. As men's hearts are moved when one man suffers to help another, so men's hearts are moved toward God when they know that in Christ he suffered for them.

6. By his suffering, Christ entered fully and completely into man's plight and in that sharing brought healing to man.

7. By his willingness to die in faithfulness to what God had to accomplish, Christ inspires men to greater faithfulness.

Helping Class Members Act

Contemplating the suffering of Christ does not merely lead to theories about what it means or how it works. The suffering of Christ reconciles men to God and frees them to live more fully and lovingly. Encourage the members of the class to indicate some of the ways in which their awareness that Christ lived and died for them will affect how they live their lives and how they treat other persons.

Planning for Next Sunday

Ask the class members to gather all the examples they can find of how men behave when they have power and authority over others.

Jesus Christ Is King

Background Scripture: Zechariah 9:9-10; John 18:33-37; Philippians 2:5-11; Revelation 19:11-16

The Main Question —Charles M. Laymon

The regular Sunday evening youth meeting at the church was interrupted by an adult who almost ran into the room to see what was happening. Instead of the sweet strains of "O Young and Fearless Prophet," the beat of rock music was coming through the walls, under the door, and out the windows.

This concerned intruder found the young people playing the rock opera *Jesus Christ Superstar*. This musical interpretation of the last days of Jesus' life in Jerusalem not only uses the rock beat but also the phrases and expressions of the "now generation."

"Isn't that sacrilegious?" asked the adult visitor. "Not at all," said a sixteen-year-old girl. "It's all about Jesus, how great he was and how people proclaimed him a superstar as he rode into Jerusalem on Palm Sunday."

This "opera" is one of the approaches to the story of Jesus that some youth find meaningful today. It falls upon many adult ears with a dull thud. Should it?

The lesson for this Sunday refers to Jesus as *King*. What does this title mean in our time when no absolute monarchies remain? How is he king? Of whom is he king? How does he exercise his kingship? Is this an empty title, or does it make a difference in our lives? Is Jesus our superstar?

The passages from the Bible that follow will help us answer these questions.

As You Read the Scripture —Claude H. Thompson

Kings have little place in our time. They seem less and less important in the politics of today's world. A king who lived over nineteen centuries ago seems even less meaningful for us. Yet that king has had a greater influence upon history than any man who ever lived. And he was a king who reigned not from a throne but from a cross.

279

Zechariah 9:9. *Rejoice greatly, O daughter of Zion! Shout aloud, O daughter of Jerusalem!* Both of these statements mean the same thing. This style of writing is known as Hebrew parallelism—for emphasis.

Israel's hope for a king was deep in her national history. In her early days Jacob gave assurance that "the scepter shall not depart from Judah, nor the ruler's staff from between his feet." (Genesis 49:10) A better known example is the people's cry for a king to the prophet Samuel (1 Samuel 8:6-9). The result of their demand was Israel's first king, Saul. The question was, however, what kind of king did Israel need? Yahweh desired to be their king, but they wanted an earthly monarch like other nations. The troubles during the monarchy—from the time of Saul until the Exile—show that having a king did not solve their problems. Yet they persisted in a hope for a king who would rule permanently and well. Thus when Zechariah said, "Lo, your king comes to you," he was expressing the hope of his people.

(Read Matthew 21:1-7 and John 12:12-16 to see how the Gospel writers incorporated this passage into their interpretation of the entrance of Jesus into Jerusalem on what we call Palm Sunday.)

Verse 10. *I will cut off the chariot from Ephraim:* The elements of war are to be destroyed: the chariot, the war horse, the battle bow. This is a king of peace. Zechariah also says that the rule of the king shall be "from the River to the ends of the earth." The river is the Euphrates, and this expression shows the great extent of the kingdom.

Philippians 2:5b-11. This passage was apparently a hymn used by the Christians long before Paul wrote his letter. The hymn so completely expressed the faith of the church regarding Jesus that Paul employed it to confirm his witness. No other passage in the New Testament describes the person of Jesus Christ quite as well as this one does.

Verse 6. *Though he was in the form of God:* The word *form* means the permanent, changeless, divine character of Jesus. Through all his experiences as Jesus of Nazareth this divine life was never forfeited. But he did not grasp it—selfishly hold on to it—if so, he would never have understood the sorry condition of human life.

Verses 7-8. *But emptied himself, taking the form of a servant:* What was Christ's by right—his experience of living within the divine life—he voluntarily gave up for a time in order to identify himself with man in trouble. Otherwise, he could never have known the depths of human need. Thus Jesus assumed the role of servant. The best example was his taking the towel and basin to wash the disciples' feet (John 13:3-9). He illustrated his own teaching: "Whoever would be great among you must be your servant." (Mark 10:43) This emptying—pouring out—of himself enabled Jesus to experience total human life, culminating in death—"even death on a cross."

Verses 9-11. *Therefore God has . . . bestowed on him the name:* The giving of a name was important in the ancient world. It designated the inner character of the person. Jesus gets a name "which is above every name"—*kurios,* Lord. It is an exalted name—one which calls forth worship and obedience. Indeed, everything—in heaven, on the earth, and under the earth—is destined to bow before him. "Jesus Christ is Lord" was the earliest Christian confession, actually a creed of commitment.

Selected Scripture

King James Version	Revised Standard Version

Zechariah 9:9-10

Zechariah 9:9-10

9 Rejoice greatly, O daughter of Zion; shout, O daughter of Jerusalem: behold, thy King cometh unto thee: he is just, and having salvation; lowly, and riding upon an ass, and upon a colt the foal of an ass.

9 Rejoice greatly, O daughter of Zion!
Shout aloud, O daughter of Jerusalem!
Lo, your king comes to you;
triumphant and victorious is he,
humble and riding on an ass,
on a colt the foal of an ass.

10 And I will cut off the chariot from Ephraim, and the horse from Jerusalem, and the battle bow shall be cut off: and he shall speak peace unto the heathen: and his dominion shall be from sea even to sea, and from the river even to the ends of the earth.

10 I will cut off the chariot from Ephraim
and the war horse from Jerusalem;
and the battle bow shall be cut off,
and he shall command peace to the nations;
his dominion shall be from sea to sea,
and from the River to the ends of the earth.

Philippians 2:5b-11

Philippians 2:5b-11

5 ... Christ Jesus:

6 Who, being in the form of God, thought it not robbery to be equal with God:

7 But made himself of no reputation, and took upon him the form of a servant, and was made in the likeness of men:

8 And being found in fashion as a man, he humbled himself, and became obedient unto death, even the death of the cross.

9 Wherefore God also hath highly exalted him, and given him a name which is above every name:

10 That at the name of Jesus every knee should bow, of things in heaven, and things in earth, and things under the earth;

11 And that every tongue should confess that Jesus Christ is Lord, to the glory of God the Father.

5 ... Christ Jesus, 6 who, though he was in the form of God, did not count equality with God a thing to be grasped, 7 but emptied himself, taking the form of a servant, being born in the likeness of men. 8 And being found in human form he humbled himself and became obedient unto death, even death on a cross. 9 Therefore God has highly exalted him and bestowed on him the name which is above every name, 10 that at the name of Jesus every knee should bow, in heaven and on earth and under the earth, 11 and every tongue confess that Jesus Christ is Lord, to the glory of God the Father.

Memory Selection: Let all the house of Israel know assuredly, that God hath made that same Jesus, whom ye have crucified, both Lord and Christ. (Acts 2:36)

Memory Selection: Let all the house of Israel therefore know assuredly that God has made him both Lord and Christ, this Jesus whom you crucified. (Acts 2:36)

The Scripture and the Main Question —Charles M. Laymon

TITLES FOR CHRIST

One day Savonarola, the monk who held Florence, Italy, in his power for a time, stood in the cathedral and announced that he was proclaiming a new ruler for the city. It was Palm Sunday, and the cathedral was crowded. The people waited breathlessly. Then Savonarola cried aloud, "The new Head is Christ! Christ seeks to become your King." And at that the whole multitude were on their feet, shouting: "Long live Jesus, King of Florence!"

The title *Superstar* for Jesus Christ, compared to this, may sound too theatrical. We are more familiar with the biblical titles, and our emotions are attached to them. Even in the Bible, however, we find a great variety of titles for Jesus; no single ascription will do.

What's in a title? This is like asking, What's in a name? Where Jesus is concerned, the names by which he is known are dynamically related to his character and to what he does for persons.

A list of these titles is revealing. He is called variously: Rabbi (John 3:2), Master (Mark 9:5), prophet (Mark 8:28), Teacher (John 13:14), Messiah (John 1:41), servant (Acts 3:26), Son of man (Mark 8:38), Savior (Acts 5:31), mediator (1 Timothy 2:5), high priest (Hebrews 4:14), Lord (Acts 2:36), judge (Acts 10:42), Son of God (Galatians 2:20), the Word (John 1:1), and King of kings and Lord of lords (Revelation 19:16).

Which of these titles do you prefer? Your answer will probably depend upon your mood and situation when you are asked this question.

THE KING OF PEACE

How appropriate it was for Dean Acheson at the time of the signing of the peace treaty with Japan to close the conference with words that had meant so much to so many persons, speaking a variety of languages: "May the peace of God which passeth all understanding be amongst us and remain with us always." The war was ended; a prayer for peace was in order.

When Jesus rode into Jerusalem on an ass on Palm Sunday, he came to tell the city that if he were her king her war would be over too. Long before this time, the prophet Zechariah had pictured the king of Israel as "triumphant and victorious," riding into the Holy City in this same humble fashion (9:9). Zechariah said that the chariot, the war horse, and the battle bow would no longer be needed after the king came. Instead, this king would "command peace to the nations . . . to the ends of the earth." (verse 10)

Two fingers of the right hand raised to form the letter *V* were used in World War II by Sir Winston Churchill to stand for final victory. During the Vietnam conflict this same sign was used for peace. Jesus is known as the king of peace. Can the peace we seek be realized apart from him? Can we change the trappings of war

282

into instruments of peace without him?

THE KING OF TRUTH

In the pursuit of war, truth sometimes seems to be lost. For the sake of safety, surprise attack, and the need to keep morale high, it appears necessary to misrepresent the facts. President Woodrow Wilson on the night before he asked Congress to declare war against Germany was talking to Frank Cobb, editor of the *New York World*. Wilson said to Cobb, "From now on we shall not be able to tell the truth."

Since Wilson made this statement a change has taken place. With our news media more highly developed it is no longer possible to keep the facts from the people. When governments try to do so, a credibility gap is created; morale and confidence in the national leadership are lowered.

We are coming to see that only truth will win out, whether in peace or war. "Give us the facts; we can take it," we say. Truth alone will provide the foundation for the future. How significant, then, to recall that Jesus once referred to himself as a king of truth (John 18:37). He had come into the world to bear witness to the truth.

KING OF OUR LIVES

Ascribing kingship to Jesus may lift and thrill us, even as it was a deeply moving experience for the pilgrims who waved palm branches before him as he entered Jerusalem. They cried, "Blessed be the King who comes in the name of the Lord!" (Luke 19:38) But his kingship must do more than give us a "charge"; it must enlist all of us in his service. Jesus must actually become the king of our lives. He must control our motives and our movements.

Richard Watson Gilder said in "The Song of a Heathen" that he would follow Jesus Christ "through heaven and hell, the earth, the sea, the air." The apostle Paul viewed Jesus' kingship in a similar way when he proclaimed: "At the name of Jesus every knee should bow, in heaven and on earth and under the earth, and every tongue confess that Jesus Christ is Lord, to the glory of God the Father." (Philippians 2:10-11)

Jesus is not yet accepted by all as the universal king. When will this be realized? No one of us can say, but it is within our power to make it true in our own lives and where we live today. What a recognition of his kingship can mean for the future opens up limitless possibilities.

Helping Adults Become Involved —Harry B. Adams

Preparation of Self and Class

This lesson marks the halfway point in the quarter. In preparing for this lesson, you will find it helpful to give some thought to what is happening to the persons who share in the class Sunday after Sunday. Are there persons in the group who are hesitant to express their ideas, or who do not seem to be part of the group? How can you help all the persons in

the group become part of the process of learning and sharing? What needs are persons bringing as they come to the class, and how can the experience of the group help to meet those needs? How can the mutual concern of all the members of the class for one another be developed?

Jesus Christ, as the one in whom God shows forth his love for the world, has been the center of attention for the previous two lessons. The discussion of the character and work of Christ continues in this lesson and in the next. The issue raised for this Palm Sunday lesson is the character of the authority Jesus exercises in the lives of men as he bears the title of king, among other titles.

Presenting the Main Question

After the first effort of the group led by Martin Luther King, Jr. to march from Selma to Montgomery was stopped by the police at the bridge, a large number of people concerned with the civil rights struggle gathered in Selma. Among them were some of the most prominent theologians and theological educators in the country.

For most of a day people stood around outside a church in Selma while the leaders of the movement conferred. There were lively debates among the theologians and others about whether the group should attempt the march to Selma again in the face of a court injunction forbidding it. As the day wore on and the crowd around the church talked and talked, many people leaned toward the view that it probably was not wise to attempt the march again.

Then Martin Luther King, Jr. appeared on the steps of the church and simply said, "We're going." The discussion stopped, and almost every person moved to begin the march from Selma to Montgomery.

Here was an incident in which one man exercised great authority over a rather large group of people. Why did people do what Martin Luther King, Jr. said they were going to do? What kind of authority did he have in that situation? Listed below are descriptions of some of the bases of authority that men exercise over others. Have the class members indicate which kind

of authority was expressed in the incident during the march from Selma.

A man has authority over others because:

1. He can hurt them in some way if they do not do what he says.
2. He has more information about the situation than others do.
3. The force of his personality simply makes persons want to do what he says.
4. He can reward them in some way if they do what he says.
5. People sense in him a moral commitment that they find impressive and persuasive.
6. He has the sheer physical power to make people do what he wants them to do.
7. He has been selected by the people to make the decisions by which they agree to abide.
8. By his previous actions on their behalf, he has gained the confidence of the people.
9. He can state the case for his views so persuasively that persons decide to do what he advocates.
10. He is an expert in one field, and therefore persons are willing to accept his views on many other issues, even though he may not have expert knowledge on them.

Developing the Lesson

Give the members of the class the opportunity to share their own insights about the ways in which men exercise power and authority over others. If you asked them to look for examples of how men behave when they have power, have them relate what they saw.

Some typical characteristics are found in persons who have authority over others, such as the following:

1. They have positions of prestige.
2. They demand certain visible signs of their authority, such as a big

office or the seat at the head of the table.

3. They are persons of considerable ego and pride.

4. They expect those over whom they have authority to "keep their place" in subtle but still recognizable ways.

5. They expect to have certain rewards or gains that other persons do not get.

Which of these characteristics did the members of the class discern as they observed persons in authority during the week?

Look with the class members at some of the titles that have been given to Jesus. One of the marks of a person in authority is often a title: president, foreman, doctor, governor, judge, general. Ask the class members to list the titles they think of in connection with Jesus. Dr. Laymon, in his section on "Titles for Christ," indicates quite a number. Spend a few moments discussing each of the titles suggested by the class and by Dr. Laymon. What does a title indicate about the character and the work of Jesus? For example, a rabbi was a teacher who instructed his people in the religion of Israel. To call Jesus a rabbi was to recognize that he taught people the ways of God and man.

Reflect on the ways in which Jesus exercised and continues to exercise his authority. Which of the ways in which men exercise their authority seem to apply to Jesus? (See above.) What kind of claim does he make on the lives of men, and what kind of power does he have over them?

Look with the class members at the passages from Zechariah and Philippians, using the help provided by Dr. Laymon and Dr. Thompson. Both passages make clear that here is an authority different from that of the man who coerces, and who demands all the glories that can accompany power.

Jesus did not exalt himself; he humbled himself. Jesus did not make men obey him, but he was obedient even unto death. The authority, the rule, the kingship of Jesus lay hold on the lives of men with the power of a love that gives and shares and suffers with men.

Consider how Jesus Christ claims men today. Invite the class members to share what it means to them to talk about Jesus as king, or as lord, or as master of their lives. How do they express their allegiance to Christ in their daily lives? What have they done or not done because they were responding to the claim that Christ makes upon them? On what occasions have they somehow felt moved to shape their lives in obedience to the call of Christ?

Helping Class Members Act

Suggest to the class members that during the coming week they seek consciously to discern what it means to acknowledge Christ as lord and king. Invite them to consider Christ's claim upon them at some point in the week when they are making a decision or dealing with another person.

Planning for Next Sunday

Ask the members of the class to bring to class next Sunday a list of the circumstances, the conditions, the factors in their lives that they find most frustrating and hardest to deal with.

Easter Is Celebration

(APRIL 22)

CLIFTON J. ALLEN [6]

Easter is the central date in the Christian calendar. It validates every preceding event; it guarantees every succeeding event.

But Easter can be forgotten. It can be just a ritual. It can be largely pagan. It can be shallow. Or Easter can be authentic; it can be celebration. Our view of Easter will indicate a great deal about our understanding of the truth of the Christian gospel. Our response to Easter will determine to a large degree the quality of the Christian life we live. The world is still waiting for Easter—perhaps because so many Christians are still so uncertain as to what Easter is all about.

Easter is the celebration of an event. Something wonderful happened. The reign of death was turned into the reign of life. Jesus Christ arose from the dead. He came out of the grave—alive—the third day after he died and was buried. Jesus Christ overcame the power of death and came forth, alive forevermore.

This experience was real. He showed himself alive by many infallible proofs (Luke 24; John 20 and 21). What an occasion for celebration! All the choirs of heaven and all the trumpets of angels and all the stars of the created universe and all the saints of the ages must have joined in hallelujahs of praise: "Death is swallowed up in victory!"

The Resurrection event is the most staggering fact in human history. And we celebrate this event in the full context of Christian faith. We can face death without fear. We know One who is the resurrection and the life— hence the glad assurance that whoever lives and believes in the living Christ will never die. The empty grave has become forever the symbol of the Resurrection age, the affirmation of the living Lord.

Easter is the celebration of a presence. The eternal "I Am" is here: the Son sent by the Father, the Bread that came from heaven, the Light that keeps on shining in the darkness of the world. At his name "every knee should bow, . . . and every tongue confess that Jesus Christ is Lord." (Philippians 2:10-11)

Easter is the thrilling awareness of Christ's continuing presence. "I am with you always" (Matthew 28:20b) is much more than a wondrous New Testament promise. It is the assurance that the Christ of God is in our midst. His presence is our joy and peace. Through his presence we can rise above— overcome or endure—tribulation, persecution, poverty, criticism, rejection, or temptation. His companionship will transform weary days into exciting opportunities, and experiences of fear and hostility into courage and forgiveness. Openness to his presence makes us open to all who walk with him in love, and hence we have fellowship with one another in the reality and enrichment and strength of Christian unity.

The reality of Easter points to a central truth about the living Christ. He has come through his Spirit to abide forever. He is present in the lives of

---

[6] Clifton J. Allen: sometime editorial secretary of the Sunday School Board of the Southern Baptist Convention.

all who believe in him and acknowledge him as Lord. He is present in his body, the church. He is present in the world—in reconciliation, in redemption, in ministry, in judgment, and in bringing to fulfillment the kingdom of God.

We can celebrate in spite of the power structures of war, hate, greed, and lust and the deceptive philosophies of atheism, secularism, and revolution. We know in experience the power of the Resurrection, the dynamic of the Spirit of holiness and truth, and the moral strength and reconciling force of the love of Jesus Christ.

Because of Easter every service of worship should involve celebration. We can celebrate the riches of grace, the hope of righteousness, and the greatness of God because of the presence of the living Christ. His word of assurance is, "Where two or three are gathered in my name, there am I in the midst of them." (Matthew 18:20) In the glory of his presence there is penitence, cleansing, renewal, aspiration, praise, and commitment. In the observance of Holy Communion, most of all, we celebrate the wonder and victory of the cross of Christ, the affirmation of his lordship, the covenant of our redemption, and the unity of our faith.

Easter is always, because of the presence of the living Lord. This means that the Christian life is meant to be a celebration of the joy of salvation. Every encounter with evil or suffering can be turned into an experience of overcoming faith. Hard work to be done in the name of Christ can be turned into exciting ventures of disciplined zeal and courageous devotion. We know the joy of Christ because we have the fullness of his Spirit.

Easter is the celebration of hope. This is the hope of glory rightly understood. It means much more than hope of life after death. This hope is the confident expectation that Christ will reign until his enemies are under his feet, and that God will bring to fulfillment his eternal purpose of redemption and cause all things in heaven and on earth to be united in Christ. We celebrate the victory as though it were already accomplished: "The kingdom of the world has become the kingdom of our Lord and of his Christ." (Revelation 11:15)

The resurrection of Christ is the guarantee of the resurrection of the dead. It is the guarantee that he is making all things new. He will not fail nor be discouraged till he has established justice in the earth. We can celebrate in joyful expectation of the time when there will be a new heaven and a new earth in which righteousness dwells.

Easter is occasion for celebration indeed. We are not blind to the ugly and frightening facts of poverty, war, injustice, anarchy, disease, hate, and human depravity. But we can face the fact of death without fear, in the assurance that, because Christ lives, we shall live also. We can live in a world of evil and suffering in the assurance that all things hold together in Christ, and that God through Christ is reconciling the world to himself.

Easter has "turned us on" because Jesus is alive, and our hearts burn within us as we feel the power of his love. Easter has filled us with excitement because Jesus has called us to be his servants in the world. Easter has painted the future in our landscape with bright colors because the living Christ is our hope and our peace.

Christ Conquered Sin and Death

Background Scripture: John 11:17-44; 1 Corinthians 15:20-28, 51-57

The Main Question —Charles M. Laymon

Why do I believe in immortality? Each member of the adult class was given a small slip of paper and asked to answer this question in a single sentence. The answers were then collected, unsigned, and read to the class. Some of them follow: "I don't know why but I do." "I believe in immortality because the Bible promises it." "I believe I shall outlast the grave because Jesus did." "I can't put it into words, but I believe it because I feel it inside." "I think I shall live after death because I want to so badly." "It doesn't make sense, this living and struggling, if death is the end."

A lot of basic wisdom is evident in these statements. They are the down-to-earth answers of persons expressed in ordinary terms. The instinct for life after death lies at the heart of each of them. They contain more insight than many lengthier statements of philosophers.

One of the reasons some persons find it difficult to believe in life after death is that they cannot picture it. A student said to me, "I don't see how the millions of people who have died can live in another world. Where does God put them all?" I replied, "If you had been asked before you were born what this world would be like, could you have pictured it?" He said, "I see what you mean. God can take care of it."

What is the significance of life beyond the grave, and where does Christ come into the picture? Christians must face immortality within this perspective. The following biblical passage will help us find the answer.

As You Read the Scripture —Claude H. Thompson

1 Corinthians 15:20. *But in fact Christ has been raised from the dead:* This is not merely Paul's witness; it is the theme of every writer of the New Testament. Apart from the fact that God raised Jesus from the dead, there would be no New Testament, no church, no Christian faith. We might even say that Christian faith is faith in the resurrection of Jesus from the dead. There is no place for the current view of some persons that resurrection is merely the experience of the post-Easter church reading back into the life of Jesus their own understanding of life. It is not valid to say that resurrection happened to the early believers but not to Jesus. This heresy must be resisted with vigor.

Since Jesus is the "first fruits of those who have fallen asleep," his resurrection assures the future life of all believers. As he said, "Because I live, you will live also." (John 14:19) The Christian looks beyond death to life beyond the reach of death because Jesus has gone before him.

Verses 21-22. *For as by a man came death, by a man has come also the*

288

resurrection of the dead: Paul refers here to the idea, expressed in Genesis, that death is the result of man's sin. There is serious question today that this idea must be taken literally. Since Adam means "man" and need not refer to a particular historical person, Paul seems to say here that death is the common heritage of all men. The idea of the solidarity of the human race—that what one does affects all and what is common to all affects each one—is a valid idea. This Paul strongly asserts.

But this chain of events was broken in the coming of Christ. However, the break is not automatic. While the involvement in sin and death is the lot of every man, our life in Christ is voluntary. To become alive in Christ, to participate in his Resurrection, requires our consent, our decision. We must choose life beyond the reach of death; we cannot inherit it apart from our surrender to Christ alive.

CHRIST CONQUERED SIN AND DEATH

Verse 23. *Each in his own order:* Christ is the *first fruits,* a term familiar to the Jews since it referred to the first fruit of the harvest. And his Resurrection anticipates his future coming—when "those who belong to Christ" shall be raised to eternal life.

Verses 24-25. *Then comes the end, when he delivers the kingdom to God:* Paul anticipates a time when all evil shall be conquered by Christ, just as death has been defeated. "Every authority and power" refers to everything opposed to God's rule among men.

Verse 26. *The last enemy to be destroyed is death:* If we accept the idea that death, physical death, is the consequence of sin, this statement is valid as it stands. But if we believe that death is a natural event, designed by God for all life, then it must be reinterpreted. I suggest that death, designed by God for every man—that is, that one generation shall live, make its contribution, then leave the stage of history—has itself been perverted by sin. Thus what was designed to be the honorable exit of every man from history by virtue of sin, which alienates man from God, is now feared.

Verses 27-28. *For God has put all things in subjection under his feet:* Paul clearly affirms that, ultimately, God's will shall prevail.

Verses 51-57. *Lo! I tell you a mystery:* If the problem of evil and death is difficult, how much more is the idea of life after death. Clearly, there will be change—as was evident in the experience of the resurrected Christ. He was the same, yet sufficiently changed so as not to be recognized.

Paul believes the basic change is that the "perishable nature must put on the imperishable." Note that immortality must be "put on." It is not simply ours because we are persons. It is a conferred gift. The Greeks believed in survival after death, but the Christian believes in resurrection—the gift of a new quality of life. Immortality, deathlessness, is attributed to God alone. But it may be conveyed to man through faith in Christ.

When immortality comes, it brings a song: "Death is swallowed up in victory." This passage, taken from Isaiah 25:8, reflects the victorious song of the faithful. This is the Easter hymn—Christ has conquered sin and death. Thus we may share in his death and also in his life beyond the reach of death. "For if we have been united with him in a death like his, we shall certainly be united with him in a resurrection like his." (Romans 6:5)

Selected Scripture

King James Version

1 Corinthians 15:20-28, 51-57

20 But now is Christ risen from the dead, and become the firstfruits of them that slept.

21 For since by man came death, by man came also the resurrection of the dead.

22 For as in Adam all die, even so in Christ shall all be made alive.

23 But every man in his own order: Christ the firstfruits; afterward they that are Christ's at his coming.

24 Then cometh the end, when he shall have delivered up the kingdom to God, even the Father; when he shall have put down all rule and all authority and power.

25 For he must reign, till he hath put all enemies under his feet.

Revised Standard Version

1 Corinthians 15:20-28, 51-57

20 But in fact Christ has been raised from the dead, the first fruits of those who have fallen asleep. 21 For as by a man came death, by a man has come also the resurrection of the dead. 22 For as in Adam all die, so also in Christ shall all be made alive. 23 But each in his own order: Christ the first fruits, then at his coming those who belong to Christ. 24 Then comes the end, when he delivers the kingdom to God the Father after destroying every rule and every authority and power. 25 For he must reign until he has put all his enemies under his feet. 26 The last enemy to be destroyed is death. 27 "For God has put all things in subjection under

26 The last enemy that shall be destroyed is death.

27 For he hath put all things under his feet. But when he saith all things are put under him, it is manifest that he is excepted, which did put all things under him.

28 And when all things shall be subdued unto him, then shall the Son also himself be subject unto him that put all things under him, that God may be all in all.

. . . .

51 Behold, I shew you a mystery; We shall not all sleep, but we shall all be changed,

52 In a moment, in the twinkling of an eye, at the last trump: for the trumpet shall sound, and the dead shall be raised incorruptible, and we shall be changed.

53 For this corruptible must put on incorruption, and this mortal must put on immortality.

54 So when this corruptible shall have put on incorruption, and this mortal shall have put on immortality, then shall be brought to pass the saying that is written, Death is swallowed up in victory.

55 O death, where is thy sting? O grave, where is thy victory?

56 The sting of death is sin; and the strength of sin is the law.

57 But thanks be to God, which giveth us the victory through our Lord Jesus Christ.

Memory Selection: I am the resurrection, and the life: he that believeth in me, though he were dead, yet shall he live: And whosoever liveth and believeth in me shall never die. (John 11:25-26)

his feet." But when it says, "All things are put in subjection under him," it is plain that he is excepted who put all things under him. 28 When all things are subjected to him, then the Son himself will also be subjected to him who put all things under him, that God may be everything to every one.

. . . .

51 Lo! I tell you a mystery. We shall not all sleep, but we shall all be changed, 52 in a moment, in the twinkling of an eye, at the last trumpet. For the trumpet will sound, and the dead will be raised imperishable, and we shall be changed. 53 For this perishable nature must put on the imperishable, and this mortal nature must put on immortality. 54 When the perishable puts on the imperishable, and the mortal puts on immortality, then shall come to pass the saying that is written:

"Death is swallowed up in victory." 55 "O death, where is thy victory? O death, where is thy sting?"

56 The sting of death is sin, and the power of sin is the law. 57 But thanks be to God, who gives us the victory through our Lord Jesus Christ.

Memory Selection: I am the resurrection and the life; he who believes in me, though he die, yet shall he live, and whoever lives and believes in me shall never die. (John 11:25-26)

The Scripture and the Main Question —Charles M. Laymon

CHRIST IS ALIVE!

A minister of my acquaintance once said that every Christian service should be opened with a particular announcement. The preacher should stand in the pulpit, face the people, and with conviction proclaim: "Christ is alive!"

I can just hear someone say, "But every Sunday isn't Easter." The answer, of course, is that the truths of Easter are valid 365 days a year. Read the sermons of the first Christian preachers such as Peter and Paul. Almost without exception they refer to the Resurrection before they close. In this way they celebrated its meaning constantly.

Let us put the question this way, What does Easter mean in the middle of August? It means just as much as it did on Easter Sunday—or it should mean as much. The fact that Jesus is alive is good news and new news daily.

Dimitrii Merezhkovskii in his book *Jesus Manifest* affirms his conviction that belief in Jesus' resurrection is the motive power that moves all who follow Christ. Concerning the origin of the resurrection faith he wrote: "From what did this faith spring? From five or six remarkably vivid hallucinations? To think so is just as absurd as to suppose that five or six sparks would make water boil in a huge caldron." The fact of the Resurrection moves Christians to new adventures every day.

The important thing is really to believe in the Resurrection for ourselves. The faith of others may provide an incentive to our own belief; but unless we are convinced ourselves, our lives cannot be lifted to Easter heights.

CHRIST THE CONQUEROR

Too often we think of the Resurrection as though it were just a magical kind of appearance and disappearance by Jesus nearly two thousand years ago. We have seen movie shots where a figure was superimposed upon a scene, only to fade away. It was almost spooky. A woman once said to me that when she thought of the risen Christ she pictured a ghost.

The New Testament has no such view of the resurrection of Jesus. He was known to the writers as one who was glorified as he overcame death and sin (1 Corinthians 15:20-21). Christ was a conqueror.

Death and sin are usually regarded as the two major enemies of man. Christ overcame the first by rising from the dead and the second by bringing forgiveness to mankind. In the New Testament he always is presented as victor in these two areas where men cannot save themselves.

Here lies the power of Jesus' resurrection. Here he accomplished something. It was not simply survival beyond the grave; more importantly it was man's salvation—renewal, forgiveness, and strength for purposeful living. A dead Jesus could not place these in our hands; a living, resurrected Christ could, and did.

LIFE AFTER DEATH

Dr. Patton of Princeton University, in illustrating the nature of faith in immortality based upon the Resurrection, said that in the Old Testament men facing death were "willing to go, but wanting to stay." In the New Testament, by contrast, they were "willing to stay, but wanting to go." Why this difference?

The words *because he lives, I too shall live* state as simply and directly

292

as possible the ground for such belief in life after death. The author of Second Timothy said it plainly when he wrote that Christ Jesus abolished death and brought life and immortality to light (1:10). And the apostle Paul felt moved to gratitude and prayer as he thought of what God had done in bringing forth Jesus from the grave: "Thanks be to God, who gives us the victory through our Lord Jesus Christ." (1 Corinthians 15:57)

All the other reasons for believing in immortality, however meaningful, pale before the fact of the Resurrection. This utterly unique event stands out above and beyond the rest. Here is more than an idea and a truth of reason; here is something that happened.

LIFE EVERLASTING NOW

When we bury our dear ones, faith in immortality makes all the difference in the world. Sorrow may remain for a time, but the sting has been removed. Realizing this, the apostle Paul was caught up in ecstasy when he cried out: "O death where is thy sting?" (1 Corinthians 15:55)

A little girl who had lost her mother in death looked up to the sky as it was filled with stars and exclaimed: "If the wrong side of heaven looks like this, what must the right side be like!" The glory of the beyond was shining through the here and now.

Christian faith in life after death transforms us and makes a difference in the way we live our present lives. It enables us to take the long look at things. We no longer measure destiny by threescore years and ten. We have already tasted immortality, for we realize that we shall live forever.

With this eternal perspective in view Paul concluded his writing on immortality by saying, "Therefore, my beloved brethren, be steadfast, immovable, always abounding in the work of the Lord, knowing that in the Lord your labor is not in vain." (1 Corinthians 15:58)

Helping Adults Become Involved —Harry B. Adams

Preparation of Self and Class

Easter! Christ the Lord is Risen today! Hallelujah! This day the church celebrates. Flowers, special music, and big crowds give a festive tone to the services. Rightly the church celebrates this day, for the church's life in the present and hope for the future are all tied up with the affirmation that "in fact Christ has been raised from the dead." (1 Corinthians 15:20)

As you prepare for this lesson, you will want to consider how you can help the class members relate the events and claims of Easter to the whole view of man and the world that has been explored during this quarter. It is the God who created and ordered the universe whose love and power is being expressed in the resurrection of Jesus Christ. Easter is God's victory over the sin, evil, and death that have distorted man and his world.

Presenting the Main Question

A person's view of death shapes the way in which he deals with life. In his play *Our Town*, Thornton Wilder stirs the imagination to awareness of how the fact of death sensitizes a person to the events of life. The scene is set in the cemetery at Grover's Corners. A young woman in her early twenties has just died and come to the cemetery. She asks if she can go back to live over just one day of her life. The stage manager warns her against the idea but finally agrees after she insists. She picks out the day of her twelfth birthday and goes back to relive that experience. Her father comes in tired from a trip out of town and pays her little attention. Her mother is so busy with cooking breakfast that she has little time to listen. The girl, knowing that her time and their time is so short, cries out to them to look at her and to cherish the precious moment together.

Some people refuse to deal with the fact of death. They turn away from any conscious consideration of death and make a determined effort to avoid any reminder that death is a reality of human existence. They act as though this life lasted forever and as though they had days without number.

Other persons let the fear of death cast a dark shadow over the whole of their life. The experience of death is an experience of the unknown, an experience that every man meets in absolute loneliness.

Still other persons fight the reality of death with a sense of bitter resentment. Death is seen as the final negation of all that they have struggled for and lived for.

Give the class members opportunity to express other views that persons have toward death. Discuss with the class members how each of the views of death influences the way in which men live and use the time that they do have.

Developing the Lesson

Consider how men go about answering questions concerning death. Even persons who try most diligently to hide from the reality of death find that they still must deal in some way

with a fact that will not go away. What kinds of evidence or argument are helpful when a man tries to puzzle out what death is and what it means? Give the class members opportunity to respond to that question, using the following as part of the discussion.

Evidence or arguments dealing with the fact and meaning of death:

1. Reports from persons who have died. There have been some claims of communication between the dead and the living; but the testimony is certainly ambiguous, open to many interpretations, and not persuasive to most people.

2. The desire for some life after physical death. Dr. Laymon cites some expressions of this deep longing. The fact that there is this longing does not *prove* that the longing will be fulfilled.

3. The bodies of men are composed of the common elements of the earth, and their bodies along with those of all other creatures simply disintegrate when the life functions cease. From this scientific fact men have argued that there really is no evidence of life after death. Physical death is simply the end of the person.

4. Man is composed of an immortal soul and a mortal body. Death is simply the freeing of the soul from the body. Yet in his experience man does not meet disembodied souls or spirits, and it is difficult for him to imagine what life would be without a body.

Explore the meaning of the resurrection of Christ as it relates to man's view of death. Using the resources provided by Dr. Laymon and Dr. Thompson, study the passages from 1 Corinthians 15 suggested for today's lesson. The affirmation of the resurrection of Jesus Christ is not a declaration of a wondrous miracle to startle men but the declaration of the power of God over the powers of death. It is witness that the God who gave life initially is the Lord over death.

Paul declares: "Lo! I tell you a mystery." (1 Corinthians 15:51) Even for the believer in the resurrection of Christ, death remains a mystery, the character of a life after death remains a mystery, and the final summation of God's purposes remains a mystery. There is no blueprint or timetable or program of events that lays bare what man confronts in death. But the Christian faces death with a hope and a quiet confidence born of the conviction of God's power and God's love, particularly as that power and love have been expressed in the resurrection of Jesus Christ. The character of God is decisive and not any evidence or argument about what happens when a man dies. As Leander Keck has written: "The central issue is not whether man has an essence that survives death but whether the God in whom he believes, however falteringly, has enough moral integrity to 'make good' with the life he himself called into existence. In the last analysis, the central theological issue in the death of man is the character of God." [7] So Paul declares: "Thanks be to God, who gives us the victory through our Lord Jesus Christ." (1 Corinthians 15:57)

Look at other meanings of the resurrection of Christ. Easter is an affirmation in the face of the death of each individual person. But the Resurrection has profound implications for other areas of man's life and experience.

Invite the class members to share

[7] "New Testament Views of Death," Liston O. Mills, ed., *Perspectives on Death* (Abingdon Press, 1969), pp. 97-98.

their ideas of the things in life that frustrate and defeat persons. You may want to note them on chalkboard or newsprint. They may include such items as the following:

1. A fear that finally everything man does really counts for nothing.

2. A certainty that it does no good to struggle for the right and the good because the struggle against evil is hopeless.

3. A sense of guilt for what he is and what he has done, which a person finds no way of dealing with.

4. A conviction that he is not worth anything and does not count for anything.

After the class members have made their own list, discuss with them what the affirmation of the resurrection of Jesus says to each of these conditions. For example, it often does seem that the power of evil is so strong that the struggle for good is hopeless. But if it was the power of evil that crucified Jesus, then it was the power of God that raised him—a victory of good over evil.

Helping Class Members Act

Easter is the celebration of a victory. Let the members of the class indicate how that victory can be reflected as they deal with the frustrations, the handicaps, the failures, the evil in their own lives and experiences.

Planning for Next Sunday

Suggest that the members of the class be alert during the coming week to all the ways they use the words *belief* or *believe, faith,* and *trust.* Ask them to be ready to report on all the experiences or relationships during the week in which they found faith to be an important factor.

Man Responds Through Faith

Background Scripture: Matthew 16:13-16; John 20:24-31;
Acts 16:25-34; Romans 10:5-13

The Main Question —Charles M. Laymon

Viktor Frankl is a world-renowned European psychologist. He has been helping people find meaning for their lives for more than a quarter of a century. He believes that this search begins when we are very young and continues throughout our life.

Frankl tells of a young girl of seventeen who came to see him about her heart but whose longing to find a purpose in life was her real problem. Commenting upon the girl's situation, Frankl said, "Who searches for meaning? Certainly an ant will not, neither will a bee. A girl, however, of 17, posing such questions and involved in such a quest proves to be a truly human being struggling for meaning."

Some people pursue the search for life's meaning through religion. Others seek for meaning through writings dealing with nature, science, or psychology. The Bible, however, remains for many the chief guidebook in this quest. Why do they select the Bible?

The answer to this question, as J. B. Phillips, the distinguished translator of the Scriptures into modern language, points out, is that here in the Bible men find a picture of people who are changed: "At the root of their being: cowards become heroes; sinners are transformed; fear, greed, envy and pride are expelled by a flood of something above and beyond normal human experience."

How does this victorious life develop? Where does it begin? Can it be explained? The biblical passages that follow will help to answer these questions.

As You Read the Scripture —Claude H. Thompson

John 20:26-29. This is one of the most moving affirmations in the New Testament. Thomas had been absent when Jesus met with his disciples following the Resurrection. But about a week later Jesus appeared again, and Thomas was there. Jesus' word was: "Peace be with you."

Verse 27. *Put your finger here, and see my hands:* When the disciples reported that Jesus had been raised from the dead, Thomas said he would not believe until he had experienced the presence of Christ alive. Here Jesus personalizes his witness. He never turns away the faintest flicker of faith. Jesus challenged Thomas to know for sure. And he did!

Verse 28. *My Lord and my God!* This is the noblest confession of faith possible. We referred last week to Lord, *kurios,* as a divine name. Thomas is satisfied with no less term to apply to Jesus. Then he adds: "My God!" Legend (or is it authentic history?) has it that Thomas went to India to witness for Christ. At any rate, there is today in that great land a church, the Mar Thoma, whose origin is so ancient it has been lost. I am prone to believe that Thomas founded that church before the end of the first century. I have been with the Mar Thoma Christians in Madras and elsewhere, and they revere this early witness to Christ as their leader.

Verse 29. *Have you believed because you have seen me?* Jesus speaks of two levels of faith—one through actual experience, the other through spiritual sensitivity. The former is forever beyond our reach, but the latter is available for all.

Romans 10:6-11. This is a portion of Paul's appeal to the Jews to abandon the old way of legalism and turn through faith to Christ. He quotes from Deuteronomy 30:12-13, showing that the true meaning of the law is not out of reach of men. But he also indicates it is not within man's ability to perform all the demands of the law. Only through faith is obedience possible. Human effort did not produce Christ as the savior of the world, nor is man able to order his own moral life.

Verse 9. *If you confess with your lips that Jesus is Lord . . . you will be saved:* This is another example of the earliest confession of faith. Read 1 Corinthians 12:3 and Philippians 2:11 for other examples of this creed. Note several elements of this confession: (1) It must be vocal. A silent witness may have its place, but God needs spokesmen for his gospel. Nothing carries more influence than a simple, sincere witness to what Christ means in one's life. One secret of the Campus Crusade, the Fellowship of Christian Athletes, and the Lay Witness Movement is the testimony as to what Christ does in persons' lives. (2) There must be faith. This is more than belief—assent. It involves surrender of one's life in obedience to Christ through repentance of our sins. This faith permits no sham. It is the inner integrity of a dedicated life. (3) There is the certainty of Jesus' resurrection. Again we meet this central theme of the gospel. It is the resurrection faith or no faith; there are no other options. The result is *you will be saved.* This is not salvation in some future life, though that is involved. Paul means a new quality of life here and now. It has the element of certainty, of joy, of contagion, of power. When John Wesley returned to England from Georgia, he wrote, "I want that faith that none can have without knowing that he hath it." And when he got it, England was reborn and the Wesleyan revival began.

Verse 11. *No one who believes in him will be put to shame:* This passage is from Isaiah 28:16, with some modification. One need not apologize for following Christ. It is an honor to walk in The Way.

Selected Scripture

King James Version	Revised Standard Version
John 20:26-29	*John 20:26-29*
26 And after eight days again his disciples were within, and Thomas with them: then came Jesus, the doors being shut, and stood in the midst, and said, Peace be unto you.	26 Eight days later, his disciples were again in the house, and Thomas was with them. The doors were shut, but Jesus came and stood among them, and said, "Peace be with you."

27 Then saith he to Thomas, Reach hither thy finger, and behold my hands; and reach hither thy hand, and thrust it into my side: and be not faithless, but believing.

28 And Thomas answered and said unto him, My Lord and my God.

29 Jesus saith unto him, Thomas, because thou hast seen me, thou hast believed: blessed are they that have not seen, and yet have believed.

Romans 10:6-11

6 But the righteousness which is of faith speaketh on this wise, Say not in thine heart, Who shall ascend into heaven? (that is, to bring Christ down from above:)

7 Or, Who shall descend into the deep? (that is, to bring up Christ again from the dead.)

8 But what saith it? The word is nigh thee, even in thy mouth, and in thy heart: that is, the word of faith, which we preach;

9 That if thou shalt confess with thy mouth the Lord Jesus, and shalt believe in thine heart that God hath raised him from the dead, thou shalt be saved.

10 For with the heart man believeth unto righteousness; and with the mouth confession is made unto salvation.

11 For the scripture saith, Whosoever believeth on him shall not be ashamed.

Memory Selection: Believe on the Lord Jesus Christ, and thou shalt be saved. (Acts 16:31)

27 Then he said to Thomas, "Put your finger here, and see my hands; and put out your hand, and place it in my side; do not be faithless, but believing." 28 Thomas answered him, "My Lord and my God!" 29 Jesus said to him "Have you believed because you have seen me? Blessed are those who have not seen and yet believe."

Romans 10:6-11

6 But the righteousness based on faith says, Do not say in your heart, "Who will ascend into heaven?" (that is, to bring Christ down) 7 or "Who will descend into the abyss?" (that is, to bring Christ up from the dead). 8 But what does it say? The word is near you, on your lips and in your heart (that is, the word of faith which we preach); 9 because, if you confess with your lips that Jesus is Lord and believe in your heart that God raised him from the dead, you will be saved. 10 For man believes with his heart and so is justified, and he confesses with his lips and so is saved. 11 The Scripture says, "No one who believes in him will be put to shame."

Memory Selection: Believe in the Lord Jesus, and you will be saved. (Acts 16:31)

The Scripture and the Main Question —Charles M. Laymon

A BASIS FOR FAITH

Faith does not come to us out of thin air. We do not stumble upon it. Neither do we believe because we are told that we ought to do so. Like a plant that sprouts and grows because we have sown the seed, just so there must be a basis for faith.

U Thant, as general secretary of the United Nations, constantly faced pessimism and disbelief. One of his chief challenges was to keep faith in the possibilities of peace. To this end he said, "We must sustain that note of hope, which our achievements in so many fields so amply justify, until it overpowers the voices of fear, cynicism and reaction." The basis for faith here was "our achievements in so many fields."

The basis of Christian faith, however, differs from U Thant's appeal. We do not believe because of our achievements. Instead, we believe because of Christ. Great as the human record is, it is not great enough to call forth such faith as Christians hold. But Christ can awaken faith; he does it daily.

In today's biblical passage it was an experience of the risen Lord that called forth faith in Thomas and the apostles. He "came and stood among them, and said, 'Peace be with you.'" (John 20:26) His living presence brought them faith. He gave them his peace, and they believed.

INQUIRING FAITH

Thomas has come down through the centuries as an example of the person who doubts. Why not, for a change, think of him as the apostle of inquiring faith? When he said that he would not believe until he had seen in Christ's hands the print of the nails and had placed his finger in the mark of the nails (John 20:25), Thomas was only affirming his need to be shown.

All Thomas had to go on as a basis for faith was the report of the other disciples that they had seen the risen Christ. In court today we would call this hearsay, and it would not be admitted as evidence. To say "someone told me that . . ." is not enough.

In Christian faith also another man's witness may be an inspiring prod to belief, but it is not a substitute for our own personal reasons for trusting Christ. The need to have sound reasons should, therefore, not be regarded as negative and doubting.

Doubt, interpreted as a function of the inquiring mind, may lead to a deeper faith than unthinking acceptance of ideas. Carl Michalson, who died in a plane crash as he was en route to speak at a large meeting of Christian educators, once said that "the doubting side of our mind knows we ought not surrender to inadequate ideas and attitudes. So it presses its weight against the ideas to see if they will really hold." This kind of doubting is not antagonistic to faith.

FAITH AND RIGHTEOUSNESS

The word *righteousness* is not found much in public or private conversation these days. It is mostly a church word. Many people are afraid to use the word because it sounds cold and forbidding. In the New Testament, however, *righteousness* is a word that is warm and friendly.

In the mountains of Tennessee a man will invite you to come up on the porch and "set a spell." When you do this, you are a member of the circle; you are accepted; you belong. It is the same with being declared righteous before God. When we come near to him in communion and fellowship, when we have the sense of belonging in the inner circle, then we are righteous. God has accepted us as kinfolk.

How does it happen? What makes it happen? Paul's answer is that faith makes a man righteous. He speaks of "the righteousness based on faith." (Romans 10:6) The Jewish view of righteousness was that it was based upon the law. The law was cold and calculating, equating performance with acceptance. Do the good deed, and you are "in"; do not do it, and you are "out."

Righteousness that is based upon faith, however, means that we are accepted in the circle of God's love because we have responded in faith to Christ. We can come into God's presence not only to "set a spell" but to abide in his love forever.

HEART KNOWLEDGE

The familiar slogan Ask the Heart —Only the Heart Knows might have come from the New Testament. The truth it asserts is thoroughly biblical. Paul said, "The word is near you, on your lips and in your heart." (Romans 10:8)

Carl F. Burke has helped many to understand the Bible better by publishing the paraphrases of some passages done by delinquent youth in such books as God Is for Real, Man and God Is Beautiful, Man. In a third volume, Treat Me Cool, Lord, Burke has a paraphrase of the eighty-sixth psalm that is filled with the inner warmth of heart knowledge. It reads, in part:

> When it seems like everybody
>   is against me
> And nothing goes right
> And people is out to get me
> Help me to know we is still
>   friends
> And that your love is here.[8]

Faith brings this kind of knowledge "if you . . . believe in your heart." (Romans 10:9)

[8] Carl F. Burke, "We Is Still Friends, Lord," *Treat Me Cool, Lord* (Association Press, 1968), p. 72.

Helping Adults Become Involved —Harry B. Adams

Preparation of Self and Class

This is the final lesson in the unit on Christian redemption. These lessons have explored how God has acted in Christ to meet and overcome the sin of man and the power of evil. The climax of God's action was reached in the resurrection of Jesus Christ.

Next week a new unit begins on the quality and character of life made possible for the Christian. The lesson today serves as the transition between what God has done and what man can become. For this lesson deals with the way in which man responds to what God has done.

The key word in this lesson is *faith*. In preparation for this lesson you will want to look again at the faith by which you live and order your life. What is it you really believe in? What

faith is being expressed as you order the priorities of your life and use the days that God has given to you? What impact does the confession of faith in Jesus Christ have on who you are as a person and on what you do?

Presenting the Main Question

What does it mean to have faith? How does one test what a man says he believes, in order to probe the depth and sincerity of his confession? The story is told of a tightrope walker who proposed to walk across a rope strung between two tall buildings. Not only was he going to walk the rope himself, but he was going to push a wheelbarrow across.

The day came for the exhibition, and a crowd gathered on the roof of the one building to watch. As the tightrope walker was ready to start, he turned to the mayor and asked him if he believed that he could push the wheelbarrow all the way over. The mayor thought for a moment and then replied that he believed he could do it. "All right," the tightrope walker said, "get in and go with me."

It is important for a man to *say* what he believes. The verbal articulation of his faith helps the person and others to define what it is that he does believe in. But what a man says he believes is confirmed or denied by what he does. His actions bear testimony to what he believes.

Look with the class members at some of the actions of men and identify what articles of faith are being expressed. Use events from the newspaper or some of the situations described below. For example, a man spends several hours a week coaching a Little League baseball team. What is he saying about what he believes? He believes that boys are important, that athletic development is significant in a person's growth, that competition is a healthy thing, that he has something to give to others, and so forth.

What are people affirming in the following acts?

1. A person spends three hours a day practicing the piano.

2. A man drives himself ruthlessly to get ahead in his business, leaving little time for his wife and family.

3. A person embezzles several thousand dollars from his employer.

4. A man plants a tree in a park in his community.

Developing the Lesson

Study the place of faith in the life of the Christian as it is set forth in the biblical passages. Use the material prepared by Dr. Laymon and Dr. Thompson as you explore with the

class John 20:26-29 and Romans 10:6-11.

Examine the difference between faith and knowledge. Give the members of the class opportunity to indicate how they think faith and knowledge are related. You will want to help the class note the following:

1. Men talk of knowledge when they are dealing with objects that can be seen and handled.

2. Men talk of knowledge when there is the possibility of proof, evidence that is persuasive to all people competent to judge it.

3. Men talk of faith when they are dealing with reality that is not open to the senses of man.

4. Men talk of faith when they are concerned about issues that are not open to proof.

Help the class members to see that faith is not blind, stupid, irrational assertion. Men have faith in things about which they cannot have full knowledge or certainty, but faith is grounded in evidence and experience. For example, no person can *prove* that another person will always be loyal to him. But a husband and a wife can believe that each will be loyal to the other. Consider with the class members what kind of evidence might make them believe such a thing. What kind of evidence is there for the faith that God loves his people?

It might be noted that in the most significant dimensions of their lives, men live by faith. No man can *prove* that another person will always love him and be loyal to him, but that faith is the basis of marriage. No man can *prove* that there is a purpose in all creation. No man can *prove* that God is and that God loves his world.

Explore the distinction that can be made between *belief* and *trust*. These two words are obviously very close in meaning, but they point to different dimensions. Belief can be used to indicate what the content of a man's faith is. Christian faith is not just "having faith." It is believing in something that can be specified and talked about. The creeds of the church express what the Christian believes. He believes in God; he believes in Jesus Christ; he believes in the Holy Spirit; he believes in the church; and so forth.

Trust is another dimension of faith. When a man has faith in another person, he may say that he *believes* that the man is honest and good and capable. If he really believes those things, then he will trust the other. When the other says something, he will accept it as true. When the other proposes a course of action, he will accept it as good and wise.

A man may say that he *believes* the airline captain is competent. He *trusts* the captain when he boards the plane.

Consider why faith is the necessary response of man if he is to share in all that God has done for him. Paul talks about the righteousness based on faith, about being justified by faith, about being saved by faith. Paul was writing in a particular context, in opposition to those who claimed that man was righteous when he obeyed the law, or justified by his own efforts at being good, or saved by the kind of life he lived.

Paul's affirmations can be distorted, of course. A man is not justified by simply having faith, regardless of what he has faith in. A man is not justified simply by saying a creed with his lips.

Give the class members opportunity to discuss how the relationship between two people is influenced by whether they believe in each other and trust each other, or whether they do not. Then discuss how man's relationship to God is changed if he believes in God and trusts in God. Only by belief and trust will a man be willing to accept what God has done for him in Jesus Christ.

Helping Class Members Act

It was suggested at the beginning of this lesson that a man's faith is demonstrated by the way in which he lives and acts. Invite the class to consider what kinds of actions speak to men of their faith in God and in Jesus Christ.

Planning for Next Sunday

Encourage the members of the class to read and think about the passage from Ephesians (2:1-10). Ask them to be alert in all their contacts during the week to identify persons who somehow seem to be living with a freshness and vitality that comes out of their relationship with Jesus Christ.

Unit VIII: The Christian Life

Horace R. Weaver

FOUR LESSONS   MAY 6–27

The four lessons of this unit on "The Christian Life" build on the other two units in this quarter—the good world that the good God made and the redemptive acts of God for man's restoration and freedom from alienation. The theme of this unit is concerned with new men and the relationships that new men have with one another and with those who have not accepted the Christian way as their style of life.

The lesson for May 6, "Christ Makes Men New," challenges us to realize that Christians are not born Christians. Men are not sons of God by the fact of being flesh and blood, in human form, but they become so as they are made new through their dedication and commitment to the Christlike God.

The lesson for May 13, "Christ Makes Men Brothers," challenges us to the truth that those persons (regardless of color or race) who are doing the will of God are brothers. This significant teaching makes Christians in Russia brothers to the approximately seventy million Christians of America. The point would be that Christians all over the world are all bound together as sons of God inasmuch as their spirits are Christ directed and moving toward his Kingdom.

The lesson for May 20, "God's Grace Sustains Me," helps adults realize that they do not live their lives alone, but that they can count on the presence of the living God to give renewed strength and added power for daily living.

The May 27 lesson, "Christ Is Our Hope," concludes this unit with the affirmation of the Christian hope that the future belongs to God. Yet God is calling us to make decisions in our present time that will affect the future too. God is counting on us as well as we are counting on him.

A list of audiovisual resources appropriate for use with the lessons of this unit may be found in the introduction to Unit VI, page 231.

LESSON 1   MAY 6

Christ Makes Men New

Background Scripture: John 1:9-13; Ephesians 2:1-10; Colossians 3:1-17

The Main Question —Charles M. Laymon

Some persons never imagine that Jesus Christ might have nothing to do with them and their lives. From their earliest memories he has always been in the picture. Like the psalmist who said of God, "Upon thee was I cast from my birth, and since my mother bore me thou hast been my God" (22:10), these persons have known that they belong to Christ from the very first.

On the dining room wall of the home in which I was born hung the famous motto: "Christ is the head of this house, the Unseen Guest at every meal, the Silent Listener to every conversation." I grew up under the influence of these words. To think of my relation to Christ was as natural as to think of my belonging to my own family.

I was surprised to learn as I grew older that everyone did not feel as strongly about Jesus Christ. His name they knew, but their relationship to him was an unknown quantity. They had historical knowledge about Jesus but did not possess any personal knowledge concerning him.

Many persons I meet today have the same perspective. This fact makes the question What has Jesus Christ to do with me? an important one—the most important question we can ask. The biblical passages for the lesson answer the question for us.

As You Read the Scripture —Claude H. Thompson

The response through faith (last Sunday's lesson) results in changed lives. The Christian faith has no message more meaningful than that men may be remade through a surrender to Jesus Christ as Lord. Elton Trueblood has an urgent message for today: "The Christian takes his stand on the fact that lives can be made new by fellowship with Christ, and he does not know of any other source of change and renewal which is equal to this." [9]

John 1:9-13. *The true light . . . was coming into the world:* Into the darkness and despair of the ancient world came the *true light*—Jesus Christ. John sets several ideas in opposition in his Gospel: life/death, good/evil, truth/error, light/darkness. Jesus is said to have so completely illuminated the darkness of time that men no longer need grope about in that darkness. He continues to be the light of the world.

Note that Jesus as the light is not produced by man's wisdom nor skill. He was *coming into the world* from the world of perfect light. Other men may have given glimpses of light, but Jesus was the light.

Verses 10-11. *He was in the world:* John insists that Jesus actually was *in the world.* His was no mere temporary appearance, nor was he only a reflection of the divine light. He experienced both the despair and the darkness of history. Again we meet the idea that Jesus was involved in the creation of the world: "the world was made through him." Yet he came as one unknown, unsought, unwanted, unloved, even by "his own people."

Verses 12-13. *To all who received him . . . he gave power to become children of God:* Yet some did believe. To believe "in his name" means something of his life was conveyed to them—through faith. Note that those who surrendered to him did *become children of God.* Jesus did not *become* the Son of God; he always *was* the Son. But we, participants in a sinful race, must *become children of God* through rebirth. We do not inherit this relationship through culture, from our family, or even through our religion; we must consent and decide to become members of the family of God. As someone has said, "We don't ooze into the Christian life; we choose into it."

Ephesians 2:1-3. *You he made alive, when you were dead:* Here is the contrast between life and death. All men are dead in sin, but there is the chance to be made alive. These words breathe the spirit of newness, of an openness for man to become a new person, to be reborn. (See John 3.)

Note the description of those in darkness and death: (1) They walk in the dark of the "course of this world." This means the evil world—alienated from

[9] D. Elton Trueblood, *A Place to Stand* (Harper & Row, 1969), p. 44.

304

God. (2) The leader is the "prince of the power of the air." Satan is referred to as possessing some supernatural power over the universe and man. (3) This evil spirit directs the "sons of disobedience" into hostility to God and his plan. (4) All men have experienced both bodily appetites and perverted mental attitudes, which militate against God. (5) God's attitude can never approve this, hence his "wrath," his displeasure.

Verses 4-5. *But God . . . out of the great love with which he loved us . . . made us alive together with Christ:* The chief characteristic of God is not wrath but love. Thus, while we were yet sinners, he loved us. The coming of Jesus into history was designed to make new men of faith out of the old men of rebellion and alienation. This action produces a fellowship with Christ in the community of faith. But the community is always created by grace, not by human abilities.

Verse 6. *[God] raised us up with him:* Resurrection is not only for Christ; it is given also to those who are in Christ.

Verse 7. *That . . . he might show the immeasurable riches of his grace:* Unmeasured privileges are provided for those who find new life in Christ.

Verses 8-9. *For by grace you have been saved through faith:* Again we are reminded that man cannot save himself. God saves him by grace, or he is not saved. No possibility for boasting of human achievement exists; salvation is through faithful surrender to Christ alive.

Verse 10. *For we are his workmanship:* Thus the new man, like original man, is created by God. The creative touch of Christ is upon every person; and his creative genius will be honored, or lost. The decision is ours. But why this new creation? "For good works." A person follows Christ not simply for convenience, comfort, or security. He walks the way of the Master in order to serve his fellow man and to produce a redemptive society on earth.

Selected Scripture

King James Version	Revised Standard Version
John 1:9-13	*John 1:9-13*
9 That was the true Light, which lighteth every man that cometh into the world.	9 The true light that enlightens every man was coming into the world.
10 He was in the world, and the world was made by him, and the world knew him not.	10 He was in the world, and the world was made through him, yet the world knew him not. 11 He came to his own home, and his own people received
11 He came unto his own, and his own received him not.	him not. 12 But to all who received him, who believed in his name, he
12 But as many as received him, to them gave he power to become the sons of God, even to them that believe on his name:	gave power to become children of God; 13 who were born, not of blood nor of the will of the flesh nor of the will of man, but of God.
13 Which were born, not of blood, nor of the will of the flesh, nor of the will of man, but of God.	

Ephesians 2:1:10

1 And you hath he quickened, who were dead in trespasses and sins;

2 Wherein in time past ye walked according to the course of this world, according to the prince of the power of the air, the spirit that now worketh in the children of disobedience:

3 Among whom also we all had our conversation in times past in the lusts of our flesh, fulfilling the desires of the flesh and of the mind; and were by nature the children of wrath, even as others.

4 But God, who is rich in mercy, for his great love wherewith he loved us,

5 Even when we were dead in sins, hath quickened us together with Christ, (by grace ye are saved;)

6 And hath raised us up together, and made us sit together in heavenly places in Christ Jesus:

7 That in the ages to come he might shew the exceeding riches of his grace in his kindness toward us through Christ Jesus.

8 For by grace are ye saved through faith; and that not of yourselves: it is the gift of God:

9 Not of works, lest any man should boast.

10 For we are his workmanship, created in Christ Jesus unto good works, which God hath before ordained that we should walk in them.

Memory Selection: If any man be in Christ, he is a new creature: old things are passed away; behold, all things are become new. (2 Corinthians 5:17)

Ephesians 2:1-10

1 And you he made alive, when you were dead through the trespasses and sins 2 in which you once walked, following the course of this world, following the prince of the power of the air, the spirit that is now at work in the sons of disobedience. 3 Among these we all once lived in the passions of our flesh, following the desires of body and mind, and so we were by nature children of wrath, like the rest of mankind. 4 But God, who is rich in mercy, out of the great love with which he loved us, 5 even when we were dead through our trespasses, made us alive together with Christ (by grace you have been saved), 6 and raised us up with him, and made us sit with him in the heavenly places in Christ Jesus, 7 that in the coming ages he might show the immeasurable riches of his grace in kindness toward us in Christ Jesus. 8 For by grace you have been saved through faith; and this is not your own doing, it is the gift of God—9 not because of works, lest any man should boast. 10 For we are his workmanship, created in Christ Jesus for good works, which God prepared beforehand, that we should walk in them.

Memory Selection: If any one is in Christ, he is a new creation; the old has passed away, behold, the new has come. (2 Corinthians 5:17)

The Scripture and the Main Question —Charles M. Laymon

WHEN CHRIST IS UNKNOWN

The French critic and writer Anatole France tells a story about Pontius Pilate, who was procurator of Judea when Jesus was crucified. Pilate was the very one who passed the death sentence on Jesus and commanded that he be placed on the cross. Years later he was asked by his friend Laelius Lamia, "Pontius, do you remember anything about Jesus who was crucified?" Pilate answered, "Jesus? Jesus—of Nazareth? I cannot call him to mind."

This, of course, is only a story; but the idea is not inconceivable. How little impression Jesus made upon some people in his own day and how little he makes upon some of our contemporaries today is surprising. Jesus, however, was not unaware that he would not be recognized by all. Did he not say that the seed that was sown in some cases would fall on hard soil and bear no crop at all, while in other cases it would multiply only thirty or sixtyfold (Matthew 13:18-23)? And did not the writer of the Gospel of John say, "He came to his own home, and his own people received him not"? (1:11)

To us who follow Christ it seems incomprehensible that persons should not respond to him. Is this lack of interest because we do not present him to the world with enthusiasm? Are we not eagerly persuasive? Do we not care enough? Are people too preoccupied, too busy to listen? Do they find our presentation of Jesus so overlaid with churchly paraphernalia—creedal, ritualistic, formal, and dull—that they are repelled rather than attracted to Christ as we proclaim him?

FINDING OUR TRUE IMAGE

The discovery of Christ, who he is and what he means for the world and ourselves, is the greatest need in life. But the finding out of who we are and who we are to become is also a necessity. The two searches belong together. When we have found Christ, we find ourselves.

E. Stanley Jones quotes Elizabeth Fry as saying before she was converted, "I feel like a contemptible fine lady, all outside and no inside."

Louisa May Alcott, author of *Little Women*, in her search for self-discovery prayed:

> Be thou my guide until I find
> Led by a tender hand,
> The happy kingdom in myself
> And dare to take command.[10]

When we are feeling such inner emptiness, the discovery of Christ becomes self-discovery. We know who we are because we have found who Christ is. John put it this way in his Gospel: "To all who received him, who believed in his name, he gave power to become children of God." (1:12)

Children of God! Here is our true image. We are not creatures meant to cringe and crawl on the face of the earth. Instead, we are God's children, intended for fellowship with him.

BORN OF GOD

When a young child rises from his crawling and walks on two feet, it is a time of rejoicing in the family circle. Walking is a major step in his maturing.

When a person comes to the discovery that he is a child of God and walks in the light of the Father's love, it is an even greater event. Call the experience a new integration of the self or a new birth or something else—something has happened. Paul speaks of the result of the experience as a "new creation." (2 Corinthians 5:17)

How does this new creation come into being? William Barclay, in *Turning to God*, says, "One man may accept Jesus Christ as Lord in one shat-

[10] Alcott, "My Kingdom."

tering moment, and . . . for another there may be an uninterrupted process and development. But in the difference there remains one common factor—there must in every life be some moment of decision.

"In the one case it will be a moment in which the direction of life is even violently reversed, in which a man breaks with the old way and accepts the new. In the second case the decision will be a decision regarding the Church. . . . It will be a moment when he deliberately takes his stand beside the Christ whom he has known for long." [11]

How can we explain what happens? It is a work of God, no less. John

[11] William Barclay, *Turning to God* (Westminster Press, 1964), p. 95.

stated this belief once and for all when he said that in such moments we are born "not of blood nor of the will of the flesh nor of the will of man, but of God." (1:13)

WHAT HAPPENS NEXT?

Men are reborn to live a new life (Ephesians 2:1-10). Inside and outside, everything changes. They are aware of the change; their family knows about it; the neighbors know; the community knows; and the world may know it too.

The true root of social change is such changed lives. Social legislation without inner renewal is like ointment applied to a sore. It may bring temporary relief from pain but not permanent cure.

Helping Adults Become Involved —Harry B. Adams

Preparation of Self and Class

This is the first lesson in the final unit of this quarter. Having looked at man's plight and God's action to get man out of his sin, this unit explores what kind of life a Christian is able to live. What kind of person does one become when he responds in faith to God's love in Jesus Christ? What actions does a person become capable of performing?

In this first lesson of the unit the concern is with the way in which Christ changes persons, enabling them to become new men and women. The interpretation here is that the new life in Christ is not something that happens totally at some given moment, even for those who have a profound experience of transformation. New life in Christ is the daily possibility of growth for all those who know him in faith. In preparing the lesson you will want to reflect on how

your own life, day by day, is influenced by your response to the love of God in Jesus Christ.

Presenting the Main Question

John Wesley wrote in his journal for May 5, 1772: "In the evening I preached in the new house at Arbroath. In this town there is a change indeed! It was wicked to a proverb; remarkable for Sabbath-breaking, cursing, swearing, drunkenness, and a general contempt of religion. But it is not so now. Open wickedness disappears; no oaths are heard, no drunkenness seen in the streets. And many have not only ceased from evil, and learned to do well, but are witnesses of the inward kingdom of God, 'righteousness, peace, and joy in the Holy Ghost.' " [12]

[12] Nehemiah Curnock, ed., *The Journal of the Rev. John Wesley, A.M.* (Charles H. Kelly, 1909), vol. V, p. 458.

Wesley saw things happening to people and to their communities when the power of God in Christ came to them. He may have been a bit too optimistic in his assessment of how what he saw as evils had been wiped out, but nonetheless it is clear that through the preaching of Wesley the gospel reached men and did change their lives.

Give the class members opportunity to respond to this statement of Wesley and to talk about the following questions:

1. In what ways can the statement by Wesley be related to people and communities today?

2. How has Jesus Christ influenced or changed persons you have known?

3. What impact does the church have on the community?

4. Why would you like or not like to live in a community that has no church?

Two or three years ago there was a significant movement in the youth culture affirming the power of Christ in the lives of young people. Quite a number of persons who had been on drugs, who had dropped out of any meaningful work or relationships, testified that Christ had brought new freedom and new meaning to their lives. In some rather remarkable instances persons who had been threatened by the disaster of hard drugs were freed from whatever it was that drove them to use drugs. It is clear that the dramatic transformation by the power attributed to Jesus Christ did not stop with the time of John Wesley.

Developing the Lesson

Explore the meaning of some of the images that are used in the biblical passages. In seeking to grasp what impact faith in Christ can have on men, it will be helpful to look more closely at the way in which the Bible talks about the changes that are made in men by Christ.

Paul writes to the people at Ephesus: "And you he made alive, when you were dead." (2:1) Paul is talking, not about life or death in terms of the organic functioning of the physical body, but about the life or death of the whole person. Have the class members look at the incidents described below and indicate whether they reflect a person who is truly alive or tragically dead.

1. A man declines to accept a position for which he is well qualified because he is almost completely lacking in confidence in himself as a person.

2. A person who had been seriously injured in a car accident due to another person's negligence is able to be concerned about how the person who caused the accident feels.

3. A person finds life dull, boring, monotonous, and without much meaning.

4. A person finds himself rejoicing in the day that has been given to him.

5. A person is able to hear and respond sensitively to persons whose life style and goals are very different from his own.

6. A person would like to support actively a low-cost housing project in his community but decides not to do so because he knows that such a proposal would cause a great deal of controversy.

After the class members have looked at these incidents, discuss with them how a person's faith in Christ would enable him to live life fully in each circumstance.

Another image used to describe the life of a Christian is *children*. Paul says that "we were by nature children of wrath" (Ephesians 2:3), while the author of John's Gospel declares that "he gave power to become children of God." (1:12) To be a child of God is to know oneself loved of God, cared for by God, sustained by God. To be a child of God is to have God expect that our lives will be used fully and creatively. Both Dr. Thompson and Dr. Laymon set forth briefly what it means to a person to become a child of God through Jesus Christ.

Paul also uses the image of following. Formerly the people to whom he wrote had followed "the course of this world," had followed "the prince of the power of the air," had followed "the desires of body and mind." (Ephesians 2:2-3) Give the class members opportunity to indicate what they think Paul means when he writes in this way. The following are some suggestions of how men follow the course of this world, and so forth.

1. They cheat or exploit others in order to get more for themselves.

2. They hurt others because of their hate or prejudice toward them.

3. They make themselves miserable with their envy and jealousy of others.

4. Their values and goals in life are set by the advertisers and image-makers of the culture.

5. Their lust drives them to use others as mere sex objects.

For those who know Christ there is another way open to them. They follow a different Lord and walk a different way—a way that leads to good works and acts of love. Again it is clear that a man does not receive God's love in Christ because he deserves it; but once his life is open to that love, his life is different. "For we are his workmanship, created in Christ Jesus for good works, which God prepared beforehand, that we should walk in them." (Ephesians 2: 10)

Sum up what it means to have new life in Christ. In the first place, new life in Christ is not just a "once-and-for-all" transformation of a person. A man's life may be radically changed by his initial commitment to Christ, but each day brings its own new possibilities for a new life. Whatever a person has been, he has the potential to live more fully and richly with Christ.

In the second place, new life in Christ has certain characteristics that can be described. It is a life in which there is meaning and purpose. It is a life in which there is hope, hope in the "immeasurable riches of his grace in kindness toward us in Christ Jesus." (Ephesians 2:7) It is a life in which a person has the security of knowing that he is loved by God. It is a life in which there is confidence of self-worth and value. It is a life in which a person knows who he is as a child of God.

Helping Class Members Act

Invite each member of the class to write on a slip of paper some action that he has wanted to do, that he felt was right to do, but that he has not felt free to do. Have the members keep their slips of paper, and ask them to see if they can open their lives to Christ until he can free them to perform the action.

Planning for Next Sunday

Ask the members of the class to be ready to report from the newspapers or from their personal experience incidents in which persons have expressed their faith in Christ as they have acted toward others.

Christ Makes Men Brothers

Background Scripture: Acts 11:4-18; Galatians 3:23-29;
Ephesians 2:11-22; 1 John 4:7-12

The Main Question —Charles M. Laymon

The pledge class of a college fraternity recently included a Negro, a Jew, and a young man who was blind. On this campus in the deep South no one thought such a thing could happen. But it did.

Of course, there were repercussions. Anonymous telephone calls and threats to burn a cross on the fraternity lawn followed announcement of the pledges. Nothing materialized, however; and life settled down to business as usual. During Greek Week this same fraternity entered the Greek Sing. And this fraternity won the contest—this, the only one on the campus with a black student in its ranks.

This college situation raises the question, How do you break down the walls that divide people from people? Other questions follow: What is involved in establishing human brotherhood? Is timing an important factor? What political and economic forces should be considered? Where does the church come into the picture? How do we re-establish communication where it has broken down between groups?

The New Testament passages that follow offer helpful answers in this area of brotherhood.

As You Read the Scripture —Claude H. Thompson

Ephesians 2:11. *Remember that at one time you Gentiles in the flesh: Gentiles,* of course, refers to all non-Jews. Apparently there were many in the Ephesian church. They were uncircumcised and hence unable to participate in full fellowship with Jews who sought to keep the law. (Study Acts 15 and Galatians 2 to see how the barrier was broken in Paul's day.)

Verse 12. *Remember that you were at that time separated from Christ:* Here are cited liabilities that the gentiles faced: (1) Before Christ came, the barrier between the circumcised and the uncircumcised was absolute. A Jew could not even enter a gentile home. (2) In contrast to the Jew the gentile had no hope of a messiah. Indeed, there was little hope for the gentile at all. (3) Gentiles were alienated from Israel, which meant they were essentially pagan. If they had a religious life at all, it was that of Rome, which had about run its course. (4) The Jews were a covenant people. (See Exodus 6:2-8.) But the gentiles, having no living God, had no covenant. (5) No hope and without a living God—the two belong together. The condition of the non-Jew was dismal; and Paul was quite able to understand it, since he had lived as a strict Jew among the gentiles of Tarsus.

Verse 13. *But now in Christ Jesus you . . . have been brought near:* Notice

311

CHRIST MAKES MEN BROTHERS

the contrast between "at that time" and *but now*. The coming of Christ had completely changed the picture. Another contrast, "far off" and *brought near*, shows the radical work of Christ. (Study Isaiah 57:19 and see verse 17 of this chapter.) "Blood of Christ" carries the idea of sacrifice—foreshadowed in the Temple offerings.

Verse 14. *For he is our peace . . . and has broken down the dividing wall:* That *dividing wall* was a reality. In the Temple it was constructed of marble with inscriptions declaring that if any non-Jew went beyond the Court of the Gentiles he would risk death. But Christ has "rent the veil in two." In him is peace, and we are both one—gentile and Jew. In a world divided by race, religion, customs, traditions—Christ is the only one who can destroy the barriers that alienate us from one another.

Verse 15. *By abolishing in his flesh the law of commandments:* Christ has produced a new humanity, neither Jew nor gentile but Christian.

Verse 16. *And might reconcile us both to God in one body:* Both Jew and gentile needed reconciliation, not only to each other, but also to God. This was accomplished at Calvary. No man can claim exemption from this need for reconciliation. And every man may find it in surrender to Christ.

1 John 4:7-12. *Beloved, let us love one another:* Love originates in God, who is here described as love. But love is no mere sentiment; it is creative action conferring worth upon others. Love is the cause and result of rebirth, making us new people in Christ. Love also creates community—a brotherhood of new people. The alternatives are clear: one either loves and is born of

God, or one is alienated from God. Verses 9 and 10 restate the truth of the Easter lesson, "Christ Conquers Sin and Death," and the lesson of last Sunday, "Christ Makes Men New."

Selected Scripture

King James Version

Ephesians 2:11-16

11 Wherefore remember, that ye being in time past Gentiles in the flesh, who are called Uncircumcision by that which is called the Circumcision in the flesh made by hands;

12 That at that time ye were without Christ, being aliens from the commonwealth of Israel, and strangers from the covenants of promise, having no hope, and without God in the world:

13 But now in Christ Jesus ye who sometimes were far off are made nigh by the blood of Christ.

14 For he is our peace, who hath made both one, and hath broken down the middle wall of partition between us;

15 Having abolished in his flesh the enmity, even the law of commandments contained in ordinances; for to make in himself of twain one new man, so making peace;

16 And that he might reconcile both unto God in one body by the cross, having slain the enmity thereby.

1 John 4:7-12

7 Beloved, let us love one another: for love is of God; and every one that loveth is born of God, and knoweth God.

8 He that loveth not knoweth not God; for God is love.

9 In this was manifested the love of God toward us, because that God sent his only begotten Son into the world, that we might live through him.

Revised Standard Version

Ephesians 2:11-16

11 Therefore remember that at one time you Gentiles in the flesh, called the uncircumcision by what is called the circumcision, which is made in the flesh by hands—12 remember that you were at that time separated from Christ, alienated from the commonwealth of Israel, and strangers to the covenants of promise, having no hope and without God in the world. 13 But now in Christ Jesus you who once were far off have been brought near in the blood of Christ. 14 For he is our peace, who has made us both one, and has broken down the dividing wall of hostility, 15 by abolishing in his flesh the law of commandments and ordinances, that he might create in himself one new man in place of the two, so making peace, 16 and might reconcile us both to God in one body through the cross, thereby bringing the hostility to an end.

1 John 4:7-12

7 Beloved, let us love one another; for love is of God, and he who loves is born of God and knows God. 8 He who does not love does not know God; for God is love. 9 In this the love of God was made manifest among us, that God sent his only Son into the world, so that we might live through him. 10 In this is love, not that we loved God but that he loved

10 Herein is love, not that we loved God, but that he loved us, and sent his Son to be the propitiation for our sins.

11 Beloved, if God so loved us, we ought also to love one another.

12 No man hath seen God at any time. If we love one another, God dwelleth in us, and his love is perfected in us.

Memory Selection: There is neither Jew nor Greek, there is neither bond nor free, there is neither male nor female: for ye are all one in Christ Jesus. (Galatians 3:28)

us and sent his Son to be the expiation for our sins. 11 Beloved, if God so loved us, we also ought to love one another. 12 No man has ever seen God; if we love one another, God abides in us and his love is perfected in us.

Memory Selection: There is neither Jew nor Greek, there is neither slave nor free, there is neither male nor female; for you are all one in Christ Jesus. (Galatians 3:28)

The Scripture and the Main Question —Charles M. Laymon

SEPARATED—ALIENATED—STRANGERS

Passing through Checkpoint Charlie en route from West to East Berlin is an awesome experience. The tragedy of separation, alienation, and estrangement weighs you down as you recall what has happened here. Death and desolation mark this spot; anguish and sorrow began—and begin —here for so many. The situation seems like a dream, yet it is all so very real when you travel across the line.

But one does not need to go to Berlin to experience what the wall represents. Estrangement can happen in any community in America where there are walls of separation between persons. Sometimes these walls are economic, political, social, and even religious. For whatever reason, whenever persons cannot know fellowship openly, a Berlin wall has been set up.

In the early days of Christianity there was, among other divisive forces, a separation between Jewish Christians and gentile Christians. At the beginning most of the Christians were converts from Judaism. Some of them felt that gentiles were still apart from God's grace in Christ. They were outsiders. This belief is reflected in the passage from Ephesians in our lesson: "Remember that you [gentiles] were at that time separated from Christ, alienated from the commonwealth of Israel, and strangers to the covenants of promise, having no hope and without God in the world." (Ephesians 2:12)

In the Book of Acts the inclusion of gentiles in the Christian community is presented as a major development. Such accounts as the going of Peter to the home of Cornelius the gentile reflect this fact. Peter was even "called on the carpet" at Jerusalem for doing this and had to defend his act before the apostles (Acts 10:1 through 11:18).

WALLS THAT CAME DOWN

We live in a day when, in the free world, there are attempts on every side to bring persons together. In the area of race we can see these attempts in the very communities where we live. Even in the theater, in some cases, the actors mingle among the audience in order to involve the spectators. And denominational union is also a lively possibility in our time.

Another attempt to relate persons to one another today is found in sensitivity groups where individuals come together in complete frankness and share their problems and their inner feelings openly. On a high level the church was once like this and can be so again if an attitude of openness and brotherhood prevails.

If walls can be built, they can also be torn down. And in the case of the early Christians the latter actually occurred. Gentiles were finally admitted into the Christian community. The first constituted council of the church, meeting in Jerusalem, formally made this decision (Acts 15).

These persons realized that "in Christ there is no east or west, in him no north or south." Gentiles had enthusiastically responded to Paul's preaching, and many new gentile converts were made on his first missionary journey outside Palestine. The Letter to the Ephesians reflects this fact: "But now in Christ Jesus you who once were far off have been brought near in the blood of Christ." (2:13) The wall between Jewish and gentile Christians had been torn down.

ONE BODY THROUGH THE CROSS

T. Z. Koo was a YMCA secretary in China. He walked eight hundred miles to get out of China in order to come to San Francisco in 1945. There he acted as a counselor to the Chinese delegation at the United Nations Conference. This Chinese gentleman made a remarkable statement: "There are differences in race, color, speech, and customs, and we can find clashing viewpoints beneath the surface in every land, but in Christ 'all things hold together.'"

The purpose of tearing down the walls that separate persons from one another is so that persons may be united into such a significant whole as Mr. Koo envisioned. This unity is not to swallow up individuality but to give added purpose to the life of each person within it.

The comparison of the church to the body was employed frequently by Paul (see 1 Corinthians 12). Each member contributes his vitality and abilities creatively to the life of the whole church. The author of Ephesians has caught this ideal of dynamic unity when he says God's purpose in Christ was to "reconcile us both to God in one body through the cross." (2:16)

The reference to the cross in this passage should not be missed. What it says is that since Christ died for all men in the kingdom of God there should be unity among all. As the title of this lesson states, Christ makes men brothers.

GOD'S LOVE AND OURS

Peter J. Ediger has paraphrased a portion of the writing of the prophet Micah in which he includes a section based on the speeches of Martin Luther King, Jr. He seems to catch the spirit of unity that lies at the heart of this lesson:

I have a dream!
I have a dream of the restructuring of our society!
I have a dream of people building on the power of love which casts out fear;
I have a dream of people building on the trust and faith which breaks down barriers;
I have a dream of people building on the hope which keeps faith and love alive in a day when prejudice and fear threaten the life of our land and our world.
I have a dream of sons of ghetto-dwellers and sons of suburbanites sitting down

together at the table of brotherhood, sharing together in the fruit of common effort and singing songs of praise to the God of all.

I have a dream of a day when little children and their fathers and their mothers will not be judged by the color of their skin but by the content of their character; when personal values will be more important than property values; when we shall see our brother's good as our own, and feel our brother's pain as our own; and we shall truly love our neighbor as ourselves.

I have a dream of nonviolence; of a society in which vengeance and retaliation are taboo; of a country which will not be ruled by bullets and by dynamite at home and which will not seek to rule by bullets and by bombs abroad; of a nation which will lead the nations of the world in turning swords into plowshares and spears into pruning hooks and bombs and bombers into bread and butter.

I have a dream of that mountain top from which we may view the promised land where valleys are exalted and mountains made low and crooked places straight.

I have a dream of a growing crescendo of voices rising out of the shame and hurt and anger of our guilt and pain and passion and singing old words with new spirit *"We Shall Overcome . . . Someday!"* [13]

God's love should make us realize that we are all one in Christ; our love must respond in a brotherhood that includes all (1 John 4:7-12).

[13] From *The Prophets' Report on Religion in North America.* Copyright 1971 by Faith and Life Press. Used by permission. Ediger states in a footnote: "Many of the thoughts in this concluding section are adapted from speeches by Martin Luther King, Jr."

Helping Adults Become Involved —Harry B. Adams

Preparation of Self and Class

The lesson last week looked at what can happen to a person when he is related through faith to Jesus Christ. In the biblical language, he is "made alive." This lesson continues the exploration of the kind of life that characterizes the person who is changed and shaped by Jesus Christ.

A person is given new life in Christ, but he is not made new to live in splendid isolation. A man's relationship to Christ has decisive influence on his relationship with other people. It is this dimension of the Christian life—a man in relation to other men—that is dealt with in this lesson.

A film and a filmstrip may serve as resources for this session: *Almost Neighbors* and *Members One of Another.* (See pages 231-32.)

Presenting the Main Question

Records of a frontier church were recently found, including minutes of the meetings of the church board in the mid-nineteenth century. From the minutes it appears that the board spent most of its time putting members out of the church, for what appeared to persons in that day to be good and sufficient reasons. What were the reasons deemed adequate to separate persons from the church of Jesus Christ? According to the records the main offenses were drinking, dancing, card playing, and fraternizing with members of another denomination.

In this day of ecumenical concern it is a bit difficult to remember the denominational exclusiveness and rivalry that literally divided the church into warring camps on the American frontier. It is tragic but true that religion has served to divide men from one another through the centuries. Consider with the class members the many ways in which men's loyalty to one religious group has served to separate them from other men, as for example the following:

1. One Protestant denomination set against other denominations.

2. Divisions within denominations over such issues as form of church government, interpretation of Scripture, creedal requirements, and so forth.

3. Separation between Protestants and Roman Catholics.

4. Division between Christians and Jews.

5. Divisions between Christians and Mohammedans, Buddhists, Hindus, and so forth.

In his Letter to the Ephesians, Paul also was writing about religious divisions. The particular issue dividing the early Christian community was whether the Jewish law had to be obeyed, "the law of commandments and ordinances." (2:15)

Many other barriers besides religious differences separate men from one another, of course. As the members of the class identify some of these barriers, list them on chalkboard or newsprint. They would include such items as the following:

> Race
> Nationality
> Class
> Sex
> Economic interest
> Language
> Geographic location
> Life style
> Age

Developing the Lesson

Consider why persons raise barriers that divide them from others. Persons have always found an identity and felt a sense of belonging as they joined together in groups. They have bound themselves together for protection, as the tribe or the nation. They have come together because of shared interests, as the union or the manufacturer's association. They have known a unity because of a shared heritage, as an ethnic group.

Persons not only join together in groups, but they also feel themselves set against others. Discuss with the class members the reasons why men are divided from one another and antagonistic toward one another. Why do black and white men find barriers between one another? Why is there conflict between Russia and the United States? Why is there a tension between the generations? Why do persons in different social classes feel uneasy with one another?

Here are some of the reasons that might be suggested.

1. People are afraid of others whom they do not know.

2. People believe that others threaten their own self-interests.

3. People have certain values that are important to them, that they feel they must protect when others do not see things as they do.

4. People have hurt and exploited one another in the past and now live with the resulting animosity and distrust.

5. People do not make the effort to try to understand how others see things and how they feel.

6. People find certain satisfaction in considering themselves better than others.

7. People are bound together more closely in their own group when they identify differences in other groups.

8. People have been conditioned by their own culture and experience to see others as their enemies.

Explore the ways in which Christ helps to break down the barriers that divide men. Review each of the reasons why men are separated from one another suggested by the class members and suggested above, and discuss how Jesus Christ breaks down the barriers or helps men overcome such divisions.

The two passages of Scripture for this lesson deal directly with the issue of division. Study the passages using the material by Dr. Laymon and Dr. Thompson. Some of the ways in which Christ unites men are indicated below:

1. Christ reconciles men to God; and when men know that both they and their brothers are no longer separated from God, they sense their unity with one another.

2. Men have been brought near to God and to one another "in the blood of Christ," created "one body through the cross." (Ephesians 2:13, 16) Paul goes on to say that this new life brings hostility to an end. When men know what Christ has sacrificed for them and for other persons, their hostility toward one another is dissipated.

3. Christ overcame the division between Jew and gentile "by abolishing in his flesh the law of commandments and ordinances." (Ephesians 2:15) In Christ the fulfillment of the letter of the law just is not important enough to separate men from one another. Christ brings a new perspective on some of the issues men use to separate themselves from others.

4. Christ brings men hope. When men have confidence in God and his future, they do not have to try to secure their own future at the expense of others.

5. Christ brings men peace. When men can be at peace with God and at peace with themselves, then it is possible for them to be at peace with their brothers.

6. Christ brings men love. When men are loved, they become confident and secure persons who can love others.

Helping Class Members Act

Consider some of the barriers that are dividing people in your community. Have the class members think about ways in which the church as a group and they as individuals can help to overcome some of these divisions.

Planning for Next Sunday

Paul states: "For I have learned, in whatever state I am, to be content." (Philippians 4:11) Ask the members of the class to think about that statement during the coming week and to apply it to their own lives as they consider these questions:

1. Would I truly want to be able to say this about myself? Why, or why not?

2. What things keep me from being content?

3. As I look at my life from the perspective of Jesus Christ, how important are these things?

God's Grace Sustains Us

Background Scripture: Isaiah 40:25-31; 2 Corinthians 4:15;
12:9-10; Philippians 4:10-13

The Main Question —Charles M. Laymon

A young adult class was discussing the purpose of religion. One member said,
"I think religion is the invention of man to overcome his insecurities." Another said, "I agree; religion is whistling in the dark." At this point still another member of the group spoke up, "Sure," he said, "religion helps you
overcome your fears; but doesn't it also challenge you to face danger? In the
crisis hour a person in the spirit of Christ may take a stand that will cost him
his job." At this, a young woman chimed in, "I am religious because all
around me I find God—in nature, in people, and in human events."

At this point the leader interjected a quotation from Robert A. Millikan,
Nobel prize winner in physics: "The . . . task of religion . . . is to develop the
conscience, the ideals, and the aspirations of mankind."

This quotation brought a different slant to the discussion and led to the
questions: What does religion do for man? What is it supposed to do? Does
it provide a channel for God's grace?

The biblical passages that follow contain some dynamic answers to these
questions.

As You Read the Scripture —Claude H. Thompson

Isaiah 40:25-26. *To whom then will you compare me:* At first reading,
this passage seems to have little reference to divine grace. Verses 25 and 26 are
in the form of questions asking the people to consider how to compare God
with any of his rivals. Looking at the heavens and considering the stars, the
question arises as to their origin. Who made them? The reply is implied in the
following questions. They came from God himself—none other. He not only
has created the vast number of them, but he has also given them names—
though we are not told what these names are. "Not one is missing," hence
there is a perfection in the operation of the constellations.

Verse 27. *My way is hid from the* LORD: It is futile to ask if our lives can be
hidden from God. Of course not! But neither is "my right disregarded by my
God." That is, God is not unconcerned; I can never escape him. Even when he
may seem hidden and uninterested in my struggles, yet the sovereign God is
still the God of all the earth—and my God.

Verse 28. *Have you not known? Have you not heard?* The author seems
almost impatient that the people seem to lack knowledge of God. *Known* and
heard what? That God is from everlasting to everlasting. That he is the creator
of all things. That he is never weary. That his ways are beyond man's ability
completely to understand. That he is ever graciously available.

319

Verse 29. *He gives power to the faint:* This is an excellent example of Hebrew poetic parallelism—repeating in the second expression the same (or similar) idea found in the first. This style was doubtless used for poetic, or musical, effect; but it had the added purpose of emphasis. At least those who are aware of their own weakness have a claim upon God for strength. Meditate upon how this unknown prophet of the Exile (often called the "Second Isaiah") must have given encouragement to dispirited captives in Babylonia! Try to imagine yourself in their position—yet believing God would never fail.

Verse 30. *Even youths shall faint and be weary:* Under captive domination even young men might be unable to resist the pressures of a strange land. The theme of fainting and exhaustion is repeated.

Verse 31. *They who wait for the* Lord *shall renew their strength:* Yet there is hope and strength for all. Those who "mount up with wings" may be the young, vigorous men. Those who "run" without weariness may be mature adults. Those who "walk and not faint" could be the aged, the infirm. But strength does not come automatically. Here is that idea of grace. Strength comes only to those *who wait for the* Lord. Grace must be accepted.

Philippians 4:10. *I rejoice . . . that . . . you have revived your concern for me:* Keep in mind that Paul is writing from prison. He had reason to be despondent, but he was not. One of the main themes of the letter is joy. Here divine grace is mediated through thoughtful friends who did not forget the prisoner. They had sent some gift to him, and now Paul replies with joyous gratitude.

Verse 11. *Not that I complain of want:* Paul refuses to entertain self-pity. If conditions are good, thank God; if not, do not complain. God never fails.

Verse 12. *I know how to be abased:* This verse is autobiographical. Paul had suffered for his faith. He had learned *how to be abased*—to be brought low in humiliation. But he also had learned how to live in abundance. Whether destitute, or in abundance, external conditions were never to determine his life. Note that three times he cites the contrasts: abased/abounding, plenty/hunger, abundance/want. Apparently this style was for emphasis, though it also implies repeated experiences.

Verse 13. *I can do all things in him who strengthens me:* Note the translation of this verse in the Jerusalem Bible: "There is nothing I cannot master with the help of the One who gives me strength."

Selected Scripture

King James Version	Revised Standard Version
Isaiah 40:25-31	*Isaiah 40:25-31*
25 To whom then will ye liken me, or shall I be equal? saith the Holy One.	25 To whom then will you compare me, that I should be like him? says the Holy One.
26 Lift up your eyes on high, and behold who hath created these things,	26 Lift up your eyes on high and see: who created these?

that bringeth out their host by number: he calleth them all by names by the greatness of his might, for that he is strong in power; not one faileth.

27 Why sayest thou, O Jacob, and speakest, O Israel, My way is hid from the LORD, and my judgment is passed over from my God?

28 Hast thou not known? hast thou not heard, that the everlasting God, the LORD, the Creator of the ends of the earth, fainteth not, neither is weary? there is no searching of his understanding.

29 He giveth power to the faint; and to them that have no might he increaseth strength.

30 Even the youths shall faint and be weary, and the young men shall utterly fall:

31 But they that wait upon the LORD shall renew their strength; they shall mount up with wings as eagles; they shall run, and not be weary; and they shall walk, and not faint.

Philippians 4:10-13
10 But I rejoiced in the Lord greatly, that now at the last your care of me hath flourished again; wherein ye were also careful, but ye lacked opportunity.

11 Not that I speak in respect of want: for I have learned, in whatsoever state I am, therewith to be content.

12 I know both how to be abased, and I know how to abound: every where and in all things I am instructed both to be full and to be hungry, both to abound and to suffer need.

He who brings out their host by number,
calling them all by name;
by the greatness of his might,
and because he is strong in power
not one is missing.

27 Why do you say, O Jacob,
and speak, O Israel,
"My way is hid from the LORD,
and my right is disregarded by my God"?

28 Have you not known? Have you not heard?
The LORD is the everlasting God,
the Creator of the ends of the earth.
He does not faint or grow weary,
his understanding is unsearchable.

29 He gives power to the faint,
and to him who has no might he increases strength.

30 Even youths shall faint and be weary,
and young men shall fall exhausted;

31 but they who wait for the LORD shall renew their strength,
they shall mount up with wings like eagles,
they shall run and not be weary,
they shall walk and not faint.

Philippians 4:10-13
10 I rejoice in the Lord greatly that now at length you have revived your concern for me; you were indeed concerned for me, but you had no opportunity. 11 Not that I complain of want; for I have learned, in whatever state I am, to be content. 12 I know how to be abased, and I know how to abound; in any and all circumstances I have learned the secret of facing plenty and hunger, abundance and want. 13 I can do all things in him who strengthens me.

13 I can do all things through Christ which strengtheneth me.

Memory Selection: My grace is sufficient for thee: for my strength is made perfect in weakness. (2 Corinthians 12:9)

Memory Selection: My grace is sufficient for you, for my power is made perfect in weakness. (2 Corinthians 12:9)

The Scripture and the Main Question —Charles M. Laymon

GOD CARES FOR NATURE

Creation began with the making of nature. Man was then created as the crown of it (Genesis 1:26-31). Ever since there has been the conviction that the God of nature and the God of human nature are one and the same. The God of the stars is the God of the heart, and he who rules the waves is he who can reign over our personal emotions. God, nature, and man are bound together in creation.

For this reason many of the psalms begin by referring to nature, and many of the prayers in the Bible do also. When the early Christians on one occasion found that Peter and John had been released by the authorities who had arrested them, they prayed joyfully, beginning their thanksgiving prayer with the words: "Sovereign Lord, who didst make the heaven and the earth and the sea and everything in them." (Acts 4:24)

Jesus also prayed to the Heavenly Father as the Lord of Nature. He once opened a brief prayer by saying, "I thank thee, Father, Lord of heaven and earth. . . ." (Matthew 11:25) More than this, Jesus heightened many persons' faith by reminding them of God's care for the birds, the grass, and the flowers (Matthew 6:26, 28-29; Luke 12:28).

The creation of the heavens by God impressed Isaiah as he wrote today's Scripture passage. The stars are a numberless host, and the Creator knows them all by name (Isaiah 40:26). Such a great God could be depended upon to have sufficient power to deliver the Jews from exile in Babylonia. He had not forgotten them; his grace would sustain them.

GOD CARES FOR MAN

We do not usually think of the grace of God in relation to the world of nature. But in a larger sense his care of nature is one with his care of man. As he sustains nature, he will also sustain man.

Benjamin Franklin has been remembered for his wise counsel. One of the first books parents used to give their children when they were old enough for serious reading was Franklin's *Autobiography*. He was eighty-one years old when he addressed the Constitutional Convention with these words: "I have lived a long time; and the longer I live, the more convincing proofs I see of this truth, that God governs in the affairs of men. And if a sparrow cannot fall to the ground without his notice, is it probable that an empire can rise without his aid?" Franklin was asserting that God makes a difference in the events of men and nations.

Isaiah, speaking in Babylonia where the Jews were held captive, also was certain of this fact. He urged his nation to "wait for the Lord" and assured the people that if they did, they would "renew their strength." Like

322

eagles, they would fly; and in running and walking they would neither grow weary nor faint (40:31). Here God's grace is love in action.

LEARNING TO TRUST GOD'S GRACE

Waiting is difficult; often nothing seems to be happening and our need is urgent. Why does God delay? we ask. Leonardo da Vinci was painting the "Last Supper" when someone chided him because he sometimes paused so long before making a stroke. He replied, "When I pause the longest, I make the most telling strokes with my brush." Such patience is often a creative expression of faith.

Most of us need to learn to be patient and trusting. It does not come easily; we chafe at the bit and crave action. The patience of trustful faith, however, may be a creative act. While we wait something is happening in us and in our situation. God is at work while we wait.

God is an expert at waiting. Some persons have regarded the patience of God as the greatest of all miracles. He waited so long for the Hebrew people to get to the point where they would accept Christ; and when he came, they still rejected him. God has waited nearly two thousand years for Christians to become C H R I S T I A N. And although some progress to this end has been made, we are far from the goal; God is still patient and waiting.

The apostle Paul was a tempestuous person. When he first became a follower of Christ, he stirred up so much furor in Jerusalem that the apostles sent him back to his home in Tarsus to cool off (Acts 9:26-30). Years later, however, as a prisoner in Rome, expecting to be martyred, Paul wrote the most positively joyful letter of his life. In this writing to the Philippian church he said, "I have learned, in whatever state I am, to be content." (4:11) Up or down, hungry or full, in plenty or want, Paul could act creatively. How can we explain this change?

THE SECRET OF VICTORY

Paul himself gave us the answer to this question. First of all, he said that he had to learn how to be patiently faithful as he trusted God's grace. At numerous times throughout the years he was anything but content with the way things were going. He had experienced beatings, stonings, and shipwrecks. He had been in and out of prison regularly, once spending a two-year imprisonment at Caesarea. His concern for the safety and growth of the churches was constantly tearing at him.

Yet gradually Paul found a way to trust. He learned that Jesus Christ was with him in his experiences and that he could count on Christ for the outcome. Now Paul could say, "I can do all things in him who strengthens me." (Philippians 4:13) This confidence in the power of God's sustaining grace is what the Christian religion gives to man.

Helping Adults Become Involved —Harry B. Adams

Preparation of Self and Class

A decisive issue in understanding the Christian life is uncovered in today's session. The issue is whether the Christian life is a gift or an achievement. Does one achieve new life by conscious effort and serious struggle? Does one make his fellow man his neighbor by stiff determination to do so? Persons have talked as though a life faithful to Christ were indeed a noble human accomplishment.

But this lesson deals with the grace of God, the free gift of God. If you will look again at the two previous lessons, you will note that it is Christ who makes men new, Christ who makes men brothers. The grace of God, his free and unmerited love, sustains men and enables them to live as persons who bear the name of Christ.

This is not to say that man sits passively waiting for God to do something. But it is to insist that the Christian life is God working through man, God acting to sustain man, God using the openness of man to his Spirit, God offering his grace to man, God enabling man to bear the burdens that he must carry.

As you prepare this lesson, think of the ways in which God's love has sustained you. You will also want to reflect on the burdens that various members of the class bear and consider how this session might help to bring God's grace to them.

Presenting the Main Question

An able young minister, just eight or ten years out of seminary, was appointed to a rather large church for a man of his age and experience. He was aggressive in developing programs, dynamic in his preaching, effective in his organizational efforts, responsible in his pastoral duties. Initially the church responded well to this attractive person and to his skillful leadership. But there was a wise and sensitive woman in the congregation who was concerned about her minister. She put her concern in these words, "From the day he arrived here, I've had the sense that he was eager for his next and bigger church."

Assuming that the woman's perception was accurate, give the class members opportunity to express their feelings about a minister who approaches his present situation with this attitude.

1. Why is it, or why is it not, a helpful stance for a minister to have in his present work?

2. What does the stance say about a minister's own personal needs?

3. What does the stance say about a minister's priorities and commitments?

4. In view of his words, "for I have learned, in whatever state I am to be content" (Philippians 4:11), what would the apostle Paul say about such an attitude?

5. What dangers do you see in Paul's words about being content? What evidence is there in Paul's own life that he was trapped by or that he avoided these dangers?

6. Why would you, or would you not, want to be able to speak Paul's words about your own life? How is the ability to speak such words related to a person's dependence on God's grace?

Developing the Lesson

Work out an understanding of the meaning of *grace* for the Christian. The title of this lesson is "God's Grace Sustains Us." Invite the members of the class to share their ideas about what it means to talk of God's grace. Some of the following dimensions may be included:

1. God's grace is expressed as his loving action toward his people.

2. God's grace is freely given, coming to those who have no merit with which to earn his love.

3. God's grace comes to men as God's compassionate care for them.

4. God's grace is shown toward his world with a joyous exuberance.

5. God's grace is exhibited as God

takes the initiative to reach out in love toward his people.

Explore with the class members what difference the sustaining grace of God makes in the lives of persons. Using the material prepared by Dr. Laymon and Dr. Thompson, study the Scripture to see what happens to persons whose lives are open to the gracious acts of God.

Some of the ways in which the grace of God changes people are suggested below.

God's grace enables persons to do the difficult tasks. Isaiah talks about the strength that is given to persons to enable them to carry on the struggles in which they are involved. Men are able to find great strength when they are giving themselves to the achievement of things that are really important. The grace of God, which assures man that there is meaning and purpose in the struggles of life, is a source of great strength.

God's grace enables persons to bear disapppointment and failure, hunger and want. Paul writes about knowing "how to be abased." (Philippians 4: 12) It has ever been the experience of man that in the time of his weakness and deprivation he finds that there is a power beyond himself that sustains him. In the powerful words of Paul to the Romans, persons come to know that nothing "will be able to separate us from the love of God in Christ Jesus our Lord." (Romans 8:39) The grace of God comes to men when they are in want, enabling them to see that what they have lost is not as crucial for the worth of a man as they once thought.

God's grace enables persons to deal with prosperity and success. So Paul writes: "I know how to abound; . . . I have learned the secret of facing plenty and . . . abundance." (Philippians 4:12) It takes a full measure of God's grace to be able to handle wealth and power. Men who succeed are tempted to rely on their own strength and cleverness, to value what they have won too highly, to be ruthless in dealing with the weaknesses and failures of those who have not succeeded as they have. The perspective on life given by Jesus Christ enables a person to deal sensitively, even with his successes.

Consider the ways in which God's grace comes to persons. Ask the class members to indicate ways in which they believe that they have experienced the grace of God in their own lives, and also the ways in which they have seen God's gracious love made known to others. You may want to list some of the ways on chalkboard or newsprint.

Have the class members look at the Scripture passages again to ask what ways God's grace is experienced there. For example, Isaiah talks of the assurance of God's power and concern as they are seen in the world created by God. Paul indicates that he is led to rejoice in God by the concern that the people in the church at Philippi have shown for him.

There are many other ways in which God's grace is experienced by men, including the following:

1. Through the Scripture.

2. Through the sacraments of the Lord's Supper and Baptism.

3. Through prayer.

4. Through taking a risk in order to serve Christ and neighbor.

5. Through extending oneself to do a job.

6. Through approaching the limits of what a man can bear in sorrow and suffering.

7. Through the words, the ministry, the life, and the presence of Jesus Christ.

Helping Class Members Act

God's grace is a free gift and cannot be earned or demanded. But a person can prepare himself and sensitize himself until he is better able to accept God's gracious love. Suggest that each member of the class accept one discipline for the coming week with the intent of making his life more open to God's grace. The discipline may involve a regular period of prayer, a reading of the Scripture, a time for sharing the days' events with another, and so forth.

Planning for Next Sunday

Ask members of the class to bring in items from the newspaper that make it difficult for people to have hope for the future, and also items that give some encouragement for the future.

LESSON 4

MAY 27

Christ Is Our Hope

Background Scripture: Acts 1:6-11; 2 Timothy 2:8-13;
1 Peter 1:3-9; 1 John 3:1-3

The Main Question —Charles M. Laymon

A popular song carried the sentiment, "I'm just a dope who is stuck with hope, and I can't get it out of my mind." The author was more descriptive of the Christian's attitude toward life than he knew. Even the apostle Paul called himself a fool for Christ's sake and said, "Love . . . hopes all things." (1 Corinthians 13:7)

Are Christians foolish because we are a people who hope? Why do we hope? What is the basis for our hope? These are fundamental questions that must be answered.

The fact is, Christian people have always hoped. The following inscription was found upon the walls of a seventeenth-century English church: "In the year 1653 when all things sacred were throughout ye nation either demonished or profaned, Sir Robert Shirley, Barronet, founded this church; whose singular praise it is to have done the best things in the worst times and hoped them in the most calamitous."

By contrast, George Bernard Shaw once cautioned against such hope. In his play *Caesar and Cleopatra* he wrote, "He who has never hoped can never despair." Yet this kind of warning has not kept Christians from continuing to hope.

Some of the basic reasons for the relentless hoping of Christians are found in the biblical passages that follow.

326

As You Read the Scripture —Claude H. Thompson

God's grace is not a temporary thing. It abides. Thus the Christian faces the future, not with despair, but with hope. The hope is centered in Christ—crucified, buried, resurrected, and returning again.

Acts 1:10-11. *While they were gazing into heaven:* This passage is Luke's account of the ascension of Christ. The facts are these: after the shocking events of Passion Week, culminating in the death and burial of Jesus, "he presented himself alive after his passion by many proofs." (Acts 1:3) But again after some days his earthly presence disappeared in what is known as the ascension.

Perhaps no New Testament report is more puzzling to modern man. How a person, known and experienced in a historical situation, could disappear *into heaven* is beyond explanation. But those who knew Jesus best were thoroughly persuaded of one thing: the events of the passion did not end the career of their Lord. Thus, while his appearances to his followers after the Resurrection soon ceased, those same followers became possessed by a dynamic fearlessness and joy never known before or since in human history.

Verse nine says "a cloud took him out of their sight." The cloud indicates a divine action. (See Revelation 11:12.) Jesus' presence with his followers did not merely fade away. This dramatized departure says that he had returned to the glory he had prior to his coming into history. Luke places this departure on the Mount of Olives. The "two men" who appeared suggest the events at the Resurrection (Luke 24:4). The "white robes" indicate messengers from God.

The message of the two men is that Jesus will return to earth victoriously. The vision of the disciples must now be turned from heaven to tasks on earth (verse 8). But the firm conviction that Jesus will come again to earth has been a permanent element in the Christian's faith throughout the centuries.

1 Peter 1:3-9. *Blessed be the God and Father of our Lord Jesus Christ!* This *blessed* is not the same as in the Sermon on the Mount; it is a prayer of praise to God. Two ideas are prominent here: a doxology for the risen Christ and the offer of new life through faith in him. This theme of new birth is basic to the New Testament message. Being "born anew to a living hope" is possible only because of "the resurrection of Jesus Christ from the dead." This belief is the only way to keep hope alive amid the struggles of a broken world. Resurrection is the central theme of all New Testament preaching.

This hope affirms an imperishable inheritance for those committed to Christ and his way. The Christian thus lives in the here and now but with a foretaste of what is to come given through the Holy Spirit. (See 2 Corinthians 1:22; 5:5; Ephesians 1:14.) In the meantime, suffering is the lot of the believer; yet he is still able to rejoice. Through his suffering his faith is tested to distinguish it from sham. While Peter knew Christ "in the flesh," those who are not so privileged may love him, believe in him, and "rejoice with unutterable and exalted joy."

1 John 3:1-3. *See what love the Father has given us:* It is God's love that calls us his children. We become children of God through acceptance of his love. There is a distinction between the Christian and "the world." While the follower of Christ must enter the world to witness, serve, and even suffer to perform the work of God, still he is a citizen of heaven. He loves the world as God loves it in order to save it (John 3:16), but the norm of his life is in Christ. After all, the world and Christ were so distinct that it brought him to the cross; but he loved it still.

While we are the children of God now, it has not yet been disclosed what blessed future there is for us. It is sufficient to know that when "he appears we shall be like him."

Selected Scripture

King James Version	Revised Standard Version
Acts 1:10-11	*Acts 1:10-11*
10 And while they looked stedfastly toward heaven as he went up, behold, two men stood by them in white apparel;	10 And while they were gazing into heaven as he went, behold, two men stood by them in white robes, 11 and said, "Men of Galilee, why do you stand looking into heaven? This Jesus, who was taken up from you into heaven, will come in the same way as you saw him go into heaven."
11 Which also said, Ye men of Galilee, why stand ye gazing up into heaven? this same Jesus, which is taken up from you into heaven, shall so come in like manner as ye have seen him go into heaven.	
1 Peter 1:3-9	*1 Peter 1:3-9*
3 Blessed be the God and Father of our Lord Jesus Christ, which according to his abundant mercy hath begotten us again unto a lively hope by the resurrection of Jesus Christ from the dead,	3 Blessed be the God and Father of our Lord Jesus Christ! By his great mercy we have been born anew to a living hope through the resurrection of Jesus Christ from the dead, 4 and to an inheritance which is imperishable, undefiled, and unfading, kept in heaven for you, 5 who by God's power are guarded through faith for a salvation ready to be revealed in the last time. 6 In this you rejoice, though now for a little while you may have to suffer various trials, 7 so that the genuineness of your faith, more precious than gold which though perishable is tested by fire, may redound to praise and glory and honor at the revelation of Jesus Christ. 8 Without having seen him you love him; though you do not now see him you believe in him and rejoice with unutterable and exalted joy. 9 As the
4 To an inheritance incorruptible, and undefiled, and that fadeth not away, reserved in heaven for you,	
5 Who are kept by the power of God through faith unto salvation ready to be revealed in the last time.	
6 Wherein ye greatly rejoice, though now for a season, if need be, ye are in heaviness through manifold temptations:	
7 That the trial of your faith, being much more precious than of gold that perisheth, though it be tried with fire, might be found unto praise and honour and glory at the appearing of Jesus Christ:	

8 Whom having not seen, ye love; in whom, though now ye see him not, yet believing, ye rejoice with joy unspeakable and full of glory:
9 Receiving the end of your faith, even the salvation of your souls.

1 John 3:1-3
1 Behold, what manner of love the Father hath bestowed upon us, that we should be called the sons of God: therefore the world knoweth us not, because it knew him not.
2 Beloved, now are we the sons of God, and it doth not yet appear what we shall be: but we know that, when he shall appear, we shall be like him; for we shall see him as he is.
3 And every man that hath this hope in him purifieth himself, even as he is pure.

Memory Selection: It is a faithful saying: For if we be dead with him, we shall also live with him: If we suffer, we shall also reign with him. (2 Timothy 2:11-12)

outcome of your faith you obtain the salvation of your souls.

1 John 3:1-3
1 See what love the Father has given us, that we should be called children of God; and so we are. The reason why the world does not know us is that it did not know him. 2 Beloved, we are God's children now; it does not yet appear what we shall be, but we know that when he appears we shall be like him, for we shall see him as he is. 3 And every one who thus hopes in him purifies himself as he is pure.

Memory Selection:
The saying is sure:
If we have died with him, we shall
    also live with him;
if we endure, we shall also reign
    with him. (2 Timothy 2:11-12)

The Scripture and the Main Question —Charles M. Laymon

A LIVING HOPE
THROUGH THE RESURRECTION
The hope of the Christian is always centered in Christ. Even though by temperament some persons are optimistic and others are pessimistic, the Christian's hope is not based upon psychological predisposition. Instead, it is grounded in God's love in Jesus Christ.

One of the famous paintings of the world is George F. Watts's canvas called "Hope." The painting shows a blindfolded woman sitting on top of the world, attempting doggedly to continue to play a lyre on which all the strings except one have snapped.

But this does not deter her. She plays on and on, plucking the last remaining string.

However, there is more courage than hope in this picture. By contrast, the Christian does not have only one string as a basis for his hoping. He has the full instrument of Christ.

The first reason for hoping in Christ that this lesson stresses is the Resurrection. As our text says, "We have been born anew to a living hope through the resurrection of Jesus Christ from the dead." (1 Peter 1:3b)

Too often for us, as we noted in the Easter lesson, the Resurrection is only a seasonable truth. When Easter has passed, we forget it. Not so with the members of the early church. Christ had overcome death itself; of this they were certain. If one's faith took this fact into account, one could continue to hope against any odds. And they did.

A LIVING HOPE THROUGH THE ASCENSION

The second reason for the hope of the Christian that this lesson presents is the ascension of Christ. The story of the final Resurrection appearance tells of his being taken from their midst and lifted to the heavens (Acts 1:9-10). Many questions can be asked in this space age that sidestep the significance of this experience for the early Christians. For example, Which way is up? Or, How far is up? These are today's questions, but they were not theirs.

The Ascension meant to the first Christians the ascendancy of Christ to a position of power and authority equal to that of God. They even began to pray to him after this in the same way that they prayed to God (Acts 7:54-60), and their prayers were answered on this basis. Here was the test of their faith.

A LIVING HOPE THROUGH CHRIST'S RETURN

The Christian hope has always been concerned with Christ's return (Acts 1:10-11). Numerous presentations of this theme have been made throughout the centuries. Some have been very specific, involving dates, places, and means. Others have been more general, not focusing upon details.

We have all heard of groups who have set the time and place of Christ's return based upon their reading of the Bible. Some have even sold their possessions and gone to the seashore or to the top of a mountain to receive him. When he did not come,

they have returned to their homes deeply disappointed, if not actually disillusioned.

Such experiences may have happened in the early church also. For this reason the Gospel of John, while not ruling out a return of Christ at the end of the age, has stressed his continued presence through the Spirit in the heart of believers (14:16-18). Here is a fact of current religious experience that we can focus upon as a ground for hoping. As a lady in one of my congregations used to say, "This can't be a bad day, for Christ lives in me today."

A LIVING HOPE THROUGH FAITH IN TOMORROW

It has been said that optimism is the consciousness of hidden reserves. No better description than this could be given of the early church and its belief in tomorrow. Its members probably expected the end of the age within their own lifetime. When this did not happen, Christians continued to believe that the outcome of the future would be on the side of Christ. In him as living Lord they had the consciousness of hidden reserves.

Here was something more stable than Dow Jones averages and the forecasts of the pollsters. When we look at ourselves, sometimes we are tempted to be pessimistic. The present, to say nothing of the future, seems beyond our reach. But our Scripture gives us a ground for hope when it says, "Beloved, we are God's children now; it does not yet appear what we shall be, but we know that when he appears we shall be like him." (1 John 3:2)

Here is our nature and our destiny. Here is the reason that we can have hope for the future in spite of all appearances to the contrary.

Helping Adults Become Involved —Harry B. Adams

Preparation of Self and Class

As you prepare this final lesson of the quarter, you will want to review the material that has been dealt with during these past three months, so that you and the class can bring the unit of study to a conclusion. The first lessons dealt with man's situation as a responsible but sinful creature in God's world. Then a series of lessons looked at the Christian affirmation of what God has done in Christ on man's behalf. The past three lessons have looked at the quality of life that comes as a person responds in faith to God's gracious love in Christ.

It is out of this background that the final lesson on hope is to be presented. The Christian affirmation of what God has done in the past has been made. The Christian conviction of the life God makes possible in the present has been examined. The Christian expectation about the future is to be explored in this lesson. As you study the Scripture and think about the lesson, you will want to be sensitive to what it is you hope for in your own life, and to reflect on what hopes sustain the members of your class.

Presenting the Main Question

Some people find it very difficult to hope, to look forward to the future with any expectation. Circumstances seem to some people to make hope simply an illusion. How can people hope when:

1. They have lost the person who shared all of life and made it meaningful for them?

2. They face squarely the threat and serious possibility that man is soon going to make his world uninhabitable?

3. They have an illness that has been diagnosed as terminal, the end to come within days or weeks.

4. They have failed at everything they have tried and see no further options open to them.

5. They contemplate the growing arsenal of weapons with which the nations of the world can destroy one another.

6. They are caught in prejudice and poverty that effectively shut them out of the mainstream of society.

7. They feel that the whole structure of life is doomed.

If you asked some of the members of the class to look for current happenings in the papers that make it difficult to have hope, have them share their findings. Give the class members opportunity to examine their feelings about the situations described above and those reported from the newspaper. Invite persons to share the concerns of their own lives that make it difficult for them to face the future with hope.

Developing the Lesson

Look at some of the things persons mean when they talk about hope. The word *hope* is used in a number of different ways, with different shades of meaning. Have the class members indicate what they think persons mean when they make statements such as the following:

1. I hope everything will turn out all right.

2. I have hope that the project will be completed successfully.

3. I hope that the Mets win the pennant.

4. I hope that man does not blow himself up with atomic weapons.

5. I hope that it does not rain tomorrow.

6. I hope I win the million-dollar sweepstake.

7. I have hope that Jim will finish college and get a job teaching at the high school.

Some of the dimensions of the way in which persons use the word *hope* in the statements above can be described as follows. Hope may be simply wishful thinking, a blind and unfounded desire to have something happen. Or hope may be an expression of an optimistic temperament, the ability to look on the bright side of every situation. Or hope may be the statement that the situation has been carefully assessed, that all factors have been weighed, and that the prospect for a successful outcome is good. Or hope may be the expression that there really is not any cause for optimism and therefore all one can do is hang on.

Explore the meaning of the hope that is offered to the Christian. The author of First Peter writes that "by his great mercy we have been born anew to a living hope." (1:3) What kind of hope is this? How does the hope of the Christian relate to the other meanings of hope described above? In seeking answers to these questions, look at what the Scripture says, using the material prepared by Dr. Thompson and Dr. Laymon.

The following aspects of the Christian hope might be noted in the course of the discussion:

1. The hope of the Christian is not grounded on any human circumstances. The Christian hope is not increased when external circumstances are going well, not threatened when things are going badly. The hope of the Christian is based on the conviction of the power and the goodness and the purpose of God as they have been made known to man in Jesus Christ. For example, it is through the resurrection of Jesus Christ from the dead that man has hope for an eternal inheritance.

2. The specific content of the hope that the Christian holds is related to the purposes of God as they have been expressed in the life of Jesus Christ. The Christian faith gives no assurance that a man's hope for prosperity will be fulfilled. Nor does it give any assurance a man's desire for good health will be granted. But there is the hope that the love of God as known in Jesus Christ will be the final, dominant power in the universe of space and time. (See Acts 1:10-11.)

3. The hope of the Christian relates both to life beyond the boundary of death and the end of time. The Christian lives in the hope that "thy kingdom come, thy will be done, on earth as it is in heaven." But, as the author of First John puts it, "Beloved, we are God's children now; it does not yet appear what we shall be." (3:2) The hope of the Christian is not simply for some appropriate state in this present order but the final fulfillment of God's purpose, a fulfillment beyond human conception or imagination except that it will be like what Christ has already made known.

Reflect on the ways in which the hope of the Christian shapes and transforms his present life. Have the class members share what they think life would be like for them if they suddenly lost all hope. What would happen to them if they had no hope? What kind of tone or quality would their existence have if they had no hope?

Then consider what quality is put into a person's life when he does have the hope that is given through Jesus Christ. The author of First John suggests, for example, that "every one who thus hopes in him purifies himself as he is pure." (3:3) What impact does the Christian hope have for the way in which a person deals with the following?

1. The prospect of his own death.
2. The decision of what is genuinely important to struggle for in this life.
3. The way in which a man faces defeat and failure.
4. The way in which a man is able to relate to others.

Helping Class Members Act

Invite members of the class to think of persons they know who seem to be close to despair or who have lost all sense of expectation about the future, and then encourage them to search for ways in which they might share with these persons the confidence that they find in the hope given to them through Jesus Christ.

Planning for Next Sunday

The lesson next Sunday begins a new series on "God's Laws for Man," based on the Ten Commandments and the law as interpreted by Christ. Ask your members to read the background Scripture for the first session, Exodus 20:1-2; Deuteronomy 5:32 through 6:3; Psalms 119:97-104; Matthew 5:17; and Mark 12:13-17, during the coming week.

Supplementary Readings on Faith

The old world in which wars between nations were possible is obsolete, but we still have to live with the menace of total destruction. We do our best to ward it off, according to our varying lights and partial judgments. If we do come safely through to a less menacing landscape, it will be of God's mercy, who was able to use the wrath of man, and the fears of man, and the sparks of light and love which enlighten every man, and so to save by love *and* fear.

. . . .

We do not believe the worst will happen. But if it did, in the moment of annihilation we should still be found believing, refusing to hate, refusing to despair. If not here, in this rebellious province of his universe, yet "somewhere else," as using an image we must say, God would still be love, and light, and life. Already I know that in this world any day may be my last, and one day will be. But beyond that are resurrection and immortal life.

. . . All we have to do is to bring out of the bag the secret which the church has always had, of living hopefully when the future is obscure. We plan for the future responsibly, knowing that the best plans often go wrong. We do not pin our final hopes on their success. We shall not think the battle is won if the danger recedes, nor yet if the world state comes. Nor shall we despair if the prospect darkens yet more. We will not despair, and we will not hate. In faith and hope and love (God help us!) we will do our best, along with anyone who will join us, or let us join them, on those terms.

—T. R. Milford, *Christian Decision in the Nuclear Age* [14]

When one looks about him at the miraculous diversity of our universe—at the miraculous world that each person, each tree, each leaf is—how can one help but believe in something greater than oneself, something that cannot be described. I think if you develop an awareness of what you are, gradually you will find God. I find Him when I awake. I go immediately to the sea and everywhere I see God, in the smallest and the largest things. I see Him in colors and designs and forms, I have the idea of God constantly. I find Him in music. What is this world, what is music but God?

Here in Puerto Rico each morning after I return from the seashore, I have breakfast and immediately afterward I go to the piano and I play two Preludes and Fugues of Bach. I have done that every day of my life for the last 79 years. I began to learn to play the piano at four.

I knew at 10 that Bach existed, and immediately I began to play the Preludes and Fugues every morning without fail, except when I was on a train or a ship, and there was no piano to play.

I see God also in Bach. Every morning of my life, I see nature first, then I see Bach. I treat music as something divine, as I treat every human being. Every human being is a miracle. The world is a miracle that only God could make.

Think how no two grains of sand are alike. How there is not one voice like another, not one nose like another, how in the millions and billions of living

14 (Fortress Press, 1967), pp. 46-47.

and non-living things in the universe, no two are exactly alike. Who but God could do that? God cannot die. God must be present all the time. Nothing can destroy that.

—Pablo Casals, "Music Is a Miracle" [15]

It is July 7, 1939. A German ship sails from Hoboken. At the railing stands a young German, Dietrich Bonhoeffer, Th.D. In sailing, he escapes from safety. And goes back to where he knows the rebellious powers have his people under control. Hitler has been ruling Germany since 1933. Jews disappear daily. Synagogues are burnt down. Concentration camps are built. The opposition is silenced.

Bonhoeffer is known to be a relentless anti-Nazi. He has written and preached against Hitler. Union Theological Seminary, in New York, impressed with his theological insights and conscious of the dangers which faced him, offered him rescue. But he wrote to the president of Union, "I have come to the conclusion that I have made a mistake in coming to America . . . I will have no right to participate in the reconstruction of Christian life in Germany after the war if I don't share the trials of this time with my people."

On board, he wrote in his diary, "Since coming on board ship my inner disruption about the future has disappeared."

Bonhoeffer was arrested by the Nazis in July, 1944, and was hanged on April 9, 1945.

—Albert H. van den Heuvel, *Meet the Man* [16]

My Lord, Thou art in every breath I take,
And every bite and sup taste firm of Thee.
With buoyant mercy Thou enfoldest me,
And holdest up my foot each step I make.
Thy touch is all around me when I wake,
Thy sound I hear, and by Thy Light I see
The World is fresh with Thy divinity
And all Thy creatures flourish for Thy sake.

For I have looked upon a little child
And seen Forgiveness, and have seen the day
With eastern fire cleanse the foul night away;
So cleaneth Thou this House I have defiled.
And if I should be merciful, I know
It is Thy mercy, Lord, in overflow.

—Kenneth Boulding, *There Is a Spirit* [17]

[15] Tacoma, Washington *News-Tribune*, December 18, 1966.
[16] (Christian Youth Publications, 1966), p. 3.
[17] (Fellowship Publications, 1943), p. 13.

FOURTH QUARTER
God's Laws for Man

UNIT IX: GUIDELINES FOR THE DISCIPLINED LIFE
Horace R. Weaver

ELEVEN LESSONS

JUNE 3–AUGUST 12

One of the strange, and almost defiant, claims of some religious people of our time is that the Ten Commandments are no longer valid. The claim is that the commandments have been completely and adequately replaced by the principle of love. For those who recognize that the Ten Commandments are like a schoolmaster for understanding the principle of love, this would be quite appropriate. But there are some who take the principle of love as permissiveness for treating the Ten Commandments as instinct and desire might dictate. These lessons are to help persons realize that there are moral and spiritual laws that are valid today even as they have been for many centuries.

As biochemists have studied the intricacies of the nature of man's biological organism, they have reached the conclusion that there are some very basic "claims" upon the physical nature of man. These "claims" are written at the time of conception and are found in what we call the DNA molecule. These molecules contain the basic structures of human life—the color of hair, facial features, and even many personality traits. Like the chemists, the prophets—and supremely Jesus Christ—have looked into the very nature of the moral and spiritual life of man and have lifted out that which God has written into the various psychological and moral structures of the human being. These moral claims were made when man was created and, like those of the DNA molecule, have been passed from generation to generation. Without them man could not live in right relationship with God or his fellow man. We are to study these innate moral structures during these eleven lessons.

The first lesson deals with man's need for the kind of authority that is now being found in the DNA molecule, and which, we feel, is also found in the teachings of the prophets and of Jesus Christ, concerning the basic structures of human life. Lessons two through ten deal with the Ten Commandments directly, with each lesson emphasizing the vital truth on which the respective commandment is based. Each law is further examined in terms of its highest interpretation—as found in the life and teachings of Jesus Christ. Jesus was concerned not with acts such as adultery or killing, but with the motivation and thoughtlife that caused the persons to commit the acts. Special attention is given to making the commandments relevant to today's living. Lesson eleven, climaxing the review of the commandments, directs attention to the Great Commandment which, said Jesus, sums up all the others.

Helpful background reading for this quarter may be found in the following books: *The Love Command in the New Testament,* Victor Paul Furnish; *Health, Healing, and Holiness,* Robert C. Leslie; *Can Man Care for the Earth?* Richard L. Heiss and Noel F. McInnis; *The Ten Commandments, An Interpretation,* Charles L. Allen; *Drugs on the College Campus,* Helen H. Nowlis; and *Drugs: A to Z,* Earl Ubell.

Listed below are several audiovisual resources that would be valuable as you prepare, not only the first unit, but also the lessons in the other unit on God's laws for man. (Each item will include a reference to the particular unit it may accompany.) These resources have been carefully selected and correlated with the major themes of the lessons. Teachers who wish to use the aids should make plans sufficiently early to insure proper scheduling and delivery. All prices are subject to change without notice. All these materials may be obtained from your denominational publishing house unless another source is denoted in the description. Because of the lapse of time between the printing of this book and the use of these materials some resources may not be available.

Conformity. 16mm film, 49 min. This film deals with the problem of conformist attitudes in American life and its inherent dangers. It is an indictment of the suffocation that "me-tooism" breeds in a nation. Rental: black and white, $12.50, from Mass Media Ministries; 2116 North Charles Street; Baltimore, Maryland 21218. (Unit IX)

The Family Next Door. 16mm film, 30 min., leader's guide. Three typical family conflicts provide the framework for this film and will undergird the efforts of the church to help interpret the factors that go to make up a happy, Christian home. Rental: black and white, $8. (Unit IX)

From Generation to Generation. 16mm film, 30 min. With a combination of art work and photography this film presents the story of the generation of life. Alternating between scenes of happy family life on a farm and diagrams presenting the reproduction cycle, we experience the oneness of all life and feel the kinship of human birth to the rest of life in the universe. Rental: color, $10. (Unit IX)

Have I Told You Lately That I Love You? 16mm film, 15 min. This film is a documentary showing a typical day in the lives of a suburban couple. Emphasis is placed upon the hollowness of family life caused by the intense desire to "get ahead" in American culture. Rental: black and white, $10, from Mass Media Ministries; 2116 North Charles Street; Baltimore, Maryland 21218. (Unit IX)

Mr. Grey. (See page 12.) (Unit IX)

The New Morality: Challenge of the Student Generation. 16mm film, 37 min. Both "hippies" and "squares" in colleges across the country reject the dogmas of the old religions and liturgies in their restless search for fresh and meaningful values both within and outside the church. "Longhairs" and crew-cut conformists comment on the nihilistic "God-is-dead" concept; Webster College president Jacqueline Grennan and Stanford University's theologians Robert McAfee Brown and Michael Novak contribute insights into the behaviorism of the cool generation. Rental: black and white, $15, from Mass Media Ministries; 2116 North Charles Street; Baltimore, Maryland 21218. (Unit IX)

None of My Business. 16mm film, 32 min. This film examines the widespread, often fallacious notions about welfare recipients. One of the fallacies is the belief that many people receiving welfare could work—if they really wanted to. The truth is that the aged, blind, totally disabled, and children too young to work account for 90 per cent of the people on welfare rolls. Rental: black and white, $8, from A-V Center; Bloomington, Indiana 47401. (Unit IX)

Of Time, Work and Leisure. (See page 12.) (Unit IX)

The Pusher. (See page 128.) (Unit IX)

The Social and Sex Attitudes in Adolescence. 16mm film, 22 min. The life stories of a young married couple are presented and contrasted in terms of their sex education and adjustment during adolescence. Rental: black and white, $5. (Unit IX)

The Top. 16mm film, 8 min. This is an animated comic parable about the attainment of material success. Antics of differing social types, mostly grotesque, who try in many ways to climb to the top, are shown. The "top" is represented graphically by a red cloudlike ceiling that seems to contain an endless supply of greenbacks. Rental: color, $12.50, from Contemporary Films; 614 Davis Street; Evanston, Illinois 60201. (Unit IX)

The Trap of Solid Gold. 16mm film, 51 min. This film tells the story of a young executive caught in the trap of living beyond his income. It raises many questions of ethics and values and will be of interest to students of modern American society as well as to adult groups. Rental: black and white, $17.50, from International Film Bureau, Inc.; 332 South Michigan Avenue; Chicago, Illinois 60604. (Unit IX)

To Adam With Love. 35mm filmstrip, 33⅓ rpm record. This filmstrip portrays the experiences of a cartoon character, Adam, who discovers through his difficulties the responsibilities of being a good steward of God's gifts in the conservation of natural resources. Sale: color, $3.50; from Lutheran Church Press; 2900 Queen Avenue; Philadelphia, Pennsylvania 19129. (Unit IX)

Trouble in the Family. 16mm film, 90 min. To study the effects of family therapy, this film examines a middle-class, suburban New England family with three children whose emotional problems are not unlike those of families across the country. Rental: black and white, $15, from Mass Media Ministries; 2116 North Charles Street; Baltimore, Maryland 21218. (Unit IX)

Worship, a Family's Heritage. 16mm film, 28 min. Newlyweds Scott and Nancy Bryson are beginning the long and challenging process of learning to know each other. Nancy is constantly frustrated at the somewhat routine and completely natural manner in which her husband accepts religion, especially family worship. Rental: color, $11; black and white, $7. (Unit IX)

The Antkeeper. (See page 127.) (Unit X)

How Long the Night. 16mm film, 27 min. The wife of an alcoholic muses over her marriage and remembers the struggles she and her husband have had. Rental: black and white, $8. (Unit X)

LSD: Insight or Insanity? 16mm film, 20 min. So much noise and violence is taking place around us in this hooked-up, tuned-in, and turned-on world that it is possible for some explosions to occur and not be heard. A fallacy gets blown to smithereens in this film, whether anybody hears it happen or not. The effect of the explosion is a thorough, shattering, and hopefully sobering one. LSD, to put it plainly, is not a shortcut to the center of being; it may instead be a roundabout route to a severe disintegration of personhood. Rental color, $15, from Mass Media Ministries; 2116 North Charles Street; Baltimore, Maryland 21218. (Unit X)

Parable. (See page 231.) (Unit X)

Right Here, Right Now. (See page 12.) (Unit X)

Why Have Law?

Background Scripture: Exodus 20:1-2; Deuteronomy 5:32 through 6:3; Psalms 119:97-104; Matthew 5:17; Mark 12:13-17

The Main Question —Charles M. Laymon

The place of law in the ordering of our lives has been seriously challenged in recent years. Some persons have become impatient with legislative change; it is frequently slow and subject to all kinds of pressure from groups seeking privileges for their own interests. Can these faults be avoided, or are they to be expected in the democratic process?

We have seen a rash of attempts by persons to take the law into their own hands and as an act of protest deliberately break it. If a law is a bad law, they say, they have a moral right to disobey it, as long as they are willing to take the consequences. Thus they will call attention to the evil character of the law, and their civil disobedience will provide a prod for change. Is this a Christian attitude?

The story is told that Henry Thoreau once refused to pay the poll tax because he felt no state had the right to tax one's existence. As a result, he was arrested. When his friend Ralph Waldo Emerson visited him in jail, he said, "Henry, why are you here?" Thoreau replied, "Ralph, why *aren't* you here?" Both men believed passionately in the freedom of the human spirit but chose different ways of asserting it. Thoreau's work on *Civil Disobedience* and Emerson's essay on *Self Reliance* have become classics, yet each was different in its approach to life and law.

Why have law? What is its purpose? What are our duties and responsibilities in relation to laws? Are men bound by bad laws? Is there more than one way to change an unworthy law? The biblical passages for this lesson will prove helpful in answering these questions.

As You Read the Scripture —George W. Frey[1]

This is the first of a series of thirteen lessons on the theme "God's Laws for Man." The basic scriptural material will be the Ten Commandments and closely related passages from the New Testament.

The Ten Commandments are found in two places in the Old Testament: Exodus 20:1-17 and Deuteronomy 5:6-21. Their present form rests upon a simpler and shorter version, which was much older. These laws were guidelines for the Hebrew people in their attempts to be obedient to the Lord God who led them out of the land of Egypt.

Exodus 20:1-2. *I am the* LORD *your God, who brought you out of the land of Egypt:* These words serve as an introduction to the Ten Commandments in both the Exodus and Deuteronomy accounts. They form an ever-recurring theme in the religion of ancient Israel. The God of the law is the God who

[1] George W. Frey: professor of Old Testament and registrar, United Theological Seminary, Dayton, Ohio.

339

acts. God's mighty act for Israel was the Exodus. This event is recalled many times. The memory of what God did for Israel in the Exodus forms a central and crucial element in her creed. Failure to keep this event alive in memory was to Jeremiah cause for spiritual infidelity (see Jeremiah 2:6). The entire faith of ancient Israel was based on this historical event in which the Lord God revealed his love for a people held in bondage. God took the initiative in acting redemptively and called a people into a covenant relationship. The Ten Commandments became early principles to help the people of the covenant realize their identity and selfhood.

Psalms 119:97-104. *Oh, how I love thy law!* This psalm is an alphabetic acrostic. Twenty-two poems of eight lines, each beginning with a different Hebrew letter, are joined together after the arrangement of the Hebrew alphabet to form a psalm of one hundred seventy-six verses. Psalms 9, 10, 25, 34, 37, 111, 112, and 145 are also alphabetic acrostics. This alphabetic arrangement obviously is unable to be observed in English translations of these psalms.

Psalms 119 is a group of reflections about the law. A reference to the law occurs in nearly every line. Just as Psalms 1 is the portrait of a person who finds genuine delight in the study of the law, so the poet in Psalms 119 points up the high respect for the law in Israel's religious life.

Verse 97 reflects the feelings of the poet well: *Oh, how I love thy law!* The word for law here is *torah,* which has wide meaning. In this context it means the religious traditions, teachings, and truths that form the rich heritage and possession of the psalmist. The law is the object of the psalmist's love and devotion.

Observe the various descriptive words referring to the law in this portion of the psalm: *commandment* (verse 98), *testimonies* (verse 99), *precepts* (verse 100), and *ordinances* (verse 102). A hurried reading of the entire psalm will indicate the frequent usage of these terms.

Note also the use of the noun *word* in the psalm. (See, for example, verses 11, 16, 89, and 105.) The Hebrew term for *word* is *dabar.* The close association of the words *dabar* and *torah* is not strange. *Dabar* carries with it the idea of purpose, plan, intent, will. *Torah* has the basic idea of instruction, plans, purposes, and the like. Both *dabar* and *torah* are used to express the purpose and will of God for Israel.

Now, observe the effects upon the person who gives serious and dedicated attention to the law: (1) he becomes wise and successful (verse 98); (2) he surpasses his teachers in understanding and insight (verse 99); and (3) he is given sustenance to live a dedicated, obedient, and disciplined life (verses 101, 103).

Interpretation of this psalm must be made in the light of its setting. This kind of psalm rises out of a time when particularism characterized Jewish religion. The righteous did not associate with evildoers. In the light of the Christian ethic of love this psalm has limitations. However, the love and dedication of the psalmist for God's law and word speaks with challenge to Christians.

Matthew 5:17. *Think not that I have come to abolish the law and the prophets:* Actually verse 18 should be read also. Jesus, as reported by Matthew, gives a lasting place to the law. The deep crucial values in the law will never become obsolete. This word of Jesus does not mean that he was blind to the hardening, deadening, and legalistic use or misuse of the law by his contemporaries. These words as preserved by Matthew do mean that Jesus recognized eternal values in the traditions of Israel and in the Ten Commandments.

Selected Scripture

King James Version

Exodus 20:1-2

1 And God spake all these words, saying,

2 I am the LORD thy God, which have brought thee out of the land of Egypt, out of the house of bondage.

Psalms 119:97-104

97 O how love I thy law! it is my meditation all the day.

98 Thou through thy commandments hast made me wiser than mine enemies: for they are ever with me.

99 I have more understanding than all my teachers: for thy testimonies are my meditation.

100 I understand more than the ancients, because I keep thy precepts.

101 I have refrained my feet from every evil way, that I might keep thy word.

102 I have not departed from thy judgments: for thou hast taught me.

103 How sweet are thy words unto my taste! yea, sweeter than honey to my mouth!

104 Through thy precepts I get understanding: therefore I hate every false way.

Matthew 5:17

17 Think not that I am come to destroy the law, or the prophets: I am not come to destroy, but to fulfil.

Revised Standard Version

Exodus 20:1-2

1 And God spoke all these words, saying,

2 "I am the LORD your God, who brought you out of the land of Egypt, out of the house of bondage."

Psalms 119:97-104

97 Oh, how I love thy law!
   It is my meditation all the day.

98 Thy commandment makes me wiser than my enemies,
   for it is ever with me.

99 I have more understanding than all my teachers,
   for thy testimonies are my meditation.

100 I understand more than the aged,
   for I keep thy precepts.

101 I hold back my feet from every evil way,
   in order to keep thy word.

102 I do not turn aside from thy ordinances,
   for thou hast taught me.

103 How sweet are thy words to my taste,
   sweeter than honey to my mouth!

104 Through thy precepts I get understanding;
   therefore I hate every false way.

Matthew 5:17

17 "Think not that I have come to abolish the law and the prophets; I have come not to abolish them but to fulfil them."

Memory Selection: Love worketh no ill to his neighbour: therefore love is the fulfilling of the law. (Romans 13:10)

Memory Selection: Love does no wrong to a neighbor; therefore love is the fulfilling of the law. (Romans 13:10)

The Scripture and the Main Question —Charles M. Laymon

THE LORD AS THE LAWGIVER

Considering law under the category of a religious subject may seem strange, but anything that affects the daily lives of persons is a religious concern. This is particularly true in our Judaic-Christian heritage, since God is viewed as the one who gave the law to the Hebrews as a basis for ordering their relationships to himself and others. The Ten Commandments are introduced with the statement, "And God spoke all these words, saying. . . ." (Exodus 20:1)

In the Bible both natural laws and civil laws are never regarded as impersonal structures to be fitted on society like a gelatin mold. Instead, they are the expressions of a Lawgiver.

In this regard I have always appreciated the statement of Archbishop William Temple in *Nature, Man and God:* "For no Law, apart from a Lawgiver, is a proper object of reverence. It is mere brute fact. . . . The reverence of persons can be appropriately given only to that which itself is at least personal."

Four hundred years earlier Richard Hooker, in *Ecclesiastical Polity*, wrote in the same vein: "Of Law there can be no less acknowledged, than that her seat is the bosom of God. . . ." And nineteen hundred years earlier the apostle Paul wrote: "Let every person be subject to the governing authorities. For there is no authority except from God." (Romans 13:1)

LOVE FOR THE LAW

When the psalmist with exuberant devotion cried out, "Oh, how I love thy law!" (119:97), he was representing Hebrew piety at its best. This statement comes from the longest psalm in the Psalter, which contains one hundred seventy-six verses in honor of the written law.

The psalmist's love for the law, however, was not blind worship of it. He had reasons for loving the law. To him the law was righteous (verse 7), good (verse 39), a source of hope (verse 43), something to sing about (verse 54), dependable (verse 86), proved (verse 140), and just (verse 149).

The purpose of law is not to limit one's life, to cramp one's style, or to enslave. Whenever laws do this, they are unworthy of the name. Edmund Burke is best known for his speech "Conciliation with America," which he delivered March 22, 1775. Here he passionately urged a policy that would recognize the rights of the American colonies. Had his pleas been heeded, the Revolutionary War might not have been fought. Burke once said, "Bad laws are the worst sort of tyranny."

On the other hand, just and decent laws bring freedom. In fact, without law there can be no true freedom. The absence of law brings anarchy, leading to mob action, violence, and the death of all human rights.

UNDERSTANDING THROUGH THE LAW

When a historian seeks to re-create the past, one of his best sources of information is the law code followed in the period he is studying. Laws relate to what people are and what they do or do not do in the society

342

to which they belong. At any given time—today, for instance—laws bring us an understanding of what is acceptable in a culture. We learn from them what a society regards as right and wrong.

The laws of God found in the Ten Commandments are in this way a direct revelation of his mind and will. This is what the psalmist felt when he wrote, "Thy commandment makes me wiser than my enemies, for it is ever with me." (119:98) The psalmist even claimed to have more understanding than his teachers because he meditated upon God's testimonies (verse 99).

The true laws of God are an expression of his nature. We know what God is like because we know the laws he has laid down for his children. He who has issued commandments against killing, committing adultery, stealing, lying, and coveting is himself righteous, just, and loving. God *is* what he requires.

KEEPING THE LAW

A student once asked how we could know that the Ten Commandments came from God. The professor answered that if everyone, everywhere, broke them for a single hour, society would be destroyed. The commandments are basic to our existence on the face of the earth; therefore they must have come from God, who created the earth.

The laws of society are made to be kept, not broken. If they are not true to God's will and man's needs, they should be changed. For this reason we have amendments, modifications, and new interpretations of old statutes continually. It is within this setting that the place of protest should be evaluated.

Laws are never static if they are worthy. Jesus said that he came not to abolish the law but to fulfill it (Matthew 5:17). He interpreted the commandments beyond their literal statement; killing became hating, and adultery became lustful thinking.

Conscience is our most valuable ally in keeping the law, both God's and man's. As someone has said, "Conscience does not make the law; it enforces it."

Helping Adults Become Involved —Howard E. Tower[2]

Preparation of Self and Class

Law. This word has different meanings for different persons. The psalmist long ago cried, "Oh, how I love thy law!" (Psalms 119:97) Many persons today, by word or action, proclaim, "How I despise the laws imposed upon me!" Others call for law and order.

As you prepare for this timely exploration, you should be quite clear what your attitude toward law is. How important is the main question?

[2] Howard E. Tower: pastor Mathewson Street United Methodist Church, Providence, Rhode Island.

A second area of preparation is to discover how members of your group feel about law in general and God's law in particular. Some ways of discovering these attitudes will be suggested below.

A third suggestion for your preparation is to read through the entire unit before planning specific lessons. This will give a sense of direction for the entire study and make preparation for individual lessons easier. Likewise, it will be helpful to read all the background Scripture.

Finally, what secular resources are available? What is being said or presented about the place of law in the press and other mass media? Two films will be helpful in this area: *The New Morality: Challenge of the Student Generation* and *Conformity.* (See page 337.) Either of these films could be used to present the main question to your class.

Presenting the Main Question

Help the group to see that the question, Why have law? implies some more basic questions. What is meant by law? Regulations that have been accepted by a particular society? Principles that seem to be the basis of the rhythm of the universe? What is the source of law? Man? God?

Perhaps this account of a true experience will open the main question for your group. In a major eastern city a group of downtown churches sponsors a learning experience for senior citizens. The six-week session each fall and spring attracts over two hundred persons between the ages of sixty-five and eighty-five. A number of serious study courses are offered. At the noon hour, as part of the luncheon experience, a town meeting forum is held. A guest speaker presents a current issue, and a question and answer period follows.

One speaker was the newly appointed chief of police. His topic, of course, was law and order. He described a recent incident in which an elderly woman was knocked down, beaten, and robbed, telling how she was even then hovering between life and death. Then proudly, he pointed out that her assailants had been apprehended and were behind bars.

In the forum hour that followed it was clear that the chief of police had struck a responsive chord with these senior citizens, whose very real concern was to be able to walk safely on their streets.

The next week the speaker was the young clergy-director of a youth coffee house. He interpreted what some of the problems of homeless, jobless youth are and how the center was seeking to meet the needs of these runaway youth, who felt the oppressive hand of the law enforcement officials of the community.

During the forum period it became evident that the senior citizens had not heard his message. For them, rejection and alienation were not the real problems these youth faced. What they needed was the strict hand of the law in home and community.

How would the senior citizens and the young people answer the question Why have law? Which answer would the members of your class be inclined to accept as valid?

Developing the Lesson

If the above illustration is used to introduce the main question, it will, no doubt, provoke discussion and the sharing of some current experiences and attitudes. In order to discover accurately the feelings of the group concerning law, you might want to distribute the following check list:

1. Laws should always be respected and obeyed. True_____ False_____
2. The only right way to change laws is by the ballot. True_____ False_____
3. When man-made laws conflict with a person's understanding of the laws of God, first loyalty must be given to God's laws. True_____ False_____
4. It is sometimes necessary to disobey a bad law to demonstrate its unfairness. True_____ False_____
5. It is all right to protest a bad law as long as the protest is nonviolent. True_____ False_____
6. Violence is sometimes required

of a person fully committed to the Christian way. True____ False____

7. God's laws change, therefore we can never say a particular law is approved by God. True____ False____

8. All good laws are based on the Ten Commandments. True____ False____

9. Jesus' law of love supersedes the Ten Commandments. True____ False____

After class members have completed the questionnaires, you may want to tabulate the answers on chalkboard or newsprint.

The second part in the development of the lesson will be the study of the Scripture. A possible method of study would be to divide the class members into three groups. Have the first group read and discuss the Exodus and Deuteronomy accounts of the giving of the law, and Psalms 119:97-104, without any aids. Let the members arrive at some agreement as to what these passages mean. They might also list unanswered questions these passages raise. The second group should study and respond to the commentary on these passages found in their denominational quarterly. The third group might examine

Dr. Laymon's and Dr. Frey's discussion of the Scripture and the main question above.

Then the three groups should share the insights gained during the discussion.

Helping Class Members Act

Suggest that members of the group take home their check lists; ponder their responses to the nine statements; and decide whether, in the light of the group discussion and their own further meditation, they want to change any of their answers.

Planning for Next Sunday

Call attention to the fact that next week's main question is related to the affirmation "God Is Supreme." Suggest that each person ponder how he feels about this assertion. If he has always assumed God to be supreme, what difference has and does this conviction make in his life? If it has made or is making no difference, does he really believe God is supreme? The main question then becomes, How do I really feel about God? Point out that the Scripture reference includes the first and second commandments. If we cannot affirm the supremacy of God, do these commandments have any relevance?

Pentecost and Its Meaning

(JUNE 10)

CHARLES B. COPHER[3]

The word *pentecost* is a Greek word that means "fiftieth day." Both Jews and Christians celebrate a religious feast titled Pentecost. The Jewish Pentecost is observed fifty days after the Feast of Passover. Christians observe the day fifty days after Easter.

Only after Greek had become the common language among Jews (c. 330 B.C.) did they give the title *Pentecost* to one of their ancient feast days. The particular feast is the second of three annual pilgrimage festivals, which were

---

[3] Charles B. Copher: Dean of Interdenominational Theological Center, Atlanta, Georgia.

345

to be celebrated in the Temple by all males (Deuteronomy 16:16). In the Old Testament the feast is called by several names. In Exodus 23:16 it is called "the feast of harvest, of the first fruits of your labor." In Exodus 34:22 it is named "the feast of weeks, the first fruits of wheat harvest." In Numbers 28:26 it is referred to as "the day of the first fruits." And again, in Deuteronomy 16:16 and in 2 Chronicles 8:13, it is called the "feast of weeks." The significance of the title "weeks" lies in the fact that the observance is dated forty-nine days, a week of weeks, after Passover (Leviticus 23:15). The outstanding feature of the feast day was the offering of the first fruits of the wheat harvest. Hence the title "first fruits." A comprehensive command, which states the meaning of the occasion and sets forth the acts of worship for the day, is recorded in Deuteronomy 26:1-15. A similar command is recorded in Leviticus 23:15-21.

In post–Old Testament times, after the destruction of the Temple by the Romans in A.D. 70, the Jews gave a new meaning and attached new ceremonies to the feast. No longer able to offer sacrifices in the Temple, the Jews associated the day with the giving of the Law to Moses. The Law was said to have been given to Moses fifty days after the first Passover had been observed in Egypt.

Just as Pentecost has been and continues to be one of three great feasts among the Jews, so it has been and continues to be one of three great feasts among Christians, the other Christian feasts being Christmas and Easter.

The first followers of Jesus were Jews. As Jews, they continued the observance of traditional feasts and customs. However, as followers of Jesus, they came to the point where they regarded Jesus as the promised Messiah, the Christ. From this point they interpreted everything in the light of their experience of Jesus Christ. Especially so did they interpret the events and meaning of what happened to them on the occasion of the first Pentecost after Jesus' death, resurrection, and ascension.

The record of what happened on that day and the disciples' interpretation are reported in Chapter 2 of the Book of Acts. This report is not altogether clear, and Christians differ in their understandings of every detail of the report. Yet some details—the really important ones—are clear. The Holy Spirit, God's eternal Spirit and Presence, symbolized by wind and fire, came upon the waiting people. They were made aware of that Spirit in an outstanding and overwhelming manner. And the operation of the Holy Spirit within them had extraordinary effects. They spoke in tongues; and although those who heard them speak had come from many lands, each land with its own language, the hearers got a message. One group among the hearers concluded that the speakers were giving testimony to the mighty works of God (Acts 2:11). Another group among the hearers concluded that the speakers were drunk from too much new wine consumed in the early morning (Acts 2:13).

The disciples themselves took their experience to mean that Jesus Christ had fulfilled promises made to them—promises now recorded in Luke 24:46-49 and Acts 1:8. And Peter, serving as spokesman on behalf of the partially respected, partially ridiculed group of disciples, explained that their experience was in fulfillment of the ancient prophecy written in Joel 2:28-32.

Later generations of Christians have retained everything associated with that first "Christian" Pentecost; and they have added new understandings, meanings, and applications. At one time it was the practice to baptize new converts on this day. In English-speaking countries the title "Whitsunday" (White Sunday) came to be applied to the day—presumably because candidates for baptism wore white robes. At other times and in other places different practices developed and continue to do so.

But what of the meaning of Pentecost? There is only one meaning—the meaning in the original report. But along with that meaning go many implications and numerous applications. And there are meanings attached to the day by Jews. From these Jewish meanings Christians may receive benefit.

Now the meaning of any feast or festival, whenever observed and really celebrated, lies in a relationship. That relationship is between the original event and the observance of it in later times. The reason behind the observance is that those participating may share in the original event. This is called "shared-history." The one who celebrates the event is there, and the event is here and now in the one who celebrates it. Such a sharing is what makes an observance a celebration. Thus Christians observe Pentecost in order to share in the experience of the first disciples who, filled with the Holy Spirit and vividly conscious of God's presence, testified to God's mighty acts.

Whenever it is celebrated, Pentecost reinspires; it renews. At the same time the Christian is reminded of the nature and mission of the church. Pentecost is a reminder that the church is itself when and only when it has the Holy Spirit operative in it and engages in the mission that Jesus Christ gives to it. Implications that flow from the indwelling of the Holy Spirit include the truth that the Spirit is not restricted to Jews alone; that God, indeed, shows no partiality (Acts 8:14-17; 10:1-35).

As we have seen, Christians have their own particular experience related to the first "Christian" Pentecost. Yet they share in the life of the Old Covenant, using the Old Testament as part of their sacred Scripture. Pentecost, as the festival of first fruits, has spiritual significance for the New Israel— the church. It reminds the church that all wealth comes from God, the Creator, and that to him belong the first fruits of labor. The Christian, like the Jew, is called upon to rejoice and give thanks for God's gifts of fruit. Furthermore, the celebration demands that Christians share God's gifts with the less fortunate (Leviticus 23:22).

Still further, Christians may find rich meaning in the present Jewish relating of Pentecost to the giving of the Law. Jesus came not to destroy the Law but to fulfill it (Matthew 5:17-18; 22:36-40). The Law does have a place in Christian life. The Christian regards certain of the specific laws as binding upon him. And as a celebration of God's giving of the Law, Pentecost is an occasion upon which the Christian may rejoice and give thanks.

God Is Supreme

Background Scripture: Exodus 20:3-6; Matthew 6:24-34; James 4:7-8

The Main Question —Charles M. Laymon

A young adult class was considering the question How should I think of God? A self-centered discussion developed, one that fixed its focus on *my* ideas, *my* views, and *my* conclusions about God. One of the group said, "This is the most important question we could ask." Another replied, "I disagree. It is more important to ask what God thinks about me."

At this point a lawyer in the class said, "You are both right; both questions are important. But there is a prior and still more significant question, What is God really like?" Do you agree?

What the lawyer was getting at is the fact that God is greater than any single individual's view of him. There is so much static in our thinking that our personal understanding of the nature of God—God as he really is—is often distorted and garbled. Some of us worship our own ideas of God rather than God as he is in himself. We need a word from God about himself.

The biblical passages for this lesson are helpful as we seek to let God tell us about himself.

As You Read the Scripture —George W. Frey

The Ten Commandments begin with a confession of faith, "I am the LORD your God." These dramatic words affirm Israel's faith in the Lord (Yahweh), who is a creative, redeeming, and sustaining personal presence in their lives.

The confession of faith in Yahweh is followed by a list of ten laws containing elementary principles for covenant living for the people of God. These laws cover the basic relationships of life in the Israelite community. The first several commandments deal with man's relationship to God, and the remaining laws have to do with man's attitude and conduct toward other persons.

Exodus 20:3. *You shall have no other gods before me:* With the Exodus event so deeply etched in the memory of Israel, it is little wonder that the first commandment affirms the supremacy of God. The phrase "before me" may be translated "to my face or before my face." This commandment does not deny the existence of other gods, but it does command Israel to worship Yahweh supremely. Israel is not to recognize or worship other deities. Yahweh and Yahweh alone is Israel's God.

Verses 4-5a. *You shall not make . . . a graven image:* This prohibition is understandable in the light of Israel's time. Neighboring religions abounded in images and figurines of all kinds. Their deities were easily represented in some human form. Furthermore there was a common belief among the ancient Near Eastern peoples that to possess an image of a god or goddess enabled the possessor to control or manipulate the god in some way. Old Testament writers make it very clear that Yahweh cannot be controlled or manipulated

348

by man's whims or fancies, much as man may wish to do so. Yahweh is free to act as he chooses. Israel is to accept God on his own terms. Israel does not make the terms or design the standards. Yahweh is Lord and Sovereign of history and demands Israel's total loyalty. God is known by his mighty acts in history and not by the production of any images or likenesses of him.

Matthew 6:24b. *You cannot serve God and mammon:* Matthew points up the great alternative—God or mammon. The word *mammon* means "money." The New English Bible translates the verse: "You cannot serve God and Money." Note, however, that the real problem is not money but the love of money. (See, for example, 1 Timothy 6:10.) Lesser gods do exist, such as money, prestige, work, success, and so forth; but none of these is God. Loving these lesser things more than God is a violation of the biblical ethic. Both Old and New Testaments indicate clearly that the divine will is disobeyed when we express our highest and finest devotion to anything or anyone other than God.

Verses 25-33. *Do not be anxious about your life:* Note the frequent use of the word *anxious* in this passage. The call is for absolute faith and trust in God's providential care. Observe the illustrations used to demonstrate the futility of anxiety—birds, flowers, and grass. Here is no anxiety! Note also the mention of food, clothes, and stature. These are still frequent causes of anxiety in persons and among nations.

Verse 33 is a jewel. No comment on its meaning is necessary save to say that it is cast in the language of positive simplicity and beauty, as is the case with so many profound religious sayings of Jesus. This verse really is the New Testament version of the first of the Ten Commandments.

Selected Scripture

King James Version	Revised Standard Version
Exodus 20:3-5a	*Exodus 20:3-5a*
3 Thou shalt have no other gods before me.	3 "You shall have no other gods before me.
4 Thou shalt not make unto thee any graven image, or any likeness of any thing that is in heaven above, or that is in the earth beneath, or that is in the water under the earth:	4 "You shall not make yourself a graven image, or any likeness of anything that is in heaven above, or that is in the earth beneath, or that is in the water under the earth; 5 you shall
5 Thou shalt not bow down thyself to them, nor serve them.	not bow down to them or serve them."
Matthew 6:24-33	*Matthew 6:24-33*
24 No man can serve two masters: for either he will hate the one, and love the other; or else he will hold to the one, and despise the other. Ye cannot serve God and mammon.	24 "No one can serve two masters; for either he will hate the one and love the other, or he will be devoted to the one and despise the other. You cannot serve God and mammon.
25 Therefore I say unto you, Take no thought for your life, what ye	25 "Therefore I tell you, do not be anxious about your life, what you

shall eat, or what ye shall drink; nor yet for your body, what ye shall put on. Is not the life more than meat, and the body than raiment?

26 Behold the fowls of the air: for they sow not, neither do they reap, nor gather into barns; yet your heavenly Father feedeth them. Are ye not much better than they?

27 Which of you by taking thought can add one cubit unto his stature?

28 And why take ye thought for raiment? Consider the lilies of the field, how they grow; they toil not, neither do they spin:

29 And yet I say unto you, That even Solomon in all his glory was not arrayed like one of these.

30 Wherefore, if God so clothe the grass of the field, which to-day is, and to-morrow is cast into the oven, shall he not much more clothe you, O ye of little faith?

31 Therefore take no thought, saying, What shall we eat? or, What shall we drink? or, Wherewithal shall we be clothed?

32 (For after all these things do the Gentiles seek:) for your heavenly Father knoweth that ye have need of all these things.

33 But seek ye first the kingdom of God, and his righteousness; and all these things shall be added unto you.

Memory Selection: Thou shalt have no other gods before me. (Exodus 20:3)

shall eat or what you shall drink, nor about your body, what you shall put on. Is not life more than food, and the body more than clothing? 26 Look at the birds of the air: they neither sow nor reap nor gather into barns, and yet your heavenly Father feeds them. Are you not of more value than they? 27 And which of you by being anxious can add one cubit to his span of life? 28 And why are you anxious about clothing? Consider the lilies of the field, how they grow; they neither toil nor spin; 29 yet I tell you, even Solomon in all his glory was not arrayed like one of these. 30 But if God so clothes the grass of the field, which today is alive and tomorrow is thrown into the oven, will he not much more clothe you, O men of little faith? 31 Therefore do not be anxious, saying, 'What shall we eat?' or 'What shall we drink?' or 'What shall we wear?' 32 For the Gentiles seek all these things; and your heavenly Father knows that you need them all. 33 But seek first his kingdom and his righteousness, and all these things shall be yours as well."

Memory Selection: You shall have no other gods before me. (Exodus 20:3)

The Scripture and the Main Question —Charles M. Laymon

NO SUBSTITUTE GODS

The first of the Ten Commandments states: "You shall have no other gods before me." (Exodus 20:3) This statement was first made in a day when men believed in the existence of many gods. The commandment asserts that there should be no substitute gods; the Lord God is to be supreme.

The sin of setting substitute gods in the place that belongs to the one, true God is not limited to the polytheistic outlook of biblical times.

While we today would regard belief in many gods as pagan, we still have our own substitute team of deities. Anything that commands our attention and loyalty more than God is a substitute deity. Many such gods currently vie for our devotion: the state, Wall Street, the automobile, social standing, the beauty cult, and so forth. All are potential gods for many and actual gods for some.

For instance, any state that practices ultimate thought control over its citizens is attempting to take the place of God in their lives. This is what made the fight of the German confessional church group against the Nazis so important. In describing this incident Daniel Day Williams has written, in his book *What Present-Day Theologians Are Thinking:* "Here it was made plain that the Church must publicly assert its primary loyalty to the God it knows in Jesus Christ, or cease to be the Christian Church." [4]

Nazism under Hitler is past history, but new and more subtle totalitarianisms continue to threaten us. A day spent before the television screen with our eyes open will confirm this fact.

No Second-Rate Images

The issue of substitute gods is the issue of giving our final loyalty and of finding our ultimate authority in something or someone in secular life. The issue of second-rate images is that of placing something between us and God. We do not literally disobey the commandment, "You shall not make yourself a graven image" (Exodus 20:4) ; but we sometimes, even in our religious practice, mistakenly stress other things rather than God. This effort may be well intentioned, but it is no less deadly.

The problem of making graven

[4] Rev. ed. (Harper, 1959), pp. 26-27.

images, in the past or in the present, is that we place something or someone less than God in the driver's seat. Often these may be only a caricature of God. For instance, some may think of God as the Cop on the Beat (conscience), the Big Daddy (a child's view), the Soft Touch (giving handouts to grabby persons), or as Mr. Meek (too sweet to judge men). Are these not misleading portraits of God?

It may also be that by insisting that everyone should follow *my* creed, *my* preacher, *my* order of service, *my* denomination, *my* view of the Bible, and *my* understanding of the sacraments one is setting up idols (images) that become more important than God.

All this does not mean that we should not have our own views of God, but that we should not make a god out of our views instead of worshiping God himself. Important as these views are, God is greater than any concept of him we may have or any means we may devise for worshiping him.

He Is Able

When we turn from substitute gods and second-rate images of God and find the true God, as Jesus knew and presented him, all life is changed. Change can take place, that is, if we respond to him in faith and trust. Such a God can be counted on; he is able to meet our needs.

This trust is the point of Jesus' words in the Sermon on the Mount, in which he counsels men to learn from the "birds of the air," the "lilies of the field," and the "grass of the field." (Matthew 6:26, 28, 30) These do not worry but count upon God to sustain them.

Sometimes such trust in the supreme God comes readily, particularly when life is going well. But at other times, when tragedy strikes or we are nervous from overwork, it may not be easy to reach out into the unseen world of spirit and take hold of a hand that is waiting to grasp ours. But we can.

This kind of faith in the God who is able has been referred to as the readiness to enter confidently into the darkness of the future. Compared to this kind of faith all our time-honored securities are illusory.

The extent to which we who live in a scientific age have come to place our trust in technological achievements rather than in God is amazing. Marvelous as these accomplishments are, they cannot mend a broken heart, bring hope in the presence of death, forgive sin, or make us honest and brave within; but God can do all this and more.

Place the Kingdom First

When we find the true God, we will discover that he takes us out of ourselves and enlists us into his service in the Kingdom he is establishing among men. Bertrand Russell wrote in *The Conquest of Happiness,* "Nothing is so dull as to be encased in self, nothing so exhilarating as to have attention and energy directed outward." Jesus was saying just this in his own way when he said, "Seek first his kingdom and his righteousness, and all these things shall be yours as well." (Matthew 6:33)

We cannot have God for ourselves only. He does not exist just to meet our personal needs. When this is all God means to us, we confirm the view of some that man invented God in order to make himself feel secure. Instead, God created men to work to bring about his Kingdom on earth.

Helping Adults Become Involved —Howard E. Tower

Preparation of Self and Class

If God is supreme for us, then it follows that his laws are unchangeable. Only our interpretation and understanding of them change. When God becomes only slightly important in our lives, then his laws have no hold upon us. Therefore, the first point of self-preparation is to examine how one feels and thinks about God. Are your major decisions made in the light of your understanding of him and your commitment to him? Or, do you think of God at only very special times, such as when you worship in the sanctuary?

The second point of preparation is to think about where the members of your group stand in relation to these important questions.

The third task is to study the in-terpretations made by Dr. Frey and Dr. Laymon. Do you agree with Dr. Frey's interpretation that the Ten Commandments grew out of Israel's confession of faith in Yahweh? Do the four topics considered by Dr. Laymon commend themselves to you?

Presenting the Main Question

The first problem you will face in making the question of the supremacy of God come to life for your group may be to lift it out of the realm of *we take that for granted.* At the outset, many persons in your group may ask, Why should we discuss whether or not God is supreme? Of course he is. Who would question that? They may also feel that a discussion of the first commandment is an academic matter. Since there is only one God, how can we have any other god before him? Who is interested in making graven images of him?

To offset any such complacent attitude you might begin by having the group members list in parallel columns events or situations that happened in the past week that give evidence that God is in charge or that seem to suggest that God is no longer in control of the world and its history.

Developing the Lesson

When the group has completed its list of evidence supporting and denying God's supremacy in the world, then, as leader, you may wish to share your feelings about God. This sharing will be particularly effective if in your own preparation you have been seized by some new faith in God's presence and power in your life or your world. Seek to guide the group in seeing that a study of the laws of God has only academic interest apart from their own experience of, and commitment to, God as the supreme power in their world and in their lives. Care should be taken to emphasize the need for new insights about and experience of God.

Move from these personal considerations of how you and your group feel about God to an exploration of the interpretation of the first commandment as presented by Dr. Frey, discussing the significance of Israel's confession of faith for their understanding and their acceptance of the Ten Commandments. This discussion should help to further strengthen the understanding of your group that the meaning of the laws of God for them is conditioned by their own faith in and belief about God's nature.

When the members of your group have come to this kind of understanding, they should be ready to think together about the interpretations given by Dr. Laymon.

A possible way of approaching this study would be to divide your group into four subgroups. Then assign one of the four sections of Dr. Laymon's exposition to each group. A member of the subgroup should read aloud the assigned section. The rest of the group should be asked to underline words of special significance or identify questions they wish to ask. The first group should then prepare a list of substitute gods they feel they and others honor today instead of the true God. Group number two would prepare to share with the class secondrate images of God they feel are held by themselves or their associates. The third group would share ways in which trust in God as the giver of life and the laws governing their lives has enabled them to handle their lives with effectiveness. The final group should try to point out ways in which their trust in God helps them try to bring into greater effectiveness his reign of righteousness.

Helping Class Members Act

It is always a little risky, if not presumptuous, to suggest action decisions in a lesson plan. The action should grow out of the experience of each individual group.

Actually, the action of the members might be very individual and very subjective. Some persons may need to spend a great deal of time in thinking further about what God really is and can be for them. Others may have difficulty seeing how a just God can be supreme in a world so full of injustice. They may need to enter into conversation during the week with trusted friends to find support for a waning faith. Still others may want to spend time during the week remembering events in their lives in which God's presence has made a difference. The follow-up action of such persons may be to witness to others about what God has done for them.

On the other hand, the group may come to the place where they want to make their corporate convictions about God and their trust in God have an impact on some local, national, or worldwide issue. Such action will give evidence that they are in fact seeking first God's kingdom and this righteousness. Or the class members may want to be a task group to make recommendations to the church council indicating ways in which their corporate worship may more adequately present their understanding and new commitment to the God they sense as supreme in their lives.

Planning for Next Sunday

Call attention to the fact that next week the group is to think about the meaning of the third commandment. Read the commandment to the class as it appears in the New English Bible: "You shall not make wrong use of the name of the LORD your God; the LORD will not leave unpunished the man who misuses his name." Ask the members of your group to ponder and compare this translation with other translations. As a specific assignment ask each person to watch for examples of misuses of God's name in conversation and common speech, in movies and television programs, and in magazines and books they may read. Be ready to share with the group the most glaring of these misuses.

LESSON 3   JUNE 17

More Than Lip Service

Background Scripture: Exodus 20:7; Matthew 5:33-37; 7:21-23; 21:28-32; Mark 7:5-8

The Main Question —Charles M. Laymon

Insincerity has long been with us; it is not primarily a twentieth-century weakness. The derivation of the word goes far back into history. Some workers in marble in ancient Rome who accidentally chipped a statue would fill in the blemish with wax of the same color as the marble they were using. These statues would then be sold as perfect specimens which, of course, they were not. To counteract this misrepresentation, honest workers invented the practice of stamping their products *sine cera,* meaning "without wax." This is how we got the word *sincere.* Insincerity then is appearing to be something one really is not. A false face is passed off for a genuine one.

The most serious accusation against the church and Christians today is that we are insincere. We do not appear to live up to the claims we make; we are not really Christian. Too much self-centered sand has gotten into the gears, so much so that it may slow us down to a dead stop.

Do you believe that we are insincere in our Christian practice? This is the question this lesson raises. The biblical background that follows is helpful in answering this question.

As You Read the Scripture —George W. Frey

The first three commandments deal with man's attitude and relationship to God. Israel believed this relationship to be basic to a true sense of brotherhood and nationhood. Mission in life is tied up with Israel's loyalty to the God who brought them into being and gave them nationhood.

Exodus 20:7. *You shall not take the name of the* LORD *your God in vain:* In ancient Hebrew society the name of a person was significant. The name actualized the individuality and distinctiveness of a person. His name and character were bound together as one and the same. Hence there was great respect for names both divine and human. This was especially the case with the name of Israel's deity, Yahweh. Respect and reverence for the name Yahweh is to be seen to this day. Our Jewish friends do not pronounce the name Yahweh; instead, they voice the word *Adonai* or use *The Shem.* The

A BUILDING CONTRACTOR TELLS HIS FOREMAN TO SKIMP ON THE AMOUNT OF CEMENT IN THE CONCRETE FOR THE SCHOOL PROJECT. THEN HE TELLS THE PRINCIPAL, "LORD KNOWS THIS IS THE BEST BUILT SCHOOL IN THIS COUNTY." IS HE TAKING THE NAME OF THE LORD IN VAIN?

word *shem* is the Hebrew word for name. Yahweh is "The Name" and is not to be voiced at all.

In Exodus 20:7 reverence for the name is applied to a very common practice in the ancient world, that of oath taking. To *take the name* is a phrase commonly used to describe the making of an oath in the name of a mutually acceptable person or witness, such as a god, a king, or a fellow citizen. Business transactions, marriages, and the like were formalized and finalized by such an oath.

This commandment is therefore a prohibition not against profanity or cursing, which is a serious moral problem in itself, but against the use of the divine name in a dishonest oath for any reason, selfish or otherwise. To take the name of a person of integrity to cover up a false or dishonest agreement brings the judgment of God and of history on a person. This commandment therefore condemns dishonesty and insincerity in every form.

Matthew 6:1. *Beware of practicing your piety before men:* The New English Bible translates this verse: "Be careful not to make a show of your religion before men."

Verses 2-4. *When you give alms, sound no trumpet before you:* Two common applications of the statement in verse 1 now follow. The first deals with giving gifts. The motivation for giving is all important. The word *hypocrites* is significant. In his translation of the passage J. B. Phillips uses the words *play actors*. Genuine piety involves more than mere role playing. Giving alms in an acceptable manner requires the total absence of fanfare. The phrase "do not let your left hand know what your right hand is doing" suggests that even your closest friends should not know what you are giving.

Verses 5-6. *When you pray, you must not be like the hypocrites:* The second application deals with the practice of prayer. Verses 5 and 6 should be read in relation to the larger context in this chapter, namely verses 7-14. Note again the use of the word *hypocrites*. Observe the guidelines for the practice of prayer. It is to be a private relationship with the Father. Verse 7, not printed in our lesson material, suggests further that prayer is to be simple, honest, and a sincere outpouring of one's soul in secret to the Father. Note the warning against prayers filled with the dramatic and with picturesque oratory. Then follows the model prayer (verses 9-13).

Mark 7:5-8. *This people honors me with their lips, but . . . in vain do they worship me:* This is a quotation from the eighth-century prophet Isaiah. (See Isaiah 29:13.) Mark is quoting from the Greek version of the Old Testament, and this accounts for the slight difference in translations. Note the question that prompts Jesus' reply and use of Scripture. Note again the use of the word *hypocrites* in verse 6. Here Isaiah and Jesus are condemning mere lip service—a dishonest practice and the problem to which the third commandment addressed itself.

Selected Scripture

King James Version	Revised Standard Version
Exodus 20:7	*Exodus 20:7*
7 Thou shalt not take the name of the LORD thy God in vain; for the LORD will not hold him guiltless that taketh his name in vain.	7 "You shall not take the name of the LORD your God in vain; for the LORD will not hold him guiltless who takes his name in vain."
Matthew 6:1-6	*Matthew 6:1-6*
1 Take heed that ye do not your	1 "Beware of practicing your piety

alms before men, to be seen of them: otherwise ye have no reward of your Father which is in heaven.

2 Therefore when thou doest thine alms, do not sound a trumpet before thee, as the hypocrites do in the synagogues and in the streets, that they may have glory of men. Verily I say unto you, They have their reward.

3 But when thou doest alms, let not thy left hand know what thy right hand doeth:

4 That thine alms may be in secret: and thy Father which seeth in secret himself shall reward thee openly.

5 And when thou prayest, thou shalt not be as the hypocrites are: for they love to pray standing in the synagogues and in the corners of the streets, that they may be seen of men. Verily I say unto you, They have their reward.

6 But thou, when thou prayest, enter into thy closet, and when thou hast shut thy door, pray to thy Father which is in secret; and thy Father which seeth in secret shall reward thee openly.

Mark 7:5-8

5 Then the Pharisees and scribes asked him, Why walk not thy disciples according to the tradition of the elders, but eat bread with unwashen hands?

6 He answered and said unto them, Well hath Esaias prophesied of you hypocrites, as it is written, This people honoureth me with their lips, but their heart is far from me.

7 Howbeit in vain do they worship me, teaching for doctrines the commandments of men.

8 For laying aside the commandment of God, ye hold the tradition of men, as the washing of pots and cups: and many other such like things ye do.

before men in order to be seen by them; for then you will have no reward from your Father who is in heaven.

2 "Thus, when you give alms, sound no trumpet before you, as the hypocrites do in the synagogues and in the streets, that they may be praised by men. Truly, I say to you, they have their reward. 3 But when you give alms, do not let your left hand know what your right hand is doing, 4 so that your alms may be in secret; and your Father who sees in secret will reward you.

5 "And when you pray, you must not be like the hypocrites; for they love to stand and pray in the synagogues and at the street corners, that they may be seen by men. Truly, I say to you, they have their reward. 6 But when you pray, go into your room and shut the door and pray to your Father who is in secret; and your Father who sees in secret will reward you."

Mark 7:5-8

5 And the Pharisees and the scribes asked him, "Why do your disciples not live according to the tradition of the elders, but eat with hands defiled?" 6 And he said to them, "Well did Isaiah prophesy of you hypocrites, as it is written,

'This people honors me with their lips,
but their heart is far from me;
7 in vain do they worship me,
teaching as doctrines the precepts of men.'
8 You leave the commandment of God, and hold fast the tradition of men."

Memory Selection: Not every one that saith unto me, Lord, Lord, shall enter into the kingdom of heaven; but he that doeth the will of my Father which is in heaven. (Matthew 7:21)

Memory Selection: Not every one who says to me, "Lord, Lord," shall enter the kingdom of heaven, but he who does the will of my Father who is in heaven. (Matthew 7:21)

The Scripture and the Main Question —Charles M. Laymon

CUSSING AND SWEARING

The words *cussing* and *swearing* carry a foul odor; they stand for a bad case of verbal halitosis. Persons who habitually cuss and swear are admitting that their vocabulary is bankrupt. They must resort to words that have a shock value in order to express what they feel and to be heard. Their use of such words often reveals a deep-seated feeling of inferiority.

When the censors allowed Rhett Butler in *Gone With the Wind* to swear on the silver screen, the door was opened to all manner of verbal vulgarity that has reached epidemic levels today. Certain popular writers of fiction have taken up the use of "four-letter words" as their personal trademarks. Even mystery story writers in some cases have departed from the fine English of Agatha Christie to major in cheap sewer words.

What has all this to do with the commandment "You shall not take the name of the LORD your God in vain"? (Exodus 20:7) Originally this prohibition reflected a belief in the magical power of a name. To use God's name in vain was to resort to the low level of magic, divination, and false swearing. The high character of God was denied, for it placed his name (nature) in bad company. Such action was taking the holy, righteous God cheaply. Using God's name in the ways described above is a similar form of blasphemy.

WHEN DO MEN TAKE GOD'S NAME IN VAIN?

We do not indulge in magic and divination, but we are tempted to take God lightly. Is not this the same thing as regarding him cheaply? We may not even use cuss words and yet be guilty of breaking this commandment.

Do you agree with the following? To desecrate and waste the beautiful earth, to despise our fellow men, to fail to take ourselves seriously, to have no hope for the future, to give up trying, to lack a passion for improving the lot of man, to be oblivious to another's need—is not each of these an expression of distrust in God and a failure to show him respect? And are these actions not, therefore, a taking of God's name in vain?

When we think of Jesus' teaching that God is a heavenly Father, taking God's name in vain becomes a refusal to live as his child.

A little boy was heard to say an ugly word. He was ashamed and placed his hand over his face. A stranger, trying to help the boy, said, "It's all right to say whatever you wish." But the lad replied, "If you were my father, you would not say that."

If men would realize that God is their father, they would cease to say and do many things that they now allow. They would practice sonship to God because they actually are his children.

To Be Seen by Men

Sometimes persons who claim to be Christian may outwardly appear to practice the religion they profess, but it is all for show. They perform certain acts to achieve a reputation for being pious, or as Jesus said, in order to be seen by men (Matthew 6:1). Is this not also a form of taking God's name in vain because their religious practice is insincere? More than lip service is required (Mark 7:5-8).

Ralph W. Sockman, famed radio preacher, once told of a little girl who filled out a New Jersey elementary school questionnaire. When asked to write down the name of the child who bragged the least about herself, she put her own name on the paper. Sockman commented, "It must have been something like that which St. Jerome had in mind when he said, 'Beware of the pride of humility.'"

Pride before God is not always that subtle. It may sometimes actually lead to flaunting one's religious achievements before others. We brag that we never miss church, that we pledge a certain amount, that we serve on numerous boards and committees, and so forth. Jesus likened such self-praise to blowing a trumpet in the synagogue to call attention to one's alms giving (Matthew 6:2). He called the persons who do so *hypocrites*. No one can be *that* good!

The church also, as an institution, may flex its muscles in order to be seen by men. When it forgets that it exists only to serve others, as Christ himself was the servant of all, the church too is taking God's name in vain. All its wealth, numbers, structure, and power do not belong to itself but to God.

To Be Seen by God

To love and honor God, rather than taking his name in vain, means to live with a constant sense of our need of him and our indebtedness to him. When one does this, he is seen and rewarded by God (Matthew 6:4).

On one occasion Francis of Assisi was invited to the home of a rich man. His host wanted to spy on Francis' praying. All night long he heard the saint say, "My God and my All, my God and my All." The simple prayer converted him to Christ then and there.

Secret piety, where God alone sees what we do, has validity. Telling others about our good deeds dulls the edge of devotion. Not letting the left hand know what the right hand is doing, as Jesus put it, releases added power and purity of purpose.

Helping Adults Become Involved —Howard E. Tower

Preparation of Self and Class

Your preparation for this third lesson in the unit will need to take into account what has happened in your group during the first two lessons. What consensus did the group achieve in answering the question Why have laws? What points of agreement did the group reach about what they can honestly affirm concerning God's supremacy? What did the members list as examples of present-day idolatry?

You might write out your answers as you think about the questions in relation to what happened during the class session. It may be even more revealing to talk with two or more members of your group during the week to discover how they are feeling and thinking after the second Sunday of study.

If you made the group assignment that was suggested in the helps for last Sunday, then part of your preparation should be to do what you asked the members of your group to do. Keep a day by day record of the misuses of God's name that you hear or see in print. About Friday or Saturday look over your diary and decide which examples or example disturbs you most. Think about why you feel disturbed.

Presenting the Main Question

Ask class members to share their examples of ways in which God's name has been misused. Add any additional examples you may have discovered. Then consider the following questions: What is the reason for the current popular misuse of God's name? Are those who so misuse God's name aware of the reasons? What is the basis upon which members of the group have judged a particular word, phrase, or presentation or interpretation of God as "taking God's name in vain"?

Developing the Lesson

One of the illustrations a member of your group may point to as evidence of the misuse of God's name might be the more frequent use of profanity in stage plays and on the screen, especially by the young. If so, one approach to the following discussion would be to call attention to both Dr. Frey's and Dr. Laymon's interpretations of the Matthew and Mark passages that place emphasis upon sincerity in religious expression. Then suggest that the charge that some youth make against professed Christians is the charge of hypocrisy. These same youth would likely say that their speech is more honest, frank, and sincere than the more restrained and proper speech of their elders. They would further maintain that they write and talk the way they feel and are. Therefore they are more honest than persons who have one kind of speech when they are in polite company, another when they are alone or with intimates, and yet another when they commit words to paper.

When you have made this kind of interpretation, ask for two volunteers: one that would defend this hypothetical position of the young, the other to seek to refute or point out its fallacies. Out of this discussion may come a more basic question, What does such a verbal or written expression reveal about the user's view of God and man?

An alternate approach might be to read to your group the following portion of Dr. Laymon's exposition: "To desecrate and waste the beautiful earth, to despise our fellow men, to fail to take ourselves seriously, to have no hope for the future, to give up trying, to lack a passion for improving the lot of man, to be oblivious of another's need—is not each of these an expression of distrust in God and a failure to show him respect?" Then ask the group members to consider what relation this question has to an understanding of the meaning of the third commandment.

Yet another approach would be to have the group members work in pairs to read Exodus 20:7 and think about this third commandment in relationship to a careful study of Matthew 6:1-6 and Mark 7:5-8. As the pairs read and discuss this Scripture, these questions might be kept in mind: Do Jesus' words interpret, fulfill, or supersede the third commandment? If a person centers his efforts and concerns on what Jesus suggests as important, does the third commandment cease to be a problem?

Helping Class Members Act

My father was a farmer. Although our farm was a one family farm, there were times such as wheat harvest when we found it necessary to hire transient farm hands. My father would not allow any farm hand to stay on the job if he heard him "take the Lord's name in vain." Even if it were only midmorning, he would pay him for the day's work and send him away.

I am certainly not suggesting this as a possible course of action for any member of your group. I am suggesting that each person in the group may decide on some action in reference to what they feel to be the misuse of God's name in our society that will be as definite a witness for their conviction as was the action of my father.

Planning for Next Sunday

The people to whom the Ten Commandments were given were peculiarly the people of God and lived in a culture that was built upon a religious base. The fourth commandment reflected the common and accepted practice of the entire people. The week began with the day we call Sunday and ended at sundown on Friday. The seventh day was the Sabbath. By contrast, ours is a pluralistic and secular culture. No one religion is accepted or practiced by all the people. Ask your class members to read the fourth commandment and the Gospel references relating to it and to consider what religious truth, if any, they speak for today's world.

Work, Rest, and Worship

Background Scripture: Exodus 20:8-11; Mark 2:23-28; Luke 4:16-23; 14:1-6; Hebrews 10:25

The Main Question —Charles M. Laymon

A group of senior highs were discussing the different ways of observing Sunday. Why do this? Why do that? Why not do this? Why not do that? The whole problem seemed so confusing, if not downright contradictory, when they looked at the pattern of Sunday behavior across the nation. What made it more difficult to understand was the different ways their parents observed Sunday. Some did one thing; some practiced other things; some allowed everything and anything. And all were "church folks," as we say.

These young people were taking the issue into their own hands—at least as far as discussing it. One young man spoke up, "Are not all days sacred? God made every day of the week." "Yes," agreed another, "aren't all days special with God?"

A third interjected, "Sunday is for living it up. Didn't Jesus say something like that?" Then a young lady replied, "Living it up? How?" And another young lady said, "Sunday is extra special for me. I even feel different on Sunday."

The whole issue was not as clear as it should have been. The adult leader

361

concluded that this was because the meaning of Sunday was no longer clear to the parents of many of the students. Honestly, is it as clear to us as it was twenty-five years ago? Are our children the only ones who are mixed up?

The questions emerge: Is there anything special about Sunday for the Christian? What? Why? Our biblical passages are helpful in answering these questions.

As You Read the Scripture —George W. Frey

The printed Scripture presents the biblical view of the Sabbath. The work-rest-worship rhythm of life is evidenced in the fourth commandment. Six days are for work, but the seventh is for rest and worship.

Exodus 20:8-11. *Remember the sabbath day, to keep it holy:* A comparison of the Exodus version of this commandment with the Deuteronomy version is interesting. (See Deuteronomy 5:12-15.) In the Exodus account the verb is *remember.* In Deuteronomy the verb is *observe.* The King James Version uses the word *keep* in Deuteronomy. The meaning of these verbs is essentially the same. The Sabbath is to be kept, reserved, and guarded as a special day in seven. The word *Sabbath* can mean either rest or seven. Another comparison of the two versions of the Ten Commandments reveals that in Exodus, God's creative acts are to be recalled and remembered (20:11), while in Deuteronomy, Israel is to remember the Exodus event (5:15).

However, both Exodus and Deuteronomy enjoin Israel to rest from work on the Sabbath and acknowledge the sovereignty of God. Note that while the Sabbath is to be a day kept to remember God's mighty acts, it is also to be a day that benefits the whole community—children, male and female servants, work animals, and even the sojourner. The sojourner was a non-Jew who lived in the community and who by this commandment received the same consideration as the others mentioned. This is a noble bit of legislation on the part of ancient Israel.

Mark 2:23-28. *The sabbath was made for man, not man for the sabbath:* Mark, along with Matthew (12:1-8) and Luke (6:1-5), records this incident in the corn field. Scholars call this passage a *paradigm* or pronouncement story. The passage is a report of a conversation Jesus had with his opponents, ending in a short saying that has sermonic or teaching value. (See verses 27-28.)

The incident referred to in verses 25-26 is found in 1 Samuel 21:1-6. Actually Ahimelech was the high priest. His son is named here perhaps because he was better known, or else Mark may be following another tradition that presents Abiathar as Ahimelech's father.

The plucking of corn on the Sabbath was forbidden by Jewish tradition. Jesus knew well that he was breaking the tradition but justified his conduct on the ground of human need. It is lawful to meet human needs on the Sabbath. Jesus also used a precedent from history to support his conduct. In citing David, he was touching upon a most beloved character of Jewish history. David ate the bread that had been placed on the holy table—bread that was to be eaten only by the priests. (See Exodus 25:30.) But David was meeting a human need.

Luke 4:16-19. *He went to the synagogue . . . on the sabbath day:* Only Luke records this visit of Jesus to the synagogue in Nazareth. Note the details of the visit given by Luke. According to Luke, Jesus attended the synagogue regularly. Part of synagogue worship consisted of lessons for the day. Visitors were frequently invited to read one of the lessons and make comments. On this occasion Jesus read the lesson, which happened to be from Isaiah 61. Jesus' reading of this majestic passage was dramatically effective. His comments were even more telling. His identification with these prophetic words caused excitement. Note the reaction. (Read verses 20-30.) Observe the dauntless courage of Jesus.

Selected Scripture

King James Version	Revised Standard Version

Exodus 20:8-11

8 Remember the sabbath day, to keep it holy.

9 Six days shalt thou labour, and do all thy work:

10 But the seventh day is the sabbath of the LORD thy God: in it thou shalt not do any work, thou, nor thy son, nor thy daughter, thy manservant, nor thy maidservant, nor thy cattle, nor thy stranger that is within thy gates:

11 For in six days the LORD made heaven and earth, the sea, and all that in them is, and rested the seventh day: wherefore the LORD blessed the sabbath day, and hallowed it.

Mark 2:23-28

23 And it came to pass, that he went through the corn fields on the sabbath day; and his disciples began, as they went, to pluck the ears of corn.

24 And the Pharisees said unto him, Behold, why do they on the sabbath day that which is not lawful?

25 And he said unto them, Have ye never read what David did, when he had need, and was an hungered, he, and they that were with him?

26 How he went into the house of God in the days of Abiathar the high priest, and did eat the shewbread, which is not lawful to eat but for the priests, and gave also to them which were with him?

Exodus 20:8-11

8 "Remember the sabbath day, to keep it holy. 9 Six days you shall labor, and do all your work; 10 but the seventh day is a sabbath to the LORD your God; in it you shall not do any work, you, or your son, or your daughter, your manservant, or your maidservant, or your cattle, or the sojourner who is within your gates; 11 for in six days the LORD made heaven and earth, the sea, and all that is in them, and rested the seventh day; therefore the LORD blessed the sabbath day and hallowed it."

Mark 2:23-28

23 One sabbath he was going through the grainfields; and as they made their way his disciples began to pluck ears of grain. 24 And the Pharisees said to him, "Look, why are they doing what is not lawful on the sabbath?" 25 And he said to them, "Have you never read what David did, when he was in need and was hungry, he and those who were with him: 26 how he entered the house of God, when Abiathar was high priest, and ate the bread of the Presence, which it is not lawful for any but the priests to eat, and also gave it to those who were with him?" 27 And he said to them, "The sabbath was made for man, not

27 And he said unto them, The sabbath was made for man, and not man for the sabbath:

28 Therefore the Son of man is Lord also of the sabbath.

Luke 4:16-19

16 And he came to Nazareth, where he had been brought up: and, as his custom was, he went into the synagogue on the sabbath day, and stood up for to read.

17 And there was delivered unto him the book of the prophet Esaias. And when he had opened the book, he found the place where it was written,

18 The Spirit of the Lord is upon me, because he hath anointed me to preach the gospel to the poor; he hath sent me to heal the brokenhearted, to preach deliverance to the captives, and recovering of sight to the blind, to set at liberty them that are bruised,

19 To preach the acceptable year of the Lord.

Memory Selection: Remember the sabbath day, to keep it holy. (Exodus 20:8)

man for the sabbath; 28 so the Son of man is lord even of the sabbath."

Luke 4:16-19

16 And he came to Nazareth, where he had been brought up; and he went to the synagogue, as his custom was, on the sabbath day. And he stood up to read; 17 and there was given to him the book of the prophet Isaiah. He opened the book and found the place where it was written,

18 "The Spirit of the Lord is upon me,
because he has anointed me to preach good news to the poor.
He has sent me to proclaim release to the captives
and recovering of sight to the blind,
to set at liberty those who are oppressed,

19 to proclaim the acceptable year of the Lord."

Memory Selection: Remember the sabbath day, to keep it holy. (Exodus 20:8)

The Scripture and the Main Question —Charles M. Laymon

SACRED UNTO GOD

Every day is sacred, as the youth said who was discussing the meaning of Sunday (see "The Main Question"). As long as this is God's earth, no day in his created order is common or ordinary. Monday, Wednesday, Friday, or Saturday—you name it, God made it.

Even so, the young girl in the same discussion who insisted that Sunday was extra special for her was speaking in line with the biblical tradition of

many centuries. Did not God say in the commandment, "Remember the sabbath day, to keep it holy"? (Exodus 20:8)

The sequence of words in the title for this lesson is unusual—"Work, Rest, and Worship." The effect is cumulative as it leads from activity to restoration, and then to adoration. In some ways the title is reminiscent of Henry Wadsworth Longfellow's definition of Sunday: "Sunday is like a stile [steps over a fence] between the fields of toil, where we can kneel and pray, sit and meditate."

What we do with Sunday, whether our actions are right or wrong, is a matter of whether our lives, under God, are enriched as a result. We should ask if our sense of God is sharper, our perception of his purpose is clearer, and our dedication to his Kingdom is deeper because of Sunday's activities.

SACRED UNTO MAN

If Sunday is to be regarded as sacred unto God, in that it makes us more conscious of his presence, it is also to be considered as sacred unto man. Did not Jesus say, "The sabbath was made for man, not man for the sabbath"? (Mark 2:27) This statement was intended to rebuff the Pharisees who were placing Sabbath regulations above the needs of persons. With them persons did not count as much as the law (Mark 2:23-24).

As a result of the way we spend Sunday we should have a sharp sense of our own significance as persons. One of Sholem Asch's characters, in his novel *East River*, says, "It is by the Sabbath that we know we are not work animals, born to eat and to labor: we are men." Someone has said that we are not working animals but worshiping animals. But do animals worship? Hardly! Men, however, can and do.

The opportunities for worship that Sunday offers provide one of our most fruitful occasions for self-discovery. In this act of the human spirit we come to know that we are persons made in God's image. No longer can we regard ourselves and our fellows cheaply.

We do not usually worship alone but in the company of others in the Christian community. The word *church* is a translation of a Greek word, *ecclesia*, which was used in the Septuagint (Greek translation of the Old Testament) to refer to the congregation of Israel gathered for worship. To this day, Sunday worship in the church is a social experience. The brotherhood is present.

HEAR THE WORD

Part of the worship experience each Sunday is the hearing of the Word of God as it comes home to us through the reading of the Scripture and the proclamation of the gospel. This was what was happening in the synagogue when Jesus read from the scroll of Isaiah and interpreted it (Luke 4:16-30).

When Alexis de Tocqueville visited America, he traveled widely, looking for the greatness of our nation in our natural resources, industry, and commerce. He did not find it there. As he said, "Not until I went into the churches of America, and heard her pulpits aflame with righteousness, did I understand the secret of her genius and power."

Not all pulpits are "aflame with righteousness," but they should be and can be. Much depends upon what the people expect from preaching. If we truly hunger for the Word as we look up to the man in the pulpit, it will make a difference in the kind of preaching we hear and our response to the message.

THE GLORY OF A GOOD HABIT

When we hear the word *habit*, we invariably think of some evil practice that grips a person and that is difficult to change. But there are good habits as well as bad habits. A large part of Christian nurture is the developing of good habits.

In the Scripture passage for today we find Luke saying of Jesus, "And he came to Nazareth, where he had been brought up; and he went to the synagogue, *as his custom was,* on the sabbath." (4:16) Behind this statement we can visualize Jesus as growing up in the synagogue and as continuing to frequent it as an adult. Even when he undertook his ministry as the Messiah, he did not consider himself above attending its services.

The popular newspaper psychologist George W. Crane once said, "Bad habits are fifth columnists. They work against us at critical times." We might turn this about and make it read: "Good habits are shock troops. They work for us at critical times."

The habit of church attendance is like this. When Sunday comes, it is not a question of shall we go or why should we go. Instead, it is a practice that we follow by habit. Attending church has become second nature with us because we find in worship the strength to meet the challenge of everyday living.

Helping Adults Become Involved —Howard E. Tower

Preparation of Self and Class

"Remember the sabbath" is a positive command. This is the way the fourth commandment begins; but like all the commandments, except the fifth, it ends with a negative demand. We are to keep the commandment by not doing any work on this special day.

How do you prepare yourself and your group to deal with this commandment that cannot be strictly observed by even the most pious person in our society? If you made the suggested assignment to your group, you have already focused attention on the fact that the commandment was given to a special people at a special time in their history. You have acknowledged that our times are very different and called upon your group to consider what truth or value for living this commandment, and the Gospel references that relate to it, suggest for living in our times. This means that some members of your group will come to this session with positive convictions to express or basic questions to ask. Your preparation will need to equip you to hear these convictions and help the group members think through their valid questions.

These suggestions may help. First, after studying the Scripture interpretation of Dr. Frey, think through two basic questions: Why was this Sabbath regulation important to the Hebrew people? What did it contribute to their religious distinctiveness? You will find help in answering these questions in the article on the Sabbath in Volume R-Z of *The Interpreter's Dictionary of the Bible.*

Second, you will want to carefully study the implications of the Gospel references: Matthew 12:1-8; Mark 2:23-28; and Luke 6:1-5. These parallel passages contain the statement of Jesus, "The sabbath was made for man, not man for the sabbath." What new interpretation of the Sabbath did Jesus provide in this saying and the incident preceding it? What misuse of the Sabbath was Jesus striking against?

Now, over against this study, place a consideration of Luke 4:16-19. As you think about this passage, consider this question: If Jesus was so critical of the manner in which the Sabbath was observed, why did he go to the synagogue regularly? What does this practice of Jesus say to us about our Sunday observance?

Presenting the Main Question

Dr. Laymon suggests as the main question for today's thinking, Is there anything special about Sunday for the Christian? What? Why? Perhaps your preparation and the thinking of some of the members of your group during this past week may suggest another question as the main question. For example, it might be one of the following: Why has Sunday observance lost its hold on our lives? Should not the rhythm of work, rest, and worship be achieved in many different ways to fit the varying life styles of a pluralistic society? How can we make our observance of a day of rest and worship more real and helpful? Perhaps you may want to focus the opening of your session on a discovery of what question is uppermost in the experience of your group, rather than focusing attention upon a predetermined question.

To select your own question or to focus on the question as stated by Dr. Laymon, the following suggestions may prove helpful.

As the members of your group gather, begin an informal conversation about the way you observed Sunday in your parents' home compared to the way you observe Sunday in your home. For example, in my parents' home on a farm in Southern Indiana, Sunday went something like this: We were awakened about 5 A.M. Father and the boys did the farm chores, including milking ten cows. Mother and the girls prepared a big breakfast. After breakfast all of us, from the youngest to the oldest, dressed in our Sunday best. The horses had been harnessed prior to breakfast. We drove the mile and a half to the church for Sunday school at 9:30, worship at 10:30. Then we drove home (usually with guests) for a big Sunday dinner. After dinner there was conversation or singing around the piano. Activities for the children included hikes in the woods to pick wild flowers or active but quiet games in the yard. One activity that was not allowed was swimming in our pond. At four o'clock the chores began. At 5:30 we ate supper, and at 6:30 we headed for the evening service at church. This was our Sunday, rain or shine, heat or cold, sleet or snow.

Today, since I am a minister, my Sundays include the regular services of the church. The free time is used doing things I like to do, or the family likes to do, ranging from taking a nap to working in my rose garden.

If you share your experience in somewhat this fashion, several of your class members should feel free to share their early Sunday customs in comparison or contrast with their present practices. The purpose of this sharing will be to identify the values and meanings in the experiences of the past and the present. Then decide what it is the group wants to focus their attention upon in their exploration of the ancient law of Sabbath observance, Jesus' interpretation of this law, and our current attitudes and practices.

Developing the Lesson

Whatever main question the group chooses, you will need some background in order to deal effectively with the question. This background should include an interpretation of the role the fourth commandment played in the long development of the Hebrew people. You could ask a group member to read a Bible dictionary article on the Sabbath and to be ready to bring to the group some of its main points, stressing the way Sabbath observance developed, its adaptation to various periods in

Israel's history, and its contribution to the uniqueness of the people of God. Or, as the leader, you may be the right person to make this presentation.

Then the group needs to deal with the Gospel references. This might be done by having the members of the class work in groups of three. The groups would consider each of the three Gospel accounts of the disciples plucking the grain on the Sabbath and try to come to agreement as to what this incident and Jesus' summation of it reveal about Jesus' attitude toward the Sabbath. Then they could study the Luke 4:16-19 reference and consider what Jesus' practice or observance of the Sabbath may have been.

Finally, the entire group will want to struggle with what positive values have issued from the Jewish observance of the Sabbath and the Christian celebration of Sunday. When these values have been identified (see Dr. Laymon's exposition), the class period might conclude with a consideration of how these values can become a part of present-day living.

Helping Class Members Act

Action may be considered in two areas. First, each member of the group will want to determine the degree to which the most helpful balance between work, rest, and worship has been achieved in his life. This kind of self-examination may, and likely should, continue into the coming week and involve discussion within the family unit and possible changes in life styles for the entire family.

Another area for action is within the church community. What changes are needed in the program of your church to improve its contribution to the God-given need for a rhythm of work-rest-worship? Is there a need for the church to provide some new worship opportunities either at varied hours on Sunday or on other days of the week?

Planning for Next Sunday

Call attention to the fifth commandment as the basis of next Sunday's study. Ask the members of your group to read Exodus 20:12; Deuteronomy 6:6-9; Ephesians 6:1-4; and 2 Timothy 1:5. As they ponder these Scriptures suggest this question: Since the fifth commandment is a positive admonition rather than a negative command, does this suggest that we need a more positive approach in family relations?

A Higher Patriotism

(INDEPENDENCE SUNDAY, JULY 1)

GEORGE A. HARTMAN[5]

As the day of national independence draws near, our hearts become strangely warmed by the emotion of patriotism. There are parades, flags, firecrackers, speeches, and the like, to produce memories and a feeling of dedication to our country. And yet, even as we speak of these things, we are deeply aware that the whole idea of patriotism is being seriously questioned in our time.

In a recent interview with a radical student from a large midwestern college the youth was asked to comment on the subject of patriotism. He immediately made an obscene gesture to show his contempt for the subject and then declared: "Patriotism is for those who are ignorant of what is going on. My loyalty is to greater concepts and wider ideals." It is tragic when a young man has become so disillusioned that he is revolted by anyone who says: "This is my country, and I love her."

We cannot help but be aware of the growing tensions connected with the emotion of patriotism. These tensions, which are sharpest at moments of public respect or contempt for patriotic symbols such as the flag, have in recent days produced a growing gap between parents and their children, between public officials and a portion of the populace. Strongly emotional discussions take place between those who believe patriotism is an automatic and unquestioning acceptance of America and her leaders and those who declare that true patriotism is more the quality of an individual's, or a people's, behavior.

Generalities and slogans are heard everywhere. One side covers its automobile bumpers with: "America: Love It or Leave It." The other side replies: "America Is Hypocritical." And with that the battle lines are drawn.

There is a standard, I believe, by which we can talk of patriotism, not as an abstraction steeped in nostalgia, but as a behavior that can be judged according to God's own norm. This standard was inscribed on the Liberty Bell by the founding fathers of this nation: "Proclaim liberty throughout all the land unto all the inhabitants thereof!"

This was not a new idea. The nation's fathers took this verse from the Bible (Leviticus 25:10, King James Version). They chose a standard that had been in the mind of our heavenly Father from the beginning. And it offers us a way to use this Independence Sunday to call for a *higher patriotism* that is full of hope and challenge for the future. At its best, this higher patriotism can represent the greatest love for our nation.

Our first challenge is to believe these words from Leviticus. They teach us that all men, by God's will, are to be free, and nations are to administer justice impartially for the benefit of each individual man, woman, and child. Liberty and justice are not for a privileged few; they are for all citizens of the land. God revealed these truths, but it has taken many centuries for a nation to come along that would try to make them a reality for her people. America was probably the first nation, and possibly the only one, to inscribe these words from Leviticus on a bell that was to ring out liberty and justice for all

[5] George A. Hartman: pastor, Divinity Lutheran Church, Columbus, Ohio.

people. They are incorporated into our common heritage as Americans, and they represent a high national goal.

If everyone in America believed these words, we would not be divided. But liberty is a precarious business. It must be constantly and actively pursued, or it erodes and finally vanishes. Therefore, we offer the second challenge—that we work with ceaseless fervor to make America's performance match her ideals as closely as possible. As citizens with the right of self-government, we have an enormous responsibility for determining that liberty will be proclaimed throughout the land to all the inhabitants thereof.

Some people want liberty and justice for themselves and are not concerned about the same for others. But love of country is inseparable from citizen action to make the country more lovable. This means voting and working to end pollution, discrimination, poverty, corruption, greed, and all else that hurts the promise and potential of America.

This also means that we will stop choosing up sides and calling one another hurtful names. It means that young and old, black and white, rich and poor, educated and uneducated, will seek to love and to work together, side by side, in understanding. We will strive to achieve together what we cannot achieve alone—the American dream and the will of God for all mankind—liberty and justice for all.

Third, let us challenge our nation to take a new look at what we call patriotic or unpatriotic. Is the one who refuses to sing the national anthem any less patriotic than the one who refuses to let the Bill of Rights apply equally to everyone? Are those who burn the flag really more unpatriotic than those who dump their garbage along America's streams and highways and despoil the countryside? Is it not time to expose all the distortions of patriotism whereby those who work and risk a great deal to correct deep injustices are accused of unpatriotic activity by some of the very forces that are eating out the heart of the nation's highest principles? And has not the time come when many of the cheap and gaudy acts of vandalism against our national shrines and symbols must be questioned and called irresponsible?

Let these challenges ring out this Independence Sunday: "Proclaim liberty throughout all the land unto all the inhabitants thereof!" If you truly believe in these American ideals, declare yourself for them for all the people. Seek a higher patriotism than that which is ordinarily practiced—a patriotism wherein a thinking and believing citizenry is dedicated to a better America, an America where liberty and justice are pursued by and for all the people.

Response to Heritage

Background Scripture: Exodus 20:12; Deuteronomy 6:6-9;
Proverbs 23:22-25; Mark 7:9-13; Ephesians 6:1-4; 2 Timothy 1:5

The Main Question —Charles M. Laymon

When the popular song "Keep the Home Fires Burning" was written, American soldiers were fighting on European soil. Its pathos gripped the hearts of American parents as they pictured their sons dreaming of hearth and home. For the soldiers, when life was breaking apart at the seams all around them, thoughts of their loved ones back in the United States kept their faith and courage alive.

We do not need to be in a war in order for youth to find hope and strength in their thoughts of home as they go out into the world on their own. But such does not happen unless the home was a place of love, trust, and understanding while they were living within the family circle.

The question then is What must a home be like if children are to find in it the heritage of faith that they will need throughout life?

The reactions of young people toward home and parents change greatly through the years, so much so, that fathers and mothers often become unduly discouraged. It has been pointed out that at age eleven children think their parents know everything; at sixteen they are not so sure; at nineteen they are convinced that they know more than their parents; at twenty-two their parents are old folks who belong to another generation and are not "with it" anymore; but at thirty they conclude that their parents were simply wonderful.

The passages from the Bible that undergird this lesson are helpful in assessing the responsibilities of parents.

As You Read the Scripture —George W. Frey

The Old Testament recognizes the central importance of the family. Any deed that results in harm to the family is a serious matter calling for justice immediately. It is not surprising therefore to find one of the Ten Commandments to be concerned with family relationships and loyalties.

Exodus 20:12. *Honor your father and your mother:* In Hebrew society the father enjoyed a unique position, but this commandment mentions the mother in the same sentence. She may not have held the high place occupied by the father, but in the Hebrew home the mother was regarded as a person with rights and privileges. The fifth commandment therefore asks that father and mother be honored. The verb translated *honor* is interesting. It carries ideas of worth, value, prestige, esteem, success, respect, and so forth. To honor a person is to respond to that person with respect, esteem, love, appreciation, and support. Honoring persons builds meaningful relationships. In addition,

371

WHAT MUST THE HOME ATMOSPHERE BE LIKE IF CHILDREN ARE TO BE ROOTED IN THE HERITAGE OF THE FAITH?

honor in the family strengthens the family and opens all members of the family to one another in love.

Note the promise to those who honor father and mother. Compare it with the penalties to persons who inflict injury to father or mother (Exodus 21:15). The death penalty is applied to those who curse a father or mother (Exodus 21:17). Observe that in both these early laws the mother is included in the legal prescriptions.

Deuteronomy 6:6-9. *And these words . . . shall be upon your heart; and you shall teach them diligently to your children:* The Book of Deuteronomy was originally written to bring about reform and renewal in the Israelite community. Thus it is not strange to note the many commands in the early chapters of the book. Such urgent instructions as heed, keep, hear, seek, know, obey, this do, remember, and so forth are common to the sermonic style of Deuteronomy. This particular passage presents a beautiful portrait of ideal family life. The home is the place where religious tradition is to be handed down. Religion is to have the central place in family conversations. Parents and children are to join in keeping religious memories alive and meaningful. *These words* refer to the teachings of the book. Actually the early chapters of Deuteronomy provide an abbreviated outline of Israel's heritage. The memories that God redeemed Israel from bondage, chose Israel to be his own because he loved Israel, and called Israel to be a peculiar people in the world constitute the basic elements in its heritage.

Ephesians 6:1-4. *Children, obey your parents. . . . Fathers, do not provoke your children to anger:* Paul builds on the Deuteronomic teaching in this passage. He alludes to the fifth commandment as "the first commandment with a promise." Note the responsibility that falls alike on fathers and children. Paul believes with Deuteronomy that the home is the custodian and transmitter of religious knowledge.

2 Timothy 1:5. *I am reminded of your sincere faith, a faith that dwelt first in your grandmother Lois and your mother Eunice:* The two letters to Timothy and the one to Titus are often called the Pastoral Letters. They deal with the very practical problems of church life at a time when the Christian churches were struggling to take root in a hostile environment. In Second Timothy, the writer encourages Timothy to keep alive the memory of his early childhood. Evidently a beautiful spirit of Christian love and faith surrounded Timothy as a child and provided him with an unforgettable heritage. (See also 2 Timothy 3:14-15.) A grandmother and a mother passed on to a growing child the rich heritage of faith in Christ. The writer urges Timothy to respond to this heritage and to keep the faith.

Selected Scripture

King James Version

Exodus 20:12

12 Honour thy father and thy mother: that thy days may be long upon the land which the LORD thy God giveth thee.

Deuteronomy 6:6-9

6 And these words, which I command thee this day, shall be in thine heart:

7 And thou shalt teach them diligently unto thy children, and shalt talk of them when thou sittest in thine house, and when thou walkest by the way, and when thou liest down, and when thou risest up.

8 And thou shalt bind them for a sign upon thine hand, and they shall be as frontlets between thine eyes.

9 And thou shalt write them upon the posts of thy house, and on thy gates.

Ephesians 6:1-4

1 Children, obey your parents in the Lord: for this is right.

2 Honour thy father and mother;

Revised Standard Version

Exodus 20:12

12 "Honor your father and your mother, that your days may be long in the land which the LORD your God gives you."

Deuteronomy 6:6-9

6 And these words which I command you this day shall be upon your heart; 7 and you shall teach them diligently to your children, and shall talk of them when you sit in your house, and when you walk by the way, and when you lie down, and when you rise. 8 And you shall bind them as a sign upon your hand, and they shall be as frontlets between your eyes. 9 And you shall write them on the doorposts of your house and on your gates.

Ephesians 6:1-4

1 Children, obey your parents in the Lord, for this is right. 2 "Honor your father and mother" (this is the

which is the first commandment with promise;

3 That it may be well with thee, and thou mayest live long on the earth.

4 And, ye fathers, provoke not your children to wrath: but bring them up in the nurture and admonition of the Lord.

first commandment with a promise), 3 "that it may be well with you and that you may live long on the earth." 4 Fathers, do not provoke your children to anger, but bring them up in the discipline and instruction of the Lord.

2 Timothy 1:5

5 When I call to remembrance the unfeigned faith that is in thee, which dwelt first in thy grandmother Lois, and thy mother Eunice; and I am persuaded that in thee also.

2 Timothy 1:5

5 I am reminded of your sincere faith, a faith that dwelt first in your grandmother Lois and your mother Eunice and now, I am sure, dwells in you.

Memory Selection: **Honour thy father and thy mother: that thy days may be long upon the land which the LORD thy God giveth thee.** (Exodus 20:12)

Memory Selection: **Honor your father and your mother, that your days may be long in the land which the LORD your God gives you.** (Exodus 20:12)

The Scripture and the Main Question —Charles M. Laymon

WHY SHOULD OUR CHILDREN RESPECT US?

In order to secure respect from children it is not sufficient simply to quote the Bible to them: "Honor your father and your mother." (Exodus 20:12) Authority—even the authority of the Bible—will not produce respect.

Respect for parents is the result of living relationships marked by love and justice. Day by day it must be built into the structure of a child's life. Respect cannot be coerced or required.

We must not confuse obedience with respect. Children, like pets, can be cowed into obedience because they fear what will happen to them if they refuse. A student once told me that he remembered the day when he calculated the results of disobeying his parents. Up to that time fear of the consequences had been the dominant

motive for obeying them. Now he figured that, if he disobeyed, his parents would spank him; but he concluded that it would be worth it. Fear had broken down as a foundation for respect.

Love and concern are the only true sources of respect and honor for parents. A soldier, when he returned from the Vietnam war, said that what had been of most help during the long months of fighting was the memory of his father's hand on his shoulder. Unable to speak words as the boy was leaving, his father had simply placed his hand upon the boy's shoulder and pressed deeply.

Children should respect their parents only if that respect is deserved. As they move from childhood, through youth, and into young adult life, they can tell.

PARENTS AS TEACHERS

Parents are a child's first teachers. The Head Start project has taught us many things about child development. One of them is that so-called backward children have usually either had backward parents or been the victims of parental neglect.

As a result of research we now know also that a child achieves half of his potential intelligence before he is four years old. Lynn Marino, in an article carried by *The Christian Home*, tells of a father who called out the names of automobiles for the amusement of his young son. The first word that the child spoke was *Volkswagen*, and that with a German accent.

These facts give new meaning to the Hebrew requirement for parents to teach the *Shema* to every child. The *Shema* says, "Hear, O Israel: The LORD our God is one LORD; and you shall love the LORD your God with all your heart, and with all your soul, and with all your might." Parents were required to teach these words diligently to their offspring (Deuteronomy 6:4-7).

Parents who teach their children to love God, either by telling them about him or by showing how they love God, are laying the foundation for an entire life of regard for God. The attitudes toward God that a child finds in the home are more important than verbal instruction. A rich heritage does not need to be put in so many words, but it does need to be expressed in outlook and action.

IT WORKS BOTH WAYS

The Book of Ephesians closes with some instructions for living the Christian life. Along with recommendations for husbands and wives, and for slaves and masters, there are words of counsel for parents and children.

Of particular interest here is the fact that the author maintains a fine balance between what each must expect and do for the other. Children must honor and obey their parents; but parents must also be considerate of their children: "Fathers, do not provoke your children to anger, but bring them up in the discipline and instruction of the Lord." (Ephesians 6:4) You see, respect works both ways.

How does one provoke his children to wrath? Is it not by expecting too much of them? Nobody is perfect, nor can one be. When standards of conduct and achievement are impossibly high, all are doomed to some failures. As adults we know this, but often children do not. Because of their failures they develop destructive guilt complexes. They do not know how to accept their inabilities or how to fail.

Excessively high demands upon children by their parents may actually lead them to commit desperate deeds. Children may cheat in school in order to get the grades their parents expect. Or they may even take their own lives rather than have to come face to face with their parents' condemnation. The high rate of suicide among teenagers is due mainly to their lack of ability to cope with failure.

PASS IT ON!

A heritage is something of value that comes to us from the past. If we do not pass it on, it dies with us. A man whose son follows him in the same profession is particularly grateful because he can transmit to the youth many things that he has learned, perhaps through pain and hardship. A minister said to me recently, "The greatest regret of my life is that my boy did not become a preacher. There was so much that I wanted to share with him, things I learned. But now—"

We may not be able to share with our children all that we have learned professionally, but we can pass on to them what we have discovered through our religious experience. This is the greatest heritage of all.

The author of Second Timothy has such a line of influence in mind when he tells the young preacher that he is thinking of the faith that "dwelt first in your grandmother Lois and your mother Eunice and now, I am sure, dwells in you." (1:5) This example inspires us to press forward into the future as followers of Christ. Our heritage is not just something for us to look upon in wonder; it summons us to pass the torch to future generations.

Helping Adults Become Involved —Howard E. Tower

Preparation of Self and Class

The fifth commandment deals with relationships within a family. This study is, therefore, very timely. A great deal is being said about the family today, much of which is negative. Children demonstrate negative feelings toward parents. Attitudes of frustration and despair are being expressed by parents. Gloomy forecasts for the future come from the research of social scientists. Yet against this present-day negativism about the family as a social unit stands the positive affirmation of the fifth commandment, "Honor thy father and thy mother."

Your assignment to your class members last Sunday called attention to this commandment and asked them to consider whether there may be too much emphasis upon the negative within their homes. This is a question you will also want to ponder.

As you think about this question and as you study the Scripture and Dr. Laymon's explication of the lesson subject, you will also need to examine what is currently being said and written about the family. What kind of family relationships are being portrayed in television programs? What do television commercials lift up as important for family happi- ness? What is the situation in the homes of your community, your church members, your class members? Do you know of particular homes that are broken or breaking up? Are you aware of children who are estranged from their parents?

A number of films relate directly or indirectly to the study of the family. If you can find one or more of the following films in your local public library or state university library, you may wish to view them as background for your preparation: *The Family Next Door, Trouble in the Family, From Generation to Generation,* and *Worship: A Family's Heritage.* (See pages 337-38.)

The film *From Generation to Generation* deepens our sense of the continuity of the human species; while the film *Worship: A Family's Heritage* gives a sense of the importance of worship or religious faith to the family.

Presenting the Main Question

Dr. Laymon quite appropriately approaches his exposition of the lesson theme from the viewpoint of the parent rather than the child. More often, in sermons or other discussions of the fifth commandment, we hear primarily of the duties this command lays upon the child in respect to his parents. Dr. Laymon's stress is put upon what the parent needs to do to merit the respect, love, and honor of his offspring. This is a sound approach since most adults are more acutely aware of their role as a parent than as a child. To place the emphasis upon the child's attitude toward his parents might turn the accusing finger of the group toward the shortcomings of the younger generation or even possibly their own children. Such problems can only be solved if both adults and children are willing to change. Therefore, the main question suggested by Dr. Laymon is valid: "What must a home be like if children are to find in it the heritage of faith that they will need throughout life?"

This question may be brought into sharp focus for your class by beginning with a reading of Deuteronomy 6:6-9. After reading this brief statement, call upon the group to meditate upon it for a minute or two in silence. Then divide your group members into subgroups of two or three persons each. Assign half the groups to talk together about the relation these words from Deuteronomy bear to the words of Exodus 20:12. Ask the remaining groups to consider in what specific ways they have been seeking to fulfill the injunction in Deuteronomy in their homes. Let the groups talk among themselves freely for four or five minutes. Then ask each group to report.

Developing the Lesson

If the above procedure is followed, by the time the sharing is completed one fact should be self-evident to the group members: The keeping of the fifth commandment is a two-way street. It involves an interchange of love and respect and honor on the part of the child for the parent, with a concern and openness and honesty on the part of the parent. This interchange will include a tension of give-and-take with the resultant pains of growth in love, in mutual understanding, and in respect.

This insight will be further strengthened by a careful examination of Paul's counsel to families in Ephesians 6:1-4. A panel of two or more persons might be used to discuss how Paul's words undergird, and grow out of, the heritage of the Hebrew people, of which heritage the fifth commandment is an important part.

This concept of a two-way relationship in keeping the law calling for respect for parents is further supported by the single verse in 2 Timothy 1:5. This verse calls attention to the importance of the continuity of the heritage of faith.

Perhaps this truth can be made more evident by involving the group in the following exercise. Let each person in your group finish this statement: What I remember most about my grandfather (or grandmother or grandparents) is _____. Next ask them to complete this sentence: What I admire (respect) my father (or mother or parents) for is _____. Some persons may not be ready to put their feelings about their parents or grandparents into words and should not be pressed to do so.

Finally, ask each person to complete this sentence: I would hope my children will be able to remember me for _____. Again, if any are not ready to put into words their hopes, suggest that they try to complete the sentence during the coming week.

You might close the discussion with the simple reminder that as parents we are passing a heritage on to our children to be remembered by them and to be an influence for good or ill in their lives.

Helping Class Members Act

At first thought it would seem that the action outcome of this lesson can and should be only a personal matter. Each person who is a parent should continue to examine his relationship to his children and decide on changes that need to be made in his life style. Or if an adult is not a parent but has living parents, he should examine his attitude toward and treatment of them. He may decide to write letters more frequently, make some long-distance calls, or visit more often.

On the other hand, upon closer examination it may become clear to your class members that there is a particular home that needs the supporting concern of the class because of a crisis situation. Or it may be that a group of parents needs to covenant together to continue to explore ways of developing a heritage of faith in a day when religion is discounted and the Christian style of life is under attack.

Planning for Next Sunday

Call attention to the theme for next Sunday, "Reverence for Human Life." Point out that the basis for this lesson subject is the four-word sixth commandment "You shall not kill." (Exodus 20:13) Could the theme of the lesson be valid without the New Testament's further interpretation of this commandment? Suggest that members think about this question as they read and study Matthew 5:21-26; James 4:1-2b; and 1 John 3:15-18.

LESSON 6   JULY 8

Reverence for Human Life

Background Scripture: Exodus 20:13; Matthew 5:21-26; 12:9-13; James 4:1-2b; 1 John 3:11-18

The Main Question —Charles M. Laymon

Evangelical humanism is the view of man that reverences him as a child of God. Although this belief is thoroughly Christian, we sometimes end up side-stepping God and bowing before human achievements only. Man is not the measure of all there is; he is not a god to be worshiped.

Still the Scriptures do call upon us to reverence human life. Anything that degrades or destroys man is sinful. Man was made in the image of the Creator, therefore no one can place a cheap price tag upon him.

An ancient proverb reads, "God sleeps in the tree, dreams in the animal, and wakes in the man." The latter part of this statement sets the perspective for this lesson.

Why then, on every hand, do we find serious threats to man's existence? War makes human beings expendable, and pollution gradually shortens our life expectancy. In capital punishment we take a human soul into our own hands, and by careless driving we spill man's blood needlessly upon our highways.

All this seems contradictory in a century when medical science has learned so much about extending our days. Social legislation for the poor and under-privileged is constantly before our lawmakers, and concern for equal justice for all is one of our national priorities.

How far should reverence for human life go? What effect should it have on the remolding of society?

The following biblical passages contain some helpful guidelines in facing this issue.

As You Read the Scripture —George W. Frey

Ancient Hebrew society experienced the uncontrolled emotions in a person that led to killing another. Killing human beings was a serious problem. Taking the life of another shattered human relations and community peace. Thus the killer had to be dealt with quickly. The sixth commandment attempted to prohibit killing.

Exodus 20:13. *You shall not kill:* This commandment is short—only two words in the original language. Nevertheless its presence attests to the concern of the legislators for the welfare of the total community. Some interpreters believe this law is a prohibition against all killing, even that of animals; but most commentators agree that the concern of this commandment is the doing to death of a human person. The sixth commandment therefore seeks to control those who would kill a person in hot haste and thereby take from him his most prized possession, namely human life.

In the Old Testament, war and the killing that accompanies battle seemingly have the approval of God. But the aim of the sixth commandment is not to cover the military conquests of Israel. Rather it deals with killing in the ordinary day by day life of the people of the community. Human life has worth and dignity. This is the major idea back of the sixth commandment. Killing another does not belong to the style of life of the people of God.

Matthew 5:21. *You shall not kill; and whoever kills shall be liable to judgment:* This verse is based on Exodus 20:13. Other laws dealing with killing are found in Exodus 21:12; Deuteronomy 17:8-13; and Leviticus 24:17. The death penalty for killing was common. Matthew 5:21 indicates that the violator shall stand trial in the Jewish court or Sanhedrin.

Verse 22. *Every one who is angry with his brother shall be liable to judgment:* Jesus deals with the inner feelings of hate, anger, and uncontrolled passions that form the prelude to killing. Likewise, Hebrew law recognized the differing conditions of killing. (See Exodus 21:13-14 and Deuteronomy 19:1-13.) *His brother* probably means a Jewish person, but the spirit of Jesus would support wider application of the words. "The council" is the Jewish court or Sanhedrin. The phrase "you fool" was a contemptuous way of speaking to or about a person. The phrase "hell of fire" refers to the valley of Hinnom south of Jerusalem. This valley in which children were once cremated in honor of Baal became a symbol of punishment for wicked persons in the future.

Verses 23-24. *First be reconciled to your brother, and then come and offer your gift:* Right relations with one's fellow man are required for sincere worship. Note how useless it is to present a gift at the altar when human relations are broken. Note the full import of this verse. It is not the worshiper's having something against another that stops him, but that other person's having something against him. The question is not who is at fault. Human relations are broken. They must be mended before worship can be effective. Reconciliation is the process of tearing away barriers and building bridges of human understanding and love. Reconciliation is the answer to passions of hate and anger.

James 4:1-2b. *What causes wars, and what causes fightings among you? . . . You desire and do not have; so you kill:* The Letter of James is a sermon in letter form that picks up much of the ethical emphasis of the Sermon on the Mount (Matthew 5 through 7). The theme of faith and love is central. These verses indicate that selfish and unrestrained desires provide the motive for killing.

1 John 3:15-18. *Little children, let us . . . love . . . in deed and in truth:* First John is written to deepen the religious life of its readers. The distinctive mark of the Christian is love. Love builds, binds, and creates. Hate divides, tears apart, and kills. Love for persons results in reverence for human life and freedom for all. Love is demonstrated by the laying down of one's life for another. When the needs of others come first for us, then it can be said we love *in deed and in truth.*

Selected Scripture

King James Version

Exodus 20:13

13 Thou shalt not kill.

Matthew 5:21-26

21 Ye have heard that it was said by them of old time, Thou shalt not kill; and whosoever shall kill shall be in danger of the judgment:

22 But I say unto you, That whosoever is angry with his brother without a cause shall be in danger of the judgment: and whosoever shall say to his brother, Raca, shall be in danger of the council: but whosoever shall say, Thou fool, shall be in danger of hell fire.

23 Therefore if thou bring thy gift to the altar, and there rememberest that thy brother hath aught against thee;

24 Leave there thy gift before the

Revised Standard Version

Exodus 20:13

13 "You shall not kill."

Matthew 5:21-26

21 "You have heard that it was said to the men of old, 'You shall not kill; and whoever kills shall be liable to judgment.' 22 But I say to you that every one who is angry with his brother shall be liable to judgment; whoever insults his brother shall be liable to the council, and whoever says, 'You fool!' shall be liable to the hell of fire. 23 So if you are offering your gift at the altar, and there remember that your brother has something against you, 24 leave your gift there before the altar and go; first be reconciled to your brother, and then come and offer your gift. 25 Make friends quickly with your ac-

altar, and go thy way; first be reconciled to thy brother, and then come and offer thy gift.

25 Agree with thine adversary quickly, whiles thou art in the way with him; lest at any time the adversary deliver thee to the judge, and the judge deliver thee to the officer, and thou be cast into prison.

26 Verily I say unto thee, Thou shalt by no means come out thence, till thou hast paid the uttermost farthing.

cuser, while you are going with him to court, lest your accuser hand you over to the judge, and the judge to the guard, and you be put in prison; 26 truly, I say to you, you will never get out till you have paid the last penny."

James 4:1-2b

1 From whence come wars and fightings among you? come they not hence, even of your lusts that war in your members?

2 Ye lust, and have not: ye kill, and desire to have, and cannot obtain.

James 4:1-2b

1 What causes wars, and what causes fightings among you? Is it not your passions that are at war in your members? 2 You desire and do not have; so you kill. And you covet and cannot obtain; so you fight and wage war.

1 John 3:15-18

15 Whosoever hateth his brother is a murderer: and ye know that no murderer hath eternal life abiding in him.

16 Hereby perceive we the love of God, because he laid down his life for us: and we ought to lay down our lives for the brethren.

17 But whoso hath this world's good, and seeth his brother have need, and shutteth up his bowels of compassion from him, how dwelleth the love of God in him?

18 My little children, let us not love in word, neither in tongue; but in deed and in truth.

1 John 3:15-18

15 Any one who hates his brother is a murderer, and you know that no murderer has eternal life abiding in him. 16 By this we know love, that he laid down his life for us; and we ought to lay down our lives for the brethren. 17 But if any one has the world's goods and sees his brother in need, yet closes his heart against him, how does God's love abide in him? 18 Little children, let us not love in word or speech but in deed and in truth.

Memory Selection: W h o s o e v e r hateth his brother is a murderer: and ye know that no murderer hath eternal life abiding in him. (1 John 3:15)

Memory Selection: **Any one who** hates his brother is a murderer, and you know that no murderer has eternal life abiding in him. (1 John 3:15)

The Scripture and the Main Question —Charles M. Laymon

TO KILL OR NOT TO KILL

In spite of the fact that the Hebrews probably exempted war and capital punishment from the commandment "You shall not kill" (Exodus 20:13), these words have prodded the consciences of Christians in time of war. Beside these words, of course, are placed Jesus' injunctions to turn the other cheek and to love one's enemies (Matthew 5:39, 44), as well as James's words on covetousness as a cause of war (James 4:1-2b).

Mark Twain is best known as a satirist. Even his novels poke fun at the ridiculous angle in some of the customs of his day. Sometimes, however, his satires took a serious vein as in the case of his "prayer" against war. In part it reads, "O Lord, our God, help us to tear their soldiers to bloody shreds with our shells; . . . help us to wring the hearts of their unoffending widows with unavailing grief; help us to turn them out rootless with their little children to wander unfriended through wastes of their desolated land. . . . We ask of one who is the Spirit of love. . . . Amen."

Christians as a whole have never regarded war, from the days of the early church, as the final answer to the issues that arise between nations. Some have participated because they felt it was the only way open to the nation in a given set of circumstances. Others have become conscientious objectors who have willingly engaged in nonmilitary service to relieve suffering on or off the battlefield. Still others have refused all forms of participation, directly or indirectly, in the war effort. And all of us who reverence life have sought, and are seeking, for means other than resorting to arms in order to settle differences between nations. The Christian's conscience will not let him rest in this quest.

GET TO THE ROOT

Jesus had a way of getting to the root of the matter, as we say, whether he was referring to the legalism of the Pharisees, the need of sinners, or the sources of killing. He internalized issues, so that our attention is focused upon basic causes rather than upon outward acts. Nowhere is this process more evident than in regard to man's destruction of his fellowman.

Take Jesus' words concerning the commandment against killing as an example: "You have heard that it was said to the men of old, 'You shall not kill. . . .' But I say to you that every one who is angry with his brother shall be liable to judgment . . . and whoever says, 'You fool!' shall be liable to the hell of fire." (Matthew 5:21-22)

We have seen deadly outbursts of violence on the streets of our cities during the last decade. The causes of some of these were obvious, but others stemmed from hidden resentments that had long been festering within the human heart.

How long men can hold a destructive resentment toward others is surprising. It has been said that Cicero so hated Clodius that two years after the death of his enemy at the Battle of Bovillae he was dating his letters "the 560th day after Bovillae." No reverence for human life is evident in this attitude.

WRONG ATTITUDES MAY BE SELF-DESTRUCTIVE

The opening of the popular television show *Mission Impossible* included the words, "This tape will self-destruct in thirty seconds." This statement might be changed slightly to read: "This attitude will self-destruct sooner than you think." It has been reported that Dr. John Hunter of England was unable to keep his temper and became so angry that he dropped dead. A blood clot in the wall of his heart was actually created by his anger.

We should reverence our own lives and those of others by controlling what we think and the attitudes we hold. In fact, if we do not have self-respect, we cannot expect others to respect us. I often think of the silence of Jesus as he stood before both Herod and Pilate. The king had no reverence for life and was interested only in being entertained by a magical performance. The procurator was concerned largely with saving his own skin as a political opportunist. Jesus would not, therefore, lower his sights by pleading for his life. He would not say a word. His dignity before those who showed no real con-

cern for him has been an inspiration to many. Jesus respected himself.

How Far Should Reverence For Human Life Go?

Strange as it may seem, we sometimes attempt to run away from God's love for us in Christ. C. S. Lewis said, in Surprised by Joy, that at one time he did not want to be captured by Christ. But he could not escape God's love. From this experience he concluded, "The hardness of God is kinder than the softness of men, and His compulsion is our liberation." When we discover God's love and his respect for persons, then we find reverence for ourselves and others.

How far should this reverence for human life go? This lesson helps us answer this question when it points out how far God himself has actually gone: "By this we know love, that he laid down his life for us; and we ought to lay down our lives for the brethren." (1 John 3:16)

Helping Adults Become Involved —Howard E. Tower

Preparation of Self and Class

If you asked the members of your class to think about the question concerning the real source of the theme of today's lesson, this exploration should also be yours. Does the four-word commandment "You shall not kill" make reverence for life imperative? Consider the contribution of the New Testament interpretation of the motivations that lead to killing and those that call for reverence for all human beings. (See the background Scripture.)

Perhaps a beginning point for your preparation should be an assessment of what is happening in your com-

munity and in your world. As I write these helps, months before you will be leading your group in their study, the following things are happening: The leaders of North Vietnam have declared that they will return American prisoners if the United States agrees to withdraw troops on a declared timetable with a complete withdrawal date stipulated. Secret negotiations are underway in Paris. Egypt and Israel are seeking a way to reopen the Suez Canal and stabilize the uneasy truce in the Near East. Four to six million Pakistani refugees are in camps in India plagued with an epidemic of cholera because of the civil war in their own country.

All these events will be history and will have contributed to your situation when you prepare for this lesson. As you catalogue what is happening in your world that seems to indicate a low estimate of the worth of human life, you will want to explore also the events that are rooted in a deep concern for the value of life. As you follow this discipline of thinking, you will likely discover the tension between those who are groping for ways to express a deep sense of the high value of persons and those whose actions stem from placing other values above human life.

Your study of the Scriptures interpreted by Dr. Frey will reveal this same struggle between those who are motivated to save life and those who are willing to kill. As long ago as three thousand years, when the Hebrew people summarized the laws they felt had come from God, they included a prohibition against killing. And yet, the whole Old Testament story reveals the fact that the people of God killed other peoples, even sometimes under the belief that they were commanded by God to do so.

But in the New Testament we have quite a different story. Jesus points not to the evil of killing but to the hate in the heart that leads to killing. James puts his finger on the desire for things that leads to fighting and taking and killing. John makes plain that love is the motive power that causes us to reverence life and to finally obey the rule against killing.

Presenting the Main Question

If you have made the kind of exploration suggested above and if the members of your group have done any thinking about the question during the week, together you might quickly bring the main question into focus. List on newsprint the happenings of the past week that give evidence to man's disregard for the sixth commandment. On another piece of newsprint list the events, attitudes, and actions that clearly indicate that many people, right now, are demonstrating their conviction that human life is sacred.

When the lists are completed, point out that in one way or another, consciously or unconsciously, each person is contributing to either the cheapening of life or the enriching of life. By his attitudes and actions he demonstrates his reverence or lack of reverence for life. So, like it or not, each class member is living out his answer to the question To what extent do I reverence human life? Therefore, the real question a committed Christian must ask is, In the light of my Christian experience and understanding of the gospel message, what must I do to make my reverence for life meet the demands and the expectations of Christ?

Developing the Lesson

Now that you have the lists on the newsprint, where do you go from this point? To continue talking about the current happenings may simply polarize the attitudes and judgments the members of the group already hold in reference to one or more of these events. Therefore, it would seem better to look for an objective set of values against which to judge the findings of the group in reference to their perception of the current happenings. A careful study of the Scripture and lesson exposition above will provide this kind of evaluation norm.

This exploration may take the following form. One work group of two or three persons might investigate how the sixth commandment became operative in the history of the Hebrew people. A beginning point would be an examination of the comparative or parallel Old Testament passages included in Dr. Frey's interpretation. In addition, use a biblical concordance to locate random passages listed under the word *kill*. The purpose of this examination would be to discover what exceptions to the sixth commandment the Hebrew people seem to have made in their history and in what ways their interpretation of the law against killing seemed to develop or change.

Another work group may explore the way in which Jesus reinterpreted the sixth commandment as revealed in Matthew 5:21-26. The objective of this study would be to determine the kind of normative standard Jesus would have us apply to our present world and community attitudes and events.

A third work group might study the James 4:1-2b reference. This group would likely have time to read the entire letter and Matthew 5 through 7 for comparative purposes. Point out that this group may discover the interrelatedness of the sixth and seventh commandments. Perhaps this group could suggest an approach to next Sunday's lesson.

A fourth work group could study Dr. Laymon's exposition above to discover points of agreement with his interpretation. They might apply his interpretations to the points in the opening listing of attitudes and actions related to reverence for life.

Time should be allotted for the work groups to share with the total group.

Helping Class Members Act

This lesson may lead to specific and corporate action. Here are some possible areas of action:

—support of pending legislation dealing with capital punishment

—identification of ways to enter into dialogue with members of a youth group to discover their sense of the value of human life

—support of specific legislation dealing with a move toward armament control or a peace settlement

—definition of attitudes toward the peacetime draft and alternate service to one's country.

Planning for Next Sunday

The work group on the study of the Letter of James may be asked to make this assignment. Or, you might suggest the group think about this question: What is the relation of our reverence for life to the injunction against adultery?

A Christian View of Sex

Background Scripture: Exodus 20:14; Matthew 5:27-32; John 8:3-11; Romans 1:24-32; 1 Corinthians 6:13b-20; Ephesians 5:21-32

The Main Question —Charles M. Laymon

At present the outlook on sex in America is undergoing significant changes. The lid has been taken off what has long been a hush-hush subject, and what traditionally had been regarded as perversion is now being considered as normal under certain circumstances. Churches have even sponsored dances for homosexuals.

A rash of X-rated movies has brought a new look at sex. What had been limited to the privacy of the bedroom is now openly spread across the movie screen. Fade-outs, which let the imagination of the viewer fill in the rest of the scene, have been supplanted by close-up views.

We also hear unusual suggestions regarding marriage. A three-year marriage vow has been urged. Even a clergyman in the Church of England has recommended the revival of a betrothal period similar to that in biblical days. This time is intended to be more intimate than the traditional engagement span. Persons of the same sex have actually taken marriage vows. Actors of fame have openly defended sexual relationships without marriage, claiming that only in such freedom can true love exist.

In this situation we must ask what Christian marriage means? Is it different from secular marriage? What is the Christian view of sex?

The biblical passages for this lesson suggest some significant answers.

As You Read the Scripture —George W. Frey

In comparison with other ancient Near Eastern codes of law the legal documents of the Old Testament give less space to problems of sex. Judging from the large number of regulations in the Babylonian, Assyrian, and Hittite law codes we may conclude that sex offenses were a real concern in these ancient cultures. While the Old Testament has fewer references to sex problems, there is unmistakable clarity about Israel's feelings in these matters. The seventh commandment is clear and to the point.

Exodus 20:14. *You shall not commit adultery:* The verb translated *commit adultery* carries the basic idea of mixing something base and impure with something holy and pure. The prophet Hosea, for example, uses the word to describe the adulteration of religious devotion by the practice of idolatry. (See Hosea 7:4.) The religious adulterer is unfaithful to God. Such spiritual adultery weakens, pollutes, corrupts, and ultimately brings ruin to persons and nations. Physical adultery has consequences no less serious and devastating than spiritual infidelity. This unholy practice can lead to broken lives, dashed hopes, and defeat.

In the seventh commandment the reference is to the act that violates the rights of womanhood, whether the woman is betrothed or married. In the Covenant Code found in Exodus 21 through 23 there is only one bit of legislation dealing directly with sexual perversion. (See Exodus 22:16-17.) But in Deuteronomy specific details are found for dealing with sex offenders. (See Deuteronomy 22:22-30.) Note in these regulations the protection given womanhood. Observe also that death by stoning is the penalty in some sex offenses. In the light of these laws we can understand the demand of the Pharisees who brought a woman "caught in adultery" to Jesus. (See John 8:1-11.)

WHAT DOES CHRISTIAN MARRIAGE MEAN? IS IT DIFFERENT FROM SECULAR MARRIAGE?

Sexual violation of womanhood brought down the wrath and judgment of the community. The incident of Amnon and Tamar illustrates the application of the moral law that was written deeply in the soul of Israel. (See 2 Samuel 13.)

Adultery involves ignoring human rights and privileges. Adulterous relations indicate lack of respect for human dignity and also the possessions of another. While a woman was not just a chattel, she was in a sense regarded as the possession or property of her husband. In the case of an unmarried girl she was the property of her father. Since property was so closely tied to the family, any violation by committing adultery against a woman became a complex offense against not only the woman but also her father or husband as the case might be. Thus committing adultery was intolerable in the community of the people of God.

Matthew 5:27-28. *Every one who looks at a woman lustfully has already committed adultery with her in his heart:* Jesus condemns both the inner disposition that leads to adultery and the act itself. This is another evidence of

Matthew's interest in Jesus' attitude toward the law of the Old Testament. He felt the continuing relevance of the Ten Commandments for the Christian community.

1 Corinthians 6:13b-20. *Do you not know that your bodies are members of Christ?* Paul's letters to the church at Corinth give us insight into the mind of this great apostle. In these letters Paul applies the gospel to the ethical and theological problems of the church at Corinth.

Corinth was a seaport located at a crossroads of world commerce. The city was open to all the vices introduced and supported by world traders. One of the problems that involved church life was sexual license. Some persons argued that sexual desire, like the desire for food, was legitimate. These verses contain Paul's reply. Observe two points: (1) The body has a higher purpose than for sex alone. The body is the dwelling place of Christ and part of Christ's own body. Sexual license renders the body unfit for the divine purpose. (2) Sex is a unifying experience between two persons. Sex compliments and completes. Promiscuity defiles the human body and violates personality. Therefore Paul advises his readers to "shun immorality." (See verse 18.)

Selected Scripture

King James Version

Exodus 20:14

14 Thou shalt not commit adultery.

Matthew 5:27-28

27 Ye have heard that it was said by them of old time, Thou shalt not commit adultery:

28 But I say unto you, That whosoever looketh on a woman to lust after her hath committed adultery with her already in his heart.

1 Corinthians 6:13b-20

13b Now the body is not for fornication, but for the Lord; and the Lord for the body.

14 And God hath both raised up the Lord, and will also raise up us by his own power.

15 Know ye not that your bodies are the members of Christ? shall I then take the members of Christ, and make them the members of an harlot? God forbid.

16 What? know ye not that he which is joined to an harlot is one

Revised Standard Version

Exodus 20:14

14 "You shall not commit adultery."

Matthew 5:27-28

27 "You have heard that it was said, 'You shall not commit adultery.' 28 But I say to you that every one who looks at a woman lustfully has already committed adultery with her in his heart."

1 Corinthians 6:13b-20

13b The body is not meant for immorality, but for the Lord, and the Lord for the body. 14 And God raised the Lord and will also raise us up by his power. 15 Do you not know that your bodies are members of Christ? Shall I therefore take the members of Christ and make them members of a prostitute? Never! 16 Do you not know that he who joins himself to a prostitute becomes one body with her? For, as it is written, "The two shall become one." 17 But he who is united body? for two, saith he, shall be one flesh.

17 But he that is joined unto the Lord is one spirit.

18 Flee fornication. Every sin that a man doeth is without the body; but he that committeth fornication sinneth against his own body.

19 What? know ye not that your body is the temple of the Holy Ghost which is in you, which ye have of God, and ye are not your own?

20 For ye are bought with a price: therefore glorify God in your body, and in your spirit, which are God's.

Memory Selection: Know ye not that your body is the temple of the Holy Ghost which is in you, which ye have of God, and ye are not your own? For ye are bought with a price: therefore glorify God in your body. (1 Corinthians 6:19-20)

to the Lord becomes one spirit with him. 18 Shun immorality. Every other sin which a man commits is outside the body; but the immoral man sins against his own body. 19 Do you not know that your body is a temple of the Holy Spirit within you, which you have from God? You are not your own; 20 you were bought with a price. So glorify God in your body.

Memory Selection: Do you not know that your body is a temple of the Holy Spirit within you, which you have from God? You are not your own; you were bought with a price. So glorify God in your body. (1 Corinthians 6:19-20)

The Scripture and the Main Question —Charles M. Laymon

RESPECT THE MARRIAGE VOW

The commandment against committing adultery (Exodus 20:14) is sometimes not fully understood. The commandment does not refer to premarital sex but to the violation of a marriage by a third party. This does not mean that premarital sex is not a sin. Not at all. What is at stake here is the preservation of the sanctity of the home. We are commanded to respect marriage vows, our own and others'.

A Christian marriage has certain particular characteristics that distinguish it from marriage in general. J. A. Davidson has defined it in these words: "A Christian marriage is in the lifelong commitment of a man and a woman to each other. It is a commitment established in authentic love and kept lively by that love. It is a commitment nourished by the devo-

tions and disciplines of Christian faith. This commitment is the cost of Christian marriage. It is worth it!" [6]

If a marriage is Christian in this sense, it is almost immune to invasion from without. A marriage does not, however, remain Christian unless the husband and wife work at it. Christian ideals must be kept in mind. Christian deeds of kindness need to be carried out within the home. Respect for each other in the Christian sense must be genuine. Forgiveness must always be a real option between the married partners. This plan should include the children that are born into such a home as well.

THE DESIRE OR THE DEED

Just as Jesus internalized the commandment against killing, he also

[6] "The Cost of Christian Marriage," *Together*, October, 1968, p. 31.

stressed the inwardness of unclean acts. Such acts begin in the lustful heart. As he said, "Every one who looks at a woman lustfully has already committed adultery with her in his heart." (Matthew 5:28)

What is meant by such lustful desires? We do possess basic sex drives that result in suggestions in the mind. But we do not need to follow raw instincts without considering the outcome. They can be modified by Christian ideals and conditioned by Christian love. What we think in regard to sex can have a great effect on what we feel in relation to sex. We are intelligent persons who need not be at the mercy of instinctive drives.

Ted McIlvenna is a specialist in the area of human sexuality. He has stated that three factors determine whether one's sexual adjustment is good or bad: " (1) how a person feels about his own body, sexual desires, and fantasies; (2) how he feels about others in this respect; and (3) his world view—whether he sees sex as good or bad." [7] Each of these is an inward matter and reminds us of Jesus' similar emphasis.

Mr. McIlvenna also commented, "These are all theological issues, . . . yet the church is terribly frightened of them." [8] Does the church have a stake here? Who is in a position to present adequately the involvement of sex with *the whole person*—physical, moral, and spiritual—except the church? Who else is doing it? the schools? the doctors? the lawyers? the courts? the parents?

UNIONS THAT DEGRADE

We cannot understand Paul's words on sexual relations in this lesson unless we begin where he begins: "Do

[7] Quoted by Linda Peak, *Christian Advocate*, January 7, 1971, p. 20.
[8] *Ibid.*

you not know that your bodies are members of Christ?" (1 Corinthians 6:15a) For him, the indwelling of Christ in the life of a Christian makes even his body something that is more than physical. What he does, therefore, with his body is a spiritual matter.

Sexual relations that are for physical satisfaction only, particularly those outside marriage, deny a person's nature in Christ. For this reason the apostle could write, "Shall I therefore take the members of Christ and make them members of a prostitute?" (verse 15b) Then he adds, "Do you not know that he who joins himself to a prostitute becomes one body with her?" (verse 16) Such a union is degrading.

Sexual union apart from love in the Christian sense is an expression of physical instinct only. It makes one less than he is in Christ. This type of union can occur in the home itself as well as in extramarital relations. A legal marriage does not, because it is legal, lift one's sights to the Christian view of sex. One has only to read the letters addressed to Ann Landers and other "advice" columnists to realize that there are sexual unions between married partners that are not on a Christian level.

Lack of Christian love and respect in the home is sometimes the cause of divorce. Elizabeth Ogg, in her book *Divorce,* says, "Some marriages are so destructive that they ought to be ended in the interests of all concerned." Do you agree?

UNIONS THAT ENRICH

A woman was being congratulated on her twenty-fifth wedding anniversary for living so long with the same man. She replied, "But he is not the same man he was when I first got hold of him." This is a humorous retort, but beneath it lies a great truth.

Neither was the woman the same woman she was when they were married. Their union in marriage had enriched the lives of each of them. Paul was not against all sexual relationships. He was certain that some unions degraded the persons involved but that other unions enriched life. Therefore he could say, "Glorify God in your body." (1 Corinthians 6:20) Sex to him was not in itself sinful.

It has been noted that there is a strong correlation between church participation and happy marriages. Divorces do occur between church members; this is undeniable. But the chances for divorce are less when the husband and wife are a part of the life of the church. Is not this because the Christian ideals for marriage relationships have made a difference in their lives?

Helping Adults Become Involved —Howard E. Tower

Preparation of Self and Class

If the work group of last session developed a plan for the consideration of the seventh commandment, their suggestion should be the starting point of your preparation. Whether the assignment for the group preparation came from them or from yourself, you may find the following suggestions helpful as you prepare to lead the group to come to grips with the issue of a Christian view of sex.

The Scripture interpretation by Dr. Frey should prove quite helpful. As you read his suggestions and seek to carry them out, consider your exploration in the light of this question: What basic attitude toward sex as a part of human experience does this commandment reveal?

Likewise, Dr. Laymon's exposition of the lesson hinges upon his attempt to look beneath the written word for the inner meaning. His search uncovers, not only the meaning implied in relationship to the time the Scripture was written, but also especially the meaning implied for today. Two questions may well be kept in mind as you examine Dr. Laymon's exposition: Do you agree with his application of the Scripture to today's situation? Do you feel Dr. Laymon makes

a complete and accurate reflection of present-day sexual attitudes and practices? What would you add or take away?

To help you deal with these last questions current sex views as portrayed in the movies and on the television screen will be a good resource. As you watch for these attitudes and practices, you will need to check them against your own experience and your knowledge of what is happening in the lives of your friends and acquaintances. It is even more urgent for you to think about what you either know, or feel you need to know, about the attitudes and practices of members of your own group.

If you have already viewed the film *From Generation to Generation,* you might recall how it deals with reverence for life as an important contribution to our sexual attitudes and practices. Two other films will be worth your reviewing: *Have I Told You Lately That I Love You?* and *The Social and Sex Attitudes of Adolescence.* (See pages 337-38.) You may be able to view one of these films at your public library. It is impossible, without knowing the nature of your group or the time available to you, to suggest how you might use films such as these during the class period. Remember, however, that sometimes a very small segment of a film can be used to focus the thinking of your group.

Presenting the Main Question

Again, if the work group last Sunday thought through and made the suggestions for the group preparation for considering this important and personal issue, you may also ask this same group to bring into focus the main question for the entire group. If this approach is taken, you, as leader, should be ready to let the group members suggest a different or modified main question for the lesson. For example, here are some restatements of the main question that might emerge: What view of the place of sex in American life is reflected in current entertainment films and television programs? How does this view, or views, differ from the biblical view? What are the new views of sex held by the younger generation? How different are these views from those held by the older generation? Is their sexual practice just more open, or is there a basic change? How do we as a group feel and think about the role of sex in our experience? What disappointments have we faced? What truths have we come upon? Do we need a norm? Can the Scriptures guide us in finding a basis for judging the healthy role of sex in our experience?

If you are taking the responsibility for introducing and making real the main question as stated by Dr. Laymon—What is the Christian view of sex?—you will need to consider how important this question is to your group. One way of doing this would be to make a two- or three-minute summary of the biblical view of the place of sex in human experience, beginning with the seventh commandment, developing Jesus' interpretation of this commandment, and concluding with Paul's concept of the human body as the temple of God. When you have completed this presentation, you might conclude with these questions: Have I rightly interpreted the Christian view of sex as you understand it? And if so, how relevant for life today do you feel this interpretation to be?

Developing the Lesson

If yours is a small group that has developed a high degree of trust, you can move from this question, or one similar to it, to a period of personal sharing. You would, of course, get a more open response if you, as leader, could share quite personally the role that physical sex has played in your life, some of the disappointments you have experienced, or ways in which your total human experience has been enriched through sexual fulfillment. Or perhaps you can begin by sharing some honest questions you have about views of sex that you have taken for granted. Or perhaps you would want to share a concern or doubt about the way in which you have interpreted to your children the role of sex in life. Whatever the sharing, it should be brief, honest, warm, and open. If you achieve this objective, others will feel free to follow; and soon you will be in the middle of an exploration of the deeper meanings of sex that are implied in the Scripture passages under study.

If this does not seem a possible approach, the following instrument might be used. Ask each class member to select the statement or statements that best reflect his experience. Then gather the questionnaires and discuss the most-selected items with the group.

1. For me the main purpose of sex-

ual relations in marriage has been the procreation of our children.

2. The sex act makes possible the fullest sense of being one with my mate and has given joy and purpose to our life together.

3. I know that the physical act of sex should enrich my whole life, but it seldom has.

4. I find talking about the experience of sex embarrassing, even with my wife or husband.

5. I sincerely hope my children find the joy of marriage that we have experienced, but I am very fearful for them.

Helping Class Members Act

Of course, first of all, the most significant action after this lesson may be a personal resolve or a decision on the part of a couple to ask for and receive counseling from the minister or another competent counselor or to be more open about sex with teen-age members of the family.

On the other hand, there may be some corporate action the group should undertake, such as monitoring television programs and films to identify attitudes toward the role of sex in human experience, organizing an intergenerational study group to explore the meaning of sex in the Christian life, or initiating action to discover what is being taught about sex in the public schools.

Planning for Next Sunday

Call attention to the fact that next Sunday you are to explore the present-day significance of the command "You shall not steal." Let the group ponder these questions: How much is included in the eighth commandment? Does stealing only mean taking something tangible that does not belong to us?

An Owner's Rights and Responsibilities

Background Scripture: Exodus 20:15; 1 Kings 21:1-9; Amos 8:4-6; Mark 12:41-44; Luke 19:1-10; Ephesians 4:28; James 2:14-17

The Main Question —Charles M. Laymon

Every now and again the question of private versus public ownership hits the front page of the daily papers. In any given year it is certain to be discussed a number of times in the editorial section. The following examples are typical: (1) The question of the rights of private interests to drill for oil offshore in Texas or California is a perennial one. Is this public or private land? Who should share in the returns? Who owns the oil under the ocean bed? (2) The question of access to shoreline beaches is an important one in a state like Florida. The law holds that public access should be available; but hotel after hotel has lined the sandy strips, and only patrons are permitted to bathe. (3) In a more personal sense, what rights to ownership does the deed to my home or farm give me? When the state wishes to run a road through my property, how long can I hold out if I desire to? And how does the state determine what is a fair value if they condemn the needed area in order to purchase it from me for public use? (4) At the heart of the debate between communism and capitalism is the issue of property ownership. Wide acres of land in Russia have been taken over by the state; and communes have been established where, theoretically, each worker owns all. But no one can make a private profit. In some cases, however, Russia has had to make room for private ownership and some profit during recent years. Why?

The subject of this lesson states the question at issue. Under God what are an owner's rights and responsibilities?

The biblical material to be studied contains some significant answers.

As You Read the Scripture —George W. Frey

Possession of land, cattle, work animals, slaves, and the like was an inherent right of a person in Old Testament times. Stealing was prohibited and penalties assessed. The eighth commandment speaks to the problem of stealing.

Exodus 20:15. *You shall not steal:* Three observations should be kept in mind as we interpret this commandment: (1) Hebrew society was much less complex than modern society. Social structures in Palestine were even less complicated than those of the Babylonians, Assyrians, or Hittites. The Code of Hammurabi, dated around the eighteenth century b.c., reveals a complex social structure. This ancient law code goes to great lengths to detail the laws and penalties for stealing. In contrast Hebrew life was more simple. Property consisted mainly of cattle, slaves, clothing, and a few agricultural tools. Later, land was added to this list. The kind of problems stealing introduced may be observed by reading Exodus 22:1, 7-8. (2) Accusations of stealing were quite uncomplicated. In a seminomadic, simple kind of pastoral life everyone knew what theft involved. Very little could be hid from a neighbor's view in this kind of society. (3) All property was closely related to the family and was preserved by the family and passed on from father to sons. A person's property was part of his personhood. It was tied to his bloodstream so to speak. Hence stealing in the Old Testament is an infringement on family rights.

Amos 8:4-6. *Hear this, you who . . . deal deceitfully with false balances:* Amos appeared like a "bolt from the blue" on Israel's fast moving scene around 750 b.c. His was an affluent society. The rich were getting richer and the poor poorer. Both groups were increasing in numbers. Amos was able to see to the core of society, and he saw its corruption. He became a champion for social justice, human rights, and absolute honesty in business and worship. This passage paints the picture vividly. The rich were taking advantage of the poor. Business practices were dishonest. Greed and selfishness ruled, and human relations suffered. Some persons could not wait until the Sabbath was over to continue their dishonest selling. Amos condemns this highhanded method of stealing and pronounces the judgment of God on Israel.

Luke 19:1-10. *For the Son of man came to seek and to save the lost:* Luke alone records the meeting of Jesus and Zacchaeus. Little is known about this man. He was a collector of taxes for the district around Jericho. This town was at the crossroads of commercial travel in the Jordan valley and was in the center of a very lush and fertile agricultural area. It is therefore likely that his position enabled Zacchaeus to amass considerable wealth. Verse 8 suggests he was a man of means.

The statement "if I have defrauded any one of anything" does not necessarily imply that Zacchaeus was dishonest. It may well be a testimony to the depth of his character and an indication that he wanted "to come clean." Jesus was impressed by a man who by profession was not popular. Collecting taxes is never a popular profession and especially when the tax is for a nation whose troops occupy one's homeland.

Luke's description of the incident is picturesque. Zacchaeus was a short fellow, but no physical handicap was going to prevent him from seeing Jesus. He climbed a sycamore tree. Note the sensitivity of Jesus. There was eyeball-to-eyeball contact. Zacchaeus lost no time in opening his home to Jesus. Luke tells us he received Jesus joyfully (verse 6). Note also the reaction of the crowd, "He has gone in to be the guest of a man who is a sinner." (verse 7) Jesus frequently broke the socially accepted customs of his day. He was more interested in helping persons than in being socially correct.

Zacchaeus quickly got to the point. If he had a streak of dishonesty in him, he was willing to make restitution. Restoring the stolen property was a basic principle in punishing a thief, and Zacchaeus offered more than the law required.

Selected Scripture

King James Version	Revised Standard Version
Exodus 20:15	*Exodus 20:15*
15 Thou shalt not steal.	15 "You shall not steal."
Amos 8:4-6	*Amos 8:4-6*
4 Hear this, O ye that swallow up the needy, even to make the poor of the land to fail,	4 Hear this, you who trample upon the needy, and bring the poor of the land to an end,
5 Saying, When will the new moon be gone, that we may sell corn? and the sabbath, that we may set forth wheat, making the ephah small, and the shekel great, and falsifying the balances by deceit?	5 saying, "When will the new moon be over, that we may sell grain? And the sabbath, that we may offer wheat for sale, that we may make the ephah small and the shekel great, and deal deceitfully with false balances,
6 That we may buy the poor for silver, and the needy for a pair of shoes; yea, and sell the refuse of the wheat?	6 that we may buy the poor for silver and the needy for a pair of sandals, and sell the refuse of the wheat?"

Luke 19:1-10

1 And Jesus entered and passed through Jericho.

2 And, behold, there was a man named Zacchaeus, which was the chief among the publicans, and he was rich.

3 And he sought to see Jesus who he was; and could not for the press, because he was little of stature.

4 And he ran before, and climbed up into a sycamore tree to see him: for he was to pass that way.

5 And when Jesus came to the place, he looked up, and saw him, and said unto him, Zacchaeus, make haste, and come down; for to-day I must abide at thy house.

6 And he made haste, and came down, and received him joyfully.

7 And when they saw it, they all murmured, saying, That he was gone to be guest with a man that is a sinner.

8 And Zacchaeus stood, and said unto the Lord; Behold, Lord, the half of my goods I give to the poor; and if I have taken any thing from any man by false accusation, I restore him fourfold.

9 And Jesus said unto him, This day is salvation come to this house, forsomuch as he also is a son of Abraham.

10 For the Son of man is come to seek and to save that which was lost.

Memory Selection: Let him that stole steal no more: but rather let him labour, working with his hands the thing which is good, that he may have to give to him that needeth. (Ephesians 4:28)

Luke 19:1-10

1 He entered Jericho and was passing through. 2 And there was a man named Zacchaeus; he was a chief tax collector, and rich. 3 And he sought to see who Jesus was, but could not, on account of the crowd, because he was small of stature. 4 So he ran on ahead and climbed up into a sycamore tree to see him, for he was to pass that way. 5 And when Jesus came to the place, he looked up and said to him, "Zacchaeus, make haste and come down; for I must stay at your house today." 6 So he made haste and came down, and received him joyfully. 7 And when they saw it they all murmured, "He has gone in to be the guest of a man who is a sinner." 8 And Zacchaeus stood and said to the Lord, "Behold, Lord, the half of my goods I give to the poor; and if I have defrauded any one of anything, I restore it fourfold." 9 And Jesus said to him, "Today salvation has come to this house, since he also is a son of Abraham. 10 For the Son of man came to seek and to save the lost."

Memory Selection: Let the thief no longer steal, but rather let him labor, doing honest work with his hands, so that he may be able to give to those in need. (Ephesians 4:28)

The Scripture and the Main Question —Charles M. Laymon

THE RIGHT AND FACT OF OWNERSHIP

When the commandment states, "You shall not steal" (Exodus 20:15),

it asserts the right of private ownership by man or men in society. The Bible bears this principle out in the various punishments it prescribes for those who steal. (See Exodus 22:1-8.)

This right of ownership is as sacred for the rich as it is for the poor. Deny the right to the affluent, and you have also taken it away from those who have little or no wealth at all. Abraham Lincoln, who came out of poverty, said, "That some should be rich shows that others may become rich." He then urged the homeless not to pull down the house of another but to "work diligently and build one for himself."

The main thrust of this lesson is not against the right of ownership. It assumes that there are both the "have-nots" and the "haves." This is realistic. Commenting upon a remark by G. K. Chesterton that he saw no reason to honor a man who at a certain point had cornered the market on soybeans, William F. Buckley, Jr., said, "On the other hand, there isn't any reason to disdain the particular skill and daring it takes to corner the soybean market."

Since ownership of this sort is a fact and will likely continue to be for a long time to come, we should seek deeper and related aspects of the subject. The right and the fact of possession are not the heart of the matter. The how, why, and to what end of ownership should be our major Christian concerns.

The Accumulation of Property

If we conclude that the ownership of property is a Christian's right and privilege, then there are certain questions that should be asked in order to face the issue responsibly. One of them is, How did I accumulate my property?

For most persons this is simply a matter of purchase. A price was asked; an offer to buy followed. Then there possibly was a counter offer followed by an agreement between the purchaser and the seller. Monies and a deed were exchanged, and the new ownership was recorded at the courthouse.

Inheritance is another way by which we come to own property. War often enlarges national holdings. And then there is theft, which the commandment condemns as a way of obtaining property.

Usually we think of housebreaking and safecracking as ways of stealing, but there are many ways to steal that are more subtle and hidden. Amos spoke of those who made "the ephah small and the shekel great" and who dealt "deceitfully with false balances." (8:5) The merchants sold with a substandard measure and bought with an overly heavy weight, which on a balance scale gave them the advantage. Note how our scales are required by law to be checked periodically, and packaged goods are examined to see if they meet the printed specifications.

More dramatic, modern methods of stealing are the "conflict of interest" situations where individuals in government use privileged information to guide them in purchasing land intended for national projects or to buy stock in industries that are slated to receive federal contracts. Putting stones in the beans and too much cereal in the dog food are as nothing compared to these more sophisticated means of thieving.

Responsibilities of Ownership

Ownership involves responsibility; it is as simple and direct as this. As soon as Zacchaeus—who must have been quite wealthy because he was "a chief tax collector, and rich"— came to grips with Jesus, he decided that he must restore four times over what he had defrauded. In addition, he gave half of what he owned to the poor (Luke 19:8).

The Jewish law required a repayment of four sheep for the theft of one (Exodus 22:1). Roman law also stipulated a fourfold restitution. Zacchaeus volunteered to go beyond this, however, by offering to give half his goods to the poor. It was this "free will" determination that marked the change in his life.

Being responsible in ownership becomes a religious concern for the Christian. He recognizes, first of all, that the earth is the Lord's. Whatever portion of its goods he has accumulated is a trust and a responsibility. J. C. Penney, who founded the Penney Stores System, felt this way about his wealth. When he died a few years ago, the press gave more space to the good he had done with his money than to the extent of his holdings.

Much has been written concerning the Rockefeller wealth and the way it was originally gained. But the descendants of John D. Rockefeller sought to handle their money responsibly. The great Rockefeller Foundation has spent millions upon millions of dollars for the public good. It sounds like the Zacchaeus story all over again.

THE JOYFUL USE OF EARTHLY GOODS

The responsibility of ownership at times weighs heavily upon those who possess much of this world's goods. They are set upon and plagued by those who solicit great gifts. Everyone has an idea as to how they can best spend their money. If these persons are Christian in their attitudes, they wish to give the money where it will do the most for the Kingdom. Deciding how to do this often keeps them awake throughout the night. But money can also be a great joy. What a privilege to be able to see wonderful projects in art, music, learning, and science begun and carried out through public gifts that one can make.

Most of us do not have to lie awake at night as we wrestle with the best way to share our wealth, for the simple reason that we have so little. Yet the responsibility and the joy of spending, giving, and sharing the small amounts that we have are ours just as much as if the total were large. Do you not think that the widow pondered long over how and where she would give her mite? How happy she would be to know that she made the right decision and has been an inspiration to many through the centuries.

Helping Adults Become Involved —Howard E. Tower

Preparation of Self and Class

The eighth commandment, like the seventh and the sixth, is concise and uncomplicated: "You shall not steal." (Exodus 20:15) Yet the theme suggested for today's study, "An Owner's Rights and Responsibilities," is less simple. It certainly implies more than refraining from seizing what belongs to another. So, also, the main question as Dr. Laymon states it and the questions you may have suggested to your class last Sunday imply a broader base of concern.

As you prepare to help the members of your class deal with the implications of the eighth commandment it will be helpful to remember that all the commandments grew out of the experience of a society that was less complicated than ours. Yet each commandment deals with a reality that is so basic to humanity that it has meaning for us in our greatly changed and changing circumstances.

No doubt you have identified the pattern of treatment that has been followed in the development of all the lessons in this unit of study. First the commandment is presented as it appears in Exodus 20. An interpretation of its impact for the experience of the Hebrew people in their early history is given. Next some further Old Testament reference is given, which shows how the meaning of the commandment developed and changed with the growing religious experience and understanding of the people of God. Then a Gospel or other New Testament reference is presented to add a dimension that is a contribution of the early Christians' understanding of the commandment. Finally, our present-day experience is examined in the light of this total biblical interpretation. Today's lesson will come into sharper focus if you examine the Scriptures in terms of this formula of approach.

The viewing of one or more of these films will illustrate the complexity of ownership and the ways of stealing today: *None of My Business, Mr. Grey,* and *The Trap of Solid Gold.* (See pages 337-38.)

Presenting the Main Question

You might introduce the main question by asking the group members to respond in turn to the question What do you think is an example of stealing today? As members of the group give their responses, list them on the chalkboard or newsprint. This listing should make clear that stealing today is much more complicated than making off with another's sheep or donkey. Let the class think about their listing. What do the various examples seem to have in common? The desire for things? A person's right to possessions? What?

Developing the Lesson

Today's lesson may be developed either by beginning with an analysis of present-day attitudes toward property and ownership or by an examination of the background Scripture.

If you elect to begin with a study of today's attitudes and practices, the following questions may be stimulating either for working as a total group or for assignment to work groups.

1. What examples of public ownership can you think of and describe?

2. Is there a difference in our attitude toward stealing from the public and stealing from individuals?

3. What subtle forms of stealing are practiced in the way we make out tax returns, the kinds of claims we make to insurance companies, and the travel expense reports we make to our employers?

4. What attitude toward ownership is evidenced by the way we do our jobs?

5. Is depriving the poor or the black man of equal opportunity to learn skills a form of stealing?

6. What are the basic differences in the view of ownership in a socialistic, a communistic, and a capitalistic society? Is there anywhere, today, a pure example of any one of these societies?

However the class deals with these or other questions they may raise, the exploration should lead to a consideration of the questions: What is the basis of ownership, private or public? How does our biblical faith help us answer this question?

The following approach to an exploration of the biblical resources may prove helpful whether the lesson begins with an exploration of the biblical view of property or the biblical study follows the exploration of present-day issues described above.

Three exploration groups may be formed. The first work group should examine the Exodus statement of the eighth commandment, giving attention to the problems related to this commandment as suggested in Exodus 22:1, 7-8. Here are some questions this group may confront:

1. What kind of experience in the life of a seminomadic society gave rise to this commandment?

2. What does Exodus 22:1 suggest concerning the seriousness with which this early society considered the act of stealing?

3. This commandment implies certain rights of ownership, but does it imply any corresponding responsibilities that go with those rights?

The second work group will examine Amos 8:4-6. Their study may be guided by questions such as these:

1. What changes had taken place in Hebrew society since the days of the Exodus commandment?

2. What forms of stealing are implied by Amos?

3. What responsibility does Amos suggest concerning the way in which a person acquires and handles property?

4. What emerging concepts of the place of ownership seem to be implied by Amos' denunciation of the rich?

The third work group will deal with Luke 19:1-10 and will confront questions like these:

1. What Old Testament concepts appear in this story about the responsibility that falls upon the person who defrauds another?

2. What new ways of stealing does the story suggest?

3. How has the social structure changed since Amos' day?

4. What do taxation and tax collection suggest about rights and responsibilities of ownership?

These three groups should be ready to report to the total group what they consider to be the message of their particular passage. When these biblical interpretations are shared, the final question should be: What do these passages say to us about the rights and responsibilities of Christian ownership today?

Helping Class Members Act

This study, if it has been effective, should lead each person to examine his own attitudes toward property—his honesty in dealing with the property he has personally and his attitude toward the property he shares in his participation in public ownership.

On the other hand, since most adult church school classes are apt to be more on the "have" side in our society than in the "have not" group, perhaps the class members will decide to help a particular person or group of persons move from the "have not" into the "have" group. Of course, such a project would require careful study prior to any specific action.

Planning for Next Sunday

Next Sunday's lesson confronts the ninth commandment: "You shall not bear false witness." Suggest the following think questions for this week:

1. What is the place of truth in advertising?

2. In what ways can truth be supported in our schools?

3. What is the role of truth in government?

Live the Truth

Background Scripture: Exodus 20:16; 23:1-3;
Proverbs 19:9; Acts 5:1-11; Ephesians 4:25-32; James 1:26; 3:1-12

The Main Question —Charles M. Laymon

In a college class studying Christian ethics the question arose as to whether it was Christian to ask a witness in a court trial to take the customary oath: "I promise to tell the truth, the whole truth, and nothing but the truth, so help me God."

One student said, "Of course it is Christian. Didn't the Ten Commandments say that we should not bear false witness?" Another countered with the remark "But didn't Jesus tell us not to swear at all? Didn't he teach that saying 'Yes' or 'No' was sufficient?"

At this point a heated discussion of truth versus untruth broke loose: What is truth anyway? Should one tell the truth if it hurts others? Is it always best for doctors to tell their patients the truth? Are lies sometimes justified? Are we lying if we keep silent when we should speak out? What about living a lie? Should the government always tell the truth in wartime?

The scriptural background for this lesson will be helpful in answering these questions.

As You Read the Scripture —George W. Frey

The effectiveness of any judicial system depends on the integrity of witnesses. Justice is established and maintained in the community only when witnesses tell the truth. The ninth commandment seeks to safeguard the process of justice so essential to the peace of the community.

Exodus 20:16. *You shall not bear false witness against your neighbor:* The verb translated *bear* may also be translated "answer" or "speak." The *neighbor* of the text may be a near one (that is, really a neighbor) or a friend. Loyalty to the God of the covenant requires that no one in the community speak a word of falsehood against another.

In Hebrew thought the relation of the spoken word to the person speaking is important. The spoken word reveals what a person really is. A word spoken carries with it something of the one who voiced that word. It becomes a living thing and an important force in person to person relations. The kind words of a person can bless, heal, and build relations. Words of slander or cursing hurt, destroy, and break human relations. Thus perjury or false witness betrays lack of inner integrity on the part of the spokesman and, at the same time, brings hurt to others.

The role of witnesses in the administration of justice in ancient Israel is carefully outlined in Deuteronomy 17:6-7; 19:15-19. Serious efforts were made to reduce perjury to a minimum.

Acts 5:1-11. *You have not lied to men but to God:* Here is a transcript

401

from a page in the life of the early church. It is the biography of two persons who thought they could live on deceit. Note the story of Ananias in contrast to that of Barnabas narrated in Acts 4:36-37. The giving of Barnabas is an illustration of voluntary sharing, while the giving of Ananias is an example of deceitful sharing. Ananias did do one noble thing; he told his wife. And she consorted in the project of deceit. His pretension of giving all proved his undoing. Neither he nor his wife was required to give all, but the deceit of pretending to proved too much. Guilt settled in upon them. Peter had a way of probing the soul. In true Old Testament fashion he said, "*You have not lied to men but to God.*" This was too much for Ananias and Sapphira. Both were destroyed by the process of deceit—a process of their own making.

This is a sobering story, to say the least. Ananias and Sapphira were respectable people. They were not guilty of murder, only of fraud or deceit. They falsified their financial situation. They lied. Yet their lack of integrity led to their deaths and a shattered community. The ninth commandment cautions against false witness against one's neighbor. The story of Ananias and Sapphira cautions against attempts to deal falsely with one's selfhood.

Ephesians 4:25. *Let every one speak the truth with his neighbor:* The contents of the Letter to the Ephesians are divided into two parts: (1) doctrinal, which deals with the purpose of the church in the world, and (2) ethical, which deals with practical matters. Here the readers are told how they ought to live as members of the church of Christ.

Verse 25 is the key to this section. This verse may have been influenced by a passage in Zechariah (8:16-17), where the ancient prophet presents a portrait of life in the ideal Jerusalem. Note, in passing, that the prophet indicates the importance of the role of truthful speech in the establishing of justice and peace in the community.

The writer of Ephesians seems to echo the idea of the corporateness of human life: "For we are members one of another." No person is an island. Every aspect of a person's existence is relational. His manner of living and speaking affects all others, either for good or ill.

This section of the letter (verses 26-32) concludes with words of caution about evil talk, falsehood, slander, malice, and the like. These things are evidences of sick persons, and their thoughts and words find no helpful place in community. True and faithful thoughts and speech open the way for Christian community and the kingdom of God.

Selected Scripture

King James Version	Revised Standard Version
Exodus 20:16	*Exodus 20:16*
16 Thou shalt not bear false witness against thy neighbour.	16 "You shall not bear false witness against your neighbor."
Acts 5:1-11	*Acts 5:1-11*
1 But a certain man named Ananias, with Sapphira his wife, sold a possession,	1 But a man named Ananias with his wife Sapphira sold a piece of property, 2 and with his wife's knowl-

2 And kept back part of the price, his wife also being privy to it, and brought a certain part, and laid it at the apostles' feet.

3 But Peter said, Ananias, why hath Satan filled thine heart to lie to the Holy Ghost, and to keep back part of the price of the land?

4 Whiles it remained, was it not thine own? and after it was sold, was it not in thine own power? why hast thou conceived this thing in thine heart? thou hast not lied unto men, but unto God.

5 And Ananias hearing these words fell down, and gave up the ghost: and great fear came on all them that heard these things.

6 And the young men arose, wound him up, and carried him out, and buried him.

7 And it was about the space of three hours after, when his wife, not knowing what was done, came in.

8 And Peter answered unto her, Tell me whether ye sold the land for so much? And she said, Yea, for so much.

9 Then Peter said unto her, How is it that ye have agreed together to tempt the Spirit of the Lord? behold, the feet of them which have buried thy husband are at the door, and shall carry thee out.

10 Then fell she down straightway at his feet, and yielded up the ghost: and the young men came in, and found her dead, and, carrying her forth, buried her by her husband.

11 And great fear came upon all the church, and upon as many as heard these things.

Ephesians 4:25

25 Wherefore putting away lying, speak every man truth with his neighbour: for we are members one of another.

edge he kept back some of the proceeds, and brought only a part and laid it at the apostles' feet. 3 But Peter said, "Ananias, why has Satan filled your heart to lie to the Holy Spirit and to keep back part of the proceeds of the land? 4 While it remained unsold, did it not remain your own? After it was sold, was it not at your disposal? How is it that you have contrived this deed in your heart? You have not lied to men but to God." 5 When Ananias heard these words, he fell down and died. And great fear came upon all who heard of it. 6 The young men rose and wrapped him up and carried him out and buried him.

7 After an interval of about three hours his wife came in, not knowing what had happened. 8 And Peter said to her, "Tell me whether you sold the land for so much." And she said, "Yes, for so much." 9 But Peter said to her, "How is it that you have agreed together to tempt the Spirit of the Lord? Hark, the feet of those that have buried your husband are at the door, and they will carry you out." 10 Immediately she fell down at his feet and died. When the young men came in they found her dead, and they carried her out and buried her beside her husband. 11 And great fear came upon the whole church, and upon all who heard of these things.

Ephesians 4:25

25 Therefore, putting away falsehood, let every one speak the truth with his neighbor, for we are members one of another.

Memory Selection: **Thou shalt not bear false witness against thy neighbour. (Exodus 20:16)**

Memory Selection: **You shall not bear false witness against your neighbor. (Exodus 20:16)**

The Scripture and the Main Question —Charles M. Laymon

WHAT IS TRUTH?

We use the word *truth* in a number of ways. What immediately comes to mind when we hear the word is the correspondence between what is said and the facts in the case. This is probably what the commandment "You shall not bear false witness against your neighbor" had in mind (Exodus 20:16). In a lawsuit, where testimony was given, "tell it like it is" was the divine requirement.

A young man was filling out a report on his summer's military experience. He was asked whether his drill sergeant had ever abused the men physically. Although he had been warned to play it safe and say nothing, he told the truth. The men had been subject to mistreatment, and he said so. Investigation led to the dismissal of the sergeant. The young man, who was subjected to considerable suffering during the investigations, said to his parents, "I answered almost by impulse. It was my bringing up at home and the influence of the church school that moved my pen to write the true answer."

Behind telling the truth we must have a sincere, unbiased, and open-minded commitment to a certain way of life. If not, we will shilly-shally because of the pressure upon us. We must live the truth day by day. Only then will bearing true witness become habitual and automatic.

THE TRUTH AND GOD

A number of persons have a stake in whether we live the truth day by day. God, ourselves, and others are involved. We cannot fail to consider the place each has. Take God, for instance. In the account of Ananias and Sapphira, Peter tells Ananias when he misrepresents the amount he has given to the common fund of the Christian community: "You have not lied to men but to God." (Acts 5:4)

Doris Forman helps us see God's place in our living the truth when she tells of the picture of Christ she and her husband placed on the living room wall of their home. Painted by Ralph Coleman, it represents Christ as looking directly into one's eyes. During the years amazing things have happened because of this picture. Guests, salesmen, the paper boy, and total strangers have opened their lives to the Formans and to God after looking at it. The picture is not magic, but it reminds persons of God so directly that in his presence they become their best selves. They are able to live the truth.

God is the Lord of all truth. This is basic to his righteousness and holiness. In administering his universe and in relating himself to his children he holds the line where truth is concerned. He "plays it straight" with us and with himself at the same time.

When we come face to face with God in our praying and daily living, we are stripped of our pretense and see ourselves as we are. We cannot wear a mask when we are in God's presence; we can only be our true selves.

THE TRUTH AND OTHERS

When men live the truth, others also are directly involved. The commandment refers to bearing false witness against one's neighbor (Exodus 20:16), and the passage from Ephesians likewise urges us to speak the truth before our neighbors, "for we are members one of another." (4:25)

Henry D. Thoreau was outspoken in his views against the ownership of slaves. He also believed in one's influence on others when it came to living the truth. Writing about his views, he said, "I know this well, that if one thousand, if one hundred, if ten men whom I could name—if ten *honest* men only—ay, if *one* HONEST man, in this State of Massachusetts, *ceasing to hold slaves*, were actually to withdraw from this co-partnership, and be locked up in the county jail therefor, it would be the abolition of slavery in America." [9] Thoreau was interested in living the truth, not simply in speaking it.

[9] Thoreau, "On the Duty of Civil Disobedience."

Martin Luther King, Jr., did just this in a situation in one American city; and the issue of racial justice became a national one.

THE TRUTH AND I

Gabriel Fackre writes concerning the frightening threat of controlling persons' minds through the use of drugs or electrode implants. The individual would be at the mercy of external forces and factors; he would not be his own man doing his own thing. This action would completely dehumanize man, who would become a robot instead of a person made in God's image.

Being human must include the high privilege and responsibility of being able both to tell the truth and to live the truth. If as individuals we do not accept the responsibility truth places upon us, we may lose the right to live it and tell it.

Helping Adults Become Involved —Howard E. Tower

Preparation of Self and Class

You have probably discovered that busy adults do very little preparation for the Sunday lesson. Because this is true, it is doubly important to present at the end of each lesson a question or questions that will linger with them and cause them to think in the midst of the busyness. In this way you can hope that the three questions suggested at the end of last Sunday's lesson may have come to class members' minds often enough during the week to bring the group together with some readiness to think deeply about what it means to live the truth in our world.

Your preparation also will need to revolve around these questions. Whenever you listen to the radio or watch television throughout the week,

jot down examples of truth and falsehood in the commercials you see and hear. Likewise, as you read newspapers and magazines, list similar examples.

The second question, about the contribution of the teaching program of the school, is a little more elusive. If you happen to be a schoolteacher, examples of truth-supporting and truth-denying experiences will be easy to come by. The same will be true if you have children in school. If neither of these represent your situation, you might recall examples of "facts" of history as you learned them in school or college that you now know were only a one-sided view of truth.

The third question, if this lesson were being presented in July of 1971, would have a ready-made example—the Pentagon Papers. In July of 1973 you, unfortunately, will likely not find it difficult to discover new examples of untruth in the affairs of the government.

As you turn to study the resources provided by Dr. Frey and Dr. Laymon, you will discover that Dr. Laymon gives a series of questions under his heading "The Main Question." Perhaps you will want to formulate one question that reflects what is implied in his series of questions. The one I came up with is What is truth, and what demands does truth place upon us if we are to be persons of integrity (wholeness) and develop a society that is healthy? This restatement of the question should aid your study of the Scripture references.

Presenting the Main Question

One way to help the class members come to some consensus about the main issue of the lesson would be to begin with a listing of the examples of truth and falsehood they have noted during the week. To avoid unnecessary repetition, it would be helpful to list the examples on chalkboard or newsprint. When members have finished reporting on their observations, add any you feel they have overlooked. Then ask members to state the most important question about truth that they need to consider.

Developing the Lesson

The development of the lesson for the remainder of your time together will grow out of and be related to what the group settles on as the main issue.

If your members have trouble selecting one issue or if discussion lags, you may want to use one of the following incidents:

A woman in her early eighties was taken to the hospital for observation and tests. After a week of X rays and other medical examinations, during which time no open or meaningful interpretation of what was happening was given to her, she underwent abdominal surgery. After two weeks of daily visitations, while she lingered between life and death, she asked her pastor, "What is wrong with me? I want to know the truth." Her pastor conferred with the surgeon, who quite frankly told him that she had undergone surgery for advanced cancer. What should the pastor tell this woman? Give reasons for your answer.

A young professional man came to his pastor and confided that he had discovered his wife was having an affair with another man. He had confronted her, and she had willingly acknowledged what she had done. She wanted to continue both as his wife and as a lover and asked him to help conceal this relationship from their nine-year-old daughter. In this kind of complex situation, what demands does truth place upon personal integrity? What are the implications of truth for the husband? for the wife? for the child?

Two teen-age boys were working part-time as parking lot attendants. The manager of the lot quite frankly asked them at the end of their first week to overcharge any customer they could. The overcharge would be split between themselves and him. If the customer noticed the overcharge, they were of course to make the right charge and apologize for their error. One boy went along with the request. The other boy continued doing his work honestly. At the end of the week the honest boy was given a choice —do as requested or be fired. He chose to quit. He had maintained his honesty, but he kept wondering whether truthfulness demanded that he report what the manager was doing to the owner of the lot. What is the full dimension of truth in this situation?

These, or any similar situations your members provide, should be considered in the light of the three Scripture references.

What demands follow from the ninth commandment? Does simply refraining from actively bearing false witness against another fulfill the demands of truth? Can one remain silent and still bear false witness?

What insight concerning truth as it involves our relationship to God is presented in the story of Ananias and Sapphira? How does this insight help us in dealing with the complex reality of truthfulness? Can we ever truly deceive God?

What about Paul's insistence that we are members one of another? Do we ever act without affecting others? What does this truth say about the extent of hurt that false witness brings to others?

Helping Class Members Act

Some new insights may come to members of the class during this lesson that will lead to more openness in their relationships within the family, a deeper realization of the importance of forthrightness in all their relationships, and a determination to help hold others accountable for falseness. But the class also may have brought to the surface some problems related to truthfulness that they may want to explore further. Members may wish to set up a number of research task groups on such areas of investigation as how to support needed legislation on truth in advertising, or how to discover what the present food and drug laws require and the degree to which they are being supported?

Planning for Next Sunday

Point to the fact that next week members are to examine the tenth commandment. Call attention to the inner, personal nature of this commandment. Ask this question: What are some of the destructive outcomes of covetousness?

The Peril of Greed

Background Scripture: Exodus 20:17; Ecclesiastes 5:10 through 6:2; Matthew 20:20-28; Luke 12:13-21; 1 Timothy 6:6-10

The Main Question —Charles M. Laymon

Scrooge and Silas Marner are well-known figures because literature has dramatized their selfishness for all to see. In this same way Lot and Jezebel of the Old Testament have become symbols of greed.

Covetousness, however, is not limited to such classic examples. Greed has choked our society like a weed that spreads beyond the bank it was intended to keep from eroding and climbs to the tops of surrounding trees, smothering their branches and killing their growth. Covetousness has forced our government to place a limit on businesses that seek to become monopolies by passing antitrust laws and forbidding price-fixing. Countries, however, can also be greedy. For many years large nations grew fat on the natural resources of smaller nations they colonized.

What is it that makes men and nations greedy? Is selfishness an ingrown tendency in all men? Does the instinct of self-preservation require that we should be covetous?

The biblical passages for this lesson provide some guidelines for facing these questions.

As You Read the Scripture —George W. Frey

The tenth commandment is detailed in its specifications. The preceding four commandments are brief, yet they speak with force and crispness to the essentials of community living. Like the previous commandments this one deals with the inner life and speaks of desires that when undisciplined lead to a shattering of personal relations.

Exodus 20:17. *You shall not covet:* The verb *covet* carries such meanings

"TAKE HEED, AND BEWARE OF COVETOUSNESS; FOR A MAN'S LIFE DOES NOT CONSIST IN THE ABUNDANCE OF HIS POSSESSIONS." (LUKE 12:15)

as delight in, wish for, desire, or plunder. Here covetousness is the desire for something that is not really one's own. In its most negative expression this would be the kind of greed that would lead a person to appropriate to himself what is rightfully and legally another's.

The commandment lists specific objects the coveting of which is prohibited. In this category are a neighbor's house, a neighbor's wife, a neighbor's male or female servant, and a neighbor's work animals. The list ends with the all-inclusive "anything that is your neighbor's." It is interesting to note that the Deuteronomic parallel (5:21) mentions "your neighbor's wife" before his "house." The word *house* frequently means the entire family, with the father as the central figure of loyalty and authority. Another interesting difference occurs in the Deuteronomic version of this commandment. In the Exodus account the verb *covet* is used both times, while in Deuteronomy the first verb is *covet* and the second verb is *desire*. The grammatical form of this latter verb suggests the translation "You shall not desire for yourself your neighbor's (or your friend's) house." Both verbs attempt to describe the inner feelings of inordinate desire for possession—lust, greed, and the willingness to plunder.

Luke 12:15-21. *A man's life does not consist in the abundance of his possessions:* This "example" story was given when some unnamed person came to Jesus with a problem. The complaint dealt with the distribution of the family estate. (See Luke 12:13.) Evidently Jesus sensed a bit of greed in the eyes of the complainer and told a story about a rich man who had everything but one. Note the personal pronouns: *"my* crops," *"my* barns," *"my* grain," *"my* goods," *"my* soul." This farmer's egocentric mood is really revealed in verse 19. Here is the portrait of a man who had built his own empire and planned to rest and enjoy it, but it crumbled as man-made things always do in time. God is Lord of life and has the final word. The ultimate payoff for greed and self-centeredness is emptiness. Life's deepest realities are found not in barns, goods, or grain but in relationships with God and man.

1 Timothy 6:6-10. *There is great gain in godliness with contentment:* This is one of many solid pieces of advice from the writer of this letter to a young preacher. To live with *contentment* is to live as God would have a person live. The desire for riches is condemned. This desire can so easily trap a person (verse 9). "Ruin and destruction" are the rewards of greed. Note, however, it is "the love of money" that is condemned here (verse 10), not money itself. The craving of wealth frequently leads to loss of commitment and heartache. The desire to be wealthy is not a priority for the Christian. The Christian's real wealth is discoverable in the divine-human relations he builds.

Selected Scripture

King James Version	Revised Standard Version
Exodus 20:17	*Exodus 20:17*
17 Thou shalt not covet thy neighbour's house, thou shalt not covet thy neighbour's wife, nor his manservant, nor his maidservant, nor his ox, nor	17 "You shall not covet your neighbor's house; you shall not covet your neighbor's wife, or his manservant, or his maidservant, or his ox, or his ass,

his ass, nor any thing that is thy neighbour's.

or anything that is your neighbor's."

Luke 12:15-21

15 And he said unto them, Take heed, and beware of covetousness: for a man's life consisteth not in the abundance of the things which he possesseth.

16 And he spake a parable unto them, saying, The ground of a certain rich man brought forth plentifully:

17 And he thought within himself, saying, What shall I do, because I have no room where to bestow my fruits?

18 And he said, This will I do: I will pull down my barns, and build greater; and there will I bestow all my fruits and my goods.

19 And I will say to my soul, Soul, thou hast much goods laid up for many years; take thine ease, eat, drink, and be merry.

20 But God said unto him, Thou fool, this night thy soul shall be required of thee: then whose shall those things be, which thou hast provided?

21 So is he that layeth up treasure for himself, and is not rich toward God.

1 Timothy 6:6-10

6 But Godliness with contentment is great gain.

7 For we brought nothing into this world, and it is certain we can carry nothing out.

8 And having food and raiment let us be therewith content.

9 But they that will be rich fall into temptation and a snare, and into many foolish and hurtful lusts, which drown men in destruction and perdition.

10 For the love of money is the root of all evil: which while some coveted after, they have erred from the faith, and pierced themselves through with many sorrows.

Luke 12:15-21

15 And he said to them, "Take heed, and beware of all covetousness; for a man's life does not consist in the abundance of his possessions." 16 And he told them a parable, saying, "The land of a rich man brought forth plentifully; 17 and he thought to himself, 'What shall I do, for I have nowhere to store my crops?' 18 And he said, 'I will do this: I will pull down my barns, and build larger ones; and there I will store all my grain and my goods. 19 And I will say to my soul, Soul, you have ample goods laid up for many years; take your ease, eat, drink, be merry.' 20 But God said to him, 'Fool! This night your soul is required of you; and the things you have prepared, whose will they be?' 21 So is he who lays up treasure for himself, and is not rich toward God."

1 Timothy 6:6-10

6 There is great gain in godliness with contentment; 7 for we brought nothing into the world, and we cannot take anything out of the world; 8 but if we have food and clothing, with these we shall be content. 9 But those who desire to be rich fall into temptation, into a snare, into many senseless and hurtful desires that plunge men into ruin and destruction. 10 For the love of money is the root of all evils; it is through this craving that some have wandered away from the faith and pierced their hearts with many pangs.

| *Memory Selection:* Take heed, and beware of covetousness: for a man's life consisteth not in the abundance of the things which he possesseth. (Luke 12:15) | *Memory Selection:* Take heed, and beware of all covetousness; for a man's life does not consist in the abundance of his possessions. (Luke 12:15) |

The Scripture and the Main Question —Charles M. Laymon

WHEN WANTING HURTS OTHERS

Greed is not just a longing for possessions. It is the desire to own at the expense of others. It is wanting what we want when we want it—REGARDLESS! It is an extreme expression of egotism. The commandment forbidding covetousness is directed against this passion (Exodus 20:17).

Even the church has been affected by greed. In the days of the Holy Roman Empire the church became a state, rich in possessions, supporting a few in luxury at the expense of the masses. Nor has the situation improved greatly in the intervening centuries. John C. Bennett, the sociologist, has stated: "The Church needs many ministers who identify themselves with the efforts of the poor to gain power to balance the thousands of ministers who, implicitly, give their blessing to the way the strong keep their power." [10]

How do we, ministers and laymen alike, give our blessing to the greed behind "the way the strong keep their power"? Is it by having fashionable churches, middle-class churches, and poverty-level churches? Is it by stressing the cult of the comfortable? Is it by substituting the liturgy of worship for the challenge of love and justice? Is it by pushing personal religion only, at the expense of social and economic outreach in the name of Christ, who thanked his heavenly Father that the gospel was preached to the poor?

WHEN WANTING HURTS ONESELF

Our attitudes and activities leave their deposit in our own personal selves. The greedy man becomes a narrow person. He resembles the fictional character of Emily, whom the author described as bounded on the north by Emily, on the south by Emily, on the east by Emily, and on the west by Emily.

The natural impulse to acquire things, which sometimes leads to greed, has been studied deeply by psychologists. In his book *Psychotherapy and a Christian View of Man*, David E. Roberts states: "We seek answers to the meaning of life by means of acquiring wealth, power, pleasure, popularity, and any number of things. . . . Far too often we strive to meet the problem by *having* something significant instead of by *becoming or being* something significant." [11] Wanting under these circumstances hurts ourselves.

The rich fool in the parable Jesus told (Luke 12:15-21) provides an example of such a person, who became greedy in his search for a false security. This is the reason God said to him: "Fool! This night your soul is required of you; and the things you have prepared, whose will they be?" (verse 20)

Whatever the reason that leads us to become greedy, however we justify

[10] In *Moral Issues and Christian Responses,* ed. Jersild and Johnson (Holt, Rinehart and Winston, 1971), p. 42.

[11] (Charles Scribner's Sons, 1959), p. 46.

411

THE PERIL OF GREED

ourselves, the end result is the same. No one really wants to become greedy. We just try to meet some basic needs in the wrong way, and we end up the loser for all our effort.

What Love of Money Means

I know an elderly woman who is extremely wealthy. In her younger days she and her husband had a hard time financially. She learned to pinch pennies as a matter of survival. Now she lives alone, clipping stock coupons and putting money in the bank. Her earlier deprivations have all but made her miserly. She once said to a friend, "I love to see it [money] pile up in my bank account."

This person's life does have another side. She recently confided to the same friend, "When I was younger, I wanted so many things desperately and could not buy them because I was so poor. Now that I am aged and could afford them, I no longer want them." Preoccupation with money (too little or too much of it) has been a concern for this woman throughout life.

The statement "the love of money is the root of all evils" (1 Timothy 6:10) is often misquoted as "money is the root of all evils," implying that possessing earthly goods in itself is evil. The passage does not say this. What it states is that the *love* of money leads to evil.

Actually, the possession of great wealth, rightly gained, is often a blessing. Who should know better how to use wealth than a Christian who is both wise and ethically sensitive?

Money, rightly spent, can do much good in the world. The love of money for money's sake, or for the power over others that it makes possible, is the destructive force that the misuse of money releases.

Possessing Nothing—Possessing Everything

Richard Eberhart has written a poem entitled "An Old Fashioned American Businessman":

I asked no quarter and I gave none.
I fought it out until eighty-one.
Intelligence guided my efforts,
Cynicism dictated my business reports.

I played one off against another,
Keeping my head well above water.
I transmuted my blood to steel
Early conquering the realm of feeling.

I taught ruthlessness by example
And hard work and steadfastness.
Now that the hated grave approaches
I wish for the love I could not give.[12]

The words in this poem tragically reveal the poverty of a businessman, who at death had nothing that really mattered. Like the rich fool, he could not take his wealth with him into the hereafter. On the other side, only spiritual values count, such as the love the businessman could not give. Materially speaking, as the passage from First Timothy states, we bring nothing into this world; and we cannot take anything out of the world (6:7).

[12] From *Collected Poems 1930-1960* by Richard Eberhart, p. 181. Copyright © 1960 by Richard Eberhart. Reprinted by permission of Oxford University Press, Inc. and Chatto & Windus Ltd.

Helping Adults Become Involved —Howard E. Tower

Preparation of Self and Class

Like the title of this lesson, "The Peril of Greed," the question sug-gested to the class for their thinking during the week implies danger. The title uses the word *peril*. The suggested question asks what *destructive* outcomes are the result of covetousness? This lesson considers a perfectly normal human response that can go so wrong that it becomes destructive, creating peril to self and others. To want is a natural human drive. To desire what others have is the result of following a drive to express ourselves through the manipulation of things.

The first requisite for preparation for this lesson is the frank recognition of the inborn drives that make us easy candidates for greed as experienced through covetousness. This human proneness to want more things than we need gave rise to the tenth commandment. Your task is to discover both what gives rise to excessive desire and the outcome of being controlled by such desire. This discovery will be the objective of your examination of the Old Testament, Gospel, and Epistle passages of Scripture, as well as the interpretation of these by Dr. Frey and the exposition of the theme by Dr. Laymon.

A helpful exercise might be to rewrite the tenth commandment so that the things we are not to covet will be stated in terms of items we might covet today. Likewise, the story of the rich fool may be rewritten in terms of a self-made, successful urban businessman.

Presenting the Main Question

If you begin your lesson with a request for examples of destructive outcomes of covetousness, you will likely have suggestions that deal with the covetousness of other persons. Urban riots may be high on the list of destructive examples. The poor are coveting what the middle class have. Most likely others will view greed as the underlying cause of war and economic exploitation.

As these examples are given, someone may honestly question what is wrong with wanting and working hard for things that contribute to the richness and enjoyment of living. If such a question arises, this will give you, as leader, an opportunity to suggest that a natural desire for possessions is not evil. The real issue is whether you are in control of your desires or they are in control of you. Seek to help your group members see the personal and internal nature of the main question. A fine line of distinction exists between wanting things that will enrich oneself and others and excessively desiring things that you do not have, should not have, or cannot have.

Developing the Lesson

To further explore the subtle nature of desire that becomes covetous and converts to greed, the class members might divide into three work groups.

The first group will work on rewording the tenth commandment to bring it up-to-date in listing things (or persons) that we should not covet. If these work groups are limited to two or three persons, the rewording might be carried on as a group process. If the task group is larger, each person may write his version of the tenth commandment. Then the task group can decide which rewrite to share with the total group.

The second work group will be asked to rewrite Luke's story of the rich fool, giving it a modern and urban setting. It may be effective to have the subgroup discuss the story, agree upon a setting, describe the kind of businessman they want to substitute for the farmer, and then build the story. Or each member of the work group may write the story as he imagines it, portraying someone he knows who aptly represents the farmer. Again the work group can decide which story to share with the class.

The third work group will endeavor to rewrite 1 Timothy 6:6-10 so that it reflects today's language and experience.

After the sharing of these rewrites the class members will be ready to discuss more clearly what these Scripture passages have communicated to them about the subtle dangers of covetousness.

As the lesson develops, the group will most likely make an immediate and unthinking response to how destructive greed and excessive desire can be when practiced by the rich or the poor, the industrialists or the labor unions. The leader's task is to help them move from this to a willingness to face the inner and personal nature, danger, and peril each of us experiences when desire gets the upper hand in our lives.

Helping Class Members Act

A number of pressing social issues are related to man's greed and covetousness:

1. The poverty cycle that cannot be broken because of the threat that "the poor"—liberated and trained in needed skills—would present to the established order.

2. Keeping minorities segregated in residential ghettos because of the fear of the suburban community that open housing would depress property values.

3. The exploitation of natural resources—oil, trees, soil—for gain.

4. The economic policy that takes out of underdeveloped countries more than we are willing to put in, because of the high return on our dollar investment.

Any one of these social issues could become the basis of group study and action. But, perhaps, if the study has helped the members of the group face squarely what desire for the things others have leads them to do, each person may be ready to revalue the worth of things and the amount of time and energy he puts into getting them. A good exercise in the coming week might be to think about ways to simplify one's desire for things so that more time will be available to enjoy being a person.

Planning for Next Sunday

Remind your class members that Jesus was asked which is the first and greatest commandment. His answer is to be the basis of next Sunday's study.

Suggest that members of the class read Deuteronomy 6:4-5 and compare this statement of the Great Commandment with Jesus' restatement of it in Mark 12:28-34 and Matthew 22:34-40, and with Paul's interpretation of the law of love in Romans 13:8-10. As these references are read, suggest that this question be in the minds of the readers: If the Great Commandment were heeded by all, which of the Ten Commandments would still be needed?

414

The Great Commandment

Background Scripture: Leviticus 19:18; Deuteronomy 6:4-5;
Mark 12:28-34; Luke 10:25-27; Romans 13:8-10

The Main Question —Charles M. Laymon

A young man was applying for a position with a large corporation. As a part of the interview he was given a list of interests and asked to arrange them in the order of their importance to him. Some of the items were easy to assign because they were superficial; others were more difficult to place. The interviewer said later that he could tell more about the young man's potential by the order in which he listed the interests than by his IQ score.

Do we have an ascending scale of values? What gets most of our attention day by day? How do we spend our money? What do we do with the time that is at our disposal?

A Christian businessman who tried to operate his stores in line with the teachings of Jesus had as his motto: "God first, others second, sales third." His success was phenomenal. Why?

In periods of national crisis the word *priorities* is frequently used. During World War II automobiles were stripped down. Gone were the chrome, the flashy paint jobs, and the yearly change of models. A new car looked as drab as an unpeeled potato. The war effort came first.

When we attempt to live as Christians, what happens to our priorities? What should happen? The biblical passages for this lesson will prove helpful in facing such questions.

As You Read the Scripture —George W. Frey

The Book of Deuteronomy has as its basic theme the renewal of religious devotion. Major emphases in the book are (1) the centralization of worship in Jerusalem, making the city the religious center of the nation; (2) the reinterpretation of the Exodus event and tradition in contemporary terms, thus making this past event central to the life of the nation; and (3) the increased stress on the unique and particular nature of Israel's self-identity, reminding them that they are "the people of God." Herein are the prescriptions for Israel's convenantal life. Herein is the second law to help the Israelites be the obedient people of God. (The word *Deuteronomy* means "second law.")

Deuteronomy 6:4. *Hear, O Israel; The* LORD *our God is one* LORD: This verse is the famous *Shema*, which is still central to Jewish religious life. The word *shema* means "hear." Note the various ways this confessional prayer may be translated. See the footnotes in the Revised Standard Version. The Deuteronomic writers intended to affirm the uniqueness of Yahweh in these words. For Israel, Yahweh and Yahweh alone is God.

Verse 5. *You shall love the* LORD *your God with . . . your heart . . . soul . . . and might:* This is how obedience and loyalty to God is to be expressed.

415

The words of this great commandment are interesting. *Heart* (*leb* in the Hebrew) means mind, will, or intellect. *Soul* (*nephesh* in the Hebrew) means vital being. *Might* (*meod* in the Hebrew) means physical energy. Love, therefore, according to Hebrew thought, is the total and complete response of a person to God. The Old Testament sees man as a unit. His intellect, emotions, and physical strength are blended into one symphonic whole. The love enjoined in this verse is thus total, complete, and full dedication to the obedience of God's will.

Mark 12:28-34. *You shall love the* LORD *your God.* . . . *You shall love your neighbor:* Both Mark and Matthew report an incident in which Jesus was asked to cite the greatest commandment. (See Matthew 22:34-40.) Mark's version includes the *Shema*, quoted from Deuteronomy 6:4. Both Mark and Matthew report that Jesus added a second commandment to the first. The second commandment dealt with loving one's neighbor as oneself. The command to love one's neighbor was really not new. Such a command appears in Leviticus 19:18: "You shall love your neighbor as yourself." The bringing together of these two commandments presents a summary of religious duty. Jesus may well have been the first to summarize the law in such concise fashion.

The Greek verb translated "love" in this passage carries the meaning of the highest kind of devotion and loyalty man is capable of expressing towards God. It is love unlimited—the full and complete giving of self to obedient living under God.

Romans 13:8-10. *Love is the fulfilling of the law:* Paul's letter to the Romans contains a complete account of his theological interpretation of the gospel. In this passage is found Paul's most positive approach to the law. The first eleven chapters of Romans contain a closely written theological argument, but a change of style occurs in Chapter 12. Paul deals with practical ethics, living the Christian life day by day. Chapter 12 points up the importance of Christian love.

Verse 8. *Owe no one anything, except to love one another:* Here is the universal obligation. The law is fulfilled and completed when love is manifested.

Verse 9. *You shall love your neighbor as yourself:* This is Paul's summary of the law. The commandments against adultery, killing, stealing, and covetousness are superseded by love of neighbor. What does it mean to *love your neighbor as yourself?* The answer is not easy. Probably a careful reading of Romans 12 and 1 Corinthians 13 may give clues. The Golden Rule (Matthew 7:12) provides an answer too. An honest awareness of who and what one is opens the way to treat others as we treat ourselves. Loving oneself here is not the kind of selfish, irrational, egocentric love that makes a person obnoxious, but an attitude of self-respect and trust that one can also apply to other persons.

Selected Scripture

King James Version	Revised Standard Version
Deuteronomy 6:4-5	*Deuteronomy 6:4-5*
4 Hear, O Israel: The LORD our God is one LORD:	4 "Hear, O Israel: The LORD our God is one LORD; 5 and you shall

5 And thou shalt love the LORD thy God with all thine heart, and with all thy soul, and with all thy might.

Mark 12:28-34

28 And one of the scribes came, and having heard them reasoning together, and perceiving that he had answered them well, asked him, Which is the first commandment of all?

29 And Jesus answered him, The first of all the commandments is, Hear, O Israel; The Lord our God is one Lord:

30 And thou shalt love the Lord thy God with all thy heart, and with all thy soul, and with all thy mind, and with all thy strength: this is the first commandment.

31 And the second is like, namely this, Thou shalt love thy neighbour as thyself. There is none other commandment greater than these.

32 And the scribe said unto him, Well, Master, thou hast said the truth: for there is one God; and there is none other but he:

33 And to love him with all the heart, and with all the understanding, and with all the soul, and with all the strength, and to love his neighbour as himself, is more than all whole burnt offerings and sacrifices.

34 And when Jesus saw that he answered discreetly, he said unto him, Thou art not far from the kingdom of God. And no man after that durst ask him any question.

Romans 13:8-10

8 Owe no man any thing, but to love one another: for he that loveth another hath fulfilled the law.

9 For this, Thou shalt not commit adultery, Thou shalt not kill, Thou shalt not steal, Thou shalt not bear false witness, Thou shalt not covet;

love the LORD your God with all your heart, and with all your soul, and with all your might."

Mark 12:28-34

28 And one of the scribes came up and heard them disputing with one another, and seeing that he answered them well, asked him, "Which commandment is the first of all?" 29 Jesus answered, "The first is, 'Hear, O Israel: The Lord our God, the Lord is one; 30 and you shall love the Lord your God with all your heart, and with all your soul, and with all your mind, and with all your strength.' 31 The second is this, 'You shall love your neighbor as yourself.' There is no other commandment greater than these." 32 And the scribe said to him, "You are right, Teacher; you have truly said that he is one, and there is no other but he; 33 and to love him with all the heart, and with all the understanding, and with all the strength, and to love one's neighbor as oneself, is much more than all whole burnt offerings and sacrifices." 34 And when Jesus saw that he answered wisely, he said to him, "You are not far from the kingdom of God." And after that no one dared to ask him any question.

Romans 13:8-10

8 Owe no one anything, except to love one another; for he who loves his neighbor has fulfilled the law. 9 The commandments, "You shall not commit adultery, You shall not kill, You shall not steal, You shall not covet," and any other commandment, are

417

and if there be any other commandment, it is briefly comprehended in this saying, namely, Thou shalt love thy neighbour as thyself.

10 Love worketh no ill to his neighbour: therefore love is the fulfilling of the law.

Memory Selection: **This commandment have we from him, That he who loveth God love his brother also. (1 John 4:21)**

summed up in this sentence, "You shall love your neighbor as yourself." 10 Love does no wrong to a neighbor; therefore love is the fulfilling of the law.

Memory Selection: **This commandment we have from him, that he who loves God should love his brother also. (1 John 4:21)**

The Scripture and the Main Question —Charles M. Laymon

One Loyalty

Most of us would be offended if we were to be called polytheists; we do not worship several gods. And yet, as we saw in a previous lesson in this series ("God Is Supreme," June 10), we sometimes substitute other interests for God and give them our supreme allegiance.

We are not as single-minded as the Kentuckian who asserted just prior to the Civil War that if the country should split, he would be loyal to the South; if the South should split, he would side with Kentucky; if Kentucky should split, he would side with his county; and if his county should split, he would stand by his town. There would be no confusion of loyalties here if it came to a showdown.

The Hebrews were also single-minded. The *Shema* (Deuteronomy 6:4) is a confession of Israel's faith; this is what she believes; here is her priority. The Hebrews were not confused. God for them was "the God of Abraham, the God of Isaac, and the God of Jacob" (Exodus 4:5) and they were loyal to him alone.

Current thinking about God is fuzzy. Many persons, if asked whether or not they believe in God, would reply: "What do you mean? What God?"

For Christians, the answer should be God is *the God and father of our Lord Jesus Christ.* Here is the distinctive identity of the God to whom we are called to give undivided loyalty. Here is our priority.

All of Me

Single-minded loyalty requires all from us: "You shall love the LORD your God with all your heart, and with all your soul, and with all your might." (Deuteronomy 6:5) The heart includes one's *mind* and *will;* the soul refers to the *self* or *vital being;* and might suggests *love in action.*

John Wesley urged his followers to get on fire with God. If they did, he assured them that men would come and watch them burn. Such depth of consecration puts conviction into what we say and sharpens our Christian witness.

In this same vein H. R. L. (Dick) Sheppard, who captured the London of his day for Christ, used to speak disparagingly of "mild and muffled enthusiasms." He said, "Causes without passion are lost causes and no movement can progress unless it can count on the white-hot energy of its ordinary adherents." [13] Dick Sheppard spoke, not of the enthusiasm of leaders mainly, but of the excited devotion of everyday Christians.

Such complete consecration to God as the Great Commandment calls for not only contributes to the interest of others in the Kingdom, but also enlarges the personalities of those who possess and express it. "We grow as we glow for Christ," said a college student.

LOVE OF GOD AND LOVE OF OTHERS

Jesus added some significant words to the passage from Deuteronomy 6: 4-5, after referring to it as the first commandment of all. He stated, "The second is this, 'You shall love your neighbor as yourself.' " (Mark 12:31) In Christian ethics the two commands cannot be separated. The author of the First Letter of John saw this truth with deep conviction when he later wrote: "If any one says, 'I love God,' and hates his brother, he is a liar; for he who does not love his brother whom he has seen, cannot love God whom he has not seen." John recalled Jesus' words on this point and added, "This commandment we have from him, that he who loves God should love his brother also." (4:20-21)

When Jesus referred to others as "your neighbor" (Mark 12:31), he opened the way for discussing the identity of one's neighbor. Who is my neighbor? This is the very same question that a lawyer asked Jesus, and in reply Jesus told the parable of the good Samaritan (Luke 10:25-37).

[13] Sheppard, "A Conspiracy of Silence."

I have always appreciated the straightforward answer made to this question by the Danish theologian Søren Kierkegaard. He said that "when we enter our closet and pray to God, and rise from prayer to go out again into the world, the very next person we meet is our neighbor." On this basis, there can be no mistaking who our neighbor really is. Such a direct approach to identifying those neighbors whom love for God leads us to love strikes down all barriers to brotherly love. Rich—poor, good—bad, white—black—yellow, where can we draw the line? The answer is nowhere.

CAN LOVE BE TAUGHT?

Can love for God and others be taught? Is nurture in religious truth possible? Evidently the author of Deuteronomy believed that love could and should be taught. He said, "You shall teach them [the words in verses 4 and 5] diligently to your children, and shall talk of them when you sit in your house, and when you walk by the way, and when you lie down, and when you rise." (Deuteronomy 6:7)

Love cannot be taught at a distance; even the distance between the pulpit and the first row of pews is too great. Mingling and fellowship are needed. This is what some of the large festival gatherings of youth today are saying to us. In spite of their extremes and excesses, youth are coming together and finding a communion of persons that, on a higher level, should be typical of their homes and churches.

Helping Adults Become Involved —Howard E. Tower

Preparation of Self and Class

Perhaps the most difficult part of preparing oneself and your class members for this lesson is the task of coming to the familiar and accepted Great Commandment with freshness and a new sense of urgency. Your group of adults have been taught again and again that the first and great commandment is to love God with their whole being and the second is to love their neighbors as they love themselves. Most of them have accepted these commandments as the standard of their lives, in word but not always in deed. It is, then, this discrepancy between profession and practice that should be the focus of the group's exploration and, therefore, your preparation.

To get yourself ready to assess this discrepancy in your own life so you may be able to motivate your class members to look deep within their lives, explore the Scripture passages. Read first the Deuteronomy 6:4-5 and Leviticus 19:18 passages, and then read Mark 12:28-34 and Matthew 22:34-40. End your reading with Romans 13:8-10. When you have finished reading, sit quietly for a few minutes. Then record any new insights that come to your mind.

As you meditate, recall that Hebrew people have been intoning the plea "Hear, O Israel: the LORD our God is one LORD; and you shall love the LORD your God with all your heart, and with all your soul, and with all your might" in gatherings for worship in all kinds of circumstances and in every corner of the world for centuries. Children in Protestant Sunday schools have learned these verses by memory since Sunday schools began. They have been taught that Jesus called this the greatest commandment and that second only to it is the demand to love our neighbor.

And yet Christians have persecuted Jews, and Jews have been suspicious of Christians. Christians have fought Christians, and Christians have exploited non-Christians. Why? Could it be that saying the words and accepting their truth may have convinced us that we are living their truth? Can any person today feel comfortable about his performance in keeping these commandments? Is answering this question really what this lesson is all about?

Presenting the Main Question

Dr. Laymon suggests that the main question for the Christian as he confronts the Great Commandment is What do I put first in my life? He seems to imply that the priorities we set for our living reveal more about the degree of love we have for both men and God than any words we may recite or insist that we believe.

You might try this approach. Ask the members of the group to formulate endings to this statement: If I could have my deepest wish granted next week, this is what it would be _____, or, this is what would happen _____. While the class members are thinking about their answers, you might complete the statement as honestly as you can. Record the answers and help the group summarize and classify them.

Now change the statement for completion to one like this: At the end of my life I would like to be remembered for _____. Again, guide the group in summing up their replies.

When these two exercises are completed and you have your lists of wished-for things, experiences, or events, ask this question: What do these expressions of our desires reveal about the influence of the Great Commandment in our lives?

Developing the Lesson

At this point in the lesson you might remind the class members of the question you left with them at the close of the last session: Which of the Ten Commandments would still be needed if the Great Commandment were heeded by all? If anyone cites any commandment that is, in his judgment, not included in the summary of the law made by Jesus, this will be the point to begin your discussion.

As the discussion moves along, no matter what the exception cited, the questions that will surface may be one or more of the following:

1. What do we mean by love?
2. How does a person show love?
3. How can you love God if you do not know what God is like?
4. How can you love your neighbor if he does not respond to your love?
5. Who is my neighbor?

Whatever questions are raised, guide the group members in determining which three or more they would like to consider in detail. Let groups of three persons talk together about the answers they feel certain about, and identify the questions for which they feel they have no answer. Give these conversation groups about five minutes to talk together, and then let each group share their answers and questions with the whole class, listing all the unanswered questions.

Now suggest that although the class members may find all the Scripture references for today's lesson very familiar, perhaps some new meaning will come if they listen to them again with quietness and openness.

Form three listening groups: one to listen to Deuteronomy 6:4-9, one for Mark 12:28-34, and one for Romans 13:8-10. Suggest that each listening group select one member to read aloud the assigned passage. Ask each group to remain in complete silence for one full minute following the reading, and then let each person share whatever thought comes to mind. Let each listening group share their thoughts until they feel they have some new shade of meaning to share with the entire class.

After the listening groups have shared their new insights with the total group, these insights should be considered for the light they shed on the questions listed earlier.

Helping Class Members Act

Dr. Laymon made reference to Søren Kierkegaard's idea that, following prayer, a person should go out into the world with the understanding that the very first person he meets is his neighbor. This may be the basis of a possible action experience for your class members.

Each member might begin the day with this prayer: Father, I want to love you with all my heart, soul, mind, and strength and to show love for my neighbor. Help me to experience that love this day. Then, following Kierkegaard's suggestion, he should consider as neighbor the very first person he contacts and respond as love dictates. See what effect this response has upon the next contact and the next throughout the entire day. Do this for a week and evaluate the degree to which obedience to the Great Commandment has improved.

Planning for Next Sunday

Call attention to the fact that in the past eleven weeks the class has explored the Ten Commandments along with the enriching New Testament interpretations of them and the meaning of both for present-day living. The study has been climaxed with a consideration of the way in which the Great Commandment fulfills and motivates the rest of the law. In a sense this unit has been completed. But in the plan of study two important considerations remain:

first, a look at the tragedy of undisciplined living and, finally, an examination of the biblical concept of
redeeming love.

Perhaps a helpful question to leave

with the group in preparation for
next Sunday might be What reactions
against our permissive and morally
loose pattern of living have you
observed?

UNIT X: DEALING REDEMPTIVELY WITH THE UNDISCIPLINED

Horace R. Weaver

TWO LESSONS   AUGUST 19–26

The first of these lessons deals with various manifestations of the undisciplined life, especially alcoholism and drug addiction. Perhaps never before in
the history of man have so many people been addicted. From glue sniffers
to heroin addicts, people are destroying their lives because of their basic
denial of who they are. Each person needs to know that his body is a "house
of God" and should be treated as a place where man meets the Holy Spirit.
The final lesson explores how wholeness can be restored to such persons
through active loving concern of members of the Christian fellowship.

Audiovisual resources appropriate for use with the lessons of this unit may
be found in the introduction to Unit IX, p. 338. Listings for the entire quarter
are given in one location to facilitate ordering well in advance of planned
viewing dates.

LESSON 1   AUGUST 19

The Undisciplined Person

Background Scripture: Proverbs 23:19-21, 29-35;
1 Corinthians 10:6-13, 31; Galatians 5:13-24

The Main Question —Charles M. Laymon

At a summer conference for youth an excited young man spoke up in his
discussion group, "Everything is going to pot." Thinking that he was making
a joke about the use of dope, his friends laughed. "No, I mean it," said the
young man. "Adults have given us a mess of a world to live in."

An article carried by *Newsweek* in 1967 titled "Anything Goes: Taboos in
Twilight" agreed with the youth: "The old taboos are dead or dying. A new,
more permissive society is taking shape, . . . a society that has lost its consensus
on such crucial issues as premarital sex and clerical celibacy, marriage, birth
control and sex education." [14]

[14] *Newsweek*, November 13, 1967, p. 74.

We can understand the confusion felt by the young man. How does one live in a world such as this, where change is so rapid and there seem to be no permanent guidelines? What is the place of self-discipline in a permissive society where "anything goes"?

The biblical passages that follow contain some help in answering these questions.

As You Read the Scripture —George W. Frey

The Book of Proverbs belongs to the wisdom literature of the Old Testament. Other examples of the wisdom movement in Israel include Job, Ecclesiastes, and several Psalms (for example, 1, 37, 49, 73, 78). Outside the canon of the Old Testament, Ecclesiasticus is a well-known wisdom book.

Wisdom writings are not peculiar to ancient Israel. The whole Near East was alive with proverbs from very early times. The earliest forms have been found in Egypt and go back as far as the third millennium B.C. In more recent years scholars have discovered a vast amount of wisdom literature produced by the Sumerians, who occupied the southern part of the Mesopotamian valley long before the time of the Babylonian Empire.

Hebrew wisdom writings came from a group of men called the sages. The sages sought to teach moral truths in the form of proverbs or clever, brief sayings. The proverb is defined as "a short, pithy saying in frequent and widespread use, expressing a well-known truth." Each saying contained a moral punch no one could miss. A casual reading of Proverbs indicates the sages dealt with everyday problems of conduct in a language of simplicity, directness, and oftentimes rare beauty. (For a good general introduction to wisdom literature, see the article on "Wisdom" in *The Interpreter's Dictionary of the Bible,* Vol. R-Z, pages 852-61.)

Proverbs 23:19. *Hear, my son, and be wise:* The sages frequently addressed the young. The word for wisdom is *hokmah.* It holds such meanings as to be firm, to exercise discipline, to deal prudently, and so forth. The possession of wisdom reveals itself in disciplined living. The wise train their minds in right thoughts.

Verses 20-21. *Be not among winebibbers, or among gluttonous eaters:* The possession of wisdom carries with it the note of restraint. Excesses of any kind are frowned upon by the sages. The wise person disciplines himself and is not given to drunkenness, overeating, or laziness. The translation of these lines in *The Jerusalem Bible* is interesting:

> Do not be one of those forever tippling wine
>   nor one of those who gorge themselves with meat;
> for the drunkard and glutton impoverish themselves,
>   and a drowsy head makes a wearer of rags.[15]

Verses 29-35. *Who has woe? Who has sorrow? Who has strife? . . . Those who tarry long over wine:* The physical agonies of the alcoholic are vividly described in these verses. He is obnoxious, obstinate, prone to argue, and a slave

[15] *The Jerusalem Bible* (Doubleday & Company, 1966).

to his own habit. His undisciplined life leads to a vicious circle. Alcoholism is a street with no end. Note the descriptive phrase in verse 35, "When shall I awake? I will seek another drink."

1 Corinthians 10:12-13. *Therefore let any one who thinks that he stands take heed lest he fall. . . . God is faithful, and he will not let you be tempted beyond your strength:* Paul is ever concerned about ethical living. Often he recalls Israel's history and seeks to press home the lessons history teaches. In the larger context from which these verses are lifted there is an allusion to the past (verses 1-4). It is a reference to the wilderness experience. The lesson is clear or should be. But there is also the contemporary reference. Paul is always relevant. He always speaks concretely to a specific situation. Thus he comes in this context to deal with a problem caused by lack of discipline. (Actually Chapter 10 should be read in its entirety.) Paul makes three points here: (1) Temptation is universal; (2) arrogance, pride, and a false sense of security may so blind a person that he falls and is victimized by his own moral blindness; and (3) God, however, in every aspect of life stands ready to offer his grace to strengthen the believer and help him back on his feet. The fidelity of God's nature is nothing short of marvelous. The spirit of faithful endurance (verse 13) is the gift of God's grace to his children.

The sages moralized, seeking to teach persons the folly of the undisciplined life. Paul goes farther. He offers the grace of God to his children and especially to those going around in the circles of their undisciplined lives. He offers the Christ of God who can and will strengthen the moral fibers for facing temptations victoriously.

Selected Scripture

King James Version	Revised Standard Version
Proverbs 23:19-21, 29-35	*Proverbs 23:19-21, 29-35*
19 Hear thou, my son, and be wise, and guide thine heart in the way.	19 Hear, my son, and be wise, and direct your mind in the way.
20 Be not among winebibbers; among riotous eaters of flesh:	20 Be not among winebibbers, or among gluttonous eaters of meat;
21 For the drunkard and the glutton shall come to poverty: and drowsiness shall clothe a man with rags.	21 for the drunkard and the glutton will come to poverty, and drowsiness will clothe a man with rags.
. . . .	. . . .
29 Who hath woe? who hath sorrow? who hath contentions? who hath babbling? who hath wounds without cause? who hath redness of eyes?	29 Who has woe? Who has sorrow? Who has strife? Who has complaining? Who has wounds without cause? Who has redness of eyes?
30 They that tarry long at the wine; they that go to seek mixed wine.	30 Those who tarry long over wine, those who go to try mixed wine.

31 Look not thou upon the wine when it is red, when it giveth his colour in the cup, when it moveth itself aright.

32 At the last it biteth like a serpent, and stingeth like an adder.

33 Thine eyes shall behold strange women, and thine heart shall utter perverse things.

34 Yea, thou shalt be as he that lieth down in the midst of the sea, or as he that lieth upon the top of a mast.

35 They have stricken me, shalt thou say, and I was not sick; they have beaten me, and I felt it not: when shall I awake? I will seek it yet again.

31 Do not look at wine when it is red,
   when it sparkles in the cup
   and goes down smoothly.

32 At the last it bites like a serpent,
   and stings like an adder.

33 Your eyes will see strange things,
   and your mind utter perverse
   things.

34 You will be like one who lies
   down in the midst of the sea,
   like one who lies on the top of
   a mast.

35 "They struck me," you will say,
   "but I was not hurt;
   they beat me, but I did not feel
   it.
When shall I awake?
I will seek another drink."

1 Corinthians 10:12-13

12 Wherefore let him that thinketh he standeth take heed lest he fall.

13 There hath no temptation taken you but such as is common to man: but God is faithful, who will not suffer you to be tempted above that ye are able; but will with the temptation also make a way to escape, that ye may be able to bear it.

Memory Selection: **Wherefore let him that thinketh he standeth take heed lest he fall. (1 Corinthians 10: 12)**

1 Corinthians 10:12-13

12 Therefore let any one who thinks that he stands take heed lest he fall. 13 No temptation has overtaken you that is not common to man. God is faithful, and he will not let you be tempted beyond your strength, but with the temptation will also provide the way of escape, that you may be able to endure it.

Memory Selection: **Let any one who thinks that he stands take heed lest he fall. (1 Corinthians 10:12)**

The Main Question —Charles M. Laymon

THE CHALLENGE OF CHANGE

Change has always affected persons. An early Greek philosopher said that one could not immerse a stick in the same river twice. The next instant new water had flowed by, leaving some changes in the stream.

The hymn writer who wrote "Change and decay in all around I see" was crying out against change.

He was thankful in the midst of change that God was changeless, and prayed, "Abide with me." Change brings stresses and sometimes forces decisions upon us that we fear to make.

It has been said that old shoes fit best. We also hear that the good old days were best. But how good were the good old days? A men's club speaker pointed out some bleak facts about the good old days. (1) In the late nineteenth century more than a million children worked twelve hours a day in factories and mines. (2) Life expectancy was fifty years in 1900. (3) A retiree in 1910 received no social security because there was none. (4) Since 1912 we have had World War I, World War II, the Korean War, and the Vietnam War; and between the first two a worldwide depression was thrown in for good measure. (5) If you were a worker in 1925, there was no minimum wage law; and your employer could require you to work as long as he pleased for as little as he pleased. These were the good old days? Some things about them were not so good.

Change can bring us good things as well as bad. Most of the above situations have been corrected. New problems have arisen. But there are new answers every day—new answers because many are regarding change as a challenge. Change calls for self-discipline in the making of new decisions, and it can lead to the creation of new persons and a new society in Christ.

DON'T PASS THE BUCK

A wag who was in a philosophical mood one day said that baseball and passing-the-buck were the two most widely played games in America. How correct was he?

Many of us find it difficult to make a decision. The results of a single error in a computerized society can be disastrous. Yet we cannot avoid the necessity to make choices. Even though we did not select our parents, decide on where we were born, or choose the kind of world we would prefer to enter, there remains a wide area where it is up to us to decide between a number of alternatives.

Men do not drift into greatness,

neither do nations. It takes disciplined decisions to move ahead. To react but passively to our environment, both social and personal, is to be less than a person.

The tragedy in communistic societies and in other types of totalitarian states is that the state takes over where personal self-discipline should rule. This can happen even in a democracy if the federal government becomes our conscience and we give up self-discipline and the right to make decisions. In group life creeping socialism is an ever present danger, because it is easier that way. Uncle Sam can become "Poppa Sam" without our realizing it.

The author of the proverb who said, "Hear, my son, and be wise, and direct your mind in the way" (23: 19) was urging men to take the path of self-discipline. They were not to pass the buck, to leave their decision-making to someone else, but to be thoughtful in directing their minds in the way of God's truth as revealed to Israel.

DEAD-END STREETS

Not everyone wants to take the responsibility of making decisions that require self-discipline. Some prefer to delegate this authority to others. It is easier to let others steer us. If something goes wrong, we can blame them.

Another group of persons runs away from situations demanding responsible thought and action by using pain deadeners, such as alcohol and drugs. Here they find either the sleep that turns off life or the euphoria that makes everything look rosy. Here also some attempt to find false courage.

One of the startling facts in all this running away from life today is the number of youth who are caught up in drugs. The turning to drugs by those who are tired, nervous, disillusioned, and ill because of the toll that years of life sometimes takes can be understood. But when young people, filled with energy and talent, use these crutches, it is doubly difficult to fathom the reason.

Some of the use of drugs by youth may be due to their desire to turn off the hurt of life. A lonely, fearful soldier in the jungles of Indochina, fighting in a war that lacks the kind of national support we have given to other wars, could easily say, "What's the use? I might as well make it a little easier."

Other young people turn to drugs merely to experiment with life. They have read about the higher levels of consciousness some drugs are said to induce and want to be "turned on." Still others use drugs because they think it is a symbol of belonging to their generation.

The tragedy is that these substitutes for facing up to life are dead-end streets. Even the writer in Prov-erbs knew this when he wrote of "those who tarry long over wine," saying, "At last it bites like a serpent, and stings like an adder." (23:32)

How to "Get With It"

Youth have a slogan they use in times when they seem to be losing their grip on life. They say, "Get with it!" This is good advice for the undisciplined person.

Some young people's groups who are fighting the use of drugs have coined another slogan: "Not High on Drugs but High on Christ." It is their way of saying that in Jesus we may find the inner resources that give us the strength to stand up to life as responsible persons.

The apostle Paul also discovered that God will enable those who turn to him to endure temptation. He said that, no matter what, God's strength is sufficient for our need in time of weakness (1 Corinthians 10:13). The truth of this promise every person may prove for himself.

Helping Adults Become Involved —Howard E. Tower

Preparation of Self and Class

As suggested in the helps for last week, there is an apparent break in our quarter's study at this point. This break involves a moving away from a consideration of the Ten Commandments in terms of the New Testament enrichment of the law and the meaning of the law for our present-day living. However, on closer examination, the break is more apparent than real.

Perhaps the first preparation task for this lesson and the one to follow is to discover how they relate to and build upon your previous study. This is important, not simply to keep some kind of logical sequence of develop-ment, but also so that a consideration of the outcome of undisciplined living is carried out in the context of the new understandings and insights achieved during the past weeks.

This part of your preparation, of necessity, will be highly personal. It will involve a careful review of the written resources, both biblical and nonbiblical, that you and your class members have used and a recalling of what has come out of the class sessions: the kinds of questions raised, the kinds of attitudes exhibited, and the experiences members have felt led to share. This review will indicate to you how to relate this lesson, dealing with the undisciplined person, to both the materials covered and the persons in your class.

A second area of preparation may be your need to place the wisdom literature of the Bible—particularly the Book of Proverbs—in its proper place in the development of Scripture. As suggested by Dr. Frey, the article in *The Interpreter's Dictionary of the Bible* will help you do this. An important thing to remember is that the pithy, wise sayings of Proverbs grew out of the Hebrew culture after many years of living with the Ten Commandments as the basis of their socioreligious culture.

Likewise, it will be helpful as you examine Paul's counsel in 1 Corinthians 10:12-13 (study the whole of Chapter 10) to remember that Paul wrote as a Jew who knew and practiced the law, but also as a Christian who was subject to the higher law of love as he found it in Christ.

Since two of the most glaring examples of undisciplined living in our society today are exhibited by the large number of persons who are alcoholics or drug addicts, you may find it worth your while to review a film dealing with each of these problem areas. There are many films on these subjects, and your local librarian may be able to help you choose the right ones. I will mention two: *How Long the Night* and *LSD: Insight or Insanity*. (See page 338.) Others are listed following the introduction to Unit IX, page 338.

Presenting the Main Question

If you asked the class members to be thinking about the question— What reactions against our permissive and morally loose pattern of living have you observed?—begin with a discussion of this question.

Instead of reporting signs of reaction to our new, freer style of living,

some members may give evidence that the mood of living is still moving in the direction of "anything goes" as long as you can get away with it. If this should happen, the group might list in parallel columns signs of "loosening up" and signs of "tightening up" on discipline, both self-discipline and externally enforced discipline.

Out of this discussion, guide the class members to formulate a main question. They may agree that Dr. Laymon expresses their feelings in his question, What is the place of self-discipline in a permissive society where "anything goes"? Or their question may move in one of these directions: How do we keep our need for, and our urge toward, freedom from degenerating into license and undisciplined living? Does the emphasis on "doing your thing" lead to self-fulfillment or self-destruction? Do we need to recover a moral base for our freedom? Are the Ten Commandments, reinterpreted in the light of our Christian faith, that needed standard?

Developing the Lesson

Whatever formulation of the main question you and the class members agree upon, you should then ask what relation the question has to the study of the past eleven weeks. The class members may readily respond to such a question and list a number of their insights that are relevant to the question as they have stated it. On the other hand, you may find that it is necessary at this point in the lesson to make a brief statement about the wisdom literature, how it developed, and how the sages of a late period in Hebrew history summed up the accumulated wisdom of the experience of their people—a people trying to fulfill the demands of the Ten Commandments.

In like manner, you may need to point out that Paul's writings, though not unrelated to the moral demands of his Hebrew heritage, certainly always went beyond that heritage. Everything Paul did and said was colored by his unique experience and relationship to Jesus Christ.

Follow your statement with an examination of the Scripture passages. This examination may be done as a class or in small work groups.

These questions may help in the exploration of the words from Proverbs: What does this passage reveal about social conditions in Israel at the time? Are some of these conditions prevalent today? Do you think the "liberated" people of that day would have considered the impact of these sayings reactionary, an attempt to return to the "good old days"?

For a consideration of the Corinthian passage (read the entire tenth chapter) these questions might serve as a guide: What temptations was Paul talking about? How do you reconcile the advice of Paul in this chapter with his insistence that love is the fulfillment of the law? Do you agree with Dr. Frey's summary of the teaching of this chapter: all face temptation; arrogance and pride may blind us all to the danger of temptation; and God's grace is extended to all? Why, or why not?

When your study of the Scripture passages is completed, consider what your discoveries suggest concerning the significance of, and the need for, disciplined living today.

Helping Class Members Act

Two questions may help each person decide what action he needs to undertake for himself: Do I make my decisions in the light of some deeply held convictions, or on the basis of the easy way out? Am I clear that personal freedom lays upon me a corresponding demand for responsible action?

For corporate or group action these issues might be explored:

1. The need for some commonly held parental standards in dealing with teen-age children in a rapidly changing culture.

2. The increasing use of drugs as a way of escape, and what to do about it.

3. The need to discover the increasing number of alcoholics and the relation of this trend to the use of beverage alcohol in social events.

4. The increase of crime in our streets and the role of police in our community.

Planning for Next Sunday

Call attention to the statement of Paul, "I do not do the good I want, but the evil I do not want is what I do." (Romans 7:19) Ask the members of your class to consider the extent to which this statement accurately describes their experience. For all who find themselves in Paul's position, here is a further question: Do we need more than law and human love to free us from this inner battle between what we are and what we want to be?

Redemptive Love in Action

Background Scripture: Matthew 12:43-45; Mark 2:13-17;
Luke 15:11-32; 1 Corinthians 9:19-23; Galatians 5:25 through 6:5

The Main Question —Charles M. Laymon

Lou Marsh was a young black man who tried to be a Christian. He desperately sought to discover God's will for his life. It was a financial struggle, but he finally graduated from Temple University and then studied for two years at Yale Divinity School, preparing for the ministry.

The question that kept bothering him was how to express his "call" in today's world. The needs of the gangs of black and Puerto Rican teen-agers in the slums of Harlem seemed to be his answer. He went there as a worker with New York City's youth board.

It was rough going, and his mother worried about him. But he assured her, "I'll be all right. I can take care of myself. Besides, somebody has to do the job."

His story does not have a happy ending, or does it? In a gang war between "the young untouchables" and "the playboys," he averted a showdown by persuading the former to abandon the fight. Four older boys, graduates of "the young untouchables," who had wanted the battle, resented Lou's influence, ambushed him, and beat him senseless. Lou died in the hospital without regaining consciousness. He was twenty-nine years old.

Was this redemptive love in action? Does every person have to die as a martyr in order to live the life of love—Christ's kind of love—for others? The Bible speaks to these questions in the following passages.

As You Read the Scripture —George W. Frey

This quarter closes appropriately with a lesson on the theme "Redemptive Love in Action." The thread that binds the Old and New Testaments together as one book is the redeeming love of God. First we see that love revealed to ancient Israel. The laws of the Old Testament demonstrate the divine love for a people God called into being and gave a purpose—redeeming the whole world. In one way or another, the whole Old Testament seeks to interpret the meaning of these laws for the people of God.

In the New Testament, God's redeeming love is seen in the life, mission, and message of Jesus. Here is a clear and compelling disclosure of redeeming love in human personality. In one way or another the New Testament writers see love in its fullest in Christ. Law and gospel meet in Christ and refocus on the Christian community. The Christian church becomes love in action.

430

Mark 2:16. *Why does he eat with tax collectors and sinners?* Why? Redeeming love is the answer. Tax collectors and sinners were the outcasts of society. They were unclean. They were not respectable people. Redeeming love does not set up such barriers. It sees all people as persons loved by the Father.

Verse 17. *I came not to call the righteous, but sinners:* To eat with someone was to enter into a significantly close relationship and implied common acceptance of one another. That Jesus would identify in such a close manner with persons regarded as scandalous was an affront of the highest order to the Pharisees. We cannot be certain whose home hosted the dinner. If Mark intended to use verses 13-14 as an introduction to this incident, then it may have been the home of Levi, son of Alphaeus. This identification of the home

JESUS TOLD THE STORY OF THE PRODIGAL SON TO DEMONSTRATE THE MEANING OF RE-
DEMPTIVE LOVE IN ACTION FOR AN UNDISCIPLINED PERSON.

may be strengthened if Luke 5:27-32 could be regarded as an account of the same event. Otherwise, "his house" in Mark 2:15 may refer to the home of Jesus. If this was the case, the offense would be all the more painful to the Pharisees. No respectable person with standing in the community would open his home to the despised of society. But Jesus did.

Jesus lost no time in answering the Pharisees' question. In clear, concise, convincing words he said, *"I came . . . to call . . . sinners."* The *sinners* were the estranged ones, who needed help, friendship, forgiveness, acceptance, redemption, and hope. The *righteous* (the right ones) already had these gifts of grace—or at least should have possessed them. Here the redeeming love of

431

God shines through Mark's story. Jesus is not only a man of action, as Mark so often pictures him, but a person filled with compassion for the lonely, hated, rejected, ugly members of society.

Galatians 5:25 through 6:5. *Bear one another's burdens, and so fulfil the law of Christ:* The main question Paul deals with in Galatians is What makes a person Christian? Is it submission to the Jewish law, especially the rite of circumcision? Or is it faith in Jesus Christ? Paul's answer is recorded in Galatians 5:6: "For in Christ Jesus neither circumcision nor uncircumcision is of any avail, but faith working through love." Faith flowing forth in love is the mark of the disciple of the Lord.

A list of adjectives describing love is found in Galatians 5:22-23. Romans 12 and 1 Corinthians 13 add to the descriptive qualities of genuine Christian love. In this passage Paul spells out still more qualities of love. Three ideas may be found here: (1) Christian love cares (6:1). All persons come under the consideration of the Christian's responsibility. Paul especially points out the man who "is overtaken in any trespass." Christian love does not sit in judgment on him but seeks to "restore him." Here is redeeming love in action. (2) The Christian is a thoroughly responsible person. He "shoulders his own pack." (See 6:5, The New Testament in Modern English.) But he also bears the burdens of others. (3) Christian love is motivated by eternal values. J. B. Phillips translates Galatians 6:4 in a meaningful way: "Let every man learn to assess properly the value of his own work and he can then be glad when he has done something worth doing without depending on the approval of others." The Christian evaluates his life style in the light of divine standards and does not wait for or need the approval of his neighbor.

The presence of this kind of love becomes a motivating force in the community, strengthening and building the fellowship of Christlike persons. Paul sums it up very aptly, "If we live by the Spirit, let us also walk by the Spirit." (5:25) When and where this happens, redeeming love is present. The peace of the community is assured, and the world will know the full value of law and gospel in a new and creative way.

Selected Scripture

King James Version

Mark 2:16-17

16 And when the scribes and Pharisees saw him eat with publicans and sinners, they said unto his disciples, How is it that he eateth and drinketh with publicans and sinners?

17 When Jesus heard it, he saith unto them, They that are whole have no need of the physician, but they that are sick: I came not to call the righteous, but sinners to repentance.

Revised Standard Version

Mark 2:16-17

16 And the scribes of the Pharisees, when they saw that he was eating with sinners and tax collectors, said to his disciples, "Why does he eat with tax collectors and sinners?" 17 And when Jesus heard it, he said to them, "Those who are well have no need of a physician, but those who are sick; I came not to call the righteous, but sinners."

Galatians 5:25 through 6:5

25 If we live in the Spirit, let us also walk in the Spirit.

26 Let us not be desirous of vain glory, provoking one another, envying one another.

1 Brethren, if a man be overtaken in a fault, ye which are spiritual, restore such an one in the spirit of meekness; considering thyself, lest thou also be tempted.

2 Bear ye one another's burdens, and so fulfil the law of Christ.

3 For if a man think himself to be something, when he is nothing, he deceiveth himself.

4 But let every man prove his own work, and then shall he have rejoicing in himself alone, and not in another.

5 For every man shall bear his own burden.

Memory Selection: Bear ye one another's burdens, and so fulfil the law of Christ. (Galatians 6:2)

Galatians 5:25 through 6:5

25 If we live by the Spirit, let us also walk by the Spirit. 26 Let us have no self-conceit, no provoking of one another, no envy of one another.

1 Brethren, if a man is overtaken in any trespass, you who are spiritual should restore him in a spirit of gentleness. Look to yourself, lest you too be tempted. 2 Bear one another's burdens, and so fulfil the law of Christ. 3 For if any one thinks he is something, when he is nothing, he deceives himself. 4 But let each one test his own work, and then his reason to boast will be in himself alone and not in his neighbor. 5 For each man will have to bear his own load.

Memory Selection: Bear one another's burdens, and so fulfil the law of Christ. (Galatians 6:2)

The Scripture and the Main Question —Charles M. Laymon

When to Keep Wrong Company

Have you heard of the coffee house ministry? It has been defined as "dialogue and doughnuts." A church sets up a coffee house where people can drop in for refreshment and fellowship. Some are established in the church building, while others are in a downtown location or even a run-down neighborhood. Persons can drop in for refreshment and talk. The subjects are as varied as the people who visit, involving both sense and nonsense. All kinds of persons with all sorts of interests are made welcome. It is not a church school class meeting—just folks getting together.

The purpose here is contact, people meeting people as they are—good, bad, or indifferent. It is not camouflaged evangelism but a sincere expression of the church's interest in persons as they are. The results are whatever they turn out to be, but God's love is always at work.

The coffee house program is not unlike the situation in today's Scripture passage. Jesus sat down to dinner with his disciples, and "many tax collectors and sinners were sitting" with him (Mark 2:15). The Pharisees and scribes criticized Jesus for his action. He was keeping the wrong company.

Jesus would not accept their criticism but defended himself with an incisive reply: "Those who are well have no need of a physician, but those who are sick; I come not to call the righteous, but sinners." (verse 17)

433

The church does not, like a country club, exist for the mutual enjoyment of its own members. It does not even belong to us, does it? It is Christ's own creation, and all should be made welcome.

WHO'S WELL?—WHO'S SICK?

Who can ever forget Dr. Thomas A. Dooley, who declined a promising medical career in America to minister to refugees in Vietnam? Wracked with pain from a terminal illness, he kept returning to the poverty-stricken sufferers in Vietnam until he could no longer move about.

In explaining why he did not choose to practice among the affluent of society, Dr. Dooley said, "All men have claims on man." Was not this the same thing Jesus said?

Our Lord's reply to the Pharisees, who objected to his eating with publicans and sinners, is a masterful combination of sarcasm and judgment. When he said that it was the sick, not the well, who needed a doctor, and then added, "I came not to call the righteous, but sinners" (Mark 2:17), he was putting his accusers in their place.

Of course it was the Pharisees who were really sick because of their attitude toward outcasts and sinners. But the wicked were sick, too. All were sick and in need of the service of the Great Physician.

In any given society it is sometimes difficult to determine who are sick and who are well. Who among us does not stand in need of prayer? Who among us does not need forgiveness daily?

WHO IS REDEMPTIVE?

Toyohiko Kagawa of Japan is another example of a redemptive person, one who allowed God's love to flow through himself to others in a healing stream. Choosing to live in the slums of Japan, this sensitive scholar and poet identified himself with those in need as Jesus did in this lesson. Kagawa contracted trachoma and ultimately all but lost his eyesight, but he would not leave the area.

Kagawa believed in nonviolent love and often contrasted it with destructive hate. He once wrote:

Love is plus
Violence is minus.
Violence is suicidal.
Love is progressive, reproductive, and eternal.[16]

Only the love that actually bends low to lift others can be redemptive. Paul put it this way when he wrote to the Galatian Christians: "Bear one another's burdens, and so fulfil the law of Christ." (6:2)

CHEAP GRACE

Another person who illustrated Jesus' kind of redemptive love toward other men was Dietrich Bonhoeffer. He frequently appears on these pages as an inspiration to faith and action. One of the expressions Bonhoeffer sometimes used was "cheap grace," which he defined as "grace without discipleship, grace without the cross, grace without Jesus Christ, living and incarnate."

Paul's definition of the Christian's responsibility rejected the idea of cheap grace. He said that each man would have to bear his own load (Galatians 6:5). This is exactly what the Christian servants of God to whom we referred in this lesson did. Lou Marsh, Tom Dooley, Toyohiko Kagawa, and Dietrich Bonhoeffer—persons after the pattern of Christ—illustrate redemptive love in action.

[16] From "Violence and Non-Resistance," *The Willow and the Bridge* (Association Press, 1947), p. 67.

Helping Adults Become Involved —Howard E. Tower

Preparation of Self and Class

Today's lesson should become a fitting climax for your three months' study of the law—as given to the people of God, as reinterpreted by Jesus Christ, and as reflected in the lives of committed Christians today. As such, today's lesson should have three dimensions. Each participant should (1) come to sense his need for the redeeming love of God as he seeks to keep God's revealed law, (2) come to realize this redeeming love is available to all, and (3) be ready to be a channel of this love to others—to be redeeming love in action.

How does a leader prepare himself and his class members for such a high aim? As suggested before, in our busy society few adults have or take time to do much through-the-week preparation. The question suggested for the consideration of the group during the week should bring the class members together this Sunday with some measure of readiness to acknowledge their own need of God's redeeming love, or with gratitude that to a measure they have experienced it! You, too, have experienced the grace of God in your life or you would not be the leader of this group. And you know you stand in constant need of God's grace. As you prepare yourself for this lesson, you will open yourself to God's love, which is freely offered to all who have faith in that love as revealed in Christ Jesus.

But what about your sincere desire that others may experience God's love also? And have you done anything to share God's redeeming love with others—those who are not of your kind?

Read and meditate upon the Gospel incident and Paul's word in his Letter to the Galatians. Ponder the interpretations of these passages by Dr. Frey and Dr. Laymon. Think about your own readiness to "eat with sinners." In other words, what have you done this week to relate in any intimate way with any person that would not be readily accepted in your work, social, or church group? Would it prepare you for the adequate leading of your group in considering "redeeming love in action" if you attempted to do one or more of the following things this week?

1. Visit a coffee house or, better still, volunteer to serve coffee for a full evening and communicate with any person who drops in and wants to talk.

2. Visit a prison and talk with a prisoner.

3. Visit a home for drug addicts.

4. Make an opportunity to talk with a militant black.

5. Attend a meeting of Alcoholics Anonymous.

You will need to exercise care that whatever contact you make is free, open, and honest, not condescending or patronizing.

Presenting the Main Question

Dr. Laymon tells of Lou Marsh, who gave his life while working in the Harlem ghetto. Then he asks a double question: "Was this redemptive love in action? Does every person have to die as a martyr in order to live the life of love—Christ's kind of love—for others?" You might begin this session with this illustration and these questions. Whatever response you receive will reveal something about where the members of your group are in their thinking and feeling in reference to the meaning and role of redeeming love in their lives and in their world.

This discussion might focus on three related questions:

1. Do I need, and how can I receive, God's redeeming love?
2. Do I really believe this love is offered to the outcasts of society?
3. How can I put this love into action?

Developing the Lesson

A possible effective approach to the further development of this lesson would be to divide your group members into three subgroups.

One group would be asked to talk together and share experiences that have convinced them of their need for God's grace and redeeming love in their lives. This sharing should go further and include the sharing of experiences in which persons have been sure that God's grace has made a difference in their lives. The conversation should focus on one or more experiences that are so unique that the conversation group feels these should be shared with the whole class.

The second conversation group would consider first the feelings they have toward "unacceptable" persons. Do their feelings often parallel the feelings expressed by the Pharisees rather than the response suggested by Jesus' action? From this discussion the group should move to share any experiences they are aware of in which the miracle of love's work took place in the life of a person who seemed beyond help or hope. If this group comes up with just one such experience to share with the entire class, their conversation and sharing will have been worthwhile.

The third group should focus their thinking and conversation upon how the kind of love they have experienced can be effectively shared with persons who have been defeated by life or who are desperately seeking to escape from life. This conversation should consider person-to-person experiences and attempts that their church or other churches have made to make God's caring love evident to the outsider: coffee houses; work with alcoholics, drug addicts, the poor, welfare recipients. Again, if one such experience can be reported to the whole class, it may stimulate the imaginations of the class members to think of new ways to put God's redeeming love into action.

The sharing period in the class should be allowed to take whatever direction is appropriate, but time should be allotted for you to lead the group in an evaluation of the quarter's study.

Helping Class Members Act

Perhaps an effective approach to further action growing out of today's lesson and the entire study would be to review with the group members the various action projects that have been initiated. Are any of these still in process? Have any of them resulted in involving other groups in the church or community? Have some been completed? With what results? Is there a need for any task groups either to start new action or to follow up on action in process?

For personal action let the group members consider these questions: In what ways has my understanding of the relevance of my Christian faith changed? What changes have I made in my style of living? Are there changes I want and need to make?

Planning for Next Sunday

If yours is a self-running group, members will, of course, set up a procedure for determining what their next period of study will be. Will it be something growing out of this study? Some other unit of study offered by your denomination? Or the next unit in the uniform series?

If your group is one that is committed to the uniform lessons for the year, you will, of course, give a brief introduction to the new quarter's study. The theme will be "The Gospel According to Paul." Members may wish to read the background Scripture during the coming week: 1 Corinthians 1:10-15 and 2 Corinthians 12:19-21.

Index of Scripture

INDEX OF SCRIPTURE

440

Index of Subjects

4966